DATE DUE			

OXFORD MONOGRAPHS ON MUSIC

TCHAIKOVSKY'S BALLETS

TCHAIKOVSKY'S BALLETS

SWAN LAKE, SLEEPING BEAUTY,
NUTCRACKER

❦

ROLAND JOHN WILEY

CLARENDON PRESS · OXFORD
1985

Oxford University Press, Walton Street, Oxford OX2 6DP

London New York Toronto
Delhi Bombay Calcutta Madras Karachi
Kuala Lumpur Singapore Hong Kong Tokyo
Nairobi Dar es Salaam Cape Town
Melbourne Auckland

and associated companies in
Beirut Berlin Ibadan Mexico City Nicosia

Oxford is a trade mark of Oxford University Press

Published in the United States
by Oxford University Press, New York

British Library Cataloguing in Publication Data

Wiley, Roland John
Tchaikovsky's ballets
1. Chaikovski, Peter Ilich—Orchestral music
I Title
782.9'5'0924   ML410.C4
ISBN 0–19–315314–9

Library of Congress Cataloging in Publication Data

Wiley, Roland John
Tchaikovsky's ballets
Bibliography: p
Includes index
1. Tchaikovsky, Peter Ilich, 1840–1893. Ballets.
I. Title
ML410.C4W53 1984   782.9'5'0924   83–23843
ISBN 0–19–315314–9

Set by Wyvern Typesetting Ltd, Bristol
Printed in Great Britain by
Billing & Sons Limited, Worcester

FOR JOHN AND RUTH

FIRST IMPRESSIONS

'. . . it is impossible . . . not to notice that the music of *Swan Lake* is pallid and monotonous in the extreme.'
> —from a review of the first performance in Moscow.

'This is the complete decline of the choreographic art! . . . As for Tchaikovsky's music, it is . . . far from suitable for ballet.'
> —from a review of the first performance of *Sleeping Beauty*.

'. . . for dancers there is rather little in it, for art absolutely nothing, and for the artistic fate of our ballet, one more step downward.'
> —from a review of the first performance of *Nutcracker*.

'The principal defect of the aforementioned ballet is its music and it is simply unbelievable that it was written by such a great master as the deceased P. I. Tchaikovsky.'
> —from a review of the first performance of *Swan Lake* in St Petersburg.

Contents

❧

Preface

❧

THIS is a study of three celebrated ballets, comprising musical analysis and accounts of the first productions. Because Tchaikovsky left us no explanations of style and structure in his music the analysis is necessarily conjectural, though the conjectures are always based on facts in the score. Because the ballets are so different a uniform approach to analysis seemed out of place: the aim has been to identify the most distinctive characteristics of each one.

Documents, in contrast, form the basis of the accounts of the first productions, which have been reconstructed, mosaic-like, from librettos, press accounts, reminiscences, historical studies, and materials used in the productions themselves. An important part of the productions is lost—the audiences who witnessed these ballets when they were new—although something of what we know of them has been sketched in the Introduction.

Of particular importance among the production materials are rehearsal scores—répétiteurs—and choreographic notations, for they illustrate more vividly than the other listed sources the difficulties of the historian's task. In their present condition they challenge the very definition of 'first production', or at least demand explanation of how this term applies to Tchaikovsky's ballets. Neither for répétiteur nor for choreographic notation is there any way of knowing whose were the many contributing hands (except in special cases), nor when, nor under what performance circumstances, remarks were entered. Yet it is certain that the répétiteurs contain several generations of remarks, some unquestionably dating from the time of the original productions, some from revivals with new casts. We know from the history of *Swan Lake* and *Nutcracker* before the Revolution that these ballets went unperformed for long periods (*Nutcracker*, for example, from 19 February 1897 to 23 April 1900). When the sets were dusted off and the dancers were back in their roles, was the work the same? Russians who vouch for the ironclad continuity of their tradition would have us think so, yet circumstances argue to the contrary. It is easy enough to distinguish a new production from the continuation of an old one, but changes are bound to occur from performance to performance, and it is to precisely this order of change—brought about by new performers and the metamorphosis of detail (whatever the commitment of the artists to preserving tradition)—that the répétiteurs bear witness. The performance tradition was simply not inviolate. The practical result is that important sources—répétiteurs, librettos, press accounts—do not always agree. The effect on terminology is to give 'first production' a freer connotation than is customarily allowed, allowing the term to embrace all relevant details of the sources which come down to us from the first performance down to a known break in tradition.

The composer's score and the study of a production, then, are not always complementary. The analyst of music tends to be predisposed in favour of the composer's text and seeks to explain and justify it; the historian of a production recognizes any number of practical considerations (to say nothing of artistic judgements made from other than musical points of view) which have the effect of disregarding or nullifying the choices the composer made. Tchaikovsky himself would have been the last person to deny the validity of these sometimes contradictory tendencies, but where he would have drawn the line between compromise and mutilation in the revision of *Swan Lake* for production in St Petersburg continues to be a matter for speculation.

Music in these ballets is therefore two things: what Tchaikovsky composed, and what his producers made of it. What Tchaikovsky composed is the subject of analysis. Of the performance versions, that for *Swan Lake* in Moscow is either lost or still in hiding; the scores as edited for performance in St Petersburg will be described in the accounts of those productions.

The complexity of these ballets has made necessary the ordering of a mass of details. While a score would be required to follow all of them, the style of the works and the aims of the producers can be understood without one. (Unless otherwise stated, bar numbers throughout the book follow those in Tchaikovsky's Collected Works.) Technical vocabulary has intentionally been limited, especially in descriptions of dances, which are offered not as a basis for reconstruction but to give some sense of pattern and movement.

The period under consideration begins in 1875—when Tchaikovsky received a commission to compose *Swan Lake*—and ends in 1895, the year Marius Petipa and Lev Ivanov revived this work. *Swan Lake* will thus be considered twice, first in the Moscow production of 1877 and again after the chapters about *Sleeping Beauty* and *Nutcracker*, a sequence that follows the chronology of the productions. In Moscow *Swan Lake* was mounted under circumstances less favourable and to performance standards generally lower than those of St Petersburg. Few details of this production come down to us, accounts of the performances are sketchy, and the quality of criticism is low. The Petipa–Minkus *La Bayadère*, produced in St Petersburg in 1877, will be described in the Introduction to allow a comparison with the exemplary state of the balletic art in St Petersburg at the time of *Swan Lake*'s modest beginnings.

The Petersburg ballet of the 1890s is so firmly associated with Marius

Petipa that writers have identified this era in Russian ballet with his name. This was a special time for Russian ballet, and much of the extraordinary success of the Petersburg versions of Tchaikovsky's ballets can surely be attributed to the combination of events and conditions attendant on their production there. It is not simply a matter of composer and choreographer being at the height of their powers, although that alone would have ensured remarkable works. Nor was this success due to the fact that the Maryinsky Theatre maintained a company of dancers with fine schooling and technical polish. These factors were of course important, but there were several others: virtually unlimited material support; the personal interest of a Director of Theatres sympathetic to ballet; knowledgeable audiences; and discriminating critics who demanded high performance standards. There was even good fortune in Petipa's occasional indisposition, for it required Lev Ivanov to deputize for him, and it is to him that we owe the exquisite nocturnal scenes in *Swan Lake*. Finally, in the 1890s there was no challenge to the pre-eminence of Petipa's style of choreography.

Changes in the imperial ballet at the turn of the century remind us of the special circumstances of the 1890s. In 1899 Ivan Vsevolozhsky stepped down after 17 years as Director of the Imperial Theatres. This cultured man, patron of Petipa and the designer of the costumes for *Sleeping Beauty* and *Nutcracker*, was succeeded by Prince Sergei Volkonsky, no less cultured but impatient to revitalize the artistic routine of the theatres, stimulate new ideas, and bring administrative reform. The last issue was the one over which he resigned barely two years later, though we remember his brief service for the even briefer appointment of a reckless young man from the provinces named Diaghilev.

Volkonsky ushered in the new century; it was he who in 1899 brought the news to Petipa that the balletmaster was to be designated by Nikolai II 'Soloist of His Imperial Majesty'. But death claimed Lev Ivanov in 1901, and then the teacher Christian Johannson in 1903 and the famous character dancer Felix Kshesinsky in 1905—each, with more than fifty years of imperial service, a patriarchal figure in the eyes of the Petersburg company. In 1901 the ballerina Pierina Legnani danced her farewell benefit performance in St Petersburg. At the time *Swan Lake* was performed there she was the last of a series of Italian virtuosos to serve in the imperial theatres and revolutionize the technique of Russian dancers. Italians had taken the ballerina's part in all Tchaikovsky's ballets at their first performances in St Petersburg, and it is no discredit to the magnificent Russians who were now fully prepared to replace them to point out that Legnani's departure marked the end of a distinctive epoch in the Maryinsky company.

The emphasis in this study is on documentary sources from the late imperial period, in preference to information gleaned from present-day revivals, which may lead to false assumptions. Also, except for *Swan Lake*, about which there is some question, no consideration has been given to the prior sources of Tchaikovsky's librettos: Perrault's tale *La Belle au bois dormant* and Hoffmann's *Nussknacker und Mausekönig* are readily available for comparison, as far as they are relevant to the understanding of Tchaikovsky's work. Except where relevant to a particular point, the position occupied by ballet in the *dukhovnaya kul'tura* ('culture of the spirit') of nineteenth-century Russia has not been discussed. The same art that appealed to the politically conservative balletomane–connoisseur was condemned by populists and revolutionaries who saw no likelihood of it being a force for social regeneration.

Nineteenth-century Russian has been translated into contemporary idiomatic English wherever possible without injustice to the spirit of the original. There is one intentional exception: texts from the choreographic notations have been translated literally, for that method better serves the rough, often ungrammatical language of the rehearsal hall, where these documents originated. Occasionally Russian words which defy precise translation, or which translated correctly seem odd at first glance, have been included in square brackets next to the English.

The sources raised many questions of spelling. Pre-Revolutionary Russian has been spelled according to the post-Revolutionary system. Russian names transliterated precisely in footnotes and bibliographic citations are spelled in the main body of the text so that the sound of the Russian variant is preserved without an eccentric appearance: Nikolai instead of Nicholas, Alexander instead of Aleksandr, Tchaikovsky instead of Chaikovskii. Names of non-Russian origin retain non-Russian spellings; names and places in *Nutcracker* follow (as did Petipa) spellings in Dumas's version of Hoffmann's tale.

In music examples and the tables setting out analyses of tonality and harmonic progressions an upper-case letter represents a major key and a lower-case a minor: thus, for example, c=C minor, C$\sharp$=C$\sharp$ major, etc. Chords are represented by roman numerals, again upper-case for major and lower-case for minor, so that I=tonic major, i=tonic minor, V^7=dominant seventh, A^6=augmented sixth (chord), ^{b}VI=flattened submediant, etc.; inversions of chords are shown in figures, so that, for example, I 6–4= second inversion of the tonic chord.

The reader will notice the use of 'balletmaster' and 'choreographer' as synonyms.

Unless otherwise specified, dates before 1918 are Old Style (twelve days behind the Western calendar in the nineteenth century, thirteen behind in the twentieth).

In the course of preparing this study I have been assisted by many individuals and the staffs of many institutions. For innumerable kindnesses I am indebted, in particular, to the following.

In the Soviet Union: the Foreign Department of the Academy of Sciences of the USSR, especially the staff of the Leningrad branch; the directors and staffs of the Central Music Library of the Theatre of Opera and Ballet named for S. M. Kirov, the State Theatre Museum named for A. A. Bakhrushin, the State Central Archive of Literature and Art, the State Historical Archive, the Leningrad Theatre Museum, the Lunacharsky State Theatre Library, the Library of the Leningrad Branch of the All-Russian Theatre Society; and to the late Natalia Roslavleva.

In the United Kingdom: the staffs of the British Library and the Victoria and Albert Museum; Dr Gerald Abraham and Dr Ann Hutchinson Guest.

In the United States: the Harvard University Libraries, especially the Harvard Theatre Collection and its Curator, Dr Jeanne T. Newlin; the International Research and Exchanges Board; the Andrew W. Mellon Foundation; the Horace H. Rackham Graduate School of the University of Michigan at Ann Arbor; and Mr George Verdak of the Indianapolis Ballet.

Three people who read the typescript deserve special thanks. Mr Clement Crisp made several valuable suggestions and corrected many infelicities in my handling of Petipa's French. Mrs Natalie Challis, of the Slavic Department of the University of Michigan at Ann Arbor, expended prodigies of expertise, patience, and goodwill in answering questions regarding translation and in discussing numerous other points. Professor John M. Ward of the Music Department, Harvard University, has guided this study from its origins in a doctoral thesis to its present form, always with discriminating judgement and excellent suggestions for improvement. The faults which remain after such distinguished assistance are my sole responsibility.

I owe my wife and son a debt of gratitude for their patience and affection, especially during the time this book was written.

List of Illustrations

✹

1. Tchaikovsky
2. Ivan Alexandrovich Vsevolozhsky. Drawing by Valentin Serov
3. Marius Petipa
4. Lev Ivanov. Drawing by Nikolai and Sergei Legat
5. *La Bayadère* (St Petersburg, 1877). Drawing of Scene 3 by K. Brozh, engraved by E. Dammyuller
6. *La Bayadère* (St Petersburg, 1877). Drawing of final scene by K. Brozh, engraved by Yu. Baranovsky
7. *Swan Lake* (Moscow, 1877). Drawing of Act II, Scene 1 by F. Gaanen, engraved by Yu. Baranovsky
8. *Swan Lake* (Moscow, 1877). Drawing of Act IV, Finale by F. Gaanen, engraved by Yu. Baranovsky
9. Detail from the répétiteur of *Sleeping Beauty*
10. Carlotta Brianza as Aurora (*Sleeping Beauty*, 1890)
11. Pavel Gerdt as Désiré (*Sleeping Beauty*, 1890)
12. Tchaikovsky's agreement with the Director of the Imperial Theatres concerning performance rights to *Nutcracker* and *Iolanthe*
13. Page from the répétiteur of *Swan Lake*
14. Pierina Legnani as Odette (*Swan Lake*, St Petersburg, 1895)
15. Pavel Gerdt as Siegfried (*Swan Lake*, St Petersburg, 1895)
16. Alexei Bulgakov as Rothbart (*Swan Lake*, St Petersburg, 1895)
17. Dancers representing snowflakes in *Nutcracker*
18. Page from the choreographic notation of Swan Lake, Scene 2

Plates 1, 2, 3, 4, 14, 15, and 16 are from the *Yearbook of the Imperial Theatres*. Plates 5, 6, 7, and 8 are from *Vsemirnaya illyustratisya*, xvii (January–June 1877). Plates 9, 12, and 13 are from the Central Music Library of the Kirov Theatre, Leningrad. Plates 10, 11, and 17 are from Y. I. Slonimsky, *P. I. Tchaikovsky and the Ballet Theatre of his Time* (Moscow, 1950). Plate 18 and the pages of choreographic notation of The Waltz of the Snowflakes from *Nutcracker* in Appendix G are reproduced by kind permission of the Harvard Theatre Collection, Cambridge, Massachusetts.

Introduction: Some Traditions

❧

BEFORE setting out, we must consider in some detail three topics which are essential preliminaries to an understanding of Tchaikovsky's ballets. Two of these—the ballet audience and the collaboration of balletmaster and composer—are liable to some misunderstanding. The third, a description of the Petipa–Minkus ballet *La Bayadère*, is not so much one tradition as a characteristic product of two: choreography combining *danse d'école* and stylized mime; and music written to order in the special collaborative manner. *La Bayadère* is a typical Petipa work of the 1870s and was produced as the choreographer Julius Reisinger was putting the finishing touches to *Swan Lake*.

(a) Composer and Balletmaster

'They tell me that during the production of a new ballet, balletmasters treat the music very unceremoniously and demand many changes and alterations. To write under such conditions is impossible.' These remarks of Tchaikovsky, conveyed to us by a specialist ballet composer in a series of reminiscences,[1] summarize the difficulties of the non-specialist who approaches ballet. In Tchaikovsky's time the first law of ballet was the balletmaster's precedence: other collaborators worked to his order, and he enjoyed complete power of veto over them. He was able to do this because he made the dances and the dances were the most unpredictable element in ballet, unwritten, largely irretrievable if forgotten, and in most cases thoroughly understood only by him. 'Both the composer and the librettist in ballet should be subordinate to the balletmaster', explains Alexander Pleshcheyev; 'pride should submit to experience'.[2]

And if, for example, one has ever seen Ivanov's steps to *Swan Lake* danced by a ballerina who was not physically similar to Pierina Legnani, for whom they were created, one understands that the need for flexibility in choreography is genuine, and that modern-day insistence on exact duplication of such individually modelled dances can be historically and artistically misguided. For Petipa a change of cast, and particularly of ballerina, might automatically call for the reshaping of a work, something to which the literature bears witness again and again. 'La Sylphide was revived for V[arvara] Nikitina', Sergei Khudekov writes. 'The author of this ballet, of course, would not have recognized his work. *La Sylphide* in its new mounting had nothing in common with its first version. Marius

Petipa adorned the old ballet with a whole series of character and classical dances in the new spirit.'[3] There are many similar examples: Petipa has to 'adjust' a revival of *La Fille du Danube*, another work danced in Russia by Marie Taglioni, to the *terre à terre* gifts of Ekaterina Vazem; and to re-create what had been aerial choreography danced by Emma Livry in *The Butterfly* at the Paris Opéra for the same dancer.[4] When his own quite ample daughter performed the leading role of Aspicia in *The Daughter of the Pharaoh* Petipa omitted Aspicia's classical dances, which 'deprived the ballet of colour and disfigured it'.[5] Later, in the same work, he made cuts and alterations to suit the talents of Virginia Zucchi.[6] Even after his official retirement he noted in his diaries fresh compositions for old works.[7]

Petipa freely acknowledged that this was common practice:

The talented balletmaster, reviving earlier ballets, will create dances in accordance with his own fantasy, his talent and the tastes of the public of his own time, and not come to expend his time and effort copying what was done by others long before. We note that in *La Fille mal gardée* Mr Taglioni changed all the previous dances, and Mr Hertel composed new music, and so too do I, without exception, every time I revive an old ballet. And then, each dancer of course performs these dances depending on her manner and capabilities.[8]

The same was true of new composition. In an anecdote Petipa once described how his judgement in a collaboration proved correct:

You know the ballet *The Vestal*. Sergei Khudekov, the famous balletomane and editor of the *Petersburg Gazette*, composed its interesting libretto and M. Ivanov, music critic of *The New Times* wrote the music . . . Khudekov invited Ivanov and me to visit him on his luxurious estate in the Ryazan government. We went there, and in the garden, in the silence, we worked peacefully. No reticence remained between us. Each of us knew what he should do. First of all the composer and I shortened Khudekov's programme. I demanded still further abbreviations; Ivanov did not support me, but the ballet was nevertheless long. Khudekov even sulked. Finally he submitted, and at rehearsal took me to one side and said: 'Marius, you were right. Shouldn't it be shortened two or three scenes?' Ivanov also agreed with him, and I made cuts, but it was not easy for me to shorten dances already produced.[9]

The priority of Petipa's opinion over those of a ballet's other creators went largely uncontested and uncriticized. Tradition provided the only authority to which he had to answer: the right of lesser artists to partici-pate, obliging him to include a certain number of dances for various ranks of soloists and the *corps de ballet*. Petipa's ballet is not unlike Metastasian opera in the rigour of its conventions.

While the balletmaster's decisions influenced all the collaborators, they particularly affected the composer. The extensive reworking of an earlier choreography as well as the final setting of steps of a new ballet often required changes in the music. In specifying precisely to Tchaikovsky his needs for the music of *Sleeping Beauty* and *Nutcracker*, Petipa was not only trying to minimize the unceremonious treatment about which the composer expressed a reservation, but was also following long-established practice. We learn, for example, from Charles Didelot's student Adam Glushkovsky that 'Didelot had his manner of uniting music with the programme of the ballet. It may be said that he was always co-participant with the composer in the creation of the music. All the large scenes of interest Didelot pondered at home, and [then] designated the music of each number: its length, tonality, tempo, orchestration . . .'[10]

One result of the balletmaster's precedence was thus the composer's subservience. But there was a reasonable need for shaping the musician's creative impulse, justified in part on technical grounds by the balletmaster's concern for the length of mimed scenes: an experienced balletmaster's conception of timing would be much surer than that of most composers, however talented. Again, Glushkovsky described Didelot's typical practice:

He would come to Messrs Cavos or Antonolini, the theatre composers. The composer sat down at his piano and Didelot without music acted out the pantomimes of certain scenes, and explained to him that for this pantomime so many bars at such a tempo, with such orchestration, were necessary . . . In ballet one gesture of pantomime may take up an entire phrase of music, and if from inexperience the composer writes thirty-two bars instead of the necessary four, it spoils the entire scene, having deprived it of speed and expressiveness.[11]

The mounting of a new work also brought pressures of a more practical kind to bear on the composer. Even the most careful balletmasters sometimes found they had miscalculated their requirements for music, or they disliked music requested in advance, and during a production required changes on the spot. Anna Petrovna Natarova, a dancer who attended rehearsals of the first production of *Esmeralda* in Russia, recalled an exchange between the choreographer Jules Perrot and the composer Cesare Pugni:

The composer Pugni arrived with his notes and showed Perrot the music he had written. Perrot in advance had designated the tempos and number of bars for each piece. Pugni had prepared it thus: at the end of one sheet was written the motive of a certain number, and if you turned the page over, there on the other side another would be written for the same number. He shows the [first] notes to Perrot; the musicians play the motive. Perrot listens. 'Now then, will this do?' 'No, it won't', says Perrot. And we, the young girls, waited impatiently for Pugni to turn over the page. This very much entertained us. 'And this?' asked Pugni. 'This is fine.'[12]

For Pugni and his colleagues, however, new composition of entire works was only one aspect of the job. Adaptation of existing music was another, especially in the earlier part of the nineteenth century when Didelot and Ivan Valberkh prepared ballets from popular operas, incorporating familiar music into a ballet score. In 1869 Minkus arranged this kind of score for Petipa's *A Midsummer Night's Dream* from Mendelssohn's music (a composer and technique used again when John Lanchbery prepared a score for Ashton's *The Dream* of 1964). Related to this was an occasional prescriptive tendency of balletmasters which went beyond specifying the length and metre of dances to include theme and motive: 'It sometimes happened that Didelot, fatigued by great exertion at rehearsal, sang in a hoarse voice to the composer musical motives which Cavos afterwards filled out, setting the music in order precisely according to the programme and the desire of the balletmaster.'[13] Yet another use of existing music was the creation of a ballet from diverse sources, a common practice in the nineteenth century. Vizentini's music for Petipa's *L'Ordre du roi* made use of music by Strauss, Delibes, Auber, Massenet, and Rubinstein.[14]

New productions of existing ballets might also require the services of a specialist in a number of ways. Frequently he would be called upon to compose dances and variations for interpolation into the old work. The use of such interpolations was widespread at the time: they were a principal vehicle for showing off the individual talents of a new dancer to a role. Often favourite dances of a ballet survived their original productions as interpolations in newer works regardless of any incongruity, in music or drama, that might result from their presence.

Once the full score was ready, a routine duty of the specialist would be to prepare a reduction for two violins (a répétiteur) for use at rehearsal. Répétiteurs are particularly valuable because they specify what music was actually performed in a given production. The procedure of reducing an orchestral score to accommodate performing forces available at rehearsal occasionally worked in reverse, when the composer would have to orchestrate a ballet from a répétiteur. When in 1848, for example, receipt of a full score of *Satanilla* from Paris was delayed, the composer Konstantin Lyadov prepared one from a rehearsal score for violin. A century later the Soviet composer Vissarion Shebalin restored the 'Sobeshchanskaya pas de deux' to *Swan Lake* with the help of a rediscovered répétiteur used in the first production.

Finally, the specialist acted as technical editor of the completed score. Besides composing interpolations without pay, Riccardo Drigo noted, there fell to his lot the almost continuous labour of correcting scores, répétiteurs, and orchestral parts, mostly in manuscript and frequently unintelligible.[15]

In the imperial theatres the balletmaster's authority over the composer was sanctioned by law. Cesare Pugni and Ludwig Minkus were recognized specialists whose job required them to compose ballet music on demand. But when the Director of Theatres issued a contract to Alexander Serov, a newcomer to the routine, it was thought necessary to specify his relationship to Petipa: 'This music must be written in conformity with the programme of the ballet . . . and by its melodies and motives conform to the character, locale and action of the ballet.' From the beginning of rehearsals Serov was obliged 'without fail to be present and, if necessary, in keeping with the demands of the choreographic stage and the declaration of the balletmaster who is mounting the ballet, to make cuts . . . or changes in the motives and additions to this music, and to make them without protest.' He was required 'to be present at the first orchestral rehearsals of the designated music for the sake of prompt changes that might be required in the orchestration.' Finally, the agreement specified that the composer could not object if the directorate 'deems it necessary to commission the composition of music for any particular *pas* from some other composer, as, for example, Mr Minkus.'[16] Tchaikovsky no doubt faced similar requirements (and was threatened once with an unwanted *pas* by Mr Minkus), though his surviving contracts, which are concerned with remuneration and performance rights, take no account of artistic matters.

What can be said of the music of these specialists? Many adverse criticisms have been levelled at them, unkind and possibly undiscriminating. Tchaikovsky himself referred to their works as 'marketplace concoctions',[17] although that was before he had tried his own hand at composing ballet. To say they were hacks and nothing more would be wrong, for in addition to meeting the stringent practical requirements imposed by the medium and its traditions, they responded to unusual artistic demands as well.

The first requirement of the specialist composer was to acknowledge the importance of the visual component in ballet. The music was to accompany something watched, it had to complement the movements of the dance. Carlo Blasis wrote: 'Ballet music and in general music . . . in dances must, so to speak, supplement [and] clarify for the audience all the mental movements which the dancer or mime artist cannot convey in gestures and the play of physiognomy.'[18]

Konstantin Skalkovsky concurred:

Music alone can give the dancer or mime that fire of expression which words inspire in the singer or actor. Music in ballet must complete in the imagination of the audience everything that is beyond the means of dance and its poses to express. Although pantomime is very expressive in itself, without the melodic sounds of music it too sometimes fails to move the soul.

Therefore excellent music for ballets is an important and not a frivolous thing. One cannot, as many think, be limited here by a hodge-podge of different polkas and marches, spiced rhythmically with the strokes of a bass drum. Of course ballet music must be lighter and less expressive then operatic music, but it must suit a multitude of varied situations, and thus itself be extremely varied.[19]

The composer–balletmaster collaboration set out to achieve a unity of sound and gesture. If it succeeded, balletomanes would praise the music as *dansante*, which, although a quality not easily defined, is wrongly condemned as trivial. According to one reviewer, in 1851, Pugni's music for Perrot's *The Naiad and the Fisherman* 'vivified the dance'.[20] Many ballet lovers of the time liked the works of specialist composers (and they still do today), possibly because they experienced them in the theatre and grew familiar with them in their proper setting.

Complementing the specialist's sensitivity to the visual was his awareness that the aural attractions of concert music could be defects in ballet. He attempted to adjust the level of inherent musical interest at any given moment to enhance the choreography, and realized that any competition of eye and ear for the audience's attention risked the weakening or loss of a desired effect. This procedure tends to produce in a ballet an inverse relationship between interest in music and interest in dance, whereby music makes its strongest impact when solo dance is the least commanding, and vice versa. The climactic moments of pure music and pure dance almost never coincide, a fact which should give pause to the analyst who seeks to judge ballet music only for its sounds.

The sources are surprisingly generous in offering explanations of what makes good ballet music. The quality most often cited is melodiousness, not simply in the sense of memorable tunes, but as a function of accompaniment. Melody is the principal measure of the *dansante* quality of ballet. Skalkovsky considered the best of Minkus's scores to be distinguished by 'a clear and lively melody, so necessary for dances'.[21] According to the ballerina Ekaterina Vazem, 'the music of Pugni . . . was melodious, [and] accompanied the dances and the mimed scenes beautifully, helping them to be comprehended by the public.'[22] And in more recent times Constant Lambert declared the superiority of *Sleeping Beauty* over *Swan Lake* because of the quality of its melody.[23] When, therefore, responsible critics found fault with melody in ballet music, they were not mere dilettantes who could not hear the tunes, but were taking exception to the quality of the fundamental conception of balletmaster and composer.

So important was melody that the other qualities of a ballet score can be ranked together in a long second place. All are accessories to the *dansante* quality determined by the melody, and either aim at simplicity and charm or grow out of the practical requirements of the medium. The importance of timing in mimed scenes has already been mentioned, but the specialist faced other requirements which could also be described as rhythmic. Balletmasters and performers alike were extremely reluctant to give up the regular metre and phrase lengths (usually in multiples of four bars) of nineteenth-century dance music. 'Dancers are not horses', Skalkovsky observes, 'and cannot jump without a measure.'[24] A practical determinant of rhythm, which called for long tracts of music divided into short units, was the physical stamina of dancers. Any formula for large-scale musical unity had to allow for frequent breaks in the continuity of the score, coming in the case of solo variations as often as every thirty-two to forty-eight bars.

Skill in orchestration was also required, not simply because the ballet orchestra was large and varied, but also because composers were expected to be sensitive to sonority. The right choice had to be made for numerous solo obbligatos, and mimed scenes were to be made suitably characterful by including descriptive elements appropriate to the action. 'If in opera Tchaikovsky always strove to concentrate on the development of fundamental dramatic conflict and avoided superfluous detail, in ballet colourful details were essential, and the composer showed in their composition inexhaustible resourcefulness.'[25] An anonymous reviewer of Minkus's farewell benefit mentioned scoring when summarizing that composer's work: 'An enormous variety of melodies, brilliant orchestration and, chiefly, consistency of musical style were guaranteed every time Minkus's name was placed on the poster.'[26]

Authorities give credit also to an extra dimension, going beyond mere technique, required of the specialist. 'Ballet music demands not only melodiousness and clear rhythm', writes Skalkovsky, 'but also consideration of the artists' means and the other conditions of the choreographic art.'[27] The Soviet historian Denis Leshkov echoed this thought when he wrote that Pugni's music depended on melodiousness, simple but beautiful harmonization, and easily remembered motives, but principally on the composer's profound knowledge of the stage conditions of ballet and the structure of the dance.[28] This special knowledge may also have been responsible for the practice on the imperial stage of changing conductors during the performance of an opera, entrusting the dances to the ballet conductor.

For what may be the most eloquent essay describing ballet music of the period we must turn again to Konstantin Skalkovsky, whose remarks, framed as the answer to a critic, deserve extended quotation:

Of course the music of ballets and of dances in operas must not be a potpourri of waltzes and polkas; Prince Trubetskoy's music in *Pygmalion* is constructed in the form of a hodge-podge, which is why it produced such a depressing effect. But the greatest delusion is to propose that contemporary programme music should be a model for ballet; that the composer of ballet need not be cowed, as in opera, by the proviso of a text, need not take into account the strength and quality of his performers; that in all of this there is nothing of concern to him, and he might freely give himself over to creation in the sphere of instrumental music and compose musical pictures one after another; and that, finally, (solo) variations of the dancers have no importance whatever in ballet music, as each lasts hardly a minute.

With such principles it is impossible to write successful ballet music, and the discord between music and subject will reveal itself to the displeasure of the public, and, it goes without saying, to the disadvantage of the composer, as the latter is writing for the pleasure of the public, and not for his own.

Dances are for those who recognize or understand that this is an important and popular branch of art, a complex affair and not a convulsive jerking of the legs and arms. It merges on the one side with painting and *plastique*; then, carrying forward into the projection of passion and animation, it adjoins also the dramatic and oratorical arts; still closer is the connection of dances with music; only with the aid of the latter do they receive their full expression, as colour enlivens a drawing.

Both dance and music, however, have their laws, their elements, and one cannot class them together, making dance only part of some kind of general musical picture.

On the contrary, in dances and, consequently, in ballet, music is only an accomplice. Music must excite, support and guide the movement of the choreographic artists, in solo or in ensembles, not at all attracting exclusive attention to itself. 'It must be', says one music theorist, justly, 'a good sister, elegant, but without pretensions, and must assist the dance, not attempting to rival it. Like a devoted friend, it ought to be heard clearly, but must not intrude; it must give pleasure, but modestly; it must accompany and animate the dances, leaving first place to the performers. Only in mimed scenes may the symphony come to the forefront, because it then clarifies, as much as can be, the feelings and passions of the mute actor. In short, as the best woman is the one of whom nothing is said, the best music for ballet is that which passes almost unnoticed, for once the public's attention is directed toward the music, it means that the music is not wholly suited to the subject, although excellent in and of itself.'

Because of this, who writes a variation for dancers, and how, are not indifferent matters. The solo for the ballerina is normally the highest expression of the ballet, its culminating point; throw out these solos, and only the sauce remains—*civet de lièvre sans lièvre*.

In the dances of the ballerina is revealed most of all the difference of schools and styles which exist in dance, as in other arts. The character of some artists—as for example [Elena] Cornalba—is virtuosity, the light victory over the greatest difficulties, boldness; the character of others—as for example Zucchi—grace and elegance, fineness and expression. The composer is obliged to take this into consideration and write music for solos accordingly. One cannot take into account just the strength with which one ballerina takes longer to circle the stage on *pointe*, and another takes less.

The ballet composer may write musical pictures well, but if for all this he is not a clear melodist, if he does not assist the performers, if he is not closely familiar with their talent and technique, then he will never attain the desired goal. We are not speaking here of the artisan aspect of the matter, which has its own significance. And for ballet music a so-called practised hand is necessary. Raphael was a great artist, but he probably would not draw stage décor as successfully as a second-rate artist involved with nothing else.

That we are right is proved by the fact that there were no protests of any kind from the balletomanes when Tchaikovsky and Glazunov wrote ballet music, even those who were in close contact with the representatives of the ballet world. No one denied these composers their right to breadth and a flair for drama, but nevertheless ballet numbers are absolutely required which have well defined dance rhythms and precisely defined forms. Otherwise dances are impossible. Even Mr Cui himself did not deny this in his interesting critique of the music of the ballet *Raymonda*.[29]

Given his reputation as spokesman and waspish polemicist for the 'Mighty Handful', César Cui's recognition of the special nature of ballet music is a striking concession (though he was objecting to the very requirements Skalkovsky noted for clear rhythm and form).[30] The nationalists were typical representatives of the fraternity of so-called serious composers who disagreed with lovers of ballet about the quality of ballet music. One critic summarized this debate, apropos of the score composed by Mikhail Mikhailovich Ivanov for Petipa's ballet *The Vestal*, by citing the classic disagreement: 'The circle of balletomanes considers the music unsuitable as ballet music, while musicians find in it only one defect: that it is too good for ballet.'[31] The balletomanes rejected the score because Ivanov, professionally trained under Tchaikovsky, as a non-specialist had ignored the requirements of the genre.

In general, the 'serious' musicians eschewed ballet music as a worthy concern. When in 1872 the Director of the Imperial Theatres S. A. Gedeonov invited Musorgsky, Cui, Rimsky-Korsakov, and Borodin to collaborate on the composition of *Mlada*, an opera–ballet, the ballet music was entrusted to Minkus. Musorgsky, moreover, in one place in his correspondence chided Alexander Dargomyzhsky for the illogicality and stupidity of the latter's *The Triumph of Bacchus*, and in another made fun of Pugni.[32] While it is possible that the nationalists' derision had roots in pride and in the theatre administration's support of Western art they thought parasitical and irrelevant, it is equally possible that snobbery and even misunderstanding played a part. None of the 'Mighty Handful' is known to have been a regular ballet-goer (in his article Cui referred to himself as an ignoramus when it came to ballet), and thus could not have been expected to understand the medium fully. Also, their aloofness may well have concealed the disappointments dealt out to them by the theatre directorate early in their careers. Whatever the reason for their antipathy, we must consider the philosophical and sociological impact of Tchaikovsky's ballet compositions in the light of it. He began by facing the prospect of ridicule, entering the province of specialists considered inferior musicians by his peers, and ended by making ballet composition a legitimate pursuit for first-rate composers. He also rescued it from the most serious problem it faced under Pugni and Minkus—that of being frozen in the stylistic clichés of the 1830s and 1840s.

The tradition of the balletmaster's precedence has had profound consequences for the history of ballet. It has created a number of vexing problems for the scholar, including the fundamental difficulty of defining precisely what constitutes a given ballet. Is a ballet its first production? The score, the libretto, or the choreography alone? Does it embrace any number of changes that will still permit the use of the original title? At what point in the history of a work's performance may it be said that changes have created a new identity for it? For similar reasons the study of ballet music is hardly less imposing: a tradition that so freely sanctions change complicates analysis, and in many instances performance scores no longer survive or are difficult to find. Recognizing the special artistic nature of ballet music—its complementary relationship to gesture—is also important to criticism. In effect, we cannot make a fair appraisal of a ballet score as a theatre piece without a knowledge of the dance.

(b) The Ballet Audience

Before turning to the investigation of a characteristic work, let us consider the audience of the imperial ballet. Was it sophisticated? What part did it play in the history of the genre?

With characteristic brio Skalkovsky wrote, in 1882:

Anyone who visits our theatre has been witness to the following phenomenon: a fifty-year-old tenor sings who has lost his voice, or a second-rate prima donna, and the public claps furiously; but let dancers appear instead, and however excellently and elegantly they dance in an opera, our public is ashamed to applaud! Another phenomenon: in a ballet some classical *grand pas d'action* is being danced; the ballerina is in good form, she executes the most difficult variations as if they were trifles, and the public glances up at her indifferently from time to time; but a popular dance is played, a gypsy or pseudo-Moorish dance, a fat old dancer with swollen legs comes out, twitches her shoulders, and our fine public claps with fervour and demands an encore.

And meanwhile abroad for some reason the Petersburg public is considered a fine judge of the choreographic art. In fact, one can say that not only the public, but also the majority of our theatre-goers, even the inveterate ones, understand precisely nothing about ballet. They look at the most brilliant *adagio* as a cow looks at a passing train.[33]

Now Skalkovsky was, after all, practically a professional theatre-goer, a member of the brotherhood for whom it was a point of honour to attend all performances of importance. He speaks with the authority of one who moulds public taste, and it is not surprising that he maintained a certain distance from the crowd. His élitist viewpoint—that of a true balleto-mane—is important to an understanding of the period, and we shall return to it.

In contrast, Pleshcheyev remarked that towards the beginning of the twentieth century ballet was the best loved entertainment not only of high society but also of the broad public;[34] before considering the matter of connoisseurship in detail it would therefore be pertinent to review the ballet audience from the standpoint of its social make-up.

There was, first of all, an element of nobility in that audience. The late Anatole Chujoy reminded us that the nineteen courts in St Petersburg, with their entourages, could themselves have filled all the theatres for every performance.[35] From here, moving down the social ladder, we work our way through the ranks of ambassadors (which included, from Spain, the Marquis Campo-Sagrada, so stout that two seats in the theatre had to be refashioned into one for him),[36] military officers, and the rich commercial class. 'Next to the aristocracy', Vazem recalled,

the grand bourgeoisie occupied a significant place in the make-up of the ballet public—railway concessionaires, factory owners, directors of banks and stock companies, tax farmers. Its male contingent was normally unremarkable to look at, but the women stood out for the magnificence of their clothes and expensive ornaments. Not in vain in the old days was the *bel-étage* of the Bolshoy Theatre called the 'diamond row', where they loved to sit, especially at benefits and other outstanding performances.[37]

Moving up the theatre—and still further down the social ladder—we would have found lesser officials, students, and, on matinée days, children.

For their part, the balletomanes have developed in retrospect a corporate identity that is more convenient than accurate. If anything, the only abiding characteristic to distinguish them as a group was their love of the art, although they do seem to have been politically conservative, supporting the autocracy. They were drawn from all social and economic classes, and their position in these respects determined the location of their seats—from the Yacht Club set in the *loges* to the guards officers in the stalls and the 'gallery balletomanes'—students exiled to the furthest balconies. But the élite among the balletomanes managed to establish among their number a new table of ranks based on seniority and connoisseurship, which to a certain extent corresponded to rankings based on wealth and position. Getting a seat at all was no easy matter: lawsuits were brought by one balletomane against another challenging the right of a subscriber to bequeath his seating priority to a relation or friend. And on particularly lavish occasions, like the benefit performance of a favourite dancer, the subscription system was suspended and the distribution of tickets placed in charge of a leading balletomane.[38]

From their reputation we know that the balletomanes were more than casual onlookers: they were eccentric, vocal, and divided. They enlivened performances with encouragement and condemnation, composed poetry, lavished gifts, and inspired respect for their critical judgements. Their most outrageous behaviour dates from the 1840s and 1850s, when they gathered at a banquet to consume one of Marie Taglioni's ballet slippers, when the young guard harnessed themselves to Fanny Elssler's carriage for a turn through the city, or, perhaps most notorious of all, when the Muscovites welcomed the Petersburg ballerina Elena Andreanova in 1848, expressing their dissatisfaction by throwing a dead cat on to the stage.

By the 1860s they had tempered somewhat the antics of those earlier years:

Ballet performances were very lively at that time. 'Parties' were formed in the public; around every artist, even soloists of the second rank, were friends and courtiers who zealously attended ballet performances, attempting, in their words, 'to make prominent' their idols. The number of 'balletomanes' grew each year, and half the audience of the Bolshoy Theatre was acquainted with one another. They egged each other on to more vocal encouragement of a favourite dancer, calling her by her diminutive: 'Go Monteku!' 'Warm it up Zhenichka!' 'Highlight Lyubov Petrovna!' They used words of which the sense was understood only by the ballet habitué. Throughout a whole performance thunderous applause and the stamping of feet broke out continuously. Such gusto in the audience was a typical peculiarity of ballet performances in Petrograd. There was nothing like it in any other European theatre. The noise and bustle among the audience had a well-known benefit. Among the artists a competition arose; loud encouragement compelled them to study and to attend dance classes diligently, without which progress in choreography in the broadest sense of the word is unthinkable.

The majority of the public that attended the ballet did not 'philosophize' about it, but looked at it as a pleasant entertainment put on by beautiful women. But in that audience a small circle of fanatic balletomanes was formed who took their ballet seriously. They subjected the merits and defects of dancers to detailed analysis. Openly expressing their opinions, they maintained among the representatives of choreography a love for moving *plastique*, explaining its beauty and even its significance among the fine arts.

In their turn the artists, listening to the voice of these true lovers of choreography, perfected themselves, striving tirelessly to accomplish the mission, established at that time, of a pure classical art.[39]

By the late 1860s and early 1870s the fraternity of balletomanes, while maintaining their élitist attitude towards the general public, fought among themselves. 'For irreconcilability they were veritable Montagues and Capulets', writes Pleshcheyev in reference to the factions that developed around rival ballerinas; 'the partisans' animosity was even expressed in little scandals, in hissing one dancer who was rival to another.'[40] Two such rivals were Adèle Grantzow and Henriette Dor:

It was said that 'Adèle enchanted' and 'Henriette astounded'. And in mime the artists did not resemble one another. Dor was a dagger-like mimic, and Grantzow was considered a direct descendant of the captivating talent of Taglioni. Comparing them in Paris, St-Léon wrote: 'Grantzow is swansdown, Dor a bullet.'

During ballet performances lively arguments took place among the public concerning these artists, and both Grantzow and Dor continuously danced on the edge of a volcano in expectation of some kind of [unpleasant] surprise from the public. Both, however, were frightened without cause. Surprises in fact followed the performances—presents and flowers were given. For Grantzow they came from the 'infernal *loge*' [of balletomanes from the Yacht Club], who considered Dor a man in a skirt. Dor had her supporters, headed by the merchant S-m, who did not begrudge the money to assure that Dor's successes were no less splendid than Grantzow's. The Dorists considered Grantzow a 'sugar-sweet German stocking-mender' who, as a true German, took up her customary occupation as soon as she returned home—knitting stockings or 'embroidering on canvas' various 'souvenirs' with which she rewarded her followers.[41]

Growing out of such rivalries was a tendency among balletomanes to enshrine works, to resist any changes in steps that conceded to easier technique or, generally, to any radical departures whatever from the performance tradition they knew. They were quick to protest against such changes (save those initiated by a favourite), a habit that stayed with them to the end. Even today some balletomanes might be described as 'precious'—inordinately sensitive to line, suavity, and charm as well as having a hawklike eye for technical detail. And some, perhaps inevitably, let affection stand in the way of objective judgement.

It is all too easy to treat the balletomanes with a light hand, as if they were harmless fanatics who gave the period a quaint charm and nothing more. Skalkovsky took care to point out that for all their eccentricities, the balletomanes were good for ballet:

If all our theatres had a circle of people who so clearly took their business to heart as our ballet lovers, then believe it, nothing but excellence for art would result. The benefit to the theatre from theatre-goers is immense, and the best West European critics bemoan the disappearance, even in Paris, of this type of adherent, together with the turning of the theatre public into a throng or flock that believes every word of the reviewers.[42]

But the vigilance of the balletomanes involved more than the simple assertion of their status as connoisseurs. All the significant critics in the St Petersburg Press were drawn from their ranks. To the extent that criticism formulated public opinion, Petersburgers were in competent hands. The balletomanes took advantage of their posts, moreover, to exert pressure on the directorate, and such a well-informed clientele could not be dismissed lightly. They pointed out the need for theatre reform, and lobbied in support of any number of demands, including the engagement of important foreign dancers. Khudekov tells this story of slightly underhand influence, another offshoot of the Grantzow–Dor rivalry of the late 1860s:

At this time balletomanes did not spare their pockets for the support of their idols. The merchant A. S. was particularly generous to Dor. There lingers in the memory of the oldtimers a special feast given by A. S-m. After dinner each of the artist-participants was given a valuable gift, and besides this the host himself distributed to the guests from the ballet world a whole handful of unset diamonds, of which the finest were presented to the two most 'influential' dancers. This was done with the aim of taking advantage of their 'influence' in order to make the directorate complete a new contract with Dor for the next year.[43]

The relationship between the balletomanes and theatre officials was not always one of conflict: there were positive collaborations also, notably the dramatically powerful librettos prepared by Khudekov for Petipa's

Roksana, Zoraya, and *The Vestal*. It was a balletomane of the 'infernal *loge*' who proposed to St-Léon the idea of *The Hunchbacked Horse*, and who assisted him in working out the content of this extremely successful work; a ballerina's husband contributed the libretto for Petipa's *The Bandits*. And the directorate, in turn, sometimes made outright concessions to the balletomanes, as when in 1871 Petipa created the ballet *The Two Stars* especially for the contrasting talents of the rivals Vazem and Alexandra Vergina.[44]

The élitism of the 1870s gradually broke down as the members of the balletomanes increased in the next decades with numbers from the *nouveau riche*. Khudekov points out the principal characteristics of the new group:

In the course of the 'Russian' period [from the mid-1870s to the mid-1880s] a new cadre of *habitué*-balletomanes was formed in the audience. Its Maecenas was Bazilevsky, who was an admirer with good intentions, and around whom gathered lovers of choreography. The talk there was all of art and of giving presents to artists. But also the intimate life of the dancers was picked to pieces, and everything having to do with the intrigues of the balletic ant-hill. In general peace and agreement reigned; the previous antagonism between parties was missing. An unctuous mood set in. They honoured all artists; they formed a kind of large family of ballet admirers, and gathered up ballet artists for dinner after performances.[45]

Of all the individuals who might be mentioned in this new generation, Fedor Ivanovich Bazilevsky perhaps best personified the less eccentric quality of the new group, together with its generosity. He patronized talent from his heart because he loved the theatre. 'I have seen', wrote Pleshcheyev, 'a subscription list [for a ballerina's gift] like the following:

N	1 rouble
X	3 roubles
Y	1 rouble
F.I.B.	395 roubles
Total	400 roubles'[46]

Bazilevsky fell ill in 1891 and died in 1895. 'With him passed, literally, "gifts from the public".'[47]

There are hints of other differences in Khudekov's assessment of the new balletomanes of the 1880s. For all the apparent conviviality, a shadow of the old élitism persisted in the somewhat haughty distinction by which the senior balletomanes distinguished themselves from the recent converts. To them the new members, whose knowledge of the art was superficial and who chased skirts, were the 'balletomanes'. By the 1890s, according to Vladimir Telyakovsky, these balletomanes had reached their peak. In the mildly sarcastic tone of the jaded administrator he describes their manner:

They entered the hall with a special confidence, exchanged a few words among themselves and with officials of the theatre administration; ushers bowed especially low to them, to which the balletomanes answered with an imperceptible upward nod of the head, the way important people normally bow.

Moving to his place, the balletomane never sat down immediately. First, if he was subscribed to the first row of the orchestra, he said a few words to the musicians, and sometimes even favoured them with a handshake. Then he leaned his elbow back against the barrier of the orchestra pit, turned and glanced back at the audience through his binoculars, in order to satisfy himself that everything was in order—that fellow balletomanes as well as his other acquaintances who came to the celebration in which his dear balletic favourite will take part were present. Then the somewhat older balletomanes offhandedly sat down as if on their sides, wearily awaiting the beginning of the ballet. Others, younger, continued to stand, even when the music of the introduction began, and took their places only just before the curtain went up. They knew this moment in the music very well, and by this, in the manner of the truly knowledgeable, they let the public know that the rite was about to begin. From the aforementioned you understood that balletomanes—these veritable proprietors of the theatre, were at home here—'in their element', and that the remaining public were timid company, having no significance for the ballet. When the curtain rose all the balletomanes, as if from the waving of a magic wand, pointed the most diverse optical instruments at the stage, and when these hit their mark—the love of their hearts—one could see smiles on their faces regardless of the optical instruments.[48]

The old guard, meanwhile, preferred to maintain a certain distance from the young and called themselves *teatraly* or 'theatre-goers', which implied long experience and more elevated motives. Pleshcheyev conceded:

I never avoided the fashionable term 'balletomane' either in ballet articles or in humorous writings about ballet festivities. But I was always opposed to it in my heart, and, if you will allow, it is even rather vulgar. The word *teatral'* sounds much better to my ear. It embraces all lovers of theatre. In the old days there were no balletomanes, but 'danceomanes'—these were one and the same but it has a much better sound. With us it got to the point that people appeared, especially the young, who did nothing and went to the ballet. It used to be asked: 'And where is X serving?' 'Ah, you see, he is a balletomane!' Out of balletomanehood there was formed a profession to which young oafs were attached . . .

In the last years before the revolution, anybody who made advances to a dancer or offered a gift to some young sylphide was called a balletomane.[49]

Becoming a genuine *teatral'* required arduous dedication. Skalkovsky claimed the title only after attending 14 performances of *La belle Hélène* (one in Armenian), 27 of *Carmen*, and 146 of *The Hunchbacked Horse*, to name but a few, after writing 1000 articles and reviews, and having been preoccupied with the theatre since his youth.[50] Becoming a balletomane, in contrast, required wealth and social position:

In general balletomanes were people with means or who were skilfully able to show that they were close to them. After all, one had to spend no small amount on dinners, subscriptions, gifts, wreaths, and flowers for the artists. One had to have a connection in the Press—and this also took money. A balletomane without money—this, of course, is nonsense: who needs him?[51]

Khudekov draws our attention to another difference between generations, in the debasement of ceremonial dinners. These had existed for decades but, like the collective make-up of the balletomanes and the word 'balletomane' itself, they changed. There is no reference at the century's end to the stylish elegance of, say, the 50th anniversary jubilee of the dancer Nikolai Goltz in 1872, with dishes appropriate to the occasion (consommé à la Didelot and pudding à la Goltz). Instead, we read of occasions monstres that took on lives of their own, with an etiquette and fascination beyond that appropriate to paying homage to a favoured dancer.[52] Feasts were prepared for artists of all calibres, but talent, according to Khudekov, was never understood on these occasions.[53]

Their eccentricities apart, the balletomanes are important historically in two ways. Firstly, they formed, during the period we are considering, a catalyst between the artists and the audience. Skalkovsky reflected:

Since the forties they have called lovers of ballet here balletomanes, i.e. maniacs of ballet; their number now grows, now dwindles, depending on fashion. To their number is joined not a few people who are lighthearted about art, but who love to gawk at attractive women, and sometimes to have dinner with them. Such parasites exist among lovers of every art, and there is nothing surprising about their presence. But that circle of true lovers, which in fact is not numerous, but which seriously admires some cleanly executed entrechat, whose members grieve at the substitution of Ivanova by Petrova in some pas, and engage in endless argument over the importance of an entrechat or the extension of the battements of this or another dancer—an argument which seems very frivolous to simple mortals—is in fact the most useful kind of person for the theatre.

Art lives by these people; they try to find young or undervalued or forgotten talents 'by the water', encourage them, bring them forward, worry, intrigue, make fools of themselves, go mad over, argue among themselves about, etc. But without them art would be in the hands of the bureaucrats only, or the artists themselves, that is, the craftsmen of art, and there would never be established that necessary connection between theatre and public, without which art cannot flourish. It seems paradoxical, but in fact it is true.[54]

Second, they helped define the era. Looking back from beyond the 1917 Revolution Pleshcheyev, in Paris, wrote:

Together with the balletomanes died the romanticism of the theatre of that epoch . . . the epoch, I would say, of the greatest choreographer Marius Petipa, to whose poetic creation and aesthetic taste even contemporary ballet, which has conquered the world stage, is wholly indebted. Of course, the choreographic art moved forward after Petipa's death, accepted new forms, progressed, but in its basis, its fundamentals still remain the covenants of Petipa, our Petersburg Noverre.[55]

The balletomane, in some sense of the word, still exists, and much of his behaviour appears to be similar to that of his imperial counterpart. We can still see him throwing flowers on the stage, the insistent youth who stamps and cheers after the lights are up and half the audience has left, and who waits at the stagedoor for his idol. But the times have changed, and gone is a special *ambiance* of the period before World War I.

(c) La Bayadère

It remains to find out something about the ballets themselves. What features made up a successful work at the time Tchaikovsky began his career in ballet? Let us look to the Petipa–Minkus *La Bayadère* for an answer. In the year of *Swan Lake*'s first performance it was *La Bayadère*, not Tchaikovsky's work, which enjoyed an overwhelming success. It remains to this day in the repertory of the Soviet ballet, and its celebrated scene the 'Kingdom of the Shades' is performed by many other companies as well. In 1877 *La Bayadère* would doubtless have been the standard against which *Swan Lake* was to be measured.

Petipa produced *La Bayadère* in his thirtieth year of imperial service. While it is true that Petipa, who was hired as a dancer and admired early in his career for his talents as a mime and partner, assisted in producing ballets from the beginning, his contribution as a choreographer remained for a long time secondary to his work as a performer. The twelve years of Jules Perrot's activity on the imperial stage (1848–59) seem to have served him as an apprenticeship, during which he composed four ballets, two *divertissements*, and dances for three operas. Of the ballets of this period attributed to him, one contained a scene by Perrot, another was produced for a private theatre, and the most substantial, *A Marriage in the Time of the Regency*, was permitted by the directorate only if producing it involved no expense to the state.[56] From all accounts, these were not such as to anticipate the creative artist to come.

He emerged as an important choreographer only in the 1860s. We have seen how unruly and even contentious the Petersburg audience was at that time in its behaviour towards dancers. Just as the 'infernal *loge*' rallied behind the principal balletmaster Artur St-Léon and the dancer Marfa Muravieva early in the decade (the Dor–Grantzow affair came later), others chose to favour Marie Petipa, Marius's wife. With a rivalry established between the two dancers conditions were ripe for Petipa to step forward as her champion in the role of balletmaster. Many of his earliest works were composed for her, but his first great ballet and a prototype for later successes was the extravagant *The Daughter of the Pharaoh*, reputedly produced in six weeks early in 1862 for the farewell benefit of Carolina Rosati. This ballet won for Petipa the official title of 'balletmaster'; it led to a very productive competition between himself and St-Léon and marked the beginning of the first distinctive period of his creative work.

In 'Marius Petipa and his Significance', an informative if not altogether flattering chapter of his *History of Dances*, Sergei Khudekov described Petipa's two stylistic periods and outlined the structure of a typical Petipa grand ballet. The periods were distinguished by subject matter. In the first, which lasted until 1888, Petipa favoured 'subjects with dramatic content, with a fable that contained a beginning, development, and a denouement arising from it.' In the second, inaugurated by *Sleeping Beauty*, he turned almost exclusively to subjects based on fairy-tales.

Regardless of period, Petipa's ballets, according to Khudekov, were 'cut to one unchanging measure' and differed only in the time and place of the action and in details of staging. The *pièce de résistance* of each ballet was the *grand pas d'action* with two to five artists, a 'complex mime-virtuoso dance with variations'. After the opening pantomime the *pas d'action* would follow the traditional format: entrance, *adagio*, variations, coda. Here virtuosity and technical difficulties prevailed, Petipa creating each dance to conform with the strengths of a particular artist. Around this centrepiece the balletmaster would arrange dances for the *corps de ballet* (wearing 'accessories which entertained the eyes and ears of the public, very diverse and sometimes even mindless, which frequently resembled the trinkets used on Italian stages'), character dances appropriate to the setting for soloists, and massive processionals which employed the entire cast.[57]

The action of *La Bayadère* certainly answers Khudekov's description of Petipa's first period. The *bayadère* Nikia and the warrior Solor have sworn eternal fidelity to each other. The Great Brahmin, however, also loves Nikia and learns of her relationship with Solor. The Rajah, moreover, has selected Solor to be the fiancé of his daughter Hamsatti, and Nikia, unaware of this arrangement, agrees to dance at Hamsatti's wedding. When the Great Brahmin tells the Rajah that Solor is in love with Nikia, they contrive to murder the *bayadère* by having her bitten by a snake concealed in the basket of flowers she holds while dancing before her rival.

In a dream Solor visits the kingdom of the shades and is reconciled with Nikia. When he wakes, preparations for his wedding to Hamsatti have begun. At the palace, the shade of Nikia appears to Solor as he and Hamsatti dance. When the Great Brahmin joins the couple's hands in marriage, the gods take revenge for Nikia's murder by destroying the palace and its occupants. In an apotheosis, the shades of Nikia and Solor are spirited off to the Himalayas.

Who wrote this story? The title-page of the libretto of *La Bayadère* makes reference to the composer and the choreographer, but not to a librettist. Petipa took advantage of this customary omission to permit the public to assume that he had composed not only the dances but also the story, which was not always true. In 1889 the playwright Konstantin

Tarnovsky claimed equal billing with Petipa on the posters of *The Talis-man*,[58] and when in 1900 a reviewer attributed the story of *La Bayadère* to Khudekov, Petipa protested but conceded that Khudekov had contributed eight lines of stage directions in a margin.[59] The origins of *La Bayadère* are further obscured, first by the similarities of setting, characters, and plot to those of *Sacountala*, a ballet produced nearly twenty years earlier by Petipa's brother Lucien in Paris; and second by the inclusion of transliterated Sanskrit words in the libretto. These seem unnecessarily erudite in this context, and surely did not originate with Petipa.

As it stands, however, the libretto displays all the characteristics cited by Khudekov as typical of Petipa. Act II began with a massive procession for which, in one sketch, the balletmaster required 36 entrances involving 216 participants.[60] There were numerous character dances and scenes portraying Indian life. The ballet opened with a festival of fire in which 'the dances of the *bayadères*, now smooth and voluptuous, now animated and charming, alternate with the wild and frenzied movements of the fakirs, who jump through the fire and who, in a state of religious intoxication, taunt their bodies with daggers and knives'.[61] Later, in a 'Hindu Dance', the performers wore little bells on their costumes, Khudekov's 'rather mind-less' accessories. The plot ensured a number of powerful encounters: the scene of jealousy between Hamsatti and Nikia, when the latter learns of Solor's engagement, was praised by critics; and the Great Brahmin's declaration of love to Nikia came in a melodramatic dialogue typical of Petipa's so-called first period:

'I love you', the Great Brahmin declares to Nikia as she dances in Act I, 'I am crazy with love for you . . . do you want me to be your protector? . . . I will make you first in the temple . . . I will force the entire people to worship you! . . . You will be the divinity of all India . . . Only . . . return my love!'

She takes his pendant from him. 'You are forgetting this', she says. 'Look at this sign, this token of the high rank that you hold . . . I do not love you and never will.' Horrified, she pushes him away.

'Ah!' the Brahmin exclaims . . . 'Remember that I will never forget this insult! . . . this mortal outrage! . . . I will use all my power to reject you! . . . And my vengeance will be fearful!'[62]

Petipa saved the best for last: the appearance of Nikia's shade at the wedding. For this *pas d'action* the choreographer fashioned a finale reminiscent of a scene in *La Sylphide*: the dancers were grouped so that the shade was visible only to her lover. This device fitted the dramatic circumstances perfectly: Hamsatti becomes increasingly apprehensive as she waits for the wedding to begin, seeming to sense something she cannot see. We know from Petipa's sketches that this scene was part of his conception of *La Bayadère* from the beginning, although Hamsatti, in an earlier idea, was to catch sight of the shade, at which point 'a distant peal of thunder' would have sounded.[63]

Spectacle was a staple of the Petipa ballet. Critics of the first perform-ance expressed their satisfaction at the evocation of the Orient in *La Bayadère*:

Everything, beginning with the superb décor of Messrs Roller, Wagner, Shishkov, and Bocharov, the lavish, ethnographically true costumes, and ending with the tiniest accessory details, glitters with magnificence, novelty, originality, and pro-duces an enchanting impression on the audience.[64]

Stage machinery played an important part in the ballet, although it was not free of defects by the opening night. During Solor's dream Nikia was to show him a castle in the sky, but in the performance the appearance of the castle was not accurately co-ordinated with Nikia's gesture, and the dancers faced downstage to look at it only after it had disappeared. Another unusual feature of the 'Kingdom of the Shades', to those who know the scene from modern revivals, will be that it was danced on a fully lighted stage. Some idea of the destruction of the Rajah's palace, even though one reviewer found that it 'went quite wretchedly', can be seen from an engraving of the scene, 'The Revenge of the Gods', published in an illustrated weekly (see Pl. 6).[65] The libretto tells us that, at the moment the Great Brahmin takes the hands of Hamsatti and Solor, '. . . a frightening peal of thunder sounds and an earthquake follows. Lightning strikes the hall, which destroys and engulfs in its debris the Rajah, his daughter, the Great Brahmin, and Solor.'[66]

Spectacle, of course, also involved virtuoso dancing from the ballerina, and Ekaterina Vazem, for whose benefit performance *La Bayadère* was first given, received ecstatic praise:

It is difficult to evaluate that perfection with which the benefit artist, Mlle Vazem, performed all the dances of her new role, both classical and character. The incomparable talent of the first ballerina of our ballet, who has no peer at the present time in all Europe, has long since reached full maturity and such a degree of perfection that it would seem impossible to go further. And meanwhile, into each of her newly performed roles Mlle Vazem, as if deliberately, puts new choreo-graphic difficulties, which she overcomes with imperceptible lightness, con-fidence, and precision. Both as these relate to elevation, which in her case is becoming broader (*plus ample*) and more ethereal, as too from the point of view of incredible speed and cleanness in the finish of her small *temps* (*petite batterie* etc.), Mlle Vazem continually has new successes, which astound the knowledgeable of the choreographic art. Finally, in the sphere of plastic poses and smooth move-ments (*adagio*), Mlle Vazem displays with each year all the more grace and finish.

The reviewer goes on to note her 'inconceivably difficult' variations in the 'Shades' scene, and called her appearance at Hamsatti's wedding 'a miracle of the choreographic art'.[67]

Less bravura, but no less spectacular, was Petipa's excellent inspiration for the entrance of the *corps de ballet* at the beginning of the 'Kingdom of the Shades'. Except for reviews, in which it was praised but not described, the earliest documentary record of this dance comes not from the first production but from a revival in the 1900–01 season. A choreographic manuscript made of the revival preserves notations for it, recorded in the system of movement notation devised by Vladimir Stepanov in the early 1890s, as revised by Alexander Gorsky. The dance has no narrative significance; the libretto provides no description of the action apart from the single word 'Dances'. The set depicts 'an enchanted place' with the outlines of a few mountains in the distance.

Petipa's choreography is striking in its simplicity. The entire dance is constructed of two basic elements: the *arabesque* for moments of repose, and short runs on *pointe* for movement around the stage. As the music begins, one dancer comes down a ramp at the back of the stage, right to left, performs an *arabesque* on the right foot, followed by a backward and leftward arching of the torso, and then moves two steps forward. In taking these last steps she makes room on the ramp for another dancer who appears immediately after and performs the same combination. The entrance proceeds thus until forty-eight women have appeared and arranged themselves in four rows of twelve across the stage.[68] Now follow various poses and turns, interspersed with travelling movements of the entire group on *pointe*.

In contrast to Vazem's dances, Petipa has made this choreography relatively free of technical complexity; herein lies it challenge. Poses *en adage*, even simple ones, when performed by so many dancers in unison are a test of the *corps de ballet*. The mistake of one dancer is immediately evident and spoils the effect of the whole. Petipa's choreography is here lucid to the uninitiated, the virtuosity of perfect execution a delight to the connoisseur.

The success of *La Bayadère* cannot be fully measured in the response of critics or the work's longevity, or even in the fact that parts of it can still delight audiences today. To these measurements we must add an appreciation of the trying moments Petipa endured backstage in the course of mounting the ballet. Vazem made no secret of her dislike for Petipa, which led to incidents at rehearsal in the late stages of production. She repeatedly rejected his steps for the *pas d'action* of the last act, bringing the choreographer to the point of despair.[69] Even more exasperating must have been the demands imposed by six subscriptions of Italian opera on available time and space at the Bolshoy Theatre. One reviewer noted that a new ballet required six months to produce,[70] during which time the balletmaster would have to show each dancer his or her part in separate rehearsals, bringing together the entire work on stage with the orchestra only shortly before the first performance.

Minkus's score for *La Bayadère* was not published when the ballet was first produced, and no orchestral score dating from that time is known to survive. Judgements about the music must therefore be made on the basis of manuscript scores and répétiteurs of diverse origins. From these, Minkus's music emerges true to the specialist tradition. The score is an accompaniment in the best meaning of the word: rhythmically clear, regularly phrased (a 'Dance of the Slaves' in alternating 4/4 and 3/4 has been deleted in the course of the work's performance history), with considerable repetition of phrases and sections no doubt anticipating the possibility of cuts in production. He responded to the libretto's call for 'harmonious, peaceful music' at the opening of the 'Kingdom of the Shades' with an idea that reflected his gift for subordination. After a cadenza for solo harp, the dance unfolds as a series of variants of this phrase (Ex. 1) alternating with a contrasting theme.

Ex. 1

Minkus maintained an association of motive with character throughout the ballet, but even themes associated with Nikia, the fakirs, and Solor recur in different keys, that for Solor being one of his most effective ideas (Ex. 2).

Ex. 2

His orchestra was large. One score from the imperial period calls for piccolo; flutes, clarinets, oboes, bassoons, and trumpets in pairs; English horn; four French horns; three trombones; tuba; harp; strings; and five percussion instruments.[71] Even with such a large ensemble, passages for full orchestra are rare. Many instruments were used for special effects or the numerous obbligato solos.

La Bayadère, therefore, displays all the characteristics of a Petipa grand ballet of the 1860s and 1870s. Its exotic setting justified lavish décor and costumes. The stage machinists responded to the audience's love of spectacle with elaborate transformations, as did Petipa with his intricate massed scenes. The balletmaster also ran the gamut of choreography —from the delicate poetry of the entrance of the shades to the brilliant virtuosity of the ballerina's solos; and from dramatically intense mimed scenes essential to the narrative, through character dances which sought to project a picturesque (if not necessarily accurate) local colour, to the abstractions of line and motion of the classical dance. Minkus's music, varied and subordinate but competent, stands directly in the specialist tradition.

As the work relates to its time La Bayadère is also typical: in concealing the identity of its author; in the competition with Italian opera for rehearsal space and for a public; and in the regrettably incomplete legacy of documents which would help us reconstruct its history. Its significance to the present study, as has been mentioned, is chronological: La Bayadère was first performed on 23 January 1877 at the Bolshoy Theatre in St Petersburg; twenty-eight days later Swan Lake was first performed at the Bolshoy Theatre in Moscow.

Swan Lake in Moscow

❧

(a) The City

AT the end of 1865 Tchaikovsky graduated from the St Petersburg Conservatory. But soon he moved to Moscow, having accepted a teaching position in Russia's second conservatory, which had recently opened there. He had never lived in the old capital.

Moscow's population in the 1860s comprised those who cherished what remained of the city's ties to the patriarchal traditions of ancient Russia, and a chic, fashionable element, West-oriented, who relished the new freedoms of the post-Nicholaevan era. To the traditionalists the reforms of Alexander II—the emancipation of the serfs, the relaxation of restrictions on the Press and on foreign travel, together with the beginning of the railways, which made easier the influx of corrupting foreign ideas—represented too much change too soon. They tended to interpret even minor differences in public behaviour since the 1850s—when, for example, students could not wear long hair and smoking was prohibited in the streets—as external manifestations of internal decay.

The Moscow to which Tchaikovsky moved nevertheless retained much of its ancient character. The multitude of onion-domed churches and the continuing esteem and awe with which Muscovites regarded monastics and *yurodivye* ('holy fools', hermits believed to possess divine attributes)[1] spoke to an almost fundamentalist religiosity with strong pagan overtones. The commercial district, or 'city', a labyrinth of long, closed, low-ceilinged buildings with arch-shaped, half-dark entrances, resembled an Asiatic bazaar, aptly reflecting Moscow's status as an ancient trading centre, and was quite unlike the Westernized mercantile establishment of St Petersburg, with its Stock Exchange and elaborate banking facilities. The street life, be it the show of an animal trainer or a barrel organ player or the amusements of the holiday fairs, still sought more to preserve the old than to sanction the new.

On Novinsky Boulevard in Butter and Bright Weeks pleasure gardens were constructed for the entertainment of the townsfolk, with booths, swings, bicycles, and old men who danced with young girls. Sellers of whipped cream, *pirozhki*, and candied apples darted through the crowd. In the booths were farces with devils,

Harlequins, Pierrots, and others. There one could even see Julia Pastrana, the bearded woman, a talking head, giants, dwarfs, and other wonders of the world.[2]

All of this simply highlights something of which Russians themselves were quite conscious: the differences between Moscow and St Petersburg, which must have been quite vivid to the young Tchaikovsky in the first weeks of his new residency. Another Muscovite, writing in the second decade of the twentieth century, described the city fifty years earlier:

At that time all Moscow bore a special stamp: not only on the buildings, which were not similar to Petersburg's, or on the streets and the movements along them, but also on Moscow's crowds and on her society in all its totality and diversity. The peculiarities of Moscow at the present time have diminished, even disappeared: there is no longer a particular Moscow outlook, a special Moscow literature, let alone a science, or even kalachi [a kind of wheat bread], saiki [rolls], and so forth, especially famous Muscovite foods in the old days but now degenerated. Finally, there is strictly speaking no true Muscovite; the present-day inhabitants of Moscow are very likely indistinguishable from Petersburgers. Both have a more or less uniform, cosmopolitan appearance. This was not true . . . when Moscow was the centre of a still powerful Slavophilism, a deep patriotism, a turn of mind which was considered purely Russian, and, mostly, the centre of a feeling supposedly individual with much to give, which repudiated almost everything that was brought to us from the 'putrified West'.[3]

The distinctive qualities of Moscow made a mixed impression on Tchaikovsky. His friend Nikolai Kashkin recalled that Moscow at first did not please its future admirer:

True, he attached great significance to the monuments of Moscow's antiquity, appreciated the picturesque views of the Kremlin and other parts of the city, but its dirty, swampy pavements and the absence of comforts for people with very limited means troubled him, and in all his sympathies he belonged to Petersburg, which had long since exceeded Moscow in these elementary amenities.[4]

Similarly, Tchaikovsky must have been disappointed with the artistic life of his new home. It had, apart from that of the Bolshoy Theatre, no symphony orchestra of professional standards. In the year of his arrival only military bands and local dance orchestras, which provided accompaniment for the masquerade balls so popular at the time, could be added to the Bolshoy ensemble when Hector Berlioz conducted there. But Moscow had found a champion to fill its musical needs in Nikolai Rubinstein, Tchaikovsky's first employer. By the time the composer arrived, Rubinstein had created a Musical Society which had not only formed the basis of a new orchestra, but by its impromptu class instruction, begun in 1863, also laid the groundwork for establishing the conservatory which now provided him with a job.

Rubinstein's efforts also show the condition of the state-operated theatres in Moscow at the time. These included, besides a Russian drama company of considerable merit in the Maly, or Small, Theatre, three companies which shared the famous Bolshoy: one sang both native and foreign opera in Russian; another was a ballet company; and the third was an Italian opera company which functioned under a contract between the state and a private impresario. Of these, by far the most successful was the Italian opera, which managed here as in St Petersburg to charm the Russians with the wonders of its singers. The Russian opera, in contrast, was suffering a serious decline at that time, and the ballet enjoyed only a moderately satisfactory existence between these extremes. It was best attended during those parts of a season when the Italian opera was silent—the Christmas holidays and Butter Week—or when it could boast a new production or the visit of a foreign ballerina. But it suffered, as did the other state companies, from the neglect of the Director of Theatres in distant Petersburg, whose energy and financial blessings were bestowed on the city where the court resided, and who considered Moscow a provincial centre. Except for coronation performances, which were given in Moscow but were bolstered by Petersburg personnel and the money appropriate to such an occasion, the Moscow theatres faced continuous artistic and financial hardships until the beginning of the twentieth century and Telyakovsky's directorship.

Financial considerations forced the ballet to share sets and properties with the opera, despite the presence at the Bolshoy of Karl Valts, a master stage machinist. The same décor that served as the interior of a castle in a ballet would turn up again in *Lucia di Lammermoor* or *Un Ballo in maschera*, or *La Favorita*, and would continue to be pressed into service until it was crumpled and threadbare.[5] A similar austerity prevailed in the wardrobe, where occasional dishonesty made matters even worse. Cases were reported of spending state money on costumes subsequently declared unusable, which had in fact been sold, in prime condition, to private persons for use at masquerade balls.[6] When *Swan Lake* was first performed a critic found the costumes 'distinguished by extreme poverty—probably there were *economic considerations*'.[7]

But the difficulties faced by the Moscow company were only partly attributable to the lack of financial help. It lacked artistic leadership as well. Between the retirement of Adam Glushkovsky and Félicité Hullin-Sor in 1839 and the appointment of Alexander Gorsky at the end of the century, there was no resident balletmaster of distinction assigned to the Moscow ballet for long enough to improve standards, and for years at a time no permanently assigned balletmaster of any kind. The 1860s, however, showed promise of a change. Between 1861 and 1864 Carlo Blasis was balletmaster at the Bolshoy. He produced three ballets, several separate *pas*, and wrote a book, but although a higher level of execution among the dancers is sometimes attributed to him he was unable to revitalize the company. There was also much contact with St Petersburg. St-Léon's contract made him responsible for both the Moscow and Petersburg companies, as a consequence of which many of his works were produced in both cities, albeit in Moscow more by his deputies than by St-Léon himself. Many famous Petersburg dancers, continuing a long-standing practice, made guest appearances in the old capital. At the height of the St-Léon–Petipa rivalry, moreover, the Director of Theatres considered transferring the latter to Moscow permanently. While the Minister of the Imperial Court rejected this idea, Petipa was nevertheless dispatched to Moscow to mount several ballets—seven between 1868 and 1870.

At the time of Tchaikovsky's arrival, then, the Moscow ballet was on the threshold of acceptable quality. According to one observer, the first soloists approached the talent of a Grantzow or a Dor. Unlike the women, the male personnel distinguished themselves by fine acting. The *corps de ballet*, however, was undistinguished:

... it was an army, like the chorus in opera, little disciplined, that worked carelessly and negligently. In the movements of the dancers of the *corps de ballet* was not observed any lightness or grace whatever, they were not together at beginnings and endings, groups formed by them were not well made and were disorderly, and those who danced 'by the water', that is, at the back of the stage, in essence only waved their arms, swung themselves back and forth, and marked time in their places. When in the course of a dance they had to run, that is, to 'flutter about' the stage, or to make a unison jump, then such a loud and extended rumble and trampling broke out that one might fear that the floor of the stage could not support the weight of the sylphides in the *corps de ballet*. Moreover, many of them—and this was observable though to a lesser degree among the *coryphées* as well—had long since achieved a rather venerable age, so that looking at their ponderous figures and quite despondent, unprepossessing faces, one could not help thinking that there was hardly a place for them in the ballet, where everything ought to be beautiful, light, graceful, young, and merry.[8]

The faults of the *corps de ballet*, stringent economies, and a borrowed repertory are among the obvious disadvantages of the satellite relationship which distinguished the Moscow ballet from the parent company in St Petersburg. Together with Tchaikovsky's initial response to Moscow and the negative attitude toward ballet music which prevailed among his peers, one wonders why he undertook the composition of *Swan Lake* at all. To explain this we must return to the milieu of the city, and to its social and artistic circles.

The Muscovites, like all Russians, had long been attracted to clubs or societies whose members shared a common interest. Moscow was dotted with them: the German or 'Schuster' Club, known for its scandals, the English Club where in the 1850s the nobility had decided issues of civic import, or the tavern operated by the merchant Egorov, which with its sawdust floors, huge iconostases, and madeira served with a slice of apple was the scene of a thousand business transactions of the city's tradesmen.[9]

Theatre artists had a similar need for a common social forum, one which could extend its hospitality not just to themselves but also to the numerous provincial artists who came to Moscow. A group of important figures in the artistic world of the city, therefore, including the playwright Alexander Ostrovsky and the indefatigable Nikolai Rubinstein, formed a club for artists, the Artistic Circle, on 14 November 1865.

The Artistic Circle accepted as members all persons involved in some branch of the arts. The group met

for the performance and consideration of works by members of the Circle; for the reading of literary works; for the exchange of ideas about works in all branches of the arts, about their theory and practice; for the performance of musical works of classical composers of all periods; to provide all artists who have come to Moscow but are not yet well known an opportunity to get acquainted with members of the public.[10]

Its membership, which by 1867 had increased to some 700, maintained a library and a gaming room, and sponsored masquerades in winter.[11] Tchaikovsky had joined on his arrival in Moscow in 1866 but did not take an active part in the Circle's musical activities, preferring instead to make the acquaintance, during dinners and cards, of Moscow's artistic set. His friendship with Alexander Ostrovsky resulted in their collaboration on the opera *The Voevoda* and the play *The Snow Maiden*.

With its opportunities for Tchaikovsky to meet potential collaborators and to discuss projects, the Artistic Circle had an important counterpart in the soirées of Marya Vasilevna Shilovskaya. This talented woman ran a miniature artistic circle of her own, where almost every evening local celebrities would gather 'at the light' (burning in her front window). Tchaikovsky's antipathy towards Moscow must have been transformed into affection as he was integråted into the city's artistic life and learned of its prospects.

Ballet artists also congregated at both the Artistic Circle and the Shilovskaya salon. They, too, with the scant prospect of increased support from St Petersburg, discussed the possibility of bringing out new works created by themselves on the local stage. One such work, *The Fern* (based on the folk-tale popularized by Gogol in 'St John's Eve', from the collection *Evenings on a Farm Near Dikanka*), is directly attributable to discussions that took place during these social evenings; it is important to an understanding of *Swan Lake*. The libretto of *The Fern* was adapted by Madame Shilovskaya's son Konstantin, who would later assist Tchaikovsky in preparing the libretto of *Evgenii Onegin*. The score was the first of many composed by Yuly Gerber, a violinist and conductor of the Bolshoy ballet orchestra, and the choreography was the work of Sergei Petrovich Sokolov, a Bolshoy dancer who created ballets there during the company's leaderless periods in the 1860s. The ballet was first performed on 27 December 1867.

The Fern was also important for what its collaborators sought to achieve: a Russian ballet created by Russians. It is thought that the idea of the ballet was stimulated by the success St-Léon had had with *The Hunchbacked Horse*, produced in Moscow the year before, and by a desire to create a ballet based on Russian folklore more authentic than that of the Frenchman. A success would not only reinvigorate the company, but might also win over the sympathy of Muscovites who perceived any ballet as a corrupt Western diversion.

The Fern, however, enjoyed only partial success, with contradictory reviews. This was not the fault of the well-intentioned collaborators so much as of the disparity between intention and realization. The legend at the basis of the story was simple enough: once a year at twelve o'clock on Midsummer's Night a magic fern blossoms in the wilderness; whoever lies in wait for the flower and finds it is led to a magnificent treasure. By the time a ballet libretto had been adapted from this the story line had become unintelligible and the action confused by cumbersome balletic conventions. The hero, Stepan, who sought the treasure in the first place so that he might be a fitting match for Nadya, ends up pledging his love to the genie of the fern, who in turn must die so that Stepan, almost as an afterthought, can return to Nadya at the end of the ballet. The *kamarinskaya*, or wedding dance, of the opening scene was certainly authentically Russian, and had to be repeated by public demand. From here, however, as the story wandered into the realms of genies and naiads, it was paralleled by un-Russian choreographic digressions in the form of dances of flowers and metals. A reviewer for *The Russian Gazette* summarized the case against *The Fern*:

If I possessed the enviable talent of Mr Yakovlev, or the magic pen of Mr Panovsky, then, of course, I would not fail to reveal my aesthetic–balletic knowledge in a magnificent article, in which I would prove that the new ballet is better than all past, existing, or future ballets, though on the other hand it isn't; that the music of the ballet is wholly national, although there is very little that is Russian in it; that the production was luxurious, although it was meagre; that Mlle so-and-so danced beautifully but not excellently, but that Mlle so-and-so danced excellently but not beautifully. But with characteristic modesty I put down my pen, leaving it to our double-talking theatre-goers to give their opinion of the ethereal lightness of our ballerinas, and the firmness of the *pointes* on which they create their inexpressive movements.[12]

In all probability *The Fern* failed because its creators were simply too inexperienced in the production of a ballet to overcome all the problems, technical and artistic, that stood in the way of success. But the work is significant in the history of the Moscow ballet regardless of its reception. It was a local production, not a borrowing from the Petersburg repertory, and while it does not itself shed any direct light on the origins of *Swan Lake*, most ballet historians believe the idea of producing *Swan Lake* originated either at the Artistic Circle or the Shilovskaya salon. Many artists who collaborated or performed in *Swan Lake* were known to have attended these gatherings: besides Tchaikovsky himself, who was music tutor to Shilovskaya's sons, these included Sergei Sokolov, Karl Valts and Yuly Gerber. Also, the Shilovskaya salon gave its habitués access to a ranking theatre official, Vladimir Petrovich Begichev, Marya Shilovskaya's husband, who as intendant determined the repertory of the Moscow imperial theatres. In 1875 he would commission the music of *Swan Lake* from his stepsons' music tutor.

While it is likely that the artists' haunts of Moscow played an important part in the creation of *Swan Lake*, they were only one factor. Another is the balletmaster who created dances for the first production. Unlike Sergei Sokolov, Julius Reisinger was not a local product; nor did he, from all appearances, sympathize with the nationalistic sentiments shared by the collaborators on *The Fern*. In fact, his participation in the creation of *Swan Lake*, his only claim to remembrance, appears in retrospect to have been almost accidental.

We first hear of Reisinger in about 1870 in connection with a ballet libretto that the machinist Karl Valts wrote and offered to the Moscow directorate. In his memoirs Valts gives no details about the formative stages of *Cinderella*, but states simply that he presented the idea to the directorate, that it was accepted, and that he commissioned the music from a composer named Mühldorfer in Leipzig. But from a letter Tchaikovsky wrote to his brother Modeste on 5 October 1870, we learn that *Cinderella* may have been his own first serious attempt at composing a ballet: 'Among other things, think that I took it upon myself to write music for the ballet *Cinderella* and that the huge four-act score must be ready in mid-December!'[13]

Other than this, and a reference to having already written part of the music made by Tchaikovsky in a letter to another brother,[14] we do not know the circumstances of his involvement with the work, or why he discontinued work on it. But *Cinderella* is nevertheless important, because it brought Reisinger to Moscow. Valts himself may have been taking credit for this development when he wrote, 'My proposal was accepted, and from Austria the balletmaster Reisinger was sent for.'[15] He goes on to describe the friendship that grew up between himself and the new choreographer, and how they would go out to a tavern near the Bolshoy for a beer between acts on ballet evenings. Why Reisinger was chosen, if not for Valts's advocacy, remains a mystery.

From an advance notice of *Cinderella* we learn something of Reisinger's work:

His chief concern is with ensembles and groups, which, it is said, will represent the acme of art. Especially significant are: in the first act, the *pas de cinq* and the large groups with shawls; in the second, the dances of the beetles and glow-worms; in the third the grand masquerade ball at the palace, in which some 200 people will be participating, and which includes the march of the fantastic and comic masks, various national dances, and an extremely original polka with little bells. The jewels on the heads of the little dancers will be decorated with bells which produce the musical scale, and one of those dancing will strike out a motive on them, which at the same time will be played in the orchestra. Then there will be a huge final galop. In the fourth act, which takes place in the fantastic world, various spirits and demons dance; in the fifth the dance of the flowers is especially effective . . .[16]

Valts claimed that *Cinderella* was successful because of his transformation scenes and special effects; a critic praised the dances but concluded that the ballet, as a whole, was not well received.[17]

After the first performances of *Cinderella* Reisinger went to Leipzig. On 1 March 1872 he sent a letter to the chief of the Moscow branch of the imperial theatres setting forth his conditions for accepting a permanent contract. These were refused. Reisinger's connection with the Moscow ballet might have been limited to guest appearances had he not been on hand in 1873 when the Minister of Court, A. V. Adlerberg, unhappy with the way the Moscow theatres were being run and particularly with the condition of the *corps de ballet*, reprimanded the Moscow theatre officials and demanded an explanation. They cited the lack of a permanent ballet-master as the main cause of the company's poor technical standards, whereupon Adlerberg, on 6 October 1873, engaged Reisinger as the Moscow balletmaster, despite his earlier rejection by theatre officials there.[18]

However expedient as an administrative measure, Reisinger's appointment appears to have been an artistic failure. His work met with a consistently hostile press. One reviewer dismissed his *Kashchei* (1873) with a single sentence: 'I made the mistake of going to see it, and it would be better not to talk about it in public.'[19] Another critic wrote, 'I have never yet had the occasion to see a choreographic novelty of such tediousness and loathsomeness on the Moscow stage.'[20] With *Stella* (1875) the scorn continued: 'The balletmaster Reisinger (I, however, seriously doubt whether he should be called "balletmaster") publicly and categorically proved his complete inability to produce ballets last year; his attempt to replace dances with featureless processions [in *Stella*] was not successful.'[21] A few months after *Stella* Reisinger began work on *Swan Lake*.

(b) The Libretto

We know the libretto of *Swan Lake* was finished before 19 October 1876, because it was published in a Moscow newspaper on that date. But we do not know who wrote it, and can only speculate with regard to its origins. It is widely accepted that the libretto originated with members of the Artistic Circle and the Shilovskaya salon. Nikolai Kashkin, writing some twenty years after the composition of *Swan Lake*, was sure that Vladimir Begichev initiated the project, less so that he actually wrote the libretto:

V. P. Begichev, former artistic manager of the Moscow Bolshoy Theatre, proposed that he [Tchaikovsky] write the ballet; Peter Ilyich gladly agreed, but at the same time insisted on a fantastic subject from knightly times. V. P. Begichev, if I am not mistaken, himself wrote the programme of the ballet *Swan Lake*. The composer approved it, and agreed to 800 roubles to write music for this subject.[22]

In his biography of Peter Ilyich, Modeste Tchaikovsky lists 'V. Begichev and Geltser' as librettists of *Swan Lake*.[23] From a letter of 9 September 1894 written by Modeste to the critic Herman Laroche we can learn something of his reason for this choice: 'According to Jurgenson's [Tchaikovsky's publisher] story, Begichev composed the libretto of *Swan Lake*, but on a copy in the possession of the theatre directorate there is a handwritten inscription: "property [*sobstvennost'*] of Geltser." Probably he copied it out, in much the same way that I copied out the subject of *Nutcracker* from the words of Vsevolozhsky . . . Judging from the stupidity of the subject and the characters' names, it is the work of one of these two.'[24] Modeste thus credits the Moscow dancer Vasily Geltser with partial authorship while conceding elsewhere that he may have been no more than a copyist. Modeste's authority has been accepted to this day despite the fact that his contention is not borne out by the evidence of anyone else.

According to the libretto, the curtain rises on Act I of *Swan Lake* to reveal Prince Siegfried celebrating his coming of age. Peasants come to congratulate him; Wolfgang, his tutor, makes advances to the peasant girls. Siegfried's mother unexpectedly arrives, and tells him that he must choose a bride the next day at a ball to be held for that purpose. Siegfried agrees, reluctantly, his mother departs, and the party starts up afresh. But night is falling; a last dance is performed; a flock of swans passes overhead, and the prince with his friend Benno leaves in pursuit of them.

Act II is set in a forest with some ruins by a lake. Siegfried and Benno have strayed far, and have no sooner decided to spend the night than they see the swans they are hunting for disappear behind the ruins. As this happens the ruins are illuminated by a magical light, which the two investigate. As they approach, Odette comes down the staircase.

She explains to the astonished hunters who she is—the unwanted stepdaughter of an evil sorceress who is trying to kill her. She is protected by her crown, which was given to her by her grandfather. If she marries, her stepmother's evil intentions will be thwarted. Siegfried, enamoured, proposes, but Odette reminds him of the ball planned for the next day and its purpose. Siegfried swears his love despite this. Dawn comes; Odette and her friends disappear into the ruins.

Act III takes place at the ball. Guests arrive and dance. Then more guests, individually announced by the herald, each group with a daughter who dances for Siegfried. After several such entrances the princess asks her son to make a choice but he cannot. Vexed, she calls Wolfgang to talk some sense into him when the fanfares sound anew: Rothbart and Odile have arrived. Siegfried is struck by Odile; he asks Benno to affirm her likeness to Odette, but his friend sees none. Infatuated, Siegfried proposes. The stage darkens, Rothbart is revealed as a demon, Odette appears in a window. Horrified, the prince runs out.

Act IV, once again by the lake, finds the swan maidens waiting for Odette, their queen. She arrives, tousled and grief-stricken. Against their advice, she lingers to spend one last moment with Siegfried, who rushes in. A storm breaks. Finding her powerless to forgive him, Siegfried, in frustration and despair, takes the crown from her head and throws it into the stormy lake. Odette dies, and both lovers are engulfed by the waters of the overflowing lake.

Because no one has ever identified with certainty the librettist of *Swan Lake*, the genesis of the story itself is another question about the first production for which there is no satisfactory answer. There are several theories, the simplest of which is that the story was put together from balletic conventions and thus, strictly speaking, had no author. Many writers have pointed out that the legends of several countries share ideas with the *Swan Lake* libretto;[25] it required neither prototype nor original conception. Germany was a common setting for nineteenth-century ballets. Siegfried, a noble prince tricked into betraying his lover, has a famous precedent in Albrecht in *Giselle* (a work that Kashkin claims was Tchaikovsky's ideal at the time of writing *Swan Lake*)[26] and the ball held so that a young man may choose a wife has a parallel in Taglioni's *La Fille du Danube*. The swan maidens can be seen as variants of wilis and sylphides, stock characters in romantic ballet. The story also has points of similarity with Auber's opera *Le Lac des fées*.

Possible as it may be to explain the libretto as an elaboration of themes taken from folklore and balletic traditions, closer scrutiny shows that other sources might have been involved. The first of three hypotheses is the work of the Soviet historian Yury Slonimsky. In his last work on *Swan Lake* we read:

Musäus's tale 'The Swans' Pond' [*Lebedinyi prud*] enriched the authors of the ballet somewhat more, the text of which contains the words 'lake of swans'. On a lakeside in the foothills of the Sudetes lives the old hermit Benno. In his youth the future knight fell in love with Princess Zoe—kinswoman of the evil ruler of an island. Exiled from the island, he found refuge by the lake. Here, in the form of a swan, comes his beloved to bathe in the lake, for it is a source of eternal youth. Benno's attempt to keep the young girl ends in failure. Many years later the knight Fridbert repeats this attempt, having heard old Benno's story (this time Zoe's daughter, the young Princess Callisto, flies to the lake). He steals the beautiful girl's swans' wings, takes from her any possibility of escape, and declares his love. The girl agrees to marriage but on the wedding day seizes her wings and disappears. The knight searches for Callisto, at last finding her on an island in the Aegean Sea, and they celebrate a luxurious wedding.[27]

There can be little doubt that Johann Karl August Musäus's 'Der geraubte Schleier' (not, as Slonimsky gives the title, 'The Swans' Pond') from the collection Die Volksmärchen der Deutschen, was at least partly used in Swan Lake. The description of the swan maidens, for example, who are transformed at night, and the idea of swans wearing crowns are close to the images of the libretto, as we read in this anonymous eighteenth-century translation:

This pool is most frequently visited by Zoe, for it is nearest home. You will not find any difficulty in distinguishing the magic from the common swans, by a crown of feathers on the top of the head. If you stand on the watch in the early hour of the morning, before the rays of the rising sun strike the surface of the water, or in the evening, when in descending to rest, its retiring light reddens the western sky, observe carefully whether any swans arrive. If you see them alight on the water or among the reeds, you will immediately perceive nymphs bathing instead of swans, and your eye will at once discover whether your mistress be there . . .[28]

Surely it was but a short step from this to a swan queen who, alone of her sisters, wears a crown. And one can also construe in the libretto's references to a magic glow at the moment of transformation and to the rose-coloured sunrise a reflection of Musäus's light that 'reddens the western sky'.

But this, it would seem, is where the likenesses end. The episode cited above accounts for barely a tenth of the story. In Musäus Benno admits to Fridbert that his monastic trappings are a sham, and that his goal of being reunited with Zoe is fired by passions of the flesh. Fridbert, for his part, enters the story a fugitive from the army who barely escapes death from hiding in a baker's oven at the wrong time. And even if his motives with Callisto are honourable in the end, he consistently achieves his aims through deceit and cunning. The only connection between these characters and Siegfried of Swan Lake would be the undesirable traits they have in common—all are somewhat self-centred and less than honourable. Here, however, Siegfried has precedents just as persuasive in James of La Sylphide and Albrecht of Giselle.

A second, more speculative hypothesis links Swan Lake through its composer to the works of Richard Wagner. The connections between Tchaikovsky and the German master have seldom been shown, for neither writers of the imperial period nor their Soviet counterparts encourage such a view. However, we know, for example, that Tchaikovsky was impressed by Wagner's conducting when the German toured Russia in 1863.[29] Between 1868 and 1876, moreover, Tchaikovsky reviewed concerts of

Wagner's music on various occasions, for the most part favourably; his career as critic ended with a report on the first Bayreuth Festival. There can be no doubt that he, like any other literate musician of the time, was familiar with Wagner's music.

More difficult to establish are his attitudes toward it, and what reason there might be to suspect the influence of Wagner on *Swan Lake*. In general Tchaikovsky seems to have favoured what he heard of *Tannhäuser* and especially *Lohengrin*. Throughout his life the Russian seemed always to admire the latter work. He referred to it as 'the crown of Wagner's creations' (1879), 'an excellent opera, written by a first-class master' (1884), and 'some of the most beautiful pages in contemporary music' (1891).[30] In contrast the music dramas, apart from certain concert excerpts (Tchaikovsky liked, for example, the 'Ride of the Valkyries'), made an indifferent and even a negative impression on him. During the time he wrote *Swan Lake* Tchaikovsky's presence was considered obligatory at soirées in the home of Karl Klindworth, who played *Der Ring des Nibelungen* for musicians scheduled to attend the first Bayreuth Festival, and in correspondence of the time he refers to Klindworth derisively as 'Wotan'. When the Russian arrived in the Bavarian town the air of pilgrimage there disgusted him, and he reported more on social than musical matters. The only work about which he mentioned details is *Das Rheingold*, and this was in a letter to his brother. Fascinated by the production devices, he found the music 'improbable nonsense through which, from time to time, flash striking details of unusual beauty.'[31]

Tchaikovsky's dissatisfaction with Wagner's tetralogy, we learn from Kashkin, was 'not so much with the music as with the general character of the subject and its bombast.'[32] He goes on to relate how Tchaikovsky admired Wagner's audacity in writing the introduction of *Das Rheingold* as the elaboration of a simple triad, a device Tchaikovsky himself had contemplated in *The Tempest* but discarded, fearing it would be too monotonous. In another passage Kashkin links the tone poem *Francesca da Rimini*, written at about the same time as *Swan Lake*, directly to *Der Ring*. *Francesca*, Kashkin claims, was salvaged from an opera project the composer had almost undertaken with a Wagnerian librettist.[33] When critics sensed a stylistic affinity between *Francesca* and *Der Ring* Tchaikovsky responded:

The remark that I wrote *Francesca* under the influence of the *Nibelungen* is very true. I myself felt it during the time I worked on the piece. If I'm not mistaken, it is especially noticeable in the introduction. Isn't it strange that I submitted to the influence of a work toward which I am in general wholly antipathetic?'[34]

All of these events—the trip to Bayreuth and its preparations, the ill-fated opera collaboration, and the composition of *Francesca*—took place between the beginning of the composition and the first performance of

Swan Lake. In particular, Tchaikovsky's acquaintance with *Der Ring* can be established at least five months before the ballet was finished, and eleven before the libretto was first published.

In the light of this, let us return to the libretto. If someone retained the name 'Benno' from the Musäus fairy-tale, then someone changed the name 'Fridbert' to 'Siegfried'. The hero's unwitting betrayal of his lover through a magic trick does not occur in Musäus, but it is common to the Siegfrieds of *Swan Lake* and *Der Ring.* Another striking feature of the libretto, its medieval German setting, provoked criticism from the editor of the newspaper in which the libretto was first published. In particular, the nobles who appeared at the ball bore names that seemed pretentious to certain Russian critics of the time—the Barons von Stein and von Roth-bart, Benno vom Sommerstein, Freiger von Schwartzfels—names recalling the Landgraf's retinue in *Tannhäuser.* We may add to these points more substantial parallels with *Lohengrin,* such as the use of the swan as a symbol of purity and innocence, the presence in both works of an evil sorceress (Ortrud and Odette's stepmother) who transforms humans into swans, and a ritual in which heralds' trumpets call forth supernatural events. It comes as no surprise that Petersburg critics remarked on the similarity between the swan theme and Lohengrin's warning to Elsa.[35] Elsa, Odette, and the Siegfrieds of both Tchaikovsky and Wagner also share a common fate: death as the result of an inadvertent betrayal.

There may, therefore, be a Wagnerian influence in the *Swan Lake* libretto, and if so, it seems probable that it came from Tchaikovsky. Modeste's condescending remark that Begichev and Geltser wrote the libretto, 'judging from the stupidity of the subject and the characters' names', may then have been ironical.

A third possibility also links the libretto to Tchaikovsky, but from a completely different angle: that *Swan Lake* is the variant of a story used by him in several earlier compositions. Gerald Abraham notes that between 1869 and 1873 Tchaikovsky had written three large theatre works in which the love of a non-mortal woman for a mortal man ended in tragedy: the opera *Undine* (1869), the opera *Mandragora* (1869–70), and *The Snow Maiden* (1873), Ostrovsky's play to which he contributed incidental music.[36] Tchaikovsky destroyed *Undine* and abandoned *Mandragora.* It is possible that he perceived in *Swan Lake* a vehicle more satisfactory than the others to present this kind of love story, which he seemed to find so attractive. We know, moreover, that the love duet in Act II of the ballet was based on discarded music from *Undine;* it is possible that Tchaikovsky began work on *Swan Lake* before destroying the opera. In a letter to Nadezhda von Meck of April 1878 he referred to burning the opera score 'about three years ago'.[37]

That a ballet on the subject of *Swan Lake* may have occurred to the composer before he began work on the earliest of these three pieces is suggested by two of Tchaikovsky's relatives, who referred to an impromptu house ballet called 'The Lake of Swans' [Ozero lebedei]. His nephew Yury Lvovich Davydov wrote:

A celebrated event was the production by Peter Ilyich of a ballet, in which my older sisters and Uncle Modeste participated. The ballet was created by Peter Ilyich, as was also the music, on the theme 'The Lake of Swans'. Of course, this was not the ballet which is given on stages now, but a children's one-act short ballet, although the principal theme—'The Song of the Swans'—was then the same as now. Peter Ilyich in his later, large composition used the theme of the children's ballet of 1871.[38]

Davydov, having been born only in 1876, had this account from his elders, but a niece of the composer, Anna Meck-Davydov, who would have been seven years old in 1871, twice confirmed the existence of this work, although she assigned it to 1867:

He [Tchaikovsky] very much loved to produce all manner of house performances. The first production, barely in my memory, was 'Swan Lake'. My sister participated; she was six. My Uncle Modeste Ilyich performed the role of the prince. I represented Cupid . . . The magnificent wooden swans on which we rocked were in the house for a long time.[39]

In the second account she again refers to the large toy swans, but with neither date nor mention of the music.[40]

Whatever its origins, the libretto of Swan Lake, as a piece of stagecraft, shows a controlling hand—in the interest of the story, in the evocation of atmosphere, and in the use of time. The last involves more than observing the unity of time, of restricting the action of the narrative to about twenty-four hours; it is a perception of the entire theatre work, from the first curtain to the last, as a continuous whole. Even the intervals in Swan Lake account for the periods elapsed between the acts at the same rate of stage time as the action of the acts themselves.

These niceties, which lend themselves to enhancement by music, point yet again to the composer's participation in the preparation of the libretto. Perhaps having his say in the libretto made Tchaikovsky ready to try his hand at composition, and prompted Kashkin to recall:

For a long time he had wanted to write a ballet, and the dances of his operas proved that he had not only an inclination toward this kind of music but a capacity for it. He waited only for an opportunity to prove his strengths in ballet music, and [Swan Lake] finally put this opportunity before him.[41]

(c) Composition and Collaboration

The composer's enthusiasm for Swan Lake is reflected in the speed with which he worked. Modeste claimed that his brother received the commission for the ballet in 1875 before leaving Moscow for the summer; on 14

August Tchaikovsky wrote to Sergei Taneyev acknowledging the commission and telling him he was already at work on the music.[42] Then, some three weeks later, he wrote to Rimsky-Korsakov telling him how he had spent his summer:

I worked very assiduously and, besides the symphony [No. 3], I wrote (in draft) two acts of a *ballet*. At the invitation of the Moscow directorate I am writing music for the ballet *The Lake of Swans*. I took on this work partly for the money, which I need, and partly because I have long wanted to try my hand at this kind of music.[43]

The last phrase, together with the underscoring of the word 'ballet', suggests the composer's sensitivity to his peer's response to the news. From a note in the holograph we know that he had finished the first three numbers of the ballet in full score by 13 October, though in correspondence he first refers to working on the orchestration only on 11 December. On 17 March 1876 he is still 'up to his neck' in the instrumentation, and after the last note of the holograph comes: 'The end!!! *Glebovo* 10 April 1876'. The entire composition thus required, whatever his other obligations, about a year.

The holograph score contains corrections of detail but nothing to shed light on the initial or intermediate stages of composition. Sketches must have existed once, judging from Tchaikovsky's mention of a draft, but they are not known to have survived.

The working relationship between Tchaikovsky and Reisinger on *Swan Lake* and the extent to which a collaboration existed at all during the time Tchaikovsky actually composed the music are not clear. Kashkin is the only contemporary who attests any collaboration: 'Of course, long consultations with the balletmaster of the Bolshoy Theatre, with whose help was worked out the programme of the dances and the entire scenario of the ballet, preceded the composition of the music.'[44]

Tchaikovsky certainly worked from a scenario, for he quoted from it in the holograph. Indeed, the scenario may have been a balletmaster's plan, the only remnants of which survive in these quotations. If, as Modeste suggested, Tchaikovsky started to compose early in 1875, the scenario must have been ready some eighteen months before the libretto was published.

But Tchaikovsky's remarks in the holograph are rarely in precise agreement with the libretto as later published. Perhaps he paraphrased the libretto, but the weight of the evidence suggests that his scenario was a different document, in some ways more informative than the libretto. Many of his comments, designed to indicate correspondence of music and stage action, are variants of the libretto without substantial differences in meaning. Others are designations of dances and their participants which a balletmaster's plan would normally contain. Tchaikovsky had to know from some source where to write a *pas de deux* or a *pas de trois*, but he also marked in the score subdivisions such as 'intrada' and 'coda'. We know only from this source that the second of the Dances of the Swans was a solo for Odette, and that the mazurka was written for soloists and the *corps de ballet*, though the programme of the first performance would list only soloists for this dance. Some rubrics in the holograph, finally, preserve details of action not retained in the published libretto. In the first act, for example, the drunken Wolfgang's flirtation with a village girl ends in a dizzying spin and fall (preserved in some modern productions), where in the libretto he ends up kissing his favourite's boyfriend. In the last act the swan maidens are teaching the cygnets to dance according to the holograph, but forcing them to dance (while waiting for Odette) according to the libretto. (Tchaikovsky's remarks are given, together with the translation of the libretto, in Appendix A.)

The balletmaster's plan—if such it was—thus outlined the story and the basic requirements for the dances. Tchaikovsky seems to have been content with this degree of specification. Perhaps he had no alternatives. Alina Bryullova recalled:

When Peter Ilyich wrote his first ballet, *Swan Lake*, he took on the task quite ignorant of the technique of balletic writing, in which the composer is entirely at the mercy of the balletmaster. The latter fixes the number of bars in each *pas*, the rhythm, the tempo, everything is strictly assigned in advance, 'and I, having leapt before I looked, began to write, like an opera, a symphony, and it came out such that not one *danseur* or *danseuse* could dance to my music, all the numbers were too long, no one could last them out. For example, one had to stand on *pointe* where I had a whole measure of *andante*'.[45]

Karl Valts confirmed Bryullova's recollection that Tchaikovsky worked without detailed knowledge of Reisinger's requirements:

Ordinarily balletmasters themselves make explicit demands of the composer as to the melodies they require. P. I. Tchaikovsky, before writing this ballet, for a long time sought someone to whom to turn for exact information about the requirements for dance music. He even asked me what he should do with dances, how long they should be, what tempo, etc. I, of course, a person little versed in this, could give him practically no advice.[46]

If nothing else, Tchaikovsky studied the work of specialists. 'He took ballet scores out of the theatre library and began to study this kind of composition in detail', Kashkin wrote; 'in general its methods were familiar to him from visiting the ballet.'[47]

On 23 March 1876 rehearsals of Act I began. Tchaikovsky wrote to Modeste the next day:

Yesterday, in the hall of the theatre school, the first rehearsal of several numbers from Act I took place. If you only knew how comical it was to see the balletmaster, who with a most serious, profound look composed dances to the sound of a violin. Besides that one could also look at the dancers, who cast smiles at the public and who took pleasure in the ready opportunity to jump and turn while carrying out their sacred duty. Everyone in the theatre was delighted with my music.[48]

For the next eleven months Reisinger choreographed *Swan Lake*. Kashkin recalled that 'during the production of the ballet on stage, some numbers were set aside as unsuitable for dancing, or were replaced by numbers from other ballets. Besides this, the balletmaster insisted on the need for a Russian Dance, the presence of which was not motivated. But the composer conceded, and the dance was written; as the piano arrangement was already printed, this number did not appear in it.'[49]

What did Reisinger do to the score, and how much did he consult with Tchaikovsky before changing it? We know that the composer spent much time in Moscow between March and the end of May, 1876, and also much of the following autumn and winter.[50] He was thus available for consultation, but no document makes reference to contact with Reisinger. The performance score and répétiteur have been lost, leaving only a poster of the first performance (translated in Appendix B) and press accounts from which to make a judgement.

Many entries on the poster have no counterpart in Tchaikovsky's holograph score. Some historians have taken this disparity between sources, and the absence of any reference on the poster to many numbers that the composer wrote, as evidence that Reisinger's performance version of *Swan Lake* involved extensive cutting of Tchaikovsky's original. Perhaps it did, but to conclude this without further consideration would be premature. It is virtually certain, for example, that the poster did not account for all the music that was played, especially the non-danced numbers. Moreover, Reisinger may have made use of the music choreographically in a way that necessitated changing the titles of separate numbers—one cannot distinguish a *pas de sept* from a *pas de six* on purely musical grounds. Because the poster refers exclusively to large units of the score, the extent of Reisinger's internal modifications of any number can only be guessed.

In the following lists, question marks indicate where poster and holograph do not agree:

Act I

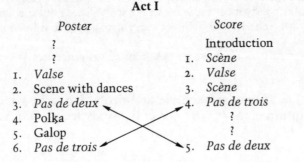

	Poster		Score
	?		Introduction
	?	1.	*Scène*
1.	*Valse*	2.	*Valse*
2.	Scene with dances	3.	*Scène*
3.	*Pas de deux*	4.	*Pas de trois*
4.	Polka		?
5.	Galop		?
6.	*Pas de trois*	5.	*Pas de deux*

Poster	Score
?	6. *Pas d'action*
?	7. *Sujet* [introduction to the *Danse des coupes*]
7. Finale	8. *Danse des coupes*
?	9. Finale

There is no reason to suspect that Reisinger omitted the introduction or the opening scene, or to doubt that the *valse* and scene with dances listed first on the poster corresponded with Tchaikovsky's Nos. 2 and 3. Even the reversal of the *pas de trois* and *pas de deux*, assuming that poster and score are referring to the same music, respresents a less striking modification than the decision of the Petersburg redactors later to transfer the *pas de deux* to the ballroom act and leave nothing in its place. The suspicious polka and galop, titles which have no counterpart in Tchaikovsky, need not necessarily connote interpolations; from a musical standpoint, two subdivisions of Tchaikovsky's No. 5, namely the *allegro* part of 5/11 and the coda, could have served Reisinger as accompaniment to the dances so named. Lastly, even though it is called a finale on the poster, the list of participants (two soloists, *coryphées*, and the *corps de ballet*) suggests a final dance rather than the finale with which Tchaikovsky ended the act. It was probably the *Danse des coupes*.

All the major numbers of the first act may thus be accounted for, leaving only the flirtation between Wolfgang and the peasant girl (No. 6 in the score), and the closing scene in which Siegfried notices the flock of swans. In both cases confirmation comes from the Press. One critic quoted the flirtation episode from the libretto when attempting to demonstrate that the story was 'of quite little sense and very much nonsense'.[51] And we have several references to the closing number in reviews. One writer referred to the swans as a 'moving white streak in the skies'. Another treated the scene as a spoof:

'Look more closely, Prince [says Benno], under the ceiling swans are flying! Wouldn't it be great to go after them?'

'No, indeed no!' intervenes the tipsy tutor, 'in the first place, these are not so much swans as poorly made pieces of wood, which I did not expect from Mr Valts, and second, Mr Tchaikovsky will get angry if you interrupt his music with your shooting!'

'Not true', whispers a lackey, 'it doesn't make any difference. It's time for the act to end!'[52]

Possibly because of the complexity of the narrative, which called for much pantomime, the theatre poster lists only four entries for Act II:

Poster	Score
?	10. *Scène*
?	11. *Scène* [entrance of the Prince, Odette; Odette's narrative]
1. Entrance of the swans	12. *Scène* [entrance of the swans]
	13. *Danses des cygnes*
	I.
?	II. [Solo for Odette]
	III. [Dances of the swans]
2. *Pas de trois* [Benno, two swan maidens]	IV.
?	
3. *Pas de deux* [Odette and Siegfried]	V. *Pas d'action* [Odette and the Prince]
	VI. *Danse générale*
?	VII. Coda
4. Finale	
?	14. *Scène* [Odette and the swans disappear in the ruins]

Because of its importance to the story, the non-danced music at either end of the act (Nos. 10–11, 15) was no doubt retained; reviewers made reference to the final number. As before, 'finale' on the poster here probably refers to a dance, most likely the Coda of the *Danses des cygnes*. Yet there is no hint on the poster of Tchaikovsky's waltz, twice repeated in the score (13/I, III, VI), which we would have to assume was not used were it not for a reviewer who included it in a list of favourite numbers: 'The expectations of the Muscovites were not undeserved. Mr Tchaikovsky's music contains some beautiful parts: the solo for violin and violoncello (*pas d'action*), *dances of the swans (waltz)* [my italics], Hungarian Dance and the concluding scene in the last act . . .'[53]

Either of the two *Danses des cygnes* still unaccounted for (No. 13/II, IV), may have served Reisinger as music for the *pas de trois* of Benno and the two swan maidens.

The five national dances, including the added Russian Dance, take up the bulk of Act III. Around them came:

Poster	Score
?	15. [Introduction]
1. Dance of the gentry and pages	16. *Danses du corps de ballet et des nains*
?	17. *Scène* (*Entrée des invités et la valse*)
?	18. *Scène* [Princess asks Siegfried to choose a bride]
2. *Pas de six*	19. *Pas de six*
3. *Pas de cinq*	?
[national dances, Nos. 20–3]	
?	24. *Scène* [finale]

Assuming that the curtain raiser (No. 15) was retained, the first entry on the poster would appear to correspond with Tchaikovsky's *Danses du corps de ballet et des nains*. It is unfortunate that the poster omits a list of participants in this dance, for knowing this would confirm or dispute the impression left on one critic: 'Instead of a crowded lively hall, as the ball of a noble princess should be, we see a broad and almost empty hall. The invited grandees presented a choice to the prince of only four girls.'[54]

The poster makes no reference to Tchaikovsky's No. 17, the Waltz of the Prospective Fiancées, which, like the Waltz of the Swans in the preceding act, is often repeated in the holograph. Our critic, however, offers a slender strand of evidence which links the music performed with the music composed. Judging from markings in the holograph, a new prospective fiancée arrived with every announcement of the herald's trumpets. On each occasion the Master of Ceremonies met the guests, who bowed to the princess and whose daughter began to dance the waltz with one of the cavaliers present. After the first three, this progression was interrupted by a complete statement of the waltz performed by the entire *corps de ballet*. Rothbart and Odile then arrived to the fourth *entrée*. Since there are four arrivals in the account of our observer, Reisinger may have arranged the scene in accordance with the music.

The *pas de six* next listed most probably corresponds to that in the score, which follows the grand waltz after a short mimed scene, itself necessary to move the action forward. One dance in Act III, described by a reviewer simply as a 'solo for oboe', was repeated by public demand; it may have been No. 19/[V], or, more likely, 19/[II]. The mere presence of a harp cadenza before the fifth variation, if tradition counts for anything, hints at this being a dance for the ballerina.

Perhaps the most baffling question raised by the poster is that of the *pas de cinq*, for which there is no counterpart, nominal or otherwise, in Tchaikovsky's score. It could have been assembled from variations unused elsewhere in *Swan Lake*, or introduced from an outside source.

Several reviewers testify to the spectacular transformation of Rothbart from man to demon and Odette's appearance in the closing scene:

All are satisfied by this and agree on the marriage of Siegfried and Odile, but Mr Valts spoils the whole affair (and spoils it very effectively, to tell the truth): the stage darkens, Odile's father appears as an evil red demon, and in the window is shown a white swan with a crown on her head. General confusion.[55]

Disagreement among the press accounts obscures our knowledge of precisely what happened in this scene. In another review we read nothing about a window: 'Mr von Rothbart changed clothes into a demon, the back of the hall was gradually concealed by a cloud with a swan in the middle of it.'[56]

The writer's intentionally prosaic reference to Rothbart's transformation as a change of clothes was an attempt at humour: did he mean that the villain threw off his cloak? Yet another account was couched in religious or mystical language: . . . 'The ballroom rose into the sky . . . in the clouds a huge swan appeared . . .'[57] The most we can learn from such evidence are hints of what actually took place.

The poster offers a single entry for Act IV :

Poster		Score
?	25.	*Entr'acte*
?	26.	*Scène* [Swan maidens await Odette]
1. *Pas d'ensemble*	27.	*Danses des petits cygnes*
?	28.	*Scène* [Odette's arrival; storm]
?	29.	*Scène* finale

Surely the *pas d'ensemble* corresponds to the only danced number in this act, the *Danses des petits cygnes*. But here as in the preceding acts the libretto describes much non-danced action that required music, and the question remains of what, if anything, Reisinger omitted from the score. Certainly not the storm and the final scene, for which a considerable amount of music was needed to accompany Karl Valts's miracles of stagecraft (see below, pp. 56–7).

If we give Reisinger the benefit of the doubt, it is possible to conclude that his performance redaction of *Swan Lake* was limited to cuts and the repositioning of parts of Tchaikovsky's score. There is little evidence for interpolation of another's music—neither in the titles on the poster, nor in remarks of critics of the first performance (who could be expected to mention a familiar dance from another ballet), nor, perhaps most persuasively, in Tchaikovsky's own response to the prospect of including somebody else's music in his ballet.

As regards collaboration, then, it seems that the two men decided on a scenario and the type and placement of dances, then went their separate ways, Tchaikovsky to prepare the score that Reisinger set only after it was finished. This would explain the disparities between the libretto and Tchaikovsky's remarks in the score, as well as those between the poster and the holograph. It would also explain Tchaikovsky's offhand description of the rehearsal—that of a spectator, not a collaborator—at which he watched Reisinger setting the dances. From an obscure manuscript account we learn, moreover, that Tchaikovsky did not prepare a répétiteur of *Swan Lake* (a normal duty of a specialist ballet composer), but rather paid someone else to do it for about one fifth of his fee.[58] Had he done it himself, we could ask for no more certain proof of his knowledge of Reisinger's editing. But this responsibility, together with the daily alterations to the score which emerged from rehearsals, fell to the lot of a musician not yet identified.

(d) Cast and Production

On 12 February 1877, the *Moscow Gazette* announced: 'Shortly, for the first time: *Swan Lake*, ballet in four acts'.

What do we know of the performance which followed eight days later? We have already considered the music and the libretto; let us turn now to the cast and a further sampling of the critical response.

New productions of ballet were rarities in the 1870s in Moscow, and *Swan Lake*, as might be expected, mustered some of the best dancers in the company. Their names, compared with those of the Maryinsky dancers of the 1890s, are unfamiliar, and thus deserve a special introduction here.

The Princess was acted by 'Nikolaeva I', presumably Olga Nikolaevna Nikolaeva, a star of the company in the 1860s who was restricted to mimed roles and character dances after a serious fall while dancing Giselle in 1869. Von Rothbart was danced by Sergei Sokolov, choreographer of *The Fern*, who was then in his twenty-ninth year of service. Wilhelm Vanner, who left Germany during the political turmoils of 1848 and who, after being released from service in Petersburg in 1854, came to Moscow the next season and stayed for thirty-five more, was a specialist in comic roles and performed the part of Siegfried's tutor Wolfgang. Baron von Stein was entrusted to another celebrated ballet actor, Fedor Andreyevich Reinshausen. His speciality was in portraying villains.[59]

The first performance of *Swan Lake* was given for the benefit of Pelagia (or Paulina) Mikhailovna Karpakova (billed as Karpakova I), who danced the part of Odette. She was not considered the company's first ballerina but second to Anna Sobeshchanskaya. Critics disagreed in their evaluation of her talents. A reviewer of Karpakova's work as a young dancer found that 'she has very little strength in her legs so that in aerial poses the artist is unsteady, wavering; there is no energy in her movements, none of the requisite speed.'[60] The ever-praising Blasis, at about the same time, declared that Karpakova's gift 'is suited to dances of a diverse kind: graceful, lively, strong, aerial, and *à terre*'.[61] Some observers were critical of her miming. Karpakova's performance of Kati in St-Léon's *Markitanka*, noted the Moscow correspondent of *The Voice*, 'is beyond the power of the young dancer, especially from the standpoint of acting and miming.'[62] A year earlier another critic had cited the 'superfluous calm of her mime' as a fishwife in Petipa's *The Daughter of the Pharaoh*.[63] Skalkovsky remarked that, while Karpakova was beautiful, 'Her dances are heavy, and she lacks expressive mime', adding that 'without special patronage she would never have advanced past *coryphée*.'[64]

In his last remark Skalkovsky was making a veiled reference to the ballerina's husband, a Greek millionaire named Millioti, whom she married in 1873. Considering that Karpakova was not the company's first ballerina, and also how rare new ballets were at this time in Moscow, it was unusual that the first performance of *Swan Lake* should be given as her benefit. In this connection it was noted:

In the production of this ballet it became clear that some kind of evil force began seriously to influence the place on stage of the highly talented A. O. Sobeshchanskaya. For her benefit she had to be content with only the fourth performance of this ballet, when in truth a new ballet should have been given to her, the leading ballerina, in its first performance.[65]

Some kind of evil force there was. From Valts we learn of influential patronage, but it was directed against Sobeshchanskaya. She enjoyed the favour of many government officials, including the Governor-General of Moscow, Vladimir Andreyevich Dolgorukov, who presented the ballerina with gifts from the family jewel chest. Sobeshchanskaya accepted Dolgorukov's gifts, but fell in love with and married Stanislav Gillert, the first Siegfried of *Swan Lake*. Gillert, Valts remarked, 'did not pretend to be an artist, still less a man', and sold the jewels. The ensuing scandal had at least two results: Sobeshchanskaya's period of service with the theatre was shortened and she was deprived of all benefit performances including the traditional farewell benefit.[66] While Valts did not record the dates of these occurrences, it is possible that Karpakova received the first performance of *Swan Lake* as her benefit not because her rich husband exerted financial pressure, but simply by default on account of the Sobeshchanskaya affair. As we shall discover, Sobeshchanskaya still had recourse to Petipa in the early months of 1877, and may herself have refused rather than have been refused the first performance. After her marriage she moved to St Petersburg, but she never danced there. She and her husband opened a soap factory which subsequently failed, whereupon she returned to Moscow, apparently by herself, and taught at the dancing school of another Moscow dancer, Lydia Mikhailovna Nelidova. Sobeshchanskaya died in Moscow in 1918.[67]

Victor Stanislav Feliksovich Gillert (billed as Gillert II) danced the part of Siegfried. Apart from this distinction, his involvement in the Sobeshchanskaya fiasco, and the dates of his service (Moscow 1875–9, St Petersburg 1889–1907) little has been recorded concerning him. He was one of two dancers to have had leading parts in both the first Moscow *Swan Lake* and the celebrated St Petersburg revival of 1895, in which he took the part of Wolfgang. (The other dancer, Alfred Bekefi, replaced Gillert as Siegfried in Moscow; he also performed in the Hungarian Dance in both cities to great acclaim.) Gillert's name is absent from the list at the head of the poster. This omission, striking because Gillert's was a leading part, may have had something to do with the Sobeshchanskaya affair, or may simply reflect a lack of seniority in the company. Except for his standing in the company there would be no reason for Reinshausen, for example, to be listed there, as his part was not an important one.

Several other dancers, not listed at the head of the poster, were import-ant for the extent and prominence of their work, though their importance is not traceable through the libretto. In Act I three women soloists appeared more often than Siegfried, the principal character: Maria Stanislavskaya, who danced in the waltz, the scene with dances, and was Gillert's partner in the *pas de deux*, the galop, and the finale; Ekaterina Karpakova, sister of the benefit artist; and Petrova III, of whom we know little more than that there were two other Petrovas senior to her in the company.

Similarly, in the lakeside acts, Mlle Mikhailova and the student Volkova featured in every number listed on the poster except the *pas de deux* for Odette and Siegfried. Volkova earned compliments from reviewers.

Mention must be made of another performer in the first production, the conductor Stepan Yakovlevich Ryabov. We know of his participation not from the poster, but principally from Modeste Tchaikovsky's condemna-tion of the production in his biography of Peter. Subsequent writers have followed Modeste in his damning of Ryabov. Modeste wrote:

The poverty of the production, meaning the décor and costumes, the absence of outstanding performers, the balletmaster's weakness of imagination, and, finally, the orchestra, although not badly constituted, had as its director Mr Ryabov, who had never before had anything to do with such a complicated score—all of this together permitted the composer with good reason to cast the blame for the failure on others.[68]

No source directly refutes Modeste's comments, but there is much to suggest that they are unfair. Ryabov, whom Valts considered a self-taught near genius,[69] compiled an impressive record of service in the Moscow ballet. At the age of eighteen he entered the imperial service as a first violin player in the Bolshoy Theatre orchestra, being promoted during the next twenty-five years to conductor of the orchestra of the Maly Theatre and then, in 1874, successor to Yuly Gerber as ballet conductor at the Bolshoy. That Ryabov conducted twenty-three of forty-seven new productions of ballet in the next twenty-five years reflects a measure of competence, as do his concert performances of Wagner and Tchaikovsky in the 1890s. He was the first member of the Moscow ballet to complete a half century of service, on which occasion Tchaikovsky's publisher Peter Jurgenson presented him with a copy of the full score of *Nutcracker*. It is possible that Modeste's condescension was rooted in Ryabov's reputation as a ballroom conductor, a capacity in which he served for over thirty years to the delight of the Muscovites.[70] As regards *Swan Lake*, Kashkin made a point of acquitting Ryabov of blame for the orchestra's inferior playing:

In our last notice, speaking of the ballet *Swan Lake*, we completely forgot to mention its execution, and meanwhile Mr Ryabov fully deserves praise for that correctness of tempo and attentiveness with which he followed the dances. Some opera conductors might benefit from keeping an eye on this ability of Mr Ryabov. As for the orchestra, it played inaccurately, and often some instruments did not play at all. In this, it is true, there is nothing surprising, since there were, as we heard, only two rehearsals.[71]

These statements of Kashkin may relate to the remarkable (but probably apocryphal) account of Soviet historian Yury Bakhrushin, who claimed that Tchaikovsky himself

conscientiously worked at rehearsals of the ballet in the capacity of concertmaster, then sat in the conductor's chair with the serious intention of conducting the orchestra at the performance. But subsequently he changed his mind, apparently, not being able to 'cut off' the dancers, that is, to end the musical phrase simultaneously with the dance phrase.[72]

The performance of Yuly Gerber in the violin solo of the love duet illustrates a problem over which Ryabov had little control:

The violin solo is excellent, although spoiled by the art of Mr Gerber. What kind of instrument does he have, for a soloist? An un-oiled theatre carriage led around the stage could provide the public no less pleasure. Thanks to Mr Gerber's violin the pleasant impression usually produced by Madame Eichenwald's harp was also lost.[73]

It would seem that Ryabov has suffered unjustly at the hands of Modeste and others who have quoted him.

One of the curiosities associated with the early productions of *Swan Lake*, one that dates from the first performance, concerns the part of Odile. The performance tradition growing from the Petersburg production of 1895 calls for Odette and Odile to be danced by the same ballerina, thus ensuring the matter of resemblance in the simplest way. On the poster of 20 February 1877, however, no dancer is listed for the part of Odile. In place of a name three asterisks are printed. The libretto describes Odile as resembling Odette, but does not specify that the resemblance is exact. Indeed, the librettist raised the possibility of a close but inexact likeness in the short episode between Siegfried and Benno in which the Prince questions his friend about Odile's similarity to Odette and receives a negative answer.

Some authorities suggest that Reisinger assigned the part of Odile to another dancer. Yury Bakhrushin contended that Odile was danced by an extra whose name would not have been acceptable for inclusion with separate billing on the poster.[74] If this was the case, the tragic effect of Siegfried's deception would have been enhanced by making clear to the audience, as it was supposedly to Benno, that Siegfried in choosing Odile acted in a delusion that was his alone. Yury Slonimsky, while admitting that it might have been thus, preferred to think that the ballerina danced both parts. He noted that the device of three asterisks was frequently used in theatre programmes of the period to indicate an artist who performed two roles in the same work.[75]

Accounts of the first performance agree with Slonimsky, although not unequivocally. Most point out the resemblance of Odile to Odette, but only one, a parody of the exchange between Siegfried and Benno, makes explicit that the two parts were danced by the same person:

'How like Mlle Karpakova she is!' exclaims Siegfried.
'Why are you so surprised?' wonders his servant: 'you see that it is she, only in another role!'[76]

From the standpoint of stage illusion it could hardly have been otherwise, for Pelagia Karpakova performed in the *pas de six*, the *pas de cinq*, and the Russian Dance of Act III. To expect the audience to accept another dancer as her double while she herself spent so much time on stage as neither Odette nor Odile would be stretching credibility beyond the very liberal normal limits of the genre.

On its opening night *Swan Lake* packed the house and brought an overall response more positive than negative. Karpakova, who danced 'lightly and elegantly' and who performed 'classical *pas* with grace and stands on *pointe* very firmly',[77] was presented with a number of bouquets and baskets of flowers. Two numbers—a variation and the Hungarian Dance from Act III—were repeated by public demand.

Most of the critics' attention was focused on three aspects of the ballet: the libretto, the music, and the choreography. In only one of eighteen notices do we read any kind words for the story: the correspondent of *The Voice* referred to it as borrowed from 'a beautiful old German fairy-tale',[78] and even this remark may have been sarcastic. For the most part the libretto, because of its German setting and its alleged stupidity, came in for sharp rebukes, which began when it was published in the *Theatre Gazette* four months before the first performance. On this occasion the editor, in a footnote, commented:

It seems to us somewhat strange that Mr Tchaikovsky chose as a subject for his ballet, the music of which is said to be charming, this fairy-tale, German, heavy, altogether unsuitable. This made necessary . . . various 'reserve stocks' [implying he could not see the necessity for the expenditure of such a large amount of production material?], indeed, 'Siegfrieds', which are tiresome when in Russian legends it is so easy to find a suitable subject for a ballet, a subject not so coarse and dull, but wholly poetic and characteristic. And from a practical standpoint, the choice of a German tale for a ballet is unfounded: Russian ballets are more interesting to a Russian public . . .[79]

The desirable social aim is more prominent in the reproach of a reviewer of the first performance who wrote, after complaining about the German subject:

A ballet with a subject taken from the life and beliefs of the people would be not only incomparably more interesting for the Russian public, but also incomparably more useful. It could be a representation of the particular mores of Russian life; it could acquaint the audience with traits of the national character, in a word, it could cease being a series of lovely but empty and sometimes absurd scenes.[80]

Indeed, it was unusual, if we accept the hypothesis that *Swan Lake* originated in the Artistic Circle or the Shilovskaya salon, for a ballet developed in circumstances of local Muscovite pride to have such a German flavour. Or was it? We have seen that Sokolov and his collaborators suffered because *The Fern*, when made into a ballet, had lost the Russian national character of the legend at the basis of the libretto. Noting this, the *Swan Lake* collaborators, ironically as it turned out, may have chosen a German setting to neutralize the criticism that they would have faced if another Russian subject had been Westernized in its adaptation for ballet. The interests of Reisinger may also have played a part.

One form that the condemnation took was in making the German aspect the butt of jokes: ' "Swans!" exclaims the Prince's friend Benno von Som . . . Sommer . . . Sommerstern . . . (Whew! you can hardly say it!).'[81]

A Petersburg reporter made fun of the libretto in this way at length, as we read in another description of Act I:

A magnificent green park. In one of its glades Mr Gillert II (also the noble Prince Siegfried) celebrates his coming of age, and on account of this orders the villagers to dance. Nothing can be done; grudgingly, but putting on a happy appearance, they begin to jump clumsily.

'But why do you dance so badly?' Mr Vanner (the Prince's tutor) asks them sternly.

'Ah, forgive us! To do otherwise to Mr Tchaikovsky's music is impossible; it is worse than marching in 3/4.'

Mr Vanner tries it out himself and is satisfied that in fact one cannot get on with Mr Tchaikovsky. The libretto, however, permits Mr Vanner to drink up a bit in honour of the Prince. After two or three manoeuvres of this kind of *Kartof-felnmusik*, the ballet begins to seem very jolly to him. He begins to jump, the villagers laugh, because they are ordered to—the public does not laugh, because the public is not aware of anything funny, since it feels so somnolent, so comfortable in this world of rather thin, drawn-out but melodious sounds . . .

Meanwhile the Prince's mother appears and says: 'Excuse me if I interrupt your party! . . .'

And what merriment indeed, under the lash, and still in 3/4 time! It turns out that the Princess wants to marry off her son.

'Anything you say, mumsy,' says Gillert II, 'I'll even marry the devil, only leave, for Christ's sake: I was having a lousy time even before you came.'

'I'm leaving, I'm leaving,' the Princess says. 'You see I explained everything that was required for the remaining acts'.[82]

Audience and reviewers alike were impressed by the fact that a composer of Tchaikovsky's stature had written music for a ballet:

... the principal hero of the present performance is Mr Tchaikovsky, who got a sore waist from bowing, and to this moment still has sore ears from the stormy 'bravos' with which his delighted public met him.[83]

This may perhaps have been the case at the end of the performance, but when it came to committing their opinions to paper the reviewers differed considerably in their estimate of the score. Taken together, the music criticisms form an interesting if predictable pattern: professional musicians (of which there were but two among the critics) drew different and sometimes opposite conclusions from non-musicians. On one point all were agreed: the ballet's principal attraction was Tchaikovsky's music: 'The theatre was positively full, which is explained solely by the interest of the public in hearing the new musical creation of one of the distinguished and quite popular Russian composers.'[84] Or, more bluntly:

Amidst the uninteresting musical junk such as the long phalanx of ballets given in recent years represents, the new ballet appears to be a bright spot on a dark background ... Mr Tchaikovsky, being one of the most prominent orchestral composers of our time, was able to put into the framework of ballet music so many purely musical virtues that the listener sitting in the theatre was drawn away in spite of himself by Mr Tchaikovsky's music from what was happening on stage.[85]

These remarks raise the principal points over which there was significant further discussion: Tchaikovsky's skill as a writer for the orchestra, and the familiar complaint of balletomanes that his music was not suited to the genre. On these points there were differences of opinion:

... we never thought and will not dare to think of being Mr Tchaikovsky's critic, let alone in such a serious work as a ballet. Fortunately, in this instance it will suit us only to repeat the conclusion, considered all but universally recognized. In *Swan Lake*, as everywhere, Mr Tchaikovsky displayed an astonishing knowledge of instrumentation—a characteristic that is being admitted by friends and enemies alike. He gave new evidence of his ability to make masterful use of orchestral forces.[86]

Yet the composer's conservatory schoolmate, Herman Laroche, in a review otherwise full of praise, found fault with the orchestration:

An abundance of means also prevails in the instrumentation. The same elegant taste, the magnificent distribution of chordal intervals in the texture which we were accustomed to encounter in the creator of *Romeo* and *Francesca*, manifests the very same defect from which, at least in my opinion, the best of his work suffers. This defect is his unwarranted love for brass and especially for percussion instruments. I know that in ordinary, common ballet music percussion is used more crudely and with less restraint than in *Swan Lake*, but this is no justification for a delicate, intellectual artist. For what do the trumpets, trombones, and kettledrums roar when in the depth of the empty stage flies a band of swans? This moment demands soft, peaceful sounds. I noted in *Swan Lake* several such moments, accompanied by noisy orchestration, despite the requirements for more appropriate, sensible characteristics. I do not think that on these occasions the composer wanted to make a concession to the tradition of ballet music; judging from other works orchestrated by him which have nothing in common with ballet, I think rather that here Tchaikovsky, as on many earlier occasions, was simply carried away by his peculiar weakness for loud sounds.[87]

In contrast, reviewers seeking to establish that *Swan Lake* was not *dansante* could not match Laroche's clarity and eloquence, and instead fell back on clichés of criticism:

The hand of a master, well acquainted with the secret resources of orchestration, is evident in the new work of Mr Tchaikovsky . . . but in general the music of the new ballet is quite monotonous and boring. For musicians, perhaps, this is a very interesting thing but for the public it is dry.[88]

In an awkward comparison another writer claimed that:

. . . it would be strange to compare Mr Tchaikovsky's score with the works of the various Minkuses, Gerbers, *et tutti quanti*; but it is impossible, at the same time, not to notice that the music of *Swan Lake* is pallid and monotonous in the extreme.

Where, then, did the theatre critics perceive the problem? We get some idea from an earlier passage in the same review:

Above all the question arises: is the ballet written for the music, or, on the contrary, the music for the ballet? Obviously, the ballet for the music. Indeed, from the technical standpoint the musical score of *Swan Lake* does not stand up to criticism: it is 'without downbeats' and not sufficiently 'motivic'. Chopin, for example, did not write his dances to be danced to, did he? The same ought to be said for Mr Tchaikovsky's music: in some places soloists and *corps de ballet* are positively at odds with the orchestra, and you see that it could not be otherwise: the melody is too . . . how can I say it? . . . confused, that is, capricious—in a word, not 'balletic'. . . . One wag expressed it thus: 'this', he said, 'is too learned, not for dances this . . .' And this statement is close to the truth.[89]

What puts us on our guard about this criticism is the extent to which the balletmaster's ineptitude prompted the conclusion that Tchaikovsky was lacking as a ballet composer. Any condemnation of the music's *dansante* quality presupposes, as this one did not, that the fault does not rest with the choreographer.

In 1877, however, Tchaikovsky had a champion who defended him against the complaints of balletomanes. Nikolai Kashkin had the singular advantage of knowing *Swan Lake* with the intimacy of someone who had just prepared a piano arrangement of the holograph score. In his review he not only defends the composer, but also claims to have raised the problem of specialist ballet composition knowing that others would misunderstand what Tchaikovsky was attempting to do. The composition of ballet music, Kashkin wrote,

. . . is in essence far from a grateful task; ballet, as it must be, consists mainly of dances, connected by the composer with more or less monotonous rhythms. Above all, in ballet the musician finds himself under the influence of the balletmaster, to whose demands, however at variance with the musical demands, he must conform. Mimed scenes allow the music some breadth, in which the composer can free himself from the narrow limitations of the dance rhythm, and receive at times an interesting programme for a symphonic picture.

And he continues a few lines later:

Mr Tchaikovsky did not strive toward the role of reformer in ballet music; his ballet, like any other, is subordinated to the conditions of the balletmaster, to a familiar succession of various *pas*, solos, and ensembles. The difference lies in the mastery of technique, the elegance of harmony, the melodic inventiveness, etc., things that comprise the elements of Mr Tchaikovsky's talent. In this respect the music of his ballet stands apart from the music of others, as there is almost no example in which such a powerful artist dedicated his talent to this kind of composition, the unfavourable conditions of which present too many inconveniences to the musician.[90]

Laroche, who saw the ballet for the first time some eighteen months later, fully agreed:

The melodies, one more plastic than the last, more harmonious and more captivating, flow as from a horn of plenty; the rhythm of the waltz, which prevails among the danced numbers, is embodied in such varied, graceful, and winning designs that never did the melodic invention of the gifted, many-faceted composer stand the test more resplendently. The music of *Swan Lake* is fully popular; what simple amateurs designate 'motives' are found in it not in less abundance but rather in greater abundance than in any ballet of Pugni. With an ease which no one would assume the learned author of so many symphonies, quartets, and overtures to have, Mr Tchaikovsky noticed the peculiarities of the ballet style, and, adapting himself to it, once again manifested that versatility which constitutes one of the most treasured properties of his compositional talent. His music is ballet music completely, but at the same time really excellent and interesting for the serious musician. Frequently after a light dance motive, transparently harmonized and which serves as material for the first 'figure' of some dance, the symphonist in the composer awakens, and on the second figure illuminates us with the succession of thick and rich chords, which for a long time remind you of that strength, not of the ballet manner, that he holds in check.[91]

Finally, the differences of opinion separating theatre-goer from professional musician did not apply to the evaluation of the character dances, where both sides offered praise and blame. The problem for their detractors, who included Laroche (who called them 'cosmopolitan', a pejorative adjective), was that they were unauthentic:

The character dances could have been a little more characteristic. Certainly we could expect this from Mr Tchaikovsky. The Russian Dance, however, is an exception (how it appeared at the ball of a German princess only Mr Reisinger knows), but the Neapolitan might have been as much Spanish as the Spanish Neapolitan.[92]

In general we must conclude that the scales of criticism tipped in Tchaikovsky's favour. And we, a century later, know what he did not know then: how unwarranted was his sensitivity to the supposedly trifling success of *Swan Lake*.

However badly Tchaikovsky fared, Reisinger fared worse. But it is even more difficult to assess the objections raised against him as choreographer than it was against Tchaikovsky as composer—not only because Reisinger's earlier failures would tend to prejudice critics against him, but also because choreography is the part of a ballet in which the shortcomings of reviewers' technical knowledge would be most sorely felt. In short, the choreography may have been bad, but the impression left by press reports may have made it seem even worse. From all appearances the inexperience of critics in matters of choreography was responsible for the absence of any technical descriptions of steps, something which the Petersburg critics could provide if they wished. The most we have is a fleeting glimpse, as in the mimed dialogue of Act II: 'At first she says "No! No! Go away, insidious man!", but then charity replaces anger, and *in a few ethereal pirouettes* [my italics] one recognizes that she also loves him . . .'[93]

These assumptions find some basis for credibility in the fact that very few critics actually discussed the choreography beyond a passing reference, preferring to devote space to other matters. In effect we have only two responses which could be described as substantial. 'Igor', the Moscow correspondent of the *St Petersburg Gazette*, wrote:

. . . Mr Reisinger's dances are weak in the extreme . . . so weak that worse, it seems, are impossible to imagine. Let us assume the majority of the 'listeners' paid not the slightest attention to them: the entire *essence* of the ballet is in the music; but what was this to Mr Reisinger, who boldly presumed to have his name printed on the programme, and still more boldly to bow before the public . . . who did not think of calling for him? Incoherent waving of the legs that continued through the course of four hours—is this not torture?[94]

The impression of a personal attack on Reisinger was carried even further by the 'Modest Observer' who reproached the balletmaster, citing passages from the libretto and noting that:

. . . the subject itself, 'as always happens in ballet', is entirely without sense and is very much nonsense; the things that charm one in a ballet—beautiful dances, the wealth of scenes, and all the diversity of transformations—are quite missing in *Swan Lake* . . . In the production of the dances Reisinger displayed, if not the art that corresponds to his speciality, then a remarkable ability to construct some sort of gymnastic exercises in place of dances. The *corps de ballet* stamp up and down in the same place, waving their arms like a windmill's vanes—and the soloists jump about the stage in gymnastic steps. The character dances in the third act came off in a more animated way; but here too these dances were not 'composed' by Mr Reisinger, but simply borrowed by him from various other ballets. Thus the 'Russian Dance', performed by Mlle Karpakova, the artist for whom the benefit was given, in all probability constitutes the fruit of the imagination of Mr Reisinger himself, for only a German can take for a Russian Dance those pirouettes that Mlle Karpakova had to manufacture.[95]

Clearly, *Swan Lake* did nothing to redeem Reisinger's reputation.

Of the décor for the first *Swan Lake* we know very little—for Acts I and III, only the names of the artists, a Mr Shangin and a Mr Gropius, respectively. Perhaps because he was a celebrity in the field, Karl Valts, who prepared the set for the lakeside acts and machines for the entire ballet, has received more attention. Valts enjoyed a long and extraordinary career at the Bolshoy Theatre in Moscow, which began in 1861, included productions for Diaghilev in Paris, and continued into the Soviet era. Famed for virtuoso feats of production (once, for *Don Giovanni*, he created seventeen scenic transformations to follow one another in rapid succession), he wrote in his memoirs of Tchaikovsky's wishes for the final scene of *Swan Lake*:

P. I. Tchaikovsky took the liveliest part in the production of its décors, and discussed them with me a great deal. Peter Ilyich gave special attention to the final act. In the storm scene, when the lake overflows its banks and floods the entire stage, a real whirlwind was built at Tchaikovsky's insistence. Branches and twigs of trees were broken, fell into the water, and were carried away by the waves. After the storm, for the apotheosis, dawn came and the landscape was illuminated by the first rays of the rising sun at the curtain.[96]

Two engravings of the lakeside, one each from Acts II and IV, are the only pictorial documents of their kind which come down to us from the first *Swan Lake* (see Pls. 7 & 8);[97] however, a critique of the first performance adds a detail to our knowledge of the setting of Act II: 'A beautiful, tranquil lake framed by high mountains and a forest. Mists hover over it (these mists, nothing more than steam, are a novelty on our stage).'[98]

Yet we should be cautious about conclusions drawn from what is shown us by the engravings. Their authenticity, for example, is open to question. The captions beneath them state: 'Sketch by our correspondent, drawing by F. Gaanen, engraving by Yu. Baranovsky'. While the engraving is very likely an accurate reproduction of F. Gaanen's drawing, we cannot know from this what Gaanen did to the correspondent's sketch, let alone how true the correspondent was to what he actually saw on stage.

The visual evidence is therefore not all reliable. The artist's sense of verisimilitude left the practical-minded viewer without a perspective of the stage (it is difficult to imagine where, if the engraving of Act II is accurate, the soloists, sixteen *coryphées*, and a *corps de ballet* of unspecified number would have danced). And at the same time the engraving exaggerates some of the fantastic elements of the story presented in the libretto: swans, swan maidens, and one dancer with wings in the process of transformation—all at once.

Parts of the engravings, in contrast, confirm Valts's memoirs and the accounts of eyewitnesses. There is clearly electrical illumination in the background for the moon, lightning, and 'the first rays of the rising sun' (though in using this Valts differed from the libretto, which simply called for the moon coming out after the storm). We can see also that the main branch of the tree in Act II broke off in Act IV to provide support for Odette and Siegfried in the water.

And water there was. The engraving of Act IV shows the lake overflowing its banks to a line near the front of the stage. Many reviewers referred to this effect—if sometimes in a jocular fashion:

. . . no sooner does Siegfried take hold of her crown than stormy waves of the lake fly up and pour over the stage, thunder and lightning occur not only in the wings but in the orchestra, and Tchaikovsky's waltz drowns in the sea of these bravura sounds just as the lovers drown in the machinist's canvas . . . Then everything clears up; in the distance weak thunderclaps are heard and the light of the moon falls on the becalmed lake.[99]

And another wrote: 'The "flood" was well made (the waves reached up to the very proscenium), only the waves in the foreground could have been taken for logs.'[100] 'It is unfortunate', we read elsewhere in agreement with this, 'that the lake at the beginning did not ripple very naturally; the waves simply crept along, and at times bobbed up and down somewhat strangely.'[101] The engraving tends to confirm this: the waves crash in from the side (perhaps the result of Valts's whirlwind), rather than follow the direction of the main body of water, which is directly in front of the audience.

To most reviewers Valts's work merited praise, though some, like the Conservatory professor Kashkin, objected to the noise the machines made, which obscured the music:

We hardly err if we say that the last scene in this quite modest libretto of *Swan Lake* probably attracted Mr Tchaikovsky, where the music plays a quite important role. But unfortunately, this best place in the ballet is virtually lost as a result of the absurd custom established on our stage to accompany every fire, flood, etc., which we represent on stage with such an unimaginable din and uproar that one might have thought himself present at a large artillery exercise or at the explosion of a powder magazine.[102]

Other critics, perhaps surfeited with miracles, found other faults: 'The havoc, rain, the storm in the lake, the flights, all this was constructed by

Mr Valts impeccably. The illusion was complete . . . It is regrettable only
that it smelled too much of gunpowder.'[103]

In what seems now to be an unusual touch, Odette and Siegfried receded
into the distance illuminated by electric light.[104]

By depicting one hunter carrying a crossbow, the engraving of Act II
finally settles a semantic question raised by many of the press accounts.
One reviewer described the weapon correctly with the obscure word
arbalet (after the French *arbalète*), while the librettist and several critics
used the term *ruzh'e*, which in twentieth-century Russian connotes a
firearm. Even if this term did not yet have such a precise meaning in the
1870s—it referred at that time to arms in general—the sarcastic tone of
many writers who reviewed *Swan Lake* left the point in doubt. Given the
freedom of producers in such matters and the imprecision of *ruzh'e*, we
might never have known, without the engraving, what was actually used.

On 26 April 1877 Anna Sobeshchanskaya made her début as Odette. By
that fourth performance new music and choreography had been added to
Swan Lake. From the conductor Stepan Ryabov we learn how Sobeshchanskaya, distrustful of Reisinger and dissatisfied with Tchaikovsky's
music, went to Petipa in St Petersburg and asked the balletmaster to create
a *pas de deux* for her. Petipa complied, as he had before when she had
complained about Reisinger's dances in *Ariadne*; for *Swan Lake* he
composed variations to music by Ludwig Minkus.

Having returned to Moscow, the ballerina informed the *Kapellmeister* that she had
acquired a *pas de deux*, which she wished to interpolate into the third act of *Swan
Lake*. When news of this found its way to Tchaikovsky, he began to protest
energetically, pointing out the embarrassment that he would suffer from the
interpolation of someone else's music in his ballet.

'Whether my ballet is good or bad', he said, 'I alone would like to take
responsibility for its music.'

After long discussions, Tchaikovsky promised to write a new *pas de deux* for the
benefit artiste.

But then a serious complication arose. The artiste did not want to change the
dance composed for her by Petipa, nor did she want to go to Petersburg again.

The possibility of calming the storm presented itself only in composing new
music for the existing dance.

Peter Ilyich took upon himself to resolve the argument in this way. Having
requested that Minkus's music be given to him, he promised to write new music
which would agree, bar for bar, note for note, with Minkus's music.

In a word, he promised to produce a *pas de deux*, to the music of which it would
be possible to perform the dance composed by Petipa, not only without any
changes, but even without rehearsals.

The music was written very quickly, and in addition pleased the benefit artiste so
much that she requested that Tchaikovsky write for her an additional variation,
which he did. In the benefit performance both of these numbers enjoyed a noisy
success with the public.[105]

It is this music, reconstructed from an accidentally rediscovered répétiteur, that has been introduced into modern productions, beginning with the revival in 1953 at the Stanislavsky and Nemirovich–Danchenko Theatre.[106] Sobeshchanskaya regularly danced the new Petipa–Minkus–Tchaikovsky *pas de deux* in place of the Act III *pas de six*.

Tchaikovsky's response to the prospect of including in his work the music of another composer argues more than anything else that the performance redaction of *Swan Lake* may have involved cuts but not interpolations. Despite Kashkin's much-quoted remark to the effect that, during the course of the ballet's run in Moscow, '... the substitution of interpolations for original numbers was made to a greater and greater degree, and towards the end almost a third of the music of *Swan Lake* was replaced with interpolations from other ballets, moreover, by very mediocre ones',[107] there seems no reason for the composer to take exception to Minkus, and not to others. Neither does Kashkin give the time at which this mutilation was supposed to have taken place. However, if it occurred—and Kashkin's integrity, if not his memory, is indisputable—a likely time would have been during the second and third Moscow productions (1880 and 1882, respectively).

Sobeshchanskaya's appearances as Odette provided her admirers with the opportunity to extol her superiority to Karpakova. D. I. Mukhin recalled that 'in the leading role of Odette Mlle Sobeshchanskaya was incomparably better than Karpakova in all respects.'[108] 'Mlle Sobeshchanskaya, for whom time does not exist,' wrote the Moscow correspondent of *The Voice*, 'to this day has no rivals. At one time she did—Muravieva, Grantzow, Dor—but these are fairies flown away, fairies from another place. Our own fairies—Karpakova, Karpakova, and Karpakova again—are still preparing for the competition. There are dancers who quickly bore their audiences, but Mlle Sobeshchanskaya is not one of them. With each year ... Mlle Sobeshchanskaya dances better and better ... Especially successful was her Russian Dance, which was repeated.'[109] Laroche, who saw her in the autumn of 1878, concurred: '... I cannot help saying that Mlle Sobeshchanskaya, who performed the leading role, is every bit as graceful and attractive as in earlier years. The public likes her very much.'[110]

Between 1877 and 1883 *Swan Lake* received the treatment usually accorded a nineteenth-century ballet. Beginning with her performance of 3 January 1878, Karpakova replaced the *pas de six* of Act III with a *pas de dix*. Whether this was a new number or the old one with four more dancers is not known.

By the end of 1879 Sobeshchanskaya, Karpakova, Gillert, and Reisinger had all left the Moscow ballet. Reisinger's successor, Joseph Peter Hansen, produced a new *Swan Lake* for his benefit performance of 13 January 1880. A student, Evdokia Kalmykova, danced the part of Odette, and Alfred

Bekefi that of Siegfried. For this production Hansen, judging by the list of dances, significantly changed the outline of the ballet's action only in the first act, where he added a seduction scene, of which nothing more is known. Of Hansen's nineteen choreographic units, fifteen clearly corresponded to Tchaikovsky's musical divisions, and some of the others may not imply a change in the music so much as a change in properties—as, for example, a *pas* with garlands danced to the composer's *pas* with cups in Act I. All the national dances were retained, as was the Sobeshchanskaya *pas de deux*.[111]

Fewer performance documents survive from Hansen's revivals than from Reisinger's first production, so our impression of his work is restricted to a few accounts. 'New dances and very effective groups promise new success for this ballet, already produced on our stage', one critic wrote. 'The public especially liked the group of the second act . . . The stage was effectively wrapped in several rows of green tulle, which represented water. The *corps de ballet*, which danced behind these waves of tulle, represented a band of bathing and swimming swans.'[112] Even the 'Modest Observer', who had castigated the first production so severely, moderated his tone: 'The ballet, which nearly failed from its first performance, is now viewed without boredom thanks to the new dances and groups of the *corps de ballet*.'[113] Nadezhda von Meck wrote to Tchaikovsky in a letter of 14–15 January:

On Sunday we heard *Swan Lake*. Such beautiful music, but the production of the ballet was very poor. I had already seen it before, but now the poster indicated that it was newly produced, with *improvements* and *embellishments* . . . Everything was ugly, and choreographically the ballet was very poor. The beautiful music of the Russian Dance was quite lost in this mixture of French and low urban dance, which was simply a conventional ballet solo with Russian characteristics here and there. Best of all was the Hungarian Dance, and the public demanded its encore. The theatre was quite full, although it was a benefit for the balletmaster Hansen and the prices were one-and-a-half times their normal levels.[114]

Hansen prepared yet another version of *Swan Lake*, which ran for four performances between 28 October 1882 and 2 January 1883. Less information survives about this production than about the first two. In the newspaper advertisements Kalmykova is listed as the featured dancer in each performance of this second Hansen production, but scholars have raised doubts concerning their accuracy. Yury Slonimsky claims that the student Lydia Geiten danced both Odette and Odile in these performances, Yury Bakhrushin that the roles were split—that Kalmykova danced Odette and Geiten Odile.[115] In the last two performances of the work before it was dropped from the repertory, 'La Cosmopolitana', an interpolation of dances not to Tchaikovsky's music, was added in Act III.[116]

All things considered, was *Swan Lake* a failure in its first productions in Moscow, as has been claimed? At a time when new ballets normally received no more than eighteen performances *Swan Lake*'s Moscow run of forty-one and of three productions in six years, is proof of the ballet's success and the interest it created. Even when mounted in Petersburg it had been performed no more than twenty times there in its first six seasons; only after thirteen years had it been given forty-one times. Further marks of success in Moscow are its selection as the opening ballet of the autumn season in 1877, and its frequent choice for benefit performances. Act IV, for example, was given at a Red Cross benefit on 10 May 1877, and Yuly Gerber requested Act III, together with all of Glinka's *A Life for the Tsar*, for his benefit performance on 8 September 1878.

   Most historians consider the Moscow productions of *Swan Lake* failures because none of them survived, while making no allowance for the almost mortal blow dealt the Moscow company by the Director of the Imperial Theatres in 1882–3. Ivan Vsevolozhsky, whose tenure was to be such a blessing for Petipa in St Petersburg, nearly brought destruction to the Moscow company. Of his positive reforms in the northern capital there will be more to say in the proper place, but his 'reform' of the Moscow ballet through retirements, firings, and reduction of funds brought the company to half its strength of the late 1870s—according to one account from 198 artists to 80.[117] In October 1883 one Moscow newspaper printed the following sad news:

The reorganization of the ballet is not final; it is a temporary measure and will take a definitive form only in two years, when the question will be decided: is ballet as an independent art necessary, or must it remain only as a necessary supplement to opera? In these two years 100,000 roubles a year is allocated to the personnel of the ballet, which figure takes into account both the régisseur and the engagement of Petersburg ballerinas. The chief régisseur, with a salary of 4,000 roubles, is the Petersburg dancer Mr Bogdanov, among whose responsibilities is the teaching of young soloists. The first dancer is Mlle Geiten, the first male dancer Mr Manokhin. Then a few second dancers of both sexes and a small number of *coryphées* and *corps de ballet*, so that in general the staff will not exceed 100 persons, whereas previously it had been almost 240.

   Besides the ballet artists being relieved of their jobs, 20 persons have received orders to report to St Petersburg, where they have been transferred.

   The remaining artists being let go, especially those among them who have not served a long time and for whom, besides payments of extraordinary one-time allotments of money, there is no guarantee [of continued work], cannot be reconciled with the thought of their dismissal. They have so insistently asked the directorate about their retention in service, *if only just to keep a job*, that finally they have forced concessions. Now again the directorate returned to the original thought: to form an examining commission of specialists and to examine all who are being retired without a pension, and to leave in service those among them who prove to be satisfactory figurants, as long as there is free money remaining in the allotment of 100,000 roubles a year for the ballet, although it was proposed originally to expend these monies in a different way.[118]

It is difficult to assess to what extent the reorganization was forced by a low degree of public interest, but with the company being deprived of a vitality, both artistic and material, unprecedented even in its traditional constraints, we cannot be surprised that *Swan Lake* did not survive, whatever its attractions.

We see therefore in the early Moscow productions of *Swan Lake* how what has become a masterpiece was in its theatrical history treated no differently than a typical Russian ballet of the nineteenth century. Tchaikovsky's collaboration on the work was recognized by his contemporaries as exceptional because the music had been written by a composer of his stature; but neither balletmasters nor ballerinas let the eminence of the composer inhibit their traditional right to modify ballets at will.

The first productions of *Swan Lake* once again demonstrate the problems associated with reconstructing the performance history of a work for which few primary sources survive, and for which the secondary sources are numerous but reflect a great variance in outlook and reliability. Certainties about the first *Swan Lake* are few , and the complex structures of possibility and likelihood which branch out from them numerous and frail.

2

The Music of *Swan Lake*

⚜

IF there is any advantage to knowing so little about the performance version of *Swan Lake* as it was produced in Moscow, it is that we are forced to consider Tchaikovsky's score undisturbed by Reisinger's changes, to reacquaint ourselves with its beauties, and to reflect on the composer's accomplishment in the history of ballet.

Comparatively few authors of the sizeable literature on Tchaikovsky and his ballets have come to grips with the music. Some of the best-known works are popular guides for the listener or ballet-goer, limited in scope to an introduction and a résumé of the action accompanied by appropriate musical examples.[1] The episodic quality of ballet music—attributable to factors such as the slow pace at which events unfold in the story and limitations on the physical stamina of dancers—is partly responsible for the tendency to describe a ballet score event by event rather than considering it as a whole. This kind of analysis may take the form of an interpretive gloss on the music:

The introduction is 'the first sketch of the beautiful and sad tale of the maiden-bird'. It begins with a lyrical theme of the oboe. Continuing with a clarinet, it grows into a melancholy song of romantic mould. This theme is related to the swan melody that first sounds at the end of Act I. Beginning from a sorrowful meditation, the narrative passes through an impassioned upsurge to dramatic protest and despair. 'In the middle section ... dark and fearsome accents enter in. The exclamations of the trombones resound sternly and ominously. A swell leads to the repetition of the opening theme (reprise–coda), performed by the trumpets, then the cellos against the background of the disquieting roll of the tympani.' The outburst of despair ends, and the pensive song of sorrowful reflection sounds anew.[2]

This example illustrates a popular and somewhat rudimentary approach, but can nevertheless serve as an introduction to the methods and conclusions of Soviet writers, who are responsible for the most carefully considered analyses in the literature. Their analysis comprises historical, stylistic, and sociological components.

Historically speaking, Tchaikovsky's ballets descended from the opera ballets and certain orchestral works of Glinka; within Tchaikovsky's own work, the ballets grew out of his essays in dance music before *Swan Lake*. One of Tchaikovsky's native gifts, according to the doctrine, was an inclination toward the composition of dance music, which found an especially fertile ground for development in the early symphonies. There the dance occupied a prominent place in certain movements, where it was subjected to symphonic treatment. It was but a short step to reciprocate by infusing an entire ballet score with symphonic elements.

Reasonable up to a point, this interpretation of history is none the less disturbing. It proposes that Tchaikovsky's achievement as a ballet composer may be measured against composers who wrote no ballet. A truer comparison would be to consider his ballets in the light of the work of specialist composers. Whatever his other accomplishments, *Swan Lake* made Tchaikovsky a specialist, as Glinka never was, and it qualified his work to be compared with the state of the art in ballet music. But this is never done; Tchaikovsky's accomplishment is thus distorted, and the specialists left unfairly disregarded. Daniel Zhitomirsky gives us a typical example of this, mentioning the specialists in passing when writing of Tchaikovsky's reforms, which

... consisted of a fundamental change in the role of music in ballet. From a practical element of secondary importance, as it was, for example, with Pugni and Minkus, ballet music became the most important, an absolutely essential component of the choreographic spectacle ... Tchaikovsky is the most significant reformer in the history of ballet music. To say the least, he connected the music with the subject of the action, with its images, development, with the general style of the piece; in its content and strength of expression Tchaikovsky's music almost always rises above the elements of subject and staging of his ballets, and is the principal factor of artistic influence.[3]

Because the composer is applying symphonic principles to ballet music, large-scale structure is assumed to be present in Tchaikovsky's ballets just as it is in his symphonies. In ballet, however, the structure is shaped by the libretto. Boris Asafiev characterized *simfonizm* (the Russian term for the use of symphonic procedures in ballet) as 'the continuity of the musical current'.[4] The coherence of the ballet is maintained as it goes along by the principle of 'through-development'—that is, the score is continuously responsive to the narrative and to the emotional states of the characters. All other points of style and technique in Soviet analysis tend to be subordinate to this very important principle.

In the Soviet view melody is a primary concern. Even where the restatement of a melody is not at issue, melodies are grouped by likenesses of intonation—by broad similarities of contour, rhythm, and expressive quality—with the implication that the stylistic likenesses parallel similarities in the story. For example, the opening of the introduction (Ex. 3), the famous swan theme (Ex. 4), and the melody sounding at the moment when Odette first appears (Ex. 5) are all smooth, lyrical melodies associated with the heroine:[5]

Ex. 3   Introduction, bars 1–4

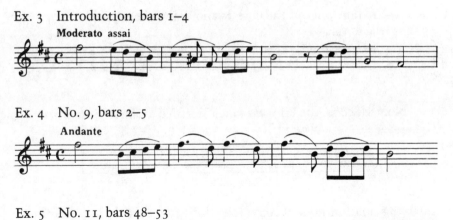

Ex. 4   No. 9, bars 2–5

Ex. 5   No. 11, bars 48–53

Comparisons of this kind can produce fascinating insights. In Act II, the only numbers Tchaikovsky associated explicitly with Odette display close intonational similarities, which prompted Tumanina to conclude that Tchaikovsky was thus offering us a portrait of the heroine.[6] The numbers are Odette's solo in the Dances of the Swans (Ex. 6) and the Interlude of the love duet (Ex. 7).

Ex. 6   No. 13/II, bars 2–4

Ex. 7   No. 13/V, bars 42–4

Similarly, Tchaikovsky confirms to us the Princess's concern over Siegfried's choosing of a bride by making the opening of her short mimed scenes (Nos. 18 and 24) a melodic variant, in 4/4 time, of the Waltz of the Prospective Fiancées (Exx. 8–9).

Ex. 8   No. 17 (Entrance of the Guests and Waltz), bars 31–7

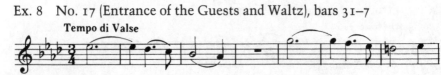

Ex. 9   No. 18 (*Scène*: the Princess takes Siegfried to the side etc.), bars 3–4

In an observation no less convincing for being speculative, Slonimsky links to Rothbart a variation of the *pas de six* (No. 19/IV)—a number for which we know nothing of the stage action—because of its striking affinities with the music of the owl in Odette's recitative[7]—powerfully march-like intonations, according to Asafiev (Exx. 10–11).

Ex. 10   *Pas de six*, Variation (4), bars 1–4.

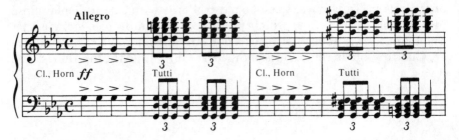

Ex. 11   No. 11, bars 176–80

Tchaikovsky also uses distinctive phrases to connect adjacent numbers. The Master of Ceremonies' sign to begin the dances—the first five notes of No. 16, the Dances of the *Corps de Ballet* and the Dwarfs—duplicates the head-motive of the refrain of the preceding introduction (Exx. 12–13).

Ex. 12   No. 16, bars 1–2

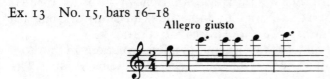

Moderato assai

Ex. 13   No. 15, bars 16–18

Allegro giusto

And the final cadence of the scene of the swans' disquiet in Act IV anticipates the opening motive of the Dances of the Little Swans which immediately follows (Exx. 14–15).

Ex. 14   No. 26, *Scène*, bars 53–6

Ex. 15   No. 27, Dances of the Little Swans, bars 1–4

The introduction of Act I promotes unity throughout the entire work in a related way. While nothing it contains is quoted later, the melodic affinity of its opening melody with the swan theme (Exx. 3–4, above), and the similarity of its powerful orchestral outburst (the *Allegro ma non troppo* at bar 36) to the music of the storm at the end of the ballet, make it an exordium in the best sense: not only does it introduce the work, but also announces in brief the essence of the tragedy to come.

Not always, however, does the attempt to relate situations in the story by means of a shared musical idea produce convincing results. The principal theme of the peasants' waltz in Act I corresponds with the refrain of Odette's recitative for the first few bars (Exx. 16–17).

Ex. 16   No. 2, *Valse*, bars 19–26

Ex. 17   No. 11, *Scène*, bars 100–6

Noting this similarity, Yury Slonimsky explained:

On the one hand the waltz characterizes the life of the hero, full of carefree diversions . . . And it is not accidental in the first dialogue of Odette and Siegfried to hear melodic turns of the waltz expounded anew. Would the composer have sought a connection of something which, it would seem, is not related? Already in the waltz the composer prepared Siegfried's break with the courtly circle and the meeting with Odette.[8]

Perhaps. But the intuitive sense of rightness about the other examples cited is absent here. And the reason why may be quite simple: the composer need not have been seeking a connection; the likeness may have been accidental. Tchaikovsky was prone to absentmindedness, even in the composition of *Swan Lake*, as we learn from an anecdote of Kashkin. Surprised at seeing the swan music of Act II in a new key, he asked the composer to explain. Tchaikovsky, to Kashkin's astonishment, had

. . . managed in the short amount of time between the composition of the first and second acts to forget the tonality and the instrumentation of the number that he had to repeat, but preserved in his memory only the general musical content and wrote the flight [music] a second time in order for it to have a complete connection with the one which followed in Act II. Possessing in essence an excellent musical memory, Peter Ilyich was very forgetful in his compositions, with some exceptions, and the occurrence with *Swan Lake* is a case in point.[9]

But there is another explanation, one which points to a flaw in the premise that the music of *Swan Lake* is continuously responsive to the story. The dogged application of this premise, which Slonimsky's rather forced explanation illustrates, presses the issue: can *all* the music of *Swan Lake* be explained by recourse to the libretto? No, if we take the libretto as the authoritative source for the story, for it gives little or no account of many parts of the score, in particular the dances. Only one dance is referred to by name—the *pas d'action* of Odette and Siegfried; others are rationalized indirectly by generalities to the effect that dances are being performed; still others, including the national dances, are not mentioned at all.

The distinction between dance and narrative inferred thus from the libretto has important choreographic and musical consequences. Narrative and dance in *Swan Lake* are comparable to recitative and aria in Metastasian opera, where action progresses in recitative and gives way to reflection in the aria. Dances are the arias (and ensembles and choruses) of *Swan Lake*—moments of choreographic reflection or the elaboration of a thought, related to the narrative but during which the story ceases to move forward.

The music follows suit. Dances are in all respects simpler than music which describes narrative: they proceed rhythmically with an audible pulse, regular periodicity in the phrases, and a major articulation every 32 to 48 bars. Textures are light, variations for solo dancers often being scored for an obbligato instrument and strings. The harmony is free of complex chords and modulations. In contrast, the music that describes narrative may be complicated, as the composer is free of his obligations to dancers. Structure and style vary in accordance with what is being described, but harmonic and rhythmic complexities and dense textures and scoring are all permitted. In short, the music may be close in its style to Tchaikovsky's symphonies and tone poems.

Slonimsky, arguing for a connection between the peasants' waltz and Odette's narration, takes no account of the fact that the first is a dance and the second an action scene. Because a dance is involved, his conclusion, which proceeds from the hypothesis that all the music of *Swan Lake* is relevant to the narrative, is weakened if not invalidated by the libretto—to say nothing of the traditional distinctions of choreographic and musical styles which Tchaikovsky observed when composing the ballet.

The orchestration of *Swan Lake*, praised so generously by critics of the first performance, deserves our attention for its merits and also as a standard against which to measure Tchaikovsky's achievements in the ballets which followed. An assessment may proceed from a number of perspectives.

In a historical context, Tchaikovsky's scoring in part draws on ante-cedents in Glinka—not in that his music sounds like Glinka's, for the ideas are quite different, but in the clarity and brightness of timbre of which he is capable. The very first bars of the ballet reflect this heritage in the choice of distinctive primary sonorities—the oboe, then the clarinet, then the cello (Ex. 18).

Ex. 18   Introduction, bars 1–12

The *entr'acte* at the beginning of Act IV is another example, as are virtually all the classical dances.

A second historical factor which conditioned Tchaikovsky's scoring in *Swan Lake* was his perception of specialist ballet music. The numerous obbligato parts of the traditional ballet solos sound forth again and again in *Swan Lake*, but perhaps nowhere more characteristically than in the violin solo of the *pas de deux* from Act I (Ex. 19).

Ex. 19   No. 5/II, bars 1–8

Similarly, the second variation of the *pas de trois* highlights the solo instrument in the plainest of textures (Ex. 20). It is one of several such examples.

Ex. 20   No. 4/III, bars 1–6

But in these and all other like passages there is something new and untraditional: Tchaikovsky, unlike his specialist colleagues, constantly elaborates his ideas. The violin solo (in its continuation) pushes forward from tradition in the evocative quality of its orchestral background (at bars 49–64—the music used for the appearance of Odette in the window of the ballroom in the Petipa–Ivanov revision), and also, if we look at the ballet orchestra of 1877 in a practical light, in the technical demands of the solo part. The music of the entire solo, moreover, traverses a number of momentary changes of style, including an almost Mahleresque juxtaposition of gypsy-like and ethereal intonations.

In the variation from the *pas de trois* Tchaikovsky was not satisfied with a single soloist, as was the habit of specialists, and so elaborated the music in the instrumental sounds: the clarinet gives way to the flute, the flute to the oboe, the oboe back again to the clarinet.

Tchaikovsky made a third concession to the specialist in the codas of the classical variation suites, which without exception are brassy, vivacious, and somewhat overblown. They constitute the most clichéd music in *Swan Lake*, and are very unlike his personal style. In the absence of the specialist tradition it is difficult to imagine them to be his.

If the scoring of *Swan Lake* owes something to history, it also owes something to the individuality of its composer. There are many signs of this, such as the fully characteristic use of the winds in arpeggios (or similar figures) as accompaniments, which occurs within a few bars of the beginning of the ballet (see bars 9–12 of Ex. 18), and the trill-like figure in the peasants' waltz (Ex. 21).

The full-throated tutti outbursts in descriptive music are very different in effect from the equally loud tuttis of the codas of the variation suites, but are far more typical of Tchaikovsky's personal style. His reliance on trombones, tubas, and percussion as the basis of these passages is evident in the storm scene and is virtually predictable in any music accompanying

Ex. 21 No. 2, bars 201–8

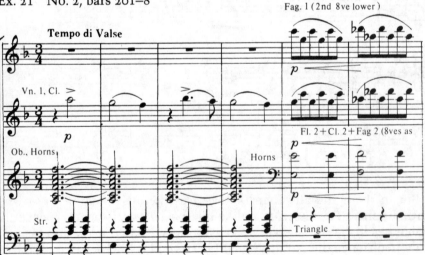

moments of crisis. In complaining of this (see Chap. 1, pp. 52–3), Laroche may have been right—Tchaikovsky did have a weakness for loud sounds. But there are considerations which mitigate his criticism as it relates to *Swan Lake*: one, already observed, is the function of the introduction as an exordium; to additional arguments we shall return presently.

Ex. 22   No. 10, bars 1–3

Orchestration, finally, lies at the heart of Tchaikovsky's marvellous talent for evocation, most prominently represented by the swan music. One cannot imagine what could better convey the image and sense of atmosphere—isolated and mysterious—of a group of swans coming to rest on a lake in the forest at nightfall than Tchaikovsky's famous oboe solo, accompanied by the harp and tremolo strings (Ex. 22).

Equally appropriate sound images are found for other situations, such as the music of the arrival of the guests in Act III, with its quiet hints of doom in the trumpets (Ex. 23), or the sadness suggested by the winds in the Dances of the Little Swans (Ex. 15, above)—granting here as elsewhere that the effect is partly attributable to the expressive connotations of the musical idea itself, its melody, rhythm, and harmony.

Ex. 23   No. 17, bars 73–80

Soviet analysis of orchestration, while including some of the ideas cited thus far, has distinctive components of its own which relate the orchestration to the drama. Some are comparatively simple, such as Tchaikovsky's use of orchestral dialogue in mimed scenes. When Odette and Siegfried first meet, one presumes that the oboe, a soprano instrument, represents Odette, and the cello in its tenor register Siegfried (Ex. 24).

The most celebrated example of this device, the reprise of the opening section of the *adagio* of Odette and Siegfried, was originally composed as a duet for soprano and baritone voices (Ex. 25).

According to Soviet theory, orchestration is at the centre of a particular kind of dynamic development, in which restatements of a theme occur

Ex. 24   No. 11, *Scène*, bars 48–63

Ex. 25   No. 13/V, bars 76–81

with ever more powerful contrasts and extensions. The development of
the swan theme in this manner continues through all four acts and reflects
the increasingly grave plight of the swan maidens. In Act I, the initial
statement (above, Ex. 22) is followed by an extension in the major mode.
The swans, as yet unthreatened, are merely being introduced (Ex. 26).

Already in Act II the extension has become more ominous; this version
will return in Act IV. Tchaikovsky uses it to frame the part of the ballet in
which the fated lovers meet, and we learn of the obstacles to their
happiness. He begins again with the music of Ex. 22 (Ex. 27).

Ex. 26   No. 9, *Scène*, bars 26–8 (first continuation of the swan theme)

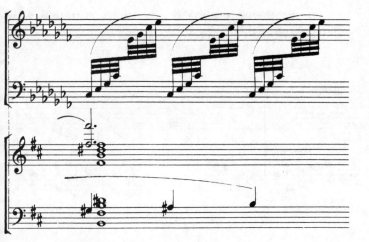

Ex. 27   No. 10, *Scène*, bars 38–43 (second continuation of the swan theme)

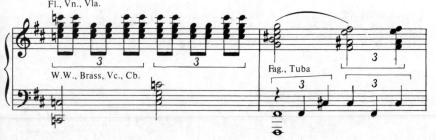

In the ballroom act the theme returns briefly twice, surrounded by intonations associated with Rothbart (Ex. 28).

Ex. 28   No. 18, *Scène*, bars 39–51

And in the final scene the swan theme sounds forth in the full orchestra as Odette and Siegfried meet their end. Respite comes only with a *subito piano*; a flock of swans appears, and the French horn which sounds at the culmination of the final *crescendo* was surely intended by the composer to coincide with the libretto's reference to 'the moon's pale rays [which] cut through the dispersing storm clouds'.

Each stage in the 'dynamic' development of the swan theme thus corresponds to a point of heightened intensity in the narrative; the theme articulates 'waves' of increasing musico-dramatic importance. But this kind of developmental procedure is not limited to music so fundamental to the story: it can shape a single number, even one which stands apart from the narrative. Indeed, the interaction of dance and symphony is nowhere more happily illustrated than in the waltzes of the ballet. Here too the devices of development are immediately apparent: the greater melodic richness of each succeeding section; the controlled increase of effect to create 'waves' of emotional impact; the sudden, artless return of an opening theme, imbued with a sense of renewal for all the contrasting ideas and development that have come between it and the first statement. All these devices make the waltz symphonic, and permit the musical content to prevail over the metrical requirements of the dance.

Soviet analytical thought is inseparable from social thought, and not wholly comprehensible without it. Indeed, the tradition of interpreting Tchaikovsky's ballets sociologically, in a manner sometimes crude and strident, sometimes eloquent or recondite, began with the reviews of the first performance of *Swan Lake*. Although Western critics tend to consider such an approach irrelevant to the lasting importance of these works, a knowledge of Soviet interpretations provides an important background to a technically-oriented analysis.

Perhaps the most striking interpretation of *Swan Lake* was written by the academician Boris Asafiev for the programme booklet of the Leningrad revival of the work in 1933. It makes extraordinary reading for present-day audiences: Tchaikovsky is portrayed as a rebel against the bourgeois society of his time, and *Swan Lake* as a document of protest, in which 'the fundamental dramatic motive of disobedience of the main hero encircled by narrowmindedness, and the growth of opposition through deepening love emotion to spontaneously impassioned indignation and destruction were carried through very logically.'[10]

Asafiev claims that the fantastic world of the swans should not be taken literally but as a conception of the sensitive artist (Siegfried in the ballet, and in turn Tchaikovsky himself):

... the two-dimensionality of the world in *Swan Lake* is not the two-dimensionality of the Philistine and the petty bourgeoisie, but the opposition between the Philistine world of the feudal and the idealized world of feeling, the 'spiritual world' solely and originally human. This is not a fairy-tale utopian world, but a psychologically real one.[11]

Rothbart, in Asafiev's view, becomes a severe and gloomy feudal potentate, accompanied either by military fanfares or by powerfully march-like intonations, while the romantic fairy-tale images of Swan Lake, he contends, 'are humanized by Tchaikovsky to such a degree that the drama of the swan and Siegfried moves [us] as a drama of actuality.'[12]

Disregarding the pressures of the era, which may have made such a view expedient (the edition here quoted was published in 1934, soon after the doctrine of Socialist Realism was proclaimed), one finds that the versatile Asafiev in this case, as so often on other subjects, set forth premises which continue to echo in the more temperate criticism of recent times. The most important of these are: (1) that meaning is infused into the story by the expressive power of music; (2) that the apparently fantastic is converted into the realistic—albeit the psychologically realistic—thus imbuing fantasy with a potential for social relevance; and (3) that the most significant assessment of music proceeds from ideological premises, leaving technical analysis for comparatively rudimentary observations.

The problem emerging from these views is not necessarily their ideological orientation, but that they discourage, under the threat of being accused of formalism, a study of stylistic subtleties which would complement the kinds of observations made so far in the present inquiry. In the case of Swan Lake these have to do with the means of coherence which unify the ballet as a single entity.

Melodic recurrence and the use of a principal key are important, apart from their contribution to coherence, because they are straightforward and unambiguous devices. Indeed, the swan theme, the waltz within the Dances of the Swans, and the principal theme of the Waltz of the Prospective Fiancées span large sections of the score and are frequently repeated. The concept of unity of key, in this case B minor, which begins and ends the ballet and closes three of the four acts, is a staple of tonal music. But the very obviousness of these devices conspires with the accusation that nineteenth-century ballet music lacks the sophistication of opera or concert music, making it difficult to speculate on the creative stimuli at the heart of the score.

If Swan Lake is a story of a prince and an evil genie and swan maidens, it is also a score of carefully chosen tonalities. While Tchaikovsky said nothing of this, he seems to have used tonality to achieve a pervasive unity which could reflect the narrative cogently and yet be as little affected as possible by the practical requirements of ballet music and the whims of the balletmaster. Judging by the music, it would seem that the composer used tonality in two distinct ways: as a consistent association with a person or circumstance; and as a means of heightening three critical focal points in the narrative by means of a particular progression.

This hypothesis is based not only on study of the score but also on remarks Tchaikovsky himself wrote in the holograph—the same remarks about narrative, already mentioned in Chapter One (pp. 39–40), which appear to be survivals from a balletmaster's plan. Tchaikovsky must have placed these signposts in the music only where he thought they were important, for they do not constitute a systematic attempt at annotation. Much of the score lacks any hint of the accompanying stage action.

The principal associations are given in the following table:

Subject	Tonality	Justification of the association
1. The swans	B minor	Principal key of the ballet; key of the scenes where the swans appear (Nos. 9, 10, 14, end of 29).
2. Siegfried	D major	Key of the opening scene, of his birthday; key of an orchestral outburst within Odette's narrative (No. 11, bars 261–4) marked by Tchaikovsky's quotation of Siegfried's 'O forgive me!' (a quotation omitted in most published scores).
3. Odette	E major/ A minor	A minor: key of her first appearance and her death; E major: key of her solo, of an interlude in the love duet, and of the coda of the Dances of the Swans (in which she doubtless made an appearance).
4. Owl/Rothbart	C major/ F minor+ F major	C major: key of owl's appearance in Odette's narrative; F minor and major: key of Rothbart's arrival and wrongdoing in Act III.
5. Odette's prospect of marriage	F♯ minor/ G♭ major	Odette tells of how she can be saved in F♯ minor (No. 11, bars 233 ff.); the love duet begins in G♭ major.
6. Siegfried's unhappiness	A♭ major	Key of Siegfried's lament ('The end of our carefree life': No. 3, bars 86 ff.); key of the Waltz of the Prospective Fiancées and of the repeat of this dance, during which he chooses Odile (No. 24, bars 38 ff.).

Tchaikovsky gives meaning to these associations by implication, through the proximity or distance of the keys in relation to one another. These relationships can easily be judged by recourse to the 'circle of fifths' (so called because, reading clockwise, each key is a perfect fifth above its predecessor on the perimeter).

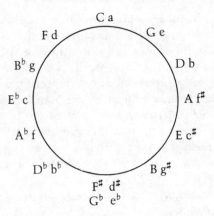

Each pair of keys (major and minor) shares the same key signature, and the two are therefore closely related. Adjacent keys are closely related, with a difference in key signature of only one accidental. Keys opposite one another are the most distant, with completely different key signatures.

The circle of fifths can tell us much about why Tchaikovsky chose the keys he did. We see, for example, that Siegfried (D major) and the swans (B minor) are closely related, as are Siegfried's unhappiness (Ab major) and Rothbart (F minor), since both these pairings are associated with a coupling of major and minor keys. Yet each pairing is distantly related to the other, being opposites on the circle of fifths. The rationale for Tchaikovsky's choice of keys in each act is now apparent: Acts I, II, and IV are dominated by the swans and are in their key; Act III, where evil triumphs, is in F minor and major. The ominous effect of the interludes between the herald's trumpets and the statements of the Waltz of the Prospective Fiancées (see Ex. 23, above) can now clearly be appreciated as announcements of the principal key of the act, anticipating the coming of Rothbart and Odile. The C major of the owl's appearance represents another diametric opposition—to the Gb major of the love duet, which represents Odette's chance to escape the evil influence. Other keys chosen by Tchaikovsky are near opposites. The distant relationship of A major to Ab major reinforces the near opposition of a number of strands of the drama:

A major	*Ab major*
The arrival of the Princess at Siegfried's party	Siegfried's dejection after his mother asks him to marry
Dances of the swans, No. 13/I and III	Dances of the swans, No. 13/VI (virtually the same music as 13/I and III)
Dances of the swans, No. 13/I and III (a waltz)	Waltz of the Prospective Fiancées

And further keys reinforce closely related characters and situations: Siegfried's D major, the swans' B minor and A major (in the dances of Act II), Odette's E major, and the F♯ minor of her promise of salvation are all adjacent on the circle of fifths.

With an awareness of these associations, we may now answer Laroche's question, 'For what do the trumpets, trombones, and kettledrums roar when a band of swans flies in the depth of the empty stage?' He did not specify the passage, but if it was in the middle of No. 10— the loudest part of the ballet to answer this description before the final scene—it would appear that his question was based on a false premise, for the point of this passage does not reside in its orchestration. Tchaikovsky uses sonority here only to emphasize the harmony, which summarizes by means of triads the conflicting pressures on Odette, namely the C major triad representing the threat of evil and the F♯ (Gb) major triad representing the promise of salvation (see Ex. 27, bars 38–41).

Tchaikovsky's assignment of keys to characters and situations in *Swan Lake* is clearly related to the drama. But it is nevertheless rather an arbitrary matter, dramatically speaking, and static, resistant to change. In contrast, the articulation of critical moments in the narrative by means of a tonal progression is a dynamic process, contributing a sense of event.

To effect this process Tchaikovsky chose the most basic device in traditional harmony, the perfect cadence, that simple progression of one triad to another a perfect fifth away. The first (the dominant) is a major triad; the second (the tonic) may be either major or minor. They progress from movement to repose: in a typical perfect cadence the dominant triad is unstable, in that the listener expects it to resolve on to the tonic.

In general, of course, Tchaikovsky uses the perfect cadence innumerable times, but there are only three occasions in the whole of *Swan Lake* when he gives it the special purpose of reinforcing the articulation of critical points in the drama: in connection with Odette and her fate; with the evil force which threatens her; and with her marriage. (The two pairs of keys listed in the table of associations for Odette and the owl/Rothbart, if construed as triads, would form a cadence if played in sequence.) The expanse of time involved in the operation of these special cadences in *Swan Lake* is very great, and the cadential process therefore very slow and frequently interrupted. Indeed, it would be inaudible if the composer did not introduce each cadence in such a way as to leave a tentative impression of preparedness to take a decisive step, and then re-create this impression near the point of resolution.

Odette appears in Act II in the key of A minor, but the chord sounding at this moment is its dominant, a triad of E major (Ex. 29).

This dominant does not immediately proceed to its resolution, and when Tchaikovsky persists in delaying it the listener's ear, in the welter of other musical activity, soon loses track of the need for resolution. Not

Ex. 29   No. 11, *Scène*, bars 39–47

until the beginning of the last scene of the ballet does the E major triad sound forth again so forcefully as the dominant of A minor, and here, finally, it does resolve itself, at the *Allegro agitato* which coincides with the final moments of Odette's life. Tchaikovsky thus marks with this special cadence the span of Odette's existence in the ballet:

> Odette appears [. . .] Odette dies
> dominant ——→ [. . .] ——→ (dominant to) tonic

The threat constantly facing Odette is treated in a similar way. As mentioned, the owl which makes an appearance in the middle of Odette's narrative is accompanied by music in C major (see Ex. 11, above); but it is soon reinterpreted as a dominant (at No. 11, bar 200). Later, in the scene where Rothbart tricks Siegfried, C major returns in the same way—as a temporary key which in the retrospect of a few moments is heard as a dominant of F minor, this time the fullblown F minor which accompanies Rothbart's treachery.

When, finally, Odette in the latter part of her narrative explains that her marriage would free her from the evil spell, Tchaikovsky accompanies the passage with yet another dominant, established by the continuously sounding C♯ in the bass (Ex. 30).

He is careful to sustain this important pitch through much of the rest of the narrative, and to produce it again for several bars without a break at the beginning and the end of the next number, the entrance of the swans. This

Ex. 30   No. 11, *Scène*, bars 218–24

dominant has to wait less time for its resolution than did the first two: Tchaikovsky resolves it at the beginning of the love duet, the point where Odette comes closest to marriage and rescue.

These special progressions may be summarized diagrammatically:

Dominant of A minor
(Odette first appears)

Dominant of F minor
(evil first appears)

Dominant of F♯ minor/ ──────────→ Tonic of G♭ major (the
G♭ major (Odette   beginning of the love
explains her salvation   duet)
through love and marriage)

Tonic of F minor (evil
materialized in Rothbart's
villainy)

Tonic of A minor
(Odette's death)

The most enigmatic and at the same time the most significant number in the entire ballet, from both an analytical and a historical standpoint, is the love duet. This *pas d'action* is the most important of several pieces of borrowed music which Tchaikovsky incorporated into the score,[13] the main section being a parody (in the musicological sense) of the duet of Undine and Huldbrand from the opera *Undine*, composed in 1869 and subsequently destroyed.[14] In the opera the water spirit Undine tells her mortal lover that he must die for having betrayed her, a situation paralleled in the ballet (Undine's declaration becoming Odette's warning).

The first part of the *pas d'action* is an *adagio* in ternary form which leads without a break into the second part, an *allegro* coda in a different key. Because of its length and contrasts of musical style the *pas d'action* as a whole has an asymmetrical structure:

> Adagio, Part I (G♭ to e♭)
> transition
> Adagio, Part IIa (E)
> transition
> Adagio, Part IIb (B)
> transition
> Adagio, Part I (reprise)
> Coda (E♭)

The transitional passages are all characterized by the same rhythmic motive:

The most unusual tonal characteristic of the number is the brevity of the opening key, G♭ major. Indeed, after the first ten bars of Part I the music turns decisively to E♭ minor. Without the introductory harp cadenza (on the dominant of G♭ major), these ten bars, and their counterparts in the reprise of Part I the entire piece could be heard in other keys, principally E♭ minor, which Tchaikovsky had not used before in the ballet. The composer entered no comments in the holograph at the point where this key is introduced, but there is reason to suppose that he used it to prepare the tragedy that follows in Act III.

The very swiftness with which E♭ minor displaces G♭ major at the beginning of the *adagio* makes the latter only a temporary key, with the inference that the happiness of Odette (which depends on Siegfried's constancy), represented by G♭ major as a key, is also temporary; and G♭ major makes no return in the ballet. Among the associative tonalities of *Swan Lake*, E♭ minor, and more particularly E♭ major, which Tchaikovsky introduces emphatically in the *allegro* coda, stands as a symbol separating the lovers: E♭ major lies between Siegfried's D and Odette's E, practically opposite both on the circle of fifths.

Later, the tonality of the coda exerts a decisive influence over the key of the next dance as a dominant preparation for it: the reprise of No. 13/I, which in No. 13/III had been repeated in the original key of A major, returns in A♭ major when repeated in No. 13/VI. This immediately follows the love duet.[15] The music first bodes ill for Odette in the disappearance of G♭ major, and ends up in the next dance by moving to the key associated with Siegfried's unhappiness. The dominant–tonic cadential progression in A♭ major thus produced between the end of the *pas d'action* and the beginning of the waltz reprise anticipates the repetitions of the same cadence between the fanfares of the herald's trumpets and the Waltz of the Prospective Fiancées. The last such cadence will bring Rothbart and Odile.

As if to underline the significance of key in the love duet and the

influence of this number over the waltz reprise, Tchaikovsky adds an aura
of alarm by introducing into the waltz an accompanimental figure not
present in its preceding appearances, drawn from the transitions of the love
duet (Ex. 31).

Ex. 31   No. 13/VI, bars 1–11

These musical events are sinister for yet another reason: they unmask a
subtle change in the ground rules by which Tchaikovsky is arranging his
tonal plan. The interpretation of the love duet and its aftermath invokes
not just the devices of associative tonality and cadential action, but also
interchange of mode (the substitution of a major key for one in the parallel
minor, and vice versa), and enharmony. Both are involved in the resolution
of the cadence between the last section of Odette's narrative and the
beginning of the love duet, where a dominant of F♯ minor moves to a tonic
of G♭ major. Change of mode is what makes relatively uneventful to the
ear the important shift in orientation from E♭ minor in the *adagio* of the
love duet to E♭ major in the *allegro* with which it ends. (Also Tchaikovsky
softens the harshness of the F minor association with evil by letting that
key mingle freely with its parallel major in Acts II and III.)

While enharmony and interchange of mode are common enough in music since 1800, they depend for their effect more on a conditioned response in the listener than do scale and cadence, which are more closely allied with acoustical principles. In the context of the drama at this point, the first two devices symbolize the intrusion of misleading external appearances into a system of thought hitherto guided by what may be called (in comparison) natural laws. Enharmony and mode change are examples of musical sleight-of-hand, and Tchaikovsky calls on them to impart a deceptive quality to the concept of evil, and to convey the uncertain, illusory basis on which rests Odette's escape from evil through marriage, her trust in Siegfried. The passage which accompanies Odette's death, unhindered by these devices, is made thereby more powerful, deliberate, and inevitable.

But what of the rest of the music, for which Tchaikovsky left no remarks in the score? It seems hardly accidental that this includes most of the music of which the libretto, likewise, takes little or no account—the dances themselves.

There are three suites of classical variations in *Swan Lake*: the *pas de trois* and *pas de deux* in Act I, and the *pas de six* in Act III. The first two (Nos. 4 and 5) are given only the slightest justification in the libretto: 'The peasants dance now in groups, now separately. Deferential Wolfgang, having drunk a little more, also joins in the dancing . . .' As for the music, we have clues which point to narrative significance, but no more. Unlike the other two *pas*, the *pas de trois* forms a closed, interrelated succession of keys which may be construed as an extended cadence formula in the key of Bb major:

Section:	Intrada	II	III	IV	V	Coda
Key:	B^b	g	E^b	c	F	B^b
Cadence formula:	I	vi	IV	ii	V	I

This tonal organization, together with the fact that Bb major is not among the important associative tonalities in *Swan Lake*, encourage the conclusion that the *pas de trois* represents a discrete 'island' of music within Act I, unrelated to the keys of narrative importance introduced up to that point.

This claim cannot be made so readily in the *pas de deux*. Narrative significance may be concealed in the facts that Siegfried danced in this number, that it began in his key, and in the elision between the opening waltz and the *andante*, and again in that between the *andante* and the *allegro* which follows. These elisions seem to say that the music following them is not to be omitted (with the possible implication that such music was important to the story). Knowing the stage action, moreover, would permit us to judge if there was any narrative significance in the opening phrase of the *andante*, which is a near quotation of the opening phrase of the entire ballet (Exx. 32–3).

Ex. 32   No. 5/II, bars 1–4

Ex. 33   Introduction, bars 1–3

There are similar hints that the *pas de six* meant something within the story. The libretto is more expansive here than it was in creating a setting for the dances in Act I: 'For some time the Prince gazes in admiration at the dancing Odile, and then himself takes part in the dances.' And, after a short dialogue between the Princess and Wolfgang, 'the dances continue, and during them the Prince shows a clear preference for Odile, who coquettishly shows off in front of him. In a moment of passion the Prince kisses Odile's hand. At that point the Princess and old Rothbart get up from their places and go to the centre, towards the dancers.'

Several features of the *pas de six* suggest that it served a narrative purpose. One has already been mentioned: the suitability of the variation in C minor (No. 19/[IV]), based on its musical style, as a dance for the evil Rothbart (see above, p. 66). The way the *intrada* begins is another: it proceeds directly from the end of the preceding number by cadential action, creating an elision similar to those in the *pas de deux*. In his choice of keys, moreover, Tchaikovsky links these dances with the rest of the act, especially in the last variation and the coda, in F minor and Ab major, respectively. Bars 5 and 6 of the last variation (the end of the introductory harp cadenza) are so similar in placement and effect to the corresponding passage in the love duet (no. 13/V, the end of bar 8) that the listener may be permitted the speculation that this dance was Odile's response or counterpart to Odette's *adagio* in Act II.

A striking coincidence of key, scoring, and metre across the entire *pas de six* forms a broad musical parallel between it and the other suite of Act I, the *pas de trois*:

No. 4, *Pas de trois*:

B♭	g	E♭	c	F	B♭
6/8	3/4	2/4	6/8	2/4	4/4
harp	oboe/bassoon	clarinet,	tutti	flute	coda;
	duet	flute			off-beat
					stress
					in
					melody

No. 19, *pas de six*:

F	B♭	g	E♭	c	f	A♭
4/4	2/4	2/4	6/8	4/4	2/4	4/4
	clarinet,	oboe/bassoon		tutti	oboe	coda;
	flute	duet				off-beat
						stress in
						melody

It is as if Tchaikovsky wanted to link all the variation suites by incorporating into the *pas de six* the tonal profile and many other likenesses from the *pas de trois* (with tonal changes appropriate to the new setting) and the subtle narrative implications of the *pas de deux*.

If parts of the variation suites can make a tenuous claim to further the story, the national dances appear to be pure *divertissement*. Their keys have all appeared earlier, but recur here without any hint of their associations elsewhere; indeed, they almost resist interpretation.[16] As a group, they are properly construed as stylish evocations of their countries, justified by balletic tradition and the expectations of the audience.

Whatever the validity of the shreds of evidence which suggest that the dances were integrated into the story, it is a fact that this music, with rare exceptions, bears little or no resemblance to the narrative music. For this reason the variation suites must be considered a separate part of the score. We must also conclude that Tchaikovsky allowed a disparity of style to exist in *Swan Lake*, arising from the juxtaposition of this style with his own more complex, more characteristic writing.

Other conclusions emerge from a scrutiny of *Swan Lake*. As regards the analysis of tonality, there is no question that Tchaikovsky knew what he was doing, only whether he was conscious of it: the coherence provided in the score by tonality is not so much recondite as subliminal. He was certainly aware of working for a balletmaster; but he was also working for himself, guided by a sure creative instinct. The tonal analysis, more than an exercise in picking out keys, forms the basis of Tchaikovsky's claim to historical accomplishment: it is no less than a great composer would be expected to do.

Yet one is reminded of Gerald Abraham's assessment of *A Life for the Tsar*, which applies also to *Swan Lake*: whatever its status as a landmark, the work is more of the past than of the future; it is of a genre that was about to fall out of fashion, to be seen as obsolete. But *Swan Lake* is more. If we find Tchaikovsky willing to conform to traditional practice in many respects, we also find him exploring and enlarging its possibilities at every turn. It is not strictly greater creative imagination as it relates to the quality of melody and harmony which separates Tchaikovsky from his specialist colleagues; it is the work of a mind constantly moving forward. For this reason, as well as in its choice of subject matter, *Swan Lake* is the last (and perhaps finest) example of the romantic ballet which originated with Adam, Taglioni, and Gauthier.

3

St Petersburg

❦

(a) Vsevolozhsky and Theatre Reform

WE have seen that *Swan Lake* was taken out of the repertory in Moscow in part because the imperial ballet in that city lost both personnel and financial support in one sweeping administrative reorganization. The Petersburg theatres were also reorganized, though not with such drastic results for the ballet,[1] and a study of Tchaikovsky's works as first produced in the Maryinsky Theatre should begin with a consideration of this theatre reform (as it was called at the time both in earnest and in derision) and its architect, Ivan Alexandrovich Vsevolozhsky (1835–1909).

Of distinguished lineage—from Ryurik through the princes of Smolensk[2]—Vsevolozhsky, like many of his ancestors, devoted himself to the service of the state. After graduating from the University of St Petersburg he worked in the Asian Section of the Department of Internal Affairs, then briefly at the Russian consulate in The Hague, and again in Petersburg as an official of special missions. Nothing about his service suggested a particular flair for directing the state theatres—though lack of aptitude or qualifications did not keep his predecessors from the post—before his assignment in 1876 to the Russian consulate in Paris. Over the next five years Vsevolozhsky developed a love for French culture and acquainted himself with the theatres of Paris and other major capitals. When Alexander III ascended the throne he appointed Vsevolozhsky Director of Imperial Theatres, from 3 September 1881.[3] Vsevolozhsky filled this post for almost eighteen years before becoming Director of the Imperial Hermitage, an appointment he held for the last ten years of his life.[4]

Vsevolozhsky's response to the theatre had its roots in his own artistic creativity. Beneath the gentle countenance lay a caricaturist of sharp eye and sure hand:

Enchantingly kind, most good, even somewhat bashful, Ivan Alexandrovich perceived with astonishing insight the humorous sides of the management, of friends, and of the most varied persons whom he encountered on his way. No one, once prominent, escaped his killing artistic verdict. It is said that Vsevolozhsky's talent for caricature spoiled his diplomatic career . . .[5]

As Director of Theatres, Vsevolozhsky applied his gift to the practical needs of opera and ballet. He prepared at least 1,087 drawings of costumes for 25 productions (including 221 for *Sleeping Beauty* and *Nutcracker* alone) and probably more which have been lost.

And in his last years,

... in his office in the [Winter] Palace looking out on the Neva, in the Imperial Hermitage he was surrounded by paintings, statues, various works of art by celebrated masters of the entire world. All the artists of the past, Italians, Spaniards, Dutchmen, cordially looked out from their golden frames at their esteemed protector. They felt the eye of their Director, a true savant of art, lovingly caress and care for them ... Here, among them, the venerable Maecenas would be revived by a youthful energy. Beauty was everything to him, and amidst the works of old masters he took delight and experienced a special artistic pleasure, a satisfaction from the beautiful.[6]

Vsevolozhsky was more than a skilled artist and connoisseur. Alexandre Benois perceived a special quality in him:

There are artists who are creators of works, and there are artists in their whole life and temperament. The first comprise an infinitely small part of humankind, but the second, perhaps, are even rarer. In any event, in the broad circle of my acquaintances I know only four persons who would be outstanding 'artists of life', and one of them was I. A. Vsevolozhsky.

Benois assesses Vsevolozhsky's manner and outlook with eloquence and insight:

I. A. Vsevolozhsky was not ... a brilliant chatterer, an obtrusive wit, or a *bon-motiste*. His conversation was distinguished by simplicity, goodwill, evenness; his witticisms and epigrams were always adorned with kind, heartfelt goodness. His small talk, a sin of the time and milieu, ... [contained] a charming note of 'self-irony', a kind of suppressed grief, a quality of disappointment ... a touch of Voltaire and Pushkin was communicated to all in the special flavour of what I. A. Vsevolozhsky said ...

Discussion never came to argument. Ivan Alexandrovich was too true to ancient seigniorial habits, and too great a philosopher of life, to permit himself to take the offensive over a difference of opinion. But this reserve did not bring forth in him anything strained and tedious; one did not have to submit to it, for one was inevitably infected by it. Everything around Vsevolozhsky, his whole environment, breathed that high-born taste, that *parfait bon goût* which is such a great rarity in our time. His office in the Hermitage was uncomfortable and cramped, with low ceilings. Its only beauty was a view of the Neva, but even this was spoiled by the small windows which had the look of stateroom portholes. Ivan Alexandrovich, however, could impart to everything a *très grand air*, a kind of seigniorial dignity, a distinctive beauty ...

Finally, I. A. Vsevolozhsky himself, to all appearances, was in astonishing harmony with his life, with his character, and with the conviction of his words. I do not know how he was in his youth, but the old man could not in any case be called aught but beautiful. There was something unusual in his face, in his rounded carriage, in his measured, just dance-like gait. He himself knew this and loved to draw caricatures of himself in which he exaggerated his physical defects: but these very features only added a special charm and even elegance to his appearance. The fact is that they were put into a kind of harmony, a kind of proportion.

His manner of greeting was characteristic. Vsevolozhsky was brought up in the traditions of the eighteenth century, in the manners of which the dance played such an outstanding role, and for him dance did not seem something light and foolish. To the contrary, he held dance in the most profound esteem, and, thanks to his understanding of the significance of dance, ballet during Vsevolozhsky's directorate rose from complete decline to unprecedented flowering. Thanks to his relationship with dance, Ivan Alexandrovich's own gestures, in particular his bows, were marked by a special elegance and even complexity, and were distinguished sharply from the whole simplified American custom of our day. And yet there is something particularly remarkable in this: there was nothing affected in the refinement and complexity of Vsevolozhsky's manners, nothing, if I may express it thus, 'of a lisp'. From head to toe, in every movement, he was a great lord and at the same time—simplicity itself.[7]

It is no surprise that Tchaikovsky, who admired refinement and shunned ostentation in people, was attracted to Vsevolozhsky as a patron, and that Vsevolozhsky, among Russians who recognized Tchaikovsky's talent before it had won him widespread fame, ranks first in offering practical opportunities for the production of his theatrical works. Virtually all the important stage works of Tchaikovsky's late years—*Sleeping Beauty*, *The Queen of Spades*, *Nutcracker*, even the famous *Swan Lake* produced after his death—and many others less known in the West today, including *Iolanthe*, *The Enchantress*, and *Mazepa*—were produced, sometimes after many tribulations, under Vsevolozhsky's auspices. His record of sympathy and support was matched only by that of Nikolai Rubinstein in the realm of Tchaikovsky's concert music.

Vsevolozhsky's own preferences in art were French in particular and retrospective in general. Benois called him the last survival of the century of Catherine, and he was not alone in making this association:

The old Hermitage transported the great *barin*-patron back to the epoch of Catherine the Great, into the midst of the brilliant old cavaliers and courtly ladies. There in that circle of refined manners, with marvellous French pronunciation, with an astonishingly acute, quick-witted word, he was his own man.[8]

Hence, no doubt, the long and fruitful relationship between Vsevolozhsky and Marius Petipa (who had only praise for him), which resulted in a number of ballets which evoked France's golden age: *L'Ordre du roi*, *Les Ruses d'amour*, and, indirectly, even *Sleeping Beauty* itself.

But running a group of theatres has its practical side. Karl Valts wrote:

I. A. Vsevolozhsky was all but the most useful Director of Theatres during the whole time of my service. A cultured, enlightened man, he possessed, besides a fine understanding of art, a sharp critical mind, which penetrated into all the details of the daily events of the theatre.[9]

Not all views of Vsevolozhsky were so benevolent. Peter Gnedich, author and playwright, claimed that Vsevolozhsky was very condescending about Ostrovsky's plays, which were extremely popular at the time, and that this truly national art took last place in his priorities:

In Petersburg he [Vsevolozhsky] rated the ballet above all else because the Tsar's family attended it most often. Then followed opera, then French drama, then German drama, and last of all—Russian drama.[10]

Telyakovsky extended the criticism to include his manner:

In his treatment of subordinates I. A. Vsevolozhsky was always very courteous and obliging, especially with artists. He promised much and managed not to do still more. He was able somehow to get around a refusal in such a way that the guilty party was not he, but someone either above or below him, that is the Minister [of the Imperial Court] or the Supervisor of the Directorate's Affairs Vladimir Petrovich Pogozhev. . . He was a true *barin*, with the tastes of a European and the cunning of a diplomat. Sincere he never was, however, nor distinguished by strong feelings, and for this reason, though he loved theatre in the main, he was not really captivated by it. The principal goals towards which he strove were to please the court and not to be taken in by any extremes.[11]

Vsevolozhsky's critics sometimes claimed that he favoured his own artistic preferences in making official policy. Had this been true Alexander's choice of a Francophile would certainly have been surprising, for the Tsar abolished the imperial Italian opera in favour of the Russian, and made clear in other ways the nationalist leaning of his attitudes towards the arts. Only in exceptional cases, albeit well-publicized ones, such as that of producing certain nationalist operas, did Vsevolozhsky waver in his commitment to Russian art, and even in this instance he claimed that his actions were a direct reflection of the imperial family's displeasure with a particular work.[12] His own choice of repertory and his overall record of achievement, despite the French and French-oriented works in which he took a substantial personal interest, vindicate Alexander's choice.

When Vsevolozhsky assumed responsibility for the imperial theatres, he was charged (as had been his predecessors) with pursuing exalted goals: not simply to provide entertainment, but to act as a beneficial influence on literature, mores, and national consciousness, to establish a school and to encourage a tradition. The condition of the theatres before he initiated his reforms, however, shows how much reality had fallen short of these aims. In the nineteenth century the post of Director of Theatres had been filled, with few exceptions, by men without the necessary experience or capacities. The resources of money and talent, which were plentiful, had been dissipated by mismanagement and the lack of leadership, with theft and waste, inadequate training, and insufficient rehearsal being some of the results. Apart from that of the highest-ranking artists, pay was low, as were fees for playwrights and composers. Performance standards consequently fell and contributed to a gradual stagnation of the repertory. In addition, the scandalous lives of some of the directors had become well known:

The history of our theatre management up to the time of Baron Kister [Vsevolozhsky's immediate predecessor] is not complicated. One head of theatres, dancing in the boudoir of a lady dancer, broke his leg; another, departing from the boudoir of a lady dancer, went to Senate Square to pacify the rebels and was killed; a third managed Russian art from the boudoir of a lady dancer for some twenty years—and so forth, endlessly.[13]

Baron Kister, however, had a particularly unenviable reputation. 'This German baron in Russian art', wrote A. S. Suvorin, 'played the role of the gardener in the greenhouse who could not make the flowers grow and instead planted cabbages and potatoes in it.'[14] Kister too enjoyed a dalliance with an artiste in his employ, but this was a minor matter compared with the widespread dislike of the man and his policies:

The retirement order of Baron Karl Karlovich Kister from the post he occupied was commented on for a week by Petersburg in many ways, or, more accurately, it was commented on by all in one accord, for there were no two opinions about the baron's work, if we disregard one special opinion—that of the baron about himself . . .
    A former Cavalry Pioneers officer, Baron Kister first served in the Botanical Garden, and then as a cashier at the Ministry of Court . . . So long as he was involved with the special affairs of the Ministry of Court, the public took little notice of Baron Kister, but when the state theatres were placed under him for several years, the name of Baron Kister became one of the most unpopular in Petersburg, thanks to his sometimes misplaced economy and his contempt for Russian art.[15]

And another wrote,

Baron Kister, like his immediate predecessors, had no particular love for the theatre, with the exception perhaps of some attraction to the French drama troupe. But at least he had a system, about which there was much talk at the time . . . It had the virtue of being well-defined: economy at any price. Like all others, this system had a certain rationale, and for people working in the theatre it had an additional meaning—that they at least knew they could rely on nothing, and ought to count only on themselves . . .
    In appearance during Kister's time everything could seem all right, even proper, but in fact everything was run in a slipshod way, not just as regards the companies which we consider models and which ought to be so, but also as regards Russian theatrical art in general.[16]

At the beginning of his term Vsevolozhsky was guided in part by complaints about Kister. On taking office he reaffirmed the goals of his predecessors, established a commission of experts to make and oversee new policies, and asked for suggestions from the public. The reforms he initiated were obscured by the arguments which they provoked, the difficulty of ascertaining what was promulgated in the ephemeral *Journal of Instructions* (an in-house publication which disseminated official policy —the dismissals of Diaghilev and Nijinsky, for example, were made official by publication in the *Journal*), and by the fact that so little of the work of Vsevolozhsky's deputies was reported accurately in the Press.[17] Included among the more sweeping measures, however, were the formation of a committee to determine repertory, the raising of salaries of all artists and workers (in some cases severalfold), and the increase of authors' fees from 2% to 10% of the box-office receipts. And there were many lesser improvements: the introduction of special drama and singing classes; the publication of *The Yearbook of the Imperial Theatres*;[18] the founding of central libraries of music, theatre, and production materials; the building of warehouses and other storage facilities; and the establishment of a photography studio within the imperial theatres. There are also reports of intangible improvements—more positive attitudes and greater willingness to co-operate at all levels—resulting from Vsevolozhsky's endearing personal attributes.

It was not long, however, before experience forced reconsideration of some of Vsevolozhsky's reforms. Certain directives had to be countermanded almost immediately. The prohibition against distribution of complimentary tickets proved embarrassing: some companies were playing to near-empty houses to the dissatisfaction both of artists and of the few who had paid for their admission. The directorate's monopoly on producing theatre posters, relinquished by the reformers, was quickly reinstated. Some of Vsevolozhsky's appointees were not successful in their new jobs, the literary–dramatic committee did not function as anticipated, some decisions were not in keeping with the goal of furthering national art (many of the leading positions in the ballet company and the Russian opera, for example, were still filled by foreigners). In addition, the reforms were criticized by some who chose to interpret negatively any equivocal results and to emphasize the inevitable drawbacks of far-reaching administrative change. For such malcontents, increasing the size of the opera orchestra simply made the singers more difficult to hear, while increasing artists' salaries was an act of unwarranted generosity. And in fact the most devastating single criticism of Vsevolozhsky's reforms, and a well-founded one, was their extraordinary cost, estimated to be at least ten times the amount needed by the economical Baron Kister.[19] Whatever his artistic and diplomatic talents, Vsevolozhsky lacked Kister's fiscal ability, and he miscalculated the degree of sacrifice his public was willing to make for reforms. His attempt to recoup expenses with higher ticket prices—and his virtual destruction of the Moscow ballet—was universally condemned.

The ballet company in Petersburg received its share of attention. Questions were raised about merging it with opera, and even about whether it should continue to be supported by the state at all. While the training and performance abilities of its artists could withstand criticism, the company nevertheless suffered from serious problems in its repertory and methods of promotion. Vacancies were filled in order of seniority—hence young artists were denied sufficient opportunities to advance. Moreover, policies regarding benefit performances worked to the detriment of the company: new works were withheld for the occasion of someone's *bénéfice* (which justified much-inflated ticket prices), while most of the season a steady diet of repertory works was given. Vsevolozhsky's reforms did not deal with these problems. Thus Skalkovsky could write, of the post-reform ballet:

The opening of ballet performances at the beginning of the 1880s was accompanied by a kind of wailing and gnashing of teeth, for in the audience of the Bolshoy Theatre, thanks to the doubling of ticket prices at ballet performances (for what reason is still unknown), very few were present: whole rows of *loges* remained completely empty or the ballet company's help sat in them with their children and live-in relatives. Tickets for the ballet became even more expensive than for opera; this was decidedly without justification considering the make-up of the public which attended the ballet, and the directorate in the end lost rather than gained from the projected price rises. The balletomanes also had a real basis for complaint. In addition to everything else, the Bolshoy Theatre [in St Petersburg] was spoiled. True, in the foyer expensive brocade curtains had been hung, and signs of some renovation were visible—but in the hall itself the electric illumination was for some reason faulty, as a result of which it became too dark. The beautiful living pictures of *Trilby* were all lost, for the illumination reached the head of one dancer, the leg of another, the back of a third, etc. What was left remained in the darkness. Astonishingly beautiful!. . . It was necessary to sit very close to the stage with huge binoculars to distinguish anything in such darkness and still find pleasure in it . . .

The stalls were so far removed from the stage [by the installation of an enlarged orchestra pit] that the dancers—technically speaking—could no longer 'fire' at their 'subjects' successfully [that is, find a visible mark to measure turns accurately], and this deprived our sylphides of liveliness, and that happy state of mind was not to be seen which ought to have resulted from the generosity of the directorate, which doubled and sometimes tripled their salaries. The salaries only of ballerinas and some balletic invalids were lowered, who danced 'out of gratitude'—a special technical term—about twenty years beyond their pension time.

Despite the facts that a ticket for the ballet doubled in cost and bureaucrats came to be in charge of dancers' *tricot* and slippers, ballet seasons did not promise anything consoling. Foreign ballerinas were not expected, and the public was left with the same ballerinas as before, who for more than ten years had been a delight to our eyes. These were of course talented artists, but it would not have been bad to see somebody new, all the more in that the public paid money not for the sake of expressing esteem for some bureaucrat, but simply out of the wish to be entertained. Only the *corps de ballet* was strengthened by several Moscow dancers. But as the Moscow *corps de ballet* at that time distinguished itself only by its fat legs, this did not especially please the balletomanes embittered by 'reforms'. . .

Ballets were given that either bored everybody or never had enjoyed the affections of the public. But as there were few dances in these works, it is natural that while awaiting a pension, dancers were more comfortable performing in them. Execution was flabby and lifeless, the company became undisciplined; some dancers became mothers, others grandmothers; a majority put on weight . . .

Production in the old ballets was horrifying . . . The breadth of the Maryinsky stage, which exceeded by eight arshins [about 19 feet] the stage of the Bolshoy Theatre (but is a third smaller in depth), did not allow the use of ballet sets [used previously at the Bolshoy[20]], for which reason sets were taken from forgotten operas. Transformations and drops also astonished the audience by their primitiveness. Nothing like it had been seen since the mystery plays of the thirteenth century! . . .

Despite the threefold leadership in the form of régisseur, balletmaster, and special assistant in charge of ballet, various old works were given in place of the announced ballets for which the public had gathered. Under these circumstances the most important *pas* and variations, without substitutions, were removed from the ballets without ceremony. This would be the same as taking out the best arias or quartets in an opera. The defects of artists could have served as a justification for this, but (in this case) many artists, including talented ones, sat with nothing to do. And why should the public care, now paying twice as much money for tickets just to subsidize petty backstage machinations? If there is no one to dance, the directorate ought to have required Messrs régisseur, balletmaster and assistant in charge of ballet to dance a *pas de trois*, and not put before the public the scraps of a performance.[21]

While nothing in this account is untrue, Skalkovsky's tone is intentionally carping because it conceals an ulterior motive: he wanted to portray the darkness of the imperial ballet's condition before the dawn of Virginia Zucchi's arrival in Petersburg. Her dancing is credited with reviving public interest in ballet after the doldrums which Skalkovsky described; her coming itself, however, is directly related to one of Vsevolozhsky's principal reforms: the encouragement of private enterprise in theatre affairs.

This reform of Vsevolozhsky ended the state's century-old, uncompromising monopoly on the activities of commercial theatres in Moscow and St Petersburg:

We came to the idea of monopoly gradually; as misappropriation [*khishchenie*] developed there began, little by little, a restriction on private spectacles. This restriction, however, never was put into law and the public did not complain of monopoly since the directorate at that time concerned itself to such a degree with the needs of the audiences that even a horse circus was maintained for several years at state expense! The monopoly of the directorate became burdensome only with Baron Kister, and during his time it received its so-to-speak unlawful formulation.

According to the law, anyone who wished to give the residents of the capital aesthetic enjoyment with the aid of music, singing, or staging was a transgressor of the financial rights of the directorate, like some sort of smuggler or bootlegger in relation to the financial monopoly of the Exchequer. Smugglers of art, it is true, were not exiled with hard labour, but to receive permission for any kind of insignificant concert was considered a matter of state importance . . .

This situation was responsible for inexplicable contradictions. Concerts were prohibited, and the government in Petersburg alone supported three state singing schools in the form of a theatre school, a conservatory, and a chapel; in other words, it was abolishing with one hand what it was building up in the other. The same kind of contradiction held sway in everything. The ballet, demanding a large troupe and elaborate staging, necessarily required large receipts as well; ballet, however, was allotted one day a week, and it was only by accident that they could find, with difficulty, a free day for the general rehearsal of a new ballet.[22]

Pleshcheyev pointed out the differences under Vsevolozhsky:

In the course of Tsar Alexander Alexandrovich's reign, theatre affairs in the capitals were completely transformed. The commission for the revision of the regulations governing the imperial theatres decided a most significant question of principle: that the imperial theatres were not commercial institutions, and must pursue moral and educational ends.

In view of this they found it possible to grant full freedom of action to private theatres. Of course, such a conclusion of the commission was met with joy, and the directorate's burdensome, absurd tax on the enterprises of impresarios passed into eternity. The monopoly of the state theatres had not only drawn on inordinate taxes, but also had paralysed the activity of entrepreneurs by other means: opening private theatres at all had not been permitted if that was perceived as being in competition with the state's box office.[23]

The issues surrounding this seemingly right-minded decision made it more complex than the settling of a long-standing grievance. Morality was on the Director's side; a controversy developed around questions of money and taste:

In general they are quite deluded who see in freedom [of enterprise] a means of uplifting theatre in Russia. Freedom, of course, will increase the number of places for spectacles and diversions, but as the instincts and tastes of the mass of public are coarse and anti-aesthetic, then the satisfaction of these instincts constitutes the most important task of private enterprise, for which excellent dividends are more important than all the aesthetics in the world. One may cite the example of Paris to confirm this, where for twenty years freedom of the theatres did not produce one serious new company, but, on the contrary, destroyed the Italian opera, which had been the favourite entertainment of the best part of Parisian snobbery. Innumerable petty *café-chanteuses* won out, who rivalled the brothels in their activity.[24]

We do not know Vsevolozhsky's view of the controversy. If he was truly committed to creating ideal theatres for the state, granting free enterprise would work to his advantage, for he could expect commercial theatres to offer the kinds of fare that the state companies had until then offered by public demand. He would gain prestige by ending the monopoly, and the attractive salaries he could offer assured him parity in any competition with private impresarios for the services of leading artists. Except for the staggering cost of this reform, granting free enterprise was beneficial for the imperial stage.

It is therefore ironic that the performances of Italian ballerinas on the boards of the Maryinsky, which brought such vitality to the state company in the renewal of public interest and in new performance techniques for Russian dancers, should have been opposed by Vsevolozhsky and Marius Petipa because these dancers' styles represented a concession to vulgar tastes incompatible with their standards. But such was the case (particularly with Virginia Zucchi, less so with her successors), as we learn from Sergei Khudekov:

An artist in his soul, Vsevolozhsky for a long time did not agree [to Zucchi's appearance in the imperial theatres], arguing that there was no place for Zucchi on the ideal stage—where choreography is in strict accord with the demands of aesthetics—because of the nature of her talent. Petipa, likewise, was not inclined to invite, in his words, this unruly Italian virtuosa, who in Paris could not manage to get invited to the Grand Opera.[25]

Skalkovsky put aside his misgivings about private enterprise in Zucchi's case, and led a vigorous campaign which won her an invitation to perform before the Tsar.[26] Tchaikovsky, who apparently thought little of Zucchi's art, must surely have been grateful for it later when he saw one of Zucchi's compatriots create the role of Aurora.[27]

One final reform has particular relevance to Tchaikovsky: Vsevolozhsky abolished the post of ballet composer. When Ludwig Minkus retired from this position in 1886 the way was clear for fresh talents to meet the challenge of writing music for ballet. Reality once again frustrated expectation, however, for most of the composers who came forward—Schenk, Fitinhof-Schell, Armsheimer, and others of similar obscurity—made contributions which did not last in the repertory. The works of Tchaikovsky and Glazunov overshadowed and to some extent compensated for the others, but even with the beauties of *Raymonda*, *Nutcracker*, and *Sleeping Beauty*, demand for new music ran well ahead of supply. As a result, compositional duties reverted back to the chief ballet conductor (with whom they had rested before the specialist post had been created in the first place), and the directorate even had recourse to Minkus again after his retirement. As we shall discover, the state's need for ballet music, Vsevolozhsky's wish to improve its artistic quality, and the amenities of a production on the imperial stage were all factors in enticing Tchaikovsky back to ballet after what he had considered the failure of *Swan Lake*.

Indeed, the conditions under which Tchaikovsky had worked on *Swan Lake* cannot compare with those Vsevolozhsky now made possible.

(b) Negotiations between the Imperial Theatres and Tchaikovsky

The first indication that Vsevolozhsky was interested in a new ballet from Tchaikovsky came on 8 November 1886, during the period that his opera *The Enchantress* was being rehearsed in Petersburg. It is a note in the composer's diary which, like many of the others, is somewhat cryptic:

At home, where everything was already packed for departure, found a letter from Vsevolozhsky with an invitation for Sunday to talk over a ballet. Fell into despair, but decided to stay and made arrangements accordingly. Rushed off to Vsevolozhsky's. Here Petipa and Frolov also showed up and we immediately started discussions. My rejection of *Salammbô*. *Undine*.[28]

The prospect of composing on the subject of Undine must have tempted Tchaikovsky, having written an opera on it, and having incorporated some of that opera into *Swan Lake*. And he agreed to the project with no sign of reluctance. To Peter Jurgenson, his publisher, he confided: 'The Directorate of the Imperial Theatres in Petersburg is commissioning from me music to the ballet *Undine* for next season. I will start work on it as soon as I finish the opera.'

He wrote to his friend Julia Petrovna Shpazhinskaya, whose husband Ippolit had written the libretto for *The Enchantress*: 'The directorate is very favourably disposed toward me. They await *The Enchantress* with impatience. [And] on very profitable terms the directorate is asking me also to write music for the ballet *Undine* for next season, on which I must get to work immediately after *The Enchantress*.' And to his sister-in-law: 'By Lent I must, as promised, present the opera *The Enchantress* to the directorate, finish its instrumentation by summer, and soon after this get down to work on the ballet *Undine*. This will bring a nice sum to me, no less than 5,000 [roubles].'[29]

All three letters were written on the same date—10 November 1886—hardly a day after the first mention of the project, and, ironically, on the day after Ludwig Minkus's farewell benefit.

That the *Undine* project has become a footnote to Tchaikovsky's career does not mean that it was not serious in 1886. Some agreement had been made: Vsevolozhsky had taken the first step towards making good on his reform; Modeste Tchaikovsky had been entrusted with the preparation of a libretto; and Peter Ilyich himself began work on the music.[30] The question, as yet not satisfactorily answered, is why the work was abandoned. Modeste wrote later that 'the programme written by me for the ballet *Undine* was not approved, by either the balletmaster M. I. Petipa or the composer'.[31] But he gives no date for the rejection, and if Yury

Slonimsky is correct in linking this with Modeste's visit to Vsevolozhsky on 15 October 1887 the matter is still not easily put aside.[32] By that time the composer would have been working on the ballet for eleven months, and it is clear that he began having doubts about the work even before the libretto was drafted. On Christmas Day 1886, in a letter to Vsevolozhsky, he expressed misgivings about meeting the promised deadline, showing his intentions for the new ballet:

Do not think that I lack the desire to write music for *Undine*. But I need sufficient leisure and strength to do it well, because this is not simply a matter of confecting some kind of ordinary ballet music; I have an ambition to write a *chef-d'oeuvre* in this genre, and more than anything else time is what I need. I therefore beg you, most respected Director, to be so good as to put forward the *Undine* project until the 1888–1889 season.[33]

Vsevolozhsky replied generously:

Of course don't trouble yourself over *Undine*. It can await the 1888–1889 season if it will be the product of your inspiration. I understand perfectly. You are too great an artist to put forward before the judgement of your contemporaries an incomplete or hastily written work. Do not hurry, and bless us with a masterpiece—a new ray in your halo of creations. *Undine* must not be a transient vision. Like *Giselle* and *Coppélia* it must live, and stay in the repertory to enchant our grandchildren as it enchanted us.[34]

It turned out to be a problem not solved simply by extending the deadline. By the time Tchaikovsky wrote to Nadezhda von Meck on 24 April 1888, he referred to *Undine* as if he had never really taken it seriously:

Everything that is written in the newspapers in regard to my new works is a *lie*. In fact at times I was contemplating and still contemplate an opera on the subject of [Pushkin's story] *The Captain's Daughter*; in fact I was also contemplating my acceptance of the directorate's proposal to write music for the ballet *Undine*, but this is only one *possibility*, and not at all a reality.[35]

On its merits, Modeste's explanation of the project's abandonment is not persuasive: the faulty libretto could have been revised. Nor does there appear to have been any ill feeling between Tchaikovsky and Vsevolozhsky: in the wake of *The Enchantress*'s decisive failure, the Director, with his customary consideration and kindness, consoled the composer and went on both to secure a state pension for him and to recommend subjects for other new works. If anything, *The Enchantress* may have doomed *Undine* by dampening, at least temporarily, Tchaikovsky's enthusiasm for composing. By the autumn of 1887 he had arranged a concert tour of several European cities, which took place at precisely the time work on *Undine*, had it continued, would have required his attention.[36] It is possible, moreover, that Tchaikovsky simply conceived a dislike for *Undine* similar to the one he unexpectedly conceived for *The Captain's Daughter* ('I suddenly and, I fear, irrevocably, cooled towards it').[37]

Vsevolozhsky, perhaps accustomed by then to the composer's volatility, did not give up but instead changed the subject. After Tchaikovsky had completed his European tour the Director wrote to him, on 13 May 1888:

I conceived the idea of writing a libretto on *La Belle au bois dormant* after Perrault's tale. I want to do the *mise-en-scène* in the style of Louis XIV. Here the musical imagination can be carried away, and melodies composed in the spirit of Lully, Bach, Rameau, etc., etc. In the last act indispensably necessary is a quadrille of all of Perrault's tales . . .[38]

No response to this letter has been preserved. Perhaps Tchaikovsky did not write one, though the wording of the next letter, written some two months later by the Director of the Petersburg Theatre School, implies that the composer had expressed an interest:

I have the honour of dispatching with this the programme of the ballet about which Ivan Alexandrovich Vsevolozhsky spoke to you. Would you be so kind as to look it over and to inform Ivan Alexandrovich or myself whether this ballet is to your taste as regards composing music to this theme? If you find it possible to fulfil the Director's wishes, your music would ensure the success of the proposed ballet.[39]

No response survives to this letter either, perhaps because Tchaikovsky was busy with other projects, or needed time to grow attracted to a new one, or simply failed to answer it.[40] With mixed curiosity and impatience Vsevolozhsky raised the matter again on 9 August:

Did you receive the libretto of the ballet *La Belle au bois dormant*? Do you find it possible to write music to this theme? In any event, if the subject is not to your taste, refuse. Perhaps next time we'll have luck.[41]

Three months to the day after the first inquiry Tchaikovsky answered Vsevolozhsky, claiming never to have received the libretto and requesting another copy. On 22 August he wrote again, from Moscow:

I hasten to inform you that the manuscript of *Sleeping Beauty* finally came, at the moment when I was getting into the carriage to go to Moscow and Kiev. I am here only for a few hours but managed to look through the scenario, and I am pleased to tell you that I am charmed, delighted beyond all description. It suits me perfectly, and I could ask for nothing better to put to music. One could not better combine for the stage the virtues of this delightful subject, and to you its author, permit me to express my sincere congratulations.[42]

As before, when *Undine* was being considered, some agreement binding Tchaikovsky to the project seems to have been made, though the absence of documents suggests that any such agreement may have been verbal. Even if the details are unknown, it appears that Vsevolozhsky, in his effort to recruit compositions to replace those of the now abolished house composers, had established a policy of remuneration. In any case Tchaikovsky was not offered the 5,000 roubles for *Sleeping Beauty* that he claimed would be his for writing *Undine*. On 12 January 1889, some three months after the letter just quoted, Vsevolozhsky sent a memorandum to the Minister of the Imperial Court:

Concerning the Payment of an Advance to the Composer Tchaikovsky

The composer Tchaikovsky, having set about composing music to the ballet *La Belle au bois dormant*, which was commissioned from him and for which he, following the example of Baron Fitinhof-Schell and Kapellmeister Drigo, agreed to receive 3,000 roubles, being at the present time in need of this money, most humbly requests this sum to be advanced to him, he being thereby obliged to produce the music commissioned from him within the time designated by the Directorate.[43]

Only after the first performance was consideration given to the quality of Tchaikovsky's score, in another memorandum from the Director to the Minister, dated 4 January 1890:

Concerning Supplementary Payment to the Composer Tchaikovsky

In view of the especially outstanding quality of the music of the ballet *Sleeping Beauty*, I consider it fair to petition respectfully before Your Excellency concerning the payment of the author of the music Tchaikovsky, that it should be supplemented in the amount of 2,000 roubles.[44]

But perhaps the most unusual step in the contractual proceedings surrounding Tchaikovsky's agreement to compose *Sleeping Beauty* was the last, signed on 13 January 1890 (that is, after the work had been performed twice). It is a standard-form contract that specifies details of performance rights and, finally, the fee Tchaikovsky received for his work:

Agreed:

This year of 1890 the [13th] day by the Director of the Imperial Theatres on the one hand and by Peter Ilyich Tchaikovsky on the other, the following conditions set forth below:

1. I, Peter Tchaikovsky, give to the Directorate of the Imperial Theatres the exclusive right of performance by the orchestras of the Imperial Theatres of the music of the newly produced ballet 'The Sleeping Beauty', composed by me.

2. The Directorate is paying me for this music 3,000 roubles at once.

3. I, Peter Tchaikovsky, do not have the right, without special permission of the Directorate, to allow the performance of the music of the ballet 'The Sleeping Beauty' on any stages within the boundaries of the Russian empire.

4. I, Peter Tchaikovsky, am obliged to submit to all existing rules and regulations relating to the production and performance of plays on the stages of the Imperial Theatres.

5. Giving to the Directorate of the Imperial Theatres in its full possession the music written by me for Russia, I, Peter Tchaikovsky, reserve to myself personally

the right of its publication, or through publishers of music, both in Russia and abroad.

6. If from my, Peter Tchaikovsky's, permission there follows the performance of my music as part of ballet presentations, in full or in part, on private stages of both capitals, then I subject myself to payment of a fine in the amount of 300 roubles for each performance.

(signed) Peter Tchaikovsky.[45]

This document does not specify (as that concerning *Nutcracker* subsequently did) that the composer will receive 10% of the receipts of each performance, and it is possible that Tchaikovsky had to be content with his single payment, the bonus, and receipts from publication. Coming as it does when all the work had been completed, the contract is unusual by modern standards, for it implies that the talents of so many collaborators on such an ambitious project had been mobilized at the outset on what appears to have been a gentleman's agreement.

(c) Vsevolozhsky, Petipa, Tchaikovsky

Vsevolozhsky was more than patron and enlightened administrator. Together with Petipa, he contributed important material to the collaboration on *Sleeping Beauty*, of which the first was the libretto. Most authorities agree that he actually wrote the text, even though no copy survives in his hand.[46] Tchaikovsky accepted, as we have seen, that Vsevolozhsky was the author. Later, in a letter to Meck, he referred to the *sujet* of the ballet as 'worked out [*obrabotan*] by the Director of Theatres himself, Vsevolozhsky.'[47]

The story of *Sleeping Beauty* as used in the ballet is well known and may be summarized as follows (a translation into English of the first edition of the published libretto appears in Appendix A).[48]

The Prologue. Six of the seven fairies have been invited to the baptism of the infant Aurora; they present gifts which foretell her attractive attributes. As the Lilac Fairy approaches the cradle with her gift, she is interrupted by a commotion in the entranceway. It is caused by the arrival of the uninvited seventh fairy, Carabosse, ugly and wicked, who as her gift wills Aurora's death when she shall later prick her finger. The Lilac Fairy now intervenes with her gift—a reprieve from death. After the misfortune predicted by Carabosse, Aurora will fall asleep for a hundred years, to be awakened to happiness by a prince's kiss.

Act I. It is Aurora's birthday, twenty years later. Four princes have come to court her. She enters, dazzling her suitors, but will not choose among them. In her dancing Aurora catches sight of a hooded old woman beating time with a knitting spindle. The Princess seizes it and continues to dance. Presently she pricks her finger, and falls as if dead. The old woman throws off her hood and is recognized as the Fairy Carabosse. The princes rush at her, swords drawn, but she disappears in a cloud of smoke and fire. At this moment the Lilac Fairy appears. She consoles the

King and Queen, and puts the entire kingdom to sleep for a hundred years. The stage is transformed as everything and everyone falls deep into slumber and the castle is overgrown with ivy, trees, and lilacs. The royal garden becomes an impenetrable forest.

Act II. A century has passed. In a forest Prince Désiré's hunting party pauses for a rest. Désiré himself arrives, but is unimpressed with the diversions of his retinue. He sends them on without him. No sooner has the hunt retired than the Lilac Fairy appears and offers to show her godson Désiré the woman of his dreams. She presents Aurora to him in a vision; impassioned, the Prince begs her to lead him to the sleeping beauty. The Lilac Fairy complies, and they embark in her boat. The journey to Florestan's castle unfolds amidst a panorama of moving scenes.

In the second scene of Act II, the clouds disperse to reveal the room where Princess Aurora lies sleeping. Désiré tries in vain to awaken her, the King and Queen, the Master of Ceremonies, until it occurs to him to kiss Aurora. The spell is broken instantly; all awaken. The King joins the hands of the young couple.

Act III. Aurora's wedding. After the entrance of the King, Queen, Aurora and Désiré, their retinues, and the fairies Diamond, Gold, Silver, and Sapphire, there follows a long procession of fairy-tale characters from Perrault's stories, culminating in the arrival of five of the seven fairies from the prologue, including Carabosse and the Lilac Fairy. An elaborate *divertissement*, involving many of these characters, takes up most of the act, at the end of which Aurora, Désiré, and the fairies of Gold and Sapphire perform a *pas de quatre*. The ballet as a whole ends with a *coda générale* and an apotheosis.

As a theatrical work the story of *Sleeping Beauty* is unusual, especially when contrasted with that of *Swan Lake.* A tension developed in the earlier ballet by means of unexpected events, the consequences of which culminated in tragedy. In *Sleeping Beauty* we know the outcome of the story by the end of the prologue, so that the rest of the ballet, without any real surprise, merely confirms the first scene. In particular, the assurance that Aurora's life will not be taken is responsible for a singular lack of tension in the story, prolonged by the *divertissement* of Act III.

Detractors of the work pointed out that it was called a *ballet-féerie,* a genre in which the audience is normally indulged with elaborate visual spectacle as compensation for weaknesses of plot and story.[49] But to accept the criticism associated with the stereotype is to attribute to Vsevolozhsky the most superficial of motives. *Sleeping Beauty* is certainly a *ballet-féerie* in name, but it strains credibility to think that Vsevolozhsky, even if he made it his business to entertain the imperial family, would marshal the finest talents of the land in Tchaikovsky and Petipa, the resources of its best theatre, and expend a phenomenal sum—estimated by Vsevolozhsky's assistant Pogozhev to be somewhat more than a quarter of the annual budget of the production department of the Petersburg theatres[50]—on a choreographic display piece without lasting meaning. This premise is not in keeping with the patience that

Vsevolozhsky displayed towards Tchaikovsky when the composer hesitated over *Undine*, or his remark that he wanted the new ballet to take its place alongside such classics as *Giselle*.

The ballet's critics failed to notice the story's potential for allegory and parable, or the deliberate simplicity which was observed by other reviewers of the first performance and by analysts of later times. Boris Asafiev perceived in the presentation of Aurora's life a cycle common to humankind: infancy, youth, love, and marriage.[51] Vsevolozhsky himself appears to have given a name to Perrault's nameless Princess—Aurora, or Dawn—and the awakening after a hundred years' sleep has connotations of rebirth and springtime clear enough to require no elaboration. It is hardly conceivable that Tchaikovsky, who had grappled with philosophical issues in many of the major works since *Swan Lake*, would agree to compose a work of such musical involvement if he saw in it no forum for philosophical deliberation. Such profligate use of his energies would not have been in keeping with his character, or with the spirit of the times.

The story of *Sleeping Beauty*, finally, contrasts with that of *Swan Lake* in its use of time. In *Swan Lake* the librettists observed the unity of time; in *Sleeping Beauty* they did not. The prologue and each act of the latter work is an isolated moment within a vast time-frame: twenty years pass between the prologue and Act I, a century between Acts I and II, and a short period between the reawakening and Aurora's wedding. A sense of timelessness results which contributes to the impression that the story of *Sleeping Beauty* lacks tension.

One of the most important differences between *Swan Lake* and *Sleeping Beauty* from the historian's point of view (and probably from Tchaikovsky's own as well) is that Marius Petipa choreographed the work. Documents left by Petipa permit a much closer look at the collaboration than was possible when Tchaikovsky worked with Reisinger. One senses that the composer viewed his work on *Sleeping Beauty* in a more serious light than *Swan Lake* because of Petipa's involvement. From Modeste Tchaikovsky we learn that

Peter Ilyich was immediately delighted both with the theme itself and with the scenario, but before embarking on the composition of the music he requested of balletmaster M. Petipa designations of the dances in the most exact way, the number of bars, the character of the music, the amount of time of each number . . . I cannot confirm it, but it seems to me that the libretto of the ballet, finished down to the finest details by M. Petipa, was received in the course of the autumn months of 1888. In any event, there is no doubt that Peter Ilyich began composing the music of *Sleeping Beauty* only upon returning from Prague [where his *Evgenii Onegin* had been produced] at the beginning of December 1888. With this in mind he decided to lock himself up in [his home at] Frolovskoe from December 20th until the middle of January, which he did.[52]

Tchaikovsky himself expressed a wish to consult Petipa in advance, which amounted to a prerequisite for his agreement to compose. To Vsevolozhsky he wrote, when accepting the proposal in principle: 'I request of you to arrange a meeting with me and Mr Petipa in order to settle details relating to music for this scenario.'[53]

He raised the matter again in a letter of 1 October 1888 to Pogozhev:

It is essential for me, before starting to compose, to discuss matters in detail with the balletmaster ... About November 1 I shall be in Petersburg for a rather extended period and during this time I shall meet and arrange matters with the balletmaster concerning *what* is necessary, *how* and *when*.[54]

Responding to this request, Vsevolozhsky wrote to the composer on 2 November:

... Petipa was here today and I requested a meeting with us on Sunday not at his place but at mine, for discussions about the ballet *La Belle au bois dormant*. If convenient, be good enough to call at one o'clock, or fix another time—I am in any case at your service.[55]

On the following Sunday, 6 November 1888, Tchaikovsky, Petipa, and Vsevolozhsky met again to discuss a new ballet—almost two years to the day after a similar meeting concerning *Undine*. On this occasion Petipa handed to Tchaikovsky instructions for the prologue. At another meeting on the following December 18, Tchaikovsky received instructions for Acts I and II, and on 22 January 1889, those for Act III (Petipa wrote these dates on the instructions).

Petipa's instructions to Tchaikovsky survive in two copies; he sent one to the composer and kept the other. These documents must be distinguished from another one, far more celebrated and widely published, which may be called the balletmaster's plan. Petipa prepared the latter early in July, 1889, in a striking format: he wrote the scenario of *Sleeping Beauty* in black ink and the musical instructions for Tchaikovsky in red. The balletmaster's plan has been variously published in Russian translation since 1940, including an appearance in the scholarly edition of Tchaikovsky's music and as a supplement to virtually every other score of *Sleeping Beauty* published in the Soviet Union; it has also been translated into English.[56] On every occasion its publication has carried the implication that it is in some way a measure of Tchaikovsky's task and accomplishment. And yet only one writer has pointed out that the balletmaster's plan differs from Petipa's instructions to Tchaikovsky, and only one other that Tchaikovsky completed the composition of the music (except for the writing-out of the orchestral score) some six weeks before Petipa prepared the balletmaster's plan.[57] It could not possibly have served the composer as a guide, and is properly studied as evidence of Petipa's changing thoughts as preparations for the production advanced.[58]

Additionally misleading about both instructions and balletmaster's plan are the suggestions first that Petipa was particularly conscientious in supplying Tchaikovsky with instructions, and second that Tchaikovsky, for his part, fulfilled Petipa's requests to the letter. Such, for example, is the impression left by Yury Bakhrushin when he wrote:

... Tchaikovsky preserved in the *temps* assigned to him almost all the dances projected by Petipa—almost in each number exactly as many bars as the balletmaster requested; one need only recall the musical character of the dances of the last act of *Sleeping Beauty* in order to satisfy oneself how precisely the composer succeeded in the task before him.[59]

But the simplest comparison of the score with the instructions gives the lie to both suggestions. True, Petipa very frequently offered guidance concerning the expressive qualities he desired in the music, but often one may fairly assume that his remarks were no more than Tchaikovsky would have imagined on his own: 'When a loud noise is heard [in the entranceway as Carabosse arrives], very animated music'; when Carabosse actually appears, 'music of a fantastic character'. Less frequent and more helpful are specifications of metre and approximate tempo. But the information which would appear to be the most valuable to a composer in Tchaikovsky's situation is that with which Petipa is most miserly: designations of the length of numbers. Modeste Tchaikovsky's remark that the balletmaster's instructions were 'finished down to the smallest details' is simply not true in this regard. Only twice in the prologue did Petipa indicate how long he wanted the music to be ('from eight to sixteen bars' at the beginning of the introduction of the *pas de six* and again at the beginning of the finale), leaving Tchaikovsky to compose nearly 1,100 additional bars without further specifications of length. The balletmaster was more generous in Acts I–III, but not enough to substantiate Modeste's claim.

Tchaikovsky did no better by Petipa. He responded with great inventiveness to the balletmaster's call for particular expressive effects, and almost invariably complied with requests for a particular metre, tempo, or scoring. As regards the length of numbers, however, he often ignored Petipa's requests. Only in a handful of instances does the music correspond exactly to Petipa's specifications, though many of the shorter dances approximate to them, especially if introductory measures are discounted. Nevertheless, there are some extraordinary disparities between the instructions and the score. In the waltz of Act I, for example, Petipa asked for 16 bars of introduction and 150 bars of waltz; Tchaikovsky gave him 36 and 261, respectively.[60] Tchaikovsky did, as a rule, supply more music than Petipa requested.

Although Petipa's instructions give the impression of firm requirements before they are compared with what Tchaikovsky wrote in response to them, the disparity between music requested and music received suggests that Tchaikovsky did not take the instructions seriously. Petipa was accustomed to having his composers close at hand; his instructions to Tchaikovsky were doubtless suggestions, subject to modifications that a specialist composer would have made in rehearsal. Tchaikovsky, unused to working in this way, instead isolated himself to concentrate on composition when he found himself free for a few weeks. It is certain that the two men conferred on changes in the music, which explains the disparities between Petipa's written instructions and the score. Without some extra information, too, Tchaikovsky could not have composed Aurora's variation in Act II, about which Petipa had written: 'Variation for the *danseuse*. (For the moment do not compose it. I must speak to the *danseuse*.)'[61]

Additional meetings to work out details of the score must have been quite frequent, as is confirmed by Petipa's daughter Vera (1885–1961), who recalled:

In the beginning father worked out the subject and created as a whole the composition of the dances, after which he entered into discussions with the composer. Peter Ilyich arrived at our house customarily in the evenings and played through his work in parts, and father listened and planned his dance fantasies in harmony with the music. Tchaikovsky's arrivals always brought us much joy, especially when the inspired sounds of his music were heard in our home. Meetings of Peter Ilyich and father took place in the drawing room at a round table, and then at the piano. The family was seated nearby in the dining room: mother required attention to the music and to her explanations, which were given in a whisper.[62]

Despite changes made at these meetings of which we have no record, Petipa's original written instructions remain valuable to the historian. Many passages in the score are directly conditioned by them, especially in the mimed scenes where Tchaikovsky included in the holograph quotations from the instructions to clarify passages for the conductor and balletmaster (as he had done in the holograph score of *Swan Lake*). Moreover, the incompleteness of Petipa's outline allows us to speculate on what Tchaikovsky contributed independently of the balletmaster's requests, particularly the music of the introduction, and the tonal plan of the entire ballet, about which Petipa wrote nothing.

Tchaikovsky composed *Sleeping Beauty* with almost Mozartean fluency. On 1 October 1888 he wrote to Pogozhev that he had not yet written a single note and would not begin before he had discussed the ballet with Petipa.[63] As Nadezhda Tumanina relates, however (taking exception to Modeste),

... Tchaikovsky did not expect the balletmaster's plan in the near future and composed the first sketches of the ballet without having the plan in hand (entrance of the fairies, waltz of the pages and girls, variations of the fairies, the beginning of the finale of the prologue). This was in October 1888 (the composer's notation in the sketches) ...

On the return trip from Prague he went again to Petersburg and received the plan of Acts I and II. At the end of December 1888 Tchaikovsky returned to Frolovskoe and was able to devote himself to the composition of the music . . .[64]

Early in January Tchaikovsky wrote to Vsevolozhsky with predictions of completion dates: 'I hope to deliver what was promised, i.e. by the beginning of the season (not later than 15 August) to deliver the *Violino répétiteur* to Petipa, and by November the entire score.'[65] This confidence was reflected in a note in one of the sketchbooks: '17 Jan[uary 1889]. Finished everything that I thought to do before departing, i.e. the first four scenes of the ballet.'[66]

A different picture of Tchaikovsky emerges from his diaries of January 1889. He finds work taxing, he is irritated with his domestic help, and, in addition to composing, he is spending time on correspondence (one day is devoted to nothing else), walking in the forest, entertaining guests, and reading Tolstoy. But he repeatedly took pleasure from the crisp winter weather, which alleviated the more trying events of the day:

4/16 January. What marvellous days we are having! The frost is not severe, it is bright, and beginning at 3 or 4 o'clock, the moon! . . .

5/17 January. Again the same astonishing, miraculous bright winter weather . . .

And on the day he finished Act II: 'Such a divine, miraculous winter day it seems there never was before. The beauty is in truth astonishing.'[67] On 23 January, the eve of his departure for Berlin, he played Act II for Vsevolozhsky.

Tchaikovsky worked at Act III during his concert tour of Western Europe (he may have sketched the opening march in Hanover), on his way back to Russia while crossing the Mediterranean (the polonaise), and while visiting relatives in Tiflis (the dances of the fairies of the precious stones, Puss in Boots, the *pas berrichon*). He finished composing *Sleeping Beauty* only at Frolovskoe in May, finding work easier when the weather turned unexpectedly wintry.[68] At the end of the last number he wrote: 'Finished the sketches 26 May 1889 in the evening at 8 o'clock. Praise God! In all [I] worked ten days in October, 3 weeks in January, and a week now! And so in all about 40 days.'[69]

The sketches completed, Tchaikovsky had finished by far the larger part of his creative work on the ballet. The time-consuming process of producing the full score from the sketches occupied him from 30 May to about 16 August 1889.

4

The Music of *Sleeping Beauty*

❧

Sleeping Beauty, like *Swan Lake*, is a work full of delights and revelations. To identify them, especially the subtler aspects of the music's structure, we must once again analyse the score, as Tchaikovsky was no more informative about the conception of his second ballet than of his first. The results of this analysis, however, will be quite different from the first because the ballets are so different. There are differences in dramatic shape and movement, and we have the added consideration of Petipa's instructions to Tchaikovsky. The advance in the composer's style from that of *Swan Lake* is another factor; the components of his style are better integrated than before, his language better developed and more mature.

(a) Thematic unity

As he had done in *Swan Lake*, Tchaikovsky in *Sleeping Beauty* links large portions of the score with recurring melodies. He restates the Lilac Fairy's theme (Ex. 34), in the manner of the swan theme, at major points in the drama (the beginning and end of the prologue, the end of Act I, the middle of Act II).

The theme associated with Fairy Carabosse receives similar treatment; Tchaikovsky often introduces it in conjunction with the Lilac Fairy's theme (Ex. 35).

Other themes are used in a similar way: Désiré's hunt music at the beginning of Act II frames the scene as the music of Siegfried's party did the opening scene of *Swan Lake*. The music of Désiré's elation (No. 16) is repeated in No. 20; and the so-called dream chords which are played as the Lilac Fairy puts the kingdom to sleep (Ex. 43, below) sound again just before she and Désiré arrive to reawaken it.

Other melodies are subject to variation within a single number. Typically these are simple variants in a faster tempo of a theme which was stated at the beginning. Tchaikovsky employs this procedure once in each act before the last: in the *adagio* of the *pas de six* (at the *allegro vivo*, bar 64 ff.); in the dances of the maids of honour and pages (when the pages dance, No. 8, bar 130 ff.), and in Aurora's *pas d'action* with Désiré (No. 15a, bar 95 ff.). In Act III he uses it often at the ends of short dances—Little Red Riding

Ex. 34   Introduction, bars 28–33

Ex. 35   Introduction, bars 1–2

Hood, the *pas berrichon*, Désiré's variation—and in the *presto* at the end of the mazurka.

As regards the relating of themes by intonational likenesses, Soviet analysts of *Sleeping Beauty* make the same kind of observations that they did in connection with *Swan Lake* (see Chapter 2, pp. 64–6). The characteristics of an important theme, when found in other themes, produce an 'image' which by its reappearance throughout the work contributes to coherence.[1]

There is also in *Sleeping Beauty* a more specific relationship between certain themes. In Act I, for example, the cries of grief after Aurora is stricken are accompanied by a melody derived from one which occurred when the four princes implored Florestan (Aurora's father) to forgive the knitters, thus linking the ill-advised request with its unfortunate outcome (Exx. 36–37).

Ex. 36   No. 9, Finale, bars 69–71

Ex. 37   No. 5, *Scène*, bars 184–6

The Lilac Fairy's music and Carabosse's theme in particular are the sources from which other musical ideas derive: they are in this sense the two most important and influential themes in the ballet, both numerically and dramatically. The first subtle transformation of the Lilac Fairy's theme occurs when she first appears on stage: Tchaikovsky makes a striking change of key from F major to A major and broadens out the melodic line to resemble Lilac's reference melody (Ex. 34, above) in the quality of its movement (Ex. 38).

He provides a similar melody for her variations in the *pas de six* (Ex. 39).

A special kind of derivation—of non-melodic characteristics—applies to the music of the panorama in Act II, an *andantino* in 6/8 with a steady pulse of semiquavers, coloured by harp arpeggios (Ex. 40). So powerfully do these features suggest the world of the Lilac Fairy (who was on stage as this music was played) that only subtle changes in orchestral sonority and the hemiola in the melody point up the extraordinary difference in the dramatic situation between this scene and the Lilac Fairy's appearances earlier in the ballet.

Ex. 38 No. 2, *Scène dansante*, bars 56–9

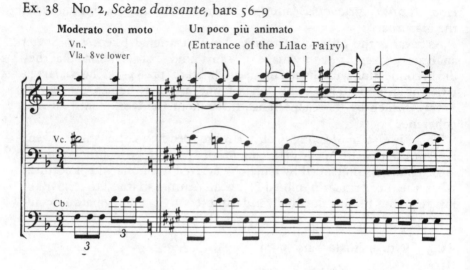

Ex. 39 No. 3, Variation VI, bars 1–6

The beginning of Carabosse's theme—especially the semitonal contrary motion of the outer voices—is the source for various passages later in the ballet. Tchaikovsky creates tension and a sense of foreboding with chromatic side-slipping coincident with Carabosse's arrival in the entrance-way (Exx. 41*a*–41*b*).

In Act I the characteristic outline of her theme returns at another critical point, as the King 'peu à peu se laisse fléchir' and forgives the knitters who have defied his law. Florestan's magnanimous gesture makes it possible for Carabosse to come to Aurora's birthday celebration; as his anger gives way to mercy we hear the distinctive chromatic lines in contrary motion (Ex. 42).

In the finale of Act I the rising chromatic fragment accompanies both the moment when Aurora pricks her finger (No. 9, bars 1–4) and the moment of her fall (bars 62–8). Both these, but particularly the first, bear a distinct resemblance to the striking dream chords which come later in the scene as the Lilac Fairy waves the entire kindgom into sleep. Carabosse's evil act,

Ex. 40   No. 17, Panorama, bars 1–5

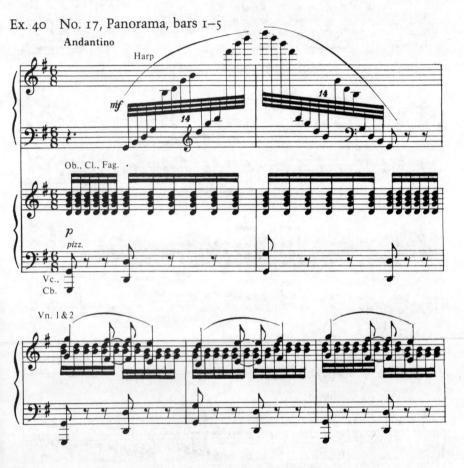

Ex. 41a   Contrary motion in Carabosse's theme

Ex. 41*b*   No. 4, Finale, bars 8–16

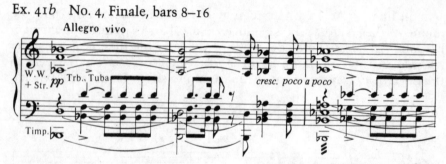

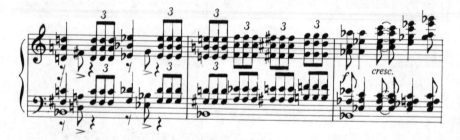

Ex. 42   No. 5, *Scène*, bars 202–4

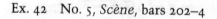

Aurora's wounding, and her death and reprieve all come together in this breathtaking moment, when 'tout le monde est pertrifié' (Ex. 43).

A gentle reminder of Carabosse's motif echoes in the fanfares which open Act II, suggesting the persistence of her wickedness even after a hundred years (Ex. 44).

Ex. 43   No. 9, Finale, bars 151–6

Ex. 44   No. 10, *Entr'acte et scène*, bars 1–6

Ex. 44 *(cont.)*

These examples are not the only themes and motives derived from the principal themes of the introduction, but they serve to demonstrate the contributions to thematic intelligibility made by the music of Carabosse and the Lilac Fairy.

(b) Rhythm and Sonority

Tchaikovsky revealed early in his career an inclination towards rhythmic complexity, which could be expressed in a variety of ways. Sometimes his melody created a rhythmic tension in relation to the implied strong and weak beats of a metre, as in the opening of the Symphony No. 1, where the time signature is 2/4 but the melody begins in 2/8 (Ex. 45).

Ex. 45   Tchaikovsky, Symphony No. 1, 1st Mvt., bars 1–8

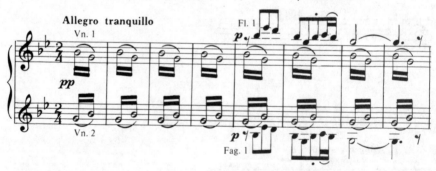

The unexpected cessation of the quaver motion at the downbeat of bar 7 creates too strong a sense of arrival for the quality of movement in the preceding two bars. The ear has been given two conflicting perceptions of the prevailing pulse, one in quavers, one in mimims; both, for the moment, are irrelevant to the time signature.

The coda of the finale of the Symphony No. 4 creates a similar effect (Ex. 46).

The timpani (like the strings in Ex. 45) set no pattern to prepare the ear for the metre which follows. And the melody, by moving in quavers on the

Ex. 46   Tchaikovsky, Symphony No. 4, 4th Mvt., bars 223–7

(strong) third beat and not on the fourth, upsets the listener's conditioned expectations of 4/4 time. When, in the last bar of the example, quavers occur on the last beat, the tension between what is expected and what occurs in the rhythm immediately disappears.

In other passages Tchaikovsky obscures the basic pulse with contrapuntal activity, or places accents in the bar to create the effect of metric displacement.

Such a composer writing music for ballet in Petipa's time ran the risk that his music might not be considered *dansante*—suitable for dancing. Tchaikovsky was surely aware of this problem, judging from the music he composed for *Swan Lake*. Apart from some mild syncopation in the waltz of Act III, the only sustained passage of dance music in *Swan Lake* of any rhythmic complexity is the episode in F♯ minor from the waltz of Act I, in which he created an effect of metric displacement. To make the dance music so rhythmically straightforward must have been done consciously.

He showed similar restraint in *Sleeping Beauty*, which is all the more remarkable given that his love of rhythmic complexity continued unabated in works written immediately before and after it. On occasion, however, we find in it a passage of 'non-balletic' Tchaikovsky. The sapphire variation of the *pas de quatre* (No. 23) anticipates the Symphony No. 6 in its 5/4 metre, though this choice originated not with the composer but, exceptionally, with the balletmaster (who ended up by reconsidering and cutting it from the production). In the rose *adagio* Tchaikovsky prepared for the tutti reprise of the main theme with an extended disruption in the flow of the 12/8 metre (Ex. 47).

We also find gentler examples, such as the beginning of the *Scène dansante* (No. 2), where the melody is phrased in a mixture of two- and three-beat groups without regard for the normal accentuation associated with triple time (Ex. 48).

There is one important exception in the work, an ensemble dance in fact, where Tchaikovsky clearly enjoys obscuring the expected beat. This also occurs in No. 2, when the pages and the young girls perform a waltz (Ex. 49).

Ex. 47   No. 8a, *Adagio*, bars 42–9

Ex. 48   No. 2, bars 1–7

Ex. 49　No. 2, *Scène dansante*, bars 102–15

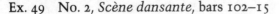

If anything, only the melody of this waltz could pass for *dansante* to a Petersburg balletomane (who might well have frowned at the two hemiolas in the first four bars), provided other elements of the texture created a suitably clear rhythmic framework. But they do not. A bass pattern with appropriately emphatic downbeat is missing, the impact of the accompanying string parts being diminished by the *pizzicato* on the first beat and the entry of the clarinets and bassoons on the second. As the piece continues, even further complexities arise from entrances on half-beats, metric displacement, and irregular patterns in the phrasing.

The careful choice of *obbligato* instruments—clarinets, bassoons, English horn, harp—in the waltz of the pages and young girls illustrates Tchaikovsky's concern for orchestral colour in *Sleeping Beauty*, already demonstrated to a lesser extent in *Swan Lake*. He also introduces in *Sleeping Beauty* a special sound idiom which he had been developing for two decades in his orchestral concert music, one comparable to those we know from the scherzos of Mendelssohn and Berlioz. We hear it in the Symphony No. 1 (3rd Mvt., especially in the introduction, bars 37–61, 86–105, etc.), in the fourth movement of the Symphony No. 3, the scherzo of the Symphony No 4, the second movement of the *Manfred* Symphony (music especially close in style to Berlioz's 'Queen Mab' from *Romeo and Juliet*), and in other works. The scherzo idiom is almost non-existent in *Swan Lake*. We hear hints of it (if anywhere) in the little variation in F♯ minor from Act II (No. 13/IV), which Lev Ivanov used for the four cygnets in the Petersburg revival. As we know nothing about what Reisinger did at this point in the Moscow production of 1877, we cannot identify anything in the action which might have led Tchaikovsky to choose it.

Tchaikovsky was pleased enough with the orchestration in *Sleeping Beauty* to say so in a letter to Meck:

When the piano arrangement is issued I will immediately send you a copy, dear friend. But I regret that you will not winter in Petersburg and will not hear my new work. I worked on its instrumentation with special love and care and invented some completely new orchestral combinations which, I hope, will be very beautiful and interesting.[2]

One such combination, used in the characterization of Fairy Carabosse, shows a special use of Tchaikovsky's scherzo idiom with grotesque effects. When we first hear the theme associated with Carabosse this is not yet clear, for it is played by the full orchestra. Tchaikovsky saves her characteristic sonority for the end of the prologue, when Carabosse is actually before us on stage (Ex. 50).

Ex. 50   No. 4, Finale, bars 37–43

The effect produced by this music—by the syncopations, grace notes, the chromatic tune, and the unconventional chord progressions—may be described by the Russian adjective *skazochnyi*, with its connotations of 'fairytale', 'fabulous', and 'fantastic'. The theme conveys Carabosse's laconic oddity and her physical lack of harmony, both reflected in the harmony of the music, which is puzzling and non-directional. The rich connotations of the theme are brought into sharp relief by the orchestration, especially the colouration of the winds.[3]

The rhythm of the waltz of the pages and the young girls and the *skazochnyi* instrumentation in *Sleeping Beauty* are important not simply because they reconcile for the first time parts of a ballet with standard patterns of Tchaikovsky's non-balletic language: the rhythmic complexity and orchestral *grotesquerie* are something more—straws in the wind, snowflakes even, blowing towards *Nutcracker*.

(c) Tchaikovsky's Transformation of the Classical Variation

Sleeping Beauty is a score filled with felicitous musical details. A number of these are, as they were in *Swan Lake*, simply adornments to the ear, ravishing touches, but many—a majority, even—contribute to the drama in some way. They are not simply examples of musical onomatopoeia, although that is an important element in *Sleeping Beauty*, but rather contribute to the overall enrichment of the score by means of a variety of musical devices. Indeed, *Sleeping Beauty* can be distinguished from *Swan Lake* by its more dramatically relevant detail, and as a result the score is more continuously related to the sense of the stage action. In particular, Tchaikovsky here lessens the distinction between music for narrative and music for classical dance, which in *Swan Lake* amounted almost to a division of styles.

This concern for the narrative or descriptive relevance of detail seems, in turn, to reflect the advance in compositional technique which separates the two works. It is easy to imagine, by the time Tchaikovsky wrote *Sleeping Beauty*, that his ability to express non-musical concepts in music was highly developed. Laroche recalled this gift of his in the shock of hearing of Tchaikovsky's death:

... he did not compose, as many (and even at times talented) Russians, 'in snatches', but in the literal sense of the word he *lived* in a world of sounds, sailing in a boundless element, and although in the last ten to twelve years it was much less productive, much more cautious and severe with itself, this internal song continued with its former strength—with a progressively growing strength, even, it seemed to me. People close to him, with whom he was not shy, know how often in conversation he suddenly would fall silent, or would not answer a question, and they were able to avoid tiring him, pestering him with 'Why are you quiet?' or 'What's the matter?'—knowing that in all probability instead of the humdrum topic of conversation there suddenly appeared before him some augmented sixth chord in *divisi* cellos, or some melody in the English horn . . . This intensive life in the world of harmony was not free of a certain strain: musical images pursued him everywhere and, as he repeatedly related to us, even in dreams they appeared to him, fantastically bound up with images and events of everyday life.[4]

Petipa's instructions, which by themselves can appear naïve and somewhat superficial in the description of effects required in the music, may have offered just the stimuli needed to spark Tchaikovsky's imagination. The intelligibility of musical detail in *Sleeping Beauty* may in fact be a direct reflection of the kind of collaboration which Petipa and Tchaikovsky enjoyed. It can be discussed only in parts of the score of which we have some knowledge of what Petipa wanted. Thus we do not know, for example, what to make of the music of the *adagio* of the *pas de six* in connection with events on stage—the libretto contains no reference to it, there are no markings in the score, and in his instructions Petipa simply wrote '*Adagio*. Short *allegro*'. Elsewhere, as in Aurora's variation in Act I, Petipa's requests were technical, as in his first call for particular instruments: 'Aurora's variation. 3/4 pizzicato for violins, cellos, and harp. (Excuse me for expressing myself so oddly.) And then lute [sic] and violin.'[5]

These suggest older conventions of music for the ballerina, as Tchaikovsky must have realized (the music of this variation is as close to the spirit of Minkus as anything else in *Sleeping Beauty*), but lacking any indication of Aurora's feelings at any given moment or of what is happening on stage he could do no more, one presumes, than respond to Petipa's request at face value.

In most other cases, Tchaikovsky enlivened the classical variations of *Sleeping Beauty* with music appropriate to the dramatic context of the dance. His accomplishment seems all the more remarkable when we consider what the audience of 1890 expected of its ballet music—namely the bravura or coquettish variations of the specialist.[6] And there is no reason to think that Petipa did not expect a score from Tchaikovsky that was conventional in many respects. For example, he was not so adventuresome in his instructions to the composer as to forgo standard genres (polkas, waltzes, galops, and the like)—the rhythmic bases of classical variations which had served him well for decades in all dramatic contexts. One can also presume that Tchaikovsky was willing to comply, but on his own level. In complying he sometimes softened the outlines of the rhythmic stereotypes of music written for classical dances, sometimes dispensed completely with those rhythms, or disguised the clichés of specialist rhythm and orchestration in some imaginative way.[7] This effort contributed to a clear stylistic consistency in *Sleeping Beauty* which we do not perceive even in a work as fine in other respects as *Swan Lake*.

The variations of the prologue, danced by the fairies who have come to bless Aurora, are remarkable for the working of Tchaikovsky's imagination on Petipa's handful of words. The composer conveyed the ingenuousness of Fairy Candide in devices as simple as the word itself: with absolutely consistent accompaniment figures and rhythmic clarity. The music is artless, moreover, in the absence of traditional rhythms. In similar fashion, Coulente is portrayed by the continuous motion, and more subtly in the devices that suggest the turning motion of the mill grinding the *fleur de farine*: the contour of the melody, the 6/8 metre, and the harmony, pivoting back and forth between G minor and Bb major on the enharmonic F#/Gb.

In Variation III, the so-called Breadcrumb Fairy Variation, Tchaikovsky responded to Petipa's phrase ('Crumbs—which are falling') with *pizzicato* strings: the scattering of the crumbs through the air in the violins, and their landing on the ground in the double basses. But here again there is something more: the striking background of trombones and tuba at the beginning catches the attention additionally by the one foreign note in the tonality of the opening phrase—the A# in bar 2. In the next statement of this phrase (bar 10) this pitch is even more prominent. And then, in the reprise, this distinctive note is missing (bar 26) at exactly the point where Tchaikovsky introduces a trill, as if to suggest that the birds had consumed the first of the fallen breadcrumbs. Tchaikovsky restores the A# in the next statement (bar 34), leaving his listeners at the end with a delicate hint of enigma.

Variation IV is the most obviously descriptive of the set: the twittering canary is represented by the twittering piccolo and flute. We hear again the trill and *pizzicato* of Variation III, but they have changed places as regards prominence, and Tchaikovsky takes care to offset the piccolo's potential for shrillness by doubling the skeleton of its line with bells.

The interruptive *ff* outbursts in the opening bars of Variation V already suggest something of the volatility of Fairy Violente, an effect continued in the main part of the dance by means of the *crescendo* and sweeping melodic gestures of bars 41–7. No doubt bearing in mind Petipa's expectation of regular phrase lengths, Tchaikovsky composed the entire variation so as to be divisible into four-bar units—almost. He elided the beginning of those sweeping gestures with the cadence of the preceding phrase, as if to show by the three-bar phrase thus produced that Violente was never to be completely under control (Ex. 51). Thus Tchaikovsky conveys Violente's fiery nature in harmony, rhythm, and sonority, together with the single odd three-bar phrase.

To Variation VI Petipa added a single word: *voluptueuse*. And in characteristic fashion the composer, for the third time in the ballet thus far, lavished *volupté* on the Lilac Fairy's music. As before, her music has breadth and spaciousness. The indivisible eight-bar phrases at the beginning contribute to this, as do the pick-up of almost two bars, the gentle dissonances of the bass against the melody, the shifts to distant Db major

Ex. 51   No. 3, *Pas de six*, Variation V, bars 34–57

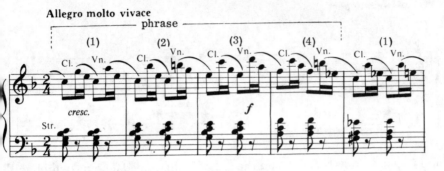

Ex. 51 (*cont.*)

of restatement

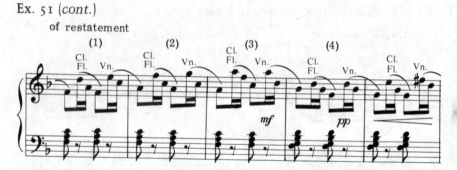

and B major (in bars 31–7), and the long dominant pedal point (which will appear again, to magnificent effect, in the Act I waltz) over which the reprise unfolds.

The six prologue variations are thus not interchangeable—they are character dances. They become more endearing when we realize that Tchaikovsky has modelled most of them on what would be hackneyed formulas in Minkus: a tarantella (Var. II), a polka (Var. IV), a galop (Var. V), and a waltz (Var. VI). He raises each form to a higher level, and conceals 'the metrically bare dance formula in the pursuit of the highest rhythmical–intonational interests.'[8]

The dances of Désiré's retinue in Act II raise another question: the evocation of period style. What is the period of *Sleeping Beauty*? Early in the negotiations Vsevolozhsky proposed to Tchaikovsky that he write melodies in the spirit of Bach, Lully, and Rameau. The glorification of Florestan as the Sun King in the apotheosis and Vsevolozhsky's wish to make the *mise-en-scène* in the style of Louis XIV are roughly in keeping with his proposal for the music, both suggesting a setting of the mid-seventeenth to mid-eighteenth century.

Petipa left Tchaikovsky full discretion to choose a period style in the music for the dances,[9] and Tchaikovsky, following an inclination already observed in his music, chose the eighteenth century.[10] The hunting scene is a balletic counterpart to the intermezzo in *The Queen of Spades*—both are stylized genre pictures, evocations within the larger dramatic framework. We sense a style change in the opening number of Act II (at bar 41) when Tchaikovsky breaks with the epic manner of the fanfares and shifts into an almost Mozartean style which anticipates the dances. By choosing a minuet and gavotte for the duchesses and baronesses, respectively, he avoids the rhythmic stereotypes of variation music. The kinds of elaborative devices used in the prologue variations are nevertheless found in these dances as well. In the *colin-maillard*, for example, the increasing bustle of the game is reflected in the complexity of texture and shorter note-values; in the dance of the marchionesses, the *pizzicato* of the darts has only sounded four bars before the clarinets begin to follow the general contour of the *pizzicato* in their tuneless, persistent warble, conveying thereby the sense of annoyance at being teased, an effect Petipa calls for in his instructions.

Tchaikovsky's treatment of variation music in *Sleeping Beauty* has both historical and aesthetic significance. It did in fact represent an advance in the history of ballet music, a more tangible one than, as could be said of *Swan Lake*, the simple fact that the score was composed by a first-rate master. According to Asafiev, *Sleeping Beauty* represented a new form for Russian music, a form of musico-choreographic action, 'the stage from which were revealed the possibilities of further evolution of the new musical form from *Nutcracker* to *The Rite of Spring* and beyond.'[11]

The aesthetic significance of the *Sleeping Beauty* variations resides in their multi-dimensionality. Tchaikovsky's music, simple in one perspective and complex in another, represents an advance in sophistication over the variations of specialists. And if there is a universal parable in the story of *Sleeping Beauty*, there is also something lifelike in the artifice of its music. Tchaikovsky enriched the metaphorical properites of the score.

(d) Tonality

In *Sleeping Beauty*, as in *Swan Lake*, Tchaikovsky's music is organized around particular tonalities to which we can assign meanings. But the associations are not maintained as strictly as before, and the keys are selected with less obvious concern for their relationship to each other in the tonal system. Moreover, the large-scale cadences of the earlier ballet are missing in *Sleeping Beauty*.

The first and most obvious departure from traditional norms in *Sleeping Beauty* is that there is no overall tonic in the work: the prologue and first act, which are symmetrical in many respects, are in one key, Act II in another, and the last act in a third. It may be inferred that the same characteristics of the ballet which justified the free treatment of time are also responsible for the freedom of key. In *Swan Lake* the conception of time was of the essence, and as the tragedy came full circle so too did the tonality; in *Sleeping Beauty* each act illuminates one situation in the story; and the sense of stasis and lack of tension within the story seem to justify the tableau-like approach to key. The succession of keys chosen by Tchaikovsky is logical, and prepared in such a way as to seem ultimately inevitable, but it is not powerfully dynamic—it lacks urgency. Without actively looking for a large-scale tonal structure we will not perceive it for what it is, just as we are but vaguely conscious of the momentum underlying the activity of surface detail in a fairy-tale.

On the basis of the introduction and the end of the finale, E major must be considered the key of the prologue. Between these two statements (putting aside for the moment all but the most important keys), the tonal progression follows an orderly sequence of rising perfect fourths, taking into account Tchaikovsky's fondness for extending the realm of a given tonic to include the keys a third above and below it (see Appendix C):

Introduction	No. 1, *Marche*	No. 2, *Scène dansante*	No. 3, *Pas de six*	No. 4, finale
E	A (c#) A (f#) A	(F) A	(V/D) B♭ – D	D E
E ⟶		A ⟶		D ⟶ [G]

While E major appears to be the overall key of the act it is important to realize that the pattern developing through the prologue suggests a different destination: G major, the logical next step in the sequence E → A → D. Indeed, Tchaikovsky anticipates an arrival in G major in the harp cadenza in the *adagio* of the *pas de six* (bars 39–41) and in the music at the beginning of the finale, when the Lilac Fairy comes forward to present her gift to Aurora. Later in the finale, G minor makes an appearance amidst a welter of other keys as the first noticeable tonal arrival after Carabosse's appearance (bars 57–67).

The reasons for expecting G major may be inferred from the events of the story. King Florestan is taking steps to ensure the continuation of his line; had Carabosse not come to the baptism the first step would have been taken without peril—Aurora, we assume, would have grown up in health and prosperity. Carabosse's coming, however, brought tribulation and interrupted, tonally speaking, a progression of keys which was moving systematically towards G. We may therefore assume that the coming of G will at some point be inevitable, when Florestan achieves his end. Realizing the importance of this tonal destination is critical to our understanding of the musical structure: the prologue has told us, in effect, where the ballet should end.

A number of similarities link the prologue with Act I, which in many respects is a replay of the prologue with princes instead of fairies, and Carabosse making good her threat. E major is again the overall key, and again we find the music being drawn towards G major. In the middle of the dance of the maids of honour there is a sudden move to the dominant of this key, in its effect very like that in the *adagio* of the *pas de six* (see No. 8, bar 199 ff.). Aurora's variation is in G, as is the coda of the *pas d'action*. Were it not again for Carabosse's intrusion, one could imagine the act ending in this key: Aurora could choose one of the four suitors and the ballet could proceed directly to the wedding. But Carabosse does intrude, with the same result as before: the celebration is thrown into turmoil and the arrival at G major is again avoided. The Lilac Fairy appears, and with her appearance the music moves instead to E major.

If there are similarities, so too are there differences, especially in the tonal plan, which may be summarized as follows:

No. 5, Scène	No. 6, Waltz	No. 7, Scène (Aurora's entrance)	(rose *adagio*)	No. 8, *Pas d'action* (maids/pages)	(Aurora)	(Coda)	No. 9, Finale
E (E^b) (e)	B^b	B^b – A	E^b	E^b	G	G – E^b	f – E
[E^b: (I)	V		I	I	III	I]	

Tchaikovsky here puts aside the pattern of perfect fourths which he used in the prologue. The act opens and closes in E, but much of the music throughout, including some of the most important, is organized around Eb as the principal key. For this reason, the act could be said to be based on the semitonal relationship of Eb to E.

Act II provides a contrast in practically every respect. It begins and ends in different keys, neither of which is E major. Instead, broadly speaking, the first scene is constructed on a cadence in Eb major:

No. 10, Entr'acte	No. 11, Blind Man's Buff	No. 12, Scène et Danses	No. 13, Farandole	No. 14, Scène (Lilac/ Désiré)	No. 15, Scène (Aurora)	No. 16, Scène (Désiré)
F – B^b	C	C to F	F	F (D^b, E) F	F–B^b–g	E^b
[E^b:			II		V	I]

Tchaikovsky announces the cadence formula of the entire scene in the fanfares which are played before the curtain is raised:

bars:	1–15	16–30	31–2
	F	B^b	E^b
[E^b:	II	V	I]

This cadence formula is more than a convenient mechanism for the musical organization of the scene: it is as perfect a mirror of the stage situation as a simple harmonic device can be. At the beginning Désiré is as far, in time and situation, from the moment of Aurora's awakening as a prolonged supertonic chord is from the moment of resolution in a cadence—in other words, the F major of the beginning is to the Eb major of the end what the Désiré of the hunting party is to the Désiré enamoured of Aurora.

Despite a key signature of two flats, most of Scene I unfolds with F major as the principal key: to the ear, the opening fanfares in F move to those in Bb as a tonic to subdominant progression, and F major returns as the key of the most substantial dance of Désiré's retinue, the farandole, which comes just before the story begins to move forward again. After the farandole F major begins to lose its identity as tonic, and, amid the more rapid rate of key change in the last part of the scene, begins to be heard in its supertonic relationship to the new key. In short, F major presides over the dramatically static hunting scene; when the dramatic momentum starts up anew, F becomes part of Eb.

The music of the second scene, which accompanies extraordinary mechanical transformations on stage, uses different harmonic ingredients for similar ends:

No. 17, Panorama	No. 18, Entr'acte (violin solo)	No. 19, Entr'acte symphonique	No. 20, Finale
G	C (e) C	C (F, f) C D^b (b^b)–V/E^b	E^b
		(entr'acte) (action)	
		[E^b: v V	I]

The dramatically static parts of the scenes are likewise static harmonically. G major is again present to remind us of the key of resolution. Here it is no longer posed near the end of the act, ready to accompany dramatic resolution but frustrated by Carabosse's mischief—a hundred years have passed and there is no longer any concern over Carabosse's curse. For this reason, possibly, Tchaikovsky felt justified in anticipating the key of Aurora's wedding in the music which carries Désiré down the river to the sleeping castle.

When the scenic marvels are past, harmonic activity and dramatic activity recommence. Here again, as in the first scene of the act, this activity results in the drive to a cadence in Eb. Because of its importance as the destination of the harmonic structure of this act, Eb must be considered the principal key.

If we consider the introduction, No. 21, to be in the dominant of the main key, Act III begins, almost predictably, in G, the long-anticipated key of resolution. Thereafter a variety of keys reflects the richness of the divertissement:

No.: 21 March	22 Polacca	23 Pas de quatre	24 Puss	25 Pas de quatre	26 Red/ Riding	27 Tom	28 Pas de deux	29 Sarabande	30 Finale
D	G	B^b–E	g	C–F	g–B^b	A	G–E	a	D–g
[G: V	I							ii	V–i]

At the close of the act Tchaikovsky takes up again and now completes the pattern of rising fourths broken off at the end of the prologue. The trials are past; Florestan's ambition has been accomplished.

We must distinguish Tchaikovsky's approach in Sleeping Beauty from that in Swan Lake. In the earlier ballet the interrelationship of principal keys was closely allied to scale—the difference between major and minor keys was important to the point where an exchange of a minor key for its parallel major (as in the replacement of Eb minor with Eb major in the love duet), with the suggestion that the two were equal, was perceived as a deception. In *Sleeping Beauty* Tchaikovsky considers as one key major and minor scales sharing a tonic, and freely substitutes one for the other.

The equivalence of a tonic major with its parallel minor is implicit in the music at the very beginning of the ballet, where Tchaikovsky states his principal keys in the tonic minor. The music begins with two terse statements of Carabosse's theme, the first in E minor, the second in Eb minor. Then the key changes resolutely to G minor. The sequence of principal keys of the entire ballet is thus announced in the first sixteen bars. The hint of the tonal destination of the ballet thus offered and the extent to which the introduction generates themes found later in the ballet combine to epitomize the whole work in the introduction in a more comprehensive way than does the introduction of *Swan Lake*.

Tchaikovsky makes more of the succession E–Eb–G than a statement of his harmonic structure. After extracting the root pitches of these triads to make a linear motive, he uses it in the form of a cadence—once, transposed, in the magnificent symphonic *entr'acte* which opens the second scene of Act II (Ex. 52).

Few musical ideas could be so apt. The chord progression above these pitches is common enough in Tchaikovsky's music. As a cadence, however, the motive in the bass is not conventional, which may be the reason why Tchaikovsky followed it with a standard cadence formula in the bass of bars 91–3; the standard formula heightens the effect of the unorthodox one. Moreover, coming just before Désiré and the Lilac Fairy enter the sleeping castle, this musical symbol of the entire ballet comes at a pivotal point in the narrative: it marks the return to life.[12]

The assignment of E minor and E major respectively to Carabosse and the Lilac Fairy parallels Tchaikovsky's choices of key in some earlier compositions. We find them, for example, in *Francesca da Rimini* (Op. 32). In this work, after the stark, unpleasant portrayal of the netherworld in elaborately extended diminished sevenths, the *allegro* subject, representing the whirlwind, is presented in E minor. Francesca's narrative, a contrast of theme and other expressive means, involves no change of key, only of mode. A similar pattern can be observed in the Symphony No. 5, in which Tchaikovsky (just before beginning *Sleeping Beauty*) chooses E minor and E major again, creating a modal contrast on the highest structural level—between the first movement and the finale. He began to sketch a programme for the work, but stopped writing when he reached the middle of the first movement. Subsequently he claimed that the work had no plan; the first thoughts, however, revealed a concern for his own submission to the 'inscrutable design of providence'.[13]

In *Sleeping Beauty* Tchaikovsky chooses E minor and E major to portray

Ex. 52 No. 19, *Entr'acte symphonique et scène*, bars 86–95

the malevolent and benevolent aspects of Aurora's destiny, personified by Carabosse and the Lilac Fairy. Indeed, he has already told us something important about the two sisters in the introduction: that they are quite different, yet in some respects the same. The difference is expressed in their themes, and the similarity implied by the common tonal centre on E. Had Tchaikovsky conceived them as opposites he might have separated the keys associated with them by a tritone, as he had those of the swans and Rothbart. But he distinguishes them by mode, to express different aspects of the same concept.

Tchaikovsky maintains these associations of Carabosse and the Lilac Fairy consistently throughout the prologue and Act I. In the prologue he places the central dramatic action of Carabosse's unexpected visit—her prediction of Aurora's death—squarely in E minor (No. 4, bars 124–75). Harmony conspires with theme at the point in Act I where the King allows the knitters to go unpunished (see Ex. 42), and at the very downbeat where the composer wrote 'Le roi peu à peu se laisse fléchir' we find, prepared by the preceding ten bars, a cadence in E minor. In this way Carabosse's influence over the unwitting King is shown: providence will not smile on him for this. But for the moment Florestan's clemency, as expressed in the music, 'disregards' the presence of E minor by continuing immediately in another key.

When Tchaikovsky follows Carabosse's E minor with the Lilac Fairy's E major in the introduction, he establishes the pattern for similar successions at the ends of the prologue and Act I. The Lilac Fairy's theme overcoming that of Carabosse symbolizes the relationship of good and evil in the ballet; it predicts the outcome of the drama, and is tantamount to a moral.

We know, however, that the Lilac Fairy's theme does not have a strict key-association beyond the prologue and first act. When she first appears to Désiré in Act II her theme is in Db major. But Carabosse is no longer a threat at this point: E major is no longer necessary as an antidote to E minor. E major is still the key which associates the Lilac Fairy with her responsibilities to Aurora; although Désiré is the more important character in Act II, the music moves immediately to that key when the Lilac Fairy brings Aurora to life in the vision scene (No. 14, bar 100 ff.).

The second principal key of the ballet, Eb major, as we have seen, becomes increasingly important in Act I. It makes only one appearance in the prologue, but goes on to become the key of Act II. In the appearance of Eb in the prologue the composer is already hinting at some special connotation: he sustains a pedal point on its dominant, over which he places a rising chromatic progression to convey both the noise in the entranceway and the first hints of dread which Carabosse's arrival will bring (No. 4, bars 8–16; see Ex. 41b above). This passage establishes further links: it recalls the terse opening of the introduction, where this key and theme were presented with a stress on the dominant; and it anticipates, by its use of a pedal point on Bb, its counterpart in Act I—the beginning of the finale, where Aurora pricks her finger (No. 9, bars 1–7).

The first clear evidence of the meaning of these relationships comes at the beginning of Act I, where we first perceive that Eb major is about to offer some challenge to the supremacy of E major. This occurs at bar 119 of the opening scene (No. 5), at the point—significantly—when the King, Queen, and four princes come on stage. This entrance, which Tchaikovsky highlights with a change of tempo and a new theme, is nevertheless short-lived, because the royal party has arrived in the midst of Catalabutte's meting out of justice to the knitting women.

The King questions his Master of Ceremonies and then flares up in anger himself, accompanied by a flurry of modulations. But soon the princes implore the King to be merciful, he relents, and the people, impressed with his magnanimity, express their happiness in the waltz. The waltz is in Bb, the dominant of Eb, and thus serves as an appropriate preparation for the

rose *adagio* in Eb. By this time the new key is firmly established. It gives
way to G, as we have seen (p. 132), but returns at the moment when Aurora
seizes the spindle from Carabosse. This action, in turn, brings us to the
beginning of the finale and presently to the Lilac Fairy's intercession and
the return to E. The entire complex of changes may be summarized as
follows:

Opening scene	Entrance of the King etc.	King is assuaged	Waltz	Rose *adagio*	Aurora's Variation	Aurora seizes spindle	Lilac's intercession
E	Eb	(e)	Bb	Eb	G	Eb	E

In this act it becomes clear that Eb major is associated with King
Florestan and his concern for the future of his realm. Hence the appropriateness of that key for his entrance and the entrance of the rivals for
Aurora's hand, one of whom, he supposes, she will marry. The waltz is an
expression of the people's delight at the King's clemency, and the rose
adagio in Eb the high point of the birthday/courtship ceremony which the
King has arranged. Later, in Act II, that key sounds first when Désiré
resolves to find Aurora, and again at the end of the act when the King joins
the lovers' hands, and the association of Eb major with Florestan's plans is
confirmed.

The return of Eb when Aurora seizes the spindle provides an explanation
for Tchaikovsky's use of this key in the prologue. Whatever Catalabutte's
negligence in omitting to invite Carabosse to the christening, the King has
ultimate responsibility—or so Tchaikovsky would seem to be telling
us—for the oversight. Thus when Carabosse appears in the entranceway
Tchaikovsky's sudden shift to Eb can be interpreted as a musical means of
linking Florestan with the misfortunes that subsequently befall his realm.
That Eb is not sustained after a strong dominant shows us how the King's
ambitions have been threatened by the arrival of the wicked fairy.

We have seen thus far that the principal keys of *Sleeping Beauty* are
allied to the story and its meanings in an intelligible way. The combination of E major and E minor represents the forces vying for control of
Aurora; Eb major represents the King's terrestrial authority and ambition;
and G, the key towards which these two are finding their way, is perfectly
compatible with them in Tchaikovsky's harmonic practice (in that both E
and Eb can serve as submediants of G).

Another key—A major—is used to suggest a connection between Aurora
and the Lilac Fairy. Of two others, C major is compatible in Tchaikovsky's
harmonic practice with all three basic keys of the ballet; F minor is not,
and the composer uses them accordingly.

The *scène dansante* (No. 2), which opens with the fairies coming
forward to pay respects to the infant Aurora, begins in F major. But the key

changes suddenly to A major at the point of the Lilac Fairy's entrance
(above, Ex. 38). As with many other striking ideas in the ballet, the
significance of this harmonic gesture is not clear at the moment it
happens; the music continues in A and thus extends the key of the march
into the *scène dansante*.

A major occurs next in Act I (No. 7), where its appearance forms several
parallels with its appearance in the *scène dansante*: both, for example,
accompany first entrances (No. 7 is Aurora's), and both approach A major
from F (No. 7, bars 7–8). Both, but especially Aurora's entrance before a
quartet of doting suitors, are obviously intended to ravish the ear (such
being the effect of the chord progression and orchestration of bars 10–14 of
No. 7). Thus the parallels between the prologue and first act create more
than a structural symmetry: they establish a relationship between the
giving of attributes to the infant Aurora and the first sight of Aurora the
young woman who displays them. Only the divine origins of Aurora's
beauty, it appears, could cause such a striking, if momentary, weakening of
the diatonic security of Florestan's realm of Eb, to which the music
immediately returns for the rose *adagio*.

C major first enters the work as a harmonic colouration within the
Lilac Fairy's theme in the introduction (bar 52). Here too, as in many
other instances, Tchaikovsky gives us in miniature a tonal relationship
which will grow in importance later, after its narrative connotations have
been clarified. Then, in the prologue, C major makes a grand entrance with
the Lilac Fairy in Variation VI of the *pas de six*. While associated with the
appropriate character, the relationship between C and E, stated in the
introduction, appears to be lost. Only at the beginning and the end of the
variation does Tchaikovsky, very subtly, show his hand. The first note of
the dance in the holograph is a G♯, hinting at the scale of E major. (In the
sole surviving rehearsal score and in at least one modern recording of
Sleeping Beauty this note has been changed to G♮—a concession to the
prevailing C major which not only produces an imbalance with the end of
the dance, but also shows a misunderstanding of Tchaikovsky's intentions.) At the approach to the final cadence the function of the C major
triad in the tonal grammar of the cadence is suddenly changed, from a tonic
to a submediant, of E (Ex. 53).

The entire variation, from the perspective of this cadence, is not in C but
in E—the Lilac Fairy's key (the cadence after the pause, to the dominant of
D, being an adjustment to prepare for the downbeat of the coda which
follows).

In these two passages Tchaikovsky assures us only that C major belongs
with E major, and that both are the province of the Lilac Fairy. The
significance of C major is shown at the end of Act I: the music moves from
E to C at the moment just before the dream chords when the Lilac Fairy
waves her wand (No. 9, bars 149–50). The key which so boldly put the

Ex. 53   No. 3, Variation VI, bars 55–60

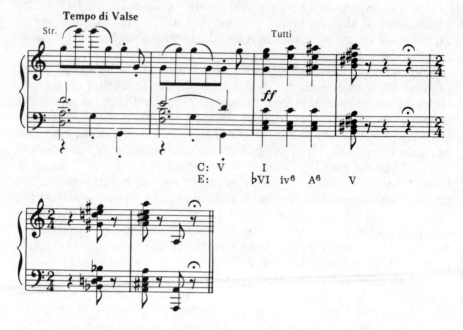

kingdom to sleep will return in the *entr'actes* that separate the scenes of Act II (Nos. 18 and 19).

The musical importance of the *entr'actes*, as might be expected, is greater than their purely practical function as music played during scene changes. The key of both—C major—relates them to the hundred years' sleep induced by the Lilac Fairy's magic. Their length and slow tempo impart a static quality appropriate to music accompanying a sleeping kingdom. And in No. 18 Tchaikovsky reminds us of Carabosse's prediction by means of an interlude in E minor (bars 26–34). Like the variant of Carabosse's motif in the hunt music (above, Ex. 44), this is a subtle, toned-down reference to music presented more stridently in the first half of the ballet. By means of these subdued, almost gentle references the composer portrays the working of time on the evil fairy's designs.

F minor is used in the finales of the prologue and Act I, immediately following (and as if in response to) Carabosse's actions. In the prologue it is the key of the music expressing the court's consternation after Carabosse predicts Aurora's death, and its use continues into the beginning of the dances of the pages and rats (No. 4, bars 176–212). After the opening bars of pedal point in No. 9, Tchaikovsky makes F minor the prevailing key of this finale. Introduced in bar 10, F minor is the key of the number from the 'sobs and cries of grief' after Aurora falls to the beginning of the Lilac Fairy's intervention. The association of F minor with evil is familiar from the music of Rothbart in *Swan Lake*, and may have influenced Tchaikovsky's choice here. Indeed, the opposition of F minor and E major and their corresponding associations with bad and good form one of the direct harmonic links between the two ballets.

In a typically subtle manner Tchaikovsky links part of Carabosse's music in F minor from the prologue with that of the first stirrings of the clouds as they begin to disperse in Act II. Using a device approaching quotation he recalls in bars 66–73 of No. 19 the key, the chord progression, and the prominent pedal note on C (but not the theme) which first occur at bars 196–203 of No. 4. He transforms the later passage in tempo, context, and scoring: Carabosse's mischief has lost its intensity and immediacy after a hundred years, but is still in operation.

Apart from the logic and consistency of Tchaikovsky's tonal associations, his harmonic scheme is convincing because key within the scheme parallels the hierarchy of earthly and supernatural power in the story. Eb major (Florestan) holds sway over terrestrial matters but gives way immediately to any higher power, benevolent or malevolent. The keys associated with Carabosse—E minor and F minor—give way in turn to E major (the Lilac Fairy). C major, as a special realm within E major associated with the hundred years' sleep, contains and subdues Carabosse's E minor and F minor in the *entr'actes* of Act II. In the end, all these keys lead to G. Appropriately, Carabosse's keys are excluded altogether from the music of Act III; Tchaikovsky deemed that they had no place at Aurora's wedding.

The conception of key in *Sleeping Beauty* is basically different from that of *Swan Lake*. In the earlier ballet Tchaikovsky selected keys to match opposites in the story in such a way as to produce a sense of contentiousness. It appears that he wished the principal keys of *Sleeping Beauty* to have no commanding interrelationship beyond their compatibility with the key of resolution. As a result the tonal structure of the ballet, in itself, leaves one with a neutral impression—when needed, Tchaikovsky creates the illusion of crisis more with sonority and volume than with key. His reasons for this may reside in the story of *Sleeping Beauty*. In the early stages of collaboration the composer expressed to Vsevolozhsky a preference for subjects 'not of this world' (*ne ot mira sego*).[14] The new world he sought was not simply that of the fairy-tale, for such would not distinguish *Sleeping Beauty* from *Swan Lake*. It was a world of inner tranquillity, free if not of evil then at least of combative violence, the fairy-tale inhabitants of which permitted Tchaikovsky to speak more eloquently of the human condition than did the gloomy characters of *Swan Lake* or the people of everyday existence.

(e) The Music of Act III

The structure, tonality, and approach to musical coherence in Act III emphasize yet another difference between *Sleeping Beauty* and *Swan Lake*: the way the ballets end. *Sleeping Beauty* not only lacks tragedy, but also comes close to lacking a sense of dénouement altogether. It would be interesting to know Vsevolozhsky's reasons for not giving a moral in the ballet comparable to those at the ends of the stories from which it was taken—why, for example, this act does not end with some reference to the Lilac Fairy, whose benevolence has made the tale come out well (especially since one final statement of her music would create structural parallels with the ends of the prologue and first act, and would musically bring the entire ballet back again to the beginning).

Whatever dramatic tension there has been has ended with the last number of Act II, and we are now celebrating the wedding of Aurora and Désiré. Apart from some purely ceremonial actions, nothing happens, the *divertissement* being rationalized as the contribution of the invited guests. Surely the prospect of composing an act full of dances presented no particular obstacle to a choreographer of Petipa's imagination and experience. And from a technical standpoint it created no problem for Tchaikovsky either. But the dramatist in him must have sensed the unusual situation: the story was over and there was still another act of music to write, most of which involved characters who had no connection whatever with the story before Act III. Indeed, by now the Lilac Fairy and Carabosse have become mere spectators, limited to a single appearance in the procession of the fairy-tales.

These changes posed a problem not so much of drama or aesthetics as of aptly conveying in music the relationship of Act III to its predecessors. Tchaikovsky solved this problem with exemplary inventiveness. First he established the key of G major, which had suggested itself as the key of resolution since the introduction. The march (itself a parallel with the prologue) and the polacca, taken as complete numbers, form a perfect cadence in G (just as the opening two numbers in Act III of *Swan Lake* had formed a perfect cadence in the key of that *divertissement*-filled act). Once this key was arrived at unambiguously the point of tonal resolution had been reached. The polacca, however, also marked the last forward movement in the drama for most of the remainder of the act. Having no further narrative to follow Tchaikovsky gave free reign to his fantasy. As regards key, what separates the initial and final statements in G in the last act may be considered a static extension of the harmony, just as the stage activity is of the dramatic action.

Tonality was not the only consideration. Tchaikovsky made the dances of Act III the most clearly picturesque of any in the ballet from the standpoint of his responses to Petipa's instructions. He also made it a summary of the earlier acts by recalling certain of their musical devices and reintroducing them in less obvious, more subjective and analogous parallels. In doing this he avoided direct links with the story, and even a sense that the process of recall is systematic. The dramatic activity of the last act in its relationship to that of the prologue and Act I is itself an analogy of the type of transformation which the composer created in the music: in all three there is a royal celebration to which special guests have been invited, but in the last act the role of the invited guests is transformed, opening a new perspective on the entire spectacle.

The *pas de quatre* (No. 23) has a number of parallels with its counterpart in the prologue, the *pas de six*. Both initiate a *divertissement* with dances of fairies after the opening ceremonies. The first substantial key in both is Bb major. Both present, at the beginning, a gentle rhythmic tension in the relationship between the melody and the prevailing metre, created when the theme begins on the last half of the bar (Ex. 54).

Ex. 54   No. 23, bars 1–7

The *entrées* which follow in the *pas de quatre* show once again Tchaikovsky's responsiveness to Petipa's instructions. Of the Gold Fairy Petipa wrote: 'Burnished gold—a gold charm', and the composer chose, almost flippantly, to set the music as a series of changing background variations, which in this case symbolize in music different views of the same object. With his customary regard for sound values, Tchaikovsky scored for the horn with a *staccato* accompaniment (bars 37–59) which conveys perfectly the required quality of mellow brilliance. The phrasing in this passage also suggests the sudden turns of a charm on its chain.

Just as a 'golden' instrument contributed to the first variation, bells are used for the Silver Fairy. Petipa wrote: 'The sound of coins must be heard.' Bells contribute to such an effect, but a striking new voice in the orchestra, first heard in the *intrada*, returns here: the piano. It is not the mere presence of a piano that is odd (Glinka in *Ruslan* and *Lyudmila* and Musorgsky in *Boris Godunov*—to name but two—had already written for it in their theatre works, and Glazunov used it later in *Raymonda*), but that it appears in *Sleeping Beauty* so unexpectedly late in the work. As it relates to this variation the new instrument is simply part of another skilful response to Petipa's words: bells and piano are an imaginative choice of sounds to represent the sound of coins. But the piano is not finished with here, and the implications of its use bear watching.

The variation of the Sapphire Fairy is next. As has been pointed out, rhythm is its most distinctive feature—the 5/4 metre represents a five-faceted sapphire, and in the orchestration the particular brilliance of the last eight bars of the dance (especially bars 36–40) is as close to the fiery gleam of the original gem as orchestral sound can come. The impression is achieved by keeping all instruments in a high register until the final cadence, by including the piano, and by replacing the horns with the brighter, more strident, cornets and trumpets.

The effect Tchaikovsky achieved at the end of the sapphire variation prepares us for the fourth *entrée*, for which Petipa left the instruction: 'Diamond—sparks, glistening like electricity.' Tchaikovsky established the beat with a solo triangle, and then let the sparks fly in the flutes, clarinet, and upper strings (Ex. 55).

The end of the last variation, like the beginning of the *intrada*, comes close to duplicating specific characteristics of its counterpart in the prologue. There, it will be remembered, the Lilac Fairy's variation began in one key and ended in another, if we attach any importance to the strong half cadence in E just before the end (see Ex. 53, above). Here, too, the last

Ex. 55   No. 23, Variation IV, bars 1–7

variation begins in one key and ends in another. The key of arrival is the same, and the cadences themselves even sound similar (Exx. 56–7). Significantly, the cadence that was interrupted in the prologue is resolved when it returns in Act III.

In the course of the variation suite, then, we encounter analogies to the prologue both general and specific. Underlying them all, it may be added, is a reminder of the principal harmonic polarity of Act I, between Eb major and E major:

Eb:	V	I	IV	VI		
	Intrada	Variation I	Variation II	Variation III	Variation IV	Coda
				E: bVI	III to V	I

C major in Variation IV is the point of contact between the two keys, continuing its role as an intermediary throughout the entire work, containing and reconciling otherwise conflicting tonalities.

Ex. 56   No. 23, Variation IV, bars 48–52

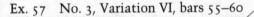

Ex. 57   No. 3, Variation VI, bars 55–60

While Carabosse has made an appearance in the procession of the fairy-tale characters, her presence is a mere formality (unless omitting to invite her to the wedding would rekindle her wrath): there is nothing more to be feared from her curse. Her sound world returns next, however, but with a different image: Puss 'n Boots and the White Cat. Petipa was nowhere more graphic in his requirements than here—'Mutual caresses, miaowing

and scratching with their claws. At the end the cry of a scratched cat . . .'
—and Tchaikovsky followed suit. There is an echo of Carabosse in the
bassoon fragments at the beginning (in double semitones no less), and in
the comical effect of the bassoon, cor anglais, and oboes throughout. These
instruments are featured again in No. 26, Little Red Riding Hood, but freed
of such grotesquerie.

For the *pas de quatre*, No. 25, Petipa wrote, 'A little *andante*: the music
represents the singing of birds'—and the *canari qui chante* returns transformed and subdued, both at the beginning of the number and again in the
second variation. Between them, the first variation, a waltz for Cinderella
and Prince Fortuné to be 'of a passionate character', catches that quality in
the short dominant extension (bars 33–40) which recalls for a moment the
same exhilarating device in the Lilac Fairy's variation and the *valse
villageoise*. The connection thus made with the Lilac Fairy's variation
might have been more evident than others described here to those watching the first performance, since Marie Petipa performed the roles of both
the Lilac Fairy and Cinderella, had this waltz not been cut in the course of
production. Tchaikovsky wrote another which was used (No. 26*b*, bar 69
ff.). It lacks the dominant extension but recalls the dance of the pages and
young girls in its capricious rhythms.

The *pas berrichon* completes the series of character dances from Perrault's tales. Once again Petipa described the action in close detail; once
again Tchaikovsky complied with music of charm and wit. The almost
Webernesque ground at the beginning nicely conveys the image of Tom
Thumb, the littlest brother, stepping about in the ogre's seven-league
boots, together with a melody which unfolds rather uncertainly, now in
triplets, now in regular duplets (Ex. 58).

Tchaikovsky seems to have sensed the forward motion of the drama
recommencing at this point: Aurora and Désiré come forward to perform a
pas de deux. Perhaps because of this the G major of their *entrée* speaks to
especially telling effect, reiterating the final tonal resolution of the ballet
which was announced at the beginning of this act. But the centrepiece of
this *pas*, and the finest example of Tchaikovsky's use of analogy in Act III,
is unquestionably the superb *adagio* which follows. Since Petipa wrote
only 'A rather large *adagio* with *fortes* and with pauses', we may assume it
was Tchaikovsky's idea to make it a retrospective of its counterpart in Act
I. It shares more with the rose *adagio*, however, than general expressive
character. The compound triple time returns, the arpeggiated chords, the
rhythmic disjunction before the final tutti (bars 49–54), and the reed
instrument solo against an accompaniment with understated downbeats,
replaced in both by the trumpet in the final statement of the main theme
(Ex. 59).

The recall, however, is not limited to the rose *adagio*. The Lilac Fairy is
brought to mind by the mingling of E major with C major, the keys of her

Ex. 58   No. 27, bars 1–19

variation in the prologue and her gesture of reprieve—the onset of the hundred-years' sleep—at the end of Act I. And parts of the orchestration are again subtly transformed, as they had been in the first *pas de quatre* of this act, by the piano, which here plays the *glissandi* which had been the harp's duty in the rose *adagio*. Another difference may be cited: instead of the overpowering sense of affirmation at the conclusion of the rose *adagio*, Aurora's *adagio* in Act III closes with a quiet restatement of its principal theme in the oboe—an epilogue with connotations of sadness and nostalgia.[15]

Ex. 59   No. 28*b*, bars 1–6

The expressive power of Aurora's *adagio* tends to overshadow the numbers which follow it, not just in the rest of the *pas de deux* but also in the remainder of the ballet. The final mazurka and the apotheosis match it in the scope of their performing forces but not in the force of sentiment. Yet to suggest, as Tumanina has,[16] that the *adagio*, whatever its claim to being an apotheosis in its own right, renders all that follows merely conventional does Tchaikovsky an injustice. There are still other ideas to be recalled. Aurora's solo variation, for example (the one piece in the entire ballet that had the distinction of being published in a Petersburg newspaper in a piano reduction),[17] returns us, especially in its violin solo, to the somewhat archaic style of her variation in Act I, and, appropriate in this last of her dances, it also recalls the key of her first appearance on stage. The sarabande, in its turn, makes a final bow to the period evocation of the dances of Désiré's hunting party. Moreover, Tchaikovsky forges a structural link with the prologue in the succession of keys which concludes Act III. Starting with the coda of the *pas de deux* he creates, here unambiguously, exactly the same sequence (accounting for mode changes) of fourth-related keys upon which he had built the prologue:

Prologue:	Introduction (Lilac)	Nos. 1–2	No. 3	
	E	A major/minor	D	g
Act III:	Coda of the pas de deux	Sarabande	Mazurka + Apotheosis	
	[No. 28]	No. 29	No. 30	

Here, of course, the key of resolution is definitive.

Many factors conspire, when considering Act III in retrospect, to suggest the possibility of an almost Aesopian double meaning in *Sleeping Beauty*, a technique of exposition associated with the tales in which it originated and also well known in nineteenth-century Russian letters. Following one line of inquiry, the work is positive in its outlook. Modelled, albeit loosely, on French courtly entertainments of the seventeenth century, *Sleeping Beauty* may be interpreted as an apostrophe to the reigning monarch, expressed through the analogy of Florestan/Louis XIV. There are hints of magnanimity in the King's forgiving the misdeeds of his subjects, and he weathers the tribulations of destiny to emerge at the end having fulfilled his original task. One presumes that some such objective motivated Vsevolozhsky, the experienced courtier, in the choice of time and setting. And the ballet is filled with glorifications of the King, though if the Director truly sought to reproduce in some way the theatre of Louis XIV, there is surely something amiss in this portrayal: Lully and his collaborators forbade the inclusion of anything not flattering to Louis XIV. Vsevolozhsky's Florestan has an incompetent Master of Ceremonies and cannot even make sure that the laws of his kindgom are obeyed—extraordinary breaches of etiquette if such a parallel were intended (especially considering how much of Russia was under martial law during Alexander III's reign). The Tsar, who reacted coolly to the new work, may well have thought that if *Sleeping Beauty* were somehow an allegory of his realm it was uncomplimentary, if not wholly undeserved.

Act III in particular sustains and enhances a second level of interpretation. The removal of the good fairies of the prologue and of the life-saving Lilac Fairy to a single procession and their replacement in the King's retinue by fairies representing wealth has a logical explanation: the new ones portend Aurora's prosperity as their sisters had her attributes. But this exchange also suggests the relegation of personal virtues to material values, and gives all too little credit to the Lilac Fairy now that the threat to Florestan's kingdom has passed.

One wonders if Tchaikovsky did not sense these disparities between exterior and interior interpretation. The introduction of the piano—significantly, perhaps, in the *pas de quatre* of precious stones—is accepted when it occurs as a means of enhancing the orchestral depiction of silver and sapphire. But when, in Aurora's *adagio*, the listener realizes that this instrument has replaced the harp, the darker, non-ethereal, material connotations of the sonorities make themselves felt. And the piano returns in the apotheosis to enhance the setting of the French tune 'Vive Henri IV!', which concludes the ballet with great pomp and ostentation.[18] After the over-loud final cadence dies away, do one's thoughts return to Aurora's majestic *adagio*, does one hear in the valedictory accents of its epilogue a reminder of a better time?

The question of allegorical interpretation, like so many others, can be pursued only in speculation. The rudiments of an assessment of Tchaikovsky's score are less conjectural. *Sleeping Beauty* is tightly organized on the largest scale both in the workings of its musical logic and in the relationship of that logic to the drama and narrative. At the same time, Tchaikovsky sustains an unfailing interest and attractiveness all through his work, lavishing upon it the full measure of his melodic and orchestral invention—and this with due regard for the conventions of the genre and the instructions of the balletmaster. The result is a work that provides marvellous entertainment and makes a philosophical statement as well. That he composed it in forty days (plus the time required to write out the score) is one of the more astonishing feats of nineteenth-century music. Whatever the excellence of his other works, Tchaikovsky never surpassed *Sleeping Beauty*.

5

Sleeping Beauty
The First Production

❦

*(a) The Music of 'Sleeping Beauty' as Performed in the Imperial
Theatres*

Tchaikovsky sent the score of each act of *Sleeping Beauty* to Petersburg as
he finished it,[1] where at least two répétiteurs (rehearsal scores) were
prepared.[2] The holograph score (Hol), the one surviving répétiteur (Rep),
and printed piano reductions of the music (PR-I, PR-II) used by Nikolai
Sergeyev, régisseur of the Petersburg ballet from 1903 to 1918, are the
principal sources from which we can learn about the performance version
of *Sleeping Beauty*.[3] All changes in the music found in these four sources
are listed in Appendix H.[4]

At some point Riccardo Drigo, ballet conductor at the Maryinsky
Theatre, began to revise the music, entering several changes in the Hol
before the copy to be used in performance, now apparently lost, was
prepared.[5] (The modifications were too numerous, and some too drastic, to
make conducting from the Hol feasible, to say nothing of the problems
posed by the composer's musical shorthand, which permitted dozens of
bars at a time to be left blank.[6]) Drigo made cuts, indicated tempo, and
added marks of expression.

For the producer of *Sleeping Beauty* the most valuable data contained in
the Hol are the tempo markings.[7] Tchaikovsky, knowing nothing of the
choreography or of the performers, had indicated tempo in accordance
with Petipa's instructions—with words alone. The metronome markings
would seem to represent Petipa's precise determinations of tempo after
going over the music; in this likelihood lies their value.

Apart from the tempo indications, cuts, and interpolations, the markings in these sources concerning music are of two kinds: verbal instructions specify a particular effect ('ritenuto', 'allargando', [to be conducted]
'in six', and the like); and the Rep in addition preserves critical evaluations
of the music, written in French ('Il faut couper dans ce morceau' is written
at the head of No. 1, 'Tâcher de passer à la valse' near the end of No. 5,
'Beaucoup trop long' at the beginning of No. 20, to cite but three). While

many people involved in the production of *Sleeping Beauty* knew French, only Petipa (whose Russian was notoriously faulty) would be expected to annotate the Rep in this language, and with comments of this kind; also, the writing appears identical to the balletmaster's. The author of these remarks—and others which relate to the production—is thus assumed to be Petipa himself.

Changes in the music increase in number from the prologue to Act III. For some reason the prologue was left virtually unchanged—perhaps Petipa and Tchaikovsky worked out the details in their meetings together.[8] In Act I two numbers were significantly modified. In Aurora's variation an interior repeat was deleted (one marked by Tchaikovsky in the Hol as being optional) and a new ending provided; in the finale the 'sobs and cries of grief' were cut.[9]

The more extensive and striking changes in Act II begin to reflect the problems of mounting a new production. Three numbers were involved: the dances of the noblewomen of Désiré's entourage (No. 12); the *pas d'action* of Aurora and Désiré (No. 15), and the *entr'acte* with violin solo (No. 18), which was to be played during the change of sets from the panorama to the sleeping castle.

The last was simply cut, as we learn in a telegram sent by Vsevolozhsky to the composer on 27 December 1889:

The first performance of the ballet is the 3rd, a gala rehearsal Tuesday the 2nd, [and] we are having a general rehearsal Saturday the 30th. Your presence is desired, all the more since, probably, you will agree to dispense with Auer's solo, [which] slows the action.[10]

Straightforward as the decision seems to have been from Vsevolozhsky's matter-of-fact announcement, making it when he did must have been dangerous. Coming one week before the first performance, it meant that changes in the score and orchestral parts were still being made at the eleventh hour:[11] Tchaikovsky had elided the *entr'acte* with the panorama which preceded it; with the *entr'acte* being omitted a new ending had to be written for the panorama.[12] The length of the ballet may have been causing concern, a consideration which may also have been responsible for many cuts in Act III. Omitting the *entr'acte* also implies the producers' confidence in the smooth operation of the stage machinery, malfunctions of which had caused several postponements of the première in the autumn of 1889.

Revisions in the dances of the noblewomen suggest a similar realization that cuts were necessary, and that they were to be made with as little disruption as possible in parts of the work that were already set (although there is some ambiguity over what was finally decided upon).

With the exception of an eight-bar cut in the Dance of the Marchionesses, the Hol preserves all four dances without change; all are assigned metronome markings. In the Rep all save the first, the Dance of the Duchesses, were cut, but not before metronome markings were entered and a pair of dancers' names added at the head of each dance. We do not know with certainty when the producers decided to cut three dances of the four, but it must have been late in the production (or for a subsequent one), judging from the way the dances are presented in the printed libretto.

The libretto is in two parts: a synopsis of the action, and a cast list with a résumé of dances. In the synopsis all four dances—of the duchesses, baronesses, countesses, and marchionesses—are listed in the order Tchaikovsky composed them. In the cast list the surnames of two performers are provided for each dance, the same names that Petipa wrote into the Rep. In the résumé of dances on the next page, however, only two dances of the noblewomen are listed, neither by title but both simply as 'variations'. Only one dancer of each pair is named here as a participant—one duchess in the first 'variation', and one baroness, one countess, and one marchioness in the second.

The inconsistencies within the libretto are thrown into sharp relief by the date of the censor's approval for publication, before which the libretto could not have been printed: 30 December 1889, the day of the *répétition générale* and four days before the first performance. If the disagreement between the cast list and the résumé of dances is a true reflection of last-minute indecision about who danced what, it confirms the anxieties which the collaborators recalled (see pp. 162–3, below). We still do not know with certainty which dance (besides the Dance of the Duchesses) was performed.[13]

In the *pas d'action* (Act II), Aurora's variation (No. 15b) was cut, and the Variation of the Gold Fairy from Act III (No. 23, Var. I) substituted for it. This change seems to have been made early, and for the ballerina, either as a result of her preference or because Petipa considered the interpolated music better suited to her gifts.[14] The substitution required Drigo to refashion the end of the preceding number.

The revised Act III, more than any other act of *Sleeping Beauty*, provides evidence of thoughtful editorial work. The opening march and the polacca were left intact.[15] From the beginning of the *divertissement* to the finale, however, there were changes in every number, the most important of which are summarized here:

1. No. 23, *pas de quatre* of precious stones. Already shortened by the removal of the Gold Fairy's music to Act II, the *pas* was shortened still more: the sapphire variation, the principal novelty (quintuple time) of which Petipa had specifically requested, was cut.[16]

2. No. 24, *pas de caractère* of Puss in Boots and the White Cat. A ten-bar introduction was added, as entrance music for the dancers. Tchaikovsky wrote it on a half folio of music paper which was bound into the Hol.

3. No. 25, *pas de quatre*. Two characters of the four, Cinderella and Prince

Fortuné, were moved to the next number. The change was one of several announced in a letter of 7 October 1889 from N. O. Christoforov, Director of the Central Music Library of the Imperial Theatres, to the composer: 'Marius Ivanovich Petipa asked me to inform you that in the third act in place of the *pas de quatre*, No. 25, he is putting a *pas de deux* for Mlle Nikitina and Mr Cecchetti, without changing the music . . .'[17]

4. No. 26, *pas de caractère* of Little Red Riding Hood and the Wolf. A new *pas de deux* was added, for Cinderella and Prince Fortuné. Petipa included a scenario of the new *pas* in Christoforov's letter of 7 October 1889.[18]

5. No. 27, *pas berrichon* for Tom Thumb and his brothers. Internal repeats were made, of eight bars near the end, then of the second half of the entire number. Permission to make them was also requested in Christoforov's letter: 'In No. 27, "Tom Thumb, his Brothers and the Ogre", Mr Drigo made a reprise at the request of Mr Petipa, and hopes that you will give your consent to this.'[19]

6. No. 28, *pas de deux* for Aurora and Désiré. The first five bars (an introduction) were retained, but in the Hol the entire *entrée* was cut.[20] Ten bars were cut from the *adagio*, an introductory bar was added and a few brief cuts were made in Aurora's variation.

In the libretto, however, No. 28 has been made a *pas de quatre* by the addition of a dance, placed after the *adagio*, for the Gold Fairy and the Sapphire Fairy (as if in compensation for the cutting of their variations from No. 23). The music of this dance cannot be identified with certainty, though the evidence suggests the *entrée* was reinstated to accompany it (the unlikely alternatives are that Tchaikovsky permitted an interpolation of someone else's music or composed a new dance that did not find its way into the principal sources). If so, the decision to expand the *pas de deux*, like that to modify the court dances in Act II, may have come late in the production, after the Hol had been laid aside in favour of copies to be used in performance.

7. No. 29, Sarabande. Unchanged in the Hol, the Rep calls for the second part of the dance (from bar 17) to be played three times instead of twice.

8. No. 30, Finale. 195 (of 452) bars were omitted, a heavy cut in the light of Petipa's remark above bar 9 of the Rep: 'Ce finale très court sans le galop de la fin.'

The large outlines of the performance score of *Sleeping Beauty* are clear. Much of the music was left intact, the prologue almost completely so. From the 1,218 bars Tchaikovsky wrote in Act I fewer than 80 were cut; 8 were added. Not before Aurora's variation in Act II do we encounter one of Petipa's few 'anti-musical changes' (Vsevolozhsky's words in a letter to Tchaikovsky),[21] the interpolation of the Gold Fairy's music from Act III. Most of the changes in the last two acts seem to have been the result of the producers' second thoughts at rehearsal, changes made, it appears, with Tchaikovsky's agreement. For much of the score we have in addition tempo designations, which probably originated with Petipa, and instructions for expressive effects, almost certainly the work of Riccardo Drigo, conductor of the first (and 190 subsequent) performance(s) of *Sleeping Beauty*.

(b) Petipa's work on Sleeping Beauty

We have observed evidence of Petipa's efforts towards a good collaboration in the attention he paid to Tchaikovsky with instructions, meetings to arrange details, and a solicitous if not reverential attitude towards changes in the score. There is also evidence, in the form of hundreds of documents, to suggest that much study went into his own contribution, the mounting of the dances and mimed scenes, which give us an insight into his choreographic methods.

After a subject was decided upon (and, probably, a libretto drafted), Petipa sought out all manner of information which might stimulate, enrich, or clarify his creative impulses. The materials used by him in this way (which have been preserved in the Petipa archive of the State Theatre Museum named for A. A. Bakhrushin in Moscow) bear witness to this stage of his work.[22]

The earliest description of the archive remains the most informative and concise:

Petipa's manuscripts can be broken down into five categories. The first is a collection of librettos of proposed ballets, written by the balletmaster himself; the second consists of plans of groups, paths of movement [khodov], and movements of various dances from ballets; the third comprises historical data and excerpts from books; the fourth, traced drawings from illustrated periodical publications, primarily French; and the fifth—the most important and significant for the ballet researcher—is his work on the creation of Sleeping Beauty.[23]

M. A. Yakovlev, a writer of the 1920s, suggested a sequence of stages of composition based on these divisions: the formulation of a libretto, the collection of historical data about the subject, the sketching of floor plans, especially for group dances, and the teaching of the new ballet to the performers.[24]

If Sleeping Beauty is typical of Petipa's methods of composition Yakovlev's hypothesis is too neat. Petipa seems continually to have refined and reconsidered his ideas. An inveterate note-taker, he sometimes wrote practical reminders to himself, for example: 'Tell Mr Efimov that it is necessary to make boots for the ogre well in advance, so Tom Thumb can rehearse in them.' And on another occasion: 'I must show my daughter the engraving of Cinderella, so as to make her understand how to put on the slipper.'[25]

The balletmaster seems also to have been constantly on the lookout for visual images which would serve his purposes. 'Request tomorrow my engraving at Mr————'s [surname effaced] to show an engraving of Little Red Riding Hood and the Wolf to Mademoiselle Zhukova I and Lukyanov [the first performers of these parts].'[26] Yury Bakhrushin cited other examples:

The balletmaster feverishly put down brilliant thoughts, historical information on scraps of paper. 'In the polonaise Tom Thumb and his brothers must come out in knitted caps (stockings).' 'Apollo, as the Sun King Louis XIV. Fairies with long trains, as drawn on the ceilings of Versailles.' 'When he [Apollo] personifies the sun, he has a cock on his shoulder and is crowned with rays of sunlight. Four white horses draw his chariot on which the signs of the zodiac are represented.' Here a remark taken from Perrault's tale 'Little Red Riding Hood', and there: 'I must see the Director and suggest to him a new assignment of roles'.[27]

As a rule, Petipa conceived choreography for a soloist in terms of that dancer's abilities. Naturally, therefore, he attached great importance to the selection of his dancers, and it is not surprising that a large number of cast lists survive among his papers:

In the *adagio* at the end of the prologue the pages must support the fairies. Strong young men are needed. Candide—Nedremskaya; Farine—in tarantella rhythm—Petrova. Breadcrumb, *pizzicato*—good enough—Kulichevskaya. Canaries—good, but fast—difficult for Johansson. Violente—Zhukova very good. The Lilac Fairy—waltz—Petipa.[28]

The ballerina's dances were Petipa's special concern, as his assistant Alexander Shiryaev explained:

Petipa worked with the ballerina separately. He carefully studied the particulars of her gifts, sought out interesting features, assiduously strove to develop them as far as possible, and constructed the dance accordingly. If it happened that he showed the ballerina a new movement, [and] she struggled and struggled with it to no avail, then he rearranged the *pas*.[29]

We cannot co-ordinate Petipa's prodigious note-taking with a particular stage of composition, but we can place the elaborate drawings of group dances somewhat more accurately. He seems to have produced most of them (allowing for an occasional inspiration not directly connected with a production in progress) in the period soon before the beginning of rehearsals, in preparation for them. According to Shiryaev, Petipa

... prepared the entire production of a new ballet at home, where he usually summoned a pianist and violinist. Ordering them to play fragments of the music repeatedly, he [then] planned the production at his table [while they played], making use of little papier-mâché figurines, especially for the ensemble dances and groups. He moved them about in the most varied combinations, which he noted down in detail on paper, making zeros for the women, crosses for the men, and various changes [of the dancers'] location with arrows, dots, lines, the significance of which he alone knew ... At rehearsal Petipa appeared with a whole pile of outlines and drawings made by him at home, and immediately began to rehearse on the basis of them.

Ordinarily Petipa worked with groups and soloists separately, and then introduced the latter into the prepared ensemble. By doing this he achieved a great saving in time. He worked with soloists as a living example, demonstrating mimed scenes. Thanks to the preparatory work at home, one act of a ballet could be produced in the course of a few days. Complete large ballets were prepared in six weeks to two months.[30]

At the beginning of 1889 the state ballet was suffering one of the periodic but temporary declines of which Petipa had seen his share. Virginia Zucchi had been released from imperial service but was still dancing in St Petersburg and drawing audiences away from the Maryinsky Theatre. Reviewing the events of the old year, on New Year's Day, 1889, the writer of an unsigned article mentioned this important change in the state ballet:

Virginia Zucchi, having three years running drawn crowds and significantly raised the level of taste in choreographic performances, was dismissed on the basis of some home-brewed consideration having nothing to do with art or the public . . .[31]

Her nominal replacement, Luigia Algizi (the writer pointed out), although talented and of a good school, did not enjoy an outstanding success. The 'Divine Virginia', meanwhile, performed to great acclaim at a private theatre in Petersburg in January and February, and returned in the summer. Newspapers chronicled her activities when she was away. Pointed comparisons between private theatres and the imperial ballet stressing differences in the attractions—and the resources—were published.

Petipa responded to this situation as he had to similar ones in the past: by staging a sumptuous new ballet. His winter offering this year was *The Talisman*, a revamped Parisian *féerie* now called a 'grand ballet in 4 acts and 7 scenes, with prologue and epilogue'. Judging from critical response, the audience was finished long before the ballet. Zucchi countered with such favourites as *La Fille mal gardée*, *Coppélia*, and Monplaisir's *Brahma*. The challenge facing Petipa and Vsevolozhsky was easier to identify than to solve: find a ballerina to compete with Zucchi, and produce a masterwork. They found a first-rate ballerina in Carlotta Brianza,[32] who arrived in the first few days of January from Moscow (where she had enjoyed a fine success the week before at her farewell benefit, performing Marguerite in a revival of Perrot's *Faust*, renamed *The Seven Deadly Sins* by the balletmaster of the Bolshoy Theatre).

The masterwork was still far from ready, and not soon to be completed. Despite the good will of Tchaikovsky, the balletmaster, and the director, a brief look at their schedules explains why there is so little information on the production of *Sleeping Beauty* before the following autumn.

From 20 December 1888 to 19 January 1889 Tchaikovsky was, from Petipa's standpoint, in virtual seclusion. When the composer arrived in Petersburg on 20 January it was for a visit of four days, during which time he saw Petipa twice: once on the 21st, and once on the 22nd for discussions about the ballet. If we assume that both men, accustomed to working under pressure, had prepared for the meetings, their deliberations must nevertheless have been adversely affected by the circumstances. The first meeting took place at a rehearsal of the ballet company, and at the second Petipa would surely have been distracted by the first performance of *The Talisman* the next day. No sooner was *The Talisman* on the boards than Tchaikovsky left for Western Europe, unavailable for consultation until May.

Tchaikovsky stopped in Petersburg on his return trip and again visited Petipa, who was no less busy than before. The balletmaster had just prepared the first two of three gala performances being given in honour of a visit by the Shah of Persia. Three days before Tchaikovsky returned Petipa had revived his ballet of 1876, *A Midsummer Night's Dream*, for a private performance in the Hermitage Theatre of the Winter Palace. The following day he supervised a performance of parts of *The Vestal* and *The Talisman* in the Maryinsky. No sooner were these responsibilities met than he had to compose a new ballet, *The Caprices of the Butterfly* (to music by Nikolai Krotkov), for the wedding of Grand Duke Pavel, the Tsar's brother. This was first performed on 5 June. By then Tchaikovsky was back again in Frolovskoe, orchestrating *Sleeping Beauty*. And there he stayed, barring three brief trips to Moscow, until 20 August, when he went not to Petersburg but south to Kamenka to visit his brother Anatole.

Despite their other responsibilities, the collaborators on *Sleeping Beauty* still made progress on the production in the first half of 1889. Petipa took one casting decision early, at Tchaikovsky's suggestion. The composer, Maria Anderson recalled,

. . . turned his attention to my performance [in *The Vestal*] and at one rehearsal of some ballet in the winter of 1889 he inquired of our balletmaster Marius Petipa: 'What is the name of that young artiste, who performed Amour in the ballet *The Vestal*?' 'Maria Anderson', answered Petipa.

I vividly remember this conversation. It took place at the front of the stage of the Maryinsky Theatre [Tchaikovsky had written 'Bolshoy Theatre' in his diary for 21 January; but Anderson was recalling this over fifty years later], close to the orchestra, five or six steps from the first wing on the right side. Peter Ilyich was in a blue jacket; as always he wore a pince-nez hanging from a little black cord. Tchaikovsky had the habit of playing with his pince-nez in his right hand during conversations.

M. Petipa was searching for somebody with his eyes. Having noticed me, he called me over with a gesture of his arm, and with the words 'ma belle'. I approached timidly and remained at some distance. They did not interrupt their conversation, which was in French, continuing as if not paying the slightest attention to my approach. From single phrases that reached me I understood that the conversation concerned the production of the new ballet *Sleeping Beauty* and, in particular, it was about me, although my name was not mentioned.

Peter Ilyich, imperceptibly, stealthily, threw a glance in my direction, apparently evaluating me as an artist. Judging by his light smile, he was satisfied with me. Several of his exclamations, clearly and precisely repeated in French, confirmed my assumption. Finishing the conversation, Peter Ilyich took several steps in my direction in his typical manner—with his body slightly inclined. Coming closer, he began to ask me various questions, mixing, as was his custom, Russian and French conversation and playing with his pince-nez.

When Peter Ilyich finished his questions, which I answered timidly and with reserve, M. Petipa, thinking that I did not understand French, began to explain to me in his broken Russo-French dialect what the conversation was about. In the 'translation' it meant that in the ballet *Sleeping Beauty* I would dance 'the little cat, as Tchaikovsky wished'.[33]

That another casting decision had been made is implied in the announcement of Brianza's new contract on 15 February 1889. She was to receive 20,000 francs for the season (which represented a rise of 1,000) and a benefit performance—*Sleeping Beauty*.[34] On 19 April we read that the new ballet was to be postponed for a year, and that a revival of *The Hunchbacked Horse* would be mounted in its place.[35] But three weeks later, on 7 May, Vsevolozhsky wrote to Tchaikovsky that the models of the sets were ready, and that Petipa had already assigned the roles; in mid-June Tchaikovsky sent the completed prologue to St Petersburg.[36]

When Petipa wrote on the balletmaster's plan, 'I have finished writing, 5 July 1889', he may well have been taking note of more than the date: the preparation of this plan may represent the first considered thinking-through of *Sleeping Beauty* permitted by his schedule since the writing of instructions for Tchaikovsky. To prepare the balletmaster's plan, Petipa simply combined the libretto with the instructions he had given Tchaikovsky. But the sum is different from the parts in a number of minor details, and some notes were added which appear in neither of the other sources. These differences seem to show that he was in fact getting to work on the practical realization of the production.[37]

He crossed out, at the beginning of Act I, the part of No. 5 in which the princes implore Florestan to be merciful to the knitters. In the margin next to the description of the Act I finale (No. 9) he wrote, 'Groups of old men, women, and children must be formed.'[38] And in connection with the *colin-maillard* (Blind Man's Buff) in Act II:

Notes for me—groups of blind man's buff—they [the women] play with the tutor. They tease him with little lances or darts. They can finish with a bourrée or farandole with peasant men and women. In this scene there must be peasant men and women who have come to offer fruit to the Prince.

At the point where the Lilac Fairy calls forth Aurora as a vision Petipa asked, for Aurora and her companions, 'Can they be in fantastic costumes?' We then see for the first time a mention of the musical requirements for the coda of the vision scene: 'For the coda—music with mutes—a 2/4 as in *A Midsummer Night's Dream*.' One wonders if this idea occurred to the balletmaster because he had revived for one of the gala performances in May his ballet of that title, with music by Mendelssohn and Minkus.

Petipa also began to sketch out the scene in which Désiré attempts to catch Aurora's shade: 'She is balanced on the branches of the trees, swims in the water of the river, or is ensconced in the masses of flowers.' This idea was apparently not realized in the production. At the end of Act II he made another change in the musical requirements given as part of his earlier instructions to Tchaikovsky. When Désiré kisses Aurora he had originally wanted the music to 'become peaceful', but he now wrote: '. . . the music makes a *crescendo*, then a pause.'

Most of the changes in Act III concern blocking. In July Petipa still wanted, for the opening march, a quadrille of Turks, Ethiopians, Africans, and Americans to precede the procession of the fairy-tale characters, harking back to the exotic *entrées* of Louis XIV's ballet. These *entrées* appear to have crossed his mind again when he had worked his way down to the sarabande. 'Perhaps no', he wrote in the margin at this point, 'I think that this [location] is for the quadrille.'

The fairy-tale characters, passing in review, were not yet in the sequence listed in the published libretto. Petipa was also having misgivings about the quartet of the Blue Bird, Princess Florine, Cinderella, and Fortuné, as we may conclude from his remark in the margin: 'Perhaps we can delete this *pas de quatre*.' His concern for the growing length of *Sleeping Beauty* is revealed by other comments: 'Very short', he wrote next to Little Red Riding Hood's dance, and 'A very short *pas de caractère*' next to the *pas berrichon*. A reference at the end of the plan to 'Air Henri IV' lets us know for the first time that the melody of the apotheosis had been decided. There is as yet no sign of the further alterations—especially in the variations of the precious stones and the mazurka—found in the music sources.

Ballet rehearsals began on 23 August 1889. Precisely when the company learned *Sleeping Beauty* during the time that the regular repertory was in production cannot be determined. As Brianza did not make her first public appearance until the beginning of October, she may have spent much of September working on her new role. 'We rehearsed the ballet some three months on the little stage of the Theatre School', she related to Pleshcheyev in Paris decades later,

'. . . in the presence of the old man Marius Petipa, Tchaikovsky, and Riccardo Drigo—composer and ballet conductor of the orchestra of the Maryinsky Theatre. Rehearsals took place to piano accompaniment, played by Drigo himself. Tchaikovsky met the wishes of the balletmaster halfway, shortening, supplementing, and changing the music according to the dances. The famous composer enchanted us with his delicacy and his extraordinary modesty, something not typical of less well-known and less talented composers.[39]

Whatever the actual schedule was, everyone worked hard. 'Petipa rehearsed *Sleeping Beauty* fervently', the dancer Nikolai Solyannikov recalled, 'the company laboured unsparingly.'[40] One reason for such intense work, it seems, was the music. According to Drigo, it was difficult for the dancers to cope with Tchaikovsky's score; the internal resistance [*vnutrennee soprotivlenie*] to it among the dancers was great, as each variation went beyond the usual formulas to which the ear was accustomed.[41] 'In Drigo's words,' Slonimsky continued, 'Petipa was at times quite undecided, when the composer had exceeded his expectations or went against them.'[42]

Alexander Shiryaev relates that, while the composer was helpful enough, the balletmaster felt he could not make the demands he customarily made of the composers he worked with:

Tchaikovsky's music presented quite a few difficulties for Petipa. He was used to working with official ballet composers—my grandfather Pugni, and Minkus, who were prepared to change the music of this or that number endlessly . . . Although Tchaikovsky and Glazunov met the balletmaster halfway, he was hesitant to make demands of them as he had of Pugni and Minkus, who at his wish reworked their compositions straightaway at rehearsal. Petipa had therefore to work quite hard on *Sleeping Beauty*. This he confessed to me.[43]

Tchaikovsky came to Petersburg for ten days in September, his first visit since May, attended orchestral rehearsals of *Sleeping Beauty*,[44] and worked closely on the music with Petipa. Pleshcheyev quotes Tchaikovsky as having said, apropos of making changes in the music during rehearsals, 'One must consider the breathing and the strengths of the performers, Petipa declared to me. I could hardly refuse the wishes of such a great master of the ballet.'[45]

During the time of the rehearsals, Vladimir Pogozhev wrote:

. . . my meetings with Tchaikovsky became more frequent, both at Vsevolozhsky's, and in the office of the theatres, in the theatre, and in my apartment. And everywhere the prevailing theme of our conversations was the discussion of some detail or another, additions, abbreviations, and small changes in the production of *Sleeping Beauty*. Much time was devoted to an inspection of costumes and décor, and later to sectional and orchestral rehearsals. Conferences and discussions with Vsevolozhsky, with Petipa, and with the conductor Drigo became part of the routine of Peter Ilyich's life.[46]

Petipa was now devoting most of his energies to the new ballet, but Tchaikovsky was caught up again in conducting; two concerts in Moscow in November, three in Petersburg, with their rehearsals, before the New Year. It is difficult to identify a period of more than a few days when the composer was free from the press of these responsibilities. Tchaikovsky spent the whole of October in Moscow, and on 10 November a Petersburg daily announced:

The new ballet *Sleeping Beauty*, as we hear, is already completely ready as regards its choreographic *mise-en-scène*. Now it is a matter only of décor and costumes, which always delay new productions on the official stage.[47]

The announcement goes on to refer to Nikitina and Cecchetti (who would perform Princess Florine and the Blue Bird, respectively), notes the date of the first performance (3 December, for Brianza's *bénéfice*), and makes known the directorate's intention to give the new ballet twelve to fifteen times before the end of the season.

With the first performance a little over three weeks away and the threat of delays, a period of anxious preparation began, one that tried the patience of all the participants. Pogozhev explains:

Despite the fact that much time was given to the production, haste, as it happens, could not be avoided. Now changes in the costumes, now additions to the décor and properties, now the adjustments of mechanical feats and the movement of the panorama, now interpolations and changes in the choreographic composition, or necessary corrections in the score and orchestral parts. Especially great was the trouble with arrangement of the magic scene of the sleeping kingdom. All this made Vsevolozhsky and Petipa, the artists, and the administration nervous, and was of course also reflected in Tchaikovsky.[48]

The composer left for Moscow on 10 November and returned to Petersburg three days later for a conducting engagement. On 22 November, the date for the first performance of *Sleeping Beauty*—3 December —was still firm; on the 30th, however, it had changed to 17 December, with Brianza's benefit to follow on Christmas Day.[49]

Tchaikovsky returned to Moscow on 22 November, returning to Petersburg at the end of the month to be present at rehearsals of *Sleeping Beauty*. On 11 December he wrote to Jurgenson, requesting the dedication of the music to be printed in large letters on the title-page of the piano reduction. 'He [Vsevolozhsky] is frightfully proud of my dedication', Tchaikovsky wrote.[50] On or about 17 December another delay appeared inevitable. In a letter to Meck, Tchaikovsky made no attempt to disguise his irritation:

It has already been almost three weeks that I have been *loafing* in Petersburg. I say: *loafing*, for I consider composition my main business, and all my efforts in regard to conducting at concerts, attending rehearsals of the ballet, etc., as something accidental, pointless, and which only shortens my life . . . The most horrible thing is that I am never alone and perpetually find myself in some abnormally excited state. This must undoubtedly, sooner or later, tell on my health. In these three weeks I continually had to attend rehearsals of my ballet, yet besides that I had to conduct at a Russian Symphony Concert. The ballet, thanks to which I have remained here so long, is put forward from day to day as a result of décor which is not yet ready, and now it is set for 3 January.[51]

By 22 December Vsevolozhsky was certain enough of the latest date to send the following memorandum, 'Concerning the Rehearsal of the Ballet Sleeping Beauty', to the Minister of the Imperial Court:

The most suitable time, considering the demands of the repertory, for the first performance of the ballet *Sleeping Beauty* seems to be 3 January 1890, with the general rehearsal of this ballet perhaps set for the morning of 2 January.

In view of the Imperial will of His Imperial Majesty to be present at the [dress] rehearsal of the aforementioned ballet, I have the honour to await Your Excellency's command with respect to the times assigned for the first performance and the general rehearsal of the ballet *Sleeping Beauty*.

In the right margin the Minister wrote: 'at 2 o'clock on 2 January', and next to this, in red, we read, '2:00 on the 2nd—remind via memorandum sent His Majesty on the evening of 1 January.'[52]

It would seem that, finally, all was in order. But events decreed otherwise: one more emergency, of an unexpected sort, had to be met. Riccardo Drigo recalled:

At the very end of December I was seriously ill with a cold and felt it beyond my powers to conduct the general rehearsal of the ballet. Tchaikovsky was in complete despair, and did not want to listen to my urging him to conduct himself. He assured me that this was quite beyond him and would completely destroy his composition. At that time his objection surprised me, but seeing his distress I could not refuse him, and—still quite ill—conducted *Sleeping Beauty*, for which I earned his sincere and friendly gratitude.[53]

The general rehearsal was itself an important social occasion. 'According to etiquette,' recalled a young student lucky enough to get a ticket,

... one had to stop in at the régisseur's office before going into the hall, already teeming, where he [the régisseur]—a true pasha, with his white beard of Methuselah and a Persian skull cap on his head—was smoking and drinking his perpetual glass of tea in this club of stars of singing and the dance; everyone loved to chatter in this vast room.

This visit has remained in my memory my whole life. Scarcely had I removed my galoshes and knocked the snow off my fur collar than I stopped myself, taken aback ...

Dare I enter? I am looking into the depth of the sumptuous room, decorated with Persian carpets, past the ballerinas in crisp tutus, at two silhouettes which make up the centre, and by the respectful deference [recul] of the artists, understood that these were 'personages' [of importance].

One of them—large, with a curved back, aquiline nose, an affable and mocking smile—wears the Star of Vladimir on the left side of his blue coat of the Director of the Imperial Theatres.

Therefore one of the imperial family is here, I thought, all proud to take part in such a brilliant assembly (in fact Emperor Alexander III was there). The other gentleman was smaller, with white hair and beard, a very pink face, an amiable and timid air. He seemed very nervous, but one could see the effort that he was making to maintain his composure.

Who is it? I tried to catch the attention of my old friend, who finally noticed me (because I was very small of stature), thick in the frothy mass of rustling tutus ...

'Levushka (petit Léon), come over so I can present you to our glory, to our pride, to Peter Ilyich Tchaikovsky!'

Flushed with emotion, in the uniform of the École des Beaux-Arts, too small, but with white gloves—so chic, I believed—carrot-coloured hair cut short, I probably seemed comical. Having emerged bravely from my amiable prison, without batting an eye, I extended my hand to the famous musician first.

'Voilà,' continued the old régisseur, amidst smiles, 'this young man adores the theatre and is already painting maquettes. The other day, talking about your *Beauty* over tea at friends of mine, he improvised décors in his own style . . . Where are they?'

And he searched in vain in the drawer of his desk.

'I find the music of *La Belle au bois dormant* excellent', I exclaimed in a voice choked with emotion, amidst general surprise shortly followed by a burst of laughter.

'Ah! You already know my ballet', Tchaikovsky marvelled, laughing, and he directed his inquisitive glance at the patriarchal beard of the régisseur . . .

Unforgettable matinée! For three hours I lived in a magic dream, intoxicated by fairies and princesses, by splendid palaces, streaming with gold, by the enchantment of the fairy-tale . . . All my being was in cadence with those rhythms, with the radiant and fresh waves of beautiful melodies, already my friends.

But what a return home! What a cruel end to the enchantment! Outside, again the densest gloom after these dazzling sights; horrible biting snow; from the Neva a glacial wind; vain attempts to find a cab, too expensive near the theatre, and finally, home; the oil lamp, sad and middle-class, hung too high.

Ah! What a contrast with the Maryinsky Theatre, all draped in beautiful blue velvets, filled with dazzling guards officers, women with low-necked gowns, resplendent, radiant, a perfumed and heterogeneous crowd, in which the red outfits and the white stockings of the valets of court, so proper, so emblazoned with imperial eagles, introduced a solemn note . . .

That evening, I believe, my vocation was decided.

So wrote Léon Bakst.[54]

'I remember . . . the general rehearsal', Brianza declared. 'Emperor Alexander III was present with all his family. They took places in the *parterre*, and in the *loges* sat artists of the opera, drama, and ballet. Some of the latter, who participated in *Sleeping Beauty*, appeared in the *loges* in costume, taking advantage of the periods when they were not on stage.' The Tsar did not actually go backstage, she observed, but normally invited a few artists to his *loge*; on this occasion he personally thanked the ballerina for her performance.[55]

Tchaikovsky noted the event in his diary. Disconsolate and hurt over Alexander's response to the ballet, he quoted the Tsar's 'Very nice' and followed it with five exclamation marks. Then, in a more forgiving tone, he wrote 'The Lord [*Gospod*'] be with him.'[56]

So enthusiastic was the public's response to the general rehearsal that Skalkovsky could write:

The new ballet *Sleeping Beauty* cannot be called new for our public because, according to the latest turn of official policy, two general rehearsals of it were given, permitting the admittance of the outside public, and since there is among us a vast majority of volunteers to watch free, even in high society, it is understandable that 'all Petersburg', as it is known [a reference to the social register], has already seen the new ballet.[57]

The performance itself, especially the complex scene changes about which there had been concern, went smoothly. 'In a word, the illusion is complete', we read in an unsigned description of the panorama on that day.[58]

(c) The First Production

The musical sources for *Sleeping Beauty* provide more than data about tempos, expressive effects, and the location of cuts and interpolations. Remarks about production—the names of dancers written into the score at the point in the music where they appear on stage, indications of dancers' floor plans in ensemble numbers, instructions for blocking and for special scenic effects—have also been added (see Pl. 18). A description of the first production can draw on yet another important source, one that can be related, on the basis of internal evidence, to the revival of *Sleeping Beauty* in 1903. This is a choreographic notation (CN), made up of prose descriptions, floor plans, and symbols of bodily movement devised by the Petersburg dancer Vladimir Stepanov.[59]

The following account is based on the musical sources, the CN, and the published libretto (translated in Appendix A), together with information from reviews and Yury Slonimsky's description of the production in *P. I. Tchaikovsky and the Ballet Theatre of his Time*.[60] A precise description of the production is, of course, impossible. Since the libretto does not list supernumeraries, of which there were dozens, and since the notators were concerned only with principal characters or others who were actually taking part in some action, it is difficult to account for all persons on stage at any given moment. The libretto, for example, calls for Aurora's cradle to be brought in by wet-nurses preceded by governesses, but the individuals involved are not named in either the cast list or the CN. Similar examples may be drawn from elsewhere in the work.

PROLOGUE

At bar 18 of No. 1 Catalabutte comes on stage. Stepping up to centre front, he announces to the assembled courtiers that the King will be arriving presently at this festival to celebrate the birth of the royal child.[61] A footman enters (bar 32) with a list of the invited guests;[62] Catalabutte meets him and receives the list. A brief exchange in mime follows:

Catalabutte: 'You have forgotten no one on the list?'

Footman: 'No.'

Catalabutte: 'So there! Make sure!'

The footman walks to rear stage centre and announces the arrival of five more couples.[63] Six pages follow them, entering from stage rear right, beginning at bar 111, and make a counter-clockwise sweep around the stage.

The King and Queen follow at bar 115. The courtiers bow. Florestan says to the Queen, 'Go and look at our sleeping child', which she does. He then summons Catalabutte and says, 'Give me the list of the invited guests.' The King and Queen inspect the list and ask if anyone has been forgotten. Catalabutte replies to this, 'I have invited them all', and Florestan returns the list to him. The Master of Ceremonies retires to front stage left. Another footman enters (at the end of No. 1) and announces the arrival of the fairies. He retires to rear stage right, the King and Queen to front left.

The first five fairies perform a 'salut du Roi' as they come in: Candide in bar 8, Fleur-de-Farine in bar 16, Breadcrumb and Violente together at bar 38, and Canari at bar 46 of No. 2, the *scène dansante*.[64] Once all five are on stage they bow to the King again and say, 'We come in order to protect [*pokrovitel'stvovat'*] your child.' They move to stage left, behind the King and Queen, as the Lilac Fairy arrives (bar 57) with a retinue of eight girls in couples.[65] 'Elle descend sur la scène' in bars 64–5, while her suite forms a line behind her. The other fairies form a semicircle between the Lilac Fairy and her suite.

The gifts are presented.[66]

As recorded in the CN, the waltz in No. 2 is an elaborate figured dance involving several characters in addition to the pages and the young girls: some children (possibly the ones who have just delivered the gifts), the Lilac Fairy's retinue, and all six fairies themselves.[67]

The first statement of the waltz theme (No. 2, bars 110–25) is taken up with an *entrée* of twelve girls (eight from the *corps de ballet* and four students) who come on in ranks of three, a student in the middle of each rank, from rear stage right. They waltz diagonally across the stage and then break away, the students making an counter-clockwise circle around the stage and back to their original location, the *corps* a clockwise one.

The Lilac Fairy's retinue takes up the second statement of the waltz (bars 126–41), crossing and re-crossing the stage twice. Their pattern begins stage right, from which, in a single file parallel with the side, they step out on left *pointe*, coming back from the other side in a series of four turns. As they perform these turns the second time, four pages (those of Violente and Breadcrumb) come on to front stage centre from the right. The men perform a combination of short jumps repeated three times and move back to half the depth of the stage (bars 142–57) before dispersing to the sides in pairs.

Then, in preparation for the return of the principal theme, the *corps de ballet* at the back and the fairies passing in front of them from stage left form two lines across the stage. Soloists and *corps* perform the steps of the return in unison, the fairies travelling independently in a zigzag pattern to stage front and back again (bars 170–86). The position of the arms is contrasted in the next phrase (raised in the back row, lowered in the front). The last sixteen bars of the waltz prepare for the final group, in which all the participants in the dance come together, the Lilac Fairy in the middle, encircled first by her sisters, then her retinue, each concentric circle closed by the dancers' joining hands. The four pages pose behind the circles, and behind them a row of women hold the pillows with the gifts.

In the libretto the entire *pas de six* (No. 3) is accounted for in the rubrics: '*Grand pas d'ensemble*. The Gifts of the Fairies', from which we learn nothing of the stage action before the variations. The only relevant comments in the Rep are written in the first ten bars: above bars 1 and 2, 'les pages présentent les cadeaux'; above bars 9 and 10 (the beginning of the *andante*), 'Les pages soutiennent les danseuses—les autres avec les présents, etc.'.

The second comment, doubtless part of the description of a group of dancers posed on stage, brings the Rep into agreement with the CN. According to the latter, Petipa took his cue from the end of the waltz and mounted the entire *adagio* as a succession of picturesque groups joined by intricate transitions. The *pas* began, however, not with the pages presenting the gifts, as the Rep has it, but with a fragment of mime. Moving to stage centre Florestan says: 'I thank you. Dance here.'

No sooner has he finished than the pose, still held from the last group of the waltz, dissolves and the dancers begin another: eighteen women (divided into sixes, on *pointe*) form a line of three rotating circles across the front of the stage, the fairies in the middle circle. The other dancers are arranged in a patttern behind them. In the second group the four pages are stationed across the front, kneeling on the left knee and each with a woman, probably one of the fairies, sitting on the right. The Lilac Fairy's retinue forms a line behind the pages. The third group's pattern contrasts with the first two, not on lines approximately parallel with the front of the stage, but all positioned on a diagonal from front stage right to rear stage left. The women perform *attitudes* and turns on *pointe*. Then the Lilac Fairy, posing on a stool, forms the centrepiece of a pattern similar to that with which the waltz had ended—surrounded by her sisters and their pages, but this time with her retinue being asked 'to lie on their right sides' across the front of the stage.

A short mimed statement precedes the final group of the *adagio*. The fairies say: 'Your little child will grow up to be a beauty and we will protect her.' The King and Queen thank them. Except for a row of children at the back of the stage, the CN does not account for the dancers in the last grouping before the *allegro vivo*. Hastily sketched, the pattern is an arrangement of dancers in parallel semicircles which open at the front of the stage.[68]

Four pages and eight girls, probably those of the Lilac Fairy's retinue, dance the *allegro vivo*, the girls now in the centre in unisons, now pairing off with the boys. At the end the boys rush forward from the back of the stage to support four of the girls in a pose, while the other four kneel.

The variations of the *pas de six* are for the 'gifts of the fairies' mentioned in the libretto. Petipa's intentions are clear from the Rep, where we read, above Variation I: 'Elle exprime et donne son caractère à l'enf[ant] qui est dans le berceau.' And then, at the head of the next four variations, 'La même idée avant de commencer', or simply 'même idée'. Three of the variations in the CN call for 'blessing' by the fairy at the beginning of the dance.

Candide begins her dance in bar 5;[69] she enters, as will her sisters, from rear left. In smooth combinations of steps and small jumps on *pointe* she dances to front right; then, travelling from stage right to stage left, she makes large, sweeping circular gestures with her body and arms, continuing in the next phrase (bars 21–8), facing Aurora but travelling backwards in a diagonal towards rear stage right. In the last seven bars she comes forward to centre front, completing her dance with a pose *en attitude*.

Fleur-de-Farine blesses Aurora as she runs by. Her floor pattern has shorter dimensions and is more restricted than Candide's spacious traversals of the stage, and her steps are more intricate and virtuoso than her sister's—short jumps, *ronds de jambe*, culminating in the last phrase with a series of eight turns.

The Breadcrumb Fairy's variation is almost entirely on *pointe*. After blessing the child she makes her way to front stage right. Then, like Candide, travelling backwards on a diagonal, she retraces part of her path in a series of short jumps. She breaks the pattern and runs again to stage right, in preparation for the principal combination of her dance: short jumps on left *pointe* with the right leg beginning *en attitude devant* and moving back to an *arabesque*, which she performs four times, facing the cradle while crossing the stage toward Aurora. A run on *pointe*, still facing the cradle but travelling to the rear in a zigzag pattern, serves as a preparation for the final phrase of the variation, in which she repeats the steps of her principal combination on the other leg.

In the variation for the 'Canari qui chante' floor patterns on diagonals prevail, most moving back and forth from the cradle. 'At all times moving the wrists' (an instruction in the CN), Aurora's next godmother enters. The initial phrases of her dance are set almost in the manner of a bird, in a series of stiff-kneed steps, the working leg to alternate sides, but ending with a double *rond de jambe* in the air; she repeats this sequence of movements as she approaches the cradle. Then, as if amazed by the sight of Aurora, she changes the quality of her movement, now softened by *demi-pliés*. The rest of her dance unfolds in tiny steps in the centre of the stage and then, in the last phrase, moving back towards the cradle. She ends with an *attitude* towards the child, then an *arabesque* facing the audience.

Unpredictable Violente waits for the first eight bars to be played before she comes on with a series of short *attitudes* on alternate legs. This initiates a variety of steps—jumps, facing movements, turns, *ronds de jambe*—changing every few bars, in keeping with her character. Midway through the music for her dance (bars 41–3) Petipa wrote: 'Elle va lui dire près tu seras gaie et tu aimeras la don [effaced] du berceau.' Suddenly she runs to the back of the stage, turns, and rushes forward on a concluding line of *pirouettes*.

One of the lingering criticisms of the first production is that Petipa erred in giving the part of the Lilac Fairy to his daughter Marie, a public favourite reputed to be a stunning beauty. Neither petite nor particularly adept at classical dance, Marie at thirty-three is said to have limited her father's choreographic options in this important role (see note 28, above, on the casting of the part). In a rare moment of gallantry, Slonimsky wrote:

Petipa's version of the Lilac Fairy's variation is without virtuoso technique. One ought not attribute this to the limited possibilities of its first executant—Marie Petipa: these played a secondary role. The intention to vary the dance character-istics of the numerous personages of the spectacle had a decisive significance. The extended, 'singing' movements with which the Lilac Fairy was provided were introduced into the work thanks to the music, which suggested *plastique*; they did not also permit making the Lilac Fairy's part technically virtuoso.[70]

By the time *Sleeping Beauty* was notated, two versions of the Lilac Fairy's variation were included, one, technically less demanding, marked 'M. Petipa', the other simply 'Variation of the Lilac Fairy'. Stylistically both fit Slonimsky's description. Marie's choreography is based on the plainest of floor plans and requires very little *pointe* work; instead, the CN calls for elegant *port de bras* and touches of mime (during a circular pass around the stage she crosses her hands on her breast in a blessing gesture). The other version features poses held on *pointe* and virtuoso combina-tions, but without sacrificing in the quality of movement the *volupté* Petipa requested for the music. At the head of this variation in the Rep we read: 'Elle lui prédit le bonheur'.

The coda is a résumé of the entire number in a series of *entrées*: first the pages in bar 5; then what appears to be the Lilac Fairy's retinue (above bar 24 Petipa wrote, 'Il faut faire les figures avec les pages, coryphées, etc.'); then, by twos in a rush of *pirouettes*, the first four fairies, crossing diagonally from opposite sides of the rear of the stage (Candide and Fleur-de-Farine in bar 37, Violente and Breadcrumb in bar 45). These dancers then form a frame for the two last entries, first Canari in bar 52 and then the

Lilac Fairy in bar 60, each escorted on stage by the quartet of pages. The *entrées* complete, all form picturesque groupings; this is followed in the CN by a short description of the close: 'The fairies take from the pages the pillows with gifts and show them to the King, saying that they are for his young daughter. The King and Queen thank the fairies. The fairies hand the pillows with the presents back to the pages.'

The King, the Queen, and Catalabutte are standing front stage left when a footman enters and announces that an evil old woman is coming in. Florestan commands that he be given the list of invited guests.

The Fairy Carabosse makes her entrance with a sweeping counter-clockwise motion around the stage from rear stage left. The King receives the list. 'Ah! You forgot to invite her, which means you have given her cause to kill our daughter.' He throws the list back at Catalabutte, who picks it up and moves across to the other side of the stage.

Carabosse walks up to Florestan and greets him; her mice and pages promenade around the stage and look at everything.[71]

Carabosse: 'You are feasting here, and you forgot me, the old woman.'

Florestan: 'I ordered all to be summoned, but he [pointing at Catalabutte] forgot to summon you.'

Carabosse: 'Ah! Excellent, I will have a word with him.'

She walks over to Catalabutte. 'You forgot to call me. I will show you.' She orders him to come over to her. 'You forgot to write me down on the list. You did not invite me to the celebration. Come over here. On your knees.' Catalabutte goes over to her, falls on his knees, and begs for mercy. Carabosse tears off his hat and throws it on the floor. Her rats pick it up and carry it into the carriage. Then three times she tears the hair from Catalabutte's head, the rats running up each time, grabbing the hair and carrying it into the carriage. [A reviewer for the *Petersburg Gazette* noted that the rats devoured the hair.] With her pages' help, Carabosse beats Catalabutte with her crutch. 'Just look at him', she says derisively, and laughs, 'See how fine he is!'

The other fairies, who have been standing halfway back on stage left, move to stage centre and form a semicircle around Carabosse, who greets them. They ask her not to be angry with the child. Carabosse, looking at them all with a fixed stare, says: 'You are feasting here—you with the tender hands, and you, little Canary, and you here, and they forgot me, but I will not be angry. You will see how I will dance here.' As her sisters retire back to stage left Carabosse summons her mice and pages, who run to the centre from all parts of the stage. She orders them to dance. [The CN preserves neither steps nor floor plans of the dances of Carabosse's retinue.]

Carabosse next walks over to the King and says, 'You listen to me. She (your daughter) will grow up, will be beautiful. Her hands will be beauti-ful.' The King and Queen are delighted. But Carabosse then says, 'Wait. She will prick her finger with a pin, lose consciousness, and die.' The King and Queen, despairing, do not know what to do.

The Queen goes to Carabosse and begs on her knees for her not to be angry with Aurora (this episode is preserved only in the CN). Carabosse, seeing the Queen's abasement, says, 'She is a queen and begs me on her knees', and laughs. The King, seeing his wife's humiliation, walks over, takes her by the hand, and leads her away from Carabosse. He says: 'You are on your knees before her; think of it—you are a queen and have debased yourself thus in front of her.'

Carabosse says once again, 'You will watch my dances.' She calls the mice and pages, and again all run in from various sides. 'You dance here.' Dance of the mice.

The wicked fairy then walks over to the cradle, but the Lilac Fairy stops her there. Carabosse's manner suddenly changes from triumphant to servile; she backs away from the cradle. The Lilac Fairy takes the offensive against her and says: 'I thank you! I thank you! I love this child so much, and you want to kill her? Listen to me, to what I say to you: she will prick her finger and fall asleep, yes! But she will not die. They will take her and carry her off.'

Carabosse: 'No!'

Lilac Fairy: 'I wish it thus.'

Carabosse is again humbled and angered.

Lilac Fairy: 'There a handsome and noble one will see her, he will kiss her on the forehead and she will awaken.'[72]

Carabosse (maliciously): 'No! No!'

Passing by the King Carabosse says, 'Remember what I told you.' She sits down in her carriage and leaves, threatening everyone with her crutch. All present threaten Carabosse.

This ends the prologue in the CN.

Despite occasional disagreements in the mass of detail provided by these documents, a coherent pattern may be observed in the structure of the choreography. The symmetry of the four numbers—mimed scene, danced number, danced number, mimed scene—is reflected in the symmetry of individual numbers. The *pas de six*, for example, has its own internal shape—initial mime, posed groupings, dances, posed groupings, concluding mime—and its own internal logic, growing out of the contrast of characteristics which the fairies impart to Aurora: the energetic Fleur-de-Farine coming just after the gentle Candide is balanced, at the other end of the variation suite, by the impetuous Violente followed by the composed Lilac Fairy. Petipa also unified some of the variations, regardless of the contrasts of the dances, with *enchaînements*, which required the dancers to face the cradle, thereby suggesting not just the giving of a blessing but also the receiving of some intangible gift—beauty or enchantment—from the child. All the variations, in turn, form a unit which contrasts in its quality of good will with the malevolence of the seventh sister expressed in the finale.

ACT I

The curtain rises to reveal eight gossiping women standing in stage centre; behind them stand two rows of onlookers, the first women, the second men. 'The gossipers are talking among themselves and walking about the entire stage knitting stockings' when Catalabutte and his servant come on stage. They look at the women, again standing in a group, and are satisfied that everything is all right; then the Master of Ceremonies goes over for a closer look.

Catalabutte: 'What are you doing here?'
Gossipers: 'We're not doing anything.'
Catalabutte: 'Why are you holding your hands behind you?'

He takes away a stocking from one of the knitters, whereupon all fall to their knees and beg him not to tell the King.

Catalabutte: 'You ought to be ashamed of yourselves; it is written that knitting is prohibited. I am having you all taken away.'

He orders his servant to carry out the command; crying, the gossipers are led off to the right as the King's pages come on from the opposite side, followed by the King and Queen, four princes (rivals for Aurora's hand), and a number of other courtiers. All on stage bow to the King. The gossipers fall on their knees before him.

Florestan (to Catalabutte): 'Tell me that all is in order here.' Catalabutte remains silent.

Florestan (to the Queen): 'Look at him—how sad he is—what is amiss with him? (to Catalabutte) What's the matter? Why are these women crying?'

Catalabutte: 'I came in and saw them knitting.'

Florestan: 'How dare they—call them over here [!]'

Catalabutte walks behind the knitters, who run over to the King, throw themselves on their knees, and beg for mercy.

Florestan (surrounded by the knitters): 'I commanded you to leave aside all such work, and you did not listen to me. (They again beg for mercy.)

No. Better not to ask. I said that you will be punished, and you shall be.'

All this time they continue tearfully to beg forgiveness. Angry, Florestan walks back and forth across the stage in agitation. The courtiers and the Queen go up behind him and soothe him; the Queen asks him to show mercy. After hearing requests for a long time Florestan agrees. The knitters run off stage; the others retire to the sides and find a place to watch the waltz.

The *valse villageoise*, which pleased the audience enough for them to call Petipa for a bow at the first performance, was remarkable for being choreographed without soloists—the *corps de ballet* and children from the theatre school danced in it—and for its elaborate groupings, which called forth the praise of critics. The notators divided the waltz into eleven parts according to the dancers' floor patterns, which were so complicated that two records were made—one of the *corps*, another of the children. The parts were numbered, and these numbers were transferred to (or possibly from) the Rep, so we can align the major sections of the choreography with the music.

Forty-eight dancers, four columns of six pairs each, move forward from the rear of the stage. Each 'cavalier holds the woman by the arm; in the woman's right hand, a small basket of flowers.' For a moment the boys hold the girls by the waist as the girls step in front of their partners on *pointe en attitude*, then let them go. These two figures take up the first thirty-two bars of the waltz (41–72).

The *corps*, still in its original formation, begins to perform facing movements when a group of children (sixteen pairs, according to Slonimsky), who had entered at bar 65, move down the centre of the stage to the front (bar 73 ff.). The children's steps are related (through the *pas ballonné*) to the steps the *corps* are performing in place. During this segment we first become aware of garlands of flowers, although the manuscript does not specify how and when they are introduced ('The cavaliers walk behind the garlands').

In preparation for the return of the main theme, all the dancers run to the rear of the stage. Then, at bars 109–40, the entire group makes its way forward slowly with a combination of *pas ballonné* and *arabesque*.

The middle part of the waltz (bars 145–76) is constructed around an elaborate posed grouping. The *corps de ballet* in couples is distributed in a large semicircle around the children, who form two concentric circles in the middle of the stage. The women of the *corps* circle around their partners and then pose in an *arabesque*; the children perform *pas ballonné* and *pas de basque*. For the second phrase of music (beginning in bar 161) the basic outlines of the group are preserved but the steps within are changed slightly: the children, now in couples, combine waltz and *balancé* in sequence while the *corps* around them raise the garlands aloft.

The last section of the waltz (beginning in bar 177), a return of the opening section with a coda, is also designed in elaborate patterns. The first is an intricate moving formation in the shape of a cross. The men form the outlines of the cross; the women, dancing in lines out to the corners of the stage in *ballonnés* and back again in waltz steps, split the angles of the cross; and the children perform *pas de basque* along its corridors. In the second pattern the men, arranged in a semicircle open at the front, hold the garlands towards the centre while the children dance in circles around the men; the women form two ranks across the front of the stage. In the third pattern, instead of rounded contours and lines spreading across the stage, the dancers form columns perpendicular to the proscenium, the women on the sides (dancing to the centre and back again), the children in the middle, and the men just outside the children. The women perform the same steps in this pattern as they had performed in the cross formation; the men catch the women and the children alternately with the garlands.

At bar 267 of the Rep Petipa wrote 'Ici j'ai fini'—that is, some thirty bars before the end—and yet the CN preserves two more floor plans. The first is a transition to the final posed group: a circle of men in the middle, framed by women front and back and men on either side. All, apparently, perform a combination of *arabesque* followed by *pas balancé*. The final posed group, celebrated in studies of *Sleeping Beauty*,[73] may not be correctly transmitted in the CN (on a sheet of paper pasted over the original, the CN accounts for twenty-four of the eighty dancers who were on stage). The design of the final posed group is based on rounded lines of dancers in progressively smaller numbers toward the front—some standing, some kneeling, some lying on the stage.

The next short *scène* (No. 7) is a transition between the big ensemble dance and the equally imposing *pas d'action* which follows. In it the audience is introduced to Aurora and the members of her suite who will take part in the *pas d'action*. At the beginning of No. 7 Florestan walks to stage centre, thanks everyone, and gives the dancers who have just finished the waltz their leave. He then goes over to the four princes, standing in a line on front stage right, and says: 'You four all love my daughter. I have agreed; you have a talk with her; whomever she shall choose will be her husband. There—she is coming here now.'

The King moves to stage left as Aurora's pages—eight children with violins—run in from the back. Then follow four young girls with mandolins, followed by four maids of honour, and then Aurora herself. The costumes of Aurora and her maids of honour are strikingly contrasted: the girls in black (dubbed 'mourning dresses' by the critic of the *Petersburg Gazette*[74]), Aurora in 'red, with gold brocade and gold lace, which goes very well on her', according to the critic D. D. Korovyakov.[75]

The Princess runs on from stage rear left to stage centre. Her dance progresses gradually from small, intricate steps which broaden to large jumps and rotary turns of the body. At the end of a series of *chaînés* she stops in front of her waiting parents.

In the mimed introduction of the *pas d'action* (the first eighteen bars of No. 8) the Queen walks over to Aurora, kisses her, and says, 'You will be so tired.' Florestan then approaches the four princes; Aurora runs up to him; he kisses her and says, as they walk back across the stage, 'You are grown up and very beautiful; these four love you and are asking for your hand. I have agreed, but you yourself must give them an answer.'

Like the waltz, the *pas d'action* (*andante maestoso*) which follows is organized around the groupings of the dancers, most of which, from the standpoint of stage action, allow each of the four princes to engage in some act of courtship. 'The first suitor [zhenikh] leads Aurora by the hand' as she performs a turn and then an *arabesque* on *pointe*. He retires and the next two do the same. For the fourth prince she adds a turn and holds the *arabesque* twice as long. The special attentions Aurora pays to the fourth suitor correspond with a remark in the CN, 'The fourth suitor is best [4i zhenikh luchshii],' and she prefers him to the others throughout the remainder of the *andante maestoso*.[76]

In the second grouping, the princes find themselves within a square of which the maids of honour, *en arabesque*, mark the corners. 'The first [prince] takes Aurora by the hand' as she holds an *attitude*, the next two likewise, and then the fourth, who supports Aurora in two turns before her *attitude*. Each prince then retires to a corner and [apparently] supports the *arabesque* of one of the maids of honour.

These long-held *arabesques* dissolve in the transition to the third grouping, in which Aurora, after a short run and turn, is herself supported by each cavalier in an *arabesque*. She performs a series of unsupported *arabesques* in the fourth group, and in the fifth one cavalier only—presumably her favourite—lifts her and then 'gradually lowers' her. The sixth group provides a frame for Aurora's turns along stage left, rear to front; across the back of the stage stand her pages, in front of them, kneeling, the young mandolin players; on the opposite side, the princes and the maids of honour.

A property is added in the seventh group. Aurora, in a circular pattern, makes a step, a turn, and a hold before receiving a flower from each prince. She graces the fourth cavalier again, this time with a double turn, and holds an *arabasque* while the Queen comes over and takes the flowers. Aurora and the fourth prince then retire to the corner of rear stage right in preparation for the eighth group. While his rivals watch, Aurora's favourite supports her, travelling on a diagonal, in two statements of a combination of steps which culminate in a double turn and *attitude*.

Aurora retraces her path alone on *pointe*; the fourth prince joins the other three. The maids of honour oblige the princes as each requests a flower, while Aurora, stage centre, displays various positions of the arms. In a penultimate group Aurora performs four turns on *pointe* in place. Kneeling, each prince gives her a flower; the Princess takes each one and throws it to her parents after running to the side. In the final group each prince supports Aurora in a turn *en attitude*, then kneels while she performs a final pair of *tours* and ends the *adagio* in an *arabesque*.

The 'Dances of the Maids of Honour and the Pages' (No. 8b), as they are called in the score, begin with the pages performing a simple dance—one clearly designed for its quaint effect. Travelling in two columns of four, the dancers move back and forth across the stage, with facing movements and turns as the columns pass through one another at the centre. Their entry takes up the first twenty bars (No. 8, bars 83–102).

The pages retire to the sides to make room for the little mandolin players, who pass once from rear to front before also moving to the sides (bars 103–10). The maids of honour form the next wave of dancers, advancing towards the front with large steps and jumps with extensions, and retiring again, always facing the audience. Then, performing turns on a diagonal, the maids of honour move out of a single file to new positions at the corners of a square (a pattern which recalls the second grouping of the rose *adagio*), thence back to their original line and on to other figures.[77]

This ensemble dance serves, in the larger span of the *pas d'action*, to separate Aurora's accompanied *adagio* from her first solo, the only choreographic excerpt from *Sleeping Beauty* to be published during Petipa's lifetime.[78] It is scored, at the balletmaster's request, for 'violins, cellos, and harp', and we now realize the reason for equipping Aurora's retinue with musical instruments: they will mime the accompaniment of her dance.[79]

Aurora enters with a sweeping run around the stage. Her dance is organized into two parts: the first features fine *pointe* work articulated by high poses and elegant *port de bras* while she traces an orderly sequence of floor patterns (zigzag, back and forth along diagonals, zigzag); the second (most probably beginning with the *allegro vivace* at bar 233) differs in its stress on roundedness (large jumps and turns in a circular pattern similar to that of her entrance).

The plan of the coda follows that of the *pas de six*: the dancers enter in reverse order of seniority. The youngest—the four mandolin players—come first, in the first thirty-two bars after bar 268, then the maids of honour at bar 300, joined by the princes. Aurora comes on in bar 355 with a flurry of turns, continuing the strand of her dance left abandoned at the end of her solo. Just before the change of time signature at bar 409 (though possibly at bar 387) 'the old witch calls Aurora'. Carabosse offers her the distaff [*pryalka*; in the libretto, *vereteno*: 'spindle'], and she accepts. The King and Queen, frightened, ask her to throw it away; she answers with a series of jumps and turns. Again they ask, and receive a similar response. Aurora dances on, performing two *sauts de basque* with *chaîné* in the last combination before she pricks her finger.

She falls. All are shocked. The King and Queen run to her, and Florestan asks, 'Who could have given her this distaff?'

All point at Carabosse. Florestan walks over to her. They tear off Carabosse's coat.[80] Again, all are shocked. The King steps back, horrified, and Carabosse follows him.

Carabosse: 'You remember—I said she would die. Ha! Ha! Ha!' She turns and walks away.

Florestan (to the princes): 'Kill her!'

Thé princes rush at Carabosse, but she disappears through a trap in the stage. Everyone scatters.

The Lilac Fairy appears from behind a magically illuminated fountain.

Florestan: 'Look. She lies there, lifeless. Save her.'

Lilac Fairy: 'All of you here will sleep one hundred years.

But she will not die. Take her over there.'

They carry the beautiful girl into the castle; the King, the Queen, and their retinue and pages all follow. The Lilac Fairy makes a magic sign with her wand and instantly everyone falls asleep—*in picturesque groups situated in the vestibule, on the terrace, along the staircase and in the garden.*[81] The fairy calls her little pages and orders them to see that no one comes near. 'You watch here that no one approaches', she commands (CN, p. 104).

The Lilac Fairy makes another sign, *and out of the earth grow lianas, huge trees, lilacs, to form an impassable thicket, which completely obscures the palace and makes it impossible to reach*. 'The obscuring of the exterior view of the castle by the forest', wrote Korovyakov, 'is produced by raising a split curtain from a hold beneath the front of the stage. Little by little the curtain conceals the stage from the audience's view, like an ordinary curtain only not from above, but from below.'[82]

According to the CN, the Lilac Fairy and her eight pages remain on stage until the regular curtain falls.

The elegance of construction and attention to detail which characterize Petipa's work in the prologue continue to be observed in Act I. His decision to build the *valse villageoise* and the rose *adagio* on successions of groupings, for example, unifies these otherwise distinctly contrasted dances. And it is clear that he wanted to reinforce choreographically the obvious parallels in the story itself (and possibly the musical ones as well)—that is, those between the prologue and Act I. This can be observed in the dances (the manner of entry in the coda) and especially in the similarities between the outer mimed scenes. We see this use of parallels, for example, in the finales: Florestan's encounter with Carabosse at the end of Act I is an exact dramatic parallel to Carabosse's encounter with the Lilac Fairy in the prologue.

But if it resembles the prologue in certain ways, the first act is different in ways that anticipate Acts II and III: in the type and extent of the ballerina's dances and in the extraordinary production devices. Petipa's normal procedure in earlier ballets had been to permit the composer a completely free rein for expressive music in mimed scenes, where classical choreography was given little stress. In variations and *pas d'action* Petipa expected the composer to yield his claim on the audience's attention. The rose *adagio* is exceptional because Tchaikovsky did not do this: his music does not simply accompany the choreography but rather matches it in intensity of expression. The unusual power and eloquence of the rose *adagio* is the result of the music and dance reinforcing (not simply complementing) each other—though critics of the time complained that Tchaikovsky exceeded the limits observed by specialist composers. As regards elaborate stagecraft, the overgrowing of the sleeping castle by the forest at the end of Act I prepares us for other magical effects to follow: the panorama in which the Lilac Fairy and Désiré sail down the river to Florestan's castle; and the transformation of the castle and its inhabitants when Désiré kisses Aurora.

At this mid-point of *Sleeping Beauty* one begins to appreciate the extent of Petipa's effort and inspiration. Skalkovsky, an inveterate balletomane, had the measure of Petipa's accomplishment in the following remark in his review—a serious passage in an otherwise characteristically irreverent critique: 'To compose and to work out in the minutest details such a huge work, yes and to teach it to a hundred people, requires much intelligence, immense taste, great knowledge, and an unusual patience and love of work.'[83]

ACT II

The CN of Act II makes the least substantial contribution to our knowledge of the first production. There is no reference in it to the opening hunting scene (No. 10 in the score), the short interlude in which Désiré expresses his wish to go to Aurora (No. 16), the panorama (No. 17), the sleeping castle (No. 19), or the closing scene (No. 20)—easily half the act as regards music. While these scenes contain little action and no dancing, such omissions contrast with the care the notators lavished on the mimed scenes of the prologue and Act I.

Notations survive for the rest of Act II, but many of them complicate the task still more. The courtly dances and the farandole, for example, are preserved in versions substantially at variance with what little is known about the 1890 performances. The dances of the apparition scene are given twice, in versions for different performing forces.

Reviewers of the first performance barely mentioned the hunting scene, though one change appropriate to the passing of time in the story between Acts I and II did not escape notice: 'The costumes of the following acts transfer the action several centuries forward [sic], and the hunt of Prince Désiré introduces us directly into the golden age of Louis XIV, with affected marchionesses and curled gentlemen.'[84]

The CN begins with No. 11, the game of Blind Man's Buff, which, though carefully blocked, is not danced. One girl binds Galifron's eyes as the others look on. She is first to hit [*udaryat'*] Galifron with her riding stick; she then runs to the side. The tutor runs after her when two others come at him heading in the opposite direction. Désiré himself next runs across the stage, on a diagonal, hitting his teacher across the shoulder with his riding stick as he passes. Another pair of girls approach Galifron stealthily and tickle his face with their muffs; the girls run off to the sides as he seizes the muffs and throws them to the ground. Yet another girl, running across the stage on a diagonal, hits him with a riding stick as she passes and runs on, laughing. Galifron catches her by the waist; she slaps him on the face. The tutor retreats, rubbing his cheek. He turns back again, only to fall prey to a last practical joke. Two rows of girls rush up and form a corridor, at the other end of which stands a newly-arrived footman; Galifron walks down the corridor, and as he reaches out to catch the girls they break away in pairs and form a new line further upstage. After the last pair has run off, Galifron falls into the footman's embrace. He tears off his blindfold and walks towards the women, threatening them and saying: 'You wait! I'll get you!' He catches the first of the girls, now standing together, arms linked, and pulls all of them around the stage. One breaks loose from the chain; Galifron chases her and grabs her by the waist. 'Don't lose control!' she warns, and the tutor begs her pardon. With this the number ends.

No. 12 begins with a pantomime.

Galifron (to the women): 'You see how bored he is. Go to him.' They do.

The women: 'Why are you sad?'

Désiré: 'I? Sad? O no!'

The women: 'Shall we dance here?'

Désiré: 'Excellent!'

Skalkovsky mentions 'very nicely produced old French dances, ending with a farandole',[85] and Korovyakov that 'The most interesting number, which bears the stamp of the epoch, the knowledge and taste of the balletmaster, is the farandole and the variations of the courtly women in Prince Désiré's hunt.'[86]

We have seen (pp. 152–3) that what courtly dances were performed, and by whom, were questions that may have been answered only in the very late stages of production. The list of dances in the libretto mentions two variations of the court ladies, and the CN preserves two, but agrees neither with libretto nor the Rep in the performing forces called for. The Dance of the Duchesses is recorded in the CN for at least three men and three women (the Rep calls for one pair of women, and the libretto for one pair of women on p. iv but for one man and one woman on p. v). The Dance of the Countesses is choreographed for a man and a woman (the Rep calls for two women), and because it is written on Nikolai Sergeyev's London stationery and dated December 1938 the dance cannot be associated directly with Petipa or with an early production of the ballet.

Slonimsky writes of Petipa's sketches of the farandole, which follows the courtly dances:

The farandole was worked out by the balletmaster quite carefully. The numerous sketches of paths and groups have the purpose of a quaint mixing of sixteen peasants with a corresponding number of courtly persons. Petipa consciously showed the idyllic relations of these and others, having in view a genre picture analogous in content to French painting.[87]

In one sketch Petipa annotates a pattern of the farandole with the remark, '40 who dance and 48 women who do not dance', as if he were anticipating a group equal in size to the *valse villageoise*.[88] But by the time he writes the balletmaster's plan he has changed his mind: the noblewomen perform the farandole with villagers of both sexes. And by the time the libretto is published the performing forces have been changed again: not all the participants are identified, but among those who are we find eight noblewomen, eight peasant girls, four huntresses, and four hunters. According to the CN, the dance begins after an unspecified number of peasants run in. For the first sixteen bars they trace, holding hands, a serpentine pattern from the back to the front of the stage. Then the girls circle round the boys. A number of elaborate figures follow, including one in which the dancers form a circle round a large stage property [possibly *tournée*, but spelled in Russian]. But there is no evidence in the CN of participation by any courtier, and, judging from the number of bars accounted for, the dance has been shortened (possibly by cutting the *presto* at the end of the piece).

At the beginning of No. 14 a footman enters and announces that game has been sighted. The order to take up lances is given; property men bring in lances and distribute them. A footman asks Galifron, 'And will you be coming with us?', to which he responds, 'No! No! I will remain here.' Désiré bids farewell to his guests. All except Désiré and Galifron leave the stage.

Désiré: 'You are not going?'

Galifron: 'No. I am tired, and I want to go home.'

Désiré: 'In that case, leave; I will stay here by myself.'

Bowing repeatedly, Galifron leaves. (The libretto calls for him to fall asleep, drunk.)

According to PR-I and PR-II, the Lilac Fairy enters in her boat at bar 50, disembarks in bar 58, and crosses the back of the stage. Approaching Désiré, she comments, 'How pensive he is.' The Prince turns to meet her, kneels, and receives her blessing.

Lilac Fairy: 'Why are you so sad? You are surrounded here by such beautiful, well-dressed women, and you do not love any of them?'

Désiré: 'None says anything to my heart. But I would love someone who pleases me.'

Lilac Fairy: 'That idea has already occurred to me. Listen. I will bring forward from over there a lovely girl, with beautiful limbs. Do you want to see her?'

Désiré: 'Yes! Yes!'

Lilac Fairy: 'Be calm. I will show her to you; you will see her and marry her.'

Walking to the depth of the stage, she makes a sign with her wand and Aurora appears through a trap door. Désiré is smitten.[89]

Aurora first appears alone at rear stage left and runs towards Désiré, who supports her in a series of turns on a diagonal across the stage. She runs to front stage left, and while her companions come in from the sides and pose *en arabesque*, facing centre, Désiré lifts Aurora in a turn. When he puts her down she runs away from him. From this point to the beginning of the next number the *corps* is almost constantly in motion, now forming lines across the back of the stage, now columns, kneeling, now moving back again to the sides; the Lilac Fairy, Aurora, and Désiré move about at the centre of the stage, conducting a mimed dialogue (the details are not recorded). The entrance scene ends with two of Aurora's companions escorting an impassioned Désiré across to stage right.

The first part of No. 15 (the *andante cantabile*) is set by Petipa as a series of groupings; the basic choreographic idea appears to have been a supported *adagio* for the ballerina unfolding against variegated formations of the *corps de ballet*, who represent Aurora's companions, in the background. The pantomimic aspect of the number makes it more distinctive than the traditional *adagio*: it is blocked as an action scene during which Désiré is frustrated in several attempts to reach Aurora. At times he is restrained by a pair of Aurora's companions, at times by the Lilac Fairy (whom he supports in poses and turns). In one grouping, during which the *corps* form two oblique lines in the rear left quarter of the stage, he pursues the Princess back and forth between the two lines. Finally, as Aurora stands at rear centre in the middle of a large semicircle of her companions, Désiré approaches the Lilac Fairy and declares his love for the beautiful apparition.

The *corps* perform the second part of the dance (No. 15*a*, bar 98 ff.) without Aurora. They advance in a line, holding each other by the waist, and then form smaller groups. The *cabriole* and the *pas de basque* are the basis of a formation in which two ranks come forward from the rear, framed by a file on either side. The dance ends with the *corps* arranged in four columns, which exchange position by means of an elaborate turning combination before moving as a group first to the rear, then to the front of the stage.

Aurora's solo, to music from Act III, is generally very softly contoured in the quality of its movement, as befits a vision: facing movements with high extensions to the side of the working leg give way to a combination of double turns, steps, and poses, ending with *chaînés*, first in a *fleurette* pattern, then on a diagonal from rear stage left.

In the first of three sections of the coda (No. 15*c*) the *corps de ballet* enter from the rear corners of the stage in lines of three. They come forward along diagonal lines which cross in the centre of the stage, and as they reach the front a second wave of dancers starts out from the rear. To produce the effect of a continuous onrush of waves of dancers, Petipa calls for them to return to the rear of the stage and re-enter until it is time for the *corps* to move into a new grouping for the second section of the coda. Aurora enters in this section, performing a series of turns as she dances towards centre front stage.[90] The coda ends with another grouping: Désiré joins Aurora and supports her in a final pair of *tours* on *pointe*, and the Lilac Fairy joins the others near the end.

The CN of Act II ends with No. 15. The next number, even though it is assigned a metronome marking in the Rep, may not have been performed. According to the balletmaster's plan, its purpose is to accompany Désiré's declaration to the Lilac Fairy of his love for Aurora. According to the CN, Désiré has already made this declaration at the end of No. 15a; if so, No. 16 would no longer be required.

No. 17, the panorama, represents by means of elaborate stage machinery the journey of the Lilac Fairy and Désiré to Florestan's castle. 'The journey is represented by the movement of two really beautifully drawn decorations', Skalkovsky wrote. 'When the castle is revealed, darkness has settled on the stage, very artfully done . . . After two or three minutes the light once again appears and reveals the interior of the sleeping beauty's castle.'[91]

The writer of a review published in a Moscow newspaper described the scene from a technical standpoint:

. . . a moving split décor [is used] which reveals several beautiful landscapes and forest scenes. The changes of scene *à vue*, between four and five of them, are very excellently and tastefully done. The curtain remains raised and an orchestral *divertissement* continues. The anterior plan of the stage gradually closes by means of two excellently executed cloud-like cloths which draw from the right side of the wings to the left. There is a profound darkness in the theatre. In a few minutes the clouds disperse and full illumination instantly lights up the new, enormous, and extremely effective scene of the castle of the sleeping *tsarevna*.[92]

Benois pointed out that the 'masterfully drawn' panorama enjoyed success with the public, but that it 'lacked a fantastic quality. It was the kind of thing that too often appeared on the stage in those days when the representation of forest places and moonlit nights was required.'[93] Nor was D. D. Korovyakov especially impressed:

. . . the moving landscape panorama in Act II called forth cheers for the machinists Messrs Berger and Bocharov, who drew the wholly characteristic and talented landscapes of the panorama, which represent wild places beside which Prince Désiré sails in a boat with the Lilac Fairy towards the enchanted castle. We must confess that, from the standpoint of scenic effectiveness and the marvels of the

machinery division of our ballet stage, neither the panorama nor the transformation [of the sleeping castle back to life] is satisfactory to us. The movement of the
split décor between the public and the stationary boat, set within the completely
immobile foreground décor, gives a very weak illusion, much less of an illusion
than provided by the movement of the background ... The transformation of a
sleeping, deathlike castle into a lively one, and the visible change of appearance of
the door of the castle into a hall, takes place during a long period of time behind a
cloudy tulle curtain and with complete darkness on the stage.[94]

Another description is given in a production scenario preserved among
Petipa's papers:

Panorama. The décor changes into night, and the scene is illuminated by the bright
light of the full moon. As the boat advances, the banks of the river change; villages,
countryside, forests, mountains are seen, and finally, the castle of the sleeping
beauty comes into view, which disappears in a bend in the river, but then reappears,
and our travellers stop in front of the large gates of the castle; they get out of the
boat, and the fairy makes a gesture with her wand.
   The gates open, and through them the vestibule is seen, the court, and the
sleeping groups of the Tsar's pages and servants. The Prince rushes forward, the
fairy follows him, the entire stage is shrouded in thick darkness and clouds.
   Musical entr'acte. When the clouds and darkness are dispersed little by little,
Aurora's room is revealed, illuminated by a phosphorescent light.
   Everything is covered with cobwebs and layers of dust. When the Prince enters,
he raises a cloud of dust, cuts through the cobwebs, and at the awakening of all the
people, all the dust and cobwebs disappear, leaving the décor clean.[95]

ACT III

Like the sources for Act II, those for Act III omit many details of the early
productions of Sleeping Beauty. In the CN the march and polacca come
down to us as lists of participants only; the sarabande and the pas de
caractère of Little Red Riding Hood are missing. Some dances in the CN
are recorded only sketchily, others probably in versions later than those
performed by the original cast. In addition, notations of six dances and the
pas berrichon are recorded by scribes whose work appears for the first time
in Act III.
   The association of Florestan with Louis XIV, made explicit in the
apotheosis, is clearly suggested by the stage décor:

... the last act takes place on an esplanade, behind which the décor reproduces
quite exactly the great palace of Versailles, with terraces, fountain, carousel
platform, grande pièce d'eau, and other magnificent embellishments of King Louis.
Incidentally, this décor requires a much greater depth of stage than there is in the
Maryinsky Theatre, so that the work of the talented Professor Shishkov does not
produce that effect which it would have had in greater perspective.[96]

   The list of entrances in the Marche (No. 21) is essentially the same in the

CN and the libretto: the King and Queen, Aurora and Désiré, and the fairies Gold, Silver, Sapphire, and Diamond. Indeed, the number of entries listed is so small for such a lengthy piece that one can appreciate Petipa's sentiment, expressed in the Rep, 'Couper la marche. Tout le monde en scène. C'est trop long.'[97]

In the polacca Aurora's godmothers and the fairy-tale characters from Perrault's other stories join the royal party.[98]

The *pas de quatre* of the precious stones (No. 23) begins the *divertissement* of fairy-tale characters which takes up most of the act. Petipa organized the choreography of this *pas* around the fairies Gold, Silver, and Sapphire together as one element of the *pas*, and the Diamond Fairy alone as another. The *intrada* begins with the first three dancing in unison and retiring at bar 35, at which point the fourth dancer comes on. The first variation, to the music Tchaikovsky had composed as a solo for the Silver Fairy, is for the three dancers; the second, to the music composed for the Diamond Fairy, is a solo. All four danced together only in the coda.

Commenting on the choreography, Korovyakov complains of the 'long familiar *cabrioles* and *entrechats*',[99] and in fact the *intrada*, as notated, shows many of these steps. The Diamond Fairy enters with a series of *cabrioles*; her dance then moves on to *terre-à-terre* combinations and a gentle turn during a run on *pointe*. What Korovyakov seems to have missed in his assessment is the overall choreographic plan of the *pas*, which moves from a bravura introduction, to softer, finer combinations (in the variations), to brilliance—jumps, including *cabrioles*—in the coda.

'Puss in Boots and the White Cat' (No. 24) was the first of the fairy-tale *pas de caractère* to achieve instant and lasting popularity. First the White Cat[100] runs on from rear stage left with a stop-and-go entrance marked every few steps by a double pose consisting of an *attitude* to the back on the right *pointe*, then *devant* on the same foot in *demi-plié*. Puss in Boots soon enters in pursuit. She tries to evade him. Both trace broad semicircles to the outside until he manages to catch her, holding her by the waist as she poses again *en attitude devant*. She breaks away, and the pursuit continues. The White Cat begins to emphasize her nervous spurts of running by stroking her face with her paw, and *pas de chat* are added. The two stalk each other. In a moment of reconciliation she strokes his head; he caresses her as he leads her by the hand in some turns. But the loving moment is short-lived; he hits her on the shoulder, and after a final caress and hold they run off stage.

As the White Cat, 'the graceful Mlle Anderson', as Skalkovsky called her, appears to have lived up to the promise expected of her when Petipa, at Tchaikovsky's suggestion, assigned her this part the previous winter (see pp. 158–9, above). 'This duet of felines', remarked the critic of the *Petersburg Gazette*, 'is performed by the legs, with cat-like sounds in the orchestra, and was repeated by Mlle Anderson and Mr Bekefi. The latter is a true cat.'[101]

In the *pas de deux* of the Blue Bird and Princess Florine which follows, the woman also runs in first. She kneels as her partner enters, the beginning and end of his path marked by poses. (The CN states, 'The cavalier enters and stands in a pose making movements with his arms.') For a moment they pose together, immobile, then the fireworks begin. She runs forward, stopping for two *pirouettes*. He follows and holds her by the waist during an *attitude* on *pointe* and in a number of supported turns which make up the bulk of their *entrée*. Petipa provides the Blue Bird with opportunities to demonstrate strength and agility in high *cabrioles* to the back and *pirouettes*, and at one point he carries his partner by the waist with one arm as he steps backward on a diagonal toward rear stage left.[102]

The entire *pas*—*entrée*, two variations, and coda—proceeds in a similar manner, in a display of virtuosity which brought praise to Varvara Nikitina and Enrico Cecchetti. 'A complete and deserved success', wrote the critic of the *Petersburg Gazette*.[103] 'The artiste brilliantly performed this *pas*, which caused a storm of applause', observed the reviewer of the *Petersburg Leaflet*.[104] And Skalkovsky summarized how the two dancers '. . . demonstrated their outstanding art. Mlle Nikitina, charmingly dressed in feathers, was light and ethereal, like "the breath from the lips of Aeolus" [an epithet of Pushkin's], Mr Cecchetti astonishingly adroit and strong.'[105]

The *pas de caractère* of Little Red Riding Hood and the Wolf was next. Since there is no reference to this *pas* in the CN, no elaboration of it in the libretto, and no account of it by critics of the first performance,[106] we must turn to the balletmaster's plan for a description:

She [Little Red Riding Hood] arrives merrily with her milk pail—3/4, 32 bars. She breaks her milk pail, she cries. The wolf arrives—she trembles—the wolf calms her—polka tempo—gentle barking—caresses her, promises her to obtain a pardon for her if she leads him to her grandmother. The *pas* ends with a waltz in a slightly faster tempo. She leaves, trembling, carried off by the wolf.

The next *pas* (No. 26b) is the new one, for Cinderella and Prince Fortuné, ordered from Tchaikovsky by Petipa in October 1889 (see p. 154 and note 18, above). Cinderella runs on to the stage, sees that she lacks a slipper, and searches for it on either side (this takes up the introductory section in 2/4). Seeing the Prince she says, 'I'll get you!' and picks up the bellows. The Prince runs in, saying 'I don't know whose slipper this is. I'll try here.' He waltzes over to her and kneels: 'How beautiful you are!' When he tries to put the slipper on her, she blows the bellows in his face, and he turns away. This sequence is repeated and begun a third time before he succeeds in fitting the slipper. They begin to dance a mazurka together, probably at bar 117, even though Petipa had requested, and Tchaikovsky had composed, a waltz.[107] Presently Cinderella throws the bellows into the wings and the dance continues unhindered until the couple exit to the side with a triple *golubets* (a stylized clicking of the heels).

'Tom Thumb, his Brothers, and the Ogre' is the last of the choreographic genre pieces, preserved in the CN mostly in floor plans and extensive written instructions. The boys run on stage, trembling with fright. Flanked by his brothers, Tom comes to the front of the stage: 'The King [that is, the ogre] wanted to kill us, but no, no!' The boys converge on Tom and rock him, thrusting him forward but not letting him go, three times. Tom runs to the rear of the stage and back again twice as his brothers run to the sides and again to the centre, clapping their hands. They next form a line seven abreast, holding on to each other's shoulders, and then a *fleurette* or star, each boy facing outward. The ogre enters and they disperse, running to the back of the stage where they form a circle, kneeling, each boy facing inward. Once on stage the ogre sits down on a bench and falls asleep. When Tom emerges from the circle of his brothers and notices this, he calls to them. They look and ask, 'What is this?' Tom answers, pointing at the ogre, 'I thought of taking his boots.' Two brothers put this idea into practice while the rest watch in delight. Only with difficulty do the young thieves carry the seven-league boots over to Tom, whereupon they line up in single file and head for the wings, making a face as they leave at the just-awakened ogre, who pursues them off stage.

The CN of the *pas de quatre* of Aurora, Désiré, and the fairies Gold and Sapphire poses the same problem within Act III that the court dances did in Act II—there is little clear description, and the authenticity of what survives is open to question. The dance performed to Tchaikovsky's wonderful duet is only sketched, in a series of alternating poses and lifts of the ballerina with short mimed episodes. The *adagio* begins with a supported turn and *attitude* on the left *pointe*, body arched back. Then the dancers step apart.

Aurora: 'I will dance with him.'

Désiré: 'I love her and will marry her.'

She embraces him. He leads her in a supported turn (*attitude* on *pointe*) and pose, again with the body arched back. They turn away from each other, to meet again further towards the rear of the stage, where he supports her in *arabesques*. He lifts her twice and carries her forward; two *pirouettes* follow each lift. They run to rear stage left and come forward again on a diagonal, pausing three times for double *pirouettes*. Stepping away from him again, she says, 'I love him and he is my betrothed.' She runs to him: more *pirouettes* and *attitudes*; at the end an *arabesque*, two turns, and a fall on to her partner's leg.

At the first performance all did not go well with the *adagio*: 'Carlotta Brianza was hardly able to finish the ballet . . . In the *pas de quatre* of the last act, during the turns, the artist scratched her entire arm above the elbow to the point of bleeding on Mr Gerdt's costume [see Pl. 11].'[108]

'In the first performance', Skalkovsky wrote,

the ballerina, performing turns, not only injured her arm, but at the conclusion she brushed against Mr Gerdt's sleeve and lost a lock of her hair. At this rate Mlle Brianza will be left bald by the end of the season. It is the same story with the other cavaliers. In the benefit performance in the second act [that is, the second scene] Aurora's suitors dance a *pas d'action* without removing their swords, as a result of which the ballerina in a fast *pirouette* brushed against Mr Bekefi's sword and tore away a piece of her dress.

These 'incidents' told upon her confidence in the dances. Mlle Brianza danced freely only when she was a step removed from her gilded partners.[109]

What happened immediately after the *adagio* cannot be exactly determined. The libretto refers to all of No. 28 as a *pas de quatre;* the CN preserves two variants of a 'Dance after the *Pas de Deux/Adagio*'. Two women, identified in one of the variants as the fairies Gold and Sapphire, perform a dance of about 38 bars in 6/8 time. In the first part of the dance their floor patterns are the same but they dance to opposite sides, and their steps are the same but on opposite legs; in the second part they are in unison. An emphasis on *cabrioles* and turns in the choreography may have been intended as a stylistic link with the earlier *pas de quatre* in which these dancers took part.

To this extent the CN agrees with the libretto: the *pas de deux* Petipa requested of Tchaikovsky was made into a *pas de quatre* by the addition of a variation for the fairies Gold and Sapphire immediately after the *adagio*. But to what music did they dance? The variations and the coda are assigned to Aurora and Désiré. Both variants of the choreography indicate that the two soloists performed to music in 6/8 time, and yet the only other music in No. 28 in this metre, the *entrée* in G major, is cut in the Hol, PR-I and PR-II.[110]

The first solo variation is Désiré's. Writing of Désiré as performed by Pavel Gerdt, who was forty-five at the time of the première,[111] Vera Petipa recalled: 'Gerdt's entrance with the ballerina in the duet of *Sleeping Beauty* was distinguished by sculptured lines and deft supports, and his brief danced numbers, thanks to his elegance, were always accompanied by applause.'[112]

A decade after the first performance there was still praise for Gerdt's work in this *pas*:

Among the ballerina's dances the *pas de deux* with Mr Gerdt stands out for its virtuoso execution. This *pas de deux* is almost the only dance in which Mr Gerdt still performs, having transferred all his dances to young dancers. Mr Gerdt in *Sleeping Beauty* dances only a few bars in all, but such beauty! One does not want to believe that Mr Gerdt has served the ballet stage for forty years . . .[113]

In the light of the appreciation of Gerdt's contemporaries for his artistry, it is unfortunate that Désiré's variation in the CN shows evidence of being the one performed by Gerdt's successor in the role, Nikolai Legat (whose name appears in the descriptions of the mimed passages in the *adagio*), in a version consistent with the revived taste for virtuosity in male dancing.[114] His dance, while not as demanding as those for the Blue Bird, nevertheless calls for *ronds de jambe* and *cabrioles* in a rapid tempo, and, at the high point, a choice between seven *entrechats septs* or seven *jetés en tournant*. It ends with a quadruple *pirouette*.

Aurora's solo, in contrast, is a *pizzicato*-style variation on *pointe* which begins *terre-à-terre*, moves on to elegant if not elevated jumps, and ends with two series of turns. In its 'choreographic coloratura' (Valerian Svetlov's term) the dance resembles her variation in Act I.

The coda aims for bravura effect. (The man's part is preserved in Legat's version.) Aurora enters, first with *pointe* work in a slashing zigzag, then circling in light *pirouettes*. Désiré comes on and joins her in a combination of *pas ballonné* and *arabesque*. Both then travel in a diagonal towards rear stage left, with short jumps on the right foot, the left extended to the back *en arabesque*. Aurora retraces her path alone in a series of turns and runs across the front of the stage to meet Désiré, whom she encircles with *pirouettes*, coming to rest in a final pose on *pointe*.[115]

Between the time of the balletmaster's plan and the first performance, the sarabande (No. 29) changed in the number and nationality of its *entrées*. In July Petipa had opened the *divertissement* 'd'après le carrousel Louis XIV' with a quadrille of Turks, Ethiopians, Africans, and native Americans. For the performance the *entrée du ballet* still included Turks and Americans, but the other two had been replaced by Romans, Persians, and Indians.[116]

The mazurka (No. 30), a *coda générale* which brings the dancers together on stage one last time, is performed to a standard step.[117] Each couple or group enters, dances several measures in the centre of the stage, and retires to the sides to make room for the next. Then the dancers who have been assembling along the sides of the stage form a circle in stage middle, framed by a large semicircle round the front of the stage. Korovyakov remarked that 'the concluding coda and sarabande seem very strange turning into a mazurka, the appropriateness of which to Versailles is rather debatable.'[118] The apotheosis, listed as the 'Gloire des Fées' in the libretto, was a magnificent *tableau vivant* representing Apollo; what characters from the ballet participated we do not know.

When the first performance was over, Pleshcheyev recalled, Tchaikovsky expressed in person to Brianza '. . . his most profound gratitude for her sharp, highly-strung dances . . . In Brianza this precision, as I heard from P. I. Tchaikovsky himself, yielded nothing to the finest watch mechanism.'[119]

The ballerina recalled: 'During the first performance . . . Tchaikovsky did not go out alone in response to the calls of the public. He went out with

Petipa and with me, and with me and Gerdt, and with other performers. On stage he tried to move us forward, and to hide himself behind us.'[120]

Tchaikovsky's appreciation of Brianza's artistry was shared by reviewers. D. D. Korovyakov praised the ballerina but expressed a reservation about the choreography: 'Mlle Brianza performed her dances brilliantly with respect to precision, strength, and grace, although in their combinations there is nothing either new or especially beautiful.'[121]

Skalkovsky was elated after her performance. 'All her dances—*entrée*, *adagio*, and variations on *pointe*—are extremely elegant, masterfully and accurately executed.'[122] Even the hard-to-please reviewer of the *Petersburg Gazette* observed that 'the most difficult *adagio*' of the first act was a mere trifle for Brianza.[123]

'I will not speak in detail of the performers', Benois declared,

The fact is, that however elegant Gerdt was in his regal part as the Prince, however brilliantly the young and very pretty Brianza performed her role, however incredibly funny Stukolkin was (in the role of Catalabutte, Marshall of the Court), however nightmarish Cecchetti in the role of Carabosse—and he was also enchanting in the dances of the 'Blue Bird'—however excellent were the dozens of other dancers who represented fairies, peasants, genies, courtiers, hunters, fairy-tale characters, etc.—all their personal mastery and the charm of each one of them combined in the beauty of the ensemble. Thus the good fortune befell me in fact to see a genuine *Gesamtkunstwerk*.[124]

Critical response to the *Gesamtkunstwerk* was mixed. 'A triumph of that art in which music, dance, and painting are combined', wrote the reviewer for *Son of the Fatherland*.[125] His colleague on the *Petersburg Gazette* claimed, of Petipa's work, 'All his dances breathe freshness and do credit to his immense taste, both in groupings and in his ability to control masses . . . The character dances are elegant and commensurate with the gifts of his excellent performers.'[126]

Criticism of *Sleeping Beauty* ranged from superficial cavils to substantial complaints. Among the superficial cavils were objections to the length of some scenes, and objections raised by Russian chauvinists: '*Ballet-féerie*! . . . A new word, used for the first time on *affiches*. But this word "féerie", as a foreign word, fully suits the new ballet, the subject of which is taken from the *foreign* tales of Perrault.'[127]

The magnificence of production connoted by the words 'ballet-féerie', magnificence towards which Vsevolozhsky and his collaborators consciously strove, brought a mixed response. Benois found that the costumes were garish in the variety of their colours, juxtaposed by a man lacking a true feeling for the harmony of colours.[128] The luxury was lost on no one:

Silk, velvet, plush, gold and silver embroidery, marvellous brocade materials, furs, plumes, and flowers, knightly armour and metal decorations—it is lavish, and the richness is showered on the adornment even of the least important characters.[129]

Skalkovsky, who had complained of the miserly attitude towards production of Vsevolozhsky's predecessor, now found himself complaining that the directorate had been spendthrift. He objected not to the expenditure as such, but to the fact that the production, because of its lavishness, had become an end in itself. Production in *Sleeping Beauty* had upset the balance of the contributory arts. The exceptional emphasis on spectacle acted to the detriment of the choreography, and when spectacle fills the hall, art suffers:

The costumes are perhaps too luxurious in their material . . . they seem too heavy for ballet . . . Of course, ballet requires lavish production and economy is out of place, because a lavish ballet will sustain more performances, draw bigger houses, and pay for itself sooner; but luxuriousness has its limits, stipulated by the nature of the art.

. . . The huge number of extras in expensive costumes and the diverse transformations constitute nothing more than a large *balagan*; such a work draws crowds, especially in the capitals where the public numbers millions. But such spectacles attract neither a constant public nor a circle of educated adherents.[130]

Korovyakov made a similar point, criticizing not the manner in which the subject of the ballet was realized, but the subject matter itself:

. . . In the strength of their poetical description Perrault's fairy-tales offer excellent material for exterior brilliance, but their internal content, in its simplicity, innocence, and childlike *naïveté*, cannot provide the food for fantasy necessary for the composition of a programme of a large ballet of the type to which our public has become accustomed in the course of many decades . . . If, indeed, the ballet will be *only spectacle*, a variegated kaleidoscope of costumes and decorations, then no magnificence of production will redeem its emptiness, lack of content, and that tedium which, towards the end, inevitably possesses every 'grown-up', not to mention an aesthetically developed audience. Risking appearing as purists in art, we cannot help regretting the means chosen by the theatre directorate in lowering the [standard of] artistry of our ballet.[131]

The balletomanes ventured an occasional assessment of the music, reflecting traditional biases. Skalkovsky's review was the most balanced:

We can note only that the music is melodious, is easily listened to, elegantly orchestrated, and pleased the public, which called out the composer several times. At places in the music, for example in the variations of the prima ballerina, the rhythm is insufficiently precise, which is very disadvantageous for the performer. Of course, rhythm imparts banality to the music, but it is necessary in dances: the latter receive clear definition from rhythm; it concentrates the attention of the public in the hoped-for place.[132]

Perhaps the best critique of the new ballet was written by Tchaikovsky's friend Herman Laroche. Laroche begins with a long disclaimer of any authority in matters choreographic, but proceeds to assert that the job of the critic is nevertheless to examine the work in all its aspects.

Sleeping Beauty was sharply criticized in the newspapers. Besides the music, with which our reviewers were not always contented, they bemoaned the absence of drama in the ballet, the fairy-tale children's subject, and finally that the story was taken from a French redaction by Perrault. Of all these charges the last, at first glance, is the weightiest. Nobody prohibits our balletmasters from representing France on the stage, as they represent ancient Greece, ancient Egypt, present-day Italy, and Montenegro. To produce a ballet from the history of medieval France or France of the last Louis would be fully legitimate and natural.

But *Sleeping Beauty* does not belong to history; it has no locale; it is a myth, belonging to the traditions of many peoples . . . The French redaction, I suggest, was chosen simply because the balletmaster of the Bolshoy Theatre, like many of his predecessors, is a Frenchman, and because our ballet, despite the purely Russian make-up of the *corps de ballet* and a majority of the soloists, lives by French traditions and nourishes itself on French literature . . . To force oneself, out of false patriotism, to represent only the mores and history of the fatherland means to deny one's fantasy the pleasure of a journey, to narrow and to limit arbitrarily the materials of works of art, to forget the glorious tradition of Pushkin's period, when 'nothing human' was 'foreign' to us.

. . . The other more general reproach of the new ballet is that it is not a drama but a 'children's tale'.

The fairy-tale, despite its prosaic form, often contains within itself the most ancient, most original myths: the basic motive of *Sleeping Beauty*, incidentally, is similar to that of the story of Brünnhilde, who is protected by fire; she is one of the innumerable embodiments of the earth which lays winter to rest and is awakened by the kiss of spring; Siegfried and Prince Désiré in this sense are one and the same . . .

Say what you wish against fairy-tales. You will do away neither with the fact that they have succeeded in taking root in our fantasy in the continuity of generations, nor with the fact that from childhood we became closely linked with them and love them, nor with the fact that we find in them some of the most profound ideas to stir humankind . . .

Laroche goes on to decry the trend towards increased violence in the theatre of his day, and the scarcity of comedy and successful works in lighter genres. He defends Petipa's choice of a children's tale, and then turns to the music, pleased

. . . that such a powerful talent as Tchaikovsky, following the general current of his time, turned to ballet and thus promotes the ennobling of musical taste in this sphere also.

. . . The Russian way in music, besides being strong in Tchaikovsky in recent years, is the issue at hand. The music completely suits the costume, the characters; in it there is a French nuance, but at the same time it savours of Russia . . .

The point is not in the local colour, which is beautifully observed, but in an element deeper and more general than colour, in the internal structure of the music, above all in the foundation of the element of melody. This basic element is undoubtedly Russian. It may be said, without lapsing into contradiction, that the local colour [in *Sleeping Beauty*] is French, but the *style* is Russian . . . The fairy-tale figures of the ancient Indo-European epic, which are transformed into *French* figures by national assimilation and transmission, once again undergo transformation under the pen of the Russian musician, acquire a new nationality, become a Russian variant. For no one variant can fully rid itself of the influence of the land, and one may thank Peter Ilyich that his development has coincided with a time when the influences of the soil became stronger among us, when the Russian soul was inspired, when the word 'Russian' ceased to be a synonym of 'peasant-like', and when the peasant-like itself was recognized in its proper place, as but *part* of being Russian.[133]

The success of *Sleeping Beauty* speaks for itself. For nearly a century it has been a standard by which the artistry of ballerinas, *corps de ballet*, and ballet orchestras has been measured. Less obvious at this distance, after a revolution in Russia and two world wars, is the influence it cast over the late imperial ballet. *Sleeping Beauty* was Petipa's greatest ballet, and the model for the subsequent major works created by him, including the superb *Raymonda* and his swan-song, *The Magic Mirror*. We hear the echo of Tchaikovsky's music, transformed in accent and colour, in the ballets of Glazunov and Stravinsky, and later in those of Asafiev, Prokofiev, and, less subtly, Shchedrin. 'By some kind of *miracle*', Benois recalled,

so many first-class artists were brought together for the creation of a genuine *chef d'oeuvre*, precious in all its details. And yet, the décor has faded, the costumes have become threadbare, the *chef-d'oeuvre* slowly disappeared after some ten to fifteen years. And no reconstruction avails. The conditions, the technical means all change, they are all forgotten, despite the most pious, it would seem, observance of traditions.[134]

The magnificent production of 1890 remains unparalleled in later stagings of the work. No impresario, save perhaps Diaghilev, has expended the money and talent that Vsevolozhsky lavished on the original. And yet, as we shall see, the Director did not rest content.

6

Nutcracker

❦

IN a letter of 25 February/9 March 1890, Tchaikovsky writes to Désirée Artôt of a ballet to follow *Sleeping Beauty*, one work in an unrealistically ambitious list of new compositions:

Now, dear Madame, you will ask me what I want to do after my opera [*The Queen of Spades*]? If the Good Lord grants me life and good health, this will be an opera on a French text by J. Detroyat and Gallet that I very much like and which I must do, having promised it to these gentlemen. And then I must absolutely take on a Russian opera of which I have had the poem in hand for two years, and which I have given my word of honour to do. And then I must do another ballet (the one this season having had a great success), and then many concertos for piano, for violin, etc., promised to my friends, among whom are some Parisians (Diémer, Taffanel [a flautist]), and then symphonies, symphonic poems, Lieder, piano pieces, etc., etc.[1]

Tchaikovsky's next reference to the new ballet comes only after the first performance of *The Queen of Spades*, the composition and production of which occupied much of his attention during the remainder of 1890. By Christmas Eve, 1890, the ballet has taken precedence over the other works he listed for Artôt; he has agreed to compose it. He writes on this day to Mikhail Ippolitov-Ivanov with discouraging news of the prospects of a production in St Petersburg of the latter's opera *Azra*:

But I must tell you frankly that for *next* year there is little hope. [Rimsky-Korsakov's] *Mlada* has been proposed, and a one-act opera and a two-act ballet [to be performed on the same evening] have been commissioned from me. Vsevolozhsky is more and more favourably disposed towards me, and absolutely will not tolerate the thought of a season without a new work of mine.[2]

If ever Tchaikovsky wrote an ill-starred work, it was *Nutcracker*. Had he known what miseries he would endure while writing it he would surely have refused; certainly when those miseries were most acute he considered withdrawing his services from the project. At the outset of the collaboration, however, prospects must have seemed bright. Fresh from the success of *Sleeping Beauty*, the same team was to produce another magnificently staged ballet based on a children's tale.

Nutcracker was ill-starred partly because Tchaikovsky was not especially enthusiastic about the scenario.[3] Vsevolozhsky, as we have seen with *Undine*, was too diplomatic a patron to insist that the composer accept a particular story. But the Director apparently chose *Nutcracker* himself, and asked Tchaikovsky to write the music.[4] And the composer agreed, although Modeste Tchaikovsky recalled that

Peter Ilyich did not experience on this occasion that urge to compose which *Sleeping Beauty* and the scenario of *The Queen of Spades* awakened in him, and the reasons for this were several. In the first place, the subject of *Nutcracker* did not much please him; *King Réné's Daughter* [the story on which *Nutcracker*'s companion-piece, the opera *Iolanthe*, was based] he chose himself, but not having a libretto [of the opera] in hand, he did not know to what extent it suited him. In the second place, Peter Ilyich grumbled at the Directorate of the Imperial Theatres for inviting foreign singers to sing in French and Italian on the Russian operatic stage.[5]

Apart from Tchaikovsky's misgivings concerning the scenario, a serious rift developed between the composer and Vsevolozhsky early in 1891. Without any reasons being given, *The Queen of Spades* had been dropped from the repertory after thirteen performances, and Tchaikovsky referred to this action as a reason for his reluctance to proceed with *Iolanthe* and *Nutcracker*, suspecting that his work was not appreciated in the highest circles. On 12 February he wrote to the Director:

Embarking on the composition of *The Daughter of King Réné* and *Casse-Noisette*, I am experiencing the feeling of a person who is being invited again into a house of which the host's behaviour revealed the previous time a disinclination to have him as guest. If the Tsar does not encourage my works for the benefit of the theatre, how can I with love, with the necessary tranquillity and pleasure, work for an institution of which he is proprietor?

. . . But you see, I have to write an opera and a ballet for next season. This is a huge work, requiring great effort, great sacrifices. Can I get down to it, when after the affront to my ego in the dropping of *The Queen of Spades* from the repertory, I can expect next season even more powerful manifestations of the sovereign's disfavour [?]!

Therefore I ask you (I have no other means of satisfying myself), personally or through the minister, to report to the Tsar that you intend to mount next season an opera and a ballet of my composition and to learn thereby whether he approves of your intention. If my surmise is groundless, if I am wrong in thinking that the Tsar is not sympathetic to the overfilling of the repertory with my works, if it pleases His Majesty that I continue to work for the theatre, then I will set about the new work with pleasure. If not, then I must, of course, decline your magnanimous proposal, for it is certainly not in me to fulfil my task with love, successfully and in accordance with your hopes in me, if my ardour for scribbling will be constantly cooled, paralysed by the awareness that the person whose encouragement and sympathy is more important than anything else in this endeavour denies me his goodwill.[6]

Taken aback, Vsevolozhsky hastened to reply, and dealt directly and tactfully with the composer's pride (though there is no indication that he ever carried out Tchaikovsky's request). He explained that the dropping of *The Queen of Spades* had to do with casting and scheduling, and went on to point out the composer's own reluctance to accept the Tsar's praise for him at the dress rehearsal of that opera. Vsevolozhsky continued:

I do not know how to reassure you . . . and how to declare to you that everything you write for us interests the Tsar's *loge* in the highest degree. On your *Daughter of King René* and on *Nutcracker* I place all my hopes for next season. This will be the chief attraction of next winter . . . A strange and unhappy character you have, dear Peter Ilyich! Why do you wish to vex and torment yourself with empty spectres? Everyone knows your value. You are indeed a Russian talent—genuine, not hollow. . .[7]

For the moment, at least, Tchaikovsky was appeased. By 25 February 1891 he could write to Modeste: '. . . I am working with all my might and am beginning to be reconciled with the subject of the ballet. I think that before my departure I will do a significant part of the first act.'[8]

True to his intention, the composer had drafted all the music up to No. 6 of Scene 1 as well as the Waltz of the Snowflakes by the time he left St Petersburg on 6 March for a conducting tour which took him to Paris and America. In the meantime, another problem was developing: contentiousness between Vsevolozhsky and Petipa. In his letter of pacification and assurance to Tchaikovsky, Vsevolozhsky relaxed his diplomatic tone for a moment in order to offer

. . . some thoughts about the ballet which do not agree with Petipa's opinions . . . He is what the French call *vieux genre*. All the solos and variations which he has conceived for Act I are without interest for the public. It is necessary now to compose a grand *ballabile* and *pas* for the ballerina, and all the variations for the various Mlles Johanssons, Zhukovas, Nedremskayas [the soloists] only weary the majority of the public.[9]

We can only guess the reasons for Vsevolozhsky's remarks, which cannot be taken wholly at face value. A *pas* for the ballerina in Act I, for example, would solve a structural problem, not a stylistic one. Why should Vsevolozhsky complain of Petipa the stylist so soon after the success of *Sleeping Beauty* and the charming *intermède* in *The Queen of Spades*, and go on to commission several more ballets in this *vieux genre* during his seven remaining years as Director? Tchaikovsky reveals a more probable cause of Vsevolozhsky's irritation in a letter he sent to the Director from Paris:

On the day of my departure from Petersburg I passed about an hour-and-a-half in conversation with M. I. Petipa in connection with *Casse-Noisette*. Having completed the discussion about business, he moved on to a detailed review of his present activities in the theatre. As far as I could make out, he brought up the subject with the purpose of drawing your attention indirectly, that is, through me, to the fact that he is very fatigued by the last season, that much lies before him in the future, and as a consequence he needs to rest and refresh himself with a trip abroad. He hasn't the means to make a trip, however, and if I am not mistaken, he wishes very much to receive an extraordinary subsidy which he cannot bring himself to request from you directly. He pointed out that [Enrico] Cecchetti has less to do and makes more than he, and, being free in the spring and summer, can earn some money outside the imperial theatre. At the end of the conversation I asked him if he wanted me to bring what he had told me to your attention in a letter. He responded in the affirmative, and so I am fulfilling his wish. To me Petipa is most likeable in all respects, and it is with the greatest of pleasure that I petition you on his behalf. If this petition is out of place and tactless, then for God's sake forgive me; but if it is possible to indulge this most kind old man, then, dear Ivan Alexandrovich, be good enough to help him in this.[10]

We do not know how Vsevolozhsky responded to this request.[11] Tchaikovsky, for his part, continued to work on *Nutcracker* while on tour—on the train to Berlin, in Paris, and in Rouen, where he stayed several days expressly for this purpose. Far from happy with the results of these efforts, Tchaikovsky expressed doubts as to whether he could finish the music for *Iolanthe* and *Nutcracker* on schedule in another letter to Vsevolozhsky:

For some time the prospect of urgent, wearisome work has begun to frighten me. Here, in Rouen, I had to call on extraordinary willpower, to make an agonizing effort in order to work. As a result what comes out is colourless, dry, hasty, and wretched. The awareness that things are not going well torments me and agonizes me to tears, to the point of sickness; a consuming depression constantly gnaws at my heart, and I have not for a long time felt as unhappy as now. I want to keep my word (for at our last meeting it seems that I positively gave my *word* to perform the work I had agreed to do, in the allotted time), and at the same time I am deeply convinced that nothing good will come out of all my excessive efforts, neither for the theatre nor for me. As always happens with very nervous and impressionable people with unbalanced natures, whose wounds are easily re-opened, everything which is now worrying and troubling me took on monstrous proportions, turned into some kind of feverish nightmare which gives me peace neither day nor night. 'Confiturembourg', 'Casse-Noisette', 'The Daughter of King Réné'—these images do not gladden me, do not excite inspiration, but frighten, horrify, and pursue me, waking and sleeping, mocking me with the thought that I shall not cope with them. Finally (for God's sake do not laugh, for I am completely serious), for the last three days I have been simply sick from despair, fright, and the most evil melancholy. In the night I suddenly decided that things cannot continue thus, and that I must grieve you by the refusal to keep my word. Dear Ivan Alexandrovich, I love you very much and can't stand it when you are angry with me—but I assure you that I just don't have the strength. Nevertheless I imagine that it is better for me to notify you in advance of the impossibility of writing an opera and ballet in time for next season, so that you can give instructions about exchanging them with something else in good time.[12]

Tchaikovsky did not, however, go on to withdraw but to request a postponement until the 1892–3 season. The day after he wrote this letter, 4/16 April, he read an announcement in a Petersburg daily of his sister's death. His request to Vsevolozhsky was even more justified in light of this latest grief.

Vsevolozhsky again displayed laudable patience:

Better for us to wait a year than to require you to write and compose operas and ballets without any inspiration and pleasure. Although the stage designs for *Casse-Noisette* are already ordered, the décor could also be painted for the season 1892–3. Only do not completely give up the task at hand. This is my most earnest entreaty to you.[13]

The Director's conciliation no doubt eased the trials of a stormy Atlantic crossing and the hectic pace of Tchaikovsky's travels in America. While the composer's dissatisfaction with *Nutcracker* never completely wore off, he overcame the dislike he felt for it during his stay in Rouen and went on to finish the score in a business-like way once back at Frolovskoe.[14] Vsevolozhsky himself seems to have been aware that the problem with *Nutcracker* was not simply another manifestation of Tchaikovsky's susceptibility to pressure and insecurity, which the Director had often encountered. In a letter of 9 August 1891 he acknowledged: 'I feel bitter remorse for having requested this ballet from you. I know that you do not find it sympathetic. Out of goodness of heart and nothing else you have not refused.'[15]

What was the problem with *Nutcracker*? There is much evidence to suggest that the story simply did not lend itself to adaptation for ballet, and that the collaborators came to realize this only after having agreed to produce it.

According to the libretto (which is normally attributed to Vsevolozhsky and Petipa but differs in some details from Tchaikovsky's instructions and the balletmaster's plan), the first act of *Nutcracker* takes place at a Christmas party. The parents of Clara and Fritz Silberhaus, and their friends, are decorating the Christmas tree; when they have finished, the children are called. Gifts are distributed, but the party is disrupted by the arrival of the children's godfather, Councillor Drosselmayer, whose entrance sets the clocks chiming and whose appearance scares the children. He has brought extravagant gifts for his godchildren, which he demonstrates to the general delight. When these extraordinary toys are put away for safe keeping Clara and Fritz are disappointed. Drosselmayer consoles them with another toy—the Nutcracker. Clara is immediately drawn to it and is dismayed when she is made to share it with Fritz, who breaks it.

The party ends, and the children are sent to bed. When all is quiet Clara comes downstairs to find the Nutcracker. She is terrified by the sound of mice. Midnight strikes, and she sees Drosselmayer's image on the face of the clock. The Christmas tree suddenly grows to an enormous height, and with this the dolls come alive. A battle ensues between the toys and the mice. After some of the toys are defeated the Nutcracker takes over and enters into combat with the Mouse King. He is about to be defeated himself when Clara throws her slipper at the Mouse King and thus enables Nutcracker to win instead. With the army of mice routed, the Nutcracker turns into a prince, who leads Clara between the branches of the Christmas tree into a winter forest. The second tableau of Act I depicts a snowstorm.

Act II takes place in the land of sweets, Confiturembourg. The inhabitants and their sovereign, the Sugar Plum Fairy, await Clara and the Nutcracker. When they arrive the Nutcracker presents Clara to his sisters and the Sugar Plum Fairy, who receive her with enthusiasm and thanks. A celebration begins, featuring a *divertissement* followed by a *pas de deux* of the Sugar Plum Fairy and her partner, Prince Coqueluche. The Nutcracker, in order to oblige Clara in her wish not to wake from what appears to her to be a dream, tells her of the 'fairy-tale wonders and the unusual customs' of Confiturembourg. The ballet ends with an apotheosis in which a beehive is depicted.

This story, while quaint, offers little promise for good theatre. It has obvious structural defects: an action-filled Act I is followed by an almost static Act II. In addition, the librettist of *Nutcracker* lost the satisfactory merging of the fantastic and everyday worlds which E. T. A. Hoffmann had taken pains to create in his prose. While the second act of the ballet may be a logical progression from the magical events which take place beneath the Christmas tree in Act I, those magical events lack compelling motivation. (The change from everyday to fantastic world also happens suddenly, without the opportunity for reflection that the act divisions provide in *Swan Lake*.) The crisis precipitated by the Mouse King and his army is not justified in the context of Clara's everyday existence (and we are given no clue to the Nutcracker's prior existence as an animate being); because Clara never returns to everyday existence from Confiturembourg, the audience is left at the final curtain asking what the point of the piece was, and what more it must know for the story to make sense. Above all, *Nutcracker* loses the element of relation to human experience that *Sleeping Beauty* gained in the process of adaptation from story to ballet. As a result, *Nutcracker* remains a simple children's tale, without significance as an allegory or a parable; it is precisely what some critics falsely accused *Sleeping Beauty* of being.

The defects of the scenario are thrown into clear relief when a ballet is based on it. The leading characters do virtually no dancing, and the leading dancers have virtually no place in the story. The emphasis on mime in the first act gives way to *divertissement* in the second, thus making them seem more disconnected dramatically. That a ballet of this length should contain only one classical *pas* for the ballerina, and this near the end of the second act, was not lost on the critics.

Soviet historians have defended *Nutcracker* by declaring it to be an apostrophe to childhood, and by doing this play down the ballet's weaknesses as drama. Asafiev, for example, proposed that to understand the composer's imagery in *Nutcracker* one should forget both the subject of the story and the scenario of this 'symphony about childhood'.[16] Julia Rozanova sums up two generations of scholarly deliberation in writing that Tchaikovsky revealed, in *Nutcracker*,

> ... a new theme in theatre music—the theme of childhood. . . [It] is a difficult theme for stage realization, and Tchaikovsky saw in Petipa's plan not a fantastic *féerie*, effective and astonishing, having only exterior points of similarity with Hoffmann's literary basis, but a serious work, profound in content. In it is revealed not only the child's soul with its special view of its surroundings, but also a decisive turning-point, a moment of qualitative change and transformation in a person on the threshold of youth, of a new discovery of the world, its joys and alarms, and before all else an enormous confidence in happiness. This psychological hidden meaning became the basic content of the music.[17]

Such a view neatly omits consideration of the most problematical character in *Nutcracker*, Councillor Drosselmayer, who, if not directly responsible for the supernatural events which threaten Clara, is in some way connected with them. For *Nutcracker* to be perceived as an essay about childhood passing into youth, it is necessary to play down Drosselmayer's frightening aspects. This is what Yury Slonimsky does, arguing that

> ... it is impossible to agree with those who stress in this music the element of 'sinister grotesque', 'Hoffmannesque terror'. The music gives one the sense that what is strange and frightening in the figure of Drosselmayer arises only in the feelings of the children.[18]

Slonimsky's interpretation is not the one Petipa wanted for Tchaikovsky's music. The balletmaster's instructions call for the cuckoo in the wall-clock to respond not just to the changing of the hour, but also to Drosselmayer's arrival, and again three times during the councillor's unwrapping of the gifts. The printed libretto retains shades of the fearsome in Drosselmayer, calling for his face to appear in the face of the clock at midnight. When some of these effects were deleted (possibly on Vsevolozhsky's account), a strong whiff of the ominous supernatural, which would have been visible to all, was lost. In the CN there is no evidence that Drosselmayer is to be portrayed as anything but a kindly old man.[19]

Other changes were made in the work between the time that Petipa gave instructions to Tchaikovsky and the time the libretto was published. 'Children's dances were loved in the highest circles,' Khudekov explained, 'for which reason Petipa, in practically all his new works, included a children's *divertissement*.'[20] In the first act of *Nutcracker* he ordered from Tchaikovsky a *divertissement* of six national dances to be performed by the children, who received national costumes as gifts, at the Christmas party. Between 5 and 29 [?] February 1891 (in the middle of which period Vsevolozhsky wrote to Tchaikovsky complaining of Petipa) the balletmaster changed his mind. On his own copy of the instructions, dated 29 February, Petipa made no reference to the national dances; he retained the galop ordered from Tchaikovsky, and added the parents' entrance, *en incroyables* (that is, dressed in fantastic costumes), and a minuet. Tchaikovsky changed his copy of the instructions to make them agree with Petipa's new version.

By assigning students of the theatre school to the important parts of Clara, Fritz, and the Nutcracker, Petipa was going beyond the tradition. Nothing prevented students from acting the parts of children, but their lack of technical attainments forced the balletmaster to refrain from composing difficult dances for them. For these he turned instead to the adults who filled the roles of secondary characters in the story.

It may be that Petipa had conceived a solution to the problems, choreographic and dramatic, posed by the scenario of *Nutcracker*, but if so he was destined not to reveal it, for after *Nutcracker* went into rehearsal on 29 September 1892 Petipa fell ill and ceased to play an active role as its choreographer.

Second balletmaster L. I. Ivanov will mount *Nutcracker* with the counsel and instructions of balletmaster M. I. Petipa, whose continuing illness prevents him from supervising rehearsals personally.

We wish the venerable balletmaster the most rapid recovery. In the production of new ballets the participation of M. Petipa, who possesses enormous taste and stage experience, is positively essential.[21]

As much as any other aspect of the production, the deputing of Lev Ivanov to produce the dances of the ballet has aroused debate, splitting generally into arguments based on period and ideology.[22] The principal point of contention in the historical assessment of Lev Ivanov is whether he was a great choreographer, or an undistinguished one given to occasional moments of inspiration. Alexander Shiryaev recalled, with regard to the second possibility, 'There were times when an idea would flash across Ivanov's mind of such originality of structure and movement, so clearly put, that you would straightway be astonished whence he drew it!'[23]

Asafiev called him 'the soul of Russian ballet at the end of the nineteenth century';[24] Anatole Chujoy (after studying Slonimsky) concluded that he was a great choreographer.[25] And yet Tchaikovsky, who worked with Ivanov on *Nutcracker*, does not refer to him once in a vast correspondence;

1. Tchaikovsky

2. Ivan Alexandrovich Vsevolozhsky

3. Marius Petipa

4. Lev Ivanov

5 & 6. *La Bayadère.* (*Top*) Scene 3: Triumphal procession in honour of the idol Badrinat. (*Bottom*) final scene: 'Revenge of the gods'

7 & 8. *Swan Lake* (Moscow, 1877). (*Top*) scene from Act II. (*Bottom*) scene from the Finale

9. A detail from the répétiteur of *Sleeping Beauty* at the beginning of No. 21

10. Carlotta Brianza as Aurora

11. Pavel Gerdt as Désiré

Сего 18 9_ года _____ ___ дня Дирекція ИМПЕРАТОРСКИХЪ Театровъ съ одной стороны и _____ съ другой, заключили между собою сіе условіе въ нижеслѣдующемъ:

1) Я _____ передаю Дирекціи ИМПЕРАТОРСКИХЪ Театровъ право представленія на сценѣ ИМПЕРАТОРСКИХЪ Театровъ въ _____ и _____ _____ оперы _____ и балета _____ мною сочиненныхъ

2) Дирекція уплачиваетъ мнѣ за каждое представленіе означенны_ пьесъ поспектакльную плату въ размѣрѣ __ % съ валоваго сбора _____

3) Я _____ обязуюсь въ продолженіе двухъ лѣтъ со дня подписанія сего условія не отдавать означенны_ пьесъ для представленія въ частныхъ сценахъ _____ разумѣя подъ этими сценами не только устраиваемыя въ чертѣ городовъ и уѣздовъ ___ но и пригородныя, загородныя, а равно въ городахъ: Павловскѣ, Царскомъ-Селѣ, Ораніенбаумѣ, Петергофѣ и Гатчинѣ.

4) За неисполненіе сего обязательства я _____ подвергаюсь уплатѣ штрафа въ размѣрѣ _____ рублей за каждое представленіе.

5) Я _____ обязуюсь подчиняться всѣмъ существующимъ правиламъ и постановленіямъ относительно постановки и представленія пьесъ на сценѣ ИМПЕРАТОРСКИХЪ Театровъ.

6) Слѣдующая мнѣ _____ поспектакльная плата должна быть выдаваема по требованію моему изъ Петербургской или Московской Конторы ИМПЕРАТОРСКИХЪ Театровъ или высылаема по мѣсту моего жительства, съ удержаніемъ почтовыхъ расходовъ; можетъ быть передана мною законнымъ порядкомъ другому лицу и переходитъ къ моимъ наслѣдникамъ на основаніи существующихъ постановленій о литературной, музыкальной и художественной собственности.

Петръ Чайковскій

ОБЪЯВЛЕНО
ВЪ ЖУРНАЛѢ РАСПОРЯЖЕНІЙ

Управляющій Конторою
Императорскихъ театровъ

12. Tchaikovsky's agreement with the Director of the Imperial Theatres concerning performance rights to *Nutcracker* and *Iolanthe*

13. A page from the répétiteur of *Swan Lake* (the beginning of the so-called swan theme)

16. Alexei Bulgakov as Rothbart

15. Pavel Gerdt as Siegfried

14. Pierina Legnani as Odette

17. Dancers representing snowflakes in *Nutcracker*

18. A page from the choreographic notation of *Swan Lake*, Scene 2: 12 children of the theatre school run on stage behind Pierina Legnani; then, flanked by the corps de ballet, they follow the pattern indicated on the floor plans

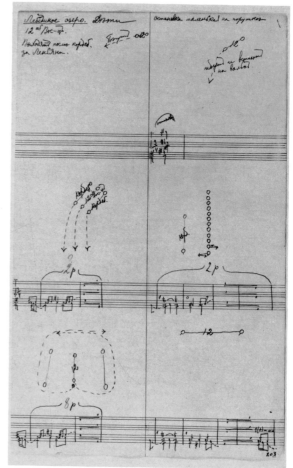

neither does Ivanov himself, ironically, mention *Nutcracker* or *Swan Lake* (the works he is remembered for by posterity) even once in his brief but touching memoirs.

In general, Soviet historians argue for his greatness—a greatness which overcame the effects of a stifling bureaucracy and the disadvantage of spending an entire career in Marius Petipa's imposing shadow. There is no question that Ivanov, unassertive to a fault, suffered discrimination in pay and opportunity for being a Russian in a foreign-dominated Russian ballet.[26] Nevertheless, his only lasting achievements, in a half-century of service, are the magnificent lakeside scenes in *Swan Lake*. Are these sufficient to allow the adjective 'great' to be applied to a career of which virtually all the remaining output is forgotten? 'Ivanov's lyrical gift was revealed unexpectedly—and thanks only to Tchaikovsky's music', remarked Krasovskaya, reaffirming Ivanov's singular but limited accomplishment. He was reputed to have an extraordinarily retentive ear and memory. 'Ivanov's musical abilities were phenomenal', wrote Shiryaev;

Once, I recall, Anton Grigorevich Rubinstein played through his ballet *The Grapevine* in the rehearsal hall. The composer had hardly left the hall before Ivanov sat down at the piano and reproduced practically all of Rubinstein's music by ear.[27]

Good though it was reputed to be, Ivanov's musicality could apparently be somewhat fickle. Several pages earlier in his memoirs, Shiryaev acknowledged that 'Ivanov himself confided to me he did not understand the music' of the Spanish Dance in *Nutcracker*—hardly a problematical piece; and Krasovskaya observed that Ivanov entrusted Shiryaev with the setting of steps to the Russian Dance in the same ballet.[28] Considering that a major contention of Soviet criticism is Ivanov's ability to produce dance movements directly stimulated by the music (as distinct from fitting the music to a preconceived dance structure, a method attributed to Petipa), such a lapse of comprehension reflects on his stature as a choreographer.

Ivanov possessed other attributes which were described by writers who had known him for some time. Pleshcheyev, for example, wrote of his personal acquaintance with Ivanov, saying that

in the theatrical milieu there are few such people, cordial and attractive in their sincerity. This good man, who never had any secret or evil backstage schemes, stood apart from every other theatrical type. Artists loved him because, having lived to almost seventy, he remained and died a colleague, a sincere colleague who recommended himself not in words but in deeds. Very few of his contemporaries survive . . .

The Petersburg stage is raised to a fitting height by its company's talents and inspiration. Ivanov of course cannot compare in talent with M. I. Petipa, but the latter rightly considered him a gifted colleague; they worked well together for a long time.[29]

And the snobbish Khudekov wrote:

As a dancer, as a mime, L. Ivanov did not stand out for any special qualities. He did not draw attention to himself, he considered himself of great 'usefulness'. Not one role did he spoil, nor did any of the roles created by him come to the forefront of attention. Everywhere he was a fitting, elegant partner of *danseuses*, striving always to remain in the shadow. Modesty was the outstanding quality of this artist, who always danced 'properly', 'correctly', not resorting to the virtuoso mannerisms of the representatives of the Italian school.

Such also was L. Ivanov as a creator of ballets. When a new ballet of this choreographer was given, everything seemed 'proper', 'fluent', as befits a good classical composition. The influence of his teacher Marius Petipa declared itself quite clearly in the 'compositions' of L. Ivanov. . .[30]

The conditions under which *Nutcracker* was first produced were hardly conducive to the improvement of Ivanov's reputation. Critics were generally so irritated by the faults of the ballet that they failed to recognize the virtues of his contribution in any substantial way. As Pleshcheyev pointed out, 'It cannot be said that Ivanov had luck as a balletmaster with regard to the subject-matter of the ballets he was assigned to produce.'[31] Ivanov's modesty, which the balletmaster himself proclaimed repeatedly in his memoirs,[32] also contributed. It lay at the basis of a retiring, phlegmatic temperament which Ivanov the choreographer—and his apologists—had to overcome.

1892 was not a particularly happy time for the second balletmaster. 'Necessity persistently tormented Ivanov', Krasovskaya explains:

Three children from the first marriage (among whom was a deaf-mute son) and three from the second were brought up on the slenderest of means. The second balletmaster time and again turned to the directorate [kontora] with requests for help. 'Finding myself at the present time in critical financial circumstances', he wrote on 10 March 1892, 'I respectfully petition the office of the imperial theatres to obtain from His Excellency the Minister of the Imperial Court a loan in the amount of one thousand two hundred roubles, with repayment at one hundred roubles monthly from the pay received by me.' Beginning with the 1880s Ivanov's affairs abound with such requests, to which satisfactory responses were not always forthcoming.[33]

On this occasion he was lent 900 roubles.

Ivanov inherited a situation in the autumn of 1892 both typical and unpromising. In finishing a ballet begun by Petipa, to what extent was his own work in *Nutcracker* original? To what extent was he made the scapegoat for defects in the work that should properly be attributed to Petipa? Indeed, can we be certain that Petipa's indisposition was not in some way linked to his realization that the defects of *Nutcracker* did not admit of easy remedy? 'To Ivanov he [Petipa] gave the less desirable part, or what he did not want to work on himself', Shiryaev recalled.[34] For Ivanov the problem was fundamental: how was one artistic temperament to realize the conceptions of another? The matter was publicly discussed, as we read in this unsigned analysis of the Petersburg ballet:

... as regards the question of ballet production, one must say that our three balletmasters (Messrs Petipa, Ivanov, and Cecchetti), in the varied character of their tendencies and tastes, recall Krylov's fable 'The Swan, the Crab, and the Pike'. And when one expects some special success from their collaboration, it is no less imaginary than in the fable itself.

M. I. Petipa is undeniably a man with an artistic nature, rich imagination, who is inventive in scenic effects, knows well the strengths of the entire company, who can place the spark of his own artistic gift in each dancer, but, having served his art for half a century, is simply unable at times, because of his physical indisposition, to devote himself completely to his calling, and limits his activity only to the supervision at the highest level of the artistic work of the other two balletmasters.

But this supervision also serves as the worst stumbling-block for the success of a venture, since what is thought up and composed by the second balletmasters loses its physiognomy [fizionomiya] in the adaptation made at the demand of the first, that is, of Mr Petipa. Although this 'adaptation' takes the worst kind of expression and alters it to the best, the result is nevertheless distorted, and the meaning of the original thought lost, the result being something unfinished, without definition and incomplete.

Speaking of works 'conceived' by the other balletmasters, I had in mind exclusively the second balletmaster L. I. Ivanov, who has devoted himself to balletic activity since 1850. He was long since able to recommend himself for being both a talented dancer and an able balletmaster, but he lacks that erudition of thought and that flight of fancy with which Mr Petipa is so well endowed.[35]

Slonimsky expands on the differences in experience and temperament between Petipa and Ivanov, which may well have exacerbated the latter's anxieties about *Nutcracker*, since fully half of the ballet consisted of mimed scenes, to say nothing of a battle scene:

For decades L. Ivanov was trained to work chiefly on the production of dances; Petipa without fail had taken on himself the régisseur's conception of the spectacle, the fine resolution of questions of pantomime—of 'action scenes'. This part of production practice was never L. Ivanov's strength. His successes always flowed from the musical reading of the danced episodes. Here [in *Nutcracker*] he was deprived of the possibility of 'growing accustomed' to the extremely complex music, to seek for a time, patiently, the key to its correct interpretation. There was little room for his original choreographic gift—Petipa's half-finished work bound him hand and foot.[36]

As work proceeded on *Nutcracker* during the autumn of 1892, Ivanov must have sensed pressures from another quarter: complaints in the Press about a decline in the company's performance standards. A reviewer of *Paquita*, for example, found the *corps de ballet* in Act I 'not completely successful; it lacked the requisite precision in the general groups, probably as a consequence of Mr Petipa's illness.'[37] We read a week later that 'Mr Petipa's illness has affected the composition of dances, and his deputies [in this case Cecchetti] compelled the *corps de ballet* to run instead of dance.'³⁸

There was, finally, some question about Antonietta Dell'Era's suitability as a ballerina. 'The heavy, large, unpretty, ungraceful dancer was much to the taste of the Germans and was firmly settled in the Berlin court theatre,' wrote Solyannikov,

But the attraction of a foreign name proved great, such that the Petersburg Press immediately came forward with enthusiastic reviews, favouring her with the epithets 'light', 'ethereal', 'astounding', etc., not taking into account the dancer's considerable weight. At first she wanted to make her début in the part of Aurora in *Sleeping Beauty*, but she changed her mind and decided to wait for the production of the new ballet *Nutcracker*, in which a role would be created for her, that of the Sugar Plum Fairy. Although this was all clearly contrary to common sense, Lev Ivanov was too good-humoured and indecisive to go against the directorate's order, and Petipa compromisingly agreed [in broken Russian] that 'madam no good . . .', but in a month Dell'Era's tour would be ending, and there was no point in arguing.³⁹

Not all the circumstances surrounding the production of *Nutcracker* were unfortunate. As early as September we read reports praising the drawings of the costumes: '. . . one more beautiful than the last, and [they] reveal their artist's excellent taste both in elegance and in the combination of colours.'⁴⁰ During the critical period of rehearsal—six weeks preceding the first performance—Tchaikovsky was in Petersburg, available for consultation.⁴¹ On 30 October he was given an advance of 1,000 roubles against performance royalties forthcoming from *Iolanthe* and *Nutcracker*,⁴² after receiving word earlier in the month of good news on other fronts: that the Institut de France had elected him a corresponding member, and that Cambridge University had the idea of offering him an honorary doctorate. The first appearance of Antonietta Dell'Era, who in fact danced Aurora before *Nutcracker* was ready, was sold out in advance, and her performance was well received.⁴³

The general rehearsal for the combined spectacle was set for 5 December. Pogozhev quotes at some length the report of the régisseur G. P. Kondratiev, who wrote mostly of *Iolanthe*:

Today, Saturday, 5 December, the general rehearsal took place. The opera lasted 1 hour, 24 minutes. The rehearsal began at 8:10 and ended at 11:55. . . . The performance was much hindered by the fact that the ballet orchestra played, not the opera orchestra. The chronic problem of all first performances is that the costumes and décor are never ready in time . . . I find it utterly superfluous to report the perfect taste and astonishing beauty of the costumes of the artists, as too of the chorus and the ballet.⁴⁴

Kondratiev's report reminds us of a factor often overlooked in the assessment of *Nutcracker*, one deserving mention before turning to a description of the first production: the ballet's relationship to *Iolanthe*, the degree to which Tchaikovsky composed *Nutcracker* anticipating how it and the opera would complement each other and interact to form an evening's entertainment. Laroche, who wrote no review of either work at the time of their first performances but discussed both in a long retrospective view of Tchaikovsky's work as a theatre composer, stressed the importance of their interdependence:

Iolanthe with *Nutcracker*, opera with ballet, were, as is well known, thought out and written with the idea of both being performed in a mixed spectacle on the same evening. In subject-matter there is between them no connection whatever . . . But two essentially distinct dramatic tasks came together in the composer's mind as a result of the circumstances that he wanted to hear them performed in consecutive order, in three or four hours, and that, therefore, in the creative process from the very beginning he imagined a certain unity of impression, and in certain features directly strove for such a unity. The unity, however, is based on contrast. *Nutcracker*—playful, merry, capricious, in places lightly caricatured, in its middle part fantastic—must have produced a clear contrast with the short, bright, touching, loving *Iolanthe*, the noisy merriment of the crowd of children with the quiet happiness of seclusion and removal from the world. The composer wanted contrast even in such details as the instrumentation of the introduction of *Iolanthe* with that of *Nutcracker*. One is without stringed instruments, the other with strings but no winds [sic]. The idea of such spectacles, as is well known, was developed and encouraged in the Paris Opera, where operas small in bulk serve as if a prologue to ballets . . . Until practical considerations make necessary the separation of the opera and the ballet, they ought to be given together. Peter Ilyich, who so often erred in practical questions in the reckoning of an effect, here turns out to be an experienced and adroit stage artist, and his ballet in a series of other ballets or excerpts does not produce that poetic and pleasing impression inherent in it [when performed] in its proper place.[45]

Of the two works, *Iolanthe* makes the more serious appeal to its audience's sensibilities. The story is brief and intense. Iolanthe is a blind princess who has been protected even from the concept of sight; she learns of her affliction from the man with whom she has fallen in love, and is cured by the power of that love. The contrast of medium and atmosphere which *Nutcracker* brings leads to an obvious rationale for the combination—the serious opera gives way to the diverting ballet—as if the whole of *Nutcracker* were to be taken by the audience as the celebration of Iolanthe's wedding, a relief from the seriousness of her story that remains free of any obligation to logic. Laroche's point is well taken—removing the opera would assuredly exaggerate the flaws of the ballet.[46]

Something in Tchaikovsky the practical man of affairs must have told him that nothing would be gained by requiring that *Iolanthe* and *Nutcracker* be performed together. When he signed an agreement with the directorate regarding fees and performance rights the works were considered separately, and *Nutcracker* enjoyed a slight advantage in royalties. This agreement, like the one concerning *Sleeping Beauty* (see Chapter 3, pp. 105–6, above), was not signed until after the first performance (see Pl. 12).

A G R E E D :

10/22 December 1892.
Of this year 1892 the day of December 8 [sic] the Directorate of the Imperial Theatres on the one hand and Peter Ilyich Tchaikovsky on the other, have agreed between ourselves the conditions as listed below:

1. I Tchaikovsky transfer to the Directorate of the Imperial Theatres the right to performance on the stage of the Imperial Theatres in St Petersburg and Moscow of the opera *Iolanthe* in one act and the ballet *Nutcracker* in two acts, composed by me.

2. The Directorate will pay me for each performance of the designated pieces a post-performance payment in the amount of 4% of the gross receipts for the opera *Iolanthe* and 6% for the ballet *Nutcracker*.

3. I Tchaikovsky pledge myself for the period of two years from the day of signing this condition not to give the designated pieces for performance on the private stages of St Petersburg and Moscow, understanding by these stages not only those which are being operated in the line of cities and *uyezds* [administrative divisions of the country], but also in the suburbs, out-of-town, as well as in the cities of Pavlovsk, Tsarskoe Selo, Oranienbaum, Peterhof, and Gatchina.

4. For not fulfilling this obligation I Tchaikovsky am subject to the payment of a fine in the amount of 2,000 roubles for each performance.

5. I Tchaikovsky am obligated to submit to all existing laws and decisions relating to production and performance on the stage of the Imperial Theatres.

6. Forthcoming to me, Tchaikovsky, must be given the post-performance payment on demand from the Petersburg or Moscow branch of the Imperial Theatres, or sent to my place of residence, with the postage deducted; it may be legally transferred by me to another person and pass on to my heirs on the basis of existing decisions about literary, musical, and artistic ownership.[47]

The documents from which the first production of *Nutcracker* may be studied are identical in type to those for *Sleeping Beauty*: the holograph score (Hol), répétiteurs (Rep-I and Rep-II), a choreographic notation (CN), the libretto, and press reviews.[48] No piano reduction of the score survives in the Sergeyev Collection. While these sources must be approached with the same caution as those for *Sleeping Beauty*, they differ from those of the earlier ballet in the kind of information they convey. The Hol and the Reps are virtually free of significant alterations to the music text, which makes a separate discussion of the performing version unnecessary. All the metronome markings in *Nutcracker*, it may be added, are Tchaikovsky's.

At the first performance, the principal dancers (excepting the prima ballerina, Antonietta Dell'Era) were essentially those of *Sleeping Beauty*. Pavel Gerdt, as Prince Coqueluche, partnered the ballerina; Maria Anderson (the White Cat in *Sleeping Beauty*) and Olga Preobrazhenskaya performed the women's leads in the dances of the mechanical dolls, partnered by Sergei Litavkin and Georgii Kyaksht. In contrast to the casting practices of many modern revivals, students (Belinskaya, Stukolkin, and Legat) were assigned the roles of Clara, Fritz, and the Nutcracker. Riccardo Drigo conducted.

ACT I

The curtain rises to reveal a table at the front of the stage, to the audience's right, at which Silberhaus, his wife, and three guests are sitting.[49] Silberhaus rises and walks to stage centre, engaging in a mimed conversation with a man [a servant?] who has just come forward from the rear of the set.

Silberhaus: 'Tell me, do you have the Christmas tree ready?'

[*Servant*]: 'No, it is not ready yet, but when it is I will tell you.'

Silberhaus walks back over to his wife and says: 'Just imagine, the Christmas tree is still not ready.'

A footman enters from rear stage right at bar 40 and announces that guests are arriving, to which Silberhaus responds, 'Show them in.'[50] They come on stage. Among them is one woman about whom Silberhaus asks his wife: 'You invited her too?' To which she replies, 'No, but she came anyway—what can be done about it?'[51]

Silberhaus now says to his wife, 'We must call the children.' The tree is proclaimed ready, and Mrs Silberhaus summons the governess and tells her to bring in the children. They enter (at bars 105–6), followed by the governess, and run to the Christmas tree. Silberhaus calls to them (at the beginning of the March, No. 2), and when they have gathered in a semicircle around him, says, pointing, 'You and you, listen to me. Over there—you will approach in twos and I will give you presents.' The children, delighted, have lined up, stage left, facing the back, by bars 13–15. Standing next to the Christmas tree, Silberhaus and an assistant begin the distribution of the gifts at bar 18, a pair of children for each two bars bowing to both the president and the assistant when they receive their presents, and moving on to form a new line, stage right.

This is the point at which Petipa had originally planned to introduce the suite of national dances. Instead, the gifts distributed, the children finish the march, starting in bar 41, by dancing, with their gifts in their hands, a number of figures in the middle of the stage. From rounded patterns the children form into files for the galop (No. 3), and move from the sides to the centre, or else change sides.[52]

The entrance of the parents *en incroyables*, which followed without a break (bars 45–60 of No. 3), is represented in the CN by two diagrams. The first shows two rows of couples entering from rear stage right and promenading back and forth across the stage. In the second, the dancers break ranks to take up positions for the *allegro*.[53]

For most of the dance all the participants perform the same or similar steps. In the first sixteen bars each dancer changes places with his or her partner, four pairs on either side of the stage. Then the women turn in their places as their partners dance to the centre and back. Reunited, the couples end this part of the dance by changing places as before. In a transitional passage they re-form into two lines parallel with the front of the stage, and stay in this pattern for the last thirty-two bars. Preceded by the two solo couples, all come forward. Only for one phrase do the men form lines along the sides, a frame for the lateral movement of the women in between; all then gather at the rear and come forward again in lines to end the dance.

Drosselmayer enters from rear stage right, and the children scatter. The councillor bows to the left and right, and, seeing the children running off, says, 'These small children were afraid of me—why is this?' Silberhaus walks over to him.

Silberhaus (greeting him): 'What? You forgot your old custom, your snuff-box.'

The president gives him a snuff-box, which the older man hands back after helping himself. Both men, through and around the arms, in the manner of a toast, take a pinch.

Drosselmayer: 'You show me these little ones. (He greets Mrs Silberhaus with an embrace and a kiss.) Tell me why these children are frightened of me.'

Silberhaus: 'It's nothing! It's nothing!'

Drosselmayer: 'I am old and unpleasant, but my heart is in the right place.' [Struck through: 'Where are those children?'

Silberhaus: 'Come here, come here' (they go after the children)] Mrs Silberhaus goes after Clara and Mr Silberhaus after Fritz.

When the children have been brought over to him, Drosselmayer says: 'You do not have to be afraid of me. I brought dolls here for you both. Do you want to see them?'

Children: 'Yes! Yes! We want to!'

Drosselmayer: 'Fine.'

The notators passed over the scene in which Drosselmayer unwraps the toys (No. 4, bars 67–98), but we have an account of it from a review of the first performance:

The entrance of the 'godfather'—Drosselmayer (Mr Stukolkin)—is accompanied by giving little Clara (student Belinskaya) and her brother Fritz (student Stukolkin) mechanical dolls, which servants bring in wrapped up in paper and tied in ribbons, and place in the middle of the stage. The wrapping is removed and beneath it turn out to be a sutler (Mlle Anderson), a soldier (Litavkin), Columbine (Preobrazhenskaya), and Harlequin (Kyaksht). The dolls stand motionless until the 'godfather' winds them with a key, and lo, each mainspring is snapped and the dolls begin automatically to move, to turn, and to dance.[54]

The dance of the first pair of dolls is not fully notated. There is only one bar of steps, but if the floor plans and markings are any indication, the dance is puppet-like, reminiscent of the dolls in *Coppélia*. After turning towards one another and bowing, the dancers follow paths that are either parallel, if moving up or down the stage, or equal and opposite, if moving laterally. Twice during the dance their angular patterns are contrasted by pairs of spring-like turns, waltzing, on an oblique line, after which they move sharply back to a position next to one another. And at the end, 'She straightens up and he stands, bent over, in a salute.'

The music for the second pair of dolls Tchaikovsky composed to order for a he-devil and a she-devil. In late February 1891 Petipa expressed (in the balletmaster's plan) a preference for the latter couple, but he—or perhaps Vsevolozhsky—had decided against them by the time of production. The choreography preserves appropriately Mephistophelian accents. Although the details are again uncertain (for the dance was recorded twice and the versions disagree), the demanding technique, the speed of execution and numerous asymmetries—in the floor plans and in departures from unison performance into passages of choreographic counterpoint—suggest a diabolical impetus. The dance requires of Columbine short jumps on *pointe* with the working leg extended forward, brief *arabesques*, and *entrechats* and *echappés*; in one phrase she holds a fan while performing a prancing step on *pointe*. Harlequin's steps are more studied in their awkwardness: at one point he struts forward, making alternate steps from the heel; at another he jumps flat-footed; and at another he makes rotary turns with the working leg extended to the side. One wonders if this dance did not stimulate the imagination of the creators of *Petrushka*, who called upon another magician to animate the Ballerina and the Moor.

At the beginning of No. 5, Drosselmayer is standing in the centre of the stage surrounded by children—seven girls on his left, six boys on his right. He calls Clara and Fritz over to him. With one arm around Clara, the other around Fritz, the councillor asks, 'Tell me, do you like the dolls?' The children respond in the affirmative. Clara and Fritz ask to be given the dolls, whereupon Drosselmayer laughs and says: 'You are little, and they are big. Come here', he continues, and takes out a nutcracker.

Children: 'What is this?'

Drosselmayer: 'You put a nut in his mouth and he cracks it.'

Fritz wants to try it, but Drosselmayer pulls back and gives the new toy to the little girl.

The CN thus presents the scene in contrast to the libretto, in which Silberhaus's refusal to let the children have their new dolls leads to their crying and Drosselmayer's gift of the Nutcracker as consolation.

The record of Clara's polka and of Fritz's noisy interruptions of her lullaby (No. 5, bars 39–171) falls short of a clear presentation of the dance. Recorded on a type of notation paper associated with an earlier generation of notations (a paper used for some of the duplicate choreographies in *Sleeping Beauty*), this may have been the work of a student. The dance is not regularly barred in the CN, and its floor plans do not clearly match the steps. It begins with two eight-bar phrases containing short steps on *pointe*, brief *attitudes*, and simple turns. Three bars in, at mid-phrase, is a direction for the right arm to be extended forward, possibly Clara's threat to Fritz not to hurt the new toy, possibly her reproach after he has done so (the arm movement is labelled *groz*, most likely an abbreviation for *grozit*: '[she] shakes her finger'). There follow eight more bars, a break, and two sixteen-bar phrases which appear to be the statements of the lullaby.

Rep-I and Rep-II, which have yielded no information about stage action since No. 2, have a few additional details: the instruction 'Il donne le casse-noisette' is given at the beginning of the *andantino* of Rep-I; 'Clara, Fritz, stu[dents]', in Russian, at the same place in Rep-II (the CN makes no reference to non-danced action at that point); and Clara's rocking of the Nutcracker at the first playing of the lullaby (bars 121 ff.).

The *L'istesso tempo* beginning at bar 172 is taken up with the adults making ready for the *Grossvatertanz*: three files of four couples each are formed (the pattern to be maintained throughout the dance), and the men bow to the ladies.[55] The dance itself is rather like a square dance. At the *allegro* (*Tempo di Grossvater*) the couples process to the rear of the stage and forward again, ending with a bow; during the *allegro vivacissimo* the couples swing each other around four times, first by the right hand, then by the left, then holding both hands.

With the recommencement of the *Tempo di Grossvater* the processional is begun anew, but it ends this time with a bow in the outer columns and the men of the centre column requesting (and receiving) a kiss from their ladies. The *allegro vivacissimo* is again taken up with the partners swinging each other around. In its third playing the *Tempo di Grossvater* brings with it a third processional, the most elaborate yet, in which the outer columns of women exchange places on the stage. The dance ends when bar 219 has been reached the third time.[56]

In Tchaikovsky's score, No. 6 begins with the dispersal of the guests, continues with Clara's venture downstairs, and ends with the miraculous growth of the Christmas tree. In the CN only the first part of this sequence is presented.

Everyone begins to leave. Silberhaus, Drosselmayer, and Mrs Silberhaus are standing in the middle of the stage.

Drosselmayer: 'It is also time for me to go.'

He bids host and hostess farewell and turns to leave, but suddenly he remembers his custom with the snuff-box. He walks back to Silberhaus, and the two conclude the evening in the way they began it—with a salutation and a pinch of snuff. The councillor leaves. Mrs Silberhaus then says 'Ah! How tired I am!' 'And I too', her husband replies. As this is being mimed, a footman crosses the stage behind them with a candelabrum. All three exit at rear stage left.

At this point the CN of Scene 1 ends, omitting everything before the Waltz of the Snowflakes. For information about the intervening numbers we may turn to the Hol, which Tchaikovsky annotates generously, the libretto, which offers a lively description of the action (but no indication of the number of performers in the complex battle scene, except to note that the students of the theatre school were joined by those from the School of the Regiment of Finnish Guards), and the Reps, which provide an idea of who appears and when.[57] In bars 56–7 of No. 6—eight bars after the beginning of the night scene—we read in Rep-I 'entrance' (of Clara, no doubt); at the beginning of the *allegro giusto* (bar 71), as she makes her way to the Nutcracker's bed, 'Noise', as if the moment at which the mice enter is marked by some sound effect. Both Reps suggest, by the word 'king' at bar 126, that the Mouse King makes an appearance in the middle of the Christmas tree's magic transformation.

The sources differ slightly in accounts of the battle scene. In agreement with the Hol at the outset, the Reps indicate, at bar 13 of No. 7, the deployment of the gingerbread soldiers. The Nutcracker enters the fray just after the beginning of 'La bataille' as marked by Tchaikovsky at bar 25, and 'the cavalry' [sic] follow at bar 52, that is, approximately where Petipa had called for the gingerbread soldiers to be devoured by the mice in the balletmaster's plan. No sooner have the cavalry arrived than 'cannon-fire' is heard (at bar 56 of Rep-II; the word is crossed out in Rep-I), repeated with the re-entry of the Mouse King at bar 73, 'the second battle'. This new fracas lasts only ten bars before 'the king stops', and at bar 98 a 'duel of the Nut[cracker] with the k[ing]' begins (Rep-I). The Hol tells us when Clara throws her slipper (that is, at bar 106).

Skalkovsky recounts the night scene as follows:

The guests disperse, the candles die out. In the dark corners of the room squeaking breaks out and on the stage mice begin to appear, armed with sharp daggers. Through the window the moon makes silver the lifeless Christmas tree, beneath which some toys remain, including the booth with a sentry and the rabbit with a drum. The crowd of mice grows and takes on a threatening aspect; the sentry in his booth comes to life and fires his musket, announcing the danger; the rabbit beats the alarm on his drum, the roofs fall away from the boxes and from them jump out the gingerbread soldiers one by one: grenadiers, hussars, artillerymen. A veritable battle ensues. One side is led by the king of the mice, the other by the courageous Nutcracker, who has turned into a prince. The mice are conquered, and the victor—the Nutcracker—kneels before his beloved Clara and leads her into the kingdom of fairy-tales.

The scene of the appearance of the mice and soldiers, and the battle itself, were not produced wholly successfully: there were many disorderly tangles and much unnecessary running about. It would be incomparably better if the formations were correct and intelligible, and the whole scene significantly shorter.[58]

The Reps offer no details of the stage activity in the journey scene, No. 8.

The celebrated Waltz of the Snowflakes is made up of an introduction (bars 1–36), the waltz proper (37–264), and a coda in 2/4 time (265–407); the Reps show a cut of sixteen bars in the coda (345–61). Neither the very beginning nor the very end was danced, as the word 'danse' appears at bar 37, and the instruction in the CN at the point corresponding to the *poco meno* (bar 343) gives, 'They [the dancers] remain in this group until the closing of the curtain, their batons quivering.' In between, the waltz unfolds in a masterful sequence of floor patterns, imaginative in design and coherent in structure.

The earlier of two notations of the waltz[59] is one of the easiest to read in the entire ballet. The assurance of the notator, whose work appears here for the first time, is reflected in the clarity of the drawings and the systematic presentation of a floor plan with the number of bars of music required to perform it. The notation is reproduced in Appendix G, together with a translation of the Russian words. The following summary gives the principal divisions of the waltz.

(1) *Entrance of the Snowflakes* (bars 37–84; Appendix G, pp. 390, 392, first four squares). Five groups of six dancers come on stage, each six divided into units of three. The dance progresses geometrically, the emphasis changing from one of circularity—waltzing turns and rotating patterns of trios of dancers—towards one based on parallel straight lines, which predominate in the last sixteen bars of this part.

(2) *Transition and Entrance of the Coryphées* (bars 85–116; Appendix G, p. 392, last two squares). All the groups begin to rotate in a pin-wheel formation (a movement introduced in the preceding part); at the same time eight *coryphées*, four from each side, enter from the back and weave a line between the circling snowflakes.

(3) *Transition and Encircled Cross* (bars 117–48; Appendix G, p. 394, first two squares). After sixteen bars of regrouping, the dancers form in this figure what may have been the *pièce de résistance* of the number, in which Ivanov summarizes, at the mid-point of the dance, his basic geometric principles: straight lines and circles, and the rotary movement with which he indicates the blizzard throughout.

(4) *Transition and Braided Figure* (bars 149–96; Appendix G, p. 394, the last four squares). A braided effect is achieved in part by the dancers in the centre and rear who perform, as the notators put it, 'dos à dos' and zigzag patterns.

(5) *Transition and Star* (bars 197–228; Appendix G, p. 396, first two squares). With this figure Ivanov creates a moving pattern in which the two sets of dancers alternate positions at the points of the star by moving back and forward from the centre. It is possible that the star in addition gives the illusion of rotation.

(6) *Transition and Round Dance* [*khorovod*] (bars 229–55; Appendix G, p. 396, squares 3–5). Five rotating circles are formed, one in each corner and one in the middle, followed by a burst of wind which makes the snowflakes swirl. In the coda the dancers at first continue as before, taking up their round dance at a run. The small circles re-form into a single large one which contracts and expands. In the final choreographic gesture of the *presto*, the dancers take each other by the hand and make a pass clockwise around the stage; at the end, a *tableau vivant*.

The downy pompoms on the white dresses [Skalkovsky writes], on the headwear in the form of rays of stars, and on the accessories in the form of clusters of wands swaying in the dancers' hands, very successfully and picturesquely represented the movements of snowflakes, while the initial grouping [of dancers] produced a fine impression of the artistic allegory of a snowdrift (see Pl. 17).[60]

The first of the many beauties of the waltz is its dynamic shape. From a static introduction Ivanov increasingly intensifies the movement through the main body of the waltz, paralleling the intensification of the tempo and metre. Instead of a bravura conclusion, which would be typical of Petipa, Ivanov follows the music to arrive at rest again—the *tableau vivant* —which not only balances the introduction in a structural sense by the absence of danced activity, but also allows the audience to reflect on the images of the dance before the curtain falls.

Ivanov uses these images to create a formal pattern in the waltz which emphasizes continuous elaboration rather than literal repetition. The result is a series of dance motives linked by common elements. The whirling rotation of the entrance of the *corps* continues when the *coryphées* make their entrance, these eight new dancers introducing a weaving pattern in the second section which is picked up again and brought out in the fourth section. In between, the encircled cross summarizes the main ideas that preceded it, and it is related to the next monumental figure, the star, not only in the commanding size of the figure itself (which filled the stage), but also in the illusion of rotation and in being enclosed by rounded lines. The star, in turn, shares with the circular formation of the coda the devices of expansion and contraction. Just before this figure, the round dance of (6) returns to the whirling rotations of (1), but with a different configuration of dancers on the stage.

The Waltz of the Snowflakes provides the basis for an assessment of Lev Ivanov the choreographer. His task was to portray a blizzard in dance. The interrelationship of the sections of the waltz reveals an imaginative sense of composition, one which seeks to reconcile unity and diversity. The patterns of the waltz demonstrate the success of Ivanov's approach to stylization, in the continuous motion of the dancers (as if they are always at the whim of the wintry breezes), and in the periodic formation of large designs appropriate to the theme, such as the circle (a whirlwind) and the star (a snowflake). Moreover, the quickly dissolving patterns in the dance are a direct reminder of the transitory images seen in a real snowstorm. When one remembers that Ivanov planned his complex choreography with simple steps—short runs, *pas balancé*, and *pas de basque*—his achievement must be considered impressive indeed.

We must leave aside the CN once again as we turn to our first glimpse of Confiturembourg (No. 10, *Scène*), for the manuscript contains no hint of it. There was probably no dancing to record. 'Strictly speaking', Skalkovsky writes, 'there is no ballet in this scene, but only a show of costumes, which flaunt luxury in their more or less remote likeness to caramels, sugar-plums, mint drops, and other products of the properties/confectioner's art.'[61]

The following scene (No. 11) contains dancing and gives the audience of *Nutcracker* a glimpse of the ballerina before the *pas de deux* at the end of the ballet. At the beginning of the scene the Sugar Plum Fairy and her prince are at the back of the stage. As they come forward he lifts her and supports her in turns. Six women (doubtless part of her retinue), three on each side, show deference to their mistress as she makes her way to the front. Once there she is surrounded by this group as she circles around the prince on *pointe*. The six form a broad semicircle as the Sugar Plum Fairy addresses them in mime: 'You listen to me. A young girl is arriving here. All of you must bow down to her. I wish it.' The major-domo enters, bows to the Sugar Plum Fairy, and announces, 'The guests are arriving', to which she responds, 'Show them in.' Clara and the Nutcracker enter from rear stage left, crossing the stage and turning forward down the centre. Stopping, they bow to the left and right. Seeing the Sugar Plum Fairy, Clara bows to her; the Fairy greets the little girl with a kiss on the head.

Sugar Plum Fairy (to the Nutcracker): 'Tell me about your adventures and I shall listen to what you say.'

Here follows a narration which was not elaborated in the CN, but which is accompanied by a recall of the battle music of Act I. When it is finished the Sugar Plum Fairy summons Clara, saying to her, 'You have a good heart—come over here.'

At this moment the Nutcracker's sisters arrive, and he embraces them. The entire royal party steps off to the right stage rear except the Sugar Plum Fairy, who comes to the centre, at a point where the CN specifies 'March' (probably a reference to bar 116), and says, 'You must all bow before them.' She calls the major-domo, who comes forward, bows, and receives her instruction: 'Begin the dancing.' He returns to the rear centre of the stage and orders this to be done.[62]

In the Spanish Dance the lead couple in the centre pass close to one another, now in sharp angular patterns, now in rounded ones as the woman dances a circle around the man. Occasionally the notators record a pose—the dancer kneeling on one knee, body thrown back, head to the side, arms rounded about the head. The secondary soloists form a background, first in the centre and then along the sides. Their movements include the *pas de basque*, a stylish hesitation or drag of the leg, and an interrupted walk in which one foot, ready to step out, at the last moment moves behind the other and receives the weight of the body while the second foot takes the step instead.

The Arabian Dance employs the same contrapuntal principle as the Spanish Dance but with different choreographic ideas. Here also pose is important—more so, perhaps, than in the Spanish Dance—in creating the basic effect of stylized Eastern languor. The soloist enters, hands behind her head, and comes to an *arabesque* as the dance begins, back arched to the rear, head to the left. The first phrase of the dance is no more than an *arabesque*, a step, and another *arabesque*. Then, standing, she 'pauses and gradually opens her arms to the side.' This broad gesture of the arms—from the back of the head upward, outward, and around to normal position—is repeated, after a turn of the body, when the steps of the dance recommence.

The phrases just described demonstrate the principal gestures of the other dancers. Characteristic through most of the dance are the moments in which a pose is held while standing still or while turning in place. These lend an appropriate static quality to the choreography, though near the end the soloist performs a series of turns while coming downstage, and is joined by a cavalier for the last pose. The other dancers, deployed to the side of the soloist, are apparently assigned simple gestures—bows, kneels, exchanges of place with partners. Near the end of the dance they come to the centre of the stage for a posed grouping—the familiar semicircles in which some dancers stand, some kneel, and some lie on the stage.

Imperfections in the CN obscure a precise view of the Chinese Dance, for the manuscript conveys conflicting information.[63] It is possible nevertheless to get a general idea of the dance. Because the steps of the Chinese Dance are more intricate than those of its companion pieces, the notators recorded them with special care. The dancers accompanying the solo couple move in a block of two rows and perform steps in unison. With great precision they perform delicate *à terre* combinations in their places, now moving laterally, now with short jumps forward, or in circles. The solo couple's dance, as before, adopts the same stylistic premises as that of the group, except at the end, where the woman soloist, like her Arabian counterpart, comes forward in a series of turns.

Ivanov brings a different conception to the Dance of the Mirlitons, or toy flutes, in that the lead dancer's part and those of the accompanying dancers interact more closely. One might say they dance together, not simply at the same time, whether in unison or in the elaborate figures which the accompanying dancers form for the soloist. In another exception to the pattern of the first three dances, the soloist does not enter until well after the others, four from either side, have come on stage and traced a rounded, hourglass-like pattern in the centre. In general, this dance makes more frequent use of *pointe* and *attitude* than its predecessors, though Ivanov is sparing in his use of turns, and tends to limit them to the ball of the foot. In one phrase the soloist, dancing in the centre as the others move towards her from the sides and back again, performs a double *rond de jambe* in the air—a virtuoso touch which has not appeared in this CN before.

The reliable Skalkovsky, after finding the Spanish Dance inept, the soloist of the Arabian Dance not suited to her part, and the Chinese Dance the best of all (it was repeated at the first performance), writes briefly about the dances omitted in the CN:

The dance of the jesters [i.e. the Russian Dance]—by students of the school—serves only as a background for the complicated *pas* of Mr Shiryaev, who performed his difficult part with striking precision . . . The dance of the *polichinelles*—led out by their jolly aunt (*mère Gigogne*, Mr Yakovlev)—is a copy of the children's harlequinade composed and produced by balletmaster Petipa during the revival of the ballet *The Wilful Wife*.[64]

From another review we learn a further detail of Shiryaev's trepak: that at one point he 'very adroitly jumped through a hoop.'[65]

A grand *ballabile* concludes the *divertissement*: the Waltz of the Flowers. As in the Waltz of the Snowflakes, the notation of this waltz conveys the choreography of a close variant of the original (a conjecture strengthened by information from the Reps). The soloists have been reduced from eight to six, the *corps* from twenty-four to sixteen. By the time it was recorded, moreover, there was no reference to a property described by a reviewer of the first performance: a golden vase containing golden flowers raised up by the *corps de ballet*.[66]

Unlike the earlier waltz, however, this one has a danced introduction, or so it would seem from the part of one page, placed after the rest of the notation for the number, entitled 'Before the Waltz, No. 13'. It is the only part of the dance to contain a notation for eight women soloists (reduced to six halfway through), and is made up of four figures. In the first the soloists, divided into columns, approach the centre from the sides; in the second, they re-position themselves into a group across the centre front of the stage, with each pair striking a different pose; in the third, they trace a circle, half of the dancers on each side, around the stage on *pointe*; in the fourth, they are placed at the side, presumably awaiting the entrance of the *corps de ballet*.

The waltz proper consists of six sections, alternating *corps* with soloists, the latters' parts by far the longer and more complex. The basic structural unit of the waltz, subject to some variation, is the thirty-two-bar period. In the first of these periods (bars 38–70) the *corps* make their entrance and arrange themselves in three columns of couples—six on each side, four in the middle. It is quite probable (though the CN does not specify this) that they bring on stage the garlands to which the CN presently refers.

The soloists, as we have seen, have already come on stage during the harp cadenzas of the first thirty-three bars, but they make their formal *entrée* into the dance, by twos, in the second section, comprising three thirty-two-bar periods. The first pair of soloists splits the columns of the *corps* on either side, and then proceeds to the centre to fill a space momentarily vacated when the middle column of the *corps* moved to the sides (bars 71–89—thirty-two bars counting an internal repeat). The second pair of soloists (in bars 90–121) comes downstage from the rear, one travelling a straight line, the other an angular one, and then return, one in a continuous straight line, the other articulating hers with turns. The *corps*, meanwhile, take their cue from the first pair of soloists: just as they had split the columns of couples on either side, now those columns themselves divide, the four forward couples passing between the four couples in the rear. An instruction accompanying this figure requires them to 'pass beneath the garland' and 'by turns pass beneath the garland'. The third pair of soloists enters (bars 122–41, thirty-two bars counting an internal repeat) on a swirling diagonal from rear stage left in an elaborate combination which includes a *cabriole*, turn, and *attitude*. In the second half of their entrance they retrace part of their path. The *corps*, in lines parallel to the diagonal, lower their garlands for most of this entrance, then reposition themselves in preparation for their interlude, the third section of the waltz.

For thirty bars (142–71) the *corps* takes over. In three phrases of eight bars each two couples waltz together at centre front while the others provide a frame. In the last six bars they move again to the sides.

In section four, the next part with soloists (bars 172–277), the CN is sketchy, with few details to clarify the part of the dance assigned to the *corps* and that to soloists. The point of the section seems to be not in the steps, which are similar to those of section two, but in the phrase-lengths and the overall shape. In the manner of a sonata-form development, section four challenges and disrupts the premises established at the beginning of the waltz: patterns are rearranged and period length is altered.[67]

The *corps de ballet* return to the forefront again at the beginning of section five (bar 278), having some bars earlier dispersed from their framing columns at the sides of the stage to form a cross by this point.[68] The lines of the cross are formed by the men on diagonals to the boundaries of the stage. The women, divided into groups of four, pass laterally through the four arms of the cross and back again, their paths marked by garlands held aloft by the men. They next retire to the sides, followed by the men. Once again in columns along the sides, the *corps* make a sweep towards the back, forming two rows of eight couples there. These rows come forward and turn outward to the sides, where they remain, garlands held high, until the final cadence.

At bar 326—twenty-eight bars from the end—the soloists make their last appearance in the waltz, in a single line dancing together for the first time. They come forward and then retire to the back again, turn on *pointe*, and kneel on one knee.

The devices Ivanov borrows from Petipa in the Waltz of the Flowers are easier to perceive than the internal rhythmic and structural complexities of his own making, a fact probably responsible for the common imperial criticism that Ivanov was dependent on the older master as a choreographer. Petipa himself, requesting music from Tchaikovsky, specifies that its length should be the same as that of the *valse villageoise* in *Sleeping Beauty*. Perhaps Petipa had planned to include choreographic likenesses to the earlier dance which, as supervisor of the production, he directed Ivanov to incorporate into the choreography. In any event, two details of the choreography are close enough to that of the *valse villageoise* to warrant mention: the use of a garland as a property, and the cross formation, through the corridors of which, formed by the men of the *corps*, other dancers pass. In *Sleeping Beauty* the other dancers were children, but Ivanov's use of the garlands—to enliven the vertical space with shape and colour, or for a coquettish embrace with a partner—is practically identical with Petipa's.

The *pas de deux* of the Sugar Plum Fairy and Prince Coqueluche (No. 14), like its counterpart in the last act of *Sleeping Beauty*, may well represent, as recorded, a revision of the original dance to accommodate the technical attainments of Pavel Gerdt's successor, Nikolai Legat, whose name is found in the CN.

The *adagio* (*andante maestoso*) divides into four parts with a transition between the second and third. Parts one and two are comparable in structure, opening with poses in place and giving way to combinations while travelling. The dance opens with three supported turns, the first from *arabesque* to *attitude*, the second *en attitude* with the cavalier walking a circle around the ballerina, the third *en attitude* with the cavalier still. The travelling portion of the first part consists of *pirouettes* performed at the ends of a short walk toward the sides of the stage. In the second part the ballerina, in place, sustains a long pose with high extensions, the working leg beginning in front, then moving to the side and back. Both dancers travel towards the sides again, the *danseuse* this time culminating the pattern with *arabesques*. Then, after an initial combination of *arabesque, pirouette,* and *arabesque,* the dimensions of the dance broaden as the dancers twice cross the stage, pausing at front stage right for a long held *arabesque*.

The third and fourth parts of the *adagio* are not parallel to each other, as are parts one and two, nor does either resemble the earlier parts in its structure. Part three begins with a preludial effect: the dancers separate and run along arched lines to the rear of the stage, where they come together again. Most of this part unfolds in three passes from back to front, enriched with *arabesques* and *pirouettes*. In the second pass the ballerina is lifted by her partner; in the third she twice performs a combination which ends in a fall and pose on the cavalier's leg.

In the last part, a mechanical device is introduced which is referred to in the CN as a *reika*.[69] This seems to have been a track or guide along which a small platform travels; placed on the platform, a dancer can be drawn along the *reika* to give the illusion of gliding across the stage. After breaking the last pose of the preceding section, the Sugar Plum Fairy and her prince move 'to the *reika*' at the rear of the stage. Then they traverse the stage 'on the *reika*' from the audience's left to its right. This part of the dance is probably that depicted in the celebrated picture of Gerdt as Prince Coqueluche drawing Varvara Nikitina as the Sugar Plum Fairy on the surface of a shawl or cloth, as if by magic.

The couple return to centre stage for the final bars of the *adagio*. The ballerina performs *petits battements* as she slowly turns, supported by the cavalier's arm. To close, she performs a variant of her earlier fall: she turns twice, comes to an *attitude*, and moves free of the cavalier for a moment. He offers her his right arm during another *arabesque*, then shifts her to his left arm and lets her down.

The man's variation is missing in the CN, and neither the Reps nor press accounts provide an idea of it. In the woman's variation—the Dance of the Sugar Plum Fairy—the sources fail us again, not so drastically, but enough to make tentative anything more than a general description.[70] Both Reps indicate that the *presto* was cut; each gives a slightly different version of the new final cadence.

Short steps on *pointe*, *petite batterie*, an occasional *attitude*, presented in different combinations, are the most numerous components of the choreography. They produce an elegant, precise, mostly *à terre* effect. Phrase-by-phrase contrasts in structure are less pronounced than they had been in the *adagio*, though there is a sense of dynamic build-up: from delicate angularity in the first part of the dance, to circular shapes, to plainer but more virtuoso movements—*pirouettes* and *ronds de jambe* —near the end.

According to the CN, the coda of the *pas de deux* begins with the ballerina spinning along the diagonal from rear stage left in alternating *pirouettes* and *chaînés*. She runs back to the corner, where she is joined by her partner to traverse the same diagonal, he supporting her in several repetitions of the *pas de bourrée* and jump, alighting *en attitude*. He next turns her in place, twice again *en attitude*, after which they cross to front stage left. He walks around her in two turns; they run to stage right, where he walks around her in yet another turn.

They now separate in preparation for the final segment of the coda, he running directly back to the mid-point of stage right, she on a diagonal to the opposite side, thrice performing a *cabriole* plus *attitude* plus *chaîné*. The final figure is a zigzag pattern in which his path always crosses behind hers, moving in the opposite direction. The step sequence features a *grand jeté*, *attitude*, and *pirouette*. Two more turns mark the final cadence.[71]

The finale recalls all the dancers of the act. The opening statement, for the *corps*, is a thirty-two-bar period of a polonaise-like procession. Beginning from the sides, a line of couples traces a pattern to the back of the stage, turning inward towards the centre, then forward to the front, then outward and back up the sides. Every few steps their path is decorated with a burst of waltzing turns.

In Rep-I we read, above bar 33, 'All dance ... with Dell'Era and the Nutcracker and Clara', as if these characters occupied some central place on stage. Dell'Era, the Sugar Plum Fairy, would soon join the *entrées*, which begin in this bar and make up the next section of the dance, a reprise of the *divertissement*.[72]

The *corps de ballet* rejoins the dancing at bar 177. Leaving the women at the sides of the stage, the men take up positions, kneeling on one knee, in four columns in the middle while buffoons from the trepak pass through the columns in a serpentine pattern. The women then join their partners, each couple enclosed by a garland from the Waltz of the Flowers. The entire group moves to the rear of the stage and again to the front before returning to the sides, where they remain until the end of the dance. They raise their garlands one last time on the final chord.[73]

Of the principal sources, only the libretto gives any description of the apotheosis, which 'represents a large beehive with flying bees, closely guarding their riches.' Eight students from the theatre school represented the bees.

After the first performance there were calls for the composer and the balletmaster. Since this occasion was not as well documented as the first performance of *Sleeping Beauty*, we know little more than that Tchaikovsky, following a widely observed custom, attended a ceremonial dinner with a number of artists and members of the theatre staff.

While they were celebrating, the reviewers of *Nutcracker* were at work, and as we read their writings we see little hint of what the ballet was to become. Most of the reasons for their displeasure have already been mentioned: the flaws of the libretto, the mixed spectacle of opera and ballet (no one, as Laroche would do later, considered the two as interrelated works), choreography derived from Petipa. In fact *Nutcracker* did not stimulate much true criticism, and of what was written about it, some is contradictory (Olga Preobrazhanskaya as Columbine was 'nice' to one observer, 'insipid' to another), some downright silly (the likening of the wordless chorus in the Waltz of the Snowflakes to the Wolf's Glen Scene in

Weber's *Der Freischütz*). In general the reviewers did not see beyond their irritations, as a sampling of their criticisms will suffice to convey.

First of all, *Nutcracker* can in no event be called a ballet. It does not comply with even one of the demands made of a ballet. Ballet, as a basic genre of art, is mimed drama and consequently must contain all the elements of normal drama. On the other hand, there must be a place in ballet for plastic attitudes and dances, made up of the entire essence of classical choreography. There is nothing of this in *Nutcracker*. There is not even a subject . . .[74]

That *Nutcracker* represented the latest stage in the decline of the Petersburg ballet was the point of a diatribe by 'Old Balletomane':

We, the old balletomanes, in times past went to the ballet for aesthetic enjoyment and in fact admired:
(1) A programme where artists could show their talent for mime;
(2) Dances, produced so that all balletic strengths [personnel] could show their choreographic art;
(3) The first *danseuse*, who in all ballets was usually assigned a leading part;
(4) Décor and costumes.
Only all of these taken together satisfied us, true adherents of pure art . . . And now? Nothing! Ballet is sliding downhill, having lost its footing, and is moving away, towards some kind of fragile and sugary *Nutcracker* . . . *Nutcracker* satisfies only in the sense of décor and costumes . . .[75]

The production was too elaborate for Tchaikovsky. The morning after the first performance, reporting his pleasure at its success to his brother Anatole, he wrote, 'The production of both [opera and ballet] was magnificent, the ballet even too magnificent. The eyes weary from this luxury.'[76] Vladimir Telyakovsky found the production to be in unimaginable bad taste, describing some of the artists in the last act as being 'dressed like fancy brioches from Fillipov's patisserie.'[77]

As regards Ivanov's dependence on Petipa, Skalkovsky observed, in addition to his remarks about *La mère Gigogne* (see p. 216, above), that the public had seen the like of the Waltz of the Snowflakes before, in Petipa's *Camargo* and *The Daughter of the Snows*.[78]

Apart from some sniping about its not being *dansante*, the music of *Nutcracker* was praised. Some reviewers found it necessary to keep the music at a distance from the story:

. . . it is a pity that so much fine music is expended on nonsense unworthy of attention, but the music in general is excellent: that designated for dances is *dansante* and that designated for the ear and for the fantasy is imaginative. Of Tchaikovsky's three ballets . . . *Nutcracker* is the best, its music indeed not for the normal ballet audience.[79]

Comparisons with *Sleeping Beauty* were inevitable. Laroche observed that Tchaikovsky made 'innocent loans from his own pocket' by using in *Nutcracker* devices of style and structure he had already used in *Sleeping*

Beauty.[80] Tchaikovsky's former student Mikhail Ivanov argued that comparisons of the two ballets should not necessarily favour *Sleeping Beauty*:

Yielding both in specifically choreographic suitability and in the sense of freshness to the music of *Sleeping Beauty*, the music of *Nutcracker* nevertheless deserves a different, much more kindly attitude with respect to the earlier work. The author's technical mastery speaks forth in brilliant fashion in this score at each step, and to enumerate those pages where Mr Tchaikovsky shows himself to be a magnificent symphonist and savant of the orchestra would take too long: such pages are too numerous.[81]

These remarks raise two central questions for analysis: In what way is the score of *Nutcracker* particularly distinguished? And how did Tchaikovsky reconcile his music with the libretto?

Tchaikovsky invents a special sound world in *Nutcracker* with his orchestration. More than a matter of pure technique, of the imaginative selection of timbres, it creates the childlike atmosphere of the ballet. One striking precedent for a combination used in *Nutcracker* comes in a work without a descriptive title: the *marche miniature* from the *Suite No. 1* for orchestra. So like *Nutcracker* is this music that one could imagine its ready transfer into the ballet had Petipa but requested a procession (for example) of the magical inhabitants of Confiturembourg. Scored for piccolo, flutes, oboes, clarinets, triangle, bells, and *divisi* violins, the *marche* is sustained at a high tessitura and a quiet dynamic for the bulk of these forces, creating a sound that anticipates many *pas*sages in the overture and march of the ballet. In particular the bells, which play the principal melody accompanied by *pizzicato* violins (at bars 58 ff.), directly anticipate the sound and treatment of the celesta of the Sugar Plum Fairy's variation.

Act I of *Nutcracker* also echoes the opening scene of *The Queen of Spades* in sound and stage action. For the theatrical device of children playing soldiers Tchaikovsky may have been indebted to Bizet (whose *Carmen* he repeatedly praised). The children in Tchaikovsky's opera are not, however, Bizet's street urchins, but children of the gentry; Fritz Silberhaus would happily have joined them, and the music which accompanies their military formations could have fitted into *Nutcracker* with ease (see pp. 230–1, below, for specific parallels of instrumentation).

As it relates to orchestration, the phantasmagorical element in *Nutcracker* has its own precedents in the *skazochnyi* timbres assigned to Fairy Carabosse—Tchaikovsky never elaborated that sound image more extensively than in his portrayal of Drosselmayer and his part marvellous, part diabolical designs. In Act I this special sound world takes on structural importance in that the traversal from the everyday reality of the party to the special reality which Clara alone perceives—for such is one way of describing the formal pattern of the act—is accompanied by increasing prominence of the low winds (bassoon and cor anglais), brass (trombone and tuba), viola, and special effects on the other instruments. We first hear these sounds with the striking of nine o'clock at bar 41 of the opening scene, in the short canon starting with the bassoon and clarinet which forms a distinctive contrast with the elegant if more conventional scoring of the music around it. The illumination of the Christmas tree 'as if by enchantment' later in this number (bars 73–8) triggers a similar response in Tchaikovsky—in which the triplet fluttering of the woodwinds corresponds to the flickering candles on the tree.

When Drosselmayer arrives, Tchaikovsky seems to take pleasure in the unabashed, undiluted oddity of his sounds, starting with the viola, accompanied by the trombones and tuba (Ex. 60).

Ex. 60   No. 4, *Scène dansante*, bars 1–8

Responding to Petipa's instructions, Tchaikovsky catches nicely, in the passage which follows this, the balletmaster's call for Drosselmayer's music to combine suggestions of the very serious with the sinister and droll. The oddity suggested at the beginning of No. 4 by the violas and trombones turns into seriousness when each note is heavily accented; the muted horns add just the right sinister effect (Ex. 61).

Ex. 61   No. 4, *Scène dansante*, bars 8–11

Another change of instrumentation a few bars after this conveys the councillor's droll aspect. Tchaikovsky substitutes horns and trumpets for violas, cellos and double basses for the low brass, and adds violins and flutes in their upper register (Ex. 62).

Ex. 62   No. 4, *Scène dansante*, bars 19–25

The beginning of the night scene in No. 6, with the ethereal combination of muted strings, flute, and harp, cannot escape Drosselmayer's influence (just as the dream scene in *Sleeping Beauty* could not escape that of Carabosse); it is mingled with quiet but distinctive collaborations of tuba, bass clarinet, and piccolo. And the sound accompanying the mysterious illumination of the Nutcracker's bed is positively Carabossian (Ex. 63).

Ex. 63   No. 6, *Scène*, bars 71–4

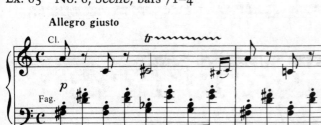

The magical growth of the Christmas tree leads us for a moment away from *grotesquerie* towards a different glance back at *Sleeping Beauty*. The impressive build-up of sound here is the equal of anything associated with the Lilac Fairy and imparts to the passage a bigness of expression exceptional for *Nutcracker*. In particular the harmonic effect created by the introduction of the flat submediant of A major at the culmination of this passage is exactly comparable in its chord grammar to the moment when the Lilac Fairy freezes Florestan's kingdom into sleep, and no less imposing (Ex. 64).

Ex. 64   No. 6, *Scène*, bars 156–60

In the battle scene (No. 7) Tchaikovsky portrays the warring parties with characteristic sounds: the toylike imagery emanating from the overture and march versus the Drosselmayeresque intonations of the army of mice. The technique is one of manipulating not only sonority but also registra-

Ex. 65   No. 7, *Scène*, bars 25–30

Ex. 65 *(cont.)*

tion and varying rhythm—higher registers and straightforward, fanfare-like rhythmic motives for the toys, lower ranges and disjunct, concocted motivic shapes for the mice, as observed in their principal theme (played by the bassoons and bass clarinet in Ex. 65).

The special orchestral colours associated with Drosselmayer cease with the battle (apart from a direct recall of the battle music in No. 11). From this point on the councillor makes his presence felt more in the tonalities than in the sonorities of the music (see pp. 235–41, below). Tchaikovsky, meanwhile, enlivens other parts of the score with picturesque orchestration. His ability to suggest the first intimations of a snowstorm at the beginning of the Waltz of the Snowflakes yields one of the most charming moments of musical landscape painting ever composed by him (Ex. 66).

'The feeling of trembling from the cold and the play of the moonlight on the delicate snowflakes', writes Laroche, 'is transmitted not only in virtuoso instrumentation but also—if my feeling can be trusted—in the very theme, its rhythm and harmony.'[82]

We need not rely exclusively on stylistic observations to discover Tchaikovsky's special concern for instrumental effects in *Nutcracker*. Some evidence is clearly documented, and the most celebrated case is first described in a letter he wrote to Jurgenson on 3 June 1891:

I have a request for you. I discovered in Paris a new orchestral instrument, something between a small piano and a glockenspiel with a divinely marvellous sound . . . It is called the 'Celesta Mustel' and it costs 1,200 francs. It can be purchased in Paris only at the inventor Mustel's. I would like to ask you to order this instrument. You will lose nothing on it, for you will lend it out for all concerts where *The Voevoda* [a symphonic poem in which Tchaikovsky planned to use it] is to be performed. And after that you will sell it to the Directorate of the Theatres, when they need it for the ballet . . . But in the meantime I would prefer it to be

Ex. 66 No. 9, *Valse des flocons de neige*, bars 1–8

shown to nobody, for I am afraid that Rimsky-Korsakov and Glazunov will get wind of it and use its unusual effects sooner than me . . .[83]

Jurgenson complied, and through the summer the instrument continued to occupy Tchaikovsky's thoughts, especially that his precedence be respected. 'For God's sake', he wrote to Jurgenson on 22 August,

. . . have a thought that no one besides myself hears the sounds of this miraculous instrument before it is played in my works, where it will be used first . . . If the instrument comes first to Moscow, then keep it away from outsiders, and if to Peter[sburg], then have Osip Ivanovich [Jurgenson] watch over it.[84]

The celesta caused Tchaikovsky another vexation—that its tuning could not be adjusted to the Petersburg *Kammerton*—but it blended well with the orchestra at its début on 7 March 1892 when the composer conducted the first performance of the *Nutcracker Suite*. Whatever his peevishness about keeping the instrument a secret, Tchaikovsky's artistic instinct, especially as it related to transforming Petipa's verbal instructions into sound, served him well: the celesta is associated with the Sugar Plum Fairy, and is perfectly suited in her variation to the task of expressing in music Petipa's call for the sound of the sprays of a fountain.

In his travels of 1891 Tchaikovsky had conducted concerts in Kiev.

Among the musicians there was a flautist and former harmony student of his, Alexander Vasilevich Khimichenko, who recalled of this occasion:

During one of the rehearsals Peter Ilyich was taking a rest in the régisseur's room. I went over to him and we began to talk about the conservatory. Peter Ilyich remembered that in Petersburg he once studied flute, but, in his words, he had forgotten everything. He expressed regret over this and asked me to show him something of the 'what's what' among interesting devices of playing. I performed for him the variations from *Carnaval* of Ciardi, and used during this an example of the device called *frulato*. Peter Ilyich was attracted to this and asked me to repeat again this manner of trilling on the chromatic scale across the entire register of the flute, which produces the impression of a cascade . . .[85]

Four days before the concert at which the celesta was first heard in Petersburg, Tchaikovsky, on the trail of *frulato*, wrote to Khimichenko:

I have a big request to make. Do you remember once in Kiev during my last visit in the régisseur's room you showed me and the others present an effect on the flute which I very much liked? It seems you called it by some Italian name, something like 'flutrando', 'flustando', that is, by some word which had the letters 't', 'r', 'l'. I would very much like to use this effect in my new ballet. Therefore I most earnestly ask you to answer me quickly the following questions:

(1) The name, the terms of this effect?
(2) How is it produced? . . .
(3) Can one or two or three flutes at once play thirds or sixths, or in sixth chords such a scale as [musical example]?

In general, enlighten me about this delightful effect, and write me several musical examples of it.[86]

Khimichenko did this, and to him belongs some of the credit for the *frulato* at the beginning of No. 11 when the cascading river of rose-oil broadens in anticipation of the arrival of Clara and the Nutcracker.

In the Hol of *Nutcracker*, at the head of No. 5, above the parts for children's trumpet and drum, with cuckoo, quail, and cymbals *ad libitum* on stage, Tchaikovsky writes: 'These instruments [the trumpets and drums] are the same as used in *The Queen of Spades* in the first scene. In the designated places the children must play them on the stage.' I. N. Ivanov, a régisseur of the Kirov Theatre, takes up the matter from there:

In the 1891–2 season [sic] we, the students of the St Petersburg Theatre School, were rehearsing the new ballet *Nutcracker*, a production of M. I. Petipa and L. I. Ivanov, music of P. I. Tchaikovsky. In this ballet all the students were used, and rehearsals went all day every day. The smallest students were used in the dances and scenes, 'children at the Christmas tree', in the first act of the ballet. When we had already learned our dances, the galop and the *Grossvater*, at one of the rehearsals we were led into the large rehearsal hall where the ballet company was rehearsing. R. Drigo, the ballet conductor, met us and gave us children's musical toys. These toys were various types and forms of children's horns, whistles, cuckoos, which would make sounds when you pressed them, rattles of metal and wood, and similar instruments, which, as we were to learn later, were specially ordered from the firm of Zimmermann and prepared in a key ordered by the composer.

R. Drigo sat at the piano and said that when he gave us a downbeat we should begin to play on the instruments. Several times we tried to do what was demanded of us, but evidently the desired results were not forthcoming, and Drigo proposed to us that we take the instruments with us and practise for the next rehearsal. The tutor who was with us asked for this not to be done, fearing the possible damage or breaking of the instruments. It was decided that we would practise before each rehearsal. On one of the following days, after dogged lessons with us in the presence of the balletmaster M. I. Petipa, and with a gentleman sitting next to him, beautifully dressed in a white suit, and who from time to time made a sign to Drigo and who had a lively discussion with M. I. Petipa—we demonstrated our success several times, trying more precisely to remember the downbeat and the required rhythm. Unfortunately, our achievements were declared unsatisfactory, and after quite a long discussion in French between M. I. Petipa, the gentleman in the white suit, and R. Drigo, the latter told us that whoever could play was permitted to; 'kak mozh' [as you can] said M. I. Petipa, smiling. At this rehearsal we realized that sitting with M. I. Petipa was the composer of the ballet *Nutcracker* and the opera *Iolanthe*—P. I. Tchaikovsky. At all subsequent rehearsals in the theatre with orchestra we saw him in the stalls, often coming up to the conductor's desk and speaking with Drigo. After the first performance of the ballet *Nutcracker*, when we sat down to eat in the school, the Inspector V. P. Pisnyachevsky came into the dining room and told us that P. I. Tchaikovsky, who was at the Director I. A. Vsevolozhsky's, asked it to be conveyed to all students that he was very pleased with the performance and the performers, he thanked all the participants very much, and was sending sweets. Two school porters brought in large baskets, and all the students of the boys' and girls' divisions and the tutors received a box of beautiful sweets. This was P. I. Tchaikovsky's last ballet, and we never had occasion to see him in the theatre again.[87]

Apparently, then, at bars 137–43 and 162–8 of No. 5 there was active support of the orchestra by the joyful noises of at least some of the children on stage. There is no indication, however, that the use of this stage band passed into the performing tradition of *Nutcracker*.

To summarize: the special orchestral effects in *Nutcracker* may be classified into three groups on the basis of the libretto: the images of childhood suggested by the overture and march; more fearsome and peculiar sounds associated with Drosselmayer; and effects associated with non-threatening magical occurrences, produced by the celesta, *frulato*, and other instruments of Confiturembourg.

If the story of *Nutcracker* and Petipa's instructions to Tchaikovsky provided opportunities for the composer to demonstrate his extraordinary talent for using the orchestra to evoke atmosphere, describe stage action, and portray character, the scenario posed problems which affected other aspects of the score. One early critic of the ballet sensed that Tchaikovsky's demonstrative concern for sonority betrayed a deficiency elsewhere. 'Mr Tchaikovsky', he pointed out, 'wrote elegant music which is distinguished by great achievements of technique and orchestration but at times not a high level of melodic invention.'[88]

While *Nutcracker* hardly lacks imaginative themes, it is undeniable that some of them are exceedingly simple, Tchaikovsky having sometimes emphasized their simplicity—plainness, even—through repetition or blatant exposure in the orchestral texture. Clara's lullaby and the Confiturembourg theme (at the opening of No. 10 and in the apotheosis) are the closest Tchaikovsky comes in *Nutcracker* to the melodies of the Lilac Fairy and the swans as regards repetition of themes in support of the drama. But these themes do not match their predecessors' ability to command the listener's attention, lacking both dramatic implications and musical character, and it is curious that Tchaikovsky chose to repeat these particular ones. (The imperfections of the libretto and the modest scope of the entire work may have deterred the composer from unifying the ballet by repeating themes first announced in the overture.) The theme which sounds as Clara and the Nutcracker arrive in Confiturembourg illustrates the combination of plain melody and pretentious exposition, as does that of the *adagio* of the *pas de deux*. Both are little more than descending octaves (Exx. 67–8).

On hearing them one involuntarily recalls and cannot help appreciating Constant Lambert's point about the quality of the ballet being related to the quality of its melody.[89] Thus the composer's dissatisfaction with the

Ex. 67   No. 11, *Scène*, bars 17–19

Ex. 68   No. 14, *pas de deux*, bars 47–8

scenario may have expressed itself in what might be considered a default of inspiration.

Laroche finds a virtue in the studied simplicity of the music of *Nut-cracker*. After quoting Tchaikovsky's admiration for a young composer who did not fear triviality, Laroche admires *Nutcracker* for the same reason:

... it will be clear that true riches do not hunger to put themselves forward as a demonstration. As for the courage not to avoid triviality, that is, the ironic tendency to be frightened away by a pleasant melody, to be embarrassed for using widely accepted accompaniments, I will remind you of the chorus without words performed in the wings during the winter scene. I think that in the first half of the 1870s our composer would never have decided to be simple to this degree. There are yet other places in the music of *Nutcracker* where this new simplicity is evident, though not in such a striking way ... The foppish and courteous little march with the sentimentally coquettish cantilena in the trio, which lies at the basis of the little overture, characterizes the surroundings and the atmosphere with a pointed-ness little suited to Tchaikovsky. If it were not for a contrapuntal variation, which spoils nothing but gives the author away, the counterfeit would be irreproachable: both the main part and the trio could have been written by Auber.[90]

Borrowed music must be taken into account in an assessment of melody in *Nutcracker*, for borrowing, like the triviality which Laroche finds so attractive, may be rooted at least in part in a lapse of inspiration.

Nutcracker contains more borrowed melodies than *Swan Lake* and *Sleeping Beauty* combined, although it is little more than half the length of either of the earlier works.[91] Petipa specifies the use of one borrowed tune, the French song 'Bon voyage, Mr Dumolet', for the parents' galop (No. 3, bars 61–118). It is one of two—the other is the carmagnole—listed by him in an early sketch of *Nutcracker*.[92] Tchaikovsky apparently chose some others on his own: *La mère Gigogne* is based on 'Giroflé, Girofla' and 'Cadet Rousselle' (Nos. 63 and 58, respectively, of Colet and Dumersan's *Chants et chansons populaires de la France*). The *Grossvater* is a German popular tune, and the Arabian Dance is based on a Georgian lullaby which Ippolitov-Ivanov notated and sent to the composer.

The origin and inspiration of the melodies are only one problematical aspect of *Nutcracker*. Turning to the pattern of the music, we discover that the libretto is responsible for choreographic deficiencies which in turn affect the score. The absence of a grand *ballabile* and classical *pas* in Act I, of which Vsevolozhsky complained, deprives this act of a traditional musical focal point. Tchaikovsky is forced to simulate one by linking together short pieces which, if judged from the perspective of the large musical numbers of the earlier ballets, are imperfect and illusory substitutes.

The middle numbers of Act I illustrate this. Charming in effect, and continuously responsive to the libretto, these numbers are nevertheless short-breathed, almost to the point of nervousness. Number 3, for example, begins with forty-four bars of *presto*, continues with sixteen of *andante*, and ends with fifty-eight of *allegro*—as it must if the demands of the action are to be satisfied with an appropriate sense of pacing. The libretto therefore precludes any sustained statement of music and dance together before the Waltz of the Flowers, since the battle scene is mimed and the choreographically exquisite Waltz of the Snowflakes is accompanied by music inspired in its understatement by the insubstantial qualities of snowflakes in nature. The need in Act I of *Nutcracker* for a musically substantial danced number directly relevant to the narrative—a pause, perhaps, but not an aside—is simply disregarded. It has no rose *adagio*.

Rhythmic complexity in dances is another aspect of Tchaikovsky's musical style which was made plain in *Sleeping Beauty* but is somewhat frustrated in *Nutcracker*. The *pas de chaises*, Drosselmayer's unwrapping of the boxes (No. 4, bars 44–98), recalls in the intricacy of its flow the waltz of the pages and young girls in the prologue of *Sleeping Beauty*. But we are not sure this number was danced. Indeed, throughout much of *Nutcracker* necessity may have prevented Tchaikovsky's giving free rein to his fascination for rhythmic involvement, because complex rhythms would not be practical in children's dances. Moreover, since rhythmic characteristics play a role in the assessment of melody, one must reconsider the simplicity of the march, Clara's polka and lullaby, the *Grossvater*, and other passages for the children in light of their participation.

Such practical considerations do not apply to the Waltz of the Snowflakes, in which Tchaikovsky carries rhythmic disjunction to the furthest point of any of his ballets. The main theme is perceived exclusively in duple time (Ex. 69).

Ex. 69   No. 9, *Valse des flocons de neige*, bars 33–45

It is possible that the eminently un-waltzlike rhythm of this waltz was responsible for Lev Ivanov's disregarding the individual bar in favour of larger spans of time.

Invention and necessity together served Tchaikovsky in finding a satisfactory method of organizing the entire ballet. Melody and orchestration contribute to that organization, as we have seen, by following the narrative, but key once again emerges as the most powerful, if subtle, organizing device of the whole score. In *Swan Lake* and *Sleeping Beauty* Tchaikovsky apparently perceived a basis for the tonal plan in the story. *Nutcracker's* dramatic faults precluded a key scheme which would be intelligible and at the same time allow itself to be allied to the libretto. (The realization of this dilemma may have caused the composer's anguish in Rouen.) Clearly, some compromise was necessary if he wished to satisfy the basic artistic requirement for tonal unity.

A scrutiny of the score suggests how he found that compromise (we must turn to the score, since Tchaikovsky explains nothing of his thinking on the subject). His procedure seems to have been to follow the narrative as far as he could, from the Christmas party to Confiturembourg; then to fashion a method of dealing with the dramatically static Act II which preserved some fidelity to the libretto while allowing a satisfactory musical sense of resolution when the curtain fell. To accomplish this he drew on devices used earlier in *Swan Lake* and *Sleeping Beauty*.

The tonal organization of *Nutcracker* is modelled on that of *Swan Lake*: it is built around keys distantly separated from one another on the circle of fifths. Hence Act I begins in Bb major, and ends, at the end of the Waltz of the Snowflakes, in E major, having abandoned the everyday reality of Silberhaus's living room. In Act II, where the narrative fails to move forward, let alone return to everyday reality, Tchaikovsky lets himself be guided by compositional dictates, and chooses to end the ballet in the same key as he began it:

Overture	Snowflakes	Confiturembourg	Apotheosis
Bb	E minor/major	E	Bb

Act I deserves attention for the method by which the main change in tonal direction takes place. The overture and first four numbers of *Nutcracker* have much in common with the prologue of *Sleeping Beauty*. Both sections represent somewhat less than a quarter of their respective ballets, and they share some large-scale tonal movements that relate to the drama. The prologue of *Sleeping Beauty* is designed around a progression of rising perfect fourths. The last step in this progression is thwarted by the drama in the unexpected arrival of the Fairy Carabosse, who throws into disarray the prospect of an uneventful baptism, and thus, musically, an arrival in the expected key. In like manner *Nutcracker*, after an initial movement by thirds between the overture and the first number, follows a pattern of perfect fourths:

Overture	No. 1	No. 2	No. 3	No. 4
Bb	D	G	G–C–F	[Bb?]

The last step in this progression, to Bb at the beginning of No. 4, is also thwarted by the drama, this time by the unexpected arrival of Drosselmayer, who throws the Christmas party into disarray. Without this surprise the celebrations in both ballets would have come to an uneventful conclusion. Because it happens, the story and the tonal plan are forced off into new directions, with the result that the expected, but suddenly withheld, harmonic arrival (coincidentally at the beginning of the fourth number in both works) must await the end of the ballet. The likenesses between Carabosse and Drosselmayer as characters and in Tchaikovsky's sound portraits of them are thus reinforced in the score by the method and positioning of their first appearances. The device is effective for its imperfection: the implicit tonal arrival, prepared and logical, is offered at a point too early for any corresponding resolution of the dramatic action to be credible. The unexpected event nevertheless provides a fresh impetus to the drama after a substantial exposition.

The keys associated with Drosselmayer warrant mention because they support the drama. From the libretto it is clear that his presence is fearsome. Indeed, because his image is to be seen in the face of the clock just before the mice appear, the fantastic events of the night scene—to say nothing of those in Confiturembourg, which develop directly out of the night scene—may be perceived as the outcome of Drosselmayer's thoughts. From the standpoint of tonal structure Drosselmayer's arrival may be expected to turn the music towards E major, the key of the magic kingdom. And so it does.

Part of the special musical image which Tchaikovsky introduces with Drosselmayer's appearance on stage—the odd rhythms and striking sonorities—is harmonic, or, more specifically, scalar. In contrast to the unequivocal cadential orientation of the music of Nos. 2 and 3, No. 4 opens in a cadentially nondescript way—the chords have points of rest, but they do not go together in patterns that produce a sense of key. Tchaikovsky surely intends this as part of his characterization of Drosselmayer, but more important for the tonal architecture of the act than this calculated indefiniteness is the scale he introduces at this point: the scale of E minor, coming when Bb major was the logical choice based on the preceding sequence of keys. For the first dozen bars of No. 4 Tchaikovsky wavers between hints of E minor and G major (the other key shared by this scale), then clearly moves to E minor in the cadence at bar 19. A new direction in the tonal plan, away from the key of the overture, has been announced. Closer analysis reveals that Drosselmayer's music does not stay consistently in E minor: to do so would spoil the effect. Tchaikovsky doubtless preferred to keep the councillor's music in a state of change for reasons of characterization, contenting himself by projecting the change which has come over the Christmas party by means of other musical devices. The rhythmic disjunction of the dances of the dolls and their keys—A major, and its parallel and relative minors—contribute to the impression of strangeness and of nonconformity to those musical norms established in the overture and first three numbers.

The keys of No. 5 are the logical continuation of the tonal premises of No. 4. The scene begins in A major as Drosselmayer presents another doll—the Nutcracker—to Clara (but notice the inflections towards E minor in bars 19–26). Echoing the movement upward by perfect fourths associated with the party dances of No. 3, Tchaikovsky here moves upward by a perfect fourth to arrive at D major for Clara's polka.

The continuation of No. 5 brings more hints of future magic, including what may be considered one of the most important: the shift out of one of the party keys, C major (found at the entrance of the *incroyables* in No. 3, and shortly to return in the interruptions of the mischievous children and the *Grossvater*), as Fritz throws down the broken Nutcracker, up a semitone to Db major when Clara retrieves the toy and consoles it. This raising of the key corresponds with Clara's heightened feelings towards the Nutcracker, and may have been intended as the moment when her imagination opens up to a state of receptivity for the miraculous events which she will presently witness.[93] This is an eminently Hoffmannesque touch—emphasizing the awareness of a new reality in a central character—and Tchaikovsky gives credence to such an interpretation of Db major by returning to it in those critical first moments after Clara comes back downstairs (No. 6: the *moderato con moto* at bar 49, from the preceding cadence in C major first to Ab, then to Db at bar 58).

The central event of No. 6, following the magical illumination of the Nutcracker's bed and the appearance of the mice, is the growing of the Christmas tree. Here Tchaikovsky permits no doubt over the arrival at A major, sustaining an association with Drosselmayer which was introduced with the dances of the mechanical dolls in No. 4. The battle scene likewise cadences in A (A minor), while maintaining the harmonic variety appropriate to its activity for 110 bars (after beginning, significantly, with another hint of E minor in bars 1–17). A logical pattern is emerging in the harmonic structure. After an unfulfilled attempt to establish Bb major through the sequential pattern of the first three numbers, Nos. 4–7 reorient the music—amid various other keys which respond to the immediate contingencies of the narrative—to A major/minor:

No. 4		No. 5	No. 6	No. 7
(e)⟶ a ⟵⟶ A		A (e)	⟶ A	(e)⟶ a
Unwrapping	1st dance	Drosselmayer gives	Christmas	Battle scene
of dolls	of dolls	Nutcracker to	tree	
		Clara	grows	

Of the subordinate tonalities used in this part of the ballet, E minor and C major are most frequently inflected, the first at Drosselmayer's arrival, at the beginning of No. 5, and again at the beginning of the battle, the second in narrative contexts associated with the everyday reality of the party. The harmonic distance of E minor from the initial Bb, and its proximity to the approaching E major of Confiturembourg, stresses by means of key relationship the importance of Drosselmayer and the implications of his visit for the rest of the ballet: when the councillor arrives, Tchaikovsky directs the tonal plan towards Confiturembourg. We have here in addition more evidence of the special meanings of E minor and E major in Tchaikovsky's thought. Just as he associates E minor with Carabosse and the threatening aspects of Aurora's fate in *Sleeping Beauty*, so in *Nutcracker* does he associate it with danger to Clara. Whereas E major is associated in *Sleeping Beauty* with the Lilac Fairy, here it is associated with Clara's deliverance from threats and fear in Confiturembourg.

The C major which serves as the principal key of the lovely journey music (No. 8) is theoretically indistinguishable from the C major of the party scene. But the expressive purposes to which Tchaikovsky puts it here and its place in the harmonic context of the middle of the ballet warrant giving it a new connotation. It is the important subordinate of E major, the triad of its flat submediant. A suggestion of ravishment inseparable from all the music between the end of the battle and the arrival of Clara and the Nutcracker in the land of sweets, music principally in the keys of C major and E major, forms a powerful link between *Nutcracker* and *Sleeping Beauty*, where the same two keys accompany the Lilac Fairy's magic in the prologue and Act I, and return in the music of Aurora's magnificent *adagio* in the last act. In *Nutcracker* the arrival in E marks the last stage in the alliance of key and narrative:

No. 8	No. 9	No. 10	No. 11
Journey	Waltz of the Snowflakes	Scene: Confiturembourg	Scene: arrival of Clara and the Nutcracker
C	e→E	E	E→C (bars 17–29)

At the end of No. 11 Tchaikovsky once again finds himself, as he had at the beginning of Act III of *Sleeping Beauty*, finished with the story without having reached a musical conclusion. As before, he solves this problem by compositional reprise: in both ballets musical ideas used in the *divertissement* recall, sometimes transformed, ideas familiar from earlier parts of the work. And in both, the classical *pas* which comes soon before the final number initiates a tonal progression which leads to the long-delayed arrival in the principal key.[94]

As regards tonal analysis, the first two numbers of the *divertissement* —the Spanish and Arabian Dances, in Eb major and G minor, respectively—are the most innocuous or the most provocative of the entire act. The first dance recalls nothing in *Nutcracker* so much as it does the variation of the Gold Fairy in *Sleeping Beauty* (for which it could easily serve if purged of its syncopations). Neither Eb major nor G minor have been used earlier in the ballet, except where Tchaikovsky took care to prepare Eb major in the preceding number (No. 11), both at the end of the number and in the return of the music of the Nutcracker's narration (bars 95–116). Such preparation admits of no ambiguity—the composer obviously wants Eb—but it does raise the question of whether this key is intended to be interpreted as some positive step in the overall harmonic development of the ballet. It is related to the Bb of the final number exactly as Drosselmayer's A major in No. 4 is related to the E major at mid-point. On the other hand, it may be intended as evidence that the harmonic discourse has in fact *stopped* developing, that Tchaikovsky has already begun to compose the music of the dramatically static *divertissement* in the way he always did—according to the whims of his instinct, without particular regard for the tonal plan.

The same question, of possible relation to keys used earlier, may be raised with regard to the Arabic Dance. Neither the Spanish nor the Arabian Dance contributes to the compositional reprise, which begins only in the next number: they are anomalies in the key pattern of the ballet. We are left, then, with either the innocuous interpretation—that Tchaikovsky chose these two keys because (as Laroche suggests) God willed it that way; or with the provocative one—that by introducing keys with no established association in the tonal plan, the composer marked the decisive break of the key scheme with the narrative, the point in the libretto after which he can no longer sustain a series of coherent tonalities responsive to the story line. If one accepts the second interpretation, these dances produce great harmonic tension where the stage activity is the most innocent—at the beginning of the traditional *divertissement*. Because this harmonic tension is produced by the key's lack of relationship to those keys associated with the narrative aspects of the ballet, it may be considered more acute than the tension produced by the tritonal relationship between the keys which organize the ballet, for the tritone at least reinforces an intelligible parallel in the story.

The remainder of *Nutcracker* tends to support the second interpretation, for signs of coherence and relationship begin recurring almost immediately after the Arabian Dance, leaving these two, in retrospect, isolated. The Chinese Dance marks the beginning of the compositional reprise by a return to the beginning of the ballet—it is the first number in Bb major since the overture.[95] The trepak, which comes next, enriches the scope of the reprise by recalling not key but rhythm—of the dance of Columbine and Harlequin. The Dance of the Mirlitons, a polka in D major, is a transformed reference to Clara's dance with the Nutcracker, another polka in D. *La mère Gigogne*, the most substantial character dance of the *divertissement*, recalls in its key the most substantial key of the part of the ballet located just opposite it—the A major of Nos. 4–7 (which occupied the beginning of roughly the second quarter of the work, as this dance does roughly the end of the third quarter). The Waltz of the Flowers echos the Waltz of the Snowflakes in scope and in the size of its roster of dancers, and the waltz of the first dolls in its relatively straightforward rhythm. It also sustains the importance of the waltz as the most important type of ensemble dance in the ballet by this appearance between the Snowflakes and the coda.

With the *pas de deux*, Tchaikovsky begins to pull the strands of compositional reprise together into a distinctive pattern with unequivocal references to the keys heard at the opening of the ballet. The entire *pas* is caught up in the process of balancing the end of the work with the beginning (see p. 149, above, for the parallel device in *Sleeping Beauty*):

Overture	Scene	March	. . .	*Pas de deux*	Coda/Apotheosis
	No. 1	No. 2		No. 14	No. 15
				adagio Coda	
B^b	D	G		G [b, e] D	B^b

There can be no doubt that Tchaikovsky tried to give *Nutcracker* a tonal unity, despite the faults of the libretto. But how did he maintain a connection with Confiturembourg, still the setting of the action when the curtain falls, as the succession of tonalities worked its way back to the key of the overture? The answer is simply by melodic recall, by re-stating in the apotheosis the Confiturembourg theme from the opening of Act II. The harmony has turned full circle, but in the land of sweets the melody lingers on.

7

Swan Lake in St Petersburg

❧

Swan Lake was not forgotten in the twelve years between its last performance in Moscow and its first in St Petersburg. After bringing out a piano
arrangement of the score at the time of the first performance,
Tchaikovsky's publisher Jurgenson added to his catalogue in the 1880s
excerpts from the ballet for various performing forces, including arrangements of three dances for two pianos, four hands, by Claude Debussy.[1]
Plans for a Petersburg production of *Swan Lake* may have predated
Nutcracker, and even *Sleeping Beauty*.

The ballet received its last performance in Moscow on 2 January 1883, in
Joseph Hansen's second version. Following his departure from Moscow,
Hansen worked briefly at the Maly Theatre in St Petersburg, and in 1884 he
accepted an appointment as balletmaster of the Alhambra Theatre in
London. On 1 December of that year he produced a one-act ballet, *The
Swans*, at the Alhambra which appears to have been a variant of the second
act of *Swan Lake*. From a contemporary account we can gain some idea of
the work:

There is only one scene . . . illustrative of a lovely bit of woodland, with in the
background a lake where some marvellously realistic swans . . . glide to and fro and
arch their necks with all the grace and dignity of the genuine article. In the lake,
too, are floating a number of nymphs, who presently emerge . . . followed by a flock
of human swans, who carry their beaks on top of their heads, who are attired in
white satin, trimmed with swan's down, and who have real feathers for their—yes,
it must be written—for their tails . . . Presently they are pursued by a band of gay
cavaliers, armed with spears. They also dance delightfully, and, if we were disposed
to jest, we might call them very appropriately 'swan-hoppers'. Their leader, it
appears, is in love with the queen of the swans, and makes no attempt to conceal
this fact . . .[2]

There is no reference to Tchaikovsky; the score of *The Swans* was
composed by the Alhambra's *chef d'orchestre* Georges Jacoby. The music
began with a three-part chorus, *bouches fermées*, followed by a dance,
probably for the nymphs, with the rubrics, 'Les sirènes couchées au fond de
l'eau. Les cygnes nageant sur le lac.' An entry of the swans was next, and
then a dance of the swans, a sequence reminiscent of *Swan Lake*. In a
mimed scene the swans expressed fright at hearing hunting horns. The

hunters, after admiring the countryside, were about to leave when they discovered the swans. The swan queen appeared at this moment. A series of variations followed for different combinations of swans and hunters. In the finale 'the queen searches for Roland [the leader of the hunters]; when she sees him in the depths of the stage, drawn towards the lake by the *rusalkas*, the queen saves him, and then takes flight with him.' The performance ended with an apotheosis: 'Above the front of the stage, the swans descend amidst long veils that represent water [as the Bolshoy stage was 'wrapped in several rows of green tulle, which represented water' in Hansen's first production of *Swan Lake* in Moscow] . . . [and] weep at the loss of their companions . . . The queen and Roland cross the lake in a boat drawn by swans.'[3]

Early in 1886—about eight months before Tchaikovsky agreed to compose *Undine*—theatre officials in St Petersburg were thinking about producing one act of *Swan Lake*, as we learn from a single exchange of letters between Jurgenson and the composer. On 27 March the publisher wrote:

Today Altani [conductor of the Moscow opera] was here. He or Pchelnikov [Intendant of the Moscow theatres] received a private letter from Vsevolozhsky in which he asked that I send him the score and parts of one act of your ballet. He requests further that you select it. He wants to give one act this summer at Krasnoe Selo [which could have meant that Lev Ivanov would have been entrusted with the choreography] before the Tsar, and, understandably, he wants to give the best one.[4]

Jurgenson suggested Act IV, but Tchaikovsky in his reply rejected this choice, insisting that Act II, 'the best in all respects', be sent instead.[5]

Two years later *Swan Lake* was being considered for production again, this time in Prague. Act II was first performed there at the National Theatre on 21 February 1888, at the second of two concerts in which Tchaikovsky conducted some of his own works.[6] He noted in his diary: 'Swan Lake. *A moment of absolute happiness.*'[7] The balletmaster, August Berger, seems to have followed the 1877 libretto, but he changed the names of Siegfried and Benno to Jaroslav and Zdenek, respectively, assigned the latter part to a *danseuse* who performed it *en travestie*, and formulated a new programme of dances:

> *Entrée dansante*
> *Valse*: Odette and the *corps de ballet*
> *Adagio*
> *Variation dansante*: Odette
> *Pas d'action*: Odette, Jaroslav, *corps de ballet*, six students
> *Valse des fleurs*
> *Grand ensemble*: Odette, *corps de ballet*, students

The ballet was given eight performances in this production.[8]

Facts and circumstantial evidence have encouraged speculation that Vsevolozhsky continued to plan a revival of Swan Lake for St Petersburg after the proposal of 1886. In 1889, over six months before the first performance of Sleeping Beauty—in fact, the day after Tchaikovsky noted the completion of that ballet in his diary—we read, among entries concerning his activities in Moscow: 'The score of Swan Lake.'[9] This reference had nothing to do with publication (another seven years would pass before the orchestral score would be printed); it may have had something to do with sending the music (which was in Moscow, at Jurgenson's) to a prospective producer.

Even as Nutcracker was being readied for production, there were signs that preparations for Swan Lake were going forward. Sketches of costumes for Odile and for a swan maiden date from 1892, drawn by the artist who created the costumes for the production when it was finally realized.[10]

While the silence of Vsevolozhsky, of Modeste, and of the composer himself is puzzling, it defies credibility to suppose that such preparations would be made if a revival were not being considered seriously, and that the composer was not aware of it. A Moscow journal announced that Swan Lake, projected for a new production in the 1894–5 season, would be given in February of 1894.[11] Twice early in 1894 such a revival was announced in the Petersburg Gazette.[12] In the light of this evidence a passage in Petipa's memoirs, thought to be a reflection of his faulty memory, warrants consideration:

The ballet Swan Lake was produced for the first time in Moscow and had no success there. Having learned of this, I went to the Director and said to him that I could not assume that Tchaikovsky's music was bad, that his part of the work had no success; the problem was not in the music but in the production of the ballet, in the dances. I asked the Director to permit me to use Tchaikovsky's work, and, making use of the subject in my own way, to produce the ballet in Petersburg.

Mr Vsevolozhsky immediately agreed with me, we approached Tchaikovsky, and Swan Lake was produced here with great success.

Tchaikovsky was delighted, and said that never with anyone but Petipa would he write ballets.[13]

If we take it that Tchaikovsky's delight was at the prospect, rather than the realization, of the production, Petipa's statement may be true. Moreover, some of the balletmaster's sketches suggest that he was at one time planning the production of those parts of Swan Lake which Ivanov subsequently realized.[14]

The composer himself may have given some thought to revising Swan Lake for a production in Petersburg. Riccardo Drigo recalled: 'While the composer was still alive I knew of his dissatisfaction with the instrumentation of the ballet, and that he intended to take up the matter, but he never managed to do this.'[15] Drigo's orchestrations of three of Tchaikovsky's piano pieces from Op. 72, used in the revival, were published with the remark, 'Numéros intercalés dans le ballet par l'auteur lui-même.' And when in 1896 *Swan Lake* was performed in Moscow at the coronation festivities of Nikolai II, Arseny Koreshchenko, a former student of Tchaikovsky who reviewed the performances, expressed the opinion that revisions in the music had been made with the composer's approval.[16]

In 1893 a ballet called *Swan Lake* was announced for production in a private theatre in Moscow. 'For July and August, at the Fantasia Garden, the ballerina Pierina Legnani has been engaged, who is to appear in the ballets *Swan Lake* and *Sita's Heart* (an Indian legend in nine scenes)', we read in the *Moskovskie vedomosti* for 9 June. On 20 June *Swan Lake* is referred to as a short ballet. Then, on 2 July: 'The planned production of the ballet *Swan Lake* will not take place.' Circumstantial evidence supports the hypothesis that this *Swan Lake* may have been Hansen's *The Swans*. The leading dancers of the Fantasia season of 1893 had performed at the Alhambra. Pierina Legnani danced there between 1888 and 1897;[17] Giorgio Saracco, balletmaster at the Fantasia, had even danced in *The Swans*: one number in the score is marked 'galop pas de deux dansé par Mlle Bessone et Sr Saracco.' Saracco, furthermore, had connections in Petersburg, where he had produced Manzotti's *Excelsior* (in 1887) and had danced with Virginia Zucchi at the Maly Theatre in 1892. In 1896 he produced *Sleeping Beauty* at La Scala (its first production outside Russia), and he acted as the representative of the Italian ballet later in the same year at Petipa's half-century jubilee at the Maryinsky Theatre.

More than any of the events just described, Tchaikovsky's death in October 1893 was responsible for stimulating efforts to revive *Swan Lake*. The first important result of these efforts was a production of Act II for a memorial concert given on 17 and 22 February 1894.

In two essays about this concert Yury Slonimsky takes a dim view of the directorate's motives for producing it, claiming that Vsevolozhsky had acted under pressure from 'socio-artistic organizations', that the decision to produce *Swan Lake* was taken in haste ('There are no traces in the documents of 1893 of the directorate's decision to revive the ballet'), and that the decision to mount the entire ballet was contingent on the success of the separate act.[18] Nowhere does he cite a report from Vsevolozhsky to the Minister of the Imperial Court, written within a month of the composer's death:

As a consequence of Your Excellency's order, I have the honour to submit for approval this draft of a programme of a performance of a concert in the Maryinsky Theatre for the erection of a monument to Peter Ilyich Tchaikovsky, and most respectfully petition Your Excellency for permission to produce the performance-concert so designated no earlier than February, 1894, since before then there will not be time, in view of the new productions of opera and ballet, for studying the musical numbers selected for performance on that evening; to which I have the honour to add that it will not be possible, in my opinion, to make use of the musical forces of the conservatory, and that the Director of Theatres will have to make do with his own.

On the next folio are listed the pieces Vsevolozhsky proposed:
(1) Act I of the opera *The Maid of Orleans*.
(2) Overture and duet, 'if found', from the opera *Romeo and Juliet*, nowhere performed before.[19]
(3) One act of the ballet *Swan Lake*, proposed for production next season.
(4) Coronation cantata, with Russian décor and costumes.[20]
This document is dated 19 November 1893.

Vsevolozhsky's report makes clear that a production of the entire ballet was already in prospect in 1893, and that the mounting of one act of *Swan Lake* was simply for the memorial concert. This seems to be borne out by the fact that no attempt was made to treat Act II as an excerpt capable of standing on its own. *The Yearbook of the Imperial Theatres* offered no synopsis of the action; reviewers at the time of the performance had only the stage action from which to recount the story of the ballet:

The subject of the whole ballet is unknown to me, but judging from the second act, it is written on the theme of an old German fairy-tale ... Prince Siegfried (Mr Gerdt), his friend Benno, and several knights enter, on a hunt. Siegfried falls in love with Odette, the queen of the swans (Mlle Legnani), and when the swans fly ashore and are transformed into girls, Siegfried, at her request, orders the hunters not to fire at them. Instead, the hunters begin to dance; at the end of the dances the enchanted maidens disperse and, in the form of swans, swim out on to the lake. Above the band of swans hovers some kind of predatory black bird with fiery eyes. From these eyes I surmised that this black bird plays an important part in the piece, made clear in those acts that were not performed.[21]

The public responded with little enthusiasm to the concerts, tickets for which were more than tripled in price.[22] No reviewer omitted mention of the ticket prices, the justification for which, apparently, was not widely known:

It is possible, however, that the public would have been reconciled with the high prices if, first, it knew that the performance was being put on especially for the benefit of a fund for the construction of a Tchaikovsky memorial (which was not printed on the posters), and not in a memorial to the composer; secondly, if contradictory announcements concerning the sale of tickets did not confuse the matter. As is well known, it was originally announced that tickets would not be sold through the central box office. Later, when it was found that sales were going badly, another announcement was issued a few days ago which said that tickets could be obtained directly from the box office of the Maryinsky Theatre. No wonder most of the public did not want to take the trouble . . .[23]

Fiscally the concert was a failure, as the hall was half empty. Artistically, especially as regards *Swan Lake*, it was a success. Another Italian ballerina had danced the first performance of a Tchaikovsky ballet, this one as if in compensation for the cancellation of the *Swan Lake* that had been scheduled for her in Moscow the previous summer. Legnani was among the last, and possibly the greatest, of the Italian ballerinas on the roster of the imperial theatres. She had made her début at the Maryinsky in the Petipa/Fitinhof-Schell *Zolushka* [Cinderella] in 1893, and stayed until 1901—the longest period of imperial service of any Italian ballerina. One reviewer wrote of her début:

Legnani turned out to be the most magnificent dancer . . . In technique she did not yield to the very best dancers whom Petersburg had just seen. Certainty in movements and absolute balance were observed by her to perfection, *pirouettes* and *fouettés* finished with astonishing exactitude. She stopped after turns with certainty, thanks to her astonishing aplomb; and the general line of the position of the body, arms, and legs was always correct. As for her appearance, she has auburn hair, is of medium height, with a pleasant expression and lively features and merry eyes. The ballerina is agile, her movements smooth, but she lacked lightness.[24]

With a technique considered unsurpassable, she was given to virtuosity. In *Zolushka* she performed two triple turns on *pointe* four times in succession, and, in the last act, thirty-two *fouettés*, for which her *Swan Lake* became famous.[25] Pleshcheyev remarked on

. . . the absence of any noticeable effort on the ballerina's part and her precision: she never makes a mistake, finishes and stops truly, recalling a statue cast in bronze . . .

In general, all dances and everything performed by the ballerina gave cause to think that Terpsichore herself appeared before us in Petersburg under the pseudonym of Legnani.[26]

Her dancing muted another long-standing complaint of Russian critics about the Italians' love of acrobatic technique:

Before Legnani, everyone here talked about the pernicious influence on our classical school of the tendency of the Italian school toward *tours de force*. But then Mlle Legnani appeared and proved that it is fully possible to unite astounding, astonishing technique with grace, beauty, and *plastique* as it relates to demands for pure, high choreographic art.[27]

Nikolai Bezobrazov added to the chorus of praise in his review of the memorial concert, and recognized Ivanov's work as well:

The incomparable ballerina Pierina Legnani danced the first role in *Swan Lake*. We do not hesitate to call Legnani incomparable—it is impossible to imagine anything more graceful, elegant, and with finer *plastique* than this ballerina . . . The *adagio* is a complete choreographic poem, and the performance of its ballerina transcends art. The smoothness of the movements, elasticity of the body, elegance of poses, involuntarily call forth delight.

. . . The production of the dances in *Swan Lake* belongs to the balletmaster L. I. Ivanov and does him great credit. Mr Ivanov revealed an abundance of the finest, most elegant taste. The balletmaster gave to all the dances a noble stamp, a consistent style.[28]

At the time of the memorial concerts, many decisions important to the revival of the complete ballet had still not been taken, possibly because preparations for the revival before Tchaikovsky's death had been informal and unhurried.[29] After the memorial concerts progress towards a revised libretto and score was more systematic and businesslike. Modeste Tchaikovsky refashioned the story with suggestions from Vsevolozhsky, who wrote to him on 17 August 1894:

I hope you will manage to avoid the last scene of the flood. These floods are trite and do not succeed well on our stage—it is sufficient to recall *Mlada*. Probably the Moscow directorate, in ordering the ballet [in 1875], had in mind using an old décor (*Le Pardon de Plöermel*) or something of the kind . . . And why does the Prince tear off the crown from the head of his beloved swan and destroy it?[30]

In his revision Modeste retained the outlines of the story but simplified the action. Siegfried emerges as a more sympathetic character than before, and the evil genie is not only better defined, but also punished in the end.

Act I remained the same as before except that Siegfried is more serious, less inclined to profligacy: the Princess no longer requires his marriage because she fears that disgrace will befall the family line if her son is left to make the choice on his own. At the end of the act the Prince leaves on the hunt with a group of his friends, not just with Benno.

Modeste substantially recast Act II. Siegfried has been separated from the other hunters when the latter discover the swans. Benno sends the rest to find the Prince, and then is accosted by the swan maidens. Apart from this scene, which is incidental to the main story line, Modeste clarified and abbreviated. Odette no longer has to mime a complicated family history: she and her friends are enchanted by an evil genie who may appear in the form of an owl or a human. But the conditions of her release are different and more complex: instead of marriage a pledge of eternal love is required, from someone who has never pledged it to another, plus the sacrifice of his life. Odette warns Siegfried of the dangers that await him at the Princess's ball, and this predictive element, thanks to the reduction in unnecessary detail in the act as a whole, emerges more clearly now than it had in the original.

There were few changes in Act III. Odette appears at the window both when Rothbart first enters and at the end of the act. The exchange between Siegfried and Benno regarding Odile's likeness to Odette was deleted, and Siegfried actually vows his love to Odile before the assembled company.

Modeste made his most significant changes in Act IV. Siegfried becomes an innocent victim of trickery rather than Odette's murderer, as he had been in 1877. Odette explains to the anxious swan maidens that Siegfried is blameless, and then decides to kill herself rather than live without him.

The evil genie tries to prevent this, but Siegfried, remembering his promise
of self-sacrifice, willingly dies also in order to break the spell. He and
Odette are united in death, and the genie falls dead.[31]

Modeste's version was itself revised when it arrived in St Petersburg.[32]
Several changes, possibly reflecting the director's opinions about passages
he thought indelicate, were made in the version of the libretto sold at
performances (see Appendix A). There was in addition a major change of
format: Acts I and II of the revision were recast as Act I, Scenes 1 and 2. The
Maryinsky editors simplified Modeste's version of the deception scene at
the ball, deleting Odile's transformation into an owl and her flight to the
window where Odette was watching. They retained only his direction that
Odile and Rothbart disappear.

Just as Modeste altered the 1877 libretto most extensively in the last act,
so the Petersburg redactors made their most significant changes in the last
act of Modeste's version. Most of these made Siegfried yet more
sympathetic, and the proceedings on stage less violent. The storm scene
was cut, as Vsevolozhsky had first recommended to Modeste.

From the beginning there had been no doubt that Riccardo Drigo would
deputize for Tchaikovsky in working with the choreographers to revise the
score. The music of Swan Lake, like the libretto, was revised twice. The
first revision consisted of cuts, additions, and re-ordering, and yielded a
score that served as a basic text for the balletmasters—what Tchaikovsky
might have written if Swan Lake had originally been composed according
to instructions from Petipa. This nouvelle version, in a piano arrangement
by Eduard Langer, was published by Jurgenson (and has been reprinted in
the West by Novello and the Tchaikovsky Foundation).

In connection with this revision, Drigo wrote to Modeste, in August
1894:

Immediately upon receipt of the new programme of Swan Lake I shall begin, with
the concurrence of Ivanov and Petipa, by preparing a series of musical numbers [to
be added to the ballet]. I will strive to do it as best I possibly can, in the hope that you
will be pleased with it.[33]

Later, in his memoirs, Drigo touched again on his revision of the work:

I was entrusted with a thankless yet utterly crucial task in the re-orchestration of a
significant part of Swan Lake of P. I. Tchaikovsky... Thus it was my lot, like a
surgeon, to perform an operation on Swan Lake, and I feared that I might not grasp
the individuality of the great Russian master.[34]

Because the orchestral score of Drigo's revision has never been
published, and no performance score used in the revival seems to be extant,
we cannot judge his orchestration except for the pieces from Op. 72
introduced into the second and third acts.[35]

Tchaikovsky's original and the nouvelle version are accessible in print for the reader who wishes to compare them in detail; a summary of the most important differences will suffice here to demonstrate the tastes and preferences of the new editors. As published, the *nouvelle version* is still in four acts and includes as appendices the piano pieces from Op. 72. In the amount of music cut from the original this version illuminates the concern of the Maryinsky editors for repetition and overstatement. They decided that many internal repeats, especially in large ensemble numbers, were not required, and made many brief cuts, often near final cadences, which had the effect of diminishing the rhetorical force of the original. The waltz of the prospective fiancées, for example, was shortened by twenty-two of its last forty-eight bars. Drigo's orchestrations also moderated what the editors plainly thought was a stentorian quality, too heavy-handed for the medium, by introducing salon music closer to accepted norms of *dansante* ballet music than had been the composer's original of 1876.

More pronounced in their effect were the deletions, radical modifications, and repositioning of numbers. In the first act the waltz and the *pas de trois* were reversed; the *pas de deux* (No. 5 in the original) was transferred to the ballroom scene. In Act II several changes were made in the dances of the swans. One dance—the return of the opening waltz (No. 13/III)—was omitted, and the order of the remaining numbers was changed. Only the first and last dances were left in their original places. The new order was:

Swans' waltz (No. 13/I)
Love duet (No. 13/V)
Dance of the Little Swans (No. 13/IV)
General Dance (No. 13/VI, transposed from Ab major to A major)
Odette's solo (No. 13/II)
Coda (No. 13/VII)

An important additional change was made: the *allegro* coda of the love duet, in Eb major, was deleted. Drigo modulated from Eb minor back to Gb major (the opening key), and added a short epilogue with the rhythmic motive of the transition (Exx. 70–1).

Ex. 70   No. 13/V, *Pas d'action*, bars 97–105

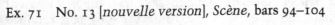

Ex. 71 No. 13 [*nouvelle version*], *Scène*, bars 94–104

Ex. 71 (cont.)

In the third act the *ballabile* (No. 16) and the *pas de six* were deleted. The waltz was extensively refashioned to bring it into conformity with the new libretto: instead of four separate entrances, one for each noble family, a single entrance sufficed for all the prospective fiancées. The scene of Rothbart's arrival with Odile was modified to permit a smooth transition to the suite of national dances, which followed a new order: Spanish, Venetian [=Neapolitan], Hungarian, Mazurka. The most extensive changes came next. The *pas de deux* Tchaikovsky had composed for Act I was interpolated here, the opening waltz being the only part retained without change. The *andante* proceeded to a new cadence so that the *allegro* in A major (No. 5/II, bars 90–164), with which Tchaikovsky had ended it, could be omitted (Exx. 72–3).[36]

Ex. 72 No. 5/II, *Pas de deux*, bars 75–90

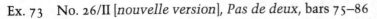

Ex. 73 No. 26/II [*nouvelle version*], *Pas de deux*, bars 75–86

After the *tempo di valse* (No. 5/III), Legnani danced a solo variation to the first of Drigo's orchestrations, 'L'Espiègle', Op. 72, No. 12. The original coda, somewhat shortened, ended the *pas*.

The last act was full of changes. The *entr'acte* was retained, but with an altered final cadence which moved the music to a new key. In place of the Scene and Dance of the Little Swans, which Tchaikovsky had placed next,

Drigo and company interpolated the orchestrated version of Op. 72, No. 11, 'Valse bluette'. Between the opening section of the Final Scene in E major and the *allegro agitato* in A minor the Maryinsky editors placed the third interpolation of orchestrated piano music, 'Un poco di Chopin', Op. 72, No. 15, which served as a *pas d'action* portraying the reconciliation of Odette and Siegfried. With the *allegro agitato* the evil genie returned. The music from here to the end of the ballet was reduced by thirty-three bars from Tchaikovsky's original, and the loud dynamics he had written at the end of the ballet were softened.

Like Modeste's libretto, Langer's *nouvelle version* was then subjected to further, less drastic alterations as the balletmasters worked out the choreography in the course of production. (Hereafter all references to the score of the Petersburg revival will be to the *nouvelle version*.) Two répétiteurs of *Swan Lake* survive,[37] and from them we can gain an idea of Drigo's additional surgical work. A complete list of the changes using the *nouvelle version* and the répétiteurs as bases, is given in Appendix H; for the present, let us again consider only the most striking.

Renamed Scene 1 of the first act, what had been Act I was shortened still more. The variation in G minor was cut from the *pas de trois*, and substantial abbreviations were made in the waltz and the polacca. The second scene followed Act II until Odette's recitative. Here, about half of the dominant elaboration of F which had followed the owl's appearance and all but five bars of the next section, over a pedal point on C♯, were

Ex. 74   No. 10 [*nouvelle version*], *Scène*, bars 193–203

(+ 57 bars to the ❋ in Ex. 75)

deleted. Although justified by the new libretto, which shortened Odette's narrative, the cut upset the formal balance of this scene by removing sections of repeated music, and also resulted in an abrupt, rather awkward progression to the final cadence of the number (Exx. 74–5).

Ex. 75   No. 10 [*nouvelle version,* further revised by Drigo], *Scène,* bars 179–91

The Maryinsky editors made one sizeable cut in the *nouvelle version* of the ballroom act. They deleted the brief return of the waltz in the final scene, which Siegfried was to have danced with Odile, and about half of the mimed scene which followed that (bars 30–91 of No. 28). Instead, there was just enough time for Siegfried to inform his mother of his choice before the stage darkened.

The last act was again much altered. A harp cadenza was introduced after the *entr'acte* (No. 29) to prepare for the 'Valse bluette'. This waltz was itself modified by a substantial repeat: after the first 119 bars, the music returned to bar 4 and proceeded through the piece again, this time to the end. The beginning of Odette's arrival music (No. 32) was preserved, but the number was broken off before the storm music. Two bars were added after bar 53, in the dominant of E major (Ex. 76).

Bars 54–96 of the *nouvelle version*—the storm music—were cut. The two added bars of dominant after bar 53 led directly into the final scene.

By the time both stages of revision had been completed, over 2,150 bars of Tchaikovsky's original score (about 36% of the music, by a bar count)

Ex. 76   No. 32 [*nouvelle version*, further revised by Drigo], bars 51–5

had been deleted. Even counting the additions from Op. 72, the score was shortened by a quarter. It is tempting to ponder, in light of this response of first-class choreographers to *Swan Lake* as composed, what Reisinger did with the score in the 1870s. If he had instincts and judgements in common with Petipa and Ivanov, he too would have cut and substituted. According to Kashkin this is what he did, in return for which he has suffered the reproach of historians, just as Petipa and Ivanov, for the same approach, have enjoyed their praise. The revisions also affirmed a cliché of balletomanic criticism: that the symphonic composer does not make the best composer of ballet music. Judging from the revisions, *Swan Lake* as Tchaikovsky composed it was too noisy, too repetitious, and insufficiently *dansante*, which is no more than the early Moscow reviewers had said of it.

While Tchaikovsky apparently thought some revision of his score was warranted, one wonders whether he would have agreed to changes that sacrificed musical coherence to choreographic expediency, and to modifications in the score more superficially logical than his own. Two of the three large-scale cadences important in the musical structure (see Chapter 2, pp. 83–5, above) were radically affected by the revision. The deletion of the part of Odette's narrative that accompanied her explanation of salvation meant that the dominant preparation for the opening of the love duet was also lost (that is, the long-term preparation which this part of her narrative represented). When Drigo altered the ending of the love duet to make the piece return to the key of the beginning, he was simply making a satisfactory close. But he struck at the heart of Tchaikovsky's musical symbols, rendering them meaningless. By ending the love duet in its principal key he took away the modulation Tchaikovsky had made to a new key. The modulation itself was a symbol of Siegfried's inconstancy, and the new key one closely related to keys associated with evil and Siegfried's misfortune from the point in Act I when he acceded to his mother's urgings for him to marry. These two revisions in particular damaged Tchaikovsky's subtle tonal plan.

When work on *Swan Lake* began—or re-began—in the autumn of 1894 cannot be established. Drigo responded in August to a letter of Modeste: 'There have been no rehearsals at all in the theatre. Our friends Ivanov and Petipa are still away from Petersburg but I hope that the huge machinery of the ballet will soon be set in motion.'[38]

Ballet rehearsals at the Maryinsky resumed on 26 August. From then until the first performance little datable information survives. Of the progress of rehearsals we know nothing, although preparations for the ballet may have been affected by the death of Alexander III on 20 October. During the period of mourning, between then and the following New Year's Day, normal public performances were cancelled.

That two choreographers shared in the creation of the Petersburg *Swan Lake* recalls the circumstances in which *Nutcracker* was produced, but here Petipa intruded on a project that Ivanov had begun. Contemporaries attributed their labours as follows:

Act I, Scene 1 (Siegfried's party)—Petipa
Act I, Scene 2 (the lakeside)—Ivanov
Act II (ballroom), except the Hungarian and Venetian Dances—Petipa
Act II, Hungarian and Venetian Dances—Ivanov
Act III (lakeside)—Ivanov, after Petipa's sketches[39]

Of the progress of Petipa's thinking we have a partial record in sketches. None is dated, but as we have seen some may have preceded the memorial concert, which, strictly speaking, would establish Petipa's precedence as the choreographer who initiated work on the production. Others clearly preserve his thoughts after February, 1894, for he noted at one point, 'The second act is already made.'[40] As before, the balletmaster's main concerns in the initial stages of a production were the assignment of dancers to parts, the sequence of dances, the floor plans of ensembles, properties, and costumes.

Once assigned, very few of the cast were changed, and only one deserves mention. Whereas Siegfried is assigned to Pavel Gerdt alone in sketches for Act I, Siegfried in the ballroom scene is listed as 'Mr Gerdt or Legat'. This may reflect Petipa's concern over giving the part of a twenty-one-year-old prince to a dancer well over twice that age. And in fact, Nikolai Legat began to replace Gerdt in certain roles at about this time (that is, in 1894). Gerdt is listed in two sketches for the mazurka, part of a conception of the ballroom scene that was later put aside: for a time Petipa considered placing the *pas de deux* of Siegfried and Odile among the national dances, just before the mazurka. This may have been an attempt to bring narrative significance to the national dances by making them part of the effect of Rothbart's bewitchment.

Petipa's conception of the waltz of the first scene was lavish. An important property was a small stool with steps, painted red and green, twenty-four of which were to be used to create different patterns, from vertical and horizontal perspectives, when dancers stood on them and struck poses. These poses, in turn, were to be embellished with baskets of flowers for the girls and batons for the boys. The batons were to be equipped with mechanisms which would make a bouquet of flowers spring out of one end at the press of a button. Twenty-four pairs of first dancers would be performing. At some point, probably near the end, Petipa planned a tableau of dancers around a maypole. He drew a maypole, and then annotated the drawing:

24 small oval baskets of flowers. From each side of the basket 3 ribbons a half arshin [14 inches] in length, each a different colour—red, blue, and yellow-gold. 4 batons—one long piece of red wood which can be carried in the hand and which will not bend. On each baton are six hooks to hold the baskets. A large pole, 7 arshins [about 16 feet] high. At its end a basket of flowers. 24 large ribbons [attached to the top of the pole] which the dancers hold while they waltz, without the large pole turning—it must remain in place. I will explain this [to the person in charge of properties]. The large ribbons are also in three colours, blue, yellow, and red.[41]

Similarly elaborate projects were planned elsewhere in the sketches. Petipa originally arranged the twelve pairs of dancers in the Venetian Dance in two sets of six, one set to dance with tambourines, the other with guitars and castanets; the swan maidens in the last act were divided into three groups distinguished by the colour of their costumes: white, black, and rose. The realities of production forced some revision of these plans.

In 1878 Laroche had written:

With other décor, in another version of the choreography which perhaps will demand some supplementary or interpolated numbers, the product of the Moscow balletmaster . . . will acquire interest besides the charming score with which the composer accompanies it . . . Generally, Petersburg could assign the roles of *Swan Lake* to such brilliant people as Moscow never dreamt of . . . For the name of the composer alone *Swan Lake* deserves to appear on our first stage, and in a magnificent production.[42]

On 15 January 1895 Laroche's prophecy was realized. Except for the tragic farewell benefit of Maria Anderson (who had seriously burned herself in a theatre fire), this was the first ballet performance after the period of mourning for Alexander III. The hall had been sold out for three days. Petipa followed the performance from his normal place behind the first wing. Drigo conducted. Gerdt and Pierina Legnani danced the leading parts. Of the indefatigable Gerdt there can be little added to what has been noted already. This dancer, who was still thought to have 'no equal among balletic cavaliers', was given credit for much of the ballerina's success, and showed in the last act his 'inimitable gift for mime'. One would have thought that at fifty Gerdt would have long since ended his career as *jeune premier*, but his age was responsible, as before, only for restrictions on his dancing. When he repeated his newest role six years after the first performance, a critic could still write, 'Mr Gerdt as always was a graceful Prince Siegfried and a magnificent cavalier of Legnani in her sometimes very risky dances.'[43]

For an account of the first production one must once again draw on the libretto, press reports, répétiteurs, and a choreographic notation.[44] The opening scene begins with the entrance of one of Siegfried's friends from rear stage right; he announces: 'Here comes the Prince, our friend. He wants to make merry, to celebrate.' Wolfgang follows, then Siegfried. After the Prince and his comrades exchange greetings, he invites them to wine. Then peasants come in from the opposite side, four women in the first row and four men in the second. They cross the stage, bow, and say: 'We are bringing these baskets of flowers to you.' Siegfried [after some unspecified intervening activity] answers: 'Dance here and make merry. Now ribbons are being brought for you.' The peasants thank the Prince. All retire to the sides to make room for the *pas de trois*,

... a captivating *pas de trois*, performed by Mlles Preobrazhenskaya and Rykhlyakova and Mr Kyaksht. This *pas* is technically difficult, is on *pointe* for the most part with double turns, and was excellently danced by the aforementioned *danseuses* and their partner.[45]

Besides technique, the *pas* as notated reveals a concern for intelligible structure. The *intrada* serves as an exposition for the entire *pas*. The opening section introduces a combination which becomes a recurring motive: *cabrioles* while travelling to the rear. Internal symmetries are suggested in the subsequent phrases as the man supports his partners in succession. At mid-point the *intrada* becomes a *pas de deux* when one of the women leaves the stage after all have paused. The second part begins with an *enchaînement* of *cabrioles* and double turns, and continues with paired phrases until the couple retires to rear stage left for a simple but striking conclusion: the woman traverses a diagonal with *pirouettes* and *chaînés*. This conclusion is also used in the variations.

The first of these, for the woman who had left the stage during the *intrada*, is in two parts. She begins with delicate, precise *pointe* work —*relevés* and *echappés*—and then is called upon to 'jump a circle on *pointe*'. The difficulty of co-ordinating music and steps may be the reason the tempo was modified: in Rep-I Tchaikovsky's *allegro semplice* has been changed to *moderato*. In the second part, her movements broaden out into larger steps and jumps, and to conclude she travels the same diagonal as her colleague, but makes twelve turns instead of eight.

Next is the man's variation. He arches across the stage from side to side—*attitude, chaîné, arabesque, cabriole*—then rests for a moment while a phrase of music ends. *Entrechats* follow, ending in a *cabriole*, and then he concludes the whole variation (at a slower tempo) with *grand jetés en tournant*, circling the stage, and a quintuple *pirouette*.

The third variation, for the other woman, is modelled on the first, and thus creates a symmetry within the entire *pas*. A display of fine *pointe* work (in this case to the side and the rear while facing front), it uses the same motive at the end—a spinning flourish of *pirouettes* and *chaînés*. Rep-I specifies tempo changes: from *allegro* to *allegretto*, and in bar one, *lento*.

The coda brings together all the important motives of the preceding dances in a final bravura statement. The woman who left the stage in the *intrada* is first to enter now, with *cabrioles*, then *pirouettes* around the stage, clockwise, to the corner of rear stage left, then more *pirouettes* across the diagonal. It is as if Petipa is compensating here for having cut short her part in the *intrada*. The man enters next (at bar 18) with a combination that recalls his variation, and then the other woman (at bar 34) with double turns. In a clear reference to the beginning of the *intrada*, all three end the coda by performing *cabrioles* while travelling to the rear, embellished after a pause with *jetés* and more *cabrioles* in place. The final pose also recalls the *intrada*, except that the man now supports both his partners at once.

Petipa creates an arch pattern in the dances of the *pas de trois*: the outer numbers are similar, the first and third variations are similar, and the man's solo in the middle constitutes the point of greatest choreographic contrast with the dances on either side. Nevertheless, the entire *pas* develops continuously as well, the later dances (particularly the coda) creating not simply balance but culmination by means of a collective or cumulative statement of what had come before.

In the CN it is not the servants at the beginning of No. 3, as the libretto specifies, but Wolfgang who sees the Princess coming and who warns the company. (Rep-II calls for a messenger to arrive.) The Princess enters (bar 30) preceded by some of her ladies-in-waiting; Siegfried greets her and kisses her hand; then, with a nod, she acknowledges the greetings of the assembly.

Princess: 'Just think. You have already grown up and must think of marriage. There [pointing to the castle] will be a ball and many beautiful girls, in beautiful dresses, with fans, and they will dance. And you must choose a bride.'

Siegfried (sadly): 'These girls say nothing to my heart, and here I would enjoy myself with my friends.'

The Princess asks him to give up this company; better to think about marriage, to which request Siegfried agrees. Satisfied with her son's promise, the Princess bids him farewell and leaves (bar 74). The Prince escorts his mother out, returns to his friends, and asks that the merriment begin anew. At the end of the scene Wolfgang begins to dance, apparently to encourage others to follow suit.

And they do, in the waltz now called the *valse champêtre*. Though certain modifications of his first thoughts were necessary, Petipa was able to realize this dance as he had anticipated in his sketches. Instead of sixty-eight dancers, the CN [in agreement with the cast list printed with the libretto] indicates forty; instead of twenty-four footstools there are sixteen. Part of the reduction in numbers may have been due to a restriction on stage space imposed by the décor for the lake, there being no intermission before the first lakeside scene in which to shift backdrops, which required the entire opening scene to be performed forward of the fourth wing.[46]

The configuration of the footstools defines the space in which the waltzing dancers perform. Petipa gives this space an illusion of size by having performers sitting, standing, or posing on the footstools, new patterns of which mark formal divisions of the dance. A second dimension of the choreography involves dancers performing within the frame. The floor patterns are familiar from Petipa's other ensemble waltzes: files of dancers changing sides, men dancing circles around their partners, now the men to the centre, now the women, waves of dancers rushing from back to front. The last design is a semicircle, the men standing on the footstools while the women dance in the centre. The closing group is constructed around the maypole which Petipa conceived as part of this dance. The CN gives little information apart from the final rubric, 'They take the ribbons', but one reviewer notes:

'At the end of the waltz a grand procession is introduced, at the high point of which ribbons are dropped in sequential order: red ribbons, blue, and yellow. The dancers pick up the ends of the ribbons, forming thereby a kind of umbrella; it turned out to be quite an effective picture.[47]

Wolfgang's flirtation scene is next. First he dances alone, then calls one of the peasant girls to his side. After a few steps together, she begins to turn him by the waist. The dizzy tutor trips and falls, to the laughter of those present, after which his partner dances away.

The polacca or dance with cups is not, like the polacca in *Sleeping Beauty*, a procession, but rather an elaborate, massive figured dance, the counterpart of the *valse champêtre*. The patterns (if not the style) are like those of a square dance: couples swinging their partners, clapping their hands; and the floor plans directly recall those of the waltz. The principal shaping device of the choreography is the reprise pattern of the music. The powerful opening section for full orchestra is danced by all the couples in a group. Each step, performed in unison, embellishes the movement of a rectangular block of dancers. The middle section (No. 7, bars 59–121), in contrast, is lighter in musical texture, its dance activity freer and less dense. Spacious lateral movement within the lines of the rectangular space is permitted as first the women and then the men dance in the centre. At the beginning of the musical reprise they again form a solid block of couples, and maintain this configuration until the end. Repositioned in a pinwheel figure, the dancers leave the stage, single file, in a sweeping circular pattern.

Critics left us little information about the polacca. Only one, 'Veteran', remarked in any detail, and he found that

> . . . the music goes in 3/4 time; the music is Spanish in character; the dances have a 6/8 rhythm. The non-coordination of the rhythm of the music with the rhythm of the dance is sharply felt. One cannot help being astonished that such an experienced balletmaster as Mr Petipa could permit such an incongruity.[48]

In the final scene Siegfried, in heavy doublet, with crossbow and sword, goes off hunting after one of his friends sees a flock of swans pass overhead. Wolfgang, who prefers bed to hunting, goes home.

The only indication of stage activity recorded in the CN for the opening of Scene 2 (No. 9) is the rubric, 'The swans swim across the stage.' The entrance of the hunters at the beginning of No. 10 is equally sketchy, showing them coming on stage, then leaving again. If the CN is a true reflection of the production, the events of No. 10 as stated in the libretto are re-ordered. First the hunters make an appearance and leave, followed by Siegfried's arrival and then Odette's. After her narrative they leave and the swan maidens enter (in No. 11); only after that does Benno return, to be encircled by the swan maidens. In his review, 'Veteran' describes the sequence of events in this order.[49]

Odette's fright during her first encounter with Siegfried is expressed in short runs punctuated by sudden stops. These sequences are interspersed with mimed statements:

> *Prince*: 'I beg you not to go away. I beg you, I beg you.'
> *Odette*: 'I am afraid of you.'
> *Prince*: 'Why?'
> *Odette*: 'You will kill me with your crossbow.'
> *Prince*: 'I will not shoot you, but will protect you.'
> She bows to him, then tries to evade him, repeatedly running and then stopping *en attitude*.
> *Prince*: 'What are you doing here?'
> *Odette*: 'I am queen of the swans.'
> *Prince*: 'I bow to you, but why are you a swan?'

Odette: 'Look there. There is a lake. My mother cried and cried. An evil magician turned me into a swan, but if someone falls in love with me and marries me, then I am saved and will not be a swan.'
Prince: 'I love you and will marry you, but show me where this genie is.'
Odette [taking a few steps]: 'He is there.'
Prince: 'I will kill him.'
He looks for his crossbow. He finds it and wants to fire, but she stops him and together they run into the wings.

Ivanov casts the first part of the entrance of the swan maidens for twenty-four members of the *corps de ballet*, who trace a serpentine pattern beginning at rear stage left. When three rows of eight are formed across the stage, they change positions slightly for several bars while making wing-like gestures with their arms, and then regroup into a triangle, the base of which is parallel to the back of the stage. At this point Benno enters. First he is surrounded by the swan maidens in a circle which expands and contracts, but in a moment, after freeing himself, he summons the other hunters. By the time they arrive the swans have formed three ranks again, at rear stage left. Twice, as the hunters are about to fire at them, a burst of four additional swan maidens, running in from the wings, stops them, and the third time Odette herself passes by, followed by twelve cygnets —students of the theatre school. (The CN at this point specifies eight students; separate records of the children's dances, preserved at the end of the manuscript, notated with Legnani as Odette, specify twelve. See Pl. 18.) By then Siegfried has also come on and at Odette's request orders his friends to desist. The dance ends when the swan maidens, in relief and gratitude, bow to Siegfried.

The swans' waltz, which 'Veteran' found 'simple and beautiful', would appear from the CN to have been more complex than the *valse champêtre* in the number of floor patterns and their frequency of change. This dance, which employs, in addition to the *corps de ballet*, children of the theatre school and separate groups of four large, four small, and two small soloists [thus designated in the CN], is recorded three times, each notation preserving the choreography for part of the performing forces. When considered together, a rich polyphony of movement is the result, in which the almost continuous activity of the *corps* is embellished by the dances of the soloists. The Reps call for *coryphées* in the opening section in A major, and four soloists in the second, in C♯ minor. Legnani and Gerdt appear at the beginning of the reprise.

The love duet that follows is a 'chef d'oeuvre in the performance of the ballerina', in which she reveals a 'brilliant technique, a lightness of movement and plasticity of pose.'[50] It is also, to describe it in Nikolai Bezobrazov's terms, a 'pas de deux à trois', because the partnering of Legnani is shared by Gerdt and Alexander Oblakov, in the part of Benno.[51]

The additional cavalier, according to legend, was to relieve Gerdt of the more strenuous requirements of his part, and was established in the performance tradition of this number.[52] When Nikolai Legat replaced Gerdt as Siegfried, he partnered the ballerina alone, for which he was reproached by the critics: '. . . not sparing his strength, he [Legat] took it upon himself to partner the ballerina in all dances. Gerdt never did this, and in the *pas d'action* of the second act the ballerina always danced with another cavalier.'[53]

By the time *Swan Lake* came to be notated the additional cavalier had been reinstated, but the rigours of partnering seem to have been more equally distributed than before. Benno walks on stage at the beginning of the harp cadenza before the love duet, and is the first in the ballerina's path of entry: he supports her in an *attitude*. But then she moves immediately to Siegfried, and throughout the dance, even though Benno several times catches her in a fall, the ballerina is lifted by Siegfried at least six times.

The *adagio* is a *tour de force* of pose and turn for Legnani. 'She was as if transformed', Khudekov wrote, '. . . preening and admiring her snow-white down, it was as if Legnani were actually experiencing these moments, filled with poetic melancholy. Languor showed in each of her graceful movements. There Legnani was at the height of understanding her art.'[54]

Of the dancing of the swan maidens in the interludes the CN provides a few sketchy floor patterns but no steps; they create different geometric shapes in the background.

The libretto says nothing, the press reports little about the remainder of this act. From the CN, however, comes confirmation of dances familiar from modern revivals, beginning with the vignette-like *pizzicato* of the four cygnets, facing front at all times with hands linked, their charming unisons of small jumps, *relevé*, *echappé*, and *pas de chat* still perilous for the under-rehearsed. It is followed by the waltz reprise, a display piece for the four *coryphées*, full of *jetés*, alighting in *arabesques* and *attitudes*, a nice foil in the broad quality of movement to the preceding dance. And then comes Legnani's solo, '. . . consisting of a whole series of turns, mostly of *ronds de jambe* and *pas de bourrée en tournant*, performed impeccably; one could not ask for more correctness and purity.'[55]

The coda begins with a number of wave-like rushes of the *corps* from back to front. Next come two groups of swan maidens (likely the four *coryphées* and the four cygnets, though the CN does not specify this), and, once positioned along the sides, all stop while the ballerina performs a variation in the middle of the number, full of turns and *changements de pieds*. All participants return to action in the last part of the coda, the *corps* performing *cabrioles* in place along the sides, the soloists crossing the front of the stage, Benno and Siegfried coming forward from the rear and joining Odette and the others in an elaborate grouping. The CN contains no record of the finale, and cannot verify the ballerina's beautiful exit, '. . . when the queen of the swans withdraws slowly, gliding on *pointe*, as if to bid *adieu* to the audience.'[56]

We must rely on the libretto for information about the opening number of Act II; the CN moves directly to the waltz of the prospective fiancées.

If the unison dances of the polacca suggest density and those of the cygnets' variation a child-like quaintness, then the unison dance of the six *invitées*, as they are aptly termed by one critic, suggests aloofness or formality. It is as if the women were not real, but abstractions or a mirage. From Siegfried's standpoint they are: the real women are spectres, the ethereal Odette a reality. This paradox may explain the costumes of the *invitées*: why would the daughters of six different local gentry come to a ball dressed the same? And why would their white dresses with trains strike the experienced Bezobrazov as inappropriate, more suited to *merveilleuses* than real people, unless he perceives a kind of otherworldly connotation in the way they are being presented?

As for the dancing, Petipa distinguishes the opening phrases of the waltz from the tutti refrain: at the beginning the dancers perform as one line of six, then make a circuit of the stage in pairs at the beginning of the tutti, or 'general waltz'. In the brief episode in F minor each dancer in turn 'does a waltz in place with the Prince, and the remaining do a *balancé* and waltz in place [while turning] in a circle.' The return of the principal theme is treated in a special way, with mazurka steps, turns, mazurka steps again, and a final bow. 'Unfortunately', writes 'Veteran', 'the performance of the waltz did not correspond to the balletmaster's thought; balance and elegance were lacking . . . in general it is fully understandable why Siegfried did not select any of these girls.'[57]

The trumpets sound; the Master of Ceremonies announces the unexpected guests. The Princess instructs that they be allowed in, rising with Siegfried and walking across the stage. Rothbart and Odile enter and greet the Princess. All are astonished.

Siegfried: 'I have seen her [before].' He approaches Rothbart and asks who Odile is.

Rothbart: 'She is my daughter.'

The Prince goes over to Odile (still referred to in the CN as Odette at this point) and says, 'I have seen you somewhere.'

Odile: 'I don't know.'

The Prince takes her by the hand and leaves the stage. The Princess and Rothbart walk over to the throne and sit down. The Spanish dancers run in.

The national dances were received by the Petersburg audience in the expected way—as pure spectacle, an opportunity to scrutinize the costumes, 'models of elegance, wonderfully chosen colour and luxury'[58], and to enjoy the art of its favourite character dancers. The Spanish and Venetian Dances left a neutral impression (the latter in part because there were no leading soloists in it), but praise of the Hungarian Dance and the mazurka was nearly unanimous. The reason in both cases was the popularity of one dancer. In the csardas 'Mlle [Marie] Petipa and Mr Bekefi danced masterfully [Bekefi had performed in this dance in the original Moscow production eighteen years before]. Mlle Petipa's costume looked particularly well on her . . .'[59] perhaps because, as another reviewer noted, she adorned it with 12,000 roubles' worth of diamonds.[60] The great success of the *divertissement* was the appearance of Felix Kshesinsky to lead the mazurka—after fifty years as a specialist, without peer among performers of this dance. According to Bezobrazov, 'The appearance of Mr Kshesinsky I, the king of the mazurka, created an absolute sensation.'[61] This dance, by 'the incomparable mazurist Kshesinsky I'[62], and the Hungarian Dance were repeated.

What came to be known as the 'Black Swan *pas de deux*', which ends the *divertissement* with glittering, steely virtuosity in the ballerina's part, is in effect, as Petipa had planned it in his sketches, a *pas de quatre demi d'action*. Odile dances, Siegfried and another cavalier (not Benno) partner her, and Rothbart acts. There is a short variation for the additional cavalier (preserved in a variant which Alexander Gorsky, who danced this part, made later as a choreographer), but none for Siegfried. The virtuoso requirements of Siegfried's part as notated in this *pas d'action* raise doubts that it was performed thus in 1895.

In the opening phrase of the *tempo di valse*, for example, the cavalier does not simply support and accompany the ballerina, whose short runs are articulated by pauses for extensions to the side which melt into *attitudes*; he performs *cabrioles* in addition. The ballerina regales the audience with turns and *sauts de basque* and displays of *port de bras*.

According to the CN, the narrative portion of the *pas* is incorporated into the *andante* (No. 26/II), though it begins during the final few bars of the preceding waltz when Odile, after traversing a diagonal in *pirouettes*, runs across the stage to Rothbart and asks, 'And what now?' He answers, 'Be silent, be silent.' At the beginning of the *andante* she dances with Siegfried, then returns to Rothbart, who approves her bewitchment of the Prince with a mimed 'Excellent!' A few bars later she goes to him again, and is reminded to be silent. Suddenly a vision of Odette, struggling to gain Siegfried's attention, appears in the window (No. 26/III, bar 49 ff.). Odile blocks Siegfried's view while Rothbart walks over to the window and drives the vision away.

For the remainder of the *pas* classical dance is given preference to mime. The first interpolated variation from Tchaikovsky's Op. 72 is a perfect counterpart to its music. Choreographically, it relieves the tension which has developed in the preceding narrative, just as the music, aided by Drigo's elegant scoring, forms a contrast with the lush Tchaikovsky sound of 1876. The dance emphasizes virtuoso steps—turns of various kinds, *echappés, ronds de jambe*—for the most part in place in the centre of the stage. In the final phrases Petipa expands the dimensions of the choreography, calling on the ballerina to perform a series of turns, on diagonals and in a *fleurette* pattern around the stage. Legnani's celebrated thirty-two *fouettés* come later, starting in bar 43 of the coda.

The ballerina's dancing in this *pas* won her great acclaim, for she '. . . flaunted her astonishing technique. Especially effective are those *renversés* which the ballerina performed in the variation of this *pas*. Mlle Legnani created a veritable furore with her miraculous dances.'[63]

'Veteran', however, found some fault:

Mlle Legnani performed her variation beautifully; the *tours* she executed were rapid and beautiful, but her arms spoiled the impression: during the execution of an *attitude en tournant* the left arm did not display a graceful roundedness and dangled awkwardly about her head. This defect is quite serious; dances are excellent only when harmony is observed in all the movements.[64]

At the end of the coda Odile runs off the stage and leaves Siegfried in the centre for the beginning of the final scene (No. 28). He walks over to the Princess and says, 'I saw here a beautiful girl and love her and ask to marry her.'

Princess: 'Excellent. But where is she?'

At that moment Odile comes out from the wings. The Princess greets her tenderly and goes into raptures over her dances.

Siegfried [approaching Rothbart]: 'I love her and want to marry her.'

Rothbart: 'You love her. Swear it.'

Siegfried ['not bringing himself' to do this]: 'No!'

Odile walks over to Rothbart and 'everything disappears'. The stage darkens and Odette appears in the window, suffering, and calls the Prince. Siegfried is horrified. When the lights come on he is lying on the floor; the Princess, motionless, is sitting on the throne.

When the curtain rises on Act III, at bar 4 of No. 29, the swan maidens are running in from opposite sides in groups of four. Soon sixteen of them have gathered at the rear of the stage, kneeling, at an angle pointing towards the front. They move around to the sides as six soloists enter from the front wings, first four and then two. The last pair makes 'three or four' circular patterns and asks, 'What have you been doing here?' To which the others reply: 'We were looking for our queen but she is not here; we called her, but in vain.'

The 'Valse bluette' which follows is intricate enough to require separate notations for the *corps* and the soloists. At first, the six soloists in the middle and the *corps de ballet* flanking them retain the same basic figure on which the entrance scene had ended, but they then move towards rear stage and back again—a variant, in its restless quality of movement, of the undulating stars and circles Ivanov had created for the snowflakes.

The first change of pattern is an important one. The *corps* form a single file in the centre of the stage, back to front. This shift from a complex figure to a plain one prepares for a new dimension to be added to the choreography: eight swan maidens in black costumes enter from rear stage right and weave their way in a serpentine line through the single file in the centre. The *corps* then form three rows across the stage, black swans forward, and move to the sides for the dances of the soloists. The rest of the waltz proceeds as a sequence of episodes alternating the *corps* with soloists; the black swans enrich the complexity of Ivanov's figures to excellent effect (one wonders if the rose-coloured swan maidens, contemplated by Petipa, would in fact have been any improvement).

Odette's anguished arrival returns the attention of swans and audience to the pressing issues of the drama (at the beginning of No. 32). Surrounded by her sisters, she explains her tragedy:

All: 'Tell us what has happened to you.'

Odette: 'There—one loved me but he deserted me and I must die.'

All: 'We beg you not to die.'

Odette: 'No, no. He abandoned me and I must die.'

The swan maidens now encircle her, protecting her and preventing her from carrying out her threat.

Siegfried enters (at the beginning of No. 33) to find six groups of swan maidens, four circles of four along the side of stage right, one circle of six opposite them, and another circle of six in the middle towards the back. Five groups are decoys, as the Prince learns to his consternation; he finds Odette in the sixth, the one in centre stage.

The last interpolated number is part of an elaborate *scène dansante* which continues to the end of the ballet. Against a changing background of picturesque groups of swan maidens, Siegfried protests his love:

Odette: 'You swore to love me.'

Siegfried: 'I do love you and I ask that we go away from here, go away.'

Odette: 'No, no, I must die.'

Siegfried: 'I love you; let us flee from here; I will marry you.'

Odette: 'No, no.'

The mimed dialogue continues during the lovers' dance, Odette one moment spinning away from Siegfried, Siegfried the next supporting Odette in turns and lifts. This mixture of narrative and dance recalls the first meeting of Odette and Siegfried in Scene 2, and also parallels the *pas de deux demi d'action* of the ballroom scene, where Odile evaded Siegfried in order to conduct a mimed dialogue with Rothbart. That the same ballerina performs both parts enhances with irony the effect of the structural likeness.

The arrival of the evil genie (at the *allegro agitato* of No. 33) disperses the swan maidens and marks the beginning of the closing scene. He separates the lovers and charges Siegfried: 'You remember; you swore there [at the ball] to love and marry. Get out of here!'

Siegfried: 'No!'

Genie [moving back slightly]: 'I shall destroy you!' He throws himself at Siegfried wrathfully.

At this moment Odette runs to Siegfried and protects him. The genie steps back in horror and threatens her also. He seizes her by the arm and throws her to the other side of the stage, then repeats to Siegfried, 'I shall destroy you!' He tries to catch the Prince, but Siegfried evades him and runs over to Odette. She protects him a second time from the onslaught of the genie, who turns and runs off the stage.

The CN ends at this point, and we must fill in the ultimate moments from other sources. According to the libretto, Odette jumps off a cliff in order to avoid being turned into a swan forever, Siegfried follows her, and the genie, thus foiled, falls dead. In a manuscript synopsis included at the end of the CN (richly glossed in an accompanying English translation), the ending is quite different:

The evil genie appears. He separates them. 'You remember, you swore to marry?'

Prince: 'No, I did not swear.'

The genie rushes at the Queen. She orders him to go away. The genie runs out and appears on the cliff.

The Queen runs to the Prince, saying farewell to him, and throws herself off the cliff. In despair the Prince follows her, and after them the genie, who is destroyed.

The apotheosis begins, and in a shell drawn by swans sails the Queen of the Swans and the Prince.

The manuscript synopsis is consistent with the events of the ballroom scene as preserved earlier in the CN, where Siegfried disobeyed Rothbart's command to swear fidelity to Odile. While it seems to have been used, this version contains a serious dramatic flaw: if Siegfried has not betrayed his trust to Odette, and if Odette is permitted such a commanding influence over the genie, then the lovers have no reason to die. Vsevolozhsky might have preferred it thus in an effort to soften the violence at the end. If so, the crisis at the end was illogical; the tragedy was unmotivated.

The apotheosis was generally found wanting. 'Veteran' described it thus: '. . . in the clouds, seated on huge swans, appear Siegfried and Odette. The apotheosis is rather absurd.'[65]

The new *Swan Lake* made a mixed impression. The décor and costumes were acknowledged as appropriate and luxurious. Legnani's dancing, excepting two rather minor complaints by 'Veteran', tended to enhance her reputation:

What a poetical ballet is *Swan Lake*! What wonderful costumes and décor, which produce the impression of something secret and lovely, what graceful swans that swim around the lake, and especially what a beautiful white swan is Mlle Legnani!

For her, it seems, there is no such thing as difficulty. Together with grace, art, precision, and confidence she joins the extraordinary strength of her steel muscles and her beautifully shaped legs. Her success was huge; she was given a multitude of flowers, and was called for repeatedly . . .[66]

In addition to curtain calls and flowers, Legnani received a gold bracelet with sapphires and diamonds, a porcelain swan with flowers, and other gifts.

Although one reviewer claimed the ballet came off 'sluggishly and monotonously',[67] and another complained that 'M Petipa's programme for the ballet is somewhat changed to the detriment of the last scene, which is stretched out by the addition of new dances',[68] the elder balletmaster held his own:

M. I. Petipa distinguished himself wonderfully well in the production of *Swan Lake*. An abundance of taste and talent is revealed in the composition of the dances of this ballet, in the masterful groupings of the *corps de ballet* and finally in the variety of the whole ensemble . . .[69]

Tchaikovsky's music failed to please critics of the first performance.

The composer himself was not satisfied with the ballet, and regretted that he wrote it without first being familiar with the requirements of ballet music; if he were alive, this ballet would probably not have been produced on the stage of the Maryinsky Theatre without preliminary alterations, as the music, excepting a few numbers, is completely unsuited for dances.[70]

Another wrote: 'The principal defect of the ballet is its music, and it is simply unbelievable that it was written by such a great master as the late P. I. Tchaikovsky.'[71]

A scrutiny of the revival tells us that choreographic concerns prevailed in the producers' decisions. Their goal was a new *Swan Lake*, of enhanced attractiveness as a danced theatrical work. If the effort caused some loss of musical coherence and some inconsistency of style (as a result of the interpolations), it was none the less responsible for gains in theatricality and in the structural clarity of the choreography. However unlike the remainder of the score, Drigo's orchestrations are effective in performance, make good theatrical sense, and reflect an editorial approach to structure in the whole work that is both consistent and intelligent.

The virtues of the revision may be observed in the new first act. Combining two acts into one offers the advantage of having the ballerina appear in every act of the ballet, but it presents risks as well: the extreme length of the first act, and an imbalance of music, narrative, and solo and ensemble dancing. Cuts reduce the first risk; re-ordering of dances sets right the balance.

Reversing the locations of the waltz and the *pas de trois* in Scene 1 is one of several changes to produce a more satisfactory distribution of balletic elements than had been the case before. In the original, two variation suites and a dance for the ballerina came before the love duet. Now the ballerina's solo is placed after the love duet, one variation suite is removed to the ballroom act, and the other, the *pas de trois*, is moved closer to the beginning of the ballet. The need for virtuoso solo dancing is satisfied in the new arrangement without endangering the love duet's freshness of effect. Indeed, the revision makes clearer and more effective the bringing together of narrative, choreographic, and musical high points in this number, so that all three can reinforce each other.

The way in which the Maryinsky editors fill the time between and around the *pas de trois* and the love duet further reveals their concern for balance. Except for the coda, all the ensemble dances in the act are placed between these numbers. This concentration of ensembles towards the beginning and in the middle of the act serves to prepare and justify the group of solo dances which comes near the end of the act in Nos. 13–17. Choreography is not the sole consideration here: the waltz and the polacca, performed by peasants in bright costumes, come earlier and are longer and more densely scored than the entrance and the waltz of the swans, which are not only shorter and lighter in musical texture, but are also performed in subdued light. In the revision, then, musical texture and dynamic, ensemble and solo dance, and bright and restful stage setting all combine with the narrative to enhance the logical progression of the action. Within this scheme numbers primarily important for their music—the introduction, the tableau spanning the first and second scenes, and the finale —come at the beginning, end, and precisely in the middle of the act.

Editing alone is inadequate to explain the wonderful impression this act, especially the lakeside scene, has made on audiences since the first performance. Two dances of this scene, the love duet and the variation of the four little swans, serve to demonstrate an artistry and a finely-tuned theatrical sense that go beyond logical organization.

There is little doubt that all the collaborators intended the love duet to be the lyrical high point of the ballet. The Maryinsky editors revised the score in such a way as to present the beauties of its music with maximum effect. This is accomplished in part by Drigo's new ending, but changes elsewhere in the ballet also contribute to the effect of this number, allowing it to speak with the fullest possible eloquence. The rearrangement of choreographic forces is partially responsible, but even more important is the omission of all music earlier in the ballet comparable to the love duet in lyric intensity, achieved by moving the so-called 'Black Swan *pas de deux*' to the ballroom act and deleting the variation in G minor from the *pas de trois*.

After the love duet, some kind of release from its musical and choreographic intensity is called for. Lev Ivanov obviously perceived this, and demonstrated in his response to this need a concern for short-term effect and long-range planning. To follow an *adagio* of great seriousness with an epigram—a brief, disarming, picturesque moment breathtaking in its *naïveté*—is a brilliant stroke. Few dances in *Swan Lake* testify more persuasively to the choreographer's sense of timing and style (to say nothing of his musicality) than the variation of the four cygnets.

Ivanov's *pas* relaxes the intensity of the love duet without appearing abrupt or stylistically incongruous, and without making any concessions to technique. Relocating the love duet may have been motivated in part by Ivanov's concern for the ballerina, that this dance be her first important solo. In addition to providing relief and contrast, the *pas* of the four cygnets makes an almost imperceptible transition from narrative to pure dance in the whole scene: it is the first in a series of dances of increasing virtuosity which will culminate in the coda, a complex ensemble with a solo variation in the middle. To end the act with a display of virtuoso dancing indulges a sophisticated audience, constitutes a timely departure from the story line, and establishes a pattern which, by its subsequent reappearance, contributes to the unity of the entire ballet. That the charm of the four little swans at first leaves us unaware of the dance's function in the structure of the entire act merely compounds its artistry.

Concern for a different kind of structural logic is reflected in the revision of Act II. Instead of making it a self-contained unit, the producers remodel it to enhance its likeness to both scenes of Act I. Several similarities between this act and the opening scene, left over from the original libretto, are allowed to stand: the atmosphere of festivity in the first number, the arrival of an unexpected guest, and the national dances with their ethnic seasoning all recall counterparts in Scene 1. Then, following the pattern of the lakeside scene, Act II stops at a decisive point in the narrative and gives way to dancing: there is a gradual build-up of choreographic virtuosity through the national dances and the *pas de deux* comparable in effect to the *grand pas de cygnes*. A brief return to narrative, accompanied by the swan theme, concludes both.

Like the second, the third act is revised to emphasize parallels with Act I, but in this case with Scene 2 alone. Ivanov introduces a clear structural parallel between the beginning of the last act and the beginning of Scene 2, namely between Nos. 11 and 12 of Scene 2 and No. 29 and the 'Valse bluette' of the last act. The first of each pair is an elaborate entrance scene for the swan maidens (for such is the use the choreographers made of the music Tchaikovsky had composed as an *entr'acte*), and the second is a waltz which blends *corps de ballet* and soloists in a *concertante* manner. These and other likenesses may be summarized as follows:

ACT I, SCENE 2	ACT III
Scene: Siegfried's first encounter with Odette	
Scene: entrance of the swan maidens	Scene: entrance of the swan maidens
Odette protects the swan maidens	
Swan's waltz	Swans' waltz (Op. 72/11)
	Scene: swan maidens protect Odette
Pas d'action: the lovers come together	Pas d'action (Op. 72/15): Siegfried's last encounter with Odette
	The lovers are reconciled
[additional dances]	[additional mimed scene]
Final scene (swan music)	Final scene (swan music)

The story of *Swan Lake*, with its striking contrast of setting and mood from scene to scene, made it eminently suitable for the collaboration of Ivanov and Petipa. Respectively they choreographed the parts of Odette and Odile, tasks especially fitted to their creative temperaments. The documents do not permit irrefutable generalizations about the choreographic styles of these two men, but do suggest tendencies in their thinking: where Petipa excelled in projecting public, formal situations, favoured abstract dance patterns, and generally sought brilliance of effect, Ivanov tended to be most effective in contexts of intimacy, preferred suggestion to declaration, and strove for impressions of profundity.

These qualities are reflected in their compositions. Petipa's framing lines tend to be fixed for the duration of a phrase or section, embellished by dancers in different poses, with the principal dance activity being carried out within them by soloists. The choreography progresses from a group through a transition to another group, so that geometric designs beautiful for their patterns and for the colour of costumes and accessories are matters of structural importance. Ivanov develops his choreography in a similar way, but achieves a different result. Often his floor patterns are not so clearly defined as Petipa's because the lines, even framing lines, are constantly active. The inside is moving outward, the outside inward; there tends to be no stable reference. The difference in choreography may be expressed in musical terms: Petipa's choreography consists of episodes in which a melody is sounding against a pedal point, Ivanov's of episodes in which several lines mingle together in free counterpoint.

In the handling of narrative content in *Swan Lake* the methods of the two may also be distinguished. The CN offers grounds for a distinction between Petipa's preference for disregarding or standing aloof from narrative in his dances and Ivanov's for imbuing dance with narrative meaning, explicity or suggested. (One should not be tempted to generalize any further than *Swan Lake* in this regard, as many of Petipa's contemporaries attested his artistry as a mimist, and he himself claimed artistic descent from Perrot.) In the ballroom *pas de deux* mime is unavoidable, and Petipa seasons Odile's dances with mimed gestures of a conventional kind. The CN gives no evidence of his requiring her to inflect her dancing mimetically. Instead, the dance conception and the mime are separate: she dances, she mimes, she dances again. Yet the effect of artificiality which this approach conveys is perfectly suited to the artificiality of the character.

Ivanov also deals with supernatural characters in the entrance of the swan maidens in Scene 2, but he, in contrast, lends persuasiveness and credibility to their dances. Whatever the librettist intended by including the episode of Benno and the swan maidens, Ivanov imparts to it an independent level of intelligibility—one might even call it psychological relevance—with suggestions of narrative. The serpentine pattern of the entrance offers something more than a way to bring twenty-four dancers on to the stage; it also suggests caution, as do the lateral movements of the three lines of eight which immediately follow. The next pattern, a wedge or triangle, suggests defensiveness, a quality enhanced by the rubric in the CN at that point: 'Simply stand (frightened)'. The immediate dispersal of the swan maidens as Benno enters is both an appropriate response of swans to seeing a hunter and an eloquent dance analogy to the flight of frightened birds. Their encircling of Benno, who is left alone after sending the other hunters to find Siegfried, comes next; by the time Benno has freed himself to hail his friends, the swan maidens are again on the defensive, having formed three close lines in the opposite corner of the stage.

Petipa's formal, detached, artificial treatment of public, ostensibly real situations forms a wonderful foil to Ivanov's talent for making credible and moving the ostensibly unreal. How well their work illustrates André Levinson's description of the essence of romantic ballet, '. . . la vanité des apparences et la vérité du rêve.'

Postlude

❧

FEW ballets have enjoyed the remarkable vitality of Tchaikovsky's. After nearly a century, *Nutcracker* may be performed throughout the Western world by more ballet companies than any other work, and the Petersburg versions of *Swan Lake* and *Sleeping Beauty* are surprisingly intact as regards music and choreography, which producers have consciously attempted to preserve. Petipa's style has evolved in the attitudes of dancers and public from old fashioned to classic. His work and Ivanov's are now considered important on their merits, and for the most part immune to fashion.

In a historical perspective, Tchaikovsky's ballets played a part in the changing attitudes of Russians towards Russian music. At the time *Sleeping Beauty* was first produced, Benois recalled, he looked on Russian music with disdain. Yet something stirred within him when he first heard this ballet, something which brought him to the theatre again:

It turned out that the music of Tchaikovsky was not only excellent and charming, but that *there was something in it* that I had *somehow always been waiting for*. And already at the second performance not the spectacle, not the dances, not the performance, not the executants captivated me, but the music conquered me, something infinitely close, part of me, something that I would call *my* music . . . After that I did not miss one performance of *Beauty* and once managed (in Butter Week, when matinées were given besides the evening performances) to go to this ballet four times in one week. Besides that, I now listened to Tchaikovsky wherever I could, at concerts and playing at home. That attraction to *Beauty* helped me soon afterward to grow fond of all of *Evgenii Onegin*, to which I had previously responded with 'distrust'.[1]

Benois goes on to declare that

The delight in *Sleeping Beauty* returned me to ballet in general, to that towards which I had grown cool, and I passed this rekindled passion along to all my friends, who gradually became 'true balletomanes'. Thus was created one of the basic conditions which prompted us a few years later to become active in the same sphere, and this activity gained for us worldwide success. I hardly err if I say that if it were not for my *violent* attraction to *Beauty* at that time (and prior to that of my attraction to *Coppélia*, *Giselle*, and *The Daughter of the Pharaoh* with Zucchi), if I had not infected my friends with my enthusiasm, then there would have been no 'Ballets Russes' and all the balletomania to which they gave birth.[2]

Perhaps immoderate in certain details, Benois's claim nevertheless provides an insight into the relationship between the late imperial ballet and the 'Saisons Russes'. So anxious are some historians to proclaim Diaghilev's modernity that the close ties of the early Russian seasons to the Petipa–Tchaikovsky generation are easily overlooked. In fact, *Carnaval* is to *Les Millions d'Arlequin* as Diaghilev–Stravinsky–Fokine is to Vsevolozhsky–Tchaikovsky–Petipa: the generation of the fathers to the generation of the sons. The family likenesses are there—in the ties of repertory (for Diaghilev produced *Swan Lake* and *Sleeping Beauty*), of approach (productions mounted in the grand manner), even in the first hints of the new emphasis on male virtuosity (the Blue Bird) and the abandoning of the trappings of classical dance (in certain of Petipa's *pas de caractère*). If anything, Diaghilev's accent on modernity hastened the elevation of the Petipa–Tchaikovsky works to classic status, for he looked back on them conscious of his sense of perspective, conscious, as Benois would have it, of his *'passé-ism'*. Suddenly, *Swan Lake* and *Sleeping Beauty* were to be revered.

Tchaikovsky's contribution may be assessed from many perspectives. In the light of the prevailing trends of specialist ballet composition, his infusion of greater sophistication and art—especially in the realms of rhythm, orchestration, and tonal structure—took ballet music out of the hands of Minkus and delivered it into the hands of Stravinsky. Within his own *oeuvre* we can follow the ballets through a process of reconciliation, the reconciliation of the consciously imposed restrictions of the specialist with the demands of his own complex language. We can also see reflected in it the gradual refinement and enrichment of his style: *Swan Lake* is to *Sleeping Beauty* what the Fourth Symphony is to the Fifth.

At that, Tchaikovsky never lost sight of the practical requirements and stylistic identity of ballet music. He made it more symphonic, but not a symphony. This was clear to the perceptive Laroche, who touched on Tchaikovsky's awareness of the special character of music for the dance:

Thanks to *Sleeping Beauty*, the name Tchaikovsky was made well known in circles which previously knew only Pugni, Minkus, Gerber, Schneitzhöffer, and perhaps Adolphe Adam. All these composers, at times fair melodists, at times virtuosos at counterpoint, responded to the composition of ballet music with a preconceived striving towards salon lightness, towards the rhythmic expressivity of banal dance. In particular the ballets of the adroit and learned Pugni are full of this assumed vulgarity and, in their turn, had an oppressive effect on the taste of balletomanes. It is a mistake to think that lovers of ballet look without listening . . . True, the ballet public proper listens with less attention, converses more loudly, and is likely more tolerant of false notes. But it certainly has its favourite effects, its favourite motives, its own tradition of form and instrumentation. The composer of *Swan Lake* already had occasion to wrestle with these customs; the composer of *Sleeping Beauty* mastered them with ease . . . And he was made a ballet composer not because he was able to adapt himself especially obligingly to requirements he was unaccustomed to, but because in the depth of his nature lay, as it were, the ability to compose dances.

. . . If Tchaikovsky had feared 'vulgarity', if he had heeded shrill affectedness, the virtuous horror of primness, the contemptuous grimace of imaginary aristocratic values—he would never have written *Sleeping Beauty*. . . He did not adapt himself to a level lower than that to which he was accustomed, he did not bow and cringe before the public. He was simply what he had to be in order to compose music for ballets . . . Obviously, after *Sleeping Beauty* he did not become pre-eminently a composer of light music, he did not become a rival of either Strauss or LeCocq. But this much is above question: that he discovered in himself a new vein, and the quarrying of this new vein had hardly begun when death overtook him.[3]

Whatever his use of complex musical devices, Tchaikovsky preserved a fundamental and ennobling simplicity in his ballets, responding without contrivance to the legitimate call for lighthearted music when it came. The honesty implicit in this approach, the gift to be simple without being simple-minded, is sensed in the musical result, and may ultimately be responsible for the fact that, even at his lightest, Tchaikovsky is never mistaken for his specialist colleagues.

In the end, Tchaikovsky's accomplishment may have been as much social as artistic. He had the authority as a composer to make Petipa, a man accustomed to getting his own way, go along with the new ballet music. And in a time and country where the success of a native composer was measured first of all in the opera house, in the concert room only after that, and not at all in the ballet theatre, Tchaikovsky made ballet composition a fit occupation. It is difficult to imagine anyone else who could have done this better—indeed, who could have done it at all.

Notes

❧

INTRODUCTION

1. Baron Boris Aleksandrovich Fitingof-Shel', 'Album of Autographs', *Moskov-skie vedomosti* [The Moscow Gazette] (5 Jan. 1899), p. 3.
2. Aleksandr Alekseevich Pleshcheev, *Sergei Lifar' ot starogo k novomu* [Sergei Lifar from Old to New] (Paris, 1938), p. 70.
3. Sergei Nikolaevich Khudekov, *Istoriya tantsev* [The History of Dances], 4 vols. (St Petersburg/Petrograd, 1913–18), iv, p. 117.
4. Khudekov, *Istoriya*, iv, pp. 106–7.
5. Khudekov, *Istoriya*, iv, p. 136.
6. Aleksandr Alekseevich Pleshcheev, *Nash balet* [Our Ballet] (St Petersburg, 2nd edn, 1899), p. 289.
7. Published in *Marius Petipa. Materialy, vospominaniya, stat'i* [Marius Petipa: Materials, Reminiscences, Articles], ed. Yurii Iosifovich Slonimskii *et al.* (Leningrad, 1971), pp. 68–112.
8. *Marius Petipa. Materialy*, p. 121.
9. Pleshcheev, *Sergei Lifar'*, pp. 68–9.
10. Adam Pavlovich Glushkovskii, *Vospominaniya baletmeistera* [Recollections of a Balletmaster] (Leningrad and Moscow, 1940), p. 178.
11. Glushkovskii, *Vospominaniya*, pp. 179, 178.
12. Anna Petrovna Natarova, 'From the Recollections of the Artist A. P. Natarova', *Istoricheskii vestnik* [Historical Messenger], xciv (Oct./Dec. 1903), pp. 430–1.
13. Glushkovskii, *Vospominaniya*, p. 179.
14. Konstantin Apollonovich Skal'kovskii, *V teatral'nom mire* [In the Theatre World] (St Petersburg, 1899), p. 141.
15. D. I. Leshkov, 'Personal Reminiscences of R. E. Drigo' (Moscow, Central State Archive of Literature and Art, *fond.* 794, *Op.* 1, *ed. khr.* 42), fol. 15.
16. Quoted in Vera Mikhailovna Krasovskaya, *Russkii baletnyi teatr vtoroi poloviny XIX veka* [Russian Ballet Theatre of the Second Half of the XIX Century] (Moscow and Leningrad, 1963), pp. 257–8.
17. *Muzykal'nye fel'etony i zametki Petra Il'icha Chaikovskogo (1868–1876 g.)* [Music Reviews and Notices of Peter Ilyich Tchaikovsky (1868–1876)] (Moscow, 1898), p. 30.
18. *Tantsy voobshche, baletnye znamenitosti i natsional'nye tantsy* [Dances in General, Ballet Celebrities, and National Dances] (Moscow, 1864), p. 46.
19. Baletoman [K. A. Skal'kovskii], *Balet, ego istoriya i mesto v ryadu izyashch-nykh iskusstv* [Ballet, its History and Place in the Fine Arts] (St Petersburg, 1882), p. 15.
20. R.Z. [?Raphael Zotov], 'Theatre Chronicle', *Severnaya pchela* [The Northern Bee], 1851, p. 126 [9 Feb.].

21. *V teatral'nom mire*, p. 243.
22. Ekaterina Ottovna Vazem, *Zapiski baleriny Sankt-Peterburgskogo bol'shogo teatra. 1867–1884* [Memoirs of a Ballerina of the St Petersburg Bolshoy Theatre. 1867–1884] (Moscow and Leningrad, 1937), p. 134.
23. Constant Lambert, *Music Ho! A Study of Music in Decline* (London, 3rd edn, 1966), p. 96.
24. *V teatral'nom mire*, p. 216.
25. *Istoriya russkoi muzyki* [History of Russian Music], ed. N. V. Tumanina *et al.*, 3 vols. (Moscow, 1957–60), ii, p. 404.
26. N., 'Farewell Benefit of L. Minkus', *Novosti i birzhevaya gazeta* [News and Stock Exchange Gazette] (11 Nov. 1886), p. 3.
27. *V teatral'nom mire*, p. 216.
28. D. I. Leshkov, 'Cesare Pugni' (Moscow, Central State Archive of Literature and Art, *fond*. 794, *Op*. 1, *ed. khr*. 39), fol. 3.
29. *V teatral'nom mire*, pp. 235–7.
30. *Novosti i birzhevaya gazeta* (9 Jan. 1898), p. 3.
31. Yakov Plyushchevskii-Plyushchik, 'On Contemporary Ballet Music; apropos of the Ballet "The Vestal" ', *Novoe vremya* [The New Times] (29 Feb. 1888), p. 2.
32. Modest Petrovich Musorgskii, *Literaturnoe nasledie* [Literary Heritage], ed. A. A. Orlova and M. S. Pekelis, 2 vols. (Moscow, 1971–2), i, pp. 48, 82.
33. *Balet, ego istoriya*, pp. i–ii.
34. Aleksandr Alekseevich Pleshcheev, '*Pod seniyu kulis . . .*' [In the Protection of the Wings] (Paris, 1936), p. 90.
35. 'Russian Balletomania', *Dance Index*, vol. vii, No. 3 (March 1948), p. 49.
36. Pleshcheev, '*Pod seniyu kulis*', p. 93.
37. *Zapiski*, pp. 193–4.
38. Pleshcheev, '*Pod seniyu kulis*', pp. 92–102.
39. Khudekov, *Istoriya*, iv, pp. 69–70.
40. '*Pod seniyu kulis*', p. 92.
41. Khudekov, *Istoriya*, iv, p. 88.
42. *V teatral'nom mire*, p. 223.
43. *Istoriya*, iv, p. 89, note **.
44. Khudekov, *Istoriya*, iv, pp. 81, 106, 108.
45. *Istoriya*, iv, p. 118.
46. *Nash balet*, p. 277.
47. *Nash balet*, p. 393.
48. Vladimir Arkad'evich Telyakovskii, *Vospominaniya* [Reminiscences] (Leningrad and Moscow, 1965), p. 416.
49. '*Pod seniyu kulis*', pp. 104, 60.
50. *V teatral'nom mire*, p. vii.
51. Telyakovskii, *Vospominaniya*, p. 419.
52. Pleshcheev, '*Pod seniyu kulis*', pp. 100–4.
53. *Istoriya*, iv, p. 141.
54. *V teatral'nom mire*, p. 115.
55. Aleksandr Alekseevich Pleshcheev, *Chto vspomnilos (za 50 let)* [What is Remembered (after 50 Years)] (Paris, 1931), p. 244.
56. Khudekov, *Istoriya*, iv, p. 70.

57. *Istoriya*, iv, pp. 149–50, 153.
58. Khudekov, *Istoriya*, iv, p. 125.
59. 'Letter to the Editor', *Peterburgskaya gazeta* [Petersburg Gazette] (7 Dec. 1900), p. 4.
60. *Marius Petipa. Materialy*, p. 171.
61. *Golos* [The Voice] (26 Jan. 1877), p. 2.
62. *Bayaderka. Balet v chetyrekh deistviyakh i semi kartinakh s apotheozom. Soch. G. Petipa. Muzyka soch. G. Minkusa. Predstavleno v I-i raz na IMPERATORSKOM Spb. Bol'shom teatre 23-go yanvarya 1877 goda* [*La Bayadère*. Ballet in Four Acts and Seven Scenes with Apotheosis. Comp. by Mr Petipa. Music comp. by Mr Minkus. Presented for the First Time at the Imperial St Petersburg Bolshoy Theatre 23 January 1877] (St Petersburg, 1877), pp. 5–6.
63. *Marius Petipa. Materialy*, p. 174.
64. *Golos* (26 Jan. 1877), p. 2.
65. *Vsemirnaya illyustratsiya* [World Illustration], xvii (Jan.–June 1877), p. 297.
66. *Bayaderka. Balet v chetyrekh deistviyakh . . .*, p. 25.
67. *Golos* (26 Jan. 1877), p. 2.
68. Harvard Theatre Collection, bMS Thr 245 (105), p. 82.
69. Vazem, *Zapiski*, pp. 166–7.
70. *Novoe vremya* (26 Jan. 1877), p. 2.
71. Harvard Theatre Collection, bMS Thr 245 (111).

CHAPTER 1

1. On holy fools, see Natalie Challis and Horace W. Dewey, 'The Blessed Fools of Old Russia', *Jahrbücher für Geschichte Osteuropas, Neue Folge*, xxii/1 (1974), pp. 1–11.
2. Aleksandr Alekseevich Pleshcheev, *Moe vremya* [My Time] (Paris, n.d.), p. 14.
3. N. V. Davydov, *Iz proshlogo* [From the Past] (Moscow, 1913), pp. 5–6.
4. Nikolai Dmitrievich Kashkin, *Vospominaniya o P. I. Chaikovskom* [Recollections of P. I. Tchaikovsky] (Moscow, 1896), p. 15.
5. Davydov, *Iz proshlogo*, p. 67.
6. D. I. Mukhin, 'My Recollections of the Imperial Theatres', *Moskovskie vedomosti* [Moscow Gazette] (13 Aug. 1901), p. 4.
7. E. Zh., '"Swan Lake" . . .', *Vsemirnaya illyustratsiya*, xvii (Jan.–June 1877), p. 334.
8. Davydov, *Iz proshlogo*, pp. 75–6.
9. Pleshcheev, *Moe vremya*, pp. 14–15.
10. P. A. Rossiev, 'The Artistic Circle in Moscow (1865–1883)', *Istoricheskii vestnik*, cxxviii (Apr.–June 1912), p. 483.
11. Iv. Zakharin (Yakunin), 'The Artistic Life of Moscow in the Seventies (Excerpts from Memoirs)', *Istoricheskii vestnik*, xc (Oct.–Dec. 1902), pp. 480–4.
12. *Russkie vedomosti* [Russian Gazette] (2 Jan. 1868), p. 3.
13. Petr Il'ich Chaikovskii, *Polnoe sobranie sochinenii. Literaturnye proizvedeniya i perepiska* [Collected Works. Literary Works and Corre-

spondence], 17 vols. (Moscow, 1953–81) [hereinafter: Collected Works Correspondence], v, p. 234.

14. Collected Works Correspondence, v, p. 235.

15. Karl Fedorovich Val'ts, *Shest'desyat pyat' let v teatre* [Sixty-Five Years in the Theatre] (Leningrad, 1928), p. 104. In one newspaper article Reisinger was referred to as 'a former figurant of the Prague theatre' (*Peterburgskaya gazeta*, 4 Nov. 1871, p. 3).

16. *Moskovskie vedomosti* (5 Dec. 1871), quoted in Krasovskaya, p. 183. The *Peterburgskaya gazeta* for 16 Nov. 1871 announced: 'They write us from Moscow that Mr Reisinger, known to nobody but engaged as balletmaster of the Moscow ballet company, has already begun rehearsals of the new ballet *Cinderella*. Mr Reisinger, as it turns out, is a strong adherent of Paul Taglioni, balletmaster of the Berlin opera theatre, since, judging from what we have managed to see at rehearsals, he is borrowing dances for *Cinderella* from the ballets of the Berlin choreographer. Mr Reisinger, for example, stuck into his ballet the whole of the dances of the nymphs from Taglioni's *Sardanapale*, and also borrowed several *pas* from the same composer's *Elinora*. The dance of the Negroes with the little bells on their heads is also taken from Taglioni.'

17. Val'ts, p. 105; Krasovskaya, p. 184.

18. Krasovskaya, p. 185.

19. *Moskovskie vedomosti* (19 Dec. 1873), p. 4.

20. *Russkie vedomosti* (30 Dec. 1873), quoted in Krasovskaya, p. 186.

21. *Moskovskie vedomosti* (21 Jan. 1875), quoted in Krasovskaya, p. 186.

22. Kashkin, *Vospominaniya*, p. 101.

23. Modest Il'ich Chaikovskii, *Zhizn' Petra Il'icha Chaikovskogo. Po dokumentam, khranyashchimsya v arkhive imeni pokoinogo kompozitora v Klinu* [The Life of Peter Ilyich Tchaikovsky. According to Documents Preserved in the Archive named for the Deceased Composer at Klin], 3 vols. (Moscow, 2nd edn 1901–3), i, p. 497.

24. Quoted in Yurii Iosifovich Slonimskii, *P. I. Chaikovskii i baletnyi teatr ego vremeni* [P. I. Tchaikovsky and the Ballet Theatre of his Time] (Moscow, 1956), p. 86.

25. See, e.g., Slonimskii, *P. I. Chaikovskii i baletnyi teatr*, pp. 90–1; Cyril W. Beaumont, *The Ballet Called Swan Lake* (London, 1952), pp. 36–40; Richard Austin, *Images of the Dance* (London, 1975), pp. 93–9.

26. *Vospominaniya*, p. 101.

27. '*Lebedinoe ozero*' *P. Chaikovskogo* ['Swan Lake' of P. Tchaikovsky] (Leningrad, 1962), p. 10.

28. *Popular Tales of the Germans*, 2 vols. (London, 1791), i, pp. 202–3.

29. *Muzykal'nye fel'etony i zametki Petra Il'icha Chaikovskogo*, p. 272; Collected Works Correspondence, viii, pp. 114–15.

30. Collected Works Correspondence, viii, p. 198; xii, p. 331; Petr Il'ich Chaikovskii, *Muzykal'no-kriticheskie stat'i* [Musico-Critical Articles] (Moscow, 1953), p. 329.

31. Collected Works Correspondence, vi, p. 64.

32. *Vospominaniya*, p. 95.

33. *Vospominaniya*, pp. 106–7. The librettist, Konstantin Ivanovich Zvantsev

(1825–90), had insisted that Tchaikovsky compose in accordance with Wagner's reform theories.

34. Collected Works Correspondence, vii, p. 201.
35. *Novosti i birzhevaya gazeta* (17 Jan. 1895), p. 3; *Novoe vremya* (17 Jan. 1895), p. 3.
36. *The Music of Tchaikovsky* (London, 1945), pp. 131–8.
37. Collected Works Correspondence, vii, p. 238.
38. *Zapiski o P. I. Chaikovskom* [Memoirs about P. I. Tchaikovsky] (Moscow, 1962), p. 26.
39. Quoted in Slonimskii, *Chaikovskii i baletnyi teatr*, p. 89.
40. Davydov, *Zapiski*, p. 92, n. 33.
41. *Vospominaniya*, p. 101.
42. *Zhizn' Petra Il'icha Chaikovskogo*, i, p. 465; Collected Works Correspondence, v, p. 410.
43. Collected Works Correspondence, v, p. 412.
44. *Vospominaniya*, p. 101.
45. Quoted in *Vospominaniya o P. I. Chaikovskom* [Recollections about P. I. Tchaikovsky] (Moscow, 2nd edn 1973), p. 132. Bryullova was the mother of Kolya Konradi, student and later ward of Tchaikovsky's brother Modeste.
46. Val'ts, p. 108.
47. *Vospominaniya*, p. 101.
48. Collected Works Correspondence, vi, p. 33.
49. *Vospominaniya*, p. 103.
50. Tchaikovsky's schedule for this period is given in *Dni i gody P. I. Chaikovskogo* [The Days and Years of P. I. Tchaikovsky], ed. V. Yakovlev (Moscow and Leningrad, 1940), pp. 127–41.
51. *Russkie vedomosti* (26 Feb. 1877), p. 2.
52. *Novoe vremya* (26 Feb. 1877), p. 2.
53. *Vsemirnaya illyustratsiya*, xvii (Jan.–June 1877), p. 334.
54. *Sovremennye izvestiya* (26 Feb. 1877), p. 1.
55. *Novoe vremya* (26 Feb. 1877), p. 2.
56. *Teatral'naya gazeta*, xxxix (22 Feb. 1877), p. 178.
57. *Sanktpeterburgskie vedomosti* [St Petersburg Gazette] (1 Mar. 1877), p. 2.
58. P. Pchel'nikov, 'Fate of a Talented Invention' (Moscow, State Central Theatre Museum named for A. A. Bakhrushin, No. 146887), fol. 8.
59. Information about the dancers was taken from Krasovskaya, pp. 136–72.
60. *Moskovskie vedomosti* (19 Sept. 1863), p. 3.
61. *Tantsy voobshche*, p. 49.
62. *Golos* (19 Oct. 1866), quoted in Krasovskaya, p. 177.
63. *Moskovskie vedomosti* (12 Jan. 1865), quoted in Krasovskaya, p. 176.
64. *Balet, ego istoriya*, p. 257. Skalkovsky's opinion is in accord with this notice from the *Peterburgskaya gazeta* (9 Nov. 1871), p. 3: 'Mlle P. M. Karpakova enjoys special favour from the directorate . . . In essence she distinguishes herself not by her choreographic art but only by her new costumes, which grow for her like mushrooms in a rainy summer . . . It seems there is not one ballet in which Paulina Mikhailovna does not participate, receiving 15 roubles for each appearance together with 900 roubles in salary. And every time, instead of applause, the public rewards her with hisses; but despite that,

this favourite of the directorate comes back again on stage as if nothing had happened.'

65. D. I. Mukhin, 'History of the Moscow Ballet', quoted in Yurii Alekseevich Bakhrushin, 'The Ballets of Tchaikovsky and their Stage History', *Chaikovskii i teatr* [Tchaikovsky and the Theatre], ed. A. I. Shaverdyan (Moscow, 1940), p. 88.
66. Val'ts, pp. 74–5.
67. 'A. I. Sobeshchanskaya', *Biryuch petrogradskikh gosudarstvennykh teatrov* [Herald of the Petrograd State Theatres] (1918), vii, pp. 53–4; *cf.* Val'ts, p. 75.
68. *Zhizn' Petra Il'icha Chaikovskogo*, i, p. 527.
69 Val'ts, p. 114.
70. This summary of Ryabov's career was taken from various notices: *Novoe vremya* (20 Jan. 1890, p. 2); *Novosti i birzhevaya gazeta* (20 Jan. 1890, p. 2; 21 Nov. 1899, p. 4); *Moskovskie vedomosti* (29 May 1892, p. 5; 13 Sept. 1899, p. 4; 20 Nov. 1899, p. 5; 22 Nov. 1899, p. 5); *Russkie vedomosti* (14 Jan. 1890, p. 4).
71. *Russkie vedomosti* (3 Mar. 1877), p. 1.
72. Yurii Alekseevich Bakhrushin, *Istoriya russkogo baleta* [History of the Russian Ballet] (Moscow, 2nd edn 1973), p. 161.
73. *Sovremennye izvestiya* (26 Feb. 1877), p. 1.
74. 'The Ballets of Tchaikovsky and their Stage History', p. 90.
75. *P. I. Chaikovskii i baletnyi teatr*, p. 106, n. 1.
76. *Novoe vremya* (26 Feb. 1877), p. 2.
77. *Vsemirnaya illyustratsiya*, xvii (Jan.–June 1877), p. 335.
78. *Golos* (1 Mar. 1877), p. 3.
79. *Teatral'naya gazeta*, c (19 Oct. 1876), p. 390.
80. *Sovremennye izvestiya* (26 Feb. 1877), p. 1.
81. *Sanktpeterburgskie vedomosti* (22 Feb. 1877), p. 2.
82. *Novoe vremya* (26 Feb. 1877), p. 2.
83. *Sanktpeterburgskie vedomosti* (23 Feb. 1877), p. 3.
84. *Teatral'naya gazeta*, xxxviii (21 Feb. 1877), p. 174.
85. *Russkii mir* [Russian World] (23 Feb. 1877), p. 1.
86. *Sovremennye izvestiya* (26 Feb. 1877), p. 1.
87. German Avgustovich Larosh, *Izbrannye stat'i* [Collected Articles], 5 vols. (Leningrad, 1974–), ii, p. 99.
88. *Teatral'naya gazeta*, xxxix (22 Feb. 1877), p. 178.
89. *Sanktpeterburgskie vedomosti* (23 Feb. 1877), p. 3.
90. *Russkie vedomosti* (25 Feb. 1877), p. 1.
91. *Izbrannye stat'i*, ii, p. 99.
92. *Sovremennye izvestiya* (26 Feb. 1877), p. 1.
93. *Teatral'naya gazeta*, xxxix (22 Feb. 1877), p. 178.
94. *Sanktpeterburgskie vedomosti* (1 Mar. 1877), p. 2.
95. *Russkie vedomosti* (26 Feb. 1877), p. 2.
96. Val'ts, p. 108.
97. *Vsemirnaya illyustratsiya*, xvii (Jan.–June 1877), p. 340.
98. *Teatral'naya gazeta*, xxxix (22 Feb. 1877), p. 178.
99. *Novoe vremya* (26 Feb. 1877), p. 2.
100. *Sanktpeterburgskie vedomosti* (1 Mar. 1877), p. 2.

101. *Sovremennye izvestiya* (26 Feb. 1877), p. 1.
102. *Russkie vedomosti* (25 Feb. 1877), p. 1.
103. *Teatral'naya gazeta*, xxxix (22 Feb. 1877), p. 178.
104. *Teatral'naya gazeta*, xxxix (22 Feb. 1877), p. 178.
105. P. Pchel'nikov, 'Recollections about P. I. Tchaikovsky', *Moskovskie vedomosti* (28 Oct. 1900), p. 4.
106. Petr Il'ich Chaikovskii, *Polnoe sobranie sochinenii* [Collected Works], xi/*b*, pp. 334–87.
107. *Vospominaniya*, p. 103.
108. Quoted in 'The Ballets of Tchaikovsky and their Stage History', p. 89.
109. *Golos* (24 Aug. 1877), p. 1.
110. *Izbrannye stat'i*, ii, pp. 99–100.
111. Information about Hansen's productions was supplied by the staff of the Tchaikovsky Home-Museum at Klin.
112. *Moskovskie vedomosti* (15 Jan. 1880), p. 4.
113. *Russkie vedomosti* (27 Jan. 1880), p. 3.
114. Peter Il'ich Chaikovskii, *Perepiska s N. F. fon Mekk* [Correspondence with N. F. von Meck], 3 vols. (Moscow and Leningrad, 1934–6), ii, p. 298.
115. Slonimskii, *'Lebedinoe ozero' P. Chaikovskogo*, p. 37; Bakhrushin, *Istoriya russkogo baleta* (2nd edn), p. 168.
116. See *Muzykal'noe nasledie Chaikovskogo* [The Musical Heritage of Tchaikovsky], ed. V. Protopopov *et al.* (Moscow, 1968), p. 162. The title 'La Cosmopolitana' may have been used as a synonym for 'potpourri', and may thus refer to dances of diverse composers. Geiten danced a 'La Cosmopolitana' in 1895 to Anton Rubinstein's music; Petipa refers to a 'La Cosmopolitana' in his diaries for 1903, supposedly to music by Pugni (*Marius Petipa. Materialy*, p. 72).
117. Slonimskii, *'Lebedinoe ozero' P. Chaikovskogo*, p. 38.
118. 'Around the Theatres', *Moskovskii listok* [Moscow Leaflet] (10 Oct. 1883), p. 2.

CHAPTER 2

1. See, e.g., Slonimskii, *'Lebedinoe ozero' P. Chaikovskogo*, pp. 15–34; Daniel' Vladimirovich Zhitomirskii, *Balety Chaikovskogo* [Tchaikovsky's Ballets] (Moscow and Leningrad, 1950), pp. 75–153; John Warrack, *Tchaikovsky Ballet Music* (London, 1979).
2. Slonimskii, *'Lebedinoe ozero' P. Chaikovskogo*, p. 15.
3. *Balety Chaikovskogo*, pp. 28–9.
4. Quoted in Yuliya Andreevna Rozanova, *Simfonicheskie printsipy baletov Chaikovskogo* [Symphonic Principles of Tchaikovsky's Ballets] (Moscow, 1976), p. 153.
5. Nadezhda Vasil'evna Tumanina, *Chaikovskii. Put' k masterstvu 1840–1877* [Tchaikovsky. Road to Mastery, 1840–1877] (Moscow, 1962), pp. 415–23.
6. *Chaikovskii. Put' k masterstvu*, p. 417.
7. *'Lebedinoe ozero' P. Chaikovskogo*, p. 26.
8. *'Lebedinoe ozero' P. Chaikovskogo*, pp. 16–17.
9. *Vospominaniya*, p. 102.

10. Igor' Glebov [Boris Vladimirovich Asaf'ev], *Lebedinoe ozero* [Swan Lake] (Leningrad, 2nd edn 1934), p. 21.
11. Glebov, *Lebedinoe ozero*, p. 14.
12. Glebov, *Lebedinoe ozero*, p. 32.
13. Tchaikovsky transferred from the opera *The Voevoda* music which became the *entr'acte* at the beginning of Act IV and the opening of the final scene, No. 29 (cf. Petr Il'ich Chaikovskii, *Polnoe sobranie sochinenii*, i/v, pp. 5–10, 31–6); the Neapolitan Dance is based on a popular tune, and the swan theme, if Yurii Davydov's inherited account is accurate, was composed for the house ballet of the late 1860s (see Chapter One, pp. 37–8). It is possible that much more of the ballet than we can verify was composed for other uses. In particular the music Tchaikovsky wrote for Valts's *Cinderella* of 1870 has ostensibly disappeared, but parts of it may live on in *Swan Lake*.
14. Our knowledge of *Undine* is based on surviving sketches: see Vladimir Vasil'evich Protopopov and Nadezhda Vasil'evna Tumanina, *Opernoe tvorchestvo Chaikovskogo* [Tchaikovsky's Operatic Works] (Moscow, 1957), pp. 46–59. In a letter to Meck of 30 April 1878 Tchaikovsky wrote that he burned the score of *Undine* 'about three years ago', which means he could still have consulted it in the early stages of composing *Swan Lake* (see Collected Works Correspondence, vii, p. 238).
15. In the first edition of the orchestral score No. 13/VI was transposed up to the key of A major, consistent with the key of Nos. 13/I and III but in a clear departure from the holograph. See P. I. Chaikovskii, *Le Lac des cygnes. Grand Ballet. Partition d'orchestre* (Moscow [1896]; reprinted New York, 1951), pp. 317–25.
16. One could interpret the Russian Dance, in A minor and danced—one presumes—by Odile, as a foreshadowing of Odette's death because of the key and character; it may even have been the dance that won Siegfried over to Odile. But this possibility must be reconciled with the facts that it was added to the score after Tchaikovsky had completed the rest of the ballet; that no comparable relevance can be attached to the other national dances; and that the libretto does not mention any of them.

CHAPTER 3

1. Evaluating the reorganization of the Moscow theatres solely on the basis of its effect on ballet is misleading. The establishment of the New Theatre for Russian drama compensated in part for the severe treatment of the ballet, and corresponds to what can be ascertained of public tastes in that city, which favoured spoken drama.
2. For an account of the family see 'Vsevolozhskie', *Entsiklopedicheskii slovar'* [Encyclopedic Dictionary], ed. F. A. Brokgaus [Friedrich Arnold Brockhaus] and I. A. Efron, vii, p. 387.
3. Slonimsky claims that Vsevolozhsky was appointed because he was 'wholly reactionary' politically and committed above all to catering to the whims of the imperial family (*P. I. Chaikovskii i baletnyi teatr*, p. 167).
4. Information about Vsevolozhsky's career and theatre reform has been taken from several sources: 'Ivan Aleksandrovich Vsevolozhskii. †29 oktyabrya

1909', *Ezhegodnik Imperatorskikh Teatrov* [Yearbook of the Imperial Theatres], 1909, instalments vi–vii, pp. 122–3; An. A., 'Vsevolozhskii, Ivan Aleksandrovich (1835–1909)', *Teatral'naya entsiklopediya* [Theatre Encyclopedia], i, col. 1035; E. Ponomarev, 'I. A. Vsevolozhskoi', *Ezhegodnik Imperatorskikh Teatrov* (1899–1900), pp. 25–[32]; V. S. Krivenko, 'I. A. Vsevolozhskoi', *Novoe vremya* (30 Oct. 1909), p. 3; 'I. A. Vsevolozhskii', *Novoe vremya* (1 Aug. 1899), p. 3; D. Boretskoi, 'Opera and Ballet During the Time of I. A. Vsevolozhskii', *Novoe vremya* (9 Aug. 1899), p. 2.

5. Krivenko, 'I. A. Vsevolozhskoi'.

6. Krivenko, 'I. A. Vsevolozhskoi'.

7. 'Ivan Aleksandrovich Vsevolozhskii', *Rech'* [Discourse] (1 Nov. 1909), pp. 2–3.

8. Krivenno, 'I. A. Vsevolozhskoi'.

9. Val'ts, p. 128.

10. *Kniga zhizni. Vospominaniya 1855–1918* [The Book of a Life. Recollections, 1855–1918], ed. V. F. Botsyanovskii (n.p., 1929), p. 142.

11. *Vospominaniya*, pp. 30–1.

12. See Telyakovskii, *Vospominaniya*, pp. 29–32; Nikolai Andreevich Rimskii-Korsakov, *My Musical Life*, trans. Judah A. Joffe (New York, 1936), pp. 296–8, 302–3.

13. Skal'kovskii, *V teatral'nom mire*, pp. 9–10.

14. Quoted in *V teatral'nom mire*, p. 9.

15. *V teatral'nom mire*, pp. 8–9.

16. Boretskoi, 'Opera and Ballet During the Time of I. A. Vsevolozhskii'.

17. Skalkovsky attacked the commission's secrecy, pointing out that budgets for the army and navy—of potential relevance to the empire's security—were published, while that of the theatres was withheld (*V teatral'nom mire*, p. 55). (Extracts from his discussions of Vsevolozhsky's reforms have been translated in the present writer's 'Three Historians of the Imperial Russian Ballet', *Dance Research Journal*, xiii/1 (1980), pp. 7–9.) The time-lag between the formulation of a proposal and its enactment into law contributes to confusion surrounding the reforms; for example, reorganization of the theatre school had priority in Vsevolozhsky's new measures from the outset, but did not find its way into the lawbooks until several years later. See *Polnoe sobranie zakonov rossiiskoi imperii* [Collected Laws of the Russian Empire], No. 5452 for the year 1888.

18. Concerning this journal, see the present writer's 'The Yearbook of the Imperial Theatres', *Dance Research Journal*, ix/1 (1976–7), pp. 30–6.

19. Skal'kovskii, *V teatral'nom mire*, p. 58.

20. Balletomanes criticized Vsevolozhsky's decision to move ballet performances from the Bolshoy to the Maryinsky Theatre. Skalkovsky points out in another passage (*V teatral'nom mire*, pp. 62–3) that although the Director's stated reason for the move was the high cost—100,000 roubles—of renovating a building declared unsafe, in fact he favoured the special interests that advocated construction of a new theatre to replace it—at an estimated cost of 7,000,000 roubles. He also observes that an Italian opera company estimated the cost of the renovations sufficient to continue operation at only 15,000 roubles. Telyakovsky claimed that Vsevolozhsky's principal mistake of his

entire tenure was the closing of the Bolshoy Theatre, and estimated 900,000 roubles as the sum required to repair the building (*Vospominaniya*, p. 29).

21. *V teatral'nom mire*, pp. 225–6, 228–9.
22. *V teatral'nom mire*, pp. 12–13.
23. Pleshcheev, *Nash balet*, p. 248.
24. Skal'kovskii, *V teatral'nom mire*, p. 73.
25. *Istoriya tantsev*, iv, p. 121.
26. *V teatral'nom mire*, pp. 121–6.
27. Slonimsky summarizes the documents showing Tchaikovsky's attitude toward Zucchi (*P. I. Chaikovskii i baletnyi teatr*, pp. 66–7).
28. *Dnevniki P. I. Chaikovskogo* [Diaries of P. I. Tchaikovsky] (Moscow and Petrograd, 1923), p. 110.
29. Collected Works Correspondence, xiii, pp. 495–6, 499.
30. See, e.g., the composer's letter to Modeste of 14 Nov. 1886 (Collected Works Correspondence, xiii, p. 505); incidental fragments 'for the ballet' among the notebooks for *The Enchantress* (cited in Slonimskii, *P. I. Chaikovskii i baletnyi teatr*, p. 165).
31. *Zhizn' Petra Il'icha Chaikovskogo*, iii, p. 288.
32. *P. I. Chaikovskii i baletnyi teatr*, p. 165 (citing an entry in Modeste's diary).
33. Collected Works Correspondence, xiii, p. 529.
34. Undated letter quoted in *P. I. Chaikovskii i baletnyi teatr*, p. 165.
35. Collected Works Correspondence, xiv, p. 416.
36. See *Zhizn' Petra Il'icha Chaikovskogo*, iii, pp. 198–238; *Dnevniki P. I. Chaikovskogo*, pp. 187–206; *Muzykal'nye fel'etony i zametki Petra Il'icha Chaikovskogo*, pp. 357–91.
37. Collected Works Correspondence, xiv, p. 429 [letter to Vsevolozhsky of 11 May 1888]. Slonimsky conjectures that Vsevolozhsky rejected *Undine* because it was expedient to produce magnificent imported ballet spectacles and, to use his hyperbole, this 'intimate romantic drama, the union of the lyrical with the fantastic, the delicate poetic and psychological content of the subject which, thanks to Tchaikovsky's personal inclinations, would undoubtedly have been deepened further in his music—all this did not correspond with the directorate's purposes with respect to ballet and could not receive the approval of the Minister of Court.' It would not respond adequately to the 'Philistine bourgeois tastes of the Tsar's milieu' which the Director satisfied with showy imports (*P. I. Chaikovskii i baletnyi teatr*, p. 169).
38. Quoted in Slonimskii, *P. I. Chaikovskii i baletnyi teatr*, p. 169.
39. *P. I. Chaikovskii i baletnyi teatr*, p. 170.
40. *P. I. Chaikovskii i baletnyi teatr*, pp. 171–2. Slonimsky gives no quarter to the possibility that Tchaikovsky's responses may have been lost, and perceives in the composer's silence a 'sharp change from waiting and restraint to an attraction to the new subject.'
41. *P. I. Chaikovskii i baletnyi teatr*, p. 170.
42. Collected Works Correspondence, xiv, p. 509.
43. 'On the Acquisition of the Music and Production of the Ballet *Sleeping Beauty*', Leningrad, Central Music Library of the Theatre of Opera and Ballet named for S. M. Kirov, vii, $\frac{54154}{delo\ 26093}$, fol. 1.

44. 'On the Acquisition of the Music and Production of the Ballet *Sleeping Beauty*', fol. 5 [a file copy]. Yury Bakhrushin gives the figure as 1,500 roubles, citing the telegram Vsevolozhsky sent to Tchaikovsky announcing the bonus ('The Ballets of Tchaikovsky and their Stage History', p. 114).

45. 'On the Acquisition of the Music and Production of the Ballet *Sleeping Beauty*', fol. 6.

46. See, e.g., Slonimskii, *P. I. Chaikovskii i baletnyi teatr*, p. 172.

47. Collected Works Correspondence, xv/a, p. 19, and letter to Shpazhinskaya, p. 123.

48. The libretto omits much of Perrault's tale *La Belle au bois dormant*, and draws from many of his other tales—in the character dances of Act III and more specifically from the beginning of *Griselidis* for the figure of Désiré and the atmosphere of the hunting scene in Act II. The Lilac Fairy may have been Vsevolozhsky's own invention, one appropriate to a man of artistic nature who had seen many springtimes in St Petersburg. For information on precedents, see Slonimskii, *P. I. Chaikovskii i baletnyi teatr*, pp. 172–4; Krasovskaya, pp. 292–4; Rozanova, *Simfonicheskie printsipy baletov Chaikovskogo*, pp. 57–60; Olga Maynard, 'The Sleeping Beauty', *Dance Magazine* (December 1972), pp. 44–64; and, for a study of the tale as folklore, Pamela L. Travers, *About the Sleeping Beauty* (New York, 1975).

49. On *ballet-féerie*, see Krasovskaya, pp. 282, 285–91; Skal'kovskii, *V teatral'nom mire*, pp. 230–3.

50. V. P. Pogozhev, 'Recollections of P. I. Tchaikovsky', in *Chaikovskii. Vospominaniya i pis'ma* [Tchaikovsky. Recollections and Letters], ed. Igor Glebov [Boris Vladimirovich Asaf'ev] (Leningrad, 1924), p. 51.

51. Or, in his exact words, 'cradle, girlhood, love, marriage' (*Izbrannye trudy* [Selected Works], 5 vols. (Moscow, 1952–7), ii, p. 182).

52. *Zhizn' Petra Il'icha Chaikovskogo*, iii, pp. 288–9.

53. Collected Works Correspondence, xiv, p. 509.

54. Collected Works Correspondence, xiv, p. 548.

55. Klin, Tchaikovsky Home Museum, No. 3468; quoted in Bakhrushin, 'Tchaikovsky's Ballets and Their Stage History', p. 103.

56. The balletmaster's plan was printed as a supplement to Bakhrushin, 'Tchaikovsky's Ballets and their Stage History', pp. 245–56; reprinted in this translation in P. I. Chaikovskii, *Polnoe sobranie sochinenii*, xii/g, pp. 368–75; trans. Joan Lawson, *The Dancing Times* (issues for December 1942), pp. 112–14; (January 1943), pp. 168–70; (February 1943), pp. 218–20; (March 1943), pp. 270–1; part of this repr. in *Dance as a Theatre Art*, ed. Selma Jeanne Cohen (New York, 1974), pp. 95–102. Slonimskii (*P. I. Chaikovskii i baletnyi teatr*, pp. 312–22) presented the balletmaster's plan in a new translation together with variants from Petipa's instructions to Tchaikovsky; the latter were published separately, in yet another Russian translation, in *Marius Petipa. Materialy*, pp. 129–36.

57. Denis Ivanovich Leshkov, *Marius Petipa* (Petrograd, 1922), p. 42, note.

58. Both documents are reprinted in Appendix D.

59. 'Tchaikovsky's Ballets and their Stage History', p. 111.

60. Any comparison of instructions and music in which a Soviet score is used would be visually misleading, because such scores include, fully written out,

music that Tchaikovsky in the holograph score indicated with repeat signs. The composer may have done this not in an attempt to disregard his instructions from Petipa but as a convenience to producers in identifying where additional music could be found if needed.

61. *Marius Petipa. Materialy*, p. 136.
62. *Marius Petipa. Materialy*, p. 249.
63. Collected Works Correspondence, xiv, p. 548.
64. Nadezhda Vasil'evna Tumanina, *P. I. Chaikovskii; velikii master* [P. I. Tchaikovsky; Great Master] (Moscow, 1968), p. 273.
65. Letter of 6 Jan. 1889 (Collected Works Correspondence, xv/a, p. 17).
66. Quoted in *Avtografy P. I. Chaikovskogo v arkhive doma-muzeya v Klinu. Spravochnik* [The Autographs of P. I. Tchaikovsky in the Archive of the Home-Museum at Klin. Catalogue], 2 vols. (Moscow and Leningrad, 1950–2), i, p. 24.
67. *Dnevniki P. I. Chaikovskogo*, pp. 219–21.
68. *Dnevniki P. I. Chaikovskogo*, p. 241.
69. Quoted in *Avtografy P. I. Chaikovskogo v arkhive doma-muzeya v Klinu*, i, p. 24. The sketchbooks which contain music for *Sleeping Beauty* have never been systematically published; Rozanova describes them in part and provides photographs of selected pages in *Simfonicheskie printsipy baletov Chaikovskogo, passim.*

CHAPTER 4

1. Thus Rozanova can write: 'An important moment in the continuity, in the logic of lyrical images is the intonational relationship of their themes. The summit and source of development, the independent epigraph, the principal musical thought of the ballet, is unquestionably the Lilac Fairy's theme. The suppleness, beauty, and balance of the melodic line, the gradual movement of the melody, its striving toward circular [*vrashchatel'nyi*] movement and, finally, the triple metre—these are the features which unify the most import-ant lyrical themes of the ballet.' She goes on to list such related themes: in addition to all those cited in the present discussion, she includes the entrance of the fairies in the *pas de quatre* (No. 23), the entrance of Aurora and Désiré (No. 28), the Gold Fairy's variation, the waltz of Act I, Aurora's variation in Act I, and the *adagio* of Aurora and Désiré (No. 28). See her *Simfonicheskie printsipy baletov Chaikovskogo*, pp. 94–5.
2. Collected Works Correspondence, xv/a, p. 169.
3. We do not know if this *grotesquerie* was part of what Tchaikovsky was referring to in his letter to Meck, but if so his claim of its being 'completely new' has not gone unchallenged. Asafiev, for example, has aptly pointed out its affinity with the music of other evil wizards, such as Chernomor in Glinka's *Ruslan and Lyudmila*. And yet there might be another influence, closer to *Sleeping Beauty* stylistically and chronologically, which Russian commentators, disinclined to credit composers outside their own national tradition, might not recognize or acknowledge. This is Wagner's music for Beckmesser in *Die Meistersinger*.
   The stories of the ballet and the opera are so different in externals that one

might easily miss the likenesses between the marker and the evil fairy. Both, for example, are supposedly endowed with power and influence, but neither can make these advantages work. In the end both are made wretched in spite of their imposing reputations.

As regards music, Beckmesser's most characteristic association in Wagner's orchestra—the so-called 'Marker Motive'—is asymmetrical, oddly harmonized, and scored for winds:

The similarity of this motive to the second phrase of Carabosse's music (Ex. 50, bars 41–3) is close indeed; in addition, Wagner, like Tchaikovsky, wrote an extensive mimed scene in which this distinctive music was the subject of an involved working-out (at the beginning of Act III, Scene 3).

When in Leipzig in January 1888, Tchaikovsky heard *Die Meistersinger* for the first time. He heard much music while on tour, but the difference here is that Wagner's opera was given at his request (see his letter to P. Tchaikovskaya of 30 Jan./11 Feb., Collected Works Correspondence, xiv, p. 358). Negotiations concerning *Sleeping Beauty* were only four months away.

4. *Izbrannye stat'i*, ii, pp. 162–3.
5. *Marius Petipa. Materialy*, p. 132. Petipa's instructions to Tchaikovsky for *Sleeping Beauty* and *Nutcracker* are reprinted on pp. 129–44 of this volume, and translated below in Appendix D.
6. For examples of traditional variation music, in which the composer was not troubled by this innovation, one need look no further than the so-called Shades Scene of *La Bayadère*, the bravura music of which has lost all contact with the setting and atmosphere of the ballet. Tchaikovsky's approach does not require ethnographic accuracy: Minkus would never have been expected to write classical variations for *La Bayadère* using Hindu instruments or style, but what he wrote quite unabashedly disregards the possibilities of musical suggestiveness present within the resources of the symphony orchestra. Though less blatantly, Tchaikovsky followed this tradition in *Swan Lake*: compare the ethnic aura of the national dances, which are true to stage illusion, with the classical variations of Acts I and III. Asafiev described the traditional practice indirectly when discussing the variations of *Sleeping*

Beauty: '. . . music not for the simple accompaniment of dances . . . by means of crudely rhythmicized melodies or, truer yet, by means of dance formulas got up into wretched melodic, harmonic, and instrumental garb' (Boris Vladimirovich Asaf'ev, *Izbrannye trudy* [Selected Works], 5 vols. (Moscow, 1952–7), ii, p. 176).

7. Asafiev makes a sharp distinction between these two techniques, stressing either distinctive dance formulas (which imply the subordination of all other musical elements to metre), or dance formulas deepened, made more complex, and transformed by symphonic development. See his *Izbrannye trudy*, ii, pp. 177–8.

8. Asaf'ev *Izbrannye trudy*, ii, p. 178.

9. About the sarabande, Petipa wrote at the end of his plan: 'J'ai donné à M. Tchaikovsky des morceaux de musique de la Sarabande. M. Petipa' (Moscow, State Central Theatre Museum named for A. A. Bakhrushin, *fond* 205, No. 107564, p. 21).

10. The hunting scene of *Sleeping Beauty* has precedents in the eighteenth-century orientation of the opening movements of the *Serenade for Strings* and the first three orchestral suites; the fourth suite, of course, comprises arrangements of Mozart. Tchaikovsky, in Laroche's words, felt an 'instinctive attraction to the classical tradition . . . He ardently loved Mozart, loved him not in theory, but energetically and successfully propagandized for him—but in Tchaikovsky's own works there was no turning back, there was nothing archaic or opposed to [his own] century . . .' (*Izbrannye stat'i*, ii, p. 163).

Alexandre Benois believed that 'Tchaikovsky was able to call forth the very atmosphere of the past with the charms of music. He was successful in re-creating the atmosphere of France in the days of the young Sun King in *Sleeping Beauty* to which only a person absolutely deaf to the summons of the past could remain indifferent. The entire hunt scene, all the courtly games and dances in the forest, and also all the turns of musical phrase which characterize Prince Désiré, possess a "genuineness" which is not at all the same thing as a clever counterfeit in imitation of antiquity, or some kind of "stylization"' (Aleksandr Nikolaevich Benua, *Moi vospominaniya* [My Recollections], 2 vols. (Moscow, 1980), i, p. 603).

11. *Izbrannye trudy*, ii, p. 176.

12. Referring to the *entr'acte* (and Carabosse's music), Benois claimed that 'this is all genuine Hoffmann, this music leads into that fantastic, terrifying sweet world which was reflected with such abundance in the stories of my favourite author, a world of captivating nightmares, a world close at hand and at the same time inaccessible . . . Tchaikovsky could not compose the music of genius of the *entr'acte* if he had not recalled that sweet languor which one feels in childhood in a half somnolent fever, when gradually one sinks into a deeper and deeper sense of non-existence, not stopping to detect precisely the echoes of the surrounding reality, which are receding further and further into the distance' (*Moi vospominaniya*, i, pp. 602–3).

13. Quoted in *Muzykal'noe nasledie Chaikovskogo*, p. 239.

14. Collected Works Correspondence, xiv, p. 505.

15. Critics of the early performances sensed an element of sadness in the last act. 'Generally all the music of the third act, despite the separate character

numbers, is less merry, less varied than it ought to be on this subject . . . Perhaps if the ballet were shorter the last act would not cause a certain weariness which it now causes . . . in part because of the music, when the ear in spite of itself begins to notice a certain lack of cheerfulness and lively animation, which in the last act, projecting a sense of general gaiety, would be especially appropriate' (M. M. Ivanov, 'Musical Observations', *Novoe vremya*, 22 Jan. 1890, p. 2).

'On this subject [*Sleeping Beauty*] Mr Tchaikovsky wrote music by no means simple in the choreographic sense, beautiful, wonderfully orchestrated, and perhaps even a little monotonous, which is noticed at the end of the ballet, where indeed a bit more *entrain* is demanded, more gaiety than the composer could give, and which is distinguished by a marked inclination toward melancholy' (from an unsigned review in *Nuvellist* (1890), ii, pp. 3–5).

16. *P. I. Chaikovskii; velikii master*, p. 280.

17. *Novoe vremya* (6 Jan. 1890), p. 4.

18. Slonimsky claims that the idea of using this tune was Vsevolozhsky's (*P. I. Chaikovskii i baletnyi teatr*, p. 195). If so, it would be reasonable to expect the idea to reach Tchaikovsky through Petipa's instructions, in which, however, there is no mention of it. That it was Tchaikovsky's own idea cannot be ruled out; he possessed a copy of a French songbook which contained it.

CHAPTER 5

1. Tchaikovsky finished the full score in the following sequence: prologue, Act I, Act III, Act II. On 18 June 1889 he explained to Alexander Siloti, who was to prepare the piano arrangement, the routing of the music: the composer would send each act to Petersburg so that copies and a répétiteur could be made; when he received it back, he would send it to Siloti (Collected Works Correspondence, xv/*a*, p. 134).

2. The surviving copy is labelled 'Copy II'. Apparently it had been one of Tchaikovsky's responsibilities to prepare the répétiteur (see his letter to Vsevolozhsky, quoted in Chapter 3, p. 112), but he failed to do so. The artisans who prepared the reduction had difficulty determining the principal melody of certain passages, which required someone—possibly Drigo—to enter corrections in the manuscript, apparently during rehearsals.

3. These sources are identified as follows:
   (*a*) Holograph score (Hol): Leningrad, Central Music Library of the Theatre of Opera and Ballet named for S. M. Kirov, Ballet No. 301.

   The score comprises 261 folios, 41 cm. × 38 cm., containing either 26 or 30 printed music staves, bound in two volumes, the first volume containing the prologue and Act I, the second Acts II and III. There are many corrections in Tchaikovsky's hand, especially in music interpolated after the manuscript was finished (such as the 'Entrée des chats', ten bars added before the (original) beginning of No. 24, and No. 26*b*, a new dance for Cinderella and Prince Fortuné). When such interpolations required parts of the original to be effaced, replacement pages in a copyist's hand were substituted (the opening of No. 27).

Some of conductor Riccardo Drigo's revisions were written on blank folios, or where space permitted on folios containing Tchaikovsky's original; others are written on loose sheets placed in the MS near the passages to which they refer.

A number of hands in addition to Tchaikovsky's and Drigo's are represented in the Hol: at least one additional hand involved in musical instructions ('accel.', 'riten.', and the like) is in larger, rougher letters than Drigo's. Others, restricted to series of numbers running across the lower half of the folios which pertain to pagination and the numbering of bars, seem to be the work of typesetters and editors preparing the music for publication.

A dispute over rights of ownership of the Hol erupted between Vladimir Pogozhev and Tchaikovsky's publisher, Peter Jurgenson. Pogozhev, who had recently supervised the building of the Central Music Library of the Imperial Theatres, claimed the right to *Sleeping Beauty* for that library, citing as the basis of his claim a new regulation according to which authors' manuscripts of works first performed in the imperial theatres were to be deposited there. Jurgenson, however, who claimed the rights to all Tchaikovsky's works by prior agreement, objected, and insisted in a letter of 17 January 1890 that the Hol be returned to him, even though he had no plans to publish it (see Pogozhev, 'Recollections About P. I. Tchaikovsky', in *Chaikovskii. Vospominaniya i pis'ma*, pp. 52–75, and Glebov's supplement, p. 89). The Hol stayed in the Central Music Library, as did the similarly disputed Hol of *The Queen of Spades*.

(b) Répétiteur (Rep): Leningrad, Central Music Library of the Theatre of Opera and Ballet named for S. M. Kirov, $\frac{\text{I } 44154}{\textit{Re Spyashch}}$.

This score, for two violins, comprises 158 folios of 12-stave music paper, 38.3 cm. × 25.3 cm., bound in one volume. It was prepared from the Hol or some other complete score, but was modified in pencil to reflect changes made in rehearsal. It is rich in remarks (in pencil and ink, French and Russian) relating to the assignment of dancers to roles and details of stage action. There is much evidence of use—worn and frayed edges, folios containing unused music folded over or pinned together, many repairs, some involving tape which obscured the original text.

The additional remarks are in several hands. Some instructions about music may have been added by Drigo, but others seem to be the work of rehearsal violinists. Remarks in French about stage action, assignment of dancers to roles, and criticism of the music are thought to be Petipa's. There are at least two unidentified scribes writing in Russian about stage action: one in thick, unambiguous letters, the other in light, delicate ones.

(c) Printed piano reductions belonging to Nikolai Sergeyev, Copy I (PR-I) and Copy II (PR-II): Cambridge, Mass., Harvard Theatre Collection, bMS Thr 245 (205).

PR-I is a complete copy (212 pp.) of the piano score in Alexander Siloti's arrangement as published by Jurgenson. It bears the following marks on its dust cover: 'SL-PR' and '11-17'. Interpolated among the printed pages are two manuscript copies of certain dances in revised versions (Nos. 24, 25, 27). Many names of dancers associated with the Moscow imperial ballet are written in it, together with annotations, in Russian and English, concerning casts and stage action.

PR-II agrees with PR-I in most of the modifications made in the music and remarks describing stage action, but it lacks printed pages 161–4, 183–94, 197–212, and all the manuscript interpolations found in PR-I.

4. The sources do not agree on the type and number of changes. The differences may relate to the time periods and locations of their use. Unlike PR-I and PR-II, the Hol and Rep never left Russia; the changes they preserve reflect modifications for performances in the imperial theatres. Of these two, the Hol would seem to be the more valuable because it was used only to prepare the first production. But it was not completely annotated; it contains the smallest number of changes of any of the sources, and no indication of some changes that were almost certainly put into practice. The Rep, judging from the names of the dancers found in it, was used only in St Petersburg, but to prepare the first production and a revival of about 1903. Except where the Rep agrees with the Hol, changes in the Rep cannot be attributed with certainty to the first production. PR-I and PR-II preserve information found in neither Hol nor Rep, but these sources were used in St Petersburg, Moscow, and London.

5. The editors of Tchaikovsky's Collected Works adopted an unsympathetic view of Drigo's modifications:

> The autograph of the score of *Sleeping Beauty* is marked all over with numerous notations in the hand of R. E. Drigo, conductor of the first performance of the ballet. We cite them as evidence of those corruptions of the author's text which were tolerated in large numbers during the first production . . . (P. I. Chaikovskii, *Polnoe sobranie sochinenii*, xii/a, p. xvii).

Yury Slonimsky absolved Petipa of responsibility for these changes:

> In the Petipa archives there are scores of his notes indicating how careful and attentive he was to music which he considered of high quality and which did not disagree with his conceptions. The cuts in 'The Sleeping Beauty' can on no account be attributed to him. They are the work of Riccardo Drigo and other conductors (*Mastera baleta* [Masters of the Ballet] (Leningrad, 1937), p. 269).

None of Drigo's critics explains the conductor's reasons for making these changes, if not to comply with Petipa's wishes.

6. Certain measures in the Hol, blank except for an alphabetical or numerical designation, indicate which earlier passages, with corresponding designations, are to be repeated. Sometimes the composer indicated the repeat of entire numbers by this method, or by means of verbal instructions.

A few details near the beginning of the Hol suggest that a passing thought had been given to conducting from this score. At the end of fol. 8^r (the end of the introduction) the printed stave-lines have been extended by hand to the edge of the paper to accommodate the change of key signature from four sharps to three (anticipating the key of No. 1); and in the last measure, 'Attacca' and 'Segue subito No. 1mo del Ballo'.

7. The editors of Tchaikovsky's Collected Works wrote: 'Metronome tempo markings in the autograph, written in later in pencil, in view of their questionable attribution to P. I. Tchaikovsky, are given within parentheses' (P. I. Chaikovskii, *Polnoe sobranie sochinenii*, xii/a, p. xix).

Of the 59 metronome markings in the Hol, only 3 found their way into the Collected Works (none appears in Siloti's piano arrangement), one of which—at the beginning of No. 23—was placed at the head of the music, without parentheses, as if it were the only one in the entire score which Tchaikovsky himself decided. Twenty-seven are confirmed in the Rep. All are listed in Appendix E.

8. Of numerous added instructions which specify expressive effects in the prologue, the most important occurs when the Lilac Fairy arrives in No. 2 (at bar 57). Here Tchaikovsky's 'poco meno animato' was changed to 'poco più animato'. It is impossible to determine what caused this change, but slowing the music, as Tchaikovsky specified, would have enhanced the likeness of the passage with the Lilac Fairy's theme in the introduction as she here makes her first appearance on stage. That all published scores preserve the change—including imperial editions of Siloti's arrangement—suggests that Tchaikovsky approved it.

There was only one cut made in the prologue: bars 68–71 of Variation V of the *pas de six*. (All reference to bar numbers are to the Collected Works edition, its reprints, or piano reductions based on it.)

9. All sources agree on these changes. The Rep preserves many others, not in the Hol, some of which may be the result of Petipa's complaints. 'Trop long' he wrote above bars 72–3 of No. 5, perhaps causing the first part of the dance of the knitters (bars 45–60) to be cut. 'Petite coupe' follows, above bar 184 of the same number, with the indication that bars 184–205 were cut. In the rose *adagio* the Rep calls for a repeat of bars 74–80, and in Aurora's variation for the deletion of the repeat sign at bar 216.

10. Quoted in Bakhrushin, 'Tchaikovsky's Ballets and their Stage History', p. 111.

11. The revision of Act II may have been complicated because the producers received essential musical materials late. Act II was the last to be scored; Tchaikovsky wrote at the end of the Hol: 'End of the 2nd Act. 16 August 89. Hoorah!' But instead of sending the music directly to the theatre (as he had proposed to do two months earlier—see note 1), he sent it to Siloti. Only after the piano reduction was made, it seems, was the score sent on to the theatre for the preparation of the Rep and copies. If Siloti and the theatre musicians required six to eight weeks for their work (a modest estimate, given the complexity of the score), the music might not have been ready for Petipa until mid October, by which time he was already setting Act III. Considering the shortness of time after Act III was ready and delays in the preparation of the stage machinery (the most complicated of which was needed for Act II), it is not difficult to understand why the revisions in the second act showed signs of haste and indecision.

12. Drigo's modification of the end of the panorama has been accepted as Tchaikovsky's in the Collected Works edition and its derivatives. If Tchaikovsky was simply informed of a change, as distinct from being requested to make the change himself, there is no justification for not restoring his original, especially in published scores and recordings. The original ending is given in Appendix H.

13. In PR-I and PR-II the Dance of the Baronesses and the Dance of the Marchio-

nesses were cut. Slonimsky states that all the court dances were cut in a revival in 1914 (*P. I. Chaikovskii i baletnyi teatr*, p. 196, n. 1).

14. All sources concur in this change, assuming that 'Segue Variation Mlle Brianza' in the Hol, at the end of No. 15*a*, implies a substitution to follow. The modified cadence of No. 15*a* is preserved on a loose folio in the Hol, and there would be no need for the 'Segue . . .' in the absence of a change, since the music which followed in the original was already a variation for Mlle Brianza.

15. In the Rep of the march the raising of the curtain was moved from bar 33 to bar 16; in the polacca the music was slowed near the end of the introduction (bars 18–21), in anticipation of the downbeat that marked the beginning of the dance proper (bar 22). Cf. the instruction Tchaikovsky provided at the comparable location in the polacca of the Suite No. 3: 'The author would like the first bar of the polacca to be taken in a *tempo très ritenuto*. Only with the second bar does the true polacca tempo begin. However, for the reprise this first bar must be taken strictly in the polacca tempo' (*Polnoe sobranie sochinenii*, xx, p. 179).

16. The editors of the Collected Works state that Variation III was deleted after the first performance, 'presumably difficult and insufficiently expressive in its five-beat rhythm . . .' (*Polnoe sobranie sochinenii*, xii/*a*, p. xviii). It may have been cut much earlier, because the Hol, surely no longer in use by the time of the first performance, shows the deletion, and because Petipa entered no dancer's name at the head of this dance in the Rep (something he did for the variations that were used).

17. Quoted in Slonimskii, *P. I. Chaikovskii i baletnyi teatr*, p. 233. We may take Christoforov's 'without changing the music' to mean 'without deleting the music originally written for Cinderella and Prince Fortuné', for the music was changed: 'ritards' and pauses were added to the opening *adagio*, the first variation was shortened, and the coda slowed from 'Presto' to 'Allegretto'.

18. The scenario has been published in two translations from the French into Russian, which differ slightly from one another:

Cinderella is forced to leave the ball and to put on her own clothes. She goes out very upset. She enters with tongs and bellows for fanning a fire. The Prince appears with a slipper, hunting for the person to whom it belongs. At the sight of Cinderella's little foot he offers her the slipper: 'It is she!' He is delighted (here follows a fitting of the slipper). Fanning the bellows, Cinderella spoils the Prince's coiffure. He follows Cinderella, confessing his love for her. Cinderella runs away from him. At the moment the Prince embraces her, she pinches his nose with her fireplace tongs. With this the *pas* ends [Slonimskii, *P. I. Chaikovskii i baletnyi teatr*, pp. 233–4].

Cinderella is as if come home from the ball and is again dressed in her old clothes. She looks very upset. She enters with tongs and bellows in order to start a fire.

The Prince appears, holding a slipper in his hand. He is searching for its owner.

He sees Cinderella's little foot, tries the slipper on her, and cries out in astonishment: 'It is she!'

With the aid of the bellows Cinderella blows the Prince's hair back into place, which had fallen down over his forehead. The Prince follows Cinderella, protesting his love. Cinderella runs out. When the Prince displays inordinate enterprise, she pinches his nose with the tongs.

With this the dance ends [*Marius Petipa. Materialy*, p. 119].

The music Tchaikovsky wrote for this (No. 26*b*), drafted with many crossings out and other signs of haste, was interpolated into the Hol. Petipa wrote requesting the composer's permission to make a small cut in it (bars 21–36) only ten days after requesting the music in the first place, a fact which attests the speed with which both men worked. Petipa's request is published in *Marius Petipa. Materialy*, p. 119.

19. Quoted in Slonimskii, *P. I. Chaikovskii i baletnyi teatr*, p. 181.
20. The Rep is inconclusive. A cut between the end of the introduction and the bottom of the page (No. 28, bars 6–14) suggests that the whole *entrée* was to be deleted, but this cut is not continued through subsequent pages to end at the beginning of the *adagio*; and these subsequent pages are marked with other cuts as if the music on either side was meant to be played. Slonimsky states that the entire *entrée* was cut (*P. I. Chaikovskii i baletnyi teatr*, p. 234).
21. Quoted in Bakhrushin, 'Tchaikovsky's Ballets and their Stage History', p. 106.
22. The collection has apparently been catalogued though no catalogue has been published. It may be that some of these papers do not warrant publication because they are piecemeal, casual—trivial, even—the kinds of remnants that one would hardly imagine the balletmaster himself wanting posterity to study. But Petipa's Russian historians have referred to the collection, and from their descriptions and samples we can get a sense of what Petipa's workshop was like.

    Part of Petipa's notes for a number of ballets has been published in *Marius Petipa. Materialy*, pp. 155–224, with commentary by Fedor Lopukhov. While it is possible to gain some idea of the intricacy of Petipa's thought from what was published, the photographs in this edition have been modified by the addition of labels, Petipa's text is given only in Russian translation (the original French in the photographs often being illegible), and the individual documents lack precise bibliographic identification. Moreover, the editors give no idea of what remains unpublished. Of Lopukhov it must be noted that whatever his credentials to speak about later productions of *Sleeping Beauty*, he was three years old when the original production was mounted, five at the time of the first *Nutcracker*, and eight when Petipa and Ivanov revived *Swan Lake*. For one critic's comments on Lopukhov's revival of *Nutcracker*, see Appendix G.
23. Boris Romanov, 'The Dancer's Notes (M. I. Petipa's Work Outside the Rehearsal Hall)', *Biryuch Gosudarstvennykh Petrogradskikh Teatrov* [Herald of the Petrograd State Theatres] (1918), vii, p. 37.
24. *Baletmeister Marius Petipa. (Ocherk iz istorii russkogo baleta)* [The Balletmaster Marius Petipa. (Essay on the History of Russian Ballet)] (Leningrad, 1924), pp. 29–30.
25. Quoted in Bakhrushin, 'Tchaikovsky's Ballets and their Stage History', p. 110.
26. Quoted in Slonimskii, *P. I. Chaikovskii i baletnyi teatr*, p. 194.
27. 'Tchaikovsky's Ballets and their Stage History', p. 107.
28. *Marius Petipa. Materialy*, p. 191. This quotation is one of two fragments of text from Petipa's notes for *Sleeping Beauty* selected by the editors of this volume; in their selection from *Swan Lake* (pp. 212–13), the reader may

observe more clearly Petipa's concern for matching dances with dancers. He apparently experienced some indecision over casting the Lilac Fairy's part; in at least three lists he assigns this part not to his daughter Marie, but to Anna Johansson (Moscow, State Theatre Museum named for A. A. Bakhrushin, *fond* 205, Nos. 106987, 106989, 106998*a*).

29. *Marius Petipa. Materialy*, p. 267.
30. *Marius Petipa. Materialy*, p. 267.
31. *Novoe vremya* (1 Jan. 1889), p. 5.
32. To suggest that Brianza was a genuine replacement for Zucchi would arouse debate both then and now. Her versatility and diligence were praised in the winter season of 1889 as she made débuts in various repertory works, and her performances of Manzotti's *Excelsior* in Paris during the summer increased her stature in Petersburg. A reviewer of her first performance in the autumn could praise her *plastique*, the strength of her legs, ethereal quality, noble elegance, precision, and virtuosity (*Novoe vremya*, 22 Sept. 1889, p. 3). With Zucchi so fresh in the minds of Petersburg balletomanes, however, it was only a matter of time before comparisons were made. One was written when she performed *Esmeralda*. Noting that Brianza had appeared in one of Zucchi's best roles, and that this constituted a kind of test for her, the reviewer summarized: 'Mlle Brianza withstood her ordeal and had success, although one cannot help noticing that her Esmeralda is only an excellent copy of the Esmeralda created by the "Divine Virginia"; we noticed nothing new or original, but with respect to dances Mlle Brianza left Mlle Zucchi behind. Of course, she has nothing of that expressivity in dances, that poetry which Mlle Zucchi had, but for that reason her performance is much lighter, livelier, and more distinctive' (*Novoe vremya*, 10 Oct. 1889, p. 3).

A year after the annual review in which Zucchi's release from imperial service was lamented, we read: '. . . Mlle Brianza is a gifted artist but no star as regards virtuosity. . . Mlle Zucchi danced at the Arcadia in the summer, but already far from as successfully as before . . .' (*Novoe vremya*, 1 Jan. 1890, p. 4).

33. Maria Karlovna Anderson, 'Meetings with P. I. Tchaikovsky', *Vospominaniya o P. I. Chaikovskom*, 2nd edn, pp. 237–8.
34. *Novoe vremya* (15 Feb. 1889), p. 3.
35. *Novoe vremya* (19 Apr. 1889), p. 3. This is probably the notice that Tchaikovsky read in Tiflis on his way home from Western Europe. Hoping that he now had sixteen months to complete *Sleeping Beauty* instead of four, he wrote asking Petipa and Pogozhev for confirmation. Vsevolozhsky replied (the letter cited in the next note), chiding the newspaper for spreading rumours.

Novoe vremya was not alone in publishing misinformation. It and others frequently had to retract, sometimes for serious mistakes, sometimes for innocent misprints (one issue contained an apology for a reference the preceding day to Pugni's music as 'pedagogic' rather than 'melodic'). In assessing what is published about delays in *Sleeping Beauty* it is difficult to know which of these terse announcements, mostly anonymous but certainly not all retracted, is true.

36. See Bakhrushin, 'Tchaikovsky's Ballets and their Stage History', p. 106. Tchaikovsky hints in his letter to Siloti of 18 June 1889 that Petipa may have

been responsible for the tone of urgency in Christoforov's letter: 'No sooner was I intending to send you the score of Act I than I received a letter from Christoforov, who requires receipt of the score directly so he can get started on a copy, making orchestral parts, and chiefly the preparation of a Violino répétiteur, which Petipa is demanding from him as soon as possible' (Collected Works Correspondence, xv/a, p. 134).

37. All quotations from the balletmaster's plan have been translated from the original: Moscow, State Theatre Museum named for A. A. Bakhrushin, *fond* 205, No. 107564 (the text is reproduced below, Appendix D).

38. 'I remember how in *Sleeping Beauty* in the final scene, after being pricked with the poisoned spindle, Aurora falls and a general commotion begins, father appealed to the children not to remain indifferent, but to include themselves in the general sorrowful experience' (Vera Petipa, quoted in *Marius Petipa. Materialy*, p. 250).

39. Quoted in Pleshcheev, *Moe vremya*, p. 147.

40. Quoted in *Marius Petipa. Materialy*, p. 263.

41. Quoted in Slonimskii, *P. I. Chaikovskii i baletnyi teatr*, pp. 180–1; specifically, Slonimsky is quoting from a report given by Boris Asafiev; it is possible that Asafiev was relating in this report the recollection of his own first-hand conversations with Drigo. Alexandre Benois recalled his brother Leonty's impression of the *répétition générale* to the effect that the music was insufficiently melodious, 'too complex and chaotic, and most of all *not dansante*. The rumour even circulated that the artists refused to dance to it, so incomprehensible did it seem to them' (*Moi vospominaniya*, i, p. 601).

42. *P. I. Chaikovskii i baletnyi teatr*, p. 181.

43. Quoted in *Marius Petipa. Materialy*, pp. 268–9.

44. He referred to the orchestral rehearsals in correspondence with Grand Duke Konstantin Konstantinovich (Collected Works Correspondence, xv/a, p. 200).

45. Quoted in Pleshcheev, *Sergei Lifar' ot starogo k novomu*, p. 25.

46. 'Recollections about P. I. Tchaikovsky', *Chaikovskii. Vospominaniya i pis'ma*, ed. Glebov, pp. 50–1.

47. *Novoe vremya* (10 Nov. 1889), p. 3.

48. 'Recollections about P. I. Tchaikovsky', in *Chaikovskii. Vospominaniya i pis'ma*, ed. Glebov, p. 51.

49. *Novosti i birzhevaya gazeta* (30 Nov. 1889), p. 3.

50. Collected Works Correspondence, xv/a, p. 217.

51. Collected Works Correspondence, xv/a, pp. 218–19.

52. 'On the Acquisition of the Music and Production of the Ballet *Sleeping Beauty*', fol. 3.

53. Leshkov, 'Personal Reminiscences of R. E. Drigo', fol. 16.

54. Léon Bakst, 'Tchaikowsky aux Ballets Russes', *Comoedia*, xv, No. 3220 (19 Oct. 1921), p. 1.

55. Quoted in Pleshcheev, *Moe vremya*, pp. 145, 148.

56. *Dnevniki P. I. Chaikovskogo*, p. 249.

57. *Novoe vremya* (5 Jan. 1890), p. 3.

58. *Syn otechestva* [Son of the Fatherland] (2 Jan. 1890), p. 3.

59. The choreographic notation (CN) of *Sleeping Beauty* (Harvard Theatre Collection, bMS Thr 245 (204)), contains notations of steps and floor patterns, and

verbal mime summaries. It comprises the following loose sheets in nine folders: 101 folios of notation paper (some blank) with 3 or 6 printed staves, 22.2 cm. × 35.5 cm., slightly frayed and discoloured from age; 4 folios of notation paper with 4 printed staves, 25.8 cm. × 39.2 cm.; 11 folios of plain white paper (8), graph paper (2), and Nikolai Sergeyev's London stationery (1), containing synopses, additional choreographic notations (some are variants of dances or parts of dances recorded on notation paper), and lists of entries for processionals in Act III.

Cataloguers' descriptions and miscellaneous scraps of paper with cataloguing information, mostly in English, are interleaved with the folios containing notation. The choreographic notations (but not the sheets with cataloguing information) have been paginated; page numbers have been assigned to each folio on the recto (the verso is unpaginated), so that only odd-numbered pages have page numbers.

The CN is part of a larger collection of dance materials once belonging to the late Nikolai Sergeyev; for a description of the collection, see the present writer's 'Dances From Russia: an Introduction to the Sergeyev Collection', *Harvard Library Bulletin*, xxiv (1976), pp. 96–112.

Stepanov's notation system has been variously published. His original treatise, *Alphabet des mouvements du corps humain au moyen des signes musicaux* (Paris, 1892), was translated by Raymond Lister: *Alphabet of Movements of the Human Body* (London, 1958). In Russian, see *Tablitsa znakov dlya zapisyvaniya dvizhenii chelovecheskogo tela po sisteme Artista Imperatorskikh S.-Peterburgskikh Teatrov, V. I. Stepanova* [Table of Signs for the Notation of the Movements of the Human Body According to the System of the Artist of the Imperial St Petersburg Theatres, V. I. Stepanov] (St Petersburg, n.d.). This explanation of Stepanov's system, by his disciple Alexander Gorsky, has been translated by the present writer in *Two Essays on Stepanov Dance Notation by Alexander Gorsky* (New York, 1978).

60. Slonimsky claims to have prepared written accounts of parts of *Swan Lake* and *Sleeping Beauty* in the 1920s, and these have been verified as true to the originals by some of the participants in the first productions. In preparing his book he submitted his work to many authorities for review, including Alexander Oblakov and Alexander Shiryaev, who performed in the first productions (*P. I. Chaikovskii i baletnyi teatr*, pp. 4–5).

61. The CN calls for Catalabutte to walk over to stage left and admire the infant Aurora in her cradle before the royal party arrives. According to the libretto, there is no cradle on stage until the wet-nurses, following the King and Queen, carry in Aurora in her cradle.

62. The libretto calls for Catalabutte to verify the list while 'surrounded by courtiers'.

63. The word *seigneurs* (in Russian), written above bar 40 in the Rep, may refer to these five couples; PR-II calls for 'guests' in bars 58 and 63. In the CN, Catalabutte sends the new arrivals to admire Aurora. Of this scene as a whole Slonimsky wrote: 'In any event in the spectacle there was neither procession with the cradle of the newborn, nor humorous or characteristic scenes—nothing except the private inventions of the actors who perform the role of Catalabutte. Everything else, in a featureless, dry, and conventional way

reproduced a procession of various courtly personages' (*P. I. Chaikovskii i baletnyi teatr*, p. 202).

64. The libretto reverses the order of fairies Breadcrumb and Canari; in the Rep, the name 'Johansson' appears above bar 46. Anna Johansson performed the part of Canari. The sequence of entrances is not clear from the CN, in which the word 'fairies' is placed above symbols of six women in two rows of three, and followed by the words: 'I—with fans, II—pages, III—'. There is no suggestion here of the staggered entrances (in time) called for in the Rep.

65. PR-I and PR-II suggest a slightly different sequence of events. They contain the following markings in No. 2: above bar 12, 'with fans'; beneath bars 26–7, 'suite of the fairy'; beneath bars 57–8, 'Lilac Fairy's pages'; above bar 73, 'Lilac Fairy'; above bar 79, '[with] censers'; above bar 85, 'with pillows'.

66. The sources disagree on the presentation of the gifts. The libretto states that a sign from Catalabutte brings pages and girls on stage with Florestan's presents for the fairies. In the CN the fairies say: 'We will give you necklaces, bracelets, rings, etc.', whereupon a group of children run on stage and kneel. In the next square we read: 'The King thanks the fairies for the gifts', and the children run off stage. The passage is hardly clarified by Sergeyev's manuscript synopsis, preserved on unnumbered, interpolated sheets at the beginning of the CN, which reads in part: 'The Lilac Fairy enters [and] bows. At this time the five [other] fairies go up to the Lilac Fairy. All say that they have brought gifts for the child, rings, bracelets, etc. They summon pages with presents on pillows and show all of this to the King and Queen. They thank the fairies for the gifts.' Slonimsky comments that the pages and girls present gifts to the fairies (*P. I. Chaikovskii i baletnyi teatr*, p. 203).

67. According to the balletmaster's plan, the fairies do not 'come down from the platform to present gifts to the child in their turn' until the beginning of the *pas de six* (Tchaikovsky wrote the quoted words in the Hol at this point). It is not clear in the libretto whether the fairies' descent occurs during or after the waltz in No. 2.

68. Cf. Lopukhov's comments about two of Petipa's sketches that are quite different from those in the CN: 'The wet-nurses carry Aurora into the centre of the group, where the Lilac Fairy is raised up on a pedestal. The Lilac Fairy also dominates the last drawing—the culmination and the end of the *adagio*' (*Marius Petipa. Materialy*, pp. 190–1).

Sergeyev's supplementary drawings of the groups of the *adagio* depict different patterns from those found in the CN proper, which require larger numbers of performers. Sergeyev too calls for the wet-nurses to bring Aurora's cradle into the middle of the last grouping of the *adagio*.

69. Our knowledge of the four-bar wait is based on information from the Rep, in which 'Elle commence' is written above bar 5.

70. *P. I. Chaikovskii i baletnyi teatr*, p. 206.

71. The members of Carabosse's suite are not listed in the libretto; in the CN there is no fixed number; and in the Rep at bar 96 (the first dance of the pages of Carabosse) we read: 'four children/mice'. Posed photographs taken at the time of the first production show four mice. The reviewer of the *Peterburgskaya gazeta* (4 Jan. 1890), p. 3, pointed out that Carabosse's wheelbarrow was drawn by six mice.

72. A variant of this passage reads: 'He will kiss her on the forehead and she will awaken and he will marry her' (CN, p. 53).

73. See, e.g., *P. I. Chaikovskii i baletnyi teatr*, pp. 213–14, and *Marius Petipa. Materialy*, pp. 202–4, for Petipa's sketches of the grouping.

74. Unsigned review, *Peterburgskaya gazeta* (4 Jan. 1890), p. 3. In the CN, PR-I, and PR-II, the maids of honour are identified by the word 'black'.

75. *Novosti i birzhevaya gazeta* (5 Jan. 1890), p. 3; Skalkovsky in *Novoe vremya* (5 Jan. 1890), p. 2, also noticed Aurora's 'very effective bright red costume, which goes beautifully with the black hair and eyes of the Italian ballerina.'

76. The CN's version of the courtship ritual thus contradicts the libretto, which states that Aurora gives preference to none. Slonimsky observed that 'one of the four princes, the strongest in supporting, the balletmaster chose as the unchanging partner of Aurora in the concluding phrases of each period. From this is created the false impression that Aurora made him her chosen one or, at least, prefers him to the others' (*P. I. Chaikovskii i baletnyi teatr*, p. 217).

77. The CN does not have an indication of the change of tempo at bar 130. The pause at the point where the maids of honour return from the square to single file may correspond to the pause at bar 129, but if so it merely emphasizes the absence of a strong choreographic articulation. Above bar 138 in the Rep is the word 'children'.

78. Aleksandr Alekseevich Gorskii, *Khoreografiya. Primery dlya chteniya* [Choreography. Examples for Reading] (St Petersburg, 1899), pp. 40–3.

79. There is a slight lack of agreement between the CN and the libretto. The latter calls for the pages and the maids of honour to accompany her on violins and lutes; there is no indication in the CN that the maids of honour ever took over this duty from the four students with mandolins.

80. The libretto calls for Carabosse to throw off her own cloak.

81. The italicized words here and in the next paragraph are taken from a production scenario included among Petipa's papers and published in Slonimskii, *P. I. Chaikovskii i baletnyi teatr*, p. 323.

82. *Novosti i birzhevaya gazeta* (5 Jan. 1890), p. 3.

83. *Novoe vremya* (5 Jan. 1890), p. 2.

84. *Novosti i birzhevaya gazeta* (5 Jan. 1890), p. 3.

85. *Novoe vremya* (5 Jan. 1890), p. 2.

86. *Novosti i birzhevaya gazeta* (5 Jan. 1890), p. 3.

87. *P. I. Chaikovskii i baletnyi teatr*, pp. 192–3.

88. Moscow, State Central Theatre Museum named for A. A. Bakhrushin, *fond* 205, No. 107391.

89. The notators recorded two versions of the appearance of Aurora's shade (the end of No. 14), and two of the dance performed to the *andante cantabile* of No. 15a. The notation recorded when Mathilde Kshesinskaya danced the part of Aurora is the more elaborate, calling for a *corps de ballet* of twenty-four instead of sixteen. The general outline and choreographic sense of both versions are the same. The notation of Aurora's variation does not mention the name of the ballerina, but Kshesinskaya (who began to perform the role of Aurora as early as 17 January 1893) danced in the coda at the time it was notated. The variants for the unidentified ballerina have been used in this description when a choice was possible because they are richer in detail, and

because they correspond with the libretto in the number of dancers in the *corps*—sixteen.

90. In the Rep 'Brianza' is written above bar 61 of the coda; PR-I and PR-II have 'Entrance of Aurora' at the same point.
91. *Novoe vremya* (5 Jan. 1890), p. 2.
92. *Russkie vedomosti* (14 Jan. 1890), p. 2.
93. *Moi vospominaniya*, i, p. 604.
94. *Novosti i birzhevaya gazeta* (5 Jan. 1890), p. 3.
95. Quoted in Slonimskii, *P. I. Chaikovskii i baletnyi teatr*, p. 324. Benois declared that the painter Ivanov 'excelled himself' in the awakening scene:

> In essence there were two décors, of which the first represented Aurora's sleeping chambers, which were immersed in total darkness; the pale moonlight made its way through the window, overgrown with cobwebs, and in the huge luxurious fireplace the coals barely smouldered; in the semi-darkness it was difficult to make out the architectural details, consistent in style with the French renaissance. And suddenly, as soon as the Prince kissed the sleeping beauty's hand [sic], the room was flooded with rays of sunlight, which penetrated into the furthest corners. When this happened, all the statues in their niches came alive in a complex play of light, and in the fireplace the fire already blazed up merrily' (*Moi vospominaniya*, i, pp. 604–5).

PR-I and PR-II provide a few details for the scene of the sleeping castle: at the beginning of No. 19, 'tulle'; at bar 78, 'I tulle'; at bar 85, 'II tulle'—all, doubtless, references to curtains—at bar 96, 'the fairy'; after the last bar, 'It is dark'. And before the first bar of No. 20: 'light'.

96. *Novosti i birzhevaya gazeta* (5 Jan. 1890), p. 3.
97. What exactly was cut we cannot learn so easily, for neither Rep nor Hol shows any evidence of modification; PR-I and PR-II call for the deletion of sixteen bars (65–72, 81–9). PR-II provides some information about stage action—the name 'Catalabutte' above bar 17; Petipa, in a sketch, provides an idea of the ballerina's costume: 'Princess Aurora—the rich, long costume of a bride (but for the performance of the duet she will put on another costume—short)' (quoted in Slonimskii, *P. I. Chaikovskii i baletnyi teatr*, p. 194).
98. The order of entries in the polacca seems to have concerned the notators more than the dancers' steps which, like those of the waltz and the mazurka, were standard unless some special treatment was required. The CN preserves only a list of entries, and this list disagrees with the order of entries provided in the other sources. PR-I and PR-II preserve the clearest and most complete list:
    Introduction (bars 1–21)
    [Cut—bars 22–9]
    Bluebeard [and his wife], Puss in Boots, and the Marquis de Carabas (bars 35–7)
    Goldilocks [and Prince Avenant] (bars 38–9)
    Peau d'âne [and Prince Charmant] (bar 46)
    Beauty [and the Beast] (bar 50)
    Cinderella [and Prince Fortuné] (bar 58)
    The Blue Bird [and Princess Florine] (bars 72–3)
    The White Cat (bar 80)
    The Wolf [and Little Red Riding Hood] (bar 87)

Ricky of the Tuft [and his Princess] (bar 95); in bar 95 of the Rep we read 'little boys'

[Cut—bars 103-10]

Tom Thumb [his brothers, the ogre, and ogress]; Fairy Carabosse (bar 111)

Fairies [Candide and Violente] (bar 119)

Fairies Breadcrumb [and Lilac] (bar 127); the libretto calls for Canari instead of Breadcrumb. Since Marie Petipa and Enrico Cecchetti had already been part of the procession, as Cinderella and the Blue Bird, by the time the Lilac Fairy and Carabosse made their appearances a double must have been provided for them

Children [unspecified] (bar 135)

99. *Novosti i birzhevaya gazeta* (5 Jan. 1890), p. 3.

100. The CN is based on Tamara Karsavina's performance of the White Cat. The critic Valerian Svetlov remarked once in a review that 'this choreographic genre piece was not in character for her' (*Birzhevye vedomosti* [Stock Exchange Gazette], 7 Apr. 1907 [evening edition], p. 3).

101. *Petersburgskaya gazeta* (4 Jan. 1890), p. 3.

102. This may be the part of the dance described by Skalkovsky when he wrote, 'With his left arm behind, in one of the groups, he threw our ballerina up on his back like a little ball' (*Novoe vremya*, 5 Jan. 1890, p. 3). 'The audience gasped when Cecchetti with his left arm threw [Nikitina] up over his back as if she were a piece of fluff' (Nikolai Aleksandrovich Solyannikov, 'Vospominaniya' [Recollections], typescript, Leningrad, Library of the All-Russian Theatrical Society [LOVTO], Inv. No. 35/r, p. 66).

103. *Peterburgskaya gazeta* (4 Jan. 1890), p. 3.

104. *Peterburgskii listok* (5 Jan. 1890), p. 3.

105. *Novoe vremya* (5 Jan. 1890), p. 3.

106. 'Mlle Zhukova I was delightful in her naïve grace in the character of Little Red Riding Hood . . .' (*Novosti i birzhevaya gazeta*, 5 Jan. 1890, p. 3); '. . . Mlle Zhukova . . . danced with expression; the red riding hood looked well on her' (*Novoe vremya*, 5 Jan. 1890, p. 3).

107. The CN indicates that a mazurka was danced; Skalkovsky confirms this in his review.

108. *Peterburgskaya gazeta* (6 Jan. 1890), p. 3.

109. *Novoe vremya* (9 Jan. 1890), p. 4. The problem was corrected not by changing the costume, but by recasting the dance.

110. Only the Rep provides any evidence that the *entrée* was used. Considering unequivocal cuts—one begins in bar 6 but is not ended—the music is reduced to thirty-four bars.

111. In some modern accounts of the Petersburg ballet of the 1890s, historians contend that the technique of male dancing was not more advanced because Pavel Gerdt was given most of the leading male roles and that he was too old to be a virtuoso. Three quotations of Yury Slonimsky illustrate this view: '. . . the performer of Désiré's part—P. Gerdt—because of his age (forty-six years), was a dancer of already quite limited possibilities'; 'In his [Petipa's] production the Prince was a routine balletic cavalier who played the role of a gallant beloved'; and 'It is clear that the composer was constrained by the

limited possibilities of P. A. Gerdt' (*P. I. Chaikovskii i baletnyi teatr*, pp. 198, 228, 234–5).

It is clear from accounts of Gerdt's contemporaries that virtuosity was not an issue in the appreciation of his artistry. Vera Petipa wrote:

In school P. Gerdt was my instructor of dance and mime. I remember how exceptionally precise and expressive his gestures were, the mime of his face, the turn of his head, the movement of his back, shoulders—all the province only of the great artists—and how absorbing his example was [quoted in *Marius Petipa. Materialy*, p. 250].

Valerian Svetlov—far from the least particular of his contemporary ballet critics—could still refer to Gerdt as 'everlasting and irreplaceable' when the dancer performed, at the age of sixty-three, the role of Florestan (*Birzhevye vedomosti*, 10 Sept. 1907 [evening edition], p. 3). And Pleshcheyev, recalling a conversation with Carlotta Brianza in the 1920s, quoted her to the effect that 'she never encountered on stage another *danseur* such as P. A. Gerdt. He was a great, singular artist' (*Moe vremya*, p. 148).

112. Vera Petipa, quoted in *Marius Petipa. Materialy*, p. 248.
113. *Peterburgskaya gazeta* (9 Nov. 1900), p. 4.
114. At the beginning of Désiré's variation in the Rep we read 'Tempo ad libitum', a possible reference to the way the music of Gerdt's dance was performed.
115. The Rep indicates 'Brianza' above bars 25–6 of the coda, suggesting a delay in her entrance.
116. The point of the sarabande was lost on some critics, who made it the butt of jokes. Only Skalkovsky and Korovyakov understood the appropriateness of the dance to the period and setting, the latter critic pointing out how 'these foreign nations were understood by the artists of Louis XIV and were represented in courtly festivities and carousels at Versailles' (*Novosti i birzhevaya gazeta*, 5 Jan. 1890, p. 3). A Moscow reviewer found the sarabande 'warmly and colourfully managed' (*Russkie vedomosti*, 14 Jan. 1890, p. 2). At some later time the dance was deleted; CN, PR-I, and PR-II make no reference to it.
117. The libretto provides no information about the entrances; the CN lists the following:
  Unidentified couples—possibly the dancers of the sarabande
  Bluebeard—part of an entrance of three couples
  Two unidentified couples
  Puss in Boots and the White Cat
  Red Riding Hood and the Wolf
  Cinderella and Fortuné
  Blue Bird and Florine
  Aurora and Désiré
  Tom Thumb, his brothers, and the ogre
118. *Novosti i birzhevaya gazeta* (5 Jan. 1890), p. 3.
119. Pleshcheev, *Moe vremya*, p. 145.
120. Quoted in Pleshcheev, *Moe vremya*, pp. 147–8.
121. *Novosti i birzhevaya gazeta* (5 Jan. 1890), p. 3.
122. *Novoe vremya* (5 Jan. 1890), p. 2.
123. *Peterburgskaya gazeta* (8 Jan. 1890), p. 3 [a review of the second performance].

124. *Moi vospominaniya*, i, p. 606.
125. *Syn otechestva* (4 Jan. 1890), p. 3.
126. *Peterburgskaya gazeta* (4 Jan. 1890), p. 3.
127. *Peterburgskaya gazeta* (3 Jan. 1890), p. 3.
128. *Moi vospominaniya*, i, p. 605.
129. *Novosti i birzhevaya gazeta* (5 Jan. 1890), p. 3.
130. *Novoe vremya* (5 Jan. 1890), p. 3. Other critics joined Skalkovsky in observing that the production obscured the ballet. The reviewer of the *Petersburg Leaflet* wrote: 'Everything is done for the eye, and for the choreography nothing at all. *Féeries* recall the book with the magnificent binding and the empty pages' (*Peterburgskii listok*, 4 Jan. 1890, p. 3). The same author continued, in the issue for the following day:

> The first conditions for making a ballet a ballet and not a *féerie* with dances, are (a) that the dances respond to the elementary demands of choreography; and (b) that these dances be, of necessity, a *direct consequence* of the programme-libretto of the ballet.
> ... There is no trace of all of this in *Sleeping Beauty*. The course of the action is not at all *illustrated* by the dances, which are dragged in for no reason at all and in most instances appear to be unexpected, in the manner of the hair that fell into the soup. For this reason members of the audience who have not read through the libretto and not become familiar with the subject matter do not understand anything whatever, lose themselves in conjecture, and, little by little, finally stop being interested and devote all their attention to the external aspect of the ballet only, [that is] whether or not the décor and costumes caress the eye [*Peterburgskii listok*, 5 Jan. 1890, p. 3].

131. *Novosti i birzhevaya gazeta* (5 Jan. 1890), p. 3.
132. *Novoe vremya* (5 Jan. 1890), p. 3.
133. *Izbrannye stat'i*, ii, pp. 138–43.
134. *Moi vospominaniya*, i, p. 606.

CHAPTER 6

1. Collected Works Correspondence, xv/*b*, p. 74.
2. Collected Works Correspondence, xv/*b*, p. 308.
3. The scenario must be distinguished from the story on which it was based. Eight years before he composed *Nutcracker*, Tchaikovsky referred to Hoffmann's story as an 'excellent tale' (letter to S. F. Flerov, 22 Jan./3 Feb. 1882, Collected Works Correspondence, xi, p. 36).
4. Vladimir Pogozhev attributes the choice of *Nutcracker* to Vsevolozhsky in 'Recollections about P. I. Tchaikovsky', in *Chaikovskii. Vospominaniya i pis'ma*, ed. Glebov, p. 79. Vsevolozhsky's letters to Tchaikovsky (see p. 197) hint that the composer agreed to write *Nutcracker* as a favour to the Director.
5. *Zhizn' Petra Il'icha Chaikovskogo*, iii, p. 427.
6. Collected Works Correspondence, xvi/*a*, pp. 50–1.
7. Quoted in *Zhizn' Petra Il'icha Chaikovskogo*, iii, pp. 429–30.
8. Collected Works Correspondence, xvi/*a*, p. 64.
9. Quoted in Slonimskii, *P. I. Chaikovskii i baletnyi teatr*, p. 241.
10. Collected Works Correspondence, xvi/*a*, p. 70.
11. It is unlikely that Petipa was granted a special leave in immediate response to

Tchaikovsky's letter. Tchaikovsky wrote to Vsevolozhsky on 13/25 March, but on 4 April Petipa produced a new ballet for the examinations of the theatre school (*Marius Petipa. Materialy*, p. 384).

12. Letter of 3/15 April 1891, Collected Works Correspondence, xvi/*a*, pp. 84–5. To Modeste he recounted his miseries, expressed relief that he had broached the matter, and affirmed his resolve:

> I was just now in such a nervous state that I wrote to Vsevolozhsky and am writing to you with a feverish nervous tremor. No! To hell with pressure, haste, moral torments . . .
> The purpose of my letter is to ask you to go to Vsevolozhsky and persuade him not to be angry with me. If he does not grasp the reasons for my determination (they all think, you know, that all I have to do is sit down and in five minutes write an opera), then explain to him that in any case I am not able to keep my promise . . . [Collected Works Correspondence, xvi/*a*, pp. 86–7].

13. Quoted in Bakhrushin, 'Tchaikovsky's Ballets and their Stage History', p. 119.

14. In letters to Modeste and to Vladimir Davydov of 25 June, and to Sergei Taneyev of 27 June 1891, Tchaikovsky writes disparagingly of the ballet (Collected Works Correspondence, xvi/*a*, pp. 155–6, 161, 165). A month later, however, he confided to Modeste: 'It is strange, when I was writing the ballet I thought that it was inconsequential, and that when I began the opera I would prove myself. And now it seems to me that the ballet is excellent, and the opera is turning out to be nothing special' (Collected Works Correspondence, xvi/*a*, p. 186). This sentiment was exceptional.

15. Quoted in Bakhrushin, 'Tchaikovsky's Ballets and their Stage History', p. 119.

16. *Izbrannye trudy*, iv, p. 107.

17. *Simfonicheskie printsipy baletov Chaikovskogo*, p. 108. Soviet analysts identify the childlike in *Nutcracker* by citing likenesses between the ballet and Tchaikovsky's *Children's Album*, Op. 39 (1878). Yury Slonimsky, for example, points out that

> It is not difficult to see in the selection and succession of pieces in the *Children's Album* something close to the scheme of Act I of *Nutcracker*: winter, children's play and diversions, to the point of hobby horses and soldiers, a sick doll, arguments over play (and perhaps over a doll), calling mama (or the governess) for help, a new or restored doll, etc.—in both [*P. I. Chaikovskii i baletnyi teatr*, p. 245].

Julia Rozanova carries Slonimsky's parallels of subject and image forward to the quotation of musical passages from the *Children's Album* which she finds similar to passages in *Nutcracker*: the polka with Clara's dance with the Nutcracker; the waltz with the final waltz of the ballet; and the sequential melody of 'Sweet Dreams' (Op. 39, No. 21) with that of the miraculous growth of the Christmas tree (*Simfonicheskie printsipy baletov Chaikovskogo*, pp. 108–10; Nadezhda Tumanina cites other likenesses between *Nutcracker* and *Sleeping Beauty* in support of the same general contention in *P. I. Chaikovskii: velikii master*, pp. 393–4). While the examples are convincing enough visually when short fragments from the two works are juxtaposed, the ear does not accept the likenesses so readily: when listening to them, the piano pieces seem to anticipate the ballet only in the most general way.

Attempting to identify the origins of the childlike aspects of Tchaikovsky's music, Boris Asafiev proposed that all intonations of childhood in Tchaikovsky's music may emerge from the composer's own experience with the sounds of the mechanical orchestrion in his father's house (*Izbrannye trudy*, iv, pp. 103–4). From this experience, Asafiev claims, come the doll-like rhythms heard in parts of the *Children's Album* and in the overture, march, the striking of nine o'clock, the dances of the mechanical dolls, and the variation of the Sugar Plum Fairy in *Nutcracker*.

18. *P. I. Chaikovskii i baletnyi teatr*, p. 253.

19. We have no direct evidence that Tchaikovsky was disturbed by these changes, yet Tchaikovsky's fascination for the bizarre in other works should not be overlooked. Relevant, for example, is Act III of the just-completed *Queen of Spades*, at the beginning of which Herman is visited by the Countess's ghost. More touching is the closing scene of *Mazepa* where Marie, witless and serene, sings a lullaby to her dying lover, unaware of his identity (a passage which anticipates the Bedlam scene in Stravinsky's *The Rake's Progress*). It is possible that part of Tchaikovsky's disenchantment with *Nutcracker* was not, as Slonimsky contends, rooted in its senselessness and banality—as a *divertissement* Act II is no less senseless than the last act of *Sleeping Beauty*—but rather in the deletion of the fantastic element.

That Tchaikovsky considered Drosselmayer an important character, perhaps the central character in the story, is implicit in the extraordinary care which he lavished on the councillor's musical portrait (see Chapter 6, pp. 222–8, below). Whatever the modifications to the libretto, the music unquestionably presents Drosselmayer as fantastic, and at times sinister. If we accept the idea that Confiturembourg is the result of Drosselmayer's meditation, the happy, escapist quality of the land of the sweets even hints at elements of sadness and nostalgia in the old man, a sadness we might expect from someone who is both aged (he lives through a period of several lifetimes in Hoffmann's story) and a magician. Hence, possibly, Alexandre Benois's admonition to his son, apropos of a new production in 1938, that the actor of Drosselmayer's part should be well acquainted with sadness (*Aleksandr Benua razmyshlyaet* ... [Alexandre Benois Reflects ...] (Moscow, 1968), p. 571). Tchaikovsky may have found in the character of Drosselmayer an opportunity for philosophical comment which helped redeem, at least for him, the scenario's deficiencies as drama.

20. *Istoriya tantsev*, iv, p. 138.

21. *Birzhevye vedomosti* (29 Sept. 1892), p. 3.

22. Questions remain as to how much of *Nutcracker* Ivanov set. Khudekov, who was close to the inner circles of the ballet, wrote that 'The production of the ballet *Nutcracker*, to Tchaikovsky's music, is attributed to L. Ivanov. This is not correct. This ballet was produced by Marius Petipa. Only one act was assigned to Ivanov, who coped with the task beautifully. . .' (*Istoriya tantsev*, iv, p. 172).

Pogozhev concurred in the distribution of labour, but not in the assessment: '. . . the composition of the choreography and the production of the second half of the ballet were entrusted to Lev Ivanovich Ivanov, far removed from Petipa both in talent and in imagination and taste' ('Recollections about P. I. Tchaikovsky', *Chaikovskii. Vospominaniya i pis'ma*, ed. Glebov, p. 82).

In the list of ballets compiled by Petipa at the time he dictated his memoirs the entry for *Nutcracker* reads: '*Casse-Noisette*, ballet féerie en deux actes et trois tableaux. Programme tiré d'un conte de E. Hoffmann par le maître de ballet Mr. Petipa, soliste de sa Majesté l'Empereur.

'Musique de Mr. P. Tschaïkowsky, mise en scène et danses composées par l'artiste émérité des théâtres impériaux, Mr. L. Ivanoff' (Moscow, State Theatre Museum named for A. A. Bakhrushin, *fond* 205, No. 138593), p. 82.

Concerning Petipa's work on the ballet, see, e.g., Slonimskii, *P. I. Chaikovskii i baletnyi teatr*, pp. 240, 260, and *Marius Petipa. Materialy*, pp. 206–9.

23. Quoted in Krasovskaya, *Russkii baletnyi teatr*, p. 370.
24. *Izbrannye trudy*, ii, p. 61.
25. 'Writings on Lev Ivanov', *Dance Perspectives*, ii (Spring, 1959), p. 56.
26. See, e.g., Krasovskaya, *Russkii baletnyi teatr*, pp. 344–8, 362–3; Yurii Iosifovich Slonimskii, 'Lev Ivanov, 1834–1901', *Mastera baleta* [Masters of the Ballet] (Leningrad, 1937), pp. 179–99; translated, with additional Soviet criticism, by Anatole Chujoy in 'Writings about Lev Ivanov', *Dance Perspectives*, ii (Spring, 1959), pp. 1–64.
27. Quoted in Krasovskaya, *Russkii baletnyi teatr*, p. 347.
28. *Russkii baletnyi teatr*, p. 367.
29. 'L. I. Ivanov. (Nekrolog)', *Novoe vremya* (13 Dec. 1901), p. 4.
30. *Istoriya tantsev*, iv, p. 172.
31. 'L. I. Ivanov. (Nekrolog)', *Novoe vremya* (13 Dec. 1901), p. 4.
32. L. I. Ivanov, 'Moi vospominaniya. Posvyashchayutsya moim tovarishcham i sosluzhivtsam' [My Recollections. Dedicated to my Colleagues and Co-workers] (Leningrad, Leningrad Theatre Museum, ORTs 5430, No. KP 7154/76; published in part as 'The Autobiography of L. I. Ivanov (My Little Reminiscences)', *Peterburgskaya gazeta*, 13 Dec. 1901, p. 5). The 'Recollections' are extensively quoted in Krasovskaya, *Russkii baletnyi teatr*, pp. 337–401, and in Slonimskii, *Mastera baleta*, pp. 171–97.
33. *Russkii baletnyi teatr*, pp. 362–3.
34. Quoted in *Marius Petipa. Materialy*, p. 268.
35. 'A Few Words about the Petersburg Ballet. (Significance of the Petersburg Ballet, the Production of Ballet Performances, and the Opening of the Ballet Season)', *Teatral* [Theatre-goer], vi, No. 83, Book 33 (September 1896), pp. 107–8.
36. *P. I. Chaikovskii i baletnyi teatr*, pp. 270–1.
37. *Novoe vremya* (14 Oct. 1892), p. 3.
38. *Novoe vremya* (21 Oct. 1892), p. 3.
39. 'Vospominaniya', pp. 73–4.
40. *Peterburgskaya gazeta* (28 Sept. 1892), p. 3; this article, as if it were a press release in praise of Vsevolozhsky, was reproduced in *Birzhevye vedomosti* the next day.
41. Nikolai Malko relates that Tchaikovsky worked closely with Drigo in the composition of *Nutcracker*; see his *A Certain Art* (New York, 1966), p. 95.

42. Leningrad, Central Music Library of the Theatre of Opera and Ballet named for S. M. Kirov, 26095 N2 $\frac{VII\ 5}{delo}$, fol. 16.

43. *Novoe vremya* (7 Nov. 1892), p. 3; (10 Nov. 1892), p. 3.

44. Quoted in 'Recollections about P. I. Tchaikovsky', *Chaikovskii. Vospominaniya i pis'ma*, ed. Glebov, p. 81.

45. *Izbrannye stat'i*, ii, pp. 258–60.

46. Tchaikovsky hinted obliquely at the interdependence of the two in a letter to Jurgenson of 2 May 1892: 'It stands to reason that the directorate will obtain the material of *Iolanthe* as well. You see one and the other together will be regarded as one large opera, and this ballet would not suit under normal conditions' (Collected Works Correspondence, xvi/*b*, p. 86). As early as 1894 there were plans of performing *Iolanthe* with another ballet, the Petipa–Drigo *The Awakening of Flora*.

47. Leningrad, Central Music Library of the Theatre of Opera and Ballet named for S. M. Kirov, 26095 N2 $\frac{VII\ 5}{delo}$, fol. 40.

48. The principal sources are identified as follows:

    (*a*) Holograph score (Hol): Moscow, State Central Museum of Musical Culture named for M. I. Glinka, *fond* 88, No. 51. The score comprises 169 folios of 24-stave music paper, 27 cm. × 34.5 cm. Only 123 folios are in Tchaikovsky's hand; the remaining 46 are a copy of the music excerpted to form the *Nutcracker Suite*. (The original folios of the suite are preserved at the Tchaikovsky Home-Museum at Klin.) The Hol is virtually free of additional marks pertaining to production and casting; nor does it contain signs of significant editorial modification.

    (*b*) Répétiteurs (Rep I and Rep II): Leningrad, Central Music Library of the Theatre of Opera and Ballet named for S. M. Kirov, $\frac{144154}{Re\ Shchel}$ (both copies are identified by the same shelf number). Rep I comprises 84 folios, Rep II 90 folios of 12-stave music paper, approximately 38 cm. × 25 cm. Rep I is in a brown binding; on the inside cover, 'No. 180'; it seems to be written by the same scribe as prepared the Rep of *Sleeping Beauty*. Rep I preserves two rare details on its first page: a name, possibly that of the copyist or arranger, and a date. 'G. Fisher' lifts this répétiteur above the utilitarian anonymity typical of this kind of document, and '7 May 1892' offers an idea of the time—seven months almost to the day before the first performance—the Rep was completed. Tchaikovsky had finished the score late in March. Rep II is in a red-brown binding; on the inside cover, 'No. 2' and the initials 'G. K.'; it is in a different, clearer, more elegant hand than Rep I.

    Another feature of Rep I warrants passing mention because it suggests when Petipa's active involvement with the production of *Nutcracker* might have ceased. Tchaikovsky annotated the Hol generously with quotations from Petipa's instructions, showing thereby which music referred to which action on stage. The Reps are faithful to the Hol in this respect and thus contain all the composer's annotations, including remarks to Drigo concerning orchestration quite irrelevant to rehearsals of the ballet with two violins. Inclusion of this information required a knowledge of French (the language of the annotations) which the copyists clearly lacked, some of their mistakes being comical to the modern reader. But comical they were not to the person who made corrections in Rep I, a person whose handwriting almost certainly identifies him as Petipa. The corrections run throughout, as if the balletmaster took time to edit the entire Rep; he even added at one point a line of text from the balletmaster's plan which Tchaikovsky had not included. In general, added remarks specifying details of the stage action and the assignment of dancers to parts, in which the Rep of *Sleeping Beauty* abounds, are fewer in *Nutcracker*; Rep I is richer in such remarks than Rep II; and in Rep I, the remarks in French cease altogether after the Waltz of the Snowflakes. If Petipa's personal involvement in the production went no further than this, Khudekov's claim that the Frenchman mounted half the ballet (see note 22, above) is thus confirmed.

(c) The choreographic notation (CN), Cambridge, Mass., Harvard Theatre Collection, bMS Thr 245 (197), comprises 116 folios of notation paper, 22.2 cm. × 35.5 cm., loosely filed in five folders. It shares general features with the CN of *Sleeping Beauty*: the folios are discoloured and frayed around the outer edges; cataloguer's descriptions and miscellaneous scraps of paper with cataloguing information are interleaved with the folios of the CN proper; it is paginated in the same way—that is, only odd-numbered pages bear a written page number. The CN of *Nutcracker* is also incomplete, lacking both action scenes (the battle, the journey, the opening tableau of Act II) and dances (the trepak, *La mère Gigogne*, and the man's variation in the *pas de deux*). It is enriched with notations which Nikolai Sergeyev seems to have added after emigrating to the West, and, perhaps most frustrating for the modern researcher, it is, in its present configuration, out of order to the point of incoherence if studied without a libretto. (The order of materials is given in Appendix F.) The cover page of the *pas de deux* from Act II is exceptional for having a date—7 November 1909. Together with evidence from the rest of the manuscript, this date allows us to propose the years 1902–9 as a time when the CN was prepared.

49. While such a small group of parents might appear odd at first, we must realize that twenty more parents are in wait backstage to appear *en incroyables*, and that the CN makes no reference to the activity around the Christmas tree.

50. The footman enters at precisely the place where Tchaikovsky wrote music illustrating the clock's striking of nine o'clock. The CN makes no reference to this anticipation of the night scene.

51. This is curious, since the woman referred to, an artist identified in the CN as 'Urakova', played the part of Marianne, Silberhaus's niece, in performances at the turn of the century.

52. A curiosity in the CN is that the end of the march is not marked as such, an unusual omission in these notations, especially, as here, because the music ends with a clear cadence. The new dance begins mid-page, and the only indication of this, apart from a change in the choreography, is the word 'galop', which has been marked through.

53. Concerning the dance of the *incroyables*, the cast list in the libretto lists ten pairs of names; the CN does not specify any number, but it does call for two lead couples to dance in front of the rest. Music was added: the Reps were

modified to repeat the first phrase of the dance (that is, bars 63–9 of No. 3, with a new bar, a first ending, interpolated between bars 69–70).

54. *Novosti i birzhevaya gazeta* (8 Dec. 1892), p. 3. Nikolai Solyannikov wrote ('Vospominaniya', p. 77) that 'Preobrazhenskaya, the charming, elegantly playful doll Columbine, enjoyed a particular success. She danced the entire number on *pointe*. This produced the characteristic of a doll-marionette: pull the string and she jumps up, her toes barely touching the floor of the stage. Columbine's dance was received with loud applause, and this number was always encored.'

55. From the Reps comes an idea of how the producers arranged the music from the options left them by Tchaikovsky: after the introduction (bars 172–86 of No. 5) the *Grossvater* proper, followed by four statements of the *allegro vivacissimo* (that is, bars 220–4); then the *Grossvater* again and four more statements of the *allegro vivacissimo*. Both Reps specify that the dance should be played '2½ times', which would mean beginning the *Grossvater* a third time and ending it, possibly, on the downbeat of bar 219. The CN provides dances for this much music.

56. The cast list within the libretto (but not the CN) includes students among the participants in this dance, and Rep II, above bar 203, specifies *vospit*. (for *vospitanniki*: 'students') without indicating the first, second or third statement of the music. A press account of the first performance referred to children getting in the way of the adults' dancing in Act I, but without specifying where.

57. A list of personnel in *Nutcracker* as produced in 1897, part of a summary of all the ballets produced at the Maryinsky Theatre that year, lists the following in addition to an unspecified number of students of the Regiment of Finnish Guards, who took the parts of mice and gingerbread soldiers:
   Female students—two dolls, two trumpeters, two drummers, six soldiers. Male students—artillery officer plus six soldiers, infantry officer plus six soldiers, the Mouse King and his retinue of four, a gingerbread officer and a sentry (Leningrad, State Historical Archive, *fond* 497, *op.* 8², *ed. xhr.* 467, fols. 3–4, 8–9).

58. *Novosti i birzhevaya gazeta* (8 Dec. 1892), p. 3.

59. The waltz is recorded twice; the version which occurs first in the CN almost certainly dates from Nikolai Sergeyev's London days—there is a reference to Sadler's Wells on its last pages—and appears to be a variant, for smaller performing forces, of the older version. Apart from one adjustment which is required in the co-ordination of music and action, the only serious question left unanswered by the CN is how to account for the fifty-nine dancers named in the cast list, when the maximum accounted for by the notators is thirty-eight.

60. *Novosti i birzhevaya gazeta* (8 Dec. 1892), p. 3.

61. *Novosti i birzhevaya gazeta* (8 Dec. 1892), p. 3. By requesting of Tchaikovsky an introduction to the scene, Petipa ensured that part of the music would be played before the curtain went up. The composer marks 'rideau' at bar 26 of No. 10, but in Rep I this word has been struck through as if to suggest the extension of the preludial portion even further into the number. Rep II follows Tchaikovsky, and further indicates 'fairies' at bar 28 and 'students' at bar 50.

These surely refer to some of the *merveilleux* listed in the libretto; the first appearance of the Sugar Plum Fairy probably coincides with the introduction of the celesta at bar 67, as Tchaikovsky instructs. The Reps agree in their call for cuts (bars 33–40 and the first statement of bars 42–9).

62. Most of the dances of the *divertissement* (No. 12) are notated twice—once to record the lead dancer or couple, once to record the remaining soloists. The trepak and *La mère Gigogne* are missing in the CN, though references to both occur later in the manuscript, in connection with the return of the dances of the *divertissement*. Both solo and choral lines of the dances move in appropriate character style but with more pronounced and virtuoso movements assigned to the principal dancers.

63. At one point, for example, an instruction in the floor plan for the dancers simply 'to run' is accompanied by movement symbols which show an elaborate combination of preparations, high steps, and poses. At another, the movement symbols call for turns not confirmed in the floor plan—an unusual inconsistency in the CN as a whole.

64. *Novosti i birzhevaya gazeta* (8 Dec. 1892), p. 3.

65. *Novoe vremya* (8 Dec. 1892), p. 3.

66. *Novoe vremya* (8 Dec. 1892), p. 3.

67. Instead of the regular thirty-two-bar periods of the preceding entrances, the first pair of soloists re-enters in the first sixteen bars of section four, and the second pair follows after another sixteen bars. To ensure the perception of this section as a new departure, rather than as a remaking of section two but on a smaller scale, Ivanov next recalls the third pair of soloists one dancer at time (the first at bar 204, the second at bar 226). Not only does he thus break the sequence of entrances by two, he also assigns irregular periods to the dancers of the third pair—twenty-two bars to the first (which includes, in bars 218–25, a short musical extension preparing for the return of the principal theme of the music), and thirty-two to the second. Having thus favoured the third pair of soloists, the first two pairs now return together, as if in compensation, as the section draws to an end (bars 258–73, the first playing of a repeated period).

Whatever the complexity of the section in its phrase structure and the assignment of dancers to it (we must recall that the passage may have been cast differently with eight soloists), an additional dimension emerges from the placing of this section within the music of the entire waltz. To understand this we must review the structure of the music, which may be summarized as follows:

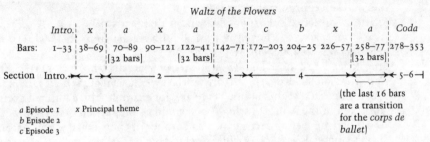

Waltz of the Flowers

	Intro.	x	a	x	a	b	c	b	x	a	Coda
Bars:	1–33	38–69	70–89	90–121	122–41	142–71	172–203	204–25	226–57	258–77	278–353
		[32 bars]			[32 bars]					[32 bars]	
Section	Intro.	⟵ 1 ⟶	⟵ 2 ⟶	⟵ 3 ⟶	⟵ 4 ⟶					⟵ 5–6 ⟶

(the last 16 bars are a transition for the *corps de ballet*)

a Episode 1   *x* Principal theme
b Episode 2
c Episode 3

If the CN accurately conveys the structure of the waltz, the boundaries of all sections of the choreography coincide with boundaries in the music except for those of section four, which ends halfway through a restatement of the principal theme. This section of the dance in effect passes through (and in a sense disregards) the beginning of the return of the principal theme in its last statement before the coda. When this important musical return begins, the choreography is at its furthest remove from the references established at the beginning of the waltz: the only period of twenty-two bars in a dance dominated by phrases of sixteen and thirty-two bars has just ended, and a pair of soloists which had been dancing as a unit before is split into two single soloists. Surely in this passage Ivanov gives us pause to reconsider the cliché of balance and symmetry which we associate with classical dance.

68. The Reps agree in placing this figure earlier in the dance, at bar 142, and calling for a circle formation here.

69. Dal' defines *reika* in part as 'a slender strip, a little plank which is planed down for the purpose of being attached to something, for setting into a narrow space' (*Tolkovyi slovar' zhivogo velikoruskogo yazyka Vladimira Dalya* [Explanatory Dictionary of the Living Great Russian Language by Vladimir Dal'], 4 vols. (St Petersburg and Moscow, 2nd edn 1882; rpt. Moscow, 1982), iv, p. 90). Alexandrov offers three words: 'lath', 'sarking', and 'tringle'—all of which connote a long, thin piece of wood to be used for various purposes (*Polnyi russko-angliiskii slovar' sostavlennyi A. Aleksandrovym* [Complete Russian-English Dictionary by A. Alexandrov] (Berlin, 1924), p. 540). To some native speakers of modern Russian, *reika* connotes a narrow guide or track, of the kind along which a sliding door would move.

70. The Reps show two generations of cuts: one cut omits the *presto* altogether and the other makes a cut within the *presto* (bars 73–80).

71. From Rep I, however, comes a hint of disagreement: above bar 4, 'Gerdt', suggesting that the cavalier entered first; then, in bar 35, 'Dell'Era', and finally, at bar 58, 'Gerdt' and 'Dell'Era' together.

72. The CN contains other lists of *entrées* which disagree with those actually notated. The list below is based on the notated entrances together with information from the Reps. *Entrées* based solely on the Reps are placed in square brackets; all the dancers (for which notations survive) enter from stage left:

Spanish Dance, principal couple (bar 33)
Chinese Dance, principal couple (bar 41)
Arabian Dance, principal soloists (bar 49)
Mirlitons, principal soloist joined by a cavalier (bar 57)
Sugar Plum Fairy and her prince [in Rep I a soloist from the Waltz of the Flowers was included] (bar 65)
[Trepak, leading dancer, and two students, or Spanish Dance, principal couple (both are listed—bar 97). Circumstantial evidence favours the return of the Spanish couple at this point. There are, for example, three notated entries for them in the waltz, of which this would be the second. Rep I shows the leader of the trepak serving also as cavalier of the soloist of the Arabian Dance some 48 bars later; while he could have been backstage, ready to re-enter in time for this, he probably could not have changed costume (from a

buffoon to an Arab) in that time. Finally, the dances with young children—*La mère Gigogne* and the trepak, like Tom Thumb in *Sleeping Beauty*, seem not to have been repeated in complex, closely integrated codas requiring brief (and no doubt pressured) vignette appearances, as here.]

['Two women', probably soloists from the Waltz of the Flowers (bar 113)]
[Chinese Dance, principal soloists (bar 129)]
[Arabian Dance, principal soloist and a cavalier (bar 145)]
[Mirlitons, principal soloist and two other soloists (bar 161)]

73. By the word 'all' in bar 209, the Reps offer a hint of what occurs in the remaining thirty-one bars of the dance. But it is only a hint, for whom 'all' consisted of is not clear. Some of the dances in the *divertissement* refer to 'Coda III', a third appearance in the finale, and it may be that these—the leaders of the Spanish and Arabian Dances, soloists from the Waltz of the Flowers, the Sugar Plum Fairy and her cavalier—fill centre stage in the last bars of the waltz. They make two passes from rear to front.

74. *Birzhevye vedomosti* (8 Dec. 1892), p. 2.
75. *Peterburgskaya gazeta* (10 Dec. 1892), p. 4.
76. Collected Works Correspondence, xvi/*b*, p. 201.
77. *Vospominaniya*, pp. 31–2.
78. *Novosti i birzhevaya gazeta* (8 Dec. 1892), p. 4.
79. *Peterburgskaya gazeta* (9 Dec. 1892), p. 4.
80. *Izbrannye stat'i*, ii, p. 273.
81. *Novoe vremya* (14 Dec. 1892), p. 2.
82. *Izbrannye stat'i*, ii, p. 274.
83. Collected Works Correspondence, xvi/*a*, pp. 129–30.
84. Collected Works Correspondence, xvi/*a*, p. 196.
85. 'Recollections from the Distant Past', *Vospominaniya o P. I. Chaikovskom*, 2nd edn, p. 86.
86. Collected Works Correspondence, xvi/*b*, p. 49.
87. Quoted in *Vospominaniya o P. I. Chaikovskom*, 2nd edn, pp. 463–4, n. 5.
88. 'Music Review', *Nuvellist* (Jan. 1893), i, p. 2.
89. *Music Ho! A Study of Music in Decline* (London, 3rd edn 1966), p. 96.
90. *Izbrannye stat'i*, ii, pp. 273–4.
91. The earlier ballets contained one borrowed melody each: 'Vive Henri IV!' from Colet and Dumersan, and a traditional Italian tune of the Neapolitan Dance in *Swan Lake*.
92. The revolutionary associations of these two songs led Fedor Lopukhov to ponder whether Petipa had originally intended *Nutcracker* as a reflection of the events of the French Revolution (*Marius Petipa. Materialy*, pp. 207–8).
93. The effect is related to the presentation of the Lilac Fairy's theme in Db major—that is, freed for a moment of its association with another key—when she first appears to Désiré in Act II of *Sleeping Beauty*.
94. In *Nutcracker*, moreover, the style change between the end of the Waltz of the Flowers and the beginning of the *pas de deux* is strong enough to suggest a shift in aspect, in expressive connotation, from spontaneity to formality. It is as if Tchaikovsky wanted to initiate at that moment a transition in the

audience's perception from the magical illusion of Confiturembourg to the reality of the houselights.

95. Tchaikovsky here invokes the same principle of harmonic structure that Schubert used in *Die schöne Müllerin*, another tritonally organized work which traverses the tonal system from Bb major to E major. In both, the tonic of the opening is recalled soon after the mid-point (in Schubert, with the twelfth song of twenty), as if to reinforce the opening key of the work more for reasons of harmonic structure than for any immediate and pressing justification in the text.

CHAPTER 7

1. Klod Debyussi [Claude Debussy], *Sobranie sochinenii dlya fortepiano* [Collected Works for Piano], 5 vols., v, pp. 203–28.
2. *The Era* (6 Dec. 1884), p. 10.
3. London, Victoria and Albert Museum, Enthoven Collection, piano arrangement of Georges Jacoby's ballet 'The Swans' (no shelf number).
4. *P. I. Chaikovskii. Perepiska s P. I. Yurgensonom* [P. I. Tchaikovsky. Correspondence with P. I. Jurgenson], 2 vols. (Moscow and Leningrad, 1938, 1952), ii, p. 37.
5. Collected Works Correspondence, xiii, p. 314.
6. In his memoirs the balletmaster Berger claimed that Tchaikovsky himself conducted *Swan Lake*; see Ladislav Hájak, *Paměti Augustina Bergra; choreografa a baletního mistra Národního Divadla v Praze a několika světových scén* [Memoirs of Augustin Berger; Choreographer and Balletmaster of the National Theatre in Prague and Various World Stages] (Prague, 1942), p. 158. Posters of the concerts indicate, however, that Tchaikovsky conducted only concert works; Adolf Čech conducted all performances of *Swan Lake* in Prague. Čech, it may be added, had conducted the first performance outside Russia of an opera by Tchaikovsky—*The Maid of Orleans* at Prague in 1882, with dances choreographed by 'balletmaster Reisinger'. In connection with Tchaikovsky's visit, see the present writer's 'Chaikovskii's Visit to Prague in 1888', *Slavic review*, xl (1981), pp. 433–43.
7. *Dnevniki P. I. Chaikovskogo*, p. 198.
8. The Národní Museum, Prague, preserves affiches for all performances of *Swan Lake* there in 1888. For a list of dates of these performances, see Fr. Ad. Šubert, *Dějiny Národního Divadla v Praze 1883–1900* [History of the National Theatre in Prague] (n.p., 1908), pp. xliv–v of the calendar of performances.
9. *Dnevniki P. I. Chaikovskogo*, p. 241.
10. Cyril W. Beaumont, *The Ballet Called Swan Lake* (London, 1952), plate between pp. 56–7.
11. *Artist. Zhurnal izyashchnykh iskusstv i literatury* [Artist. Journal of the Fine Arts and Literature], vi, No. 33 (Jan. 1894), p. 199.
12. Quoted in Krasovskaya, *Russkii baletnyi teatr*, p. 377.
13. *Memuary Mariusa Petipa, soloista Ego Imperatorskogo Velichestva i baletmeistera Imperatorskikh teatrov* [Memoirs of Marius Petipa, Soloist of His

Imperial Majesty and Balletmaster of the Imperial Theatres] (St Petersburg, 1906), p. 72.

14. *Marius Petipa. Materialy*, pp. 210, 215–17.

15. 'Personal Recollections of R. E. Drigo', fol. 16.

16. *Moskovskie vedomosti* (8 May 1896), p. 4.

17. Ivor Guest, 'The Alhambra Ballet', *Dance Perspectives*, iv (Autumn, 1959), p. 34.

18. *P. I. Chaikovskii i baletnyi teatr*, p. 129; *'Lebedinoe ozero' P. I. Chaikovskogo*, p. 42.

19. Probably the duet later published in *Polnoe sobranie sochinenii*, lxii, pp. 211–63.

20. 'On the Imperial decision to put on two performances of a concert-spectacle in the Maryinsky Theatre in February 1894, the proceeds from one of which will be put toward the erection of a monument to the deceased composer Peter Ilyich Tchaikovsky, and from the other toward the opening of a subscription for the establishing of a capital fund for financial aid', Leningrad, State Central Music Library of the Theatre of Opera and Ballet named for S. M. Kirov, VII 54154 *delo* 26094, fols. 1–2 [copies].

21. *Novoe vremya* (19 Feb. 1894), p. 3.

22. The most expensive *loge* in the Maryinsky Theatre, normally 15 roubles 70 copecks at that time, was 55 roubles for the memorial concert; a seat in the furthest balcony, normally 22 copecks, was now 1 rouble 50 copecks. These were the same prices as were charged for tickets to *Der Ring des Nibelungen*.

23. *Peterburgskii listok* (18 Feb. 1894), p. 3.

24. Skal'kovskii, *V teatral'nom mire*, pp. 209–10. Krasovskaya (*Russkii baletnyi teatr*, pp. 460–1) cites the same review as being Bezobrazov's, from the *Peterburgskaya gazeta* of 6 Dec. 1893.

25. According to Solyannikov ('Vospominaniya', p. 86), Legnani performed not thirty-two but twenty *fouettés* at the first performance of *Swan Lake* in 1895, and won an ovation after repeating the number.

26. *Novosti i birzhevaya gazeta*, 18 Oct. 1896, p. 3; *Nash balet*, 2nd edn, p. 380.

27. *Sanktpeterburgskie vedomosti* (17 Jan. 1895), p. 3. Acknowledging her technical attainments, Solyannikov wrote:

> It cannot be said that Legnani was a great artist: an unremarkable exterior, no talent as a mime, insufficient culture, a provincial manner, the habit of holding the skirt of her ballet dress with her thumb and index finger . . . a certain sharpness and angularity—these are qualities of hers which were reflected in the roles she performed, especially at the beginning of her tenure on the Petersburg stage. But with the years Legnani's dancing gradually became more feminine and plastic, it took on more spiritual qualities under the strong artistry of the Petersburg ballet ['Vospominaniya', p. 83].

28. *Peterburgskaya gazeta* (18 Feb. 1894), p. 3.

29. Slonimsky insists that the directorate was reluctant to commit itself to mounting the entire ballet, citing as evidence of its cautiousness the fact that a formal agreement concerning performance rights was not signed by Modeste and Vsevolozhsky until August 1894, some six months after the memorial concert (*P. I. Chaikovskii i baletnyi teatr*, pp. 130–1). As we have seen in the case of *Nutcracker*, however, Tchaikovsky himself did not sign

such an agreement until after the first performance. The dates of these agreements clearly do not establish the time of the directorate's intention to proceed with a production.

30. Quoted in Slonimskii, *P. I. Chaikovskii i baletnyi teatr*, pp. 131–2.

31. This version of the libretto was published by Jurgenson with the first edition of the orchestral score: *Le Lac des cygnes* (Moscow [1896]; rpt. New York [1951]), pp. ii–vi.

32. An MS libretto of the complete *Swan Lake*, claimed by its cataloguers to be in the hand of Modeste Tchaikovsky, was received by the directorate of the imperial theatres on 26 Sept. 1894. It is possibly a revision which reflects Vsevolozhsky's preferences: it is divided into three acts and four scenes; there is a brief reference to a storm, but none to a flood (Leningrad, Lunacharsky State Theatre Library, *otdel* iv, *shkaf* 22, *polka* 6, *mesto* 1, No. 19060).

33. Quoted in Slonimskii, *P. I. Chaikovskii i baletnyi teatr*, p. 131. Tchaikovsky's holograph reflects the Petersburg redaction only in the first lakeside scene—a new ending for the love duet, cuts in Odette's recitative and elsewhere—as if to suggest it was used for the memorial concert (or the projected 1886 performance) but not in connection with revisions for the revival of the complete work.

34. 'Personal Recollections of R. E. Drigo', fols. 16–17.

35. Drigo's orchestrations were published separately by Jurgenson; they were reprinted as an appendix to the reprint of the orchestral score (see note 31, above). His orchestration may in fact have been limited to these interpolations. The performance score presently in use at the Kirov Theatre in Leningrad is a copy of the Jurgenson orchestral score (with the stamp of the Central Music Library of the Imperial Theatres still visible), with changes added to reflect the Petersburg redaction. An incomplete manuscript orchestral score of early Soviet provenance now in the Harvard Theatre Collection (fMS Thr 186, 2–3) also preserves Tchaikovsky's orchestration.

36. The original *allegro* survives in some modern productions, and, although rescored, has been wrongly attributed to Drigo (as, for example, in the piano arrangement published by the Tchaikovsky Foundation). In the score used in performances at the Kirov Theatre this music appears with the rubric 'Variation of Chabukiani'.

37. Leningrad, Central State Music Library of the Theatre of Opera and Ballet named for S. M. Kirov, $\frac{I\,44154}{re\,Leb}$ (both copies are identified by the same shelf number). Rep I consists of 149, Rep II of 150 folios of 12-stave notation paper, approximately 38 cm. × 25 cm. Both are signed with an elaborate monogram which appears to be made of the Cyrillic counterparts of the initials 'V. V. P.'. Neither Rep is dated. Rep I, in a thick green cardboard binding, shows more evidence of wear than Rep II; many corners are reinforced with tape, edges are frayed, and pages are falling out of the binding. Rep II, in a thick brown cardboard binding, seems to have been copied from Rep I or some similar source; it shows no particular signs of use and wear, and contains fewer additional markings pertaining to stage action than Rep I. As those markings pertain to the names of performers, the names of dancers in Rep II are in some

cases those of an earlier generation than the names in Rep I.

38. Quoted in Slonimskii, *P. I. Chaikovskii i baletnyi teatr*, pp. 131–2.

39. Pleshcheev, *Nash balet*, 2nd edn, p. 397; Nikolai Bezobrazov in the *Peterburgskaya gazeta*, 16 Jan. 1895, p. 3, and 23 Nov. 1898, p. 3; Lopukhov, recalling comments of Alexander Shiryaev, in *Marius Petipa. Materialy*, pp. 210, [224] (see also Shiryaev, *Marius Petipa. Materialy*, p. 269).

40. *Marius Petipa. Materialy*, p. 212.

41. *Marius Petipa. Materialy*, p. 214.

42. *Izbrannye stat'i*, ii, pp. 98, 100.

43. *Novoe vremya* (16 Jan. 1901), pp. 4–5.

44. The choreographic notation (CN), Cambridge, Mass., Harvard Theatre Collection, fMS 186 (11–13), comprises 105 folios, approximately 22.2 cm. × 35.5 cm., loosely filed in 10 folders. Except for two unruled pages, on which a variant of the Neapolitan Dance is notated, the entire manuscript is written on paper printed with either 3 or 6 Stepanov notation staves. This CN shares general characteristics with those of *Sleeping Beauty* and *Nutcracker*: the paper is discoloured and frayed. A thorough description of the contents of this CN, on 8 typewritten sheets, in English, is filed in the first of the 10 folders. At the end of the CN, in folders with separate bibliographic identifications [fMS Thr 186 (12) and (13)], there is a manuscript synopsis of the action of *Swan Lake* in Russian, and a typewritten description of the action in English.

 The CN of *Swan Lake* was probably begun before 14 January 1901, for it contains in Act III references to Gerdt and Legnani (who danced the parts of Siegfried and Odette for the last time on that date). The latest imperial period notations appear to be of the Spanish Dance in Alexander Gorsky's version, which was first performed in Petersburg in 1913. Judging from the dancers' names in the manuscript and the dates on which they performed the roles assigned to them there, most of the ballet seems to have been recorded between 30 April 1906 and 10 April 1907. The first lakeside scene and the ballroom *pas de deux*, for example, were recorded in the performance of Vera Trefilova, and there is evidence that this part of the CN, like parts of those of *Sleeping Beauty* and *Nutcracker*, is not absolutely true to the first production.

 The CNs of the last act are out of sequence in their present configuration, and some notations are ambiguously identified (the last interpolation from Op. 72 is labelled '6/8' instead of the correct '3/8', and at the end of the CN, unmarked as to their proper location in the ballet, are to be found records of the children's dances from the first lakeside act.

45. *Peterburgskaya gazeta* (16 Jan. 1895), p. 3.

46. Lopukhov's commentary on Petipa's sketches, *Marius Petipa. Materialy*, pp. 212–13.

47. *Novosti i birzhevaya gazeta* (17 Jan. 1895), p. 3.

48. *Novosti i birzhevaya gazeta* (17 Jan. 1895), p. 3.

49. *Novosti i birzhevaya gazeta* (17 Jan. 1895), p. 3.

50. *Novosti i birzhevaya gazeta* (17 Jan. 1895), p. 3.

51. *Peterburgskaya gazeta* (18 Feb. 1894), p. 3.

52. This version of the dance continued for a time after Nikolai Sergeyev had produced *Swan Lake* in London. See, e.g., Cyril W. Beaumont and Russell

Sedgwick, *The Swan Lake Ballet as Presented by the Sadler's Wells Ballet* (London, 1947), Plates VIII and X.

53. *Novosti i birzhevaya gazeta* (6 Apr. 1901), p. 3.
54. *Istoriya tantsev*, iv, p. 134.
55. *Novosti i birzhevaya gazeta* (17 Jan. 1895), p. 3.
56. Mathilde Feliksovna Kshesinskaya [H. S. H. The Princess Romanovsky-Krassinsky], *Souvenirs de la Kschessinska, Prima-Ballerina du Théâtre Impérial de St Petersbourg* (Paris, 1960), p. 108.
57. *Novosti i birzhevaya gazeta* (17 Jan. 1895), p. 3.
58. *Sanktpeterburgskie vedomosti* (17 Jan. 1895), p. 3.
59. *Novosti i birzhevaya gazeta* (17 Jan. 1895), p. 3.
60. *Peterburgskaya gazeta* (16 Jan. 1895), p. 3.
61. *Peterburgskaya gazeta* (16 Jan. 1895), p. 3.
62. *Sanktpeterburgskie vedomosti* (17 Jan. 1895), p. 3.
63. *Peterburgskaya gazeta* (16 Jan. 1895), p. 3.
64. *Novosti i birzhevaya gazeta* (17 Jan. 1895), p. 3.
65. *Novosti i birzhevaya gazeta* (17 Jan. 1895), p. 3.
66. *Novoe vremya* (16 Jan. 1895), p. 3.
67. *Peterburgskii listok* (16 Jan. 1895), p. 3.
68. *Novosti i birzhevaya gazeta* (17 Jan. 1895), p. 3.
69. *Peterburgskaya gazeta* (16 Jan. 1895), p. 3.
70. *Novosti i birzhevaya gazeta* (17 Jan. 1895), p. 3.
71. *Peterburgskii listok* (17 Jan. 1895), p. 4.

POSTLUDE

1. *Moi vospominaniya*, i, p. 602.
2. *Moi vospominaniya*, i, pp. 606–7.
3. *Izbrannye stat'i*, ii, pp. 269–70.

APPENDIX A

Scenarios of Tchaikovsky's Ballets
Translated from the First Editions of their Librettos

I. 'SWAN LAKE' (Moscow, 1877). *Source: Teatral'naya gazeta*, c (19 Oct. 1876), pp. 390–1. A second edition (of 1,200 copies) was issued by the Moscow printer I. I. Smirnov in time for sale at performances. Included below in square brackets are remarks, some of which are variants of this text, written by Tchaikovsky in the holograph score.

ACT I

The action takes place in Germany. The décor of the first act depicts a magnificent park, in the depth of which a castle is visible. Crossing the stream is a pretty little bridge. On stage is the young sovereign Prince Siegfried, who is celebrating his coming of age. The Prince's friends are sitting at small tables and drinking wine. [The theatre represents part of a magnificent park; in the depth of the stage is seen a castle. A pretty little bridge is thrown across the river. Prince Siegfried with his friends are sitting at tables and drinking wine.] Peasants and, of course, peasant girls, who arrive to congratulate the Prince, dance at the wish of the slightly tipsy old Wolfgang, the young Prince's tutor. The Prince treats the dancing men to wine, but Wolfgang pays court to the peasant women, and gives them ribbons and bouquets. [A crowd of townsfolk approaches to congratulate the Prince. His tutor Wolfgang orders them to entertain his charge with dances. The Prince commands that wine be served. Servants carry out the order. Flowers and ribbons are given out to the women.]

The dances become more animated. A messenger runs in and announces to the Prince that the Princess, his mother, wishing to converse with him, now herself deigns to come here. The news throws the merriment into confusion, the dances cease, the peasants retire to the background, servants hasten to take away the tables, to hide the bottles, etc. The honourable tutor, realizing he is serving as a bad example to his student, tries to assume the look of a businesslike and sober man. [A messenger runs in and announces that the Princess–mother is arriving presently. The servants put everything in order. The tutor tries to assume the appearance of a sober man.]

And lo, the Princess finally appears, accompanied by her suite. [Entrance of the Princess . . .] All the guests and peasants bow to her respectfully. The young Prince, and behind him his drunken and staggering tutor, go to meet the Princess.

The Princess, noting her son's embarrassment, explains to him that she came not to break up the party, to disturb him, but because she had to discuss with him his marriage, for which the day of his coming of age was selected. [She talks to him about marriage etc.] 'I am old', the Princess continues, 'and therefore I want you to marry while I am still alive. I want to die knowing that you did not disgrace our famous family line by your marriage.'

The Prince, as yet not inclined towards marriage, annoyed at his mother's proposal but ready to reconcile himself to it, asks her respectfully: whom has she chosen for him as a lifetime companion?

'I have not yet chosen anybody', his mother answers, 'because I want you to do this yourself. Tomorrow I will have a grand ball, at which will gather nobles and their daughters. From these you will have to choose the one that pleases you, and she will be your wife.' Siegfried sees that the matter is not yet especially unpleasant, and therefore answers, 'I will never be disobedient to you, mama.'

'I have said everything that I must,' the Princess answers to this, 'and I shall leave. Make merry, don't hesitate.' [The Princess departs.]

On her departure the Prince's friends circle around him, and he tells them the sad news. 'The end of our good times—farewell, dear freedom', he says. [The Prince says: 'The end of our carefree life' etc.]

'There is still a lot of time', his knight Benno reassures him. 'Right now, for the moment put the future aside when the present smiles on us, when it is ours.'

'That's true', the Prince answers, laughing.

[The knight Benno consoles him. All sit down and the celebration begins anew.] The binge [*kutezh*] starts anew. The peasants dance now in groups, now separately. Deferential Wolfgang, having drunk a little more, also joins in the dancing, in such a funny, jesting way of course that everybody bursts out laughing. [The tutor, having become somewhat drunk, dances and excites general merriment by his awkwardness.] Having finished dancing, Wolfgang takes to courting but the peasant girls laugh and run away from him. One of them he especially likes, and as a preliminary to declaring his love he wants to kiss her. But the cheat avoids him and, as always happens in ballets, instead of kissing her he kisses her suitor. [The tutor turns around . . . and falls!] Wolfgang's perplexity. General laughter of those present.

But night is falling quickly; it is getting dark. One of the guests proposes to dance with cups in hand. [It is beginning to get dark. One of the guests proposes to dance a last dance with cups in hand.] Those present carry out his proposal with pleasure. From a distance appears a flying band of swans. [Subject. A flight of swans appears as a line in the sky etc.]

'But it would probably be difficult to find them', says Benno egging on the Prince, showing him the swans.

'That's nonsense', answers the Prince, 'I will certainly find them. Hand me my crossbow.'

'That's not necessary', Wolfgang dissuades, 'you don't have to: it's time to sleep.'

The Prince gives the appearance that indeed, perhaps it is not necessary, and it is time to sleep. But as soon as the old man leaves, calmed down, Siegfried calls his servant, takes his crossbow, and quickly runs out with Benno in the direction the swans flew.

ACT II

A mountainous, wild locale, with forest on all sides. In the depth of the stage—a lake, on the shore of which, to the right of the audience, are some buildings which are falling down, a kind of chapel. Night. Moonlight.

Around the lake a band of white swans with cygnets is swimming. [The swans are swimming around the lake.] The flock swims in the direction of the ruins. In front, a swan wearing a crown on its head.

The Prince and Benno come on to the stage, exhausted. [Entrance of the Prince.] 'I cannot go further', says the latter, 'I don't have the strength. Can we not rest?'

'Perhaps', answers Siegfried. 'Must we not have gone far from the castle? Here, maybe, we ought to spend the night . . . Look', he points to the lake, 'there is where the swans are. Quickly, the crossbow!' [The Prince notices the swans.]

Benno gives him the crossbow; the Prince no sooner takes aim than the swans instantly disappear. [The Prince wants to fire . . . the swans disappear.] At the same moment the interior of the ruins is illuminated by some kind of extraordinary light.

'They flew away! It's a shame . . . But look—What's that?' and the Prince points out to Benno the illuminated ruins.

'Strange!' says Benno, astonished. 'This place must be enchanted.'

'Let's go and investigate', answers the Prince and heads towards the ruins. Just as he approaches the place a girl in a white dress, wearing a crown of precious stones, appears on the steps of the staircase. [The appearance of Odette.] She is illuminated by the moonlight.

The astonished Siegfried and Benno retreat from the ruins. Shaking her head sadly the girl asks the Prince: 'Why do you pursue me, knight? What have I done to you?' [The girl says to the Prince: 'Why do you pursue me?' etc.]

The Prince answers in confusion: 'I didn't think . . . didn't expect . . .'

The girl walks away from the steps, calmly comes up to the Prince, and putting her hand on his shoulder, says with reproach: 'The swan that you wanted to kill—it was I!'

'You? A swan? It cannot be!'

[Odette's narrative.]

'Yes, listen . . . My name is Odette, my mother is a good fairy; against her father's will she fell in love with a noble knight and married him, but he destroyed her, and she was no more. My father married another, forgot about me, but my wicked stepmother, who was a witch, hated me and nearly killed me. But my grandfather took me in. The old man loved my mother very much and cried so about her that from his tears this lake was formed. He himself went to a place there in the deepest part and concealed me from people. Now, not long ago he began to indulge me, and is giving me full freedom to make merry. Thus by day with my friends we transform ourselves into swans, and merrily fly through the air, high, almost to heaven itself; and by night we play and dance here near our dear little old man. But my stepmother even now leaves neither me nor my friends in peace.'

At this moment the sound of an owl rings out.

'Did you hear? . . . This is her ominous voice', says Odette, looking around alarmed. 'Look, there she is!'

In the ruins appears a huge owl with eyes lit-up. [The appearance of the owl.]

'She would have destroyed me long ago', Odette continues. 'But grandfather follows her vigilantly, and keeps me from harm. With my marriage the witch loses her chance to injure me, but until then only this crown saves me from her wickedness. [*Odette*: 'with my marriage' etc.] And that is all, my story is not long.'

'O forgive me, beautiful one, forgive!' says the agitated Prince, falling on his knees. [*Prince*: 'O forgive me' etc.]

From the ruins run out rows of young girls and children [The swans appear in a line etc.]; all turn to the young hunter with reproaches, saying that for the sake of empty amusement he nearly deprived them of that which they held dearest of all things.

The Prince and his friend are in despair.

'Enough', says Odette, 'Stop. You see, he is good, he grieves, he is sorry for me.' [*Odette*: 'Enough, stop, he is good' etc.]

The Prince takes his crossbow, and having quickly broken it, throws it away, saying, 'I swear henceforth never to raise my hand to kill a bird of any kind!' [The Prince breaks his crossbow.]

'Be at ease, knight. Let us forget everything and make merry together.' [*Odette*: 'Be at ease, knight' etc.]

Dances begin, in which the Prince and Benno take part. The swans now form beautiful groups, now dance singly. The Prince is constantly around Odette; during the dances he falls madly in love with her, and implores her not to reject his love (*Pas d'action*). Odette laughs and does not believe him.

'You do not believe me, cold, cruel Odette.'

'I am afraid to believe you, noble knight, afraid that your imagination is only deceiving you. Tomorrow at your mother's ball you will see many beautiful young girls and you will fall in love with another; you will forget about me.'

'O, never! I swear on my knightly honour!'

'Then listen: I will not hide from you that you please me. I have also fallen in love with you, but a terrible foreboding possesses me. It seems to me that the intrigues of this witch, preparing you for some kind of test, will ruin our happiness.'

'I challenge the whole world to battle! You, you alone I will love my whole life! And no magic of this witch will ruin my happiness!'

'Very well, tomorrow our destiny must be decided: either you will never see me again, or I myself will obediently place my crown at your feet. But enough. Time is passing, dawn is coming. Farewell—until tomorrow!'

Odette and her friends disappear in the ruins. [Odette and the swans disappear in the ruins etc.] Dawn breaks out in the sky; on the lake a band of swans swims out, and above them, ponderously flapping its wings, flies a huge owl.

ACT III

A magnificent hall in the Princess's castle. All is prepared for the festival.

Old Wolfgang gives the last orders to the servants. [The old man Wolfgang gives orders to the servants. The guests arrive.] The Master of Ceremonies meets and places the guests. The herald who appears announces the arrival of the Princess with the young Prince, who enter accompanied by their courtiers, pages, and dwarfs. [Arrival of the Prince, Princess, and her suite, pages, dwarfs, etc.] Amiably exchanging bows with the guests, they take the place of honour prepared for them. The Master of Ceremonies, at a sign from the Princess, gives the order to begin the dances. [The Master of Ceremonies gives a sign to begin the dances.] The guests, men and women, form various groups [*Ballabile*]; the dwarfs dance. [The dwarfs dance.] The sound of trumpets proclaims the arrival of new guests. The Master of Ceremonies goes to meet them, and the herald announces their names to the Princess. An old count with his wife and young daughter come in. They bow respectfully to their host and hostess, and the daughter, at a sign from the Princess, takes part in the dances. [The sound of trumpets announces the arrival of new guests. The Master of Ceremonies goes to meet them, and the herald announces their names to the Prince. An old count comes in with his wife and daughter. They bow to the host and hostess, and the daughter dances the waltz with one of the cavaliers.] Then the trumpet sounds anew, again the Master of Ceremonies and the herald perform their duties: new guests enter . . . The Master of Ceremonies places the old people, and the girls are invited to dance by the Princess. [Again the sound of trumpets and the arrival of guests. The old people are seated, and the daughter dances the waltz at the invitation of one of the guests.] After several such entrances the Princess calls away her son to the side and asks him which of the girls produced a pleasant impression on him. [Again the same scene (at bar 120 of No. 17; at bar 148) General waltz; (at bar 184) Here the entire *corps de ballet* dances the waltz . . . The Princess takes her son to the side and asks which of the girls pleases him etc.]

The Prince sadly answers her, 'So far none of them pleases me, dear mother.'

Vexed, the Princess shrugs her shoulders, calls Wolfgang, and angrily tells him her son's words. The tutor attempts to speak to his pupil but the trumpets sound again, and von Rothbart enters the hall with his daughter Odile. [Entrance of Baron Rothbart and Odile.] At the sight of Odile the Prince is struck with her beauty; her face reminds him of his swan/Odette. He calls his friend Benno and asks him, 'Doesn't she look like Odette?' [The Prince is struck by the likeness of Odile to Odette and asks Benno about this.]

'To my eyes not in the least . . . You see your Odette everywhere', answers Benno.

For some time the Prince gazes in admiration at the dancing Odile, and then himself takes part in the dances. The Princess is delighted, calls Wolfgang, and asks him if this guest, apparently, is creating an impression on her son? [The Princess is happy that Odile pleases her son and asks Wolfgang about this.]

'O yes', answers Wolfgang, 'wait for a moment, the young Prince is not a stone; he will shortly fall in love.'

Meanwhile the dances continue, and during them the Prince shows a clear preference for Odile, who coquettishly shows off in front of him. [The Prince invites Odile to dance the waltz.] In a moment of passion the Prince kisses Odile's hand. [The Prince kisses Odile's hand.] At that moment the Princess and old Rothbart get up from their places and go to the centre, towards the dancers. [The Princess and Rothbart go to the centre.]

'My son', says the Princess, 'you may kiss the hand only of your bride.' [The Princess says that Odile must be the Prince's bride.]

'I am ready, dear mother.'

'What does her father say about this?' asks the Princess.

Von Rothbart triumphantly takes his daughter's hand and gives it to the young Prince. [Rothbart triumphantly takes his daughter's hand and gives it to the Prince.]

The stage instantly darkens, the cry of an owl rings out, the clothes fall from von

Rothbart and he appears in the form of a demon. [Instantly the stage darkens etc.] Odile bursts out laughing. With a noise the window flies open, and in it is seen a white swan with a crown on her head. In horror the Prince throws down the arm of his new fiancée, and clasping his hand to his heart runs out of the castle.

ACT IV

The décor of Act II. Night.

Odette's companions await her return; some of them are wondering where she could have gone. [Odette's girlfriends are wondering where she has gone.] They are sad without her, and they try to amuse themselves by dancing and making the young swans dance. [The swan maidens are teaching the cygnets to dance.]

But now Odette runs in, her hair tousled in disorder under her crown and dispersed on her shoulders; she is in tears and despair. [Odette runs in and tells her friends of her sorrow.] Her friends surround her and ask, 'What happened to you?'

'He did not keep his vow, he did not pass the test!' says Odette.

Her friends indignantly urge her to think no more of her betrayer.

'But I love him', Odette says sadly.

'Poor thing, poor thing! Let us fly quickly. Here he comes.' ['There he comes', Odette's friends tell her etc.]

'He?!' Odette says with alarm and runs towards the ruins; but she suddenly stops and says, 'I want to see him for the last time.'

'But you will be destroyed!'

'O no! I will be careful. Be off, sisters, and wait for me.'

All go into the ruins. Thunder is heard . . . At first separate rolls, and then ever closer and closer; the stage darkens from the gathering clouds, which from time to time are illuminated by lightning. The lake begins to sway. [The stage darkens, a storm breaks out. Thunder rings out.]

The Prince runs on to the stage. [The Prince runs in.]

'Odette . . . here!' he says and runs to her. 'O forgive me, forgive me, dear Odette!' ['O, forgive me', says the Prince. Final scene.]

'It is not in my power to forgive you; all is finished. We are seeing each other for the last time!'

The Prince entreats her passionately; Odette remains inexorable. She looks around timidly at the agitated lake and, freeing herself from the Prince's embrace, runs towards the ruins. The Prince catches up with her, takes her by the hand, and in despair says, 'Not this way. No! Willing or unwilling, you will always remain with me!'

He quickly takes the crown from her head and throws it into the stormy lake, which already has overflowed its banks. Over her head flies the owl, which with a cry carries off in its claws Odette's crown, which the Prince threw off.

'What have you done?! You have destroyed yourself and me. I am dying', says Odette, falling into the Prince's arms, and, through the noise of the peals of thunder and the noise of the waves, the sad last song of the swan is heard. [Odette falls into the Prince's arms.]

One after another the waves run up against the Prince and Odette, and soon they disappear under the water.

The storm quiets. In the distance the weak rolls of thunder are hardly perceptible; the moon's pale rays cut through the dispersing storm clouds, and on the calm lake appears a band of white swans. [Appearance of the swans over the lake.]

★

II. 'SLEEPING BEAUTY'. *Source*: *Sleeping Beauty. Ballet-féerie in 3 Acts with Prologue* [Libretto] (St Petersburg, 1890), pp. 1–22.

PROLOGUE

Scene 1

The Christening of Princess Aurora

A banquet in one of the halls of the King's palace. At the right a platform for the King and Queen, and for the fairies—godmothers of the Princess Aurora. At the rear of the stage, an entranceway.

Courtiers: ladies and cavaliers form groups in expectation of the entrance of the King and Queen. The masters of ceremonies show them to their places and explain the procedure, how in this instance to offer congratulations to the King and Queen, as also to the influential fairies, invited in the capacity of godmothers to the baptismal feast of Princess Aurora.

Catalabutte, surrounded by courtiers, verifies the list of invitations sent to the fairies. Everything has been done in accordance with the King's order and is ready for the festivities. The court is full; from minute to minute the entrance of the King and Queen is expected, as well as the arrival of the invited fairies.

The sound of trumpets. Entrance of the King and Queen, preceded by pages; behind them the nannies and wet-nurses of Princess Aurora carry a cradle in which the royal child sleeps. As soon as the King and Queen take their places on the platform, on either side of the cradle, the masters of ceremonies announce the arrival of the fairies.

Entrance of the fairies—*Candide*, *Fleur de Farine*, *Violente*, *Canaries*, and *Breadcrumb*. The King and Queen meet them and show them to their places on the platform.

Entrance of the *Lilac* Fairy, Princess Aurora's principal godmother. She is surrounded by her subordinate spirits, who carry large fans, censers, and who bear their sovereign's mantle.

At a signal from *Catalabutte* pages and young girls bring forward gifts on brocade pillows, gifts designated by the King for the godmothers of his daughter, and they explain to each fairy that it is for her. The fairies leave the platform in order to present gifts to their goddaughter in their turn.

Grand pas d'ensemble
Gifts of the Fairies

When her turn comes the *Lilac* Fairy approaches the cradle to present her gift, as suddenly a loud noise is heard at the entrance; a page runs in and informs *Catalabutte* that a new fairy, whom they forgot to invite to the feast, is already at the castle gate. This is the evil fairy *Carabosse*—the most powerful and evil in the entire land. *Catalabutte* has completely lost his presence of mind. How could he have forgotten her, he, the personification of accuracy? Trembling with fear he approaches the King in order to tell him of his mistake. The King and Queen are very upset; this mistake may bring with it much unhappiness in the fate of their dear child. The fairies also seem upset by this.

Carabosse appears in a wheelbarrow drawn by six large rats; ugly dirty pages accompany her. The King and Queen beseech her to forgive *Catalabutte's* indiscretion; he will be punished according to her command. *Catalabutte*, neither dead nor alive, throws himself at the knees of the evil fairy, begging her for forgiveness and promising to serve her faithfully to the end of his days.

Carabosse laughs at him mockingly and entertains herself by plucking out tufts of his hair and throwing them at the rats, who devour them. Soon *Catalabutte's* head is completely bald.

'Although I am not *Aurora's* godmother', says Carabosse, 'I nevertheless want to give her something.'

The good fairies entreat her to forgive the master of ceremonies' unexpected forgetfulness, and not to poison the happiness of this best of kings.

But *Carabosse* only laughs. Her gaiety quickly passes to her ugly pages, and even to her rats. The good fairies turn away from their sister with repugnance.

'*Aurora*, thanks to the gifts of her six godmothers', says *Carabosse*, 'will be the most beautiful, the most seductive [*soblaznitel'naya*—cf. Petipa's *séduisante*], the most clever of all the princesses in the world. I do not have the power to deprive her of these qualities, but in order that her happiness never be disturbed—you see how good I am—she will fall asleep the first time she pricks her finger or hand, and her slumber will be forever.' The King, Queen, and entire court are dumbfounded.

Carabosse makes signs with her wand over the cradle, pronouncing magic words and, happy at the trick she has played on her sisters, begins to guffaw; her gaiety is transferred to all her ugly retinue.

But the *Lilac* Fairy, who had yet to present a gift to her goddaughter and was standing screened by Aurora's cradle, now comes forward. *Carabosse* looks at her with suspicion and wickedness. The good fairy leans over the cradle: 'Yes, you will fall asleep, my little *Aurora*, as our sister *Carabosse* wishes', the *Lilac* Fairy says, 'but not forever. The day will come when a prince, under the influence of your beauty, will kiss you on the brow, and you will awaken from your long slumber, in order to become the bride of this prince, in order to live in happiness and contentment.'

Carabosse, enraged, sits down in her wheelbarrow and disappears. The good fairies surround the cradle, as if wishing to protect their goddaughter from their evil sister.

(*Scene*)

End of Prologue

ACT I

Scene 2

Princess Aurora's Four Suitors

A park in the castle of King Florestan XIV. To the right is the castle's entrance. The higher parts of the castle are lost in the greenery of the trees. In the depth of the stage a marble fountain.

Aurora is twenty. *Florestan* is happy that Fairy *Carabosse*'s prediction has not come true. *Catalabutte*, whose hair has not grown back, appears in a comical nightcap—he fines some villagers for working in front of the castle with needles, and reads them a declaration that prohibits the use of needles and pins within a hundred-mile radius of the royal residence, then sends them to prison under guard.

The King and Queen are shown on a terrace of the castle in the company of four princes, suitors of Princess Aurora. The King asks what the peasants who had been sent off to prison had done wrong. *Catalabutte* explains the reason for the arrest and shows the material evidence. The King and Queen are horrified. 'Let the guilty suffer for their offences and never more see the light of God's world.' The princes beg mercy for the guilty. Not one tear must be shed in *Florestan*'s kingdom on *Aurora*'s twentieth birthday. The King pardons the peasants—but with the condition that their work be burned by the executioner in a public place. General rejoicing. Dances of the peasants. 'Long live King *Florestan*, long live Princess *Aurora*!' The princes have not seen Princess Aurora, but each of them has a medallion with her portrait. They are all burning with the wish to be her favourite and express this to the King and Queen, who assure them that they gave full freedom of choice to their beloved daughter, and that whomever she loves will be their son-in-law and successor to the kingdom.

Entrance of *Aurora*. She runs in accompanied by her maids of honour who carry bouquets and wreaths. The four princes, astonished at her beauty, attempt to gain her favour, but Aurora dances between them, giving preference to none.

(*Pas d'action*)

Competition among the princes. *Aurora*'s coquetry. The King and Queen urge her to make a choice. 'I am still so young', she says, 'let me yet take advantage of my freedom.'—'Do as you know best, but remember that the interests of the state demand your marriage, in order that you may bear a successor to the throne. *Carabosse*'s prediction worries us very much.' 'Don't worry about her prediction coming true—I must pierce my hand or finger, and I never take into my hand either spindles or needles. I sing, dance, and make merry, but never work.'

The four princes encircle her and ask her to dance among them, as it is rumoured that she is the most graceful girl in all the world.

Aurora agrees to grant their wish. She dances to the accompaniment of lutes and fiddles played by the young girls and pages. The four princes are delighted with her, and she increases her efforts to be lighter and more graceful in order to please them. Not only do the princes and the court admire her, but also the gathering of peasants follows her aerial flights with curiosity. General delight. General dances. Suddenly *Aurora* notices an old woman, who is beating time with a spindle. She takes the spindle from her and with it continues to dance, now as with a sceptre, now imitating the work of spinners, attempting to excite the full admiration of the four courtiers. Suddenly her dances are interrupted, and in horror she looks at her hand, pricked and bloodstained by the spindle.

As if mad, she throws herself from side to side and finally falls unconscious. The King and Queen rush to their beloved daughter, and at the sight of the Princess's wounded hand, understand the full weight of the misfortune that has befallen them.

The old woman to whom the spindle belonged throws off her cloak. She is recognized as *Carabosse*, who laughs at the despair of *Florestan* and the Queen. The four princes unsheath their swords and rush towards her, but *Carabosse* with a diabolical laugh disappears in a cloud of smoke and fire. The four princes with their suite run out, frightened. At this moment in the depth of the stage a fountain is illuminated with a magic light and the *Lilac* Fairy appears in the fountain. 'Be consoled', she says to the despairing parents: 'your daughter is sleeping and will sleep for a hundred years, but in order that nothing about her happiness shall change, you will fall asleep. Her awakening will be a signal for your awakening; return to the castle, I will watch over you.' They place the sleeping girl on a sedan chair and carry her out, accompanied by the King and Queen and the highest dignitaries of the court. The cavaliers, pages, and guards bow before this procession. The fairy waves her wand in the direction of the castle and all these groups on the threshold and on the staircase suddenly fall asleep, as if stunned. Everything falls asleep, including the flowers and the splashes of the fountain; ivy and creepers grow out from the earth and cover themselves and the castle and the sleeping people. Trees and large bushes of lilacs grow up magically under the influence of the fairy, and transform the royal garden into an impenetrable forest. The fairy's subordinates group themselves around her, and she orders them to guard the castle so that no one dare disturb the tranquillity of those whom she is protecting.

(Scene)

End of Act I

ACT II

Scene 3

Prince Désiré's Hunt

A forest place; a broad river flows in the depth of the stage. The thick forest stretches into the far distance. To the right of the audience, cliffs, covered with vegetation. The landscape is filled with bright sunlight.

At the opening of the curtain the stage is empty, sounds of hunting horns are heard, then Prince Désiré's hunt, who are pursuing animals in a nearby forest. The hunters enter and settle down on the grass to lunch. Soon Prince *Désiré* appears with his tutor *Galifron* and several courtiers of the King, his father. Lunch is prepared for the Prince and his suite. Hunters and ladies, in order to divert the Prince, dance, shoot at archery, and play at various games. *Galifron* urges his student to join the courtiers and particularly to be amiable with the ladies, as he will have to choose a wife for himself from the gentry of his own homeland. Among the neighbouring kings there are only sons and not one princess of the royal blood to whom he could be married. *Galifron* takes advantage of the opportunity to show him all the noble young women of the country.

Dance of the Duchesses
Dance of the Marchionesses
Dances of the Countesses
Dance of the Baronesses

All these young women try to please the Prince, but *Désiré*, glass in hand, and with a little smile on his lips, looks at the futile effort of this group of excellent young girls; his heart has still not begun to speak, he still has not met the object of his dreams, and he will not marry before meeting the girl he seeks.

The hunters approach to report to the Prince that a bear has been trapped, and that if the Prince wanted to kill it, this was his certain chance. But the Prince is tired: 'Hunt without me', he tells his retinue, 'I want to rest here; this place pleases me.' The hunt and court move away, and *Galifron*, who had drained not just one bottle, falls asleep near the Prince.

Just as the hunt moves away a boat of mother-of-pearl, with decorations of gold and precious stones, appears on the river. From it on to the shore steps the *Lilac Fairy*, who is also the godmother of Prince *Désiré*. The Prince bows before the good fairy, who graciously turns to him and asks him what is in his heart. 'Are you not yet in love?' she asks him. 'No', the Prince answers, 'the noble young ladies of my homeland do not captivate me, and I prefer to remain a bachelor than marry a woman only for reasons of state.' 'If so', the fairy says, 'I will show you your future wife: she is the most beautiful, the most enchanting [*ocharovatel'naya*—cf. Petipa's *séduisante*] and most intelligent of all princesses in the world.' 'Where can I see her?' 'I will call her spectre, and if you like her, you may fall in love with her.' The fairy waves her wand to the side of the cliffs, which open and show *Aurora* with her girlfriends, sleeping. At another sign from the fairy, *Aurora* rises with her friends and appears on stage. Rays of the rising sun illuminate her with a rose-coloured light.

The Prince, entranced, follows this vision, which evades him. A dance now full of languor, now lively, delights him more and more. He wants to catch her, but she evades his arms, appearing where he did not expect her, and finally she disappears in the cleft of the rocks.

Insane with love, the Prince throws himself at the knees of his godmother. 'Where is this heavenly creature to be found, whom you showed me? Lead me to her. I want to see her and press her to my heart.'

'Let us go', says the fairy and leads him to her boat, which immediately moves along its path. *Galifron* continues to sleep.

The boat moves quickly and the landscape becomes more and more wild (panorama).

Evening comes; soon night begins to fall—the moon illuminates the boat with a silver light; in the distance the castle is seen, which again disappears in a bend in the river. But then finally the castle appears again—the goal of their journey. The Prince and the fairy get out of the boat. The fairy, with a wave of her magic wand, makes the gates open; the entrance hall is seen, where the guards and the pages are sleeping. The Prince runs in with the fairy. The stage is all obscured by dense clouds, and peaceful music is heard.

Musical entr'acte

Scene 4

Sleeping Beauty's Castle

When the clouds disperse a room appears where Princess *Aurora* is seen on a large bed beneath a canopy; the King and Queen are sleeping opposite her in two armchairs; the court ladies, cavaliers, and pages sleep standing up, leaning against one another and making up sleeping groups. A layer of dust and cobwebs covers the furniture and the people. The candlelight is asleep; the fire in the stoves is asleep. The scene is illuminated by phosphorous light. To the left of the bed a door is opening, and the fairy enters with the Prince. The Prince rushes to the bed, calls in vain to the Princess, stirs the King, Queen, and *Catalabutte*, who sleeps on a stool at the King's feet. Nothing helps, but only raises clouds of dust. The fairy remains an unconcerned observer of the Prince's despair. Finally he rushes to the sleeping beauty and kisses her on the forehead.

The magic spell disappears; *Aurora* awakens and with her the entire court; the dust and cobwebs disappear, candles illuminate the room, the fire flares up in the fireplace. The Prince implores the King to agree to the marriage with his daughter. 'Such is her destiny', answers the King and joins the hands of the two young people.

End of the Second Act

ACT III

Scene 5

The Wedding of Aurora and the Prince
The Esplanade of Florestan's Castle

Entrance of the King, Queen, the newly-weds with their suite, and the fairies: Diamond, Gold, Silver and Sapphire.

Polonaise

Procession of the Fairy Tales

1. Bluebeard and his wife
2. Puss in Boots
3. Marquis de *Carabas*, in a sedan chair, with his lackeys
4. Goldilocks and Prince *Avenant*
5. Donkey-skin and Prince *Charming*
6. Beauty and the Beast
7. Cinderella and Prince *Fortuné*
8. The Blue Bird and Princess *Florine*
9. The White Cat, carried in on a pillow
10. Little Red Riding Hood and the Wolf

11. *Ricky of the Tuft* and Princess Aimée
12. Tom Thumb and his brothers
13. The Ogre and Ogress
14. Fairy *Carabosse* in a wheelbarrow drawn by rats
15. Fairy *Candide* and her genies
16. Fairy *Violente* and her genies
17. The chariot of Fairy *Canaries* and her suite
18. The *Lilac* Fairy drawn by four large genies

Divertissement

Pas de quatre

Diamond Fairy
Gold Fairy
Silver Fairy
Sapphire Fairy

Pas de caractère: Puss in Boots and the White Cat
Pas de deux: The Blue Bird and Princess *Florine*
Pas de caractère: Little Red Riding Hood and the Wolf
Pas de caractère: Cinderella and Prince *Fortuné*
Pas berrichon: Tom Thumb, his brothers, and the Ogre
Pas de quatre: Aurora, Désiré, the Gold and Sapphire Fairies

Entrance of the ballet

Sarabande: Roman, Persian, Indian, American, and Turkish

General coda

Apotheosis
(*Gloire des Fées*)

★

III. 'NUTCRACKER'. *Source: Nutcracker (Casse-Noisette). Ballet-féerie in two acts and three scenes* [Libretto] (St Petersburg, 1892), pp. 7–20.

ACT I

Scene 1

The theatre represents a room in Silberhaus's home

First Tableau

A Christmas tree in Silberhaus's home; the relatives are busy decorating the tree; the guests are chatting merrily; servants are distributing various drinks and refreshments; the guests all arrive. Finally the Christmas tree is decorated and lighted. Mr Silberhaus asks his niece Marianne to fetch the children; the latter hastens to fulfil his wish.

Second Tableau

The door is opened and Marianne leads in the children, having arranged them in pairs. The children, at the sight of the tree, rush towards it and admire the brilliant sight with enthusiasm: gold and silver apples, nuts, confections, and other delicacies hanging from the tree's branches. Silberhaus's children thank their parents for their kindness. The guests, pleased with the festivities, watch the children's joy with a smile. Silberhaus passes out gifts to the children, which really delight them; they dance while one of the host's relatives plays the piano.

Third Tableau

New guests arrive; the company greets them merrily; dances begin; the children, in order not to interfere with the dancers, take seats around the Christmas tree.

Fourth Tableau

The wall clock begins to strike; an owl pops out of it and flaps its wings; with the last stroke Drosselmayer appears in the doorway. The children, at the sight of him, run off to the sides. Drosselmayer, having stood for a moment in the doorway, comes into the room, where he cheerfully greets Silberhaus and his wife. Having excused himself to his amiable hosts for being late, Drosselmayer requests permission to see Silberhaus's children soon, especially his goddaughter Clara. After greeting the children he orders the servants to bring the gifts intended for the children, and footmen roll in two large dolls wrapped up in paper. All present are somewhat astonished at this and make fun of his conceits; Drosselmayer unwraps the paper, and out of it come two dolls, one of which represents a sutler, the other a recruit in the French army. He winds them up with a key and they dance. Guests and children admire the dolls. Out of other papers Drosselmayer takes a Harlequin and Columbine. The children are delighted; they thank their good godfather and cannot tear themselves away from the charming toys, but Silberhaus, fearing for the safety of the expensive gifts, orders the footmen to put them away in the study. Clara and Fritz cry. Drosselmayer, wishing to console them, takes out of his pocket the cleverest doll—a Nutcracker—and makes it crack nuts. The children forget their tempers and rejoice in their new toy.

   Clara and Fritz quarrel over it; Drosselmayer announces at that point that the Nutcracker belongs to all and must crack nuts for all. Clara unwillingly gives up the Nutcracker to Fritz, who makes it crack the largest nuts, so that finally it breaks its jaws. With vexation Fritz throws the toy to the floor; Clara runs over to the Nutcracker, takes it into her arms, and begins to rock it as if it were a sick little child. Meanwhile Fritz and the other children form their own orchestra and make a frightful noise. Clara entreats the mischievous children not to make a noise, and to give the injured Nutcracker a chance to fall asleep. At first the children honour her request, but soon proceed as before; Clara then puts the Nutcracker down in the bed of her favourite doll, and wraps him in a.blanket. Silberhaus proposes a general dance to his guests, at which time he gives the order to move the furniture to make a broad space for the dancers. At the conclusion of the dances Mrs Silberhaus reminds her husband that it is time for the children to go to bed. Clara wants to take the Nutcracker with her but her father will not permit it. Marianne leads

Silberhaus's children out. The guests thank their host and hostess for the pleasure afforded the children and for the happy reception and then gradually disperse. After a time the hall is left empty and is illuminated only by the moonlight falling through the window.

Fifth Tableau

Clara, worried about her dear Nutcracker, cannot fall asleep and, convinced that everyone in the house has retired, decides to have a look at her dear injured one. She goes over to the bed and tenderly looks at the Nutcracker. Suddenly she hears behind the chairs and behind the cupboard the quiet rustle, bustle, and scratching of mice; she becomes so frightened that she wants to run, but at this very moment the clock begins to strike and she sees that not an owl appears on the clock but godfather Drosselmayer himself, who with a sardonic smile looks down on her and, having spread out the flaps of his caftan [sic], is waving them, exactly as an owl does its wings. The rustle and bustle increase from all sides; out of the cracks, under the ledges, peep out a multitude of bright little eyes—the room is filled with mice. Clara, scared, runs to the bed of her injured Nutcracker, seeking protection there.

Sixth Tableau

The moon, hidden by clouds for a time, again begins to shine through the window, illuminating Clara with its light. The Christmas tree grows and reaches enormous proportions; the dolls begin to stir. Toy rabbits diligently sound the alarm, sentries in their boxes salute with rifles and then fire. The dolls run about in fright, waving their arms, and think how best to get away. A detachment of gingerbread soldiers appears and forms into ranks. In the enemy detachment of mice a special enthusiasm is noticeable. The battle begins and the army of mice, driving back the gingerbread soldiers from their position, is left victorious. Triumphing in their victory, the mice return with pieces of the gingerbread soldiers, which they devour then and there.

Seventh Tableau

The Nutcracker, seeing the failure of the gingerbread army, rises quickly from his bed, disregarding his wound, and orders the toy rabbits quickly to sound the alarm again. Dancers [plyasuny] in the capacity of army doctors appear and order the soldiers to pick up the wounded on stretchers, and the dolls diligently bandage the injured; in response to the alarm, boxes of tin soldiers open; out of them quickly comes the Nutcracker's army and forms a square. At this moment the Mouse King appears with his honour guard and boldly orders an attack on the enemy. The army of mice, sensing the presence of its king and wishing to excel, attacks the square several times, but falls back with many casualties.

Eighth Tableau

The Mouse King enters into single combat with the Nutcracker and is surely about to kill him. But at this point Clara, seeing the danger which threatens her beloved, instinctively takes the slipper from her foot and throws it with all her might at the

Mouse King's back. The situation is quickly reversed; in this instant the Nut-cracker, taking advantage of his enemy's blunder, wounds him; together with the other mice, the Mouse King runs off. The Nutcracker, with bloodstained sword in his hand, goes over to Clara, falls on his knees, is transformed into a beautiful prince, and asks her to follow him. Clara, happy to see the Nutcracker alive and well, gives him her hand. They walk over to the Christmas tree and are lost in its branches.

Scene 2

The hall is transformed into a forest of fir trees in winter. Snow begins to fall in large flakes, and raises whirlwind and blizzard. Gradually the storm quiets and the winter landscape is illuminated by soft moonlight; in the moonlight the snow sparkles like diamonds.

ACT II

The Palace of Sweets: Confiturembourg
First Tableau

The Sugar Plum Fairy with Prince Coqueluche* stands in a sugar kiosk, adorned by dolphins, out of whose mouths pour fountains of currant syrup, orgeat, lemonade, and other refreshing and sweet drinks. The sovereign fairy awaits the arrival of Clara with Prince Nutcracker. Everything is ready for the celebration and the meeting of the newly-arrived. The Sugar Plum Fairy and the Prince step down from the kiosk. The fairies and the confections, picturesquely grouped, bow before her, and silver soldiers salute her. She asks them all to try to entertain the intelligent and dutiful Clara, who deserves the most joyful reception: all with joyfulness and readiness express the desire to oblige their sovereign.

Second Tableau

The major-domo, having seen the approach of the guests, quickly arranges the little moors and pages; the heads of the latter are made of pearl, their bodies of rubies and emeralds, their legs of pure gold; they hold flaming torches in their hands. Clara and the Nutcracker calmly sail along the river in a gilded nutshell. As the guests step ashore the silver soldiers salute them, little moors in costumes made of iridescent hummingbird feathers take Clara by the hand and carefully help her disembark. At this moment the sugar kiosk on the rose-coloured river begins to melt from the rays of the scorching sun, the fountains stop gushing, and the kiosk disappears. The Sugar Plum Fairy with Prince Coqueluche amiably meet Clara and the Nutcracker, all around them bow to them with deep esteem. The major-domo, showing his respect, greets Prince Nutcracker on his successful return to the palace of Confiturembourg. Clara, astonished and delighted, admires the magnificence

* In Russian *koklyush*, following the French *coqueluche*, means 'whooping cough'. It was probably not the librettist's intention for the Prince's name to have this connotation, but rather the familiar usage, as in the phrase *être la coqueluche*: 'to be the idol [of the public]', or 'favourite'.

and richness of the city which stretches out broadly before her eyes. The princesses, sisters of the Nutcracker, on seeing their beloved brother, run to him and embrace him tenderly. The Nutcracker, touched by the reception, leads Clara by the hand and presents her to his sisters, adding that to her alone is he indebted for his miraculous rescue. The Sugar Plum Fairy, hugging Clara, praises her heroic deed, and the deeply moved princesses hasten to express their gratitude to Clara, and tenderly embrace her. Meanwhile the good Sugar Plum Fairy makes a sign to the major-domo to begin the celebration, who in turn makes a sign and the moors carry in a table covered with various confections and fruits. The Sugar Plum Fairy with Prince Coqueluche and with her suite withdraw, in order not to interfere with the unrestrained merriment of the newly-arrived. The major-domo seeks to entertain the guests with a beautiful *divertissement*, made up of dances according to a programme drawn up earlier by the Sugar Plum Fairy.

Third Tableau

The Sugar Plum Fairy again appears with her retinue and Prince Coqueluche. Seeing her wishes being carried out by the intelligent and efficient major-domo, she herself wants to take part in the celebration. In delight Clara looks at the events going on around her, dazzled at the sight of the enchanting spectacle; she thinks she is seeing all this in a dream; it seems to her that it would be terrible to wake up now. Prince Nutcracker, radiating joy that he was able to please his young and pretty rescuer, tells her of the fairy-tale wonders and the unusual customs of the kingdom of the sweets.

Apotheosis

The apotheosis represents a large beehive with flying bees, closely guarding their riches.

*

IV. 'SWAN LAKE', St Petersburg, 1895. *Source: Swan Lake. Fantastic Ballet in 3 Acts and 4 Scenes* [Libretto] (St Petersburg, 1895), pp. 9–22.

ACT I
Scene 1
A park before a castle

Benno and his comrades are waiting for Prince Siegfried, in order to celebrate merrily his coming of age. Prince Siegfried enters, accompanied by Wolfgang. The feast begins. Peasant girls and young men arrive to congratulate the Prince, who directs the men to help themselves to wine, and gives ribbons to the girls. The slightly drunk Wolfgang sees to the execution of his student's order. Dances of the peasants.

Servants run in and announce the arrival of the Princess–mother. This news upsets the general merriment. The dances are stopped, servants hurry to remove the tables and to conceal the traces of festivity. The young men and Wolfgang feign abstinence. The Princess enters, preceded by her retinue; Siegfried goes to meet his mother, greeting her deferentially. She tenderly reproaches him for trying to deceive her, for she well knows that he is celebrating now, and she came not to keep him from festivities with his circle of friends, but to remind him that the last day of his bachelorhood has begun, and that tomorrow he must be married. To the question: who is the bride? the Princess answers that this will be decided at a ball the next day, to which she has summoned all the young girls worthy of becoming her daughter and his wife. He himself will select the one that pleases him most.

Having decided to let the interrupted party continue, the Princess departs.

The Prince is pensive; giving up his free and easy bachelor's life saddens him. Benno persuades him that a concern for the future does not make for a very agreeable present. Siegfried gives a sign for the resumption of the festivities. The celebration and dancing are renewed. Wolfgang, completely drunk, makes everybody laugh at his participation in the dances.

Night is beginning to fall. One more farewell dance and it is time to disperse. Dance with cups.

A band of swans flies over. The young men are not yet asleep. The sight of the swans makes them think of ending this day with a hunt. Benno knows where the swans fly at night. Having left behind the drunken Wolfgang, Siegfried and the young men depart.

Scene 2

A rocky, wild place. In the depth of the stage a lake. At the right, on the shore, the ruins of a chapel. A moonlit night.

First Tableau

A band of white swans swims around the lake. In front, a swan with a crown on its head.

Second Tableau

Benno enters with several friends from the Prince's retinue. Having noticed the swans they prepare to fire at them, but the swans swim away. Benno, having sent his companions to inform the Prince that they found the flock, remains alone. The swans, transformed into beautiful young girls, surround Benno, who is staggered by the magic phenomenon and is powerless against their charms. His companions return ahead of the Prince. At their arrival the swans fall back. The youths are about to shoot at them. The Prince enters and is also taking aim, but at this moment the ruins are illuminated by a magic light and Odette appears, pleading for mercy.

Third Tableau

Siegfried, struck by her beauty, forbids his comrades to shoot. She expresses her thanks to him and explains that she, Princess Odette, and the young girls subject to her are the unhappy victims of a wicked genie who bewitched them. By day they are condemned to take the form of swans and only at night, near these ruins, can they regain their human form. Their master, in the form of an owl, watches over them. His dreadful spell will continue until somebody falls truly in love with her, for life. Only a person who has not sworn his love to any other can be her deliverer and return her to her previous state. Siegfried, enchanted, listens to Odette. At this moment an owl flies in, and having transformed itself into the evil genie appears in the ruins; having listened to the conversation, it disappears. Horror takes hold of Siegfried at the thought that he could have killed Odette when she was in the form of a swan. He breaks his bow and throws it away in indignation. Odette consoles the young Prince.

Fourth Tableau

Odette calls all her friends and with them attempts to divert him with dances. Siegfried is all the more enchanted by Princess Odette's beauty and offers to rescue her. He has never sworn his love to anybody and because of this may deliver her from the owl's magic. He will kill him and free Odette. The latter answers that this is impossible. The destroyer of the evil genie will come only at that moment when some infatuated man sacrifices himself out of love for Odette. Siegfried is ready to do this also; for her sake he would be glad to die. Odette believes in his love, believes that he never vowed his love to someone else. But tomorrow is the day when a whole throng of beautiful girls will come to his mother's court, and he will be obliged to choose one of them for his bride. Siegfried says that he will be married only when she, Odette, appears at the ball. The unhappy girl answers that this is impossible because at that time she can only fly around the castle in the form of a swan. The Prince vows never to betray her. Odette, moved by the youth's love, accepts his vow but warns that the evil genie will do everything to make him swear fidelity to another. Siegfried still promises that no magic will take Odette from him.

Fifth Tableau

Dawn is breaking. Odette takes leave of her beloved, and with her friends disappears into the ruins. The dawn's light brightens. On the lake again swims out a flock of swans, and above them, waving its wings heavily, flies a large owl.

ACT II

A magnificent hall. Everything is prepared for the feast.

First Tableau

The master of ceremonies gives last minute orders to the servants. He meets and places the arriving guests. The entrance of the Princess and Siegfried in the vanguard of the court. Procession of the brides and their parents. General dance. Waltz of the Prospective Fiancées [val's nevest].

Second Tableau

The Princess–mother asks her son which of the young girls most pleases him. Siegfried finds them all delightful, but does not see any to whom he could swear eternal love.

Third Tableau

Trumpets announce the arrival of new guests. Von Rothbart enters with his daughter Odile. Siegfried is astonished by her likeness to Odette and greets her enthusiastically. Odette, in the form of a swan, appears at the window, warning her loved one of the evil genie's magic. But he, captivated by the beauty of the new guest, neither sees nor hears anything but her. The dances begin anew.

Fourth Tableau

Siegfried's choice is made. Confident that Odile and Odette are one and the same, he chooses her as his bride. Von Rothbart triumphantly takes the hand of his daughter and gives it to the young man, who in the presence of everyone pronounces a vow of eternal love.

At this moment Siegfried sees Odette in the window. He understands that he has become the victim of deception, but it is already too late: the vow is pronounced, Rothbart and Odile disappear. Odette forever must remain in the power of the genie, who in the form of an owl appears above her in the window. In a burst of despair the unhappy Prince flees. General confusion.

ACT III

A deserted place near the swan lake. In the distance the magic ruins. Cliffs. Night.

First Tableau

Swans in the form of girls anxiously await Odette's return. In order to shorten the time of restlessness and anguish, they try to divert themselves with dances.

Second Tableau

Odette rushes in. The swans greet her joyfully, but despair overcomes them when they learn of Siegfried's betrayal. All is ended; the evil genie triumphed and there is no deliverance for the unfortunate Odette: she is condemned to be the slave of evil spells forever. It would be better, while still in the form of a girl, to perish in the waves of the lake than to live without Siegfried. Her friends try in vain to console her.

Third Tableau

Siegfried runs in. He is searching for Odette in order to fall at her feet and beg forgiveness for his unintended betrayal. He loves her alone and made his vow of fidelity to Odile only because he saw Odette in her. Odette, at the sight of her beloved, forgets her sorrow and both give themselves over to the joy of meeting.

Fourth Tableau

The appearance of the evil genie interrupts the momentary enchantment. Siegfried must fulfil his vow and marry Odile, and Odette with the coming of dawn will forever be changed into a swan. Better to die while there is time. Siegfried vows to die with her. In terror the evil genie disappears. Death out of love for Odette is his destruction. The unhappy girl, having embraced Siegfried for the last time, runs to the cliff to throw herself from its height. The evil genie in the form of an owl hovers over her in order to change her into a swan. Siegfried rushes to Odette's assistance and together with her throws himself into the lake. The owl falls, dead.

Apotheosis

Affiche of the First Performance of *Swan Lake*, in English Translation

1877

Imperial Moscow Theatres

In the Bolshoy Theatre

On Sunday, 20 February

For the Benefit of the Dancer

Mlle Karpakova I

For the First Time

SWAN LAKE

Grand ballet in 4 acts, composed by balletmaster Mr Reisinger. Music composed by P. I. Tchaikovsky. Machines and electric illumination by Mr Valts. Men's costumes—Mr Simone, women's—Mlle Voronenko. Footwear—Mr Pirone. Flowers—Mlle Deladvez. Wigs and coiffures—Mr Silvan.

DÉCOR

Act I—Mr Shangin. Act II—Mr Valts. Act III—Mr Gropius.
Act IV—Mr Valts.

Roles will be performed as follows: Odette, Mlle Karpakova I; Princess, Mlle Nikolaeva I; von Rothbart, Mr Sokolov; Wolfgang, Mr Vanner; von Stein, Mr Reinshausen.

Mr Gerber will play the violin solo.

To dance:

In the first act:

1. Mlles Stanislavskaya, Karpakova II, Petrova III, Nikolaeva II, *coryphées:* Mlles Vladimirova, Gureva, Esaulova I, Gavrilova, Andreanova III, Ivanova III, Semenova II, Rei, N. Lebedeva, Dmitrieva, Kondrateva, Brandukova II, and the *corps de ballet*—waltz.
2. Mlles Stanislavskaya, Karpakova II, Petrova III, Nikolaeva II, Messrs Gillert II, Nikitin, Litavkin, and Ershov—Scene with Dances.

3. Mlle Stanislavskaya and Mr Gillert II—*Pas de deux*.
4. Mlles Karpakova II, Nikolaeva II, and Petrova III—Polka.
5. Mlle Stanislavskaya, Mr Gillert II, *coryphées*, and *corps de ballet*—Galop.
6. Mlles Karpakova II, Nikolaeva and Petrova III—*Pas de trois*.
7. Mlle Stanislavskaya, Mr Gillert II, *coryphées*, and *corps de ballet*—Finale.

In the second act:

8. Mlle Mikhailova, student Volkova, *coryphées*: Mlles Smirnova, Lvova, Andreanova I, Semenova II, Dmitrieva, Rei, Gureva, Andreanova III, Brandukova I, Leonteva II, Ezhova, Osipova I, Ivanova III, Brandukova II, Kvartalevskaya, Gavrilova, and *corps de ballet*—Entrance of the swans.
9. Mlle Mikhailova, student Volkova, and Mr Nikitin—*Pas de trois*.
10. Mlle Karpakova I and Mr Gillert II—*Pas de deux*.
11. Mlles Karpakova I, Mikhailova, student Volkova, Messrs Gillert II, Nikitin, *coryphées*, and *corps de ballet*—Finale.

In the third act:

12. Dance of the gentry and pages.
13. Mlle Karpakova I, students Savitskaya, Mikhailova, Dmitrieva, Vinogradova, and Mr Gillert II—*Pas de six*.
14. Mlles Karpakova I, Manokhina, Karpakova II, Andreanova IV, and Mr Gillert II—*Pas de cinq*.
15. Mlle Nikolaeva II and Mr Bekefi—Hungarian Dance.
16. Mlle Stanislavskaya and Mr Ermolov—Neapolitan Dance.
17. Mlle Karpakova I—Russian Dance.
18. Mlles Alexandrova and Manokhina—Spanish Dance.
19. Mlles Volkova I, Leonteva II, Egorova, Petrova III, Messrs Gillert I, Gulyaev, Litavkin, and Kondratiev—Mazurka.

In the fourth act:

20. Mlle Mikhailova, student Volkova, *coryphées*, and 16 students—*Pas d'ensemble*.

The action takes place in Germany.

Curtain at 7.30 p.m.

Tickets may be purchased from 9.00 a.m. at the box office of the Bolshoy Theatre.

Dramatis personae:

Odette, good fairy	Mlle Karpakova I
Sovereign Princess	Mlle Nikolaeva
Prince Siegfried, her son	Mr Gillert II

Wolfgang, his tutor . . . . Mr Vanner
Benno von Sommerstern, friend of the Prince . . . . Mr Nikitin
von Rothbart, evil genie in the guise of a guest . . . . Mr Sokolov
Odile, his daughter, resembling Odette . . . . Mlle * * *
Master of Ceremonies . . . . Mr Kuznetsov
Baron von Stein . . . . Mr Reinshausen
The baroness, his wife . . . . Mlle Polyakova
Freiger von Schwartzfels . . . . Mr Titov
His wife . . . . Mlle Gorokhova I
Court gentlemen, friends of the Prince:
   1.   . . . . Mr Litavkin
   2.   . . . . Mr Gulyaev
   3.   . . . . Mr Ershov
Herald . . . . Mr Zaitsev
Messenger . . . . Mr Alekseyev
Peasant girls:
   1.   . . . . Mlle Stanislavskaya
   2.   . . . . Mlle Karpakova II
   3.   . . . . Mlle Nikolaeva II
   4.   . . . . Mlle Petrova III
    Gentry of both sexes, heralds, guests, pages, peasants, servants, swans, and cygnets.

Tchaikovsky's Harmony

I. *Some Typical Features of Chord Grammar and Tonality*

Tchaikovsky was fond of extending the concept of a tonic to embrace mediant and especially submediant triads of a key. When in the second movement of the Sixth Symphony (to choose an especially clear example) the opening section in D major moves to the middle section in B minor (supported, in this case, by a pedal point on D), the effect is one not of modulation from one key to a second so much as a colouristic extension of the first.

A special instance of tonic extension to the submediant involves a change of mode, namely the juxtaposition of a tonic in the major with a submediant borrowed from the minor. A typical example from the concert music written at the time of *Swan Lake* is the final cadence of the first movement (the last dozen bars) of the Third Symphony.

In *Swan Lake* and especially the later ballets Tchaikovsky used this succession to create an effect of poignancy. Sometimes enharmony is involved, as in the shift from Db major to A (=Bbb) major in the Dances of the Little Swans:

Another favoured progression involves enharmonic reinterpretation in its typical occurrence, namely the re-spelling of the pitches of a dominant seventh chord in a given key to create an augmented sixth chord in the key a semitone lower (or vice versa). The device constitutes a pivot chord to permit rapid modulation by semitones, as the following example illustrates:

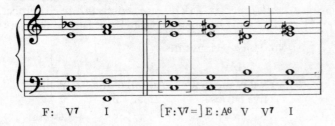

F: V⁷   I   [F:V⁷=] E : A⁶ V   V⁷   I

In *Sleeping Beauty* Tchaikovsky uses this distinctive enharmony before the end of the first bar, that is, in the first three chords of the work:

The first and third chords sound alike in their pitches, but the difference in their implied resolutions as spelled—the first to E and the second to F—is reflected in the structure of the whole ballet by the juxtaposition of E and F as keys in the middle of the work, that is, between the end of Act I and the beginning of Act II.

II. *The Prologue of* Sleeping Beauty (an elaboration of the diagram given in Chapter 4, p. 132).

Tchaikovsky uses the flat submediant and enharmony to enrich the progression of keys by a rising perfect fourth on which the prologue of *Sleeping Beauty* is constructed.

	Introduction	
	E	V⁷/A
	(Lilac Fairy)	(Anticipation of the *Marche*)
	Bars: 28–65	66–76

No. 1, *Marche*

A	iii/A	A	vi/A	V/A	(B♭)	A
Ritornello	Catalabutte, 1st *récit*	Ritornello	Catalabutte, 2nd *récit*	Ritornello theme		Coda
Bars: 1–31	32–44	48–78	79–109	115–27	136–9	140–7

Two details of No. 1 that predict harmonic events in Nos. 2 and 3 warrant mention: (1) the juxtaposition of F major and F♯ minor as submediant areas of A major in bars 20–3 (especially the introduction of F major as the flat submediant of A major); and (2) the highlighting of B♭ major just before the final cadence. Much of *Sleeping Beauty* is thus inflected—a key stated briefly in a given number is justified by Tchaikovsky with a more substantial restatement later in the work.

	No. 2, *Scène dansante*		
	♭VI/A	V → I/A	A
	Arrival of the first five fairies	Arrival of the Lilac Fairy	Waltz
	Bars: 1–56	57–95	96–210

The inflection of F major in the *Marche* is justified by the opening section of this *Scène*; the modulation from F to A is achieved by Tchaikovsky's enharmonic pivot:

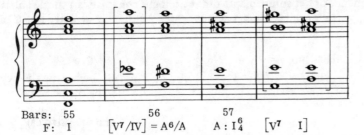

Bars: 55   56   57
F: I   [V⁷/IV] = A⁶/A   A : I⁶₄   [V⁷   I]

This cadence is similar to the closing cadence of No. 1 in that the chord progression prepares for a move to Bb, as if Tchaikovsky were going to repeat the striking gesture at the end of the *Marche* before moving on to a full stop in A major. He avoids the Bb triad, but when Bb is suggested the listener may experience a flash of recognition strong enough to recall the preceding number.

Both *Marche* and *Scène dansante* are heard in the overall key of A major, which was established by the perfect cadence between the end of the introduction and the downbeat of the *Marche*. All the subsidiary key areas of Nos. 1 and 2 are related by a third to A, and are treated by Tchaikovsky as extensions of that tonic.

The first four bars of No. 3, the *pas de six*, comprise a transition from A major to D major. The chords are:

	f♯	B	e	A⁷
	[vi/A=]			
	iii/D	V/ii/D	ii/D	V⁷/D
Bars:	1	2	3	4–6

Of these, the first constitutes a pivot chord, equally at home in A major and D major; the rest form a strong half-cadence in D, emphasized by three full bars of harp cadenza on the dominant seventh. This must suffice to establish the new key (or to announce the key towards which the entire *pas* will move), for immediately after the V⁷/D Tchaikovsky avoids sounding the D triad by introducing a V⁷/Bb (that is, precisely the same chord as gave colour and seasoning to the cadence at the end of the *Marche* and the modulation from F to A in the *Scène dansante*). The principal keys of the remainder of the *pas de six* are:

Adagio	Variations:	I	II	III	IV	V	VI	Coda
Bb		Bb	g	D	D	F	C(E)	D

The strength of Bb after the initial movement to D weakens for a time the precedence of D as tonic, and bears out hints of the importance of Bb in Nos. 1 and 2. But as we proceed through the variations, and especially the coda, D emerges pre-eminent again, and Bb, in retrospect, becomes its flat submediant. The progression from Bb to D in the course of the *pas de six* thus forms a structural parallel with the *Scène dansante*, which also stressed the flat submediant at the beginning. The prominence of flat submediant key areas in Nos. 2 and 3 may be related to the narrative as a means of conveying the special quality of ravishment associated with the presence of supernatural characters at Aurora's baptism. The use of F major and

Bb major as subsidiary key areas also brings the music close to the tonal realm of
Florestan (who has invited the fairies to the baptism in part for reasons of state).
The sequence of flat submediants in the prologue constitutes a subtle anticipation
of the cadence formulas in Eb major on which Act II is constructed (see Chapter 4,
pp. 133–4):

	No. 2	No. 3	No. 4
	F (=^{b}VI/A)	B^b (=^{b}VI/D)	E^b (=^{b}VI/G–E^b being the key implied by the pedal point in bars 8–17, before Carabosse arrives)
E^b:	II	V	I

Other details within the *adagio* of the *pas de six* link it with the surrounding
numbers. The progression from F to A at bars 24–6 is strikingly similar to the
entrance of the Lilac Fairy in No. 2. The dominant chord adorned with harp
cadenzas at bars 39–41 recalls the sound of the introduction of No. 3 but looks
forward in its key to the G major which is supposed to come in the finale but does
not. The conjecture that something expected is not forthcoming is strengthened by
the fact that two other keys inflected as this one is—Bb in Nos. 1 and 2, and D
earlier in No. 3—do in fact lead to substantial statements after their brief initial
references.

The orderly and consistent progress of keys through the first three numbers
breaks down in No. 4 as a direct reflection of the disorder on stage which attends
Carabosse's arrival. That the finale begins in D affirms the importance of this key;
it forms an element of continuity with the *pas de six*. And for these first few bars
one can even sense the coming of G: the ability of the D triad to resolve to G as its
dominant, but followed instead by an unexpected dominant seventh of its flat
submediant, not the tonic triad of G major, makes the opening bars of No. 4 similar
in chord function to their counterparts in No. 3:

No. 3. D: ——————→ V^7–V^7/^{b}VI
No. 4. G: V ——————→ V^7/^{b}VI

But Carabosse changes all this. The scene represents a different approach to
musical coherence. So complex do the tonalities become, and so rapid the rate of
harmonic change, that theme and stage action take precedence over key in the
moment-to-moment logic. The scene from Carabosse's entrance may be sub-
divided as follows:

1. Introduction: noise in the vestibule (V/Eb, 8–17) and confusion of the court (to
   V/d, 17–36).
2. First section based on Carabosse's theme (37–80):
   (a) Carabosse appears (c♯–e, 37–40);
   (b) King and Queen beg Carabosse (rapid key change, 41–56);
   (c) Catalabutte falls at Carabosse's feet (g, 56–66);
   (d) Carabosse's wrath (g–bb, 67–75).
3. Dialogue of Carabosse and the good fairies (B–F♯, 81–95).

4. Second section based on Carabosse's theme (96–123):
   (a) Carabosse's laugh (c♯–e, 96–111);
   (b) Cadential theme (to e, 112–23).
5. Carabosse's prediction (e, 124–75).
6. Consternation of the court (f, 176–203).
7. Dances of Carabosse's pages and rats (204–31):
   (a) Carabosse's theme (f–g♯, 204–19);
   (b) Cadential theme (g♯, 220–31).
8. Lilac Fairy's intervention (E, 232–93).

We discover in the finale (if we seek out the tonalities, which the composer often obscures) more evidence of Tchaikovsky's tendency to modulate by third: c♯ to e, g to bb, f to g♯ [=ab]. The difference here is that the sense of extended or expanded tonic, which characterized his third-related tonal movements in the rest of the prologue, is missing. Modulation in the finale is too frequent and abrupt. Yet the composer is careful to select, in those passages where the tonality is stable for a time, keys which are important in the tonal plan of the entire ballet:

> E minor—Carabosse's prediction.
> F minor—response to Carabosse's evil (consternation of the court).
> E major—intervention and reprieve of the Lilac Fairy.

Coherence is best served by thematic recurrence—an especially important device given that the stage action and the rapid tonal change leave the impression that the finale is through-composed. Tchaikovsky uses Carabosse's theme (given in Chapter 4, Ex. 50) in the manner of a ritornello—when the wicked fairy first appears, when she responds to her sisters' begging for clemency, and when her pages and rats dance. More subtly, he gives strength to the musical structure of the number with repetitions of music *en bloc*, or nearly so:

> Bars 67–72=bars 37–42 transposed;
> Bars 204–31=bars 96–123 transposed;
> Bars 96–111=a thematic variant of bars 37–42, and are in the same key.

III. *Odette's Narration in* 'Swan Lake' (No. 11, bars 100–274).

In composing Odette's narration Tchaikovsky appears to have adhered to the libretto (or a scenario closely related to it) much more closely than the rubrics in the score permit us to certify. The following points are based on a co-ordination of libretto and score by means of the articulations they have in common.

Tchaikovsky divided the music of the narration into three parts, and mirrored the rising intensity of Odette's story, together with the appearance of the owl between the second and third parts, by setting each section in a key a semitone higher than the last. Except for the music accompanying the appearance of the owl, all the sections are unified by one melody and its variants:

Allegro vivo

The key progression is as follows:

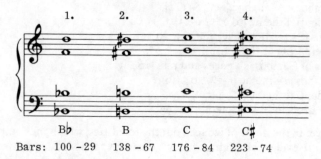

1. Odette's narration begins: 'My mother was a good fairy . . .'
2. ['But my grandfather took care of me . . .']
3. The appearence of the owl.
4. Odette: 'With my marriage [the witch will lose her power over me . . .]'

Of these, only No. 2 in the diagram is conjectural in the sense that there is no rubric in the score at the point where Bb gives way to B. But it is a logical point to begin the next phase of Odette's story, having to do with her grandfather, for it occurs about midway between the beginning of her narration and the owl's appearance.

Tchaikovsky anticipated the appearance of C and its associations with the owl, the stepmother, and evil, in the first section of the narration. The music, in Bb, moves to the dominant seventh of C (in the libretto this segment of the explanation ends with a reference to Odette's stepmother, who hated and ill-treated her). Tchaikovsky resolves this dominant not to C but to B after invoking his favourite method of enharmonic modulation:

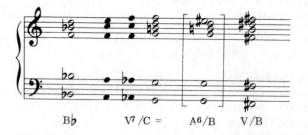

Here, as in the love duet (see Chapter 2, pp. 86–8), the acoustical sleight-of-hand suggests the inextricability of the swans and their fate. At the end of the second episode, the tonal symbols of the swans and the threat to their well-being are juxtaposed directly in the succession of B and C. The appearance of the owl coincides with the first orchestral tutti of the scene. The music following the owl's appearance, which at first suggests that the C triad is a tonic, clearly becomes an elaboration of F, ending with a hint of resolution:

This passage would appear to correspond with another reference to the step-mother in the libretto: 'My stepmother leaves neither me nor my friends in peace.' The music resolves deceptively to Db at bar 222, and this pitch becomes enharmonically the C♯ pedal point of the music of Odette's final section of pantomime. As the progression from B to C symbolizes a threat *of* evil, so the progression from C to C♯ symbolizes a threat *to* evil, in that Odette's marriage would break the stepmother's spell. All the striking semitonal shifts are thus intelligible responses to the libretto.

There is one other noteworthy semitonal shift in this series, a brief one which occurs within the C♯ section. The music moves abruptly to a full orchestral tutti on a D major triad (No. 11, bar 261), where the composer has written in the holograph a line of Siegfried's text, 'O forgive me!', a line not reproduced in any edition of the score. The music quickly returns to C♯, but the temporary move to D, so clearly linked with Siegfried, reinforces his association with that key established when the curtain rose on Act I.

IV. *The Entrance of the Swan Maidens*

The number following Odette's narration, No. 12, provides music for the entrance of the swan maidens. It includes music for the entrance proper, followed by a tripartite section for the mimed scene in which Odette directs the swan maidens to cease chastizing the huntsmen for their thoughtless sport, Siegfried destroys his crossbow, and Odette invites the young men to join them in dances. The entrance section begins as Odette's recitative had ended, with a pedal point on C♯, then moves through various chromatic sequences to bar 53. When Odette begins her mimed passage, 'Enough, stop; you see that he is good, he grieves . . .', the music moves briefly to B minor and then to C♯ minor again. Siegfried throws down his crossbow and Odette offers her invitation without departing from this key. The harmonic effect of the entire scene, despite the ornamental digressions of the entrance music, is one of extending the C♯ pedal with which No. 11 had ended, an effect enhanced by the unassertive final cadences at the ends of Nos. 11 and 12.

The strength of C♯ minor thus established permitted Tchaikovsky to make an effortless change of key at the beginning of No. 13, the Dances of the Swans. Indeed, A major, the key of Dance I, because it is the submediant of C♯ minor, need not represent a change of key at all if we interpret it as an example of Tchaikovsky's practice of extending tonics. To perceive no modulation enhances the sense of resolution of the special cadence at the beginning of the love duet, especially since

Tchaikovsky, by restricting the keys of the intervening dances to A major, E major, and F♯ minor, would never have left the realm of C♯ minor. According to this rationale the F♯ minor of Dance IV becomes the first chord of the formula leading to an arrival in Gb major:

End of No. 12	No. 13/I	13/II	13/III	13/IV	[harp cadenza]	13/V
c♯	A	E	A	f♯	[V/G♭]	G♭
c♯: i	VI	III	VI	iv=		
				G♭: i	V	I

V. *Tonality in Act IV of* 'Swan Lake'

Act IV is the shortest and, as it contains but one dance, choreographically the most austere in *Swan Lake*. The preponderance of the mimed scenes links it with Act II, and may be responsible also for musical likenesses with the earlier lakeside act. Tchaikovsky abandons here the two simple devices he had used to unify its predecessors: a framing tonality (granting in the case of Act III that Nos. 15 and 16 together form a cadence in the tonic major of the act), and the repetition of whole numbers or large parts of them.

The complex tonal structure of this act may be perceived in the large as a rising sequence of keys related by semitone, reminiscent of the structure of Odette's narration:

No. 25	No. 27	No. 29
Entr'acte	Dances of the Little Swans	Final Scene
A minor	B♭ minor	B minor

On a smaller scale, Tchaikovsky prepares harmonically for these large movements. Number 26, the scene in which Odette's friends await her, shares a rhythmic motive with No. 25 and ends with a pedal point on the pitch Bb, which provides a smooth movement into the following dances. The key of No. 27 acts in turn as a minor dominant of Eb minor, the key of the beginning of the storm scene. Then the storm music works its way towards B, the dominant of the E with which No. 29 begins. It is here that the dominant chord on E, associated with Odette, resolves to A minor at the *allegro agitato*, coincident with her death following a closing dialogue with Siegfried. Odette falls as the storm forces the lake to overflow its banks, and the music comes to its last forceful dominant: the F♯ major triad, which resolves into the final statement of the swan music.

Within the music of the storm and final scenes some of the keys, stated but briefly, reinforce associations established in prior occurrences. The Eb minor at the opening of No. 28 affirms the interpretation of ill tidings assigned to it at the time of its initial appearance in the love duet. That number contains further references to earlier associations in the short interlude, marked 'con passione' in the score (bars 40–53), which is probably the music Tchaikovsky intended to accompany the mimed scene in which the swan maidens warn Odette of the danger of seeing Siegfried again. Odette's decision to see Siegfried is reflected in the progression of keys: the interlude begins in B, the key of the swans, and ends in D, Siegfried's key. This D major, however, leads again into the harmonically complex storm music, which is based on a series of seventh chords and moves to a drum roll on B, the dominant preparation for the beginning of the final scene.

The final scene opens in one of Odette's keys, E major, over the root of which Tchaikovsky superimposes a triad of F:

No. 29, reduction of bars 1–8.

Even at the end, Odette's music is dominated by the triad associated with evil.

Marius Petipa's Scenarios for
'Sleeping Beauty' and 'Nutcracker'

I. *Petipa's Instructions to Tchaikovsky* (from *Marius Petipa. Materialy, vospominaniya, stat'i* [Leningrad, 1971], pp. 129–44).

II. *Petipa's Balletmaster's Plans* (from documents preserved in the Petipa archive of the State Theatre Museum named for A. A. Bakhrushin in Moscow, *fond* 205; the plan for *Sleeping Beauty* used here was copied from Document 107564, and that for *Nutcracker* from No. 106942. Occasional corrections in spelling, capitalization, and wording have been made. In the balletmaster's plan for *Sleeping Beauty*, the scenario was written in black ink, the musical instructions in red.)

*

I*a. Petipa's Instructions to Tchaikovsky for 'Sleeping Beauty'.*

SLEEPING BEAUTY

[PROLOGUE]

No. 1. At the rise of the curtain a salon march for the entrance of the lords and ladies.

No. 2. For Catalabutte's little recitative, the march becomes somewhat more serious.

No. 3. Fanfares—broad grandiose music.

No. 4. 3/4, *grazioso*.

No. 5. 3/4, more broadly.

No. 6. 3/4, quite lively and *dansante* (pages and young girls enter dancing).

No. 7. A short introduction for the *pas de six* (8–16 bars).

No. 7. *bis. Adagio.* Short *allegro.* Variations:
    Candide
    Coulante, finest wheat flour
    Breadcrumbs falling
    Canary singing
    Violente, 2/4 tempestuous
    Lilac Fairy, voluptuous [*voluptueuse*] variation
    Coda—2/4, abrupt, lively.

No. 8. From 8 to 16 bars, when the Lilac Fairy wants to approach the cradle.

No. 9. When a loud noise is heard—a quite lively movement.

No. 10. Music of a fantastic character.

No. 11. She sneers mockingly, and entertains herself by pulling out tufts of Catalabutte's hair. Music appropriate to the situation.

No. 12. 'I am not a godmother.' The music changes and becomes tender . . .

No. 13. Tender when the fairies counsel her to forgive.

No. 14. Carabosse laughs . . . her gaiety passes over to her pages and mice. (A light hiss.)

No. 15. For the little recitative, diabolically sarcastic music.

No. 16. She pronounces the magic words. A short, grotesquely fantastic dance for the ugly pages.

No. 17. The Lilac Fairy, who still has not offered her gift. Tender and rather derisive music.

No. 18. Carabosse in a rage. Violent, energetic music. A group around the cradle.

End of the prologue

ACT I
Scene 2

No. 1. At the rise of the curtain young peasant boys and girls form groups. They finish hanging garlands of flowers for the occasion of Aurora's birthday. Joyful music—48 b[ars].

No. 2. Scene and dance. Gossip of the knitting women. 2/4 from 32 to 48 bars.

No. 3. Entrance of Catalabutte. He is pleased at the sight of peasants with flowers. From 16 to 24 b[ars].

No. 4. His face changes appearance at the sight of the old women with the knitting needles. His anger grows, and he orders them taken to prison. 32 bars.

No. 5. The King, Queen, and four princes appear on the terrace of the castle. Music of appropriate noble character. 8 bars for the entrance on to the terrace, then 4 bars for the question and 4 bars for the answer. Four times in all. For example, one question: 'Where are these women being taken?' Four bars. Answer: 'I am taking them to prison.' Four b[ars]. Question: 'What crime have they committed?' Four b[ars]. Catalabutte shows them the evidence. 4 b[ars]. The King is in a fright, is enraged: 'Let them endure the deserved punishment!' Energetic music for 24 b[ars].

No. 6. The princes urge clemency for the guilty. For this admonition 16 b[ars]. They mollify the King.

No. 7. General rejoicing. 16 bars in order to take places and begin the waltz *cantabile* (smooth).

The *corps de ballet* with large and small hoops of flowers, which they prepared for Aurora's name-day [sic].

Waltz of 150 b[ars].

No. 8. The four princes have still not seen Princess Aurora. Their ardent wish is to cause her to love them. Each to himself admires a medallion with a likeness of the young Princess. Music which expresses a tender agitation, 24 b[ars], making a transition into

No. 9. Aurora's entrance. 2/4, coquettish, pointed—32 b[ars]. End with 6/8, *forte*, 16 b[ars].

No. 10. *Pas d'action*. Grand *adagio* of a very animated character (*mosso*). Rivalry of the princes. The music expresses their jealousy, then Aurora's coquetry. For the conclusion of the *adagio*, broad grandiose music.

No. 11. *Allegro* for the maids of honour. 48 b[ars], concluding with a polka *temps* for the pages.

No. 12. Aurora's variation. 3/4, *pizzicato* for violins, cellos, and harp. (Excuse me for expressing myself so oddly.) And then lute and violin.

No. 13. Coda. 2/4, vivace—96 b[ars].

No. 14. Suddenly Aurora notices the old woman. With a spindle she beats time in 2/4; then a transition to

No. 15. 3/4, a gay and very songful motive. When counting in 3/4 begins, Aurora seizes the spindle, which she waves like a sceptre—32 b[ars]. Suddenly (a pause) pain! Blood! 8 bars of 4/4, *largo*.

No. 16. Horror—2/4, *vivace*—she no longer dances—it is some kind of mindless turning, as if she had been bitten by a tarantula. At the end she falls as if dead. (For the circling no more than 24 b[ars].)

No. 17. When she falls as if dead, *tremolo* for several bars. Sobbing and cries of despair of all present.

No. 18. At this moment the old woman throws off her cloak. For this hurried movement a chromatic* scale in the entire orchestra.

No. 19. All recognize the Fairy Carabosse, who laughs at the despair of Florestan and the Queen. The princes draw their swords and rush at her. (Short, powerful, and expressive music, ending with a diabolical passage when Carabosse with a hellish laugh disappears in smoke and fire.) The four princes and their retinues disperse in terror.

No. 20. At this moment a fountain at the back of the stage lights up. A tender, fantastic, and magic melody. This number must be long, in order to last to the end of the act.

ACT II

Scene 3

No. 1. Hunting fanfares resound. Hunters and huntresses come on stage and disperse to rest, gathering to eat on the grass. Hunt music, with a transition into a quite short motive of rest.

The Prince appears just as this motive sounds.

No. 2. The royal courtiers propose to the ladies a game of blind man's buff and tag. The latter agree. 2/4, *vivace*, 72 b[ars].

No. 3. Another motive. Galifron takes advantage of the occasion to have the women pass in front of the Prince; one after another they process in front of him before engaging in other dances. 24 bars.

No. 4. Dance of the duchesses. They are noble and proud—24 bars.

No. 5. Dances of the baronesses. They are arrogant and conceited [*spesivy*—cf. Petipa's *guindées*]—24 b[ars].

No. 6. Dance of the countesses. They are coquettish and amusing—24 b[ars].

No. 7. Dance of the marchionesses. They are mischievous. Armed with little

---

* In the margin: 'diatonic'.

darts they tease the other women. 32 bars. Then they propose to dance a farandole in the manner of local peasants. Farandole.

No. 8. Coda. From 48 to 64 bars in mazurka rhythm.

No. 9. Whippers-in enter and say that a bear has been surrounded. A hunter's folk tune, gradually dying away in the distance. 48 b[ars].

No. 10. The hunt has hardly moved off when a boat made of mother-of-pearl appears. Fantastic, poetic music in a *largo* tempo. 48 bars.

No. 11. With a new wave of the fairy's magic wand Aurora appears and rushes on stage. 6/8 for 24 b[ars]. A voluptuous *adagio*. Coquettish *allegro*—3/4 for 48 b[ars]. Variation for Aurora.

Coda in 6/8, concluding in 2/4. This is one *pas*.

No. 12. 'Where is that divine being you showed to me?' Very agitated, passionate music. 32 bars for the transition into the panorama.

No. 13. The boat is under way. The length of the music depends on the extent of the panorama.

No. 14. With a wave of her wand the fairy orders the gates to be opened. The entranceway is visible. A thick mist enshrouds the stage. A tender melody is heard. 32 bars of *largo*.

No. 15. Musical *entr'acte*.

Scene 4

Sleeping Beauty's Castle

No. 16. When the clouds and mists disperse, mysterious music—24 bars (*largo*).

No. 17.* A short, fantastic scene for bats, big flies, and gnats. Muted instruments, 2/4—64 b[ars].

No. 18. The door opens to the left of the bed. The music is still mysterious—16 b[ars].

No. 19. Désiré runs to the bed. Agitated music. 24 b[ars].

No. 20. Finally he rushes wildly over to the sleeping beauty and kisses her forehead. The music makes a *crescendo*. At the moment of the kiss it dies down.

No. 21. The spell is broken. The music expresses astonishment, then joy and happiness. It retains its excitement and ardour to the end of the act.

ACT III

Scene 5

No. 1. Entrance and procession of the King and the newly-weds, who are present at court. A march, broad music, 48 bars.

No. 2. A grand danced polonaise from 80 to 96 bars, for the procession of the fairy-tales.

Divertissement.

No. 3. *Pas de quatre.*

Fairies of burnished gold, silver, sapphires, and diamonds. *Allegro* in 6/8, quite brilliant—64 b[ars]. The four entrances (variations), each from 24 to 32 bars.

---

* No. 17 is completely struck through.

1) Burnished gold—a gold charm.
2) Silver—the sound of coins must be heard. In polka time.
3) Sapphire—five points, music in quintuple time.
4) Diamond—sparks, glistening like electricity, 2/4, quick.
5) Short coda in the same character as the diamond variation, in 2/4, 48 b[ars].
Pas de deux.
Goldilocks and Prince Avenant. (Probably this *pas de deux* will not be used.)
Note (it ought not to be composed).
No. 4. *Pas de caractère.*
Puss in Boots and the White Cat.
Mutual caresses, miaowing, and scratching with their claws. At the end the cry
of a scratched cat. For the beginning love music in 3/4. At the end, accelerated 3/4
and miaowing. (This *pas* must not be long.)
No. 5. *Pas de quatre.*
Cinderella and Prince Fortuné.
The Blue Bird and Princess Florine.
A little *andante.* The music represents the singing of birds. Variations for
Cinderella and Prince Fortuné of a passionate character. 32 b[ars]. Variations for the
Blue Bird and Princess Florine. 2/4 singing of birds. 24 bars. Little coda in 64 b[ars].
They kiss, like birds.
No. 6. *Pas de caractère.*
Little Red Riding Hood and the wolf.
She runs in merrily with a milk pail. 2/4 *spiccato.* 32 bars. The pail breaks. She
cries. The wolf appears. She trembles. The wolf terrifies her (in polka time—cloy-
ing), consoles her, promises to obtain a pardon for her if she leads him to her
grandmother. The *pas* ends with several polka *temps* speeded up (the wolf carries
her out, trembling).
No. 7. *Pas Berrichon.*
Tom Thumb and his brothers.
All seventeen [sic] enter in one line. First the smallest, Tom Thumb, puts on the
ogre's boots. They rejoice over this brilliant victory. For their entrance 16 b[ars] in
2/4. They move in gigantic steps. After these 16 b[ars] the music becomes very
merry; they dance and laugh. At the end the growling of the ogre reaches them.
They dash off as fast as their legs can carry them, pursued by the ogre.
No. 8. *Pas de deux.*
Aurora and Désiré.
For their entrance 32 b[ars] of brilliant music in 6/8. A rather large *adagio* with
fortes and with pauses.
Variation for the cavalier in 6/8, 48 b[ars] (*forte*).
Variation for the *danseuse.* (For the present don't compose it. I must speak with
the *danseuse.*)
Coda in 2/4 of a very effective character. From 80 to 96 bars.
No. 9. Sarabande. Quadrille performed by the Turks, Ethiopians, Africans, and
Americans, 3/4—48 b[ars]. (A pompous and measured dance.)
No. 10. General coda.
        Mazurka.
Charming, exuberant music, capable of making anyone dance.
No. 11. Apotheosis.

Music appropriate to the situation—broad, grandiose.

Apollo in the costume of Louis XIV, illuminated by the sun and surrounded by fairies.

*End**

★

IIa. *The Balletmaster's Plan for 'Sleeping Beauty'*

[Note: the first entry in each pair is the scenario, the second lists Petipa's requirements for music.]

[Title-page]

10 Juillet 1889

Programme
La Belle au bois-dormant
Ballet fantastique en cinq tableaux

M. Petipa

[Page 1]

J'ai fini d'écrire le 5 Juillet 1889

1er Tableau

PROLOGUE

Le baptême de la Psse. Aurore

Une salle de festin au palais du Roi Florestan XIV. Estrade à droite pour le Roi, la Reine et les fées marraines de la *Psse.* Aurore.

Porte du vestibule au fond.

(1) Des dames et les seigneurs sont groupés dans la salle attendant l'arrivée du Roi et de la Reine. Des maîtres de cérémonie indiquent à chacun sa place en recommandant de bien suivre le programme indiqué pour offrir les félicitations et les souhaits d'usage au Roi et à la Reine, ainsi qu'aux puissantes fées invitées à la fête du baptême de la *Psse.* Aurore en qualité de marraines.

(1) Au lever du rideau, marche de salon pour les entrées des dames et [des] seigneurs.

(2) Catalabutte, entouré des serviteurs de la cour, vérifie la liste des invitations envoyées aux fées. Tout a été exécuté selon les ordres du Roi. Tout est prêt pour la fête,—le Roi et la Reine peuvent venir dans la salle du festin; —la cour y est au complet, et les fées sont attendues d'un moment à l'autre.

(2) Pour le petit récit de Catalabutte, la marche devient un peu sérieuse —demi-comique.

<hr>

* At the bottom of the last page: 21 January 1889.

(3) Fanfares. Le Roi et la Reine font leur entrée, précédés des pages et suivis des gouvernantes et des nourrices de la *Psse*. Aurore, portant le berceau où dort l'enfant royal.

(3) Fanfares—musique large et grandiose.

A peine le Roi et la Reine ont-ils pris place sur l'estrade, ayant entre eux le berceau, que les maîtres de cérémonies annoncent l'arrivée des fées.

Entrée des fées

(4) Candide, Fleur de Farine, Violente, Canari, Miettes [qui tombent] sont les premières à entrer dans la salle.

(4) Un 3/4 gracieux.

Le Roi et la Reine vont les recevoir et les font monter sur l'estrade.

[Page 2]

(5) Entrée de la Fée des lilas—marraine principale d'Aurore. Elle est entourée de ses génies familiers portant de grands éventails, des parfums, et soutenant le manteau de leur maîtresse. A un signe de Catalabutte, les pages . . .

(5) Le 3/4 plus large.

(6) et des jeunes filles accourent en portant sur des coussins de brocart les présents que le Roi destine aux marraines de sa fille. Ils forment des groupes charmantes et indiquent à chacune des fées les présents qui lui sont destinés.

(6) Le 3/4 assez animé et dansant. Les pages et les jeunes filles viennent en dansant.

(7) Les fées descendent de l'estrade. A leur tour elles vont faire des dons à leur filleule.

(7) Petite introduction pour le pas de six.

Pas de six

Adage suave
Petit Allégro
Candide
Coulante. Fleur de farine
Miettes—qui tombent
Canari—qui chante
Violente—2/4 échevelé
La Fée des lilas—variation voluptueuse
Coda—2/4 piqué et vif.

(8) La Fée des lilas veut à son tour s'approcher du berceau pour faire son don à Aurore,—

(8) Huit à seize mesures quand la Fée des lilas veut s'approcher du berceau.

(9) Quand on entend un grand bruit dans le vestibule. Un page accourt et informe Catalabutte qu'une nouvelle fée qu'on avait oubliée d'inviter à la fête vient d'arriver à la porte du château. C'est la Fée Carabosse, la plus puissante et la plus méchante de la contrée. Catalabutte est consterné.—Comment

[Page 3]

a-t'il pu l'oublier—lui l'exactitude même. Tout tremblant, il s'approche du Roi pour lui avouer son erreur—sa faute. Le Roi et la Reine sont très inquiets. Le manque de mémoire du principal maître d'hôtel peut causer de grands malheurs et influer sur le sort de leur chère enfant.—Les fées elles-mêmes ne semblent pas rassurées.

(9) Quand on entend un grand bruit—Mouvement très animé.

(10) Carabosse paraît dans une brouette traînée par six gras rats. Elle est suivie de pages difformes et ridicules.—Le Roi et la Reine la supplient de pardonner la maladresse de Catalabutte. On lui infligera la punition que Carabosse voudra bien indiquer. Catalabutte, plus mort que vif, se précipite aux pieds de la méchante fée. Qu'elle daigne seulement l'épargner il est prêt à la servir fidèlement jusqu'à la fin de ses jours.

(10) Musique d'un caractère fantastique.

(11) Carabosse ricane, et s'amuse à lui arracher des mèches de cheveux, qu'elle jette à ses rats et qu'ils dévorent.—Bientôt la tête de Catalabutte est complètement dénudée.

(11) Elle ricane et s'amuse à lui arracher des mèches. Musique en situation. Les pages rient d'un air caustique.

(12) 'Je ne suis pas la marraine d'Aurore', dit Carabosse, 'mais je veux quand même lui faire un don.'

(12) —Je ne suis pas la marraine. La musique change et devient calme.

[Page 4]

(13) Les bonnes fées recommandent le pardon de l'oubli involontaire du maître d'hôtel, la suppliant de ne point empoisonner le bonheur du meilleur des Rois.

(13) La musique devient douce quand les fées recommandent le pardon.

(14) Carabosse ne fait qu'en rire—son hilarité gagne ses pages monstrueux et même ses rats.

Les bonnes fées se détournent avec répugnance de leur sœur.

(14) Carabosse ne fait qu'en rire. Petit sifflement.

(15) 'Aurore sera, grâce aux dons de ses six marraines,' dit Carabosse, 'la plus belle, la plus séduisante, la plus spirituelle princesse de l'univers. Je n'ai pas le pouvoir de lui enlever ces qualités. Mais pour que son bonheur ne soit jamais troublé—vous voyez comme je suis bonne—elle s'endormira la première fois qu'elle se piquera le doigt ou la main et son sommeil sera éternel!'

(Le Roi, la Reine et toute la cour sont consternés.)

(15) Pour ce petit récit—musique satirique, diabolique.

(16) Carabosse étend sa baguette sur le berceau en proférant des mots magiques, puis heureuse du mauvais tour fait à ses sœurs les bonnes fées—elle éclate de rire. Gaieté folle des monstres de sa suite.

(16) —Proférant des mots magiques. Petite danse fantastique et grotesque pour ces pages difformes.

(17) Mais la Fée des lilas, qui n'avait pas encore offert son don à sa filleule et qui s'était dissimulée derrière le berceau d'Aurore, sort de sa cachette. Carabosse la regarde avec méfiance et colère.

[Page 5]

La bonne fée se penche vers le berceau. 'Oui tu t'endormiras, ma petite Aurore comme l'a voulu notre sœur Carabosse,' dit Lilas—mais pas pour toujours. Il viendra un jour un Prince qui épris de ta beauté déposera un baiser sur ton front—et tu sortiras de ton long sommeil pour devenir la compagne de ce Prince et pour vivre heureuse et contente.'

(17) La Fée des lilas qui n'avait pas encore offert son don. Musique douce et un peu ricaneuse.

(18) Carabosse furieuse remonte dans sa brouette et disparaît. Les bonnes fées se

groupent autour du berceau et semblent protéger leur filleule contre la méchante sœur.

(18) Carabosse furieuse. Musique énergique et endiablée. Groupe autour du berceau. *Tableau.*

Fin du prologue

[Page 6]

ACTE I

2ème Tableau

Les quatres fiancés de la Psse. Aurore

Le parc du château de Florestan XIV. A droite du spectateur l'entrée du château. Les étages supérieurs se perdent dans le feuillage des arbres. Une fontaine de marbre dans le style du XVII siècle au fond de la scène. *

(1) Aurore a atteint ses 20 ans. Florestan, heureux de voir les prédictions de la Fée Carabosse ne se réalisant pas est dans la joie.

(1) Au lever du rideau les jeunes villageois et villageoises forment des groupes en finissant de travailler à de hautes guirlandes de fleurs pour la fête de la jeune Aurore. Musique joyeuse.

(2) Scène de commérages.

(2) Scène et danse de commérages des tricoteuses. 32 à 48 mesures—2/4.

(3) Catalabutte, dont les cheveux n'ont jamais repoussé depuis et qui porte une perruque ridicule, est en train de mettre à l'amende quelques villageoises qui munies de leurs aiguilles sont venues travailler

(4) —devant le château. Il leur fait lire une pancarte interdisant l'emploi d'aiguilles ou d'épingles sur une superficie de 100 lieues autour de la résidence royale. Il les fait reconduire sous escorte en prison.

(3) Entrée de Catalabutte. Il est heureux en apercevant les villageoises. Il les remercie.

(La musique change—mouvement de colère.)

(4) La figure change en voyant les vieilles travailler et munies de leurs aiguilles. En leur faisant lire une pancarte.—Sa colère augmente et il ordonne de les mettre en prison.

[Page 7]

(5) Le Roi et la Reine paraissent sur la terrasse du château. Les quatre princes, aspirants à la main d'Aurore, les accompagnent. Le Roi demande quel méfait a été commis par les villageoises qu'on emmène en prison. Catalabutte fait part de la cause de l'arrestation et montre les pièces de conviction. Le Roi et la Reine sont épouvantés. 'Qu'elles subissent la peine de leur crime et qu'elles ne revoient jamais le jour. [Crossed out: Les Princes Charmant, Avenant, Fleur-des-pois et Fortuné implorent la grâce des coupables. Pas une larme ne doit couler dans le royaume de Florestan le jour où Aurore aura atteint les 20 ans. Le Roi se laisse fléchir. Les villageoises sont graciées, mais leur travail sera brûlé en place publique par le bourreau.

Allégresse générale, danses et rondes villageoises. Vive le Roi Florestan! Vive la *Psse*. Aurore!]

---

* In the upper left margin of the page: 'J'ai changé de ce qui est écrit sur le programme.'

(5) Le Roi, la Reine et les 4 *Pces*. paraissent sur le terrasse. Musique noble et caractéristique. 4 mesures pour la demande et 4 mesures pour la réponse—cela se dit 4 fois. Un 2/4 large. Par example:—Demande: où conduisez-vous ces femmes? 4 mesures. Réponse: En prison, 4 mesures. Demande: Quel méfait a été commis par ces villageoises? 4 mesures. Catalabutte montre les pièces de conviction. 4 mesures. (32 à 48 mesures.)

Colère du Roi qui est épouvanté. Qu'elles subissent la peine de leur crime. Musique énergique.

(6) Les princes Charmant, Avenant, Fleur-des-pois et Fortuné implorent la grâce des coupables. Pas une larme ne doit couler dans le royaume de Florestan le jour où Aurore aura atteint ses 20 ans. Le Roi se laisse fléchir.

[Page 8]

(6) Les princes implorent la grâce des coupables. Pour cette prière, 24 mesures. Le Roi se laisse fléchir.

(7) Allégresse générale, danses et rondes villageoises. Vive le Roi Florestan, vive la *Psse*. Aurore!

(7) Allégresse générale. 8 à 16 mesures pour se placer.

Valse cantabile (coulante) 150 mesures.

Corps de ballet. [In pencil: pas de cerceaux—(Du nouveau)]

(8) Les quatre princes n'ont jamais vu la *Psse*. Aurore, mais ils sont tous en possession de médaillons contenant le portrait de la fille du Roi. Ils sont tous pris d'un ardent désir de se faire aimer et l'expriment à Florestan et à la Reine. Ceux-ci les assurent qu'ils donnent liberté entière à leur fille de fixer son choix. Celui qu'elle aimera sera leur gendre et héritier du royaume.

(8) Les quatres Princes n'ont jamais vu la *Psse*. Aurore. Musique qui exprime une douce agitation, ardent désir de se faire aimer. Chacun de son côté admire le médaillon contenant le portrait de la jeune *Psse*. 24 mesures.

(9) Entrée d'Aurore—Elle accourt suivie de ses demoiselles d'honneur portant des bouquets et des couronnes. Les quatre Princes sont frappés de sa beauté. Chacun d'eux veut se faire valoir et se faire aimer d'elle. Mais Aurore danse au milieu de ses amoureux, sans donner la préférence à aucun.

(9) 16 à 24 mesures qui s'enchaînent avec l'autre mouvement pour l'entrée d'Aurore. Une 2/4 piqué, coquet—32 mesures et finir avec 16 mesures par un 6/8 forté.

(10)   *Pas d'action*

[Page 9]

Grand adage très mouvementé (Mosso). Rivalité des Princes. Un moment la musique exprime la jalousie, puis la coquetterie d'Aurore. Ensuite musique large et grandiose pour finir.

(11) Allégro pour les demoiselles d'honneur—48 mesures et finir par un tempo de polka pour les pages.

(12)   *Variation d'Aurore*

Un pizzicato pour violon, violoncelle et harpe, ou bien, luth et violon.

(13)   *Coda*

2/4 vif (vivace) 96 mesures.

Ce qui se passe dans l'adage du pas d'action.

Rivalité des Princes—coquetterie d'Aurore. Le Roi et la Reine l'exhortent à fixer son choix.

'Je suis encore si jeune', répond Aurore, 'Laissez-moi jouir de la vie et de ma liberté.'

'Fais comme tu voudras, mais songe que la raison d'État veut que tu sois mariée et que tu donnes un héritier à mon pays. La prédiction de Carabosse ne laisse pas de nous tourmenter.'

'Rassurez-vous, mon père. Pour que la prédiction s'accomplisse il faudrait que je me pique la main. Je chante, je danse, je m'amuse—mais je ne travaille jamais.'

Les quatre Princes l'entourent et lui adressent leur prière de danser en leur presence car elle est, dit-on, la plus gracieuse jeune fille, dont on ait jamais ouï parler.

Aurore, avec sa bonté naturelle, veut bien remplir leur désir. Elle danse tandis que ses demoiselles d'honneur et ses pages jouent du luth et du violon. Les 4 *Pces*. viennent tour à tour la complimenter et, pour mériter leur suffrage, elle redouble de grâce et de légèreté.

[Page 10]

Ce ne sont pas seulement les princes et la cour qui l'admire, toute la population de la ville et des villages, jeunes et vieux, suivent avec curiosité les méandres de son vol aérien. Délire et danse générale.*

(14) Tout à coup Aurore aperçoit une vieille qui, avec son fuseau, semble battre la mesure de ses pas légers.

(14) Tout à coup Aurore aperçoit une vieille qui, avec son fuseau, bat la mesure à 2/4 et qui passe en battant toujours de son fuseau à un mouvement à 3/4 gai et très chantant. Lorsque commence le 3/4, Aurore saisit la quenouille qu'elle brandit —comme un sceptre. Elle provoque l'admiration de tout le monde. 24 mesures de valse. Mais subitement (temps d'arrêt) douleur! Son sang coule! 8 mesures à 4 temps—large. Dans sa terreur ce n'est plus une danse qu'elle exécute, c'est un vertige de folie comme piqué par la tarentule! Elle finit par tomber inanimée! Ce vertige ne doit durer que 24 à 32 mesures. Un trémolo de quelques mesures avec des sanglots et des cris de douleur!! Père, Mère!!

Mais alors la vieille à la quenouille rejette son manteau. Pour ce moment précipite, gamme chromatique par tout l'orchestre.

On reconnaît la Fée Carabosse qui se rit du désespoir de Florestan et de la Reine. Les Princes dégaînent et se jettent sur elle. Musique vigoureuse et courte pour finir avec un mouvement diabolique lorsque Carabosse avec un rire infernal disparaît dans un tourbillon de feu et de fumée. Les 4 princes et leur suite [s'en]fuient épouvantés.

A ce moment, la fontaine du fond s'illumine. Ici, une musique douce, fantastique et magique. Ce numéro est long, pour aller jusqu'à la fin de l'acte.

[Page 11]

(14) J'ai fini d'écrire le programme.

Elle se saisit de cette quenouille qu'elle brandit tantôt comme un sceptre, tantôt imitant le travail des fileuses, elle trouve un nouveau plaisir à provoquer l'admira-

---

* In the upper left margin of this page: 'Il faut faire des groupes de vieillards, femmes et jeunes enfants.'

tion de ses quatre soupirants. Mais subitement, sa danse est interrompue, elle regarde sa main transpercée par le fuseau et que son sang rougit. Dans sa terreur ce n'est plus une danse qu'elle exécute, c'est un vertige de folie qui la saisit. Elle se précipite d'un côté et d'un autre et finit par tomber inanimée. Le Roi et la Reine se sont precipités sur leur fille chérie—en voyant la main blessée de la *Psse*. ils comprennent toute l'étendue de leur malheur. Mais alors la vieille à la quenouille rejette son manteau. On reconnaît la Fée Carabosse que se rit du désespoir de Florestan et de la Reine. Les quatre Princes dégaînent et se jettent sur elle pour la transpercer de leurs épées, mais Carabosse, avec un rire infernal, disparaît dans un tourbillon de feu et de fumée. Les quatre Princes et leur suite [s'en]fuient épouvantés. A ce moment la fontaine du fond s'illumine d'une lumière magique—la Fée des lilas paraît au milieu des jets d'eau.

(15) 'Consolez vous', dit-elle aux parents éplorés—'Elle dort et elle dormira 100 ans. Mais pour que rien ne soit changé, à son bonheur, vous dormirez avec elle. Son réveil sera le signal du vôtre. Rentrez au château. Je veille à vôtre sécurité.'

On dépose la Princesse endormie sur un brancard et on l'emporte suivie du Roi, de la Reine et des principaux personnages de la cour. Les seigneurs, les pages et les gardes s'inclinent au passage de ce cortège. Mais la Fée étend sa baguette dans la direction du château. Tout ce monde groupé sur le perron et sur l'escalier est tout à coup pétrifié. Tout s'endort, jusqu'aux fleurs et aux eaux de la fontaine, des lierres et des lianes poussent

[Page 12]

de dessous la terre et couvrent le château et les hommes endormis. Des arbres et des massifs de lilas, dont la croissance magique est due à la puissance de la Fée, transforment le jardin royal en une forêt impénétrable. Les génies familiers de la Fée des lilas se groupent autour d'elle. Celle-ci leur recommande de veiller à ce qu'aucun profane ne vienne troubler le repos de sa protégée.

Tableau

Fin du 1ᵉʳ acte

ACTE II

3ᵉᵐᵉ Tableau

La chasse du Prince Désiré

(1) Site boisé. Une large rivière serpente au fond du tableau. Une forêt épaisse s'étend à perte de vue. A droite du spectateur des rochers couverts de végétation. Un soleil radieux éclaire le paysage.

Au lever du rideau personne en scène. On entend les fanfares d'une chasse. C'est celle du *Pce*. Désiré qui poursuit les loups et les lynx des forêts voisines. Les chasseurs et les chasseresses entrent en scène et se disposent au repos en faisant une collation sur le gazon.

Bientôt survient le Prince Désiré avec son précepteur Galifron et quelques seigneurs de la cour du Roi son père. On dispose la collation pour le prince et ses compagnons.

(1) On entend les fanfares d'une chasse.

Musique de chasse qui passe à un motif de repos assez court.

(2–3) Les chasseurs et les chasseresses pour amuser le jeune prince forment des rondes, jettent des javelots, tirent de l'arc et inventent les jeux les plus divers.

(2–3) Les seigneurs de la cour du Roi proposent de jouer aux jeux de colin-maillard, main-chaude, etc. Un 2/4 vif de 48 à 60 mesures.

[Page 13]

Galifron engage sa pupille à se joindre à sa cour et surtout à être aimable envers les dames. Car c'est parmi la noblesse de son pays qu'il doit choisir une épouse. Tous les Rois, voisins de son futur royaume n'ont que des fils. Il n'y a pas une seule Princesse de sang royal dont il pourrait faire sa femme.*

(4) Galifron profite de la circonstance pour faire défiler des demoiselles nobles de la contrée.

(4) Autre motif—Galifron profite de la circonstance.

16 mesures avant de commencer la danse.

24 mesures pour chaque danse de ces dames.

(5) —24 mesures. Danse des duchesses—nobles et orgueilleuses.

(6) —24 mesures. Danse des baronnes—arrogantes et guindées.

(7) —24 mesures. Danse des comtesses—coquettes et ridicules.

(8) —24 mesures. Danse des marquises—espiègles. Elles prennent des petits javelots pour asticoter ces dames et ces messieurs.

(9) La marquise propose de danser une farandole comme les villageoises du pays. Une farandole pour coda—48 à 64 mesures—temps lourd de mazurka.

[Petipa has drawn a line around the following: Notes p. moi—Des groupes de colin-maillard. Elles jouent avec le précepteur. Elles l'asticotent avec de petites piques ou javelots. Elles peuvent finir par une bourrée ou farandole avec des villageois et villageoises.

Il faut en scène des villageois et villageoises qui sont venus offrir des fruits au Prince.]

Toutes ces demoiselles s'évertuent de plaire au Prince. Mais Désiré, le verre en main, se rit des efforts inutiles de cette nuée de jolies filles. Son cœur n'a pas parlé—il n'a pas encore rencontré la femme de ses rêves. Il n'épousera personne avant d'avoir trouvé celle qu'il cherche.

Cela se dit pendant les danses

[Page 14]

(10) Les piqueurs viennent annoncer qu'un ours a été cerné dans sa tanière. Si le Prince veut le tuer, c'est un coup de fusil sûr et certain.

Mais le Prince se sent fatigué. 'Chassez sans moi', dit-il aux seigneurs, 'je veux encore me reposer dans cet endroit qui me plaît.'

Les seigneurs et la cour s'éloignent et Galifron, qui a vidé plus d'une bouteille de champagne, s'endort à côté du Prince.

(10) Les piqueurs viennent annoncer qu'un ours a été cerné. Un 2/4 vif qui finit doucement en s'éloignant. 48 mesures.

(11) A peine la chasse s'est éloignée, qu'une embarcation de nacre incrustée d'or et de pierreries paraît sur la rivière. La Fée des lilas, qui est aussi la marraine du *Pce*. Désiré, en descend. Le Prince se prosterne devant la bonne Fée, qui le relève avec bienveillance et le questionne sur l'état de son cœur.

'Tu n'aimes encore personne?' lui demande-t-elle. 'Non', répond le Prince, 'les

_____

* In upper left margin of the page: 'Pendant les jeux.'

demoiselles nobles de mon pays n'ont pas su captiver mon cœur—et je préfère rester vieux garçon que d'épouser une femme par raison d'état.'

'Si c'est ainsi', reprend la Fée, 'je te désignerai ta future compagne, elle est la plus belle, la plus séduisante, la plus spirituelle Princesse de l'univers.'

'Mais où puis-je la voir?'

'Je vais faire apparaître son ombre. Vois si elle te plaît et si tu peux l'aimer.'

(11) A peine la chasse s'est éloignée, qu'une embarcation de nacre paraît. Musique fantastique, poétique. Musique large, 48 à 64 mesures.

(12) La Fée des lilas étend sa baguette du côté du rocher qui s'entrouvre et laisse voir Aurore et ses compagnes endormies. A un nouveau geste de la Fée, Aurore se lève avec ses femmes et s'élance sur la scène. Les rayons du soleil couchant l'éclairent d'une lumière rose.*

[Page 15]

(12) A un nouveau geste de la Fée, Aurore se lève et s'élance sur la scène. Adage voluptueux. Petit Allégro coquet. Variation pour Aurore, et petite coda. Pour la coda—musique avec sourdine—2/4 comme dans le songe d'une nuit d'été.

(12 bis) Tout cela se passe pendant la danse d'Aurore et ses compagnes:

Désiré, frappé d'admiration, suit cette ombre qui lui échappe toujours. La danse tantôt langoureuse, tantôt vive l'enchante de plus en plus. Il veut la saisir, mais elle glisse entre ses mains et reparaît là où il ne la cherchait pas. Se balançant sur les branches des arbres, [crossed out: nageant dans l'eau de la rivière ou couchée dans les massifs des fleurs.]† Puis enfin il la revoit dans le creux du rocher, où elle disparaît définitivement. Fou d'amour, Désiré se précipite aux pieds de sa marraine.

(13) 'Où se trouve l'être divin que vous m'avez fait voir? Conduisez-moi près d'elle, je veux la voir, la presser contre mon cœur!'

(13) Où se trouve l'être divin que vous m'avez fait voir? Musique très agitée, passionnée. 48 mesures pour arriver au panorama.

(14) 'Viens', dit la Fée et elle fait monter le Prince dans sa barque qui se met à descendre le courant de la rivière, tandis que Galifron continue son sommeil.

Panorama

(14) La barque avance. Musique selon le temps que durera le panorama.

(14 bis) Panorama: La barque avance avec rapidité—le paysage devient de plus en plus sauvage, le jour baisse; bientôt il fait nuit—la lune éclaire le sillage de la barque en pailliettes argentées. On aperçoit au loin un château qui disparaît de nouveau à un coude de la rivière. Mais le voilà enfin ce château—but du voyage.

[Page 16]

Le prince et la Fée descendent de la barque.

(15) La Fée d'un geste de la baguette magique fait ouvrir la grande porte. On aperçoit le vestibule où dorment des gardes et des pages. Le Pce. Désiré s'y précipite suivi de la Fée.‡

(15) La Fée d'un geste de sa baguette magique fait ouvrir la grande porte. 24 mesures.

---

* In the margin to the left of No. 12: 'Peuvent-ils mettre des costumes fantastiques?'
† Above the words 'couchée dans le': 'Peut-être bon.'
‡ Upper left margin (page 16): 'Fin du panorama.'

(16) La scène est envahie par d'épaisses vapeurs. On entend une douce musique.
(16) La scène est envahie par d'épaisses vapeurs. On entend une douce musique.

Entracte musical

4ème Tableau

Le château de la belle au bois dormant

(1) Quand les nuages et les vapeurs se dissipent on aperçoit la chambre où repose la Princesse Aurore, sur un grand lit à baldaquin. Le Roi Florestan et la Reine dorment en face de leur fille dans deux fauteuils. Les dames de la cour, les seigneurs et les pages appuyés les uns contre les autres ronflent à qui mieux mieux. Des couches de poussière et des toiles d'araignées couvrent les meubles et les personnages. Les lumières dorment, le feu dans la cheminée dort aussi, une lumière phosphorescente éclaire le tableau.

(1) Quand les nuages et les vapeurs se dissipent—musique mystérieuse—48 mesures.

[Page 17]

(2) Une porte à gauche du lit s'ouvre—Désiré et la Fée pénètrent dans le sanctuaire.

(2) Une porte à gauche du lit s'ouvre. Musique toujours mystérieuse. 14 mesures.

(3) Désiré se précipite vers le lit—mais il a beau appeler la Princesse—secouer le Roi et la Reine ou Catalabutte endormi sur un tabouret aux pieds du Roi—rien n'y fait et il ne soulève que des nuages de poussière. La Fée reste témoin impassible du désespoir de Désiré.

(3) Désiré se précipite vers le lit. Musique agitée. 48 mesures.

(4) Enfin celui-ci se précipite sur la belle endormie et la baise au front. Point d'arrêt.

(4) Enfin celui-ci se précipite sur la belle endormie et la baise au front. La musique va crescendo, puis temps d'arrêt.

(5) Le charme est rompu. Aurore se réveille. Toute la cour aussi. Poussière et toiles d'araignées disparaissent, les lumières éclairent la chambre, le feu pétille dans la cheminée.

Désiré supplie le Roi de lui accorder la main de sa fille. 'Telle est sa destinée', répond le Roi—et il unit les mains des deux jeunes gens.

(5) Le charme est rompu. La musique exprime l'étonnement, la surprise, la joie et le bonheur. Tous s'embrassent en se revoyant. Jusqu'à la fin—musique chaude et brillante.

Fin du 2ème acte

[Page 18]

ACTE III

5ème Tableau

Les Noces de Désiré et d'Aurore
L'esplanade du château de Versailles

(1) Entrée et cortège du Roi et des Fiancés—salués par les courtisans.
Marche—musique large—48 mesures.

Divertissement
Entrée du ballet

1: d'après le carrousel Louis XIV

(2) Quadrille—Turque
Quadrille—Éthiopien
Quadrille—Africain
Quadrille—Américain

Cortège des contes des fées

(3) Grande polonaise dansée—80 à 96 mesures pour faire défiler les contes des fées.
  (1) Barbe-bleu et sa femme
  (2) Le chat botté
  Le Marquis de Carabas dans sa chaise à porteurs et ses valets
  (3) Cendrillon et le *Pce.* Fortuné
  (4) La belle et la bête
  (5) L'oiseau bleu et la *Psse.* Florine
  (6) La chatte blanche, portée sur un coussin de velours cramoisi par 4 grands
    valets
  (7) La belle aux cheveux d'or et le *Pce.* Avenant
[Page 19]
  (8) Peau d'âne et le *Pce.* Charmant
  (9) Chaperon rouge et le loup
  (10) Riquet à la houppe et la *Psse.* Aimée
  (11) Le Petit Poucet et ses frères
  (12) L'ogre et l'ogresse
  (13) La Fée Carabosse, dans sa brouette aux rats
  (14) Les bonnes fées—du Prologue
  (15) La Fée des lilas et sa suite
  (16) Quatre fées
  La Fée or-fin
  La Fée argent
  La Fée saphir
  La Fée diamant
Défilé devant le Roi et les fiancés, révérences.

Divertissement des pas

(1) Pas de quatre. Fées or-fin—argent—saphir—diamant.
Allegro 6/8 assez brillant—64 mesures.
  4 Variations de 24 et 32 mesures.
  (1) Or-fin—charmeuse dorée
  (2) Argent—on doit entendre sonner l'argent—temps de polka
  (3) Saphir—les cinq facettes—musique à 5 temps
  (4) Diamant—étincelles brillantes comme l'électricité—2/4 vif
  (5) Petite coda dans le même caractère du 2/4 du diamant—48 mesures
[Page 20]
(2) Pas de caractère. Le chat botté et la chatte blanche.
  Des miaulements réciproques, des caresses, et des coups de griffes. Pour la fin,
égratignures et le cri du chat. Pour commencer un 3/4 amoureux et pour finir un 3/4
précipite de miaulements. (Le pas ne doit pas être long.)

(3) Pas de quatre classique.* Cendrillon et le *Pce*. Fortuné. L'oiseau bleu et la *Psse*. Florine.

Petit andante—la musique exprime le chant de l'oiseau.

Une variation pour Cendrillon et le *Pce*. Fortuné—32 mesures d'un temps passionné.

Une variation pour l'oiseau bleu et la *Psse*. Florine—un 2/4 le chant de l'oiseau—24 mesures. Petite fin de 64 mesures. Ils se becquètent.

(4) Le petit chaperon rouge et le loup.†

Pas de caractère—très court.

Elle arrive gaîment avec son pot-au-lait. 3/4—32 mesures. Elle casse son pot-au-lait—elle pleure. Arrive le loup—elle tremble—le loup la tranquillise—temps de polka—aboiement doucereux—la caresse, lui promet de lui faire obtenir son pardon, si elle le conduit chez sa vieille mère. Le pas finit avec le temps de valse un peu plus précipité. Elle part tremblant et emportée par le loup.

(5) Pas Berrichon.‡

Pas de caractère très court.

Le petit poucet et ses frères.

Ils arrivent 7 d'une seule file. Le premier, le plus petit poucet [sic], porte les bottes de l'ogre. Ils sont joyeux de cette éclatante victoire. Pour l'entrée un 2/4—16 mesures. Ils arrivent à grandes enjambées. Après les 16 mesures, le 2/4 devient très gai et il rient aux éclats et dansent autour des bottes. À la fin, ils entendent le grognement de l'ogre. Le petit poucet tout tremblant met les bottes, et les 6 autres se tenant par la file, ils fuient à toutes jambes poursuivis par l'ogre.

[Page 21]

(6) Pas de deux classique.

Aurore et Désiré.

Pour l'entrée un 6/8 brillant—32 mesures.

Un adage assez grand et large, avec des fortés et des temps d'arrêts.

Une variation pour Désiré. 6/8—48 mesures, forté.

Une variation pour Aurore. Ne pas composer de suite.

Coda—2/4 a *gd.* effet—80 à 96 mesures.

(7) Coda générale.

—Sarabande de caractère.§

Musique entrainante, bouillante, à faire sauter toute le monde.

Apothéose

Musique en situation—large, grandiose.

Air Henri IV.

Apollon en costume de Louis XIV, éclairé par le soleil entouré des fées.

Fin¶

*

* In the left margin next to No. 3: 'Peut-être passer ce pas de 4.'

† In the left margin next to No. 4: 'Cette description ne va pas—Elle ne casse pas le pot-au-lait qu'elle n'a même pas. Voir les contes de Perrault.'

‡ At the beginning of No. 5, in the right margin: '(L'ogre doit avoir un lorgnon)'.

§ In the left margin next to No. 7: 'Peut-être non. Je pense que c'est pour le quadrille.'

¶ At the end of the Balletmaster's Plan: 'J'ai donné à Mr. Tchaikovsky des morceaux de musique de la Sarabande. M. Petipa.'

Ib. Petipa's Instructions to Tchaikovsky for 'Nutcracker'.

NUTCRACKER

Ballet in two acts and three scenes

ACT I

The curtain rises on a large drawing room, illuminated by only one candelabrum.

No. 1. The President with his wife and guests are decorating the Christmas tree. Peaceful and tender music—64 bars. The clock strikes nine, and with each stroke the owl on the clock flap its wings. All is ready; it is time to call the children. All this occurs within the 64 bars of music.

No. 2. The tree, as if by magic, lights up brightly by the fire of the candles. Sparkling music, 8 b[ars].

No. 3. The doors open. For the children's entrance noisy and jubilant music. 24 b[ars].

No. 4. The astounded and delighted children stop as if rooted to the ground. Several measures of childlike *tremolo*.

No. 5. The President orders a march to be played. March in 64 bars. Each child receives a gift and a party favour with a costume. The children, playing, change clothes; all this happens during the march.

No. 6. Dances: (1) Chinese Dance—24 b[ars]. (2) Spanish Dance—32 b[ars]. (3) Italian Dance, tarantella—32 b[ars]. (4) English Dance—giga in 2/4, very rapid—48 bars. (5) A jester dances a Russian trepak—from 16 to 24 b[ars]. (6) Coda—French cancan, the last figure a quadrille. Furious galop for the children—48 b[ars].*

No. 7. The general liveliness is interrupted by the appearance of Councillor Drosselmayer. For his entrance the clocks chime and the owl greets him, flapping its wings. Very serious, rather sinister and even droll music. *Largo* from 16 to 24 b[ars].

The children hide behind their parents' legs. They are calmed, seeing that the councillor brought toys. Here the music gradually changes character, 24 b[ars]. It becomes less sad, brighter, and finally merry.

No. 8. The President's children wait impatiently for the gifts godfather Drosselmayer will distribute. [Crossed out: 'When the councillor gets ready to give the toys to Silberhaus's children, the owl in the clock greets each gift with a flapping of its wings, forcing the clock to strike.'] The latter orders two boxes to be brought in. From one he takes out a large head of cabbage—this is Clara's gift. [Crossed out: 'The owl beats his wings, and the clock strikes 4 times.'] From the other, a large pie—this is for Fritz. [Crossed out: 'the same flutters its wings—4 bars.'] Seeing

---

* Written in the left margin opposite No. 6: 'All these dances follow one another without a break.'

All dances listed in No. 6 are struck out. In the text and parentheses in margins Tchaikovsky's remark: 'Little galop for the children'—crossed out. 'Galop for the children and entrance of the parents dressed as *Incroyables*. Entrance of the parents dressed as *Incroyables*, 16 bars of rococo (*tempo menuetto*).' Crossed out: 'Short galop reinstated.' Then: 'Bon voyage, M. Dumolet.' Crossed out: '16 or 24 bars.'

such uninteresting gifts, children and parents are disappointed. All exchange glances . . . For this moment only 4 b[ars] of chords, expressing surprise.*

No. 9. Drosselmayer, smiling, orders both presents to be placed in front of him—8 bars of music. He winds them up—still another 8 bars of music in which is heard the squeaking of the keys that wind up the mechanism of the toys. To the children's great joy, a large doll emerges from the head of the cabbage, and from the pie—a soldier. 16 more bars of mazurka for this small scene.

No. 10. *Pas de deux*. Leave is given until 10 o'clock. A sharp, disjunct waltz with clear rhythm. 48 b[ars].

No. 11. Drosselmayer orders two large snuff-boxes to be brought in, from which jump out a boy-devil and a girl-devil. 16 bars of music of transition to the following dance.

Diabolical dance of the mechanical dolls. Quite lively, syncopated dance in 2/4—48 b[ars].

No. 12. Clara and Fritz are now happy. They thank their godfather and want to carry off their toys. A merry, graceful *andantino*, 16 b[ars]. Their parents prohibit this. They cannot play with such beautiful toys. The *andantino* becomes more serious—8 b[ars]. Clara cries! Fritz is carrying on. This takes place in the music of the last eight bars. In order to console them, the old councillor takes a third toy out of his pocket. It is a Nutcracker. At least they can play with this. A more lively *andantino*—another 8 b[ars].

No. 13. Clara is delighted with the little fellow. Here begins a polka. Clara asks for what purpose the gift is intended. The councillor takes a hazel nut and cracks its shell with the aid of the Nutcracker. In the music the 'crack-crack' rings out, all within the polka. Fritz, having heard the nut crack in the jaws of the Nutcracker, grows interested in it and wants his turn to crack nuts with it. Clara does not want to give him the Nutcracker. The parents remind her that the Nutcracker does not belong to her alone. Clara gives her beloved to her brother and looks on in horror as he forces it to crack two hazel nuts. Then he shoves such a large walnut into its mouth that crack! His teeth are broken . . . All this occurs during the polka—48 b[ars].

No. 14. With a laugh Fritz throws away the toy—8 bars of very lively music. Clara picks it up and consoles her beloved with caresses. 8 more bars of less vivacious and more tender music. She takes her doll out of her bed and puts the Nutcracker in its place. This is done during these eight bars.

No. 15. Lullaby.

16 measures for the lullaby, which is interrupted by eight bars of fanfares on the horns, trumpets, and other brasses. This is Fritz and his friends teasing Clara. 16 more bars of lullaby, and again the same noisy interference of the instruments—8 bars.

No. 16. In order to put an end to this disorder, the President proposes his guests dance the *Grossvater*. 8 bars to introduce this dance.

No. 17. *Grossvater*. (The music can be found at the music store.)†

No. 18. The guests thank the President and his wife and leave. The children are

---

* Written in the left margin, underlined by Tchaikovsky: 'For No. 8 the music must be rather serious. 8 bars and pause to show the head of cabbage. Then 8 bars again (to repeat) and pause for the pie.'

† In the margin: 'I would prefer the dance of the *incroyables*.'

ordered off to bed. Clara asks permission to take the sick Nutcracker with her. Her parents refuse. She leaves, sad, having carefully tucked in her beloved. A gracious march, ending with a *diminuendo* from 24 to 32 b[ars].

No. 19. The stage is empty. Night. The moonlight coming through the window illuminates the drawing room. 8 bars of mysterious and tender music.

Clara, in her nightgown, cautiously returns. Before going to sleep she wanted to see her dear invalid. For her entrance 8 more b[ars] of more mysterious music. She is frightened. 2 bars representing how she is trembling. She goes over to the Nut-cracker's bed, from which, it seems to her, is emitted a fantastic light. 8 bars of fantastic and still mysterious music. The clock strikes midnight. A pause in the music. During the time that the clock strikes midnight Clara looks at the clock, and notices with horror that the owl has been transformed into Drosselmayer, who looks back at her with a mocking smile. She wants to flee but her strength fails her. This is done on a *tremolo*. After the strokes of the clock, a *tremolo* for the representation of horror.

No. 20. In the night silence she hears the scratching of mice. She makes an effort to go away, but the mice surround her on all sides. After the *tremolo* a fast 4 bars representing the scratching of the mice, and 4 more bars for their hissing. Possessed by terror, Clara wants to take her unhappy Nutcracker and run! But her fright is too great, she sinks into a chair. Everything disappears. After the hissing of the mice 8 more bars in a fast tempo, ending with a chord (this when she sinks powerless on the chair).

No. 21. The Christmas tree becomes huge. 48 bars of fantastic music with a grandiose *crescendo*.

No. 22. A sentry on watch cries out: 'Who goes there?' The mice do not answer. Two bars for the cry 'Who goes there?' and 2 bars of silence. The sentry fires. One or two bars. The dolls are in a tumult. 2 bars of fright. The sentry awakens the rabbit-drummers. 8 bars for awakening and 8 bars for an alarm signal, then 4–8 bars to get into formation. Battle—2/4 for 48 b[ars].* The mice are victorious and devour the gingerbread soldiers. 8 bars after the 48 b[ars] of battle, in order that the mice's teeth be heard chewing on the gingerbread.

No. 23. The Mouse King appears. His troops greet him loudly. For his entrance sharp, spiteful music which offends the ear. Then rings out 'Kuik, Kuik!' ('hoorah'). For the entrance of the King 8 b[ars] and 4 for the cries of 'hoorah' (Kuik, kuik).

No. 24. The Nutcracker summons his old guard. 'To arms!' he cries. 4 bars, and 8 b[ars] to get into military formation.

No. 25. The second battle begins. Again 2/4. A salvo of guns rings out. A hail of grapeshot, volley of guns, piercing cries. 96 b[ars].

No. 26. In order to defend the Nutcracker, Clara throws her slipper at the Mouse King, then falls, senseless. 2 bars for the piercing cry and 6 for the whistling of the mice, which disappear. This takes place at the end of the 96 b[ars].

No. 27. The Nutcracker turns into an enchanting prince. One or two chords. He runs to aid Clara, who regains consciousness. Here begins emotional music, which changes into a poetic *andante*, and ends in a grandiose fashion. 64 bars. The décor changes. A fir forest in winter. Gnomes with torches are standing around the

---

* Written in the margin: 'During the battle the dolls move away from the tree and set about making bandages.'

Christmas tree to pay homage to the prince, Clara, and the dolls, who are placed around the tree. A grouping. All this takes place within the *andante* of 64 bars.

No. 28. Snow is falling. Suddenly thick, light, white snowflakes begin to move (60 dancers). They swirl around continuously; in the third quarter of the waltz they form a snowball, then a strong burst of wind breaks up the snowball and forces the dancers to spin around.

End

The snow which falls in thick flakes is illuminated by electricity. Scene.

For No. 28 a whirling waltz. In the third quarter of the waltz a furious burst of wind causes all the dancers to spin around.

End of the second tableau

ACT II

No. 1. The magic castle of Confiturembourg. The most fantastic décor. The backdrop and wings represent palms of gold and silver spangles on cloth. At the back of the stage fountains gushing lemonade, orangeade, orgeat, and currant syrup.

For the beginning of the act, before the raising of the curtain, an introduction: becoming with the raising of the curtain quite grandiose, making a transition to No. 2.

No. 2. Among these fountains on the river of rose-oil stands out a pavilion of barley-sugar. Within its bannered columns are seen the Sugar Plum Fairy and her retinue. On stage at the rise of the curtain the following characters are seen: caramels, marzipans, gingerbreads, nougats, dragées, sticks of barley-sugar, peppermints, hard candy [*sucre candi*], pralines, currants [*raisins de Corinthe*], pistachios, macaroons, and small silver soldiers who guard the castle. In the middle of the stage a little man dressed in brocade stands immobile. This is the master of ceremonies.

Andante quasi allegretto, 16 b[ars], making a transition to No. 3.

No. 3. The Sugar Plum Fairy appears with her retinue. A grouping in the fantastic pavilion. They come down on to the stage. All the confections bow.

The music in the course of the next 16 bars becomes tender and caresses the ear.

No. 4. The river of rose-oil swells noticeably, and from its restless waves appear Clara and the Prince in a boat made of shells, studded with stones glittering in the sun. It is drawn by two gold dolphins with raised heads, who spray into the air spouts of rose-coloured crystal, which fall back as rain tinted in all the colours of the rainbow.

Six charming moors with parasols covered with little bells, in caps of gold mussel shells and in costumes of hummingbird feathers, jump down to the ground and lay down a carpet of angelica, studded with peppermints, on which the groom and bride complete their entrance. The Sugar Plum Fairy is prepared to meet them. The silver soldiers present arms, and all the fantastic people make a *grande révérence* in greeting. The little man in the gold brocade bows respectfully before the Nutcracker and exclaims, 'Oh, good prince, at last you are here! Welcome to Confiturembourg!'

Here, it seems to me, arpeggios. The music broadens and swells like an agitated river. A faster *andante* to the end of this number, from 24 to 32 bars.

No. 5. Twelve small pages appear, who carry in their hands, in place of torches, clusters of burning aromatic herbs. Their heads are of pearl; the torsos of six are of rubies; the other six are of emeralds. With all this they trot out on their little legs fashioned with the greatest care out of gold. Behind them follow four doll-sized women, but so richly dressed, so magnificently appointed with jewels that Clara recognizes without error that they are the princesses of Confiturembourg. All four, at the sight of the Nutcracker, throw themselves on his neck in an outburst of tender feelings, and exclaim simultaneously, in one voice: 'Oh, my prince! Oh, my glorious prince! Oh, my brother! Oh, my glorious brother!'

For this entrance music, 3/4 of a quite agitated character, from 24 to 32 bars.

No. 6. The Nutcracker is very moved. Having taken Clara by the hand, he turns with emotion to the princesses: 'My dear sisters, this is Mlle Clara Silberhaus, to whom I am indebted for my life, for if she had not thrown her slipper at the Mouse King at the moment when I was losing the battle, then I would already now either be lying in the grave, or, even worse, would have been eaten up by the Mouse King.'

8 bars of broad, and very moving 2/4, then 16 bars of ardent and war-like music.

No. 7. 'Oh, dear Mlle Silberhaus, O noble rescuer of our dear and beloved prince and brother!'

Here broad music in 2/4 becomes faster and more agitated under the influence of the story of the rescue of the Nutcracker. 16 bars.

No. 8. At a sign from the Sugar Plum Fairy there appears on stage, as if by magic, a sparkling table covered with preserves etc. The little man orders that chocolate be served.

Continuation of the same 2/4. The trumpets of the small silver soldiers sound—8 bars and 8 bars—to serve chocolate. This serves as a short introduction to the *pas*.

No. 9. *Divertissement.*

Chocolate. Spanish Dance in 3/4—from 64 to 80 bars.

1st dance.

No. 10. Coffee. Arabia. The kingdom of Yemen. Coffee mocha. Oriental Dance. From 24 to 32 bars of charming and voluptuous music.

2nd dance.

No. 11. Tea. *Allegretto* in 3/4. In the Chinese taste, little bells etc. 48 bars.

3rd dance.

No. 12. For the end, a trepak. 64 bars of fast music in 2/4.

4th dance.

No. 13. Dance with little fifes. Polka tempo. From 64 to 96 bars. They dance, playing on little fifes made of reed, both ends of which are stopped with a piece of gold-beater's skin.

5th dance.

No. 14. Dance of 32 buffoons and Mother Gigogne and her children, who are creeping out from behind her skirt. Leisurely and very accented, in 2/4—64 bars. Transition to music in 3/4—48 b[ars] for the entrance of Mother Gigogne and her children, jumping out from behind her skirt. Then again 2/4, but in a somewhat faster tempo, from 32 to 48 b[ars]. At the end, a group with Mother Gigogne, surrounded by buffoons.

6th dance.

No. 15. *Grand ballabile.* Waltz of flowers and large garlands. 8 bars for the introduction, then the same number of bars as in the *valse villageoise* in *Sleeping Beauty* (2nd scene). The little man claps his hands, and 36 dancers appear, arrayed in flowers. They carry a large bouquet of angelica, which they offer to the groom and bride. No sooner have they given it to them than the dancers, as is accepted in opera, take positions and begin to dance.

7th dance.

No. 16. *Pas de deux.*

The Sugar Plum Fairy with Prince Coqueluche. An *adagio* intended to produce a colossal impression—48 bars. Variation for the *cavalier*—48 b[ars] in 6/8. Variation for the *danseuse*, 32 bars of *staccato* in 2/4. In this music it is as if drops of water shooting out of fountains are heard. End with a very fast 24 bars.

Coda. Still lively music in 2/4—88 bars.

8th dance.

No. 17. Grand general coda for all participants on stage, as too for those who already have completed their *pas*. 128 bars of very brilliant and fiery music in 3/4.

No. 18. *Apotheosis.*

Illuminated fountains etc. Grandiose *andante* from 16 to 24 bars.

End

★

II*b. The Balletmaster's Plan for 'Nutcracker'.*

[Page 1]　　　　　　　　　　　*Casse-noisette*

*Ballet en 2 actes et 3 tableaux**

Au tirer du rideau, le *gd.* salon n'est éclairé qu'avec un seul candélabre.

(1) Le Président avec sa femme et ses invités ornent l'arbre de Noël. Musique douce et silencieuse. 64 m.

Il sonne neuf heures: à chaque coup de l'horloge la chouette fait un mouvement avec ses ailes. Tout est prêt, il est temps d'appeler les enfants.

Tout cela se passe sur les 64 m.

(2) L'arbre s'éclaire à giorno comme par enchantement.

Musique pétillante de 8 m.

(3) La porte s'ouvre: musique bruyante et joyeuse pour l'entrée des enfants. 24 m.

(4) Les enfants s'arrêtent saisis d'étonnement et d'admiration.

Un trémolo enfantin de quelques m.

(5) Le Président ordonne de jouer une marche.

Marche de 64 m. Chaque enfant reçoit des cadeaux. Tout cela se fait sur la marche.

(6) Galop pour les enfants. 48 m.

(6 bis) Entrée des invités habillés en incroyables. 16 m. *pr* l'entrée. Puis danse rococo—temps de menuet—Bon voyage cher Dumolet.

(7) L'entraînement général est interrompu par l'arrivée du Conseiller Dros-

---

* Upper left margin: 'Copie de ce qui j'ai donné à Mr. Tchaikovsky.'

selmayer. Pour son entrée, la grande horloge sonne et la chouette l'accueille avec des battements d'ailes. Musique très sérieuse, un peu effrayante et même comique. Un mouvement large, 16 à 24 m.

Les enfants vont se blottir près des parents, ils se rassurent en voyant qu'il porte des joujoux. Ici la musique change petit à petit de caractère.

24 m. elle devient moins triste, plus claire et enfin passe à la gaieté.

(8) Les deux enfants du Président attendent avec impatience la distribution des cadeaux du parrain Drosselmayer. Pour ce No. 8, musique assez grave de 8 m., et temps d'arrêt pour montrer le chou! Les mêmes 8 m.—reprise—pour le pâté et aussi temps d'arrêt.

pas de caisses

Celui-ci fait apporter deux caisses: de l'une il retire son *gd* chou, c'est le cadeau de Claire. De l'autre un *gd* pâté, c'est pour Fritz. En voyant des cadeaux aussi peu interessants les enfants et les parents ont l'air désillusionné. Pour ce moment seulement 4 m. avec des accords d'étonnements—tous se regardent.

[Page 2]

(9) Drosselmayer en souriant ordonne qu'on porte devant lui les deux cadeaux. 8 m. d'un temps de mazourka. Il les montre—8 autres mesures de mazourka qui font entendre le grincement de la clef qui monte les joujoux. A la grande joie des enfants, une grande poupée sort du chou, et du pâté un soldat. Encore 16 m. de mazourka pour cette petite scène.

(10) Pas de deux. La permission de 10 heures.

Une valse piquée, saccadée et bien rhythmée—48 m.

(11) Drosselmayer fait apporter 2 *gdes.* tabatières d'où sortent un diable et une diablesse/arlequin et colombine. 16 m. pour donner le temps d'entrer dans l'autre pas.

Pas diabolique des poupées à ressorts. Un 2/4 assez vif et syncopé—48 m.*

(12) Claire et Fritz maintenant sont enchantés, ils remercient le parrain et veulent emporter les joujoux.

Andantino gracieux, joyeux, 16 m.

Les parents les leur défendent; on ne joue pas avec des cadeaux aussi beaux. L'andantino devient plus sérieuse. 8 m. Claire pleure! Fritz fait le capricieux. Cela se passe sur les dernières 8 m.

Pour les consoler le vieux conseiller retire de sa poche un troisième cadeau: un Casse-noisette, avec cela on peut jouer. L'andantino plus animé avec 8 m. encore.

(13) Claire du coup est enchantée du petit bonhomme. Ici commence un temps de polka. Claire demande au conseiller la destination du cadeau? Celui-ci prend une noisette et la fait casser par le Casse-noisette. On entend la musique qui fait Carrac-carrac, knak-knak toujours sur le temps de polka. Fritz, en entendant le knak-knak du bonhomme, s'intéresse à lui. Fritz veut à son tour lui faire casser des noisettes. Claire ne veut pas le lui donner. Les parents font observer à la petite Claire, que le Casse-noisette ne lui appartient pas à elle seule. Claire cède son favori à son frère et regarde avec effroi comment Fritz lui fait casser 2 noisettes; puis il lui fourre dans la bouche une si grande noix, que les dents du Casse-noisette se cassent. Trak! . . . Tout cela se fait sur la polka—48 m.

* In the left margin next to No. 11: 'C'est à voir. J'aime mieux les diables que Columbine et Arlequin.'

[Page 3]

(14) Fritz jette le jouet en riant! 8 m. d'une musique très animée.

Claire le prend et avec des caresses tâche de consoler son favori. 8 autres mesures moins animées et plus caressantes. Elle enlève la poupée du lit et y pose le bonhomme. Cela se fait sur les 8 m.

(15) La Berceuse.

16 m. pour la berceuse qui est interrompue par 8 m. d'une fanfare de cors, de trompettes, et autres instruments de cuivre. C'est Fritz et ses amis qui lui font cette plaisanterie. La berceuse reprend encore 16 m.—même vacarme des instruments—8 m.

(16) Pour couper court à ce tumulte, le Président prie ses invités de danser le Gross-Fater.

8 m. pour entrer dans cette danse.

(17) Gross-Fater.

(18) Les invités remercient le Président, sa femme et s'en vont. On ordonne aux enfants d'aller se coucher. Claire demande la permission d'emporter avec elle le Casse-noisette malade. Les parents refusent. Elle s'en va toute chagrine après avoir bien enveloppé son favori. Une marche gracieuse qui finit en diminuendo. 24 à 32 m.

(19) La scène est vide. Il se fait nuit. La lune [non] éclaire le salon [non] par la fenêtre. 8 m. d'une musique douce et mystérieuse. Claire en toilette de nuit revient avec précaution; avant de s'endormir elle a voulu revoir son malade chéri. Encore 8 m. plus mystérieuses pour son entrée. Elle a peur! 2 m. de frissons, elle s'avance vers le lit du Casse-noisette qui lui semble produire une lumière fantastique. 8 m. d'une musique fantastique et encore mystérieuse. Minuit sonne. Temps d'arrêt pour la musique. Pendant que minuit sonne, elle regarde l'horloge et voit avec effroi que la chouette s'est transformée en Drosselmayer qui la regarde avec son sourire moqueur. Après la sonnerie, un petit

[Page 4]

trémolo d'effroi. Elle veut s'enfuir mais les forces lui manquent. Cela se passe sur le trémolo.

(20) Dans le silence de la nuit elle entend les souris qui grattent. Elle fait un effort pour s'en aller, mais les souris apparaissent de tous côtés. Après le trémolo, de suite 4 mesures pour faire entendre le grattement des souris et 4 autres mesures pour leur sifflement. Alors saisie d'effroi! elle veut emporter le pauvre Casse-noisette et s'enfuir! Mais la frayeur est trop grande; elle s'affaise sur une chaise. Tout disparaît. Après le sifflement des souris, encore 8 m. d'un mouvement accéléré et qui se termine par un accord! C'est lorsqu'elle s'affaise sur un siège.

(21) La porte s'ouvre et l'arbre devient /paraît/ immense. 48 m. d'une musique fantastique, d'un crescendo grandiose.

(22) La sentinelle qui fait guet crie—qui vive? Les souris ne répondent pas. 2 m. pour crier 'qui vive' et 2 m. de silence. La sentinelle tire un coup de fusil. Une ou 2 m. Les poupées son effarouchées.* 2 m. d'effroi. La sentinelle réveille les lapins à tambours. 8 m. pour se réveiller et 8 m. pour battre l'alarme, puis 4 à 8 m., pour se ranger en bataille.

Combat—2/4 de 48 m. Les souris triomphent—c'est après les 48 m. de combat 8

---

* In the left margin next to No. 22: 'Pendent le combat, les poupées sont descendues de l'arbre et vont faire de la charpie.'

m.—et dévorent les soldats à pain d'épice. Pour entendre manger les pains d'épice avec les dents des souris.

(23) Le roi des souris arrive. Son armée l'acclame! Pour son entrée, une musique aigre et rageuse dont le son blesse l'ouïe en toute, un couis, couis/hourra. Pour l'entrée du roi 8 m., et 4 pour le hourra!/couis couis.

(24) Casse-noisette appelle sa vieille garde. Il crie 'Aux armes!!'—4 m., et 8 m. pour se ranger encore en bataille.

(25) Une seconde bataille commence. Encore un 2/4. On entend une bordée d'artillerie et une volée de mitraille, [des] fusillades et des cris perçants. 96 m. [Page 5]

(26) Claire pour défendre Casse-noisette, jette son soulier* sur le roi des souris, puis elle tombe évanouie. 2 mesures pour un cri aigu et 6 m. pour le sifflement des souris qui disparaissent. Cela s'exécute sur la fin des 96 m.

(27) Casse-noisette se change en Prince—reconnaissant—un ou 2 accords. Il va porter des soins à Claire qui revient à elle. Ici commence une musique pathétique qui s'enchaîne avec son andante poétique et qui se termine d'une manière grandiose. 64 m. Le décor change. Une forêt de sapins en hiver.

(28) La neige commence à tomber. Soudain! survient une avalanche de neige comme des flocons blancs et légers. 60 danseuses. Elles tourbillonnent sans fin; en trois quarts de la valse, elles forment une pelote, une boule de neige, puis une forte rafale de vent détache la boule de neige qui fait tourbillonner les danseuses.

Fin

La neige qui tombe à gros flocons est éclairée par la lumière électrique.

Tableau

Pour le No. 28. Une valse tourbillonnante. Au trois quarts de la valse, un coup de vent impétueux fait tourbillonner toutes les danseuses.

[Page 6]   *Casse-noisette*
ACTE II

[On the left side of the page:] No. 1. Pour le commencement de l'acte avant le lever du rideau, une introduction qui s'entraîne avec le lever du rideau et qui devient plus grandiose pour le No. 2.

[On the right side of the page:] Le palais enchanté de Confiturembourg. Décor des plus fantastiques.

La toile de fond et les coulisses représentent des palmes, or, argent en paillettes sur tulle.

Au fond, des fontaines de limonade, d'orangeade, d'orgeat et de sirop de groseille.
(2) [On the left side of the page:] Un andante quasi allegretto de 16 m., qui l'enchaine aussi avec le No. 3.

[On the right side of the page:] Au milieu de ces fontaines, on voit sur le fleuve d'essence de rose, un kiosque de sucre d'orge avec colonnes à transparent où l'on aperçoit la Fée dragée avec sa suite. Les personnes qui sont en scène au lever du rideau sont: des caramellas [sic], massepains, pain d'épice, cannelles-nougats,

---

* Written below the word 'soulier': 'pantoufle'.

dragées, sucre d'orge, pastilles de menthe, sucre candi, pralines, raisins de Corinthe, pistaches, macarons et des petits soldats d'argent qui tiennent la garde du palais.

Au milieu de la scène, reste planté un petit homme habillé d'une robe de brocart d'or. C'est le maître des cérémonies.

(3) [On the left side of the page:] La musique devient douce et harmonieuse pendant 16 autres mesures.

[On the right side of the page:] La Fée dragée apparaît avec sa suite dans le kiosque fantastique. 'Groupe.' Ils descendent sur la scène. Tous les bonbons s'inclinent.

(4) [On the left side of the page:] Je pense ici, des arpèges? La musique s'élargit et gonfle comme les flots agités. Andante plus accéléré jusqu'à la fin de ce morceau de 24 à 32 m.

[On the right side of the page:] Le fleuve d'essence de rose se gonfle visiblement, et de ses flots agités, paraît Claire et le Prince bienfaisant sur un char de coquillages couvert de pierreries étincelant au soleil, et trainé par des dauphines d'or qui relèvent la tête et lancent en l'air des gerbes brillantes de cristal rose qui retombent en pluie diaprée de toutes les couleurs de l'arc-en-ciel.

Six charmants maures avec des parasols garnis de sonnettes et avec des bonnets en écaille de dorade et des habits en plumes de colibri, sautent à terre et placent un tapis d'angélique tout parsemé de pastilles de menthe, sur lequel les fiancés font leur entrée.

[Page 7]

La Fée dragée va les recevoir.

Les soldats d'argent leur présentent les armes, et tout ce monde fantastique fait la *gde.* révérence. Le petit homme au brocart d'or s'incline respectueusement devant le Casse-noisette en lui disant: Oh! cher Prince, vous voilà donc enfin! Soyez le bienvenu à Confiturembourg.

(5) [On the left side of the page:] Pour cette entrée une musique, à 3/4 assez agité, 24 à 32 m.

[On the right side of the page:] Douze petits pages arrivent, portant dans leurs mains des brins d'herbe aromatique, allumés en guise de flambeaux, leurs têtes sont composées d'une perle; six d'entre eux ont le corps fait de rubis, et six autres d'émeraudes, et avec cela ils trottent fort joliment sur deux petits pieds d'or ciselés avec le plus grand soin. Ils sont suivis de quatre dames de la taille d'une poupée, mais si splendidement vêtues, si richement parées, que Claire ne peut méconnaître en elles les princesses royales de Confiturembourg. Toutes quatre en apercevant Casse-noisette, s'élancent à son cou avec la plus tendre effusion, s'écriant en même temps et d'une seule voix: O mon prince! mon excellent prince . . . O mon frère! mon excellent frère!

(6) [On the left side of the page:] Un 2/4 large et très pathétique de 8 m., puis 16 mesures assez guerrières et chaudes.

[On the right side of the page:] Casse-noisette est fort touché, et prenant Claire par le main, il dit pathétiquement, en s'adressant aux quatre princesses: Mes chères sœurs, voici, Mlle Claire Silberhaus que je vous présente; c'est elle qui a sauvé ma vie; car si, au moment où je venais de perdre la bataille, elle n'avait pas jeté sa pantoufle au roi des souris, je serais maintenant couché dans le tombeau, ou, qui pire est encore, dévoré par le roi des souris.

(7) [On the left side of the page:] Ici le 2/4 large, devient pressé, agité de l'heureuse délivrance de Casse-noisette—16 mesures.

[On the right side of the page:] Ah! chère Mlle Silberhaus, o noble libératrice de notre cher et bien aimé prince et frère.

[Page 8]

(8) [On the left side of the page:] Suite de même 2/4. Les trompettes des petits soldats d'argent se font entendre, 8 m., et 8 m. pour finir.

[On the right side of the page:] La Fée dragée fait un signe, et une table resplendissante de confitures, etc.... paraît sur la scène comme par enchantement.

[Continuing on the left side of the page:] et 8 m. pour servir le chocolat. Comme petite introduction du pas.

[On the right side of the page:] Le petit homme ordonne qu'on serve le chocolat.

Divertissement

(9) 1ère danse. Le chocolat, pas espagnole. Un 3/4 de 64 à 80 m.*

(10) 2ème danse. Le café. Arabie, royaume d'Yemen. Café de moka, danse orientale, 24 à 32 mesures d'une musique voluptueuse et charmeuse.

(11) 3ème danse. Le thé. Un 3/4 Allegretto—type chinois—clochettes, etc. 48 m.

(12) 4ème danse. Pour finir, la danse du Trépak, avec cerceaux. Un 2/4 pressé—64 m.

(13) 5ème danse. Danse des mirlitons. Temps de polka. 64 à 96 m. Ils dansent en jouant avec une flûte faite d'un roseau bouché à ses extrémités par un morceau de baudruche.

(14) 6ème danse. Pas des 32 polichinelles et de la mère Gigogne avec ses petits enfants qui sortent de sa jupe.

Un 2/4 très accentué et pas pressé de 64 m. qui s'enchaîne avec un 3/4 de 48 m. pour l'entrée de la mère Gigogne et de ses enfants qui sautent de sa jupe; puis, le 2/4 reprend un peu plus vite pendant 32 à 48 m. A la fin, groupe avec la mère Gigogne au milieu des polichinelles.

[Page 9]

(15) 7ème danse. Grand ballabile. Valse des fleurs avec de gdes. guirlandes. 8 m. pour entrer dans la valse ensuite, même longueur de mesures comme la Valse villageoise dans la Belle au bois dormant (2me tableau). Le petit homme frappe entre ses deux mains, et 36 danseuses habillés en fleurs, ainsi que 36 danseurs, arrivent en portant un grand bouquet d'angélique qu'ils présentent aux fiancés. A peine l'ont ils donné, que comme cela se pratique dans les opéras, les danseuses et danseurs prennent leurs positions, et commencent à danser.

(16)† 8ème danse. Pas de deux. Fée dragée avec le Prince bienfaisant.

Adage colossal d'effets—48 m.

Une variation pour le danseur. 6/8—48 m.

Une variation pour la danseuse. Un 2/4 piqué, 32 m. où l'on peut aussi entendre

---

* Throughout the *divertissement*, Petipa listed the dances on both sides of the page. Since the left column consisted only of the numbers, the two sides have been consolidated in the present list.

† Crossed out at this point: 'Coda du pas. No. 17/9ème danse.'

les gouttes des eaux qui jaillissent des fontaines, puis finir avec 24 m. très accélérées. Coda. Encore un 2/4* vif de 88m.

(17) 9ème danse. Grande coda générale par tout le monde qui est en scène et ceux qui ont déjà dansé le pas. 128 m. d'un 3/4 très entraînant et chaud.

(18) Apothéose. Fontaines avec de couleurs, fontaines lumineuses etc., etc. Andante grandiose de 16 à 24 m.

Fin†

* After '2/4' but crossed out: 'très entraînant et chaud.'
† At foot of page: 'Le 29 fev. j'ai écrit cela, c'est très bien.'

Metronome Markings in the Holograph Score
of *Sleeping Beauty*

[There are no such markings in the prologue.]

ACT I

No. 5. Beginning: [♩ =] 152.
     Moderato (bar 119): [♩ =] 108.

No. 7. Beginning: [♩ =] 72.
     Allegro qiusto (bar 19): [♩♩ =] 144.

No. 8. *Allegro maestoso* (bar 19): [♩. =] 52.
     Dances of the Maids of Honour and Pages (bar 83): [♩ =] 144.
     Pages (bar 130): [♩ =] 168.
     Aurora's variation (bar 168): ♪ = 184.
       Meno mosso (bar 199): ♪ = 132.
       Allegro vivace (bar 233): [♩ =] 184.
     Coda (bar 264): [♩ =] 160.
       Poco più mosso (bar 314): [♩ =] 176.
       Tempo primo (bar 355): [♩ =] 160.

No. 9. Finale: [♩ =] 152.
     Allegro vivo (bar 29): [♩ =] 168.
     Andante con moto (bar 69): [♩ =] 88.

ACT II

No. 10. ♩ = 132.
     Un poco più tranquillo (bar 41): ♩ = 112.

No. 11. ♩ = 138.

No. 12. Dance of the Duchesses: ♩ = 92.
     Dance of the Baronesses: ♩ = 144.
     Dance of the Countesses: ♩. = 104.
     Dance of the Marchionesses: ♩ = 126.

No. 13. Beginning: ♩ = 138.
     Tempo di mazurka: ♩. = 72.

No. 14. ♩. = 132.
     Allegro vivace (bar 100): ♩. = 100.

No. 15.   *Pas d'action*:   ♩. = 66.
          Allegro (bar 98):   ♩. = 84.
          Aurora's variation: ♩ = 120.
          Coda: ♩ = 160.
No. 16.   ♪ = 144.
No. 17.   ♪ = 138.
No. 18.   ♩ = 80.
No. 19.   *Andante misterioso*:   ♩ = 76.
          Allegro (bar 100):   ♩ = 144.
No. 20.   ♩ = 144.
          Un pochetto più tranquillo (bar 22):   ♩ = 116.
          A tempo (bar 30):   ♩ = 144.

ACT III

No. 21.   ♩ = 116.
No. 22.   At bar 22:   ♩ = 108.
No. 23.   *Allegro non tanto*:   ♩ = 92.
              Variation II: ♩ = 152.
              Variation III: ♩ ♩. = 63.
              Variation IV: ♩ = 160.
              Coda: ♩ = 160.
No. 24.   ♩ = 92.
No. 25.   *Adagio*:   ♩ = 56.
          Variation II: ♩ = 80.
          Coda: ♩ = 152.
No. 26.   ♩ = 108.
No. 27.   ♩ = 132.
No. 28.   *Entrée*:   ♩. = 72.
          Adagio: ♩. = 50.
          Coda: ♩ = 160.
No. 30.   Apotheosis: ♩ = 69.

Present Order of Materials in the Choreographic Notation of *Nutcracker*

	Pages in notation	Position in musical score
1. Scene of Drosselmayer's entrance.	3–[4]	No. 4, bars 1–66
2. First dance of the mechanical dolls.	5–7	No. 4, bars 99–154
3. Opening scene of Act I.	9–[12]	No. 1
4. Children at the Christmas tree.	13–[14]	No. 2
5. Children's galop, parents' entrance *en incroyables*.	[14]–19	No. 3
6. Parents' dance *en incroyables* —two lead couples.	21–3	No. 3, bars 61–118
7. Second dance of the mechanical dolls.	25–[26]	No. 4, bars 155–238
8. Scene: Drosselmayer and the children.	29–[30]	No. 5, bars 1–38
9. Clara and the Nutcracker.	[unnumbered]	No. 5, bars 39–171
10. Introduction and *Grossvatertanz*.	33–5	No. 5, bars 172–225
11. Scene: dispersal of the guests.	37–[38]	No. 6, bars 1–48
12. Waltz of the Snowflakes.	39–45	No. 9
13. Arabian Dance [later version?]	51–[52]	No. 12*b*
14. Waltz of the Snowflakes [later version?]	53–7	No. 9
15. Waltz of the flowers [later version?]	59–61	No. 13
16. Spanish Dance (soloists).	65–5*a*	No. 12*a*
17. Spanish dancers in the final waltz.	[66]	No. 15, bars 33–40
18. Chinese dancers in the final waltz.	67–[68]	No. 15, bars 41–8, 129–44
19. Arabian dancers in the final waltz.	69–[70]	No. 15, bars 49–56, 145–60
20. Mirlitons in the final waltz.	71	No. 15, bars 57–64, 161–76
21. Spanish Dance (soloists).	73–[74]	No. 12*a*

	Pages in notation	Position in musical score
22. Arabian Dance (lead soloist).	77–9	No. 12*b*
23. Arabian Dance (soloists).	81–[82*a*]	No. 12*b*
24. Chinese Dance (soloists).	83–[84]	No. 12*c*
25. Chinese Dance (lead couple).	87–[88]	No. 12*c*
26. Mirlitons.	89–[92]	No. 12*e*
27. Waltz of the Flowers (*corps de ballet*).	93–[98]	No. 13
28. Waltz–coda.	99–[100]	No. 15
29. List of entries for the Waltz coda.	101	No. 15, bars 33– 176 [?]
30. Waltz–coda (another version, showing ending).	105–7	No. 15
31. Waltz of the Flowers (soloists).	109–15	No. 13
32. Introduction to the Waltz of the Flowers.	117	No. 13, bars 1–38
33. Dance of students, 2/4, Act II [not identified].	119–[120]	?
34. Coda of the *pas de deux*.	123–[124]	No. 14[*d*]
35. Scene: arrival of the Nutcracker and Clara in Confiturembourg.	131–[136]	No. 11
36. *Pas de deux*, 'Adagio'.	139–43	No. 14[*a*]
37. *Pas de deux*, woman's variation.	147–9	No. 14 [*c*]
38. Waltz–coda, entry for the Sugar Plum Fairy and her cavalier.	151	No. 15, bars 65–96
39. Waltz–coda, another entry for the Sugar Plum Fairy and her cavalier.	[152]	No. 15, bars 209– 39[?]

APPENDIX G

The Waltz of the Snowflakes from *Nutcracker*

I T is rare in the documentary study of choreography to find both a production record of a dance no longer performed and an eye-witness account, itself of sufficient detail and authority to be used as a source by scholars. It is more remarkable still when the eye-witness has recalled the production over thirty years after the first performance.

Akim L'vovich Volynsky's 'A Wretched Housepainter' (published in *Zhizn' Iskusstva* [The Life of Art] (20 Feb. 1923), vii, pp. 4–5 is a criticism of a staging of *Nutcracker* based on his recollection of Lev Ivanov's original production.* He takes his title from a line of Pushkin, rendered approximately: 'I don't find it funny when a wretched housepainter sullies the Madonna of Raphael', from which he draws parallels—between the rehearsal coach [*repetitor*] and the wretched housepainter, between Ivanov and Raphael. Volynsky invokes the great poet again after describing Ivanov's work, with which, 'in its elegance, in the intelligence and finish of each element, perhaps only Pushkin's verses can contend.'

Translation cannot do full justice to Volynsky's remarkable language, with its elaborate imagery, now poetic, now graphic, now alliterative, now enriched with the vocabulary of the *danse d'école*. His description of the Waltz of the Snowflakes is especially lovely because he describes the choreography using the images of a natural snowstorm.

We are fortunate that Volynsky, of all the late imperial balletomanes, came to write this article. Eccentric in dress and behaviour, he was a writer with a refreshingly lucid grasp of the artistic effects of Ivanov's work (in contrast, say, to the acerbic matter-of-factness of a Skalkovsky or the even-handedness of a Pleshcheyev). The first part of this appendix is devoted to a translation of pertinent parts of Volynsky's description; his castigation of the revised dances is quoted when it reflects his views concerning Ivanov. The production record, which is reproduced after Volynsky's article in photographs, with diplomatic transcriptions of the Russian text, boasts no such literary pretensions. Of all the dances in the choreographic notation of *Nutcracker* it is, if not completely unambiguous, the clearest and most intelligible (see also Chapter 6, pp. 212–14, above).

These sources complement each other. The notators, by drawing the patterns of the dance with an eye towards reproducing the choreography, clarify parts of Volynsky's sometimes rhapsodic prose. Volynsky, in contrast, provides information that the floor plans convey at best imperfectly, by inference—Lev Ivanov's mastery as a matter of artistic effects perceived. Together, the two accounts bring us as close to the dance as documents can.

---

* Volynsky does not specify which production he saw, but it is surely the revival by Lopukhov and Shiryaev which had first been performed at the Kirov Theatre on 4 February 1923.

At the beginning of his article Volynsky claimed to be one of Ivanov's most fervent admirers:

He is an astonishing genius, fundamentally pure and honest, full of moderation and effortless tact, harmoniously clear, but with periodic undercurrents of Slavic melancholy and introspection . . . In *Nutcracker* Lev Ivanov demonstrated his remarkable musicality . . . There is nothing in the music of *Nutcracker*, not one rhythm, not one bar which would not flow into dance. All on stage effervesces incessantly, in the peaceful splash of the gentlest patterns, with bursts of glowing, happy children's laughter, of children's delights, thrills and chagrin a moment later. And all of this wrapped in the aromas of a Christmas tree, with the crackling here and there of twigs catching fire from the candles. Indeed, a genuine, freshly-cut Christmas tree, an illuminated, coniferous Flora, in the style and spirit bequeathed to us by our Russian children's memories—and not some schematic representation [of a tree] . . .

As for the second scene of this act [in the production being reviewed], the celebrated Dance of the Snowflakes, it was truly a profanation of our dearest recollections. Every feature of Lev Ivanov's production was thought out and deeply felt in the greatest degree. He gathered together the barely perceptible sparkles of frost, the hachures and patterns of snow crystals, monograms and arabesques of the *plastique* of frost into one well-proportioned, artistically finished vision . . . In the production of Lev Ivanov the dancers appear in white dresses in lines of three people, with bits of down on their heads and dresses. In their hands they have ice-like stalactites, also trimmed with light snow. These charming details, which introduced the brightness and enchantment of the frosty element into the scene, were nowhere to be found on the present occasion . . . This is how it was presented by Lev Ivanov. Khorovods of three women cut across the stage in zigzags, forming various figures: little stars, little circles, quickly moving, wind-tossed lines—parallel and intersecting. One section of the dancers forms a cross, large and long, with an interior circle of other snowflakes. In front of them, facing the audience, eight wintry sylphides dance in the rhythm of the waltz, making rapid and soft *pas de basque*. The circle rotates in one direction, the cross in the opposite. And still nothing but classical dance is used, ponderous *temps* alternating with their velvety conclusions. This wonderful scene was completely rejected by the latest rehearsal coach . . . It is the true corruption of Raphael's Madonna by the hand of a coarse, wretched housepainter!

Other scenes of *Nutcracker*, in this last part of the first act, were also cast off with barbarous ruthlessness. Lev Ivanov depicted a figure similar to the [Cyrillic] letter ' П '. Before our eyes is a thick, conjoined line of four rows [of dancers], and lines at the sides of two rows. The dancers in the upper rows intertwine their arms to form a circle. The lines at the sides fall away, only to rush after one another, also gathering together and weaving themselves into little circles. And the dances are still based on those same fine little steps of the balleticized march, which the *pas de basque* is. Hardly noticeable little jumps—adhering, soft, downy—moistening the earth in snowy footsteps. Finally, the last picture of this moment. The snowflakes form a large star, with dancers moving inward and outward. A choreographic iamb is introduced into the dance, [a step] based on the realistic moving away [*sdvig*, possibly sidestepping] and protractedly smooth flexion of the returning leg. The star is quickly transformed into a large *khorovod*. The circle now opens, now closes. The snowstorm twists the huge group, this pyramid of dancers, into a circle. Snow falls. The snowflakes tremble. The icicles also wave gently in the air from side to side.

The first, and apparently the older, of two records of the Waltz of the Snowflakes (Harvard Theatre Collection, bMS Thr 245 (197), pp. 41–5) is reproduced below. The accompanying transcription provides an English translation of the Russian words and abbreviations; only those parts of a floor plan containing text have been transcribed.

THE WALTZ OF THE SNOWFLAKES

CHOREOGRAPHIC NOTATION
AND TRANSCRIPTION

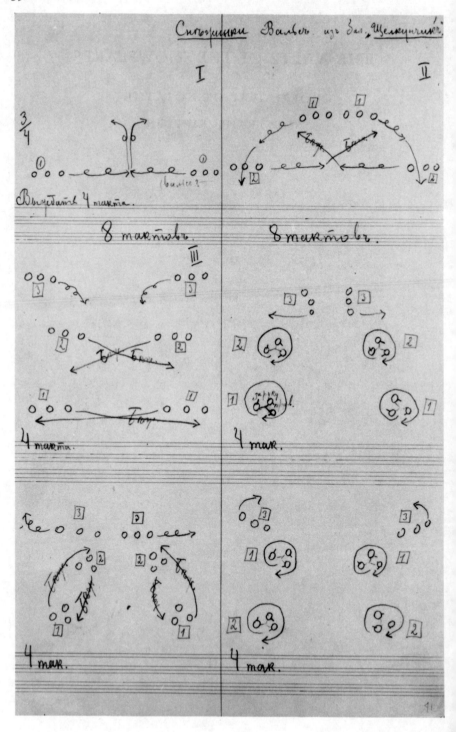

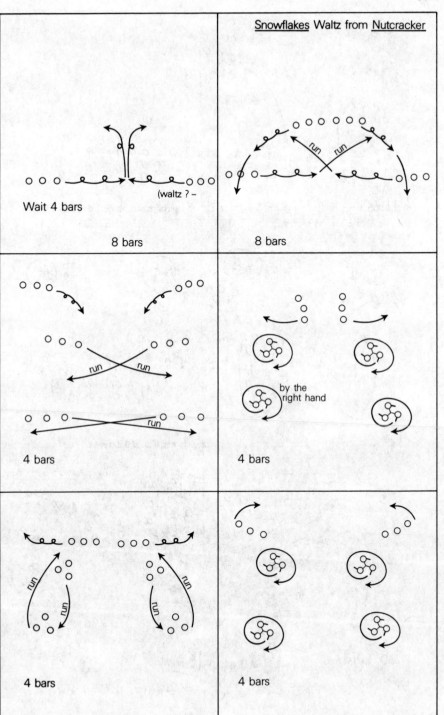

Snowflakes Waltz from Nutcracker

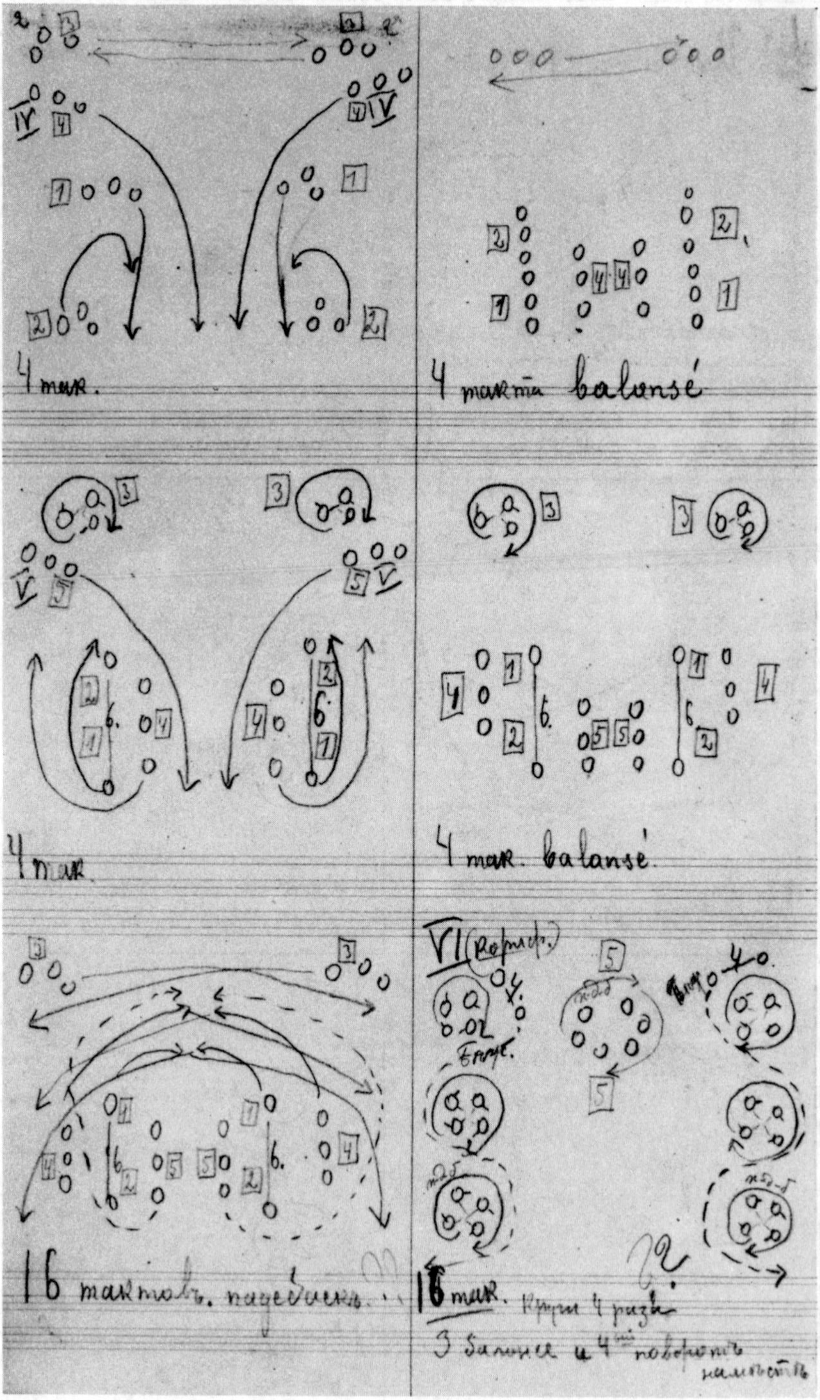

4 такт.

4 такта balansé

4 такт.

4 так. balansé.

16 тактовъ перемѣны.

16 так. крути 4 разъ

3 балансе и 4-й поворотъ намѣстѣ

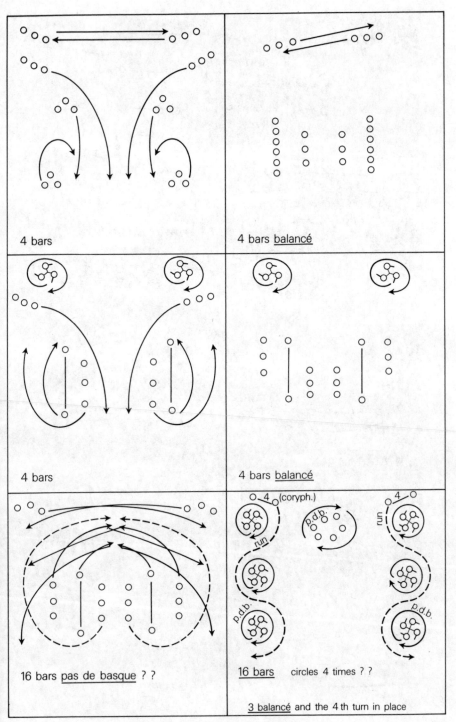

4 bars

4 bars _balancé_

4 bars

4 bars _balancé_

16 bars _pas de basque_ ? ?

16 bars   circles 4 times ? ?

3 balancé and the 4 th turn in place

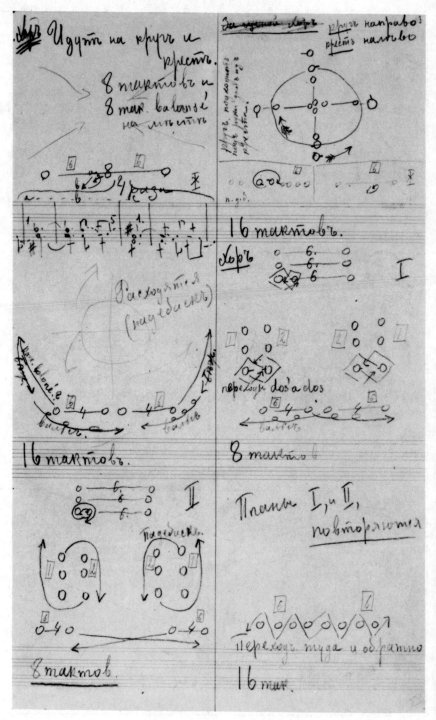

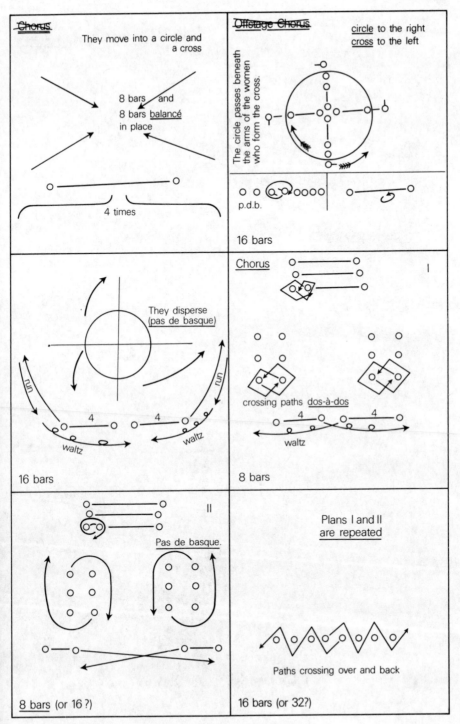

Chorus

They move into a circle and a cross

8 bars and
8 bars *balancé*
in place

4 times

Offstage Chorus

circle to the right
cross to the left

The circle passes beneath the arms of the women who form the cross.

p.d.b.

16 bars

They disperse
(pas de basque)

run   run

4   4

waltz   waltz

16 bars

Chorus   I

crossing paths dos-à-dos

4   4

waltz

8 bars

II

Pas de basque.

8 bars (or 16?)

Plans I and II
are repeated

Paths crossing over and back

16 bars (or 32?)

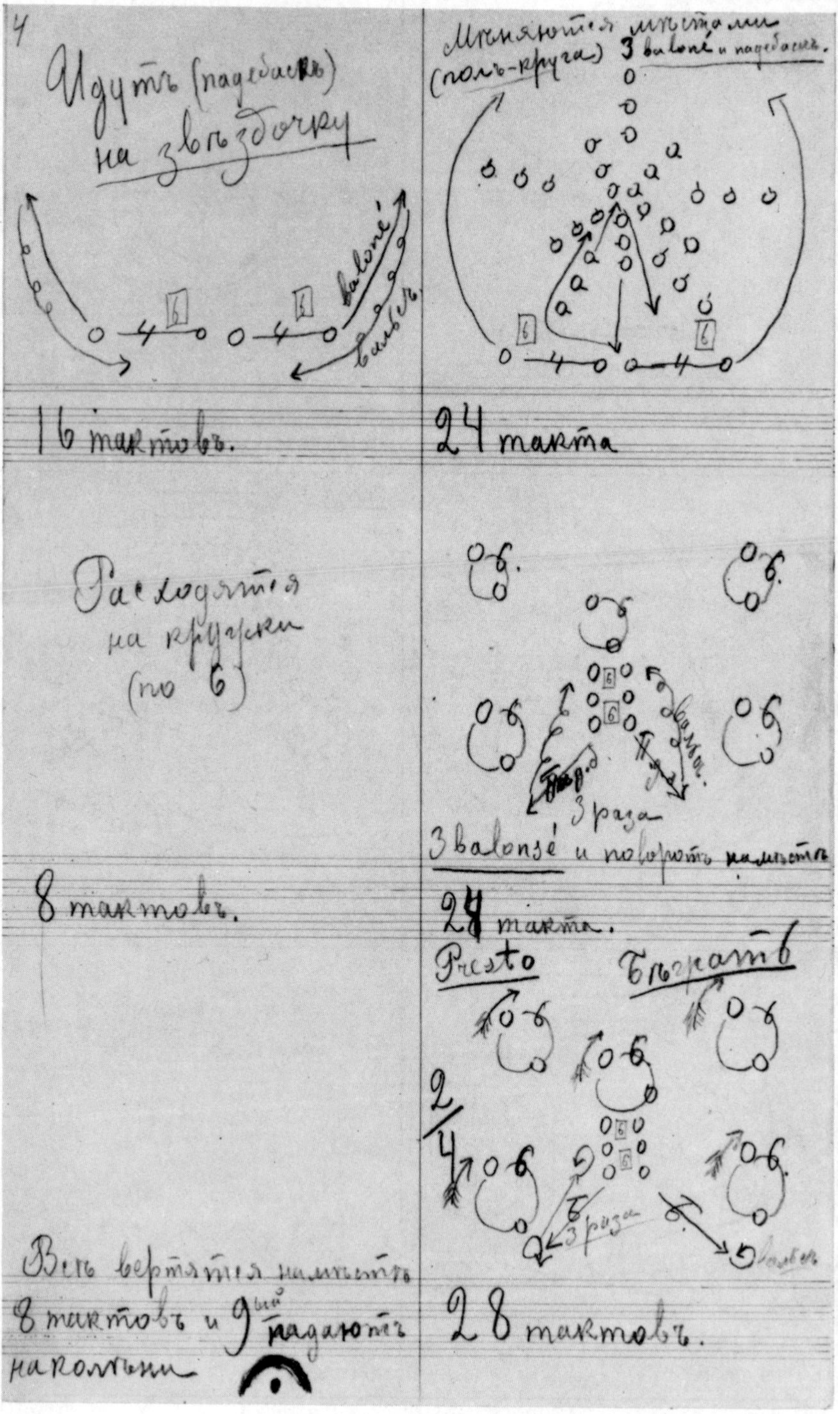
4
Идутъ (падебаскъ) на звѣздочку
balonsé
вальсъ
16 тактовъ.
Мѣняются мѣстами (полъ-круга)
3 balonsé и падебаскъ.
24 такта
Расходятся на кружки (по 6)
8 тактовъ.
вальсъ
3 раза
3 balonsé и поворотъ на мѣстѣ
24 такта.
Presto
Бѣгать
2/4
3 раза
вальсъ
Всѣ вертятся на мѣстѣ
8 тактовъ и 9ый падаютъ на колѣни
28 тактовъ.

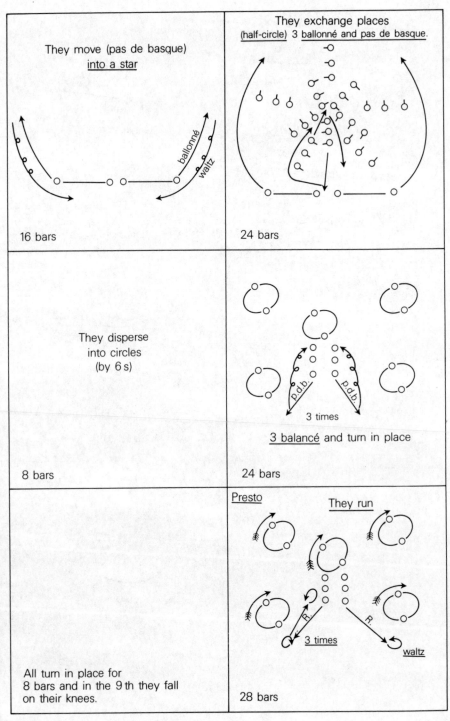

They move (pas de basque)
into a star

ballonné
waltz

16 bars

They exchange places
(half-circle) 3 ballonné and pas de basque.

24 bars

They disperse
into circles
(by 6 s)

8 bars

p.d.b.

3 times

3 balancé and turn in place

24 bars

All turn in place for
8 bars and in the 9th they fall
on their knees.

Presto

They run

R.

R.

3 times

waltz

28 bars

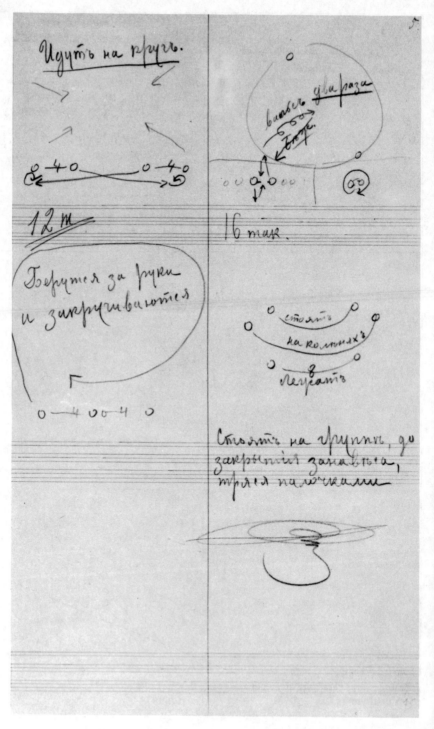

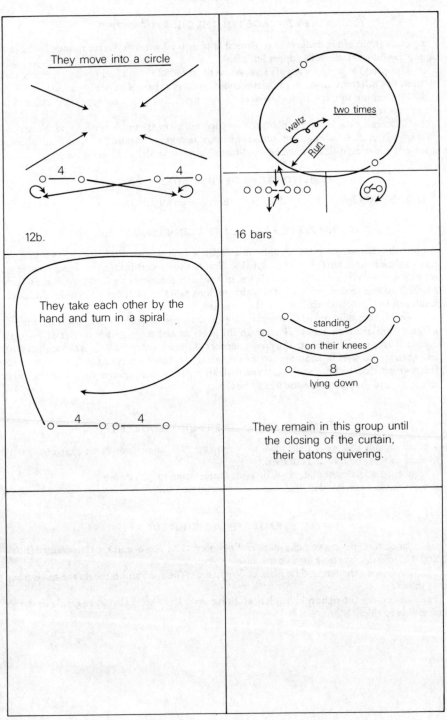

They move into a circle

4   4

12b.

two times

waltz

Run

16 bars

They take each other by the
hand and turn in a spiral

4   4

standing

on their knees

8

lying down

They remain in this group until
the closing of the curtain,
their batons quivering.

NOTES TO PAGE 1 OF THE CHOREOGRAPHY

1. Each group of six dancers (two threes) is identified with an Arabic numeral within a square (within a circle in the upper left plan).

2. The query in the upper left plan (as well as those found on pp. 2 and 3 of the notation) was written in a different hand, and suggests confusion on the part of a later régisseur.

3. Concerning the first three plans, cf. Volynsky: '. . . the dancers appear . . . in lines of three people . . .'

4. Concerning the last three plans of this page and all of the following page, cf. Volynsky: 'Khorovods of three women cut across the stage in zigzags, forming various figures: little stars, little circles, quickly moving wind-tossed lines—parallel and intersecting.'

NOTE TO PAGE 2 OF THE CHOREOGRAPHY

1. In the right lower plan, 'p. d. b.' is an abbreviation for *pas de basque*.

NOTES TO PAGE 3 OF THE CHOREOGRAPHY

1. In the right upper plan, 'p. d. b.' is an abbreviation for *pas de basque*. Regarding the figures presented in this plan, cf. Volynsky: 'Part of the dancers form a cross, large and long, with an interior circle of other snowflakes. In front of them, facing the audience, eight wintry sylphides dance in the rhythm of the waltz, making rapid and soft *pas de basque*. The circle rotates in one direction, the cross in the opposite.'

2. The right middle and left lower plans appear to correspond to Volynsky's recollections of a figure similar to the letter 'Π', though his account and the notation do not agree in all details. Three rows constitute the cross-member of the letter where Volynsky recalled four, and there is no sign in the notation of this group of dancers forming a circle with arms intertwined. But the lines at the sides do rush after one another (groups 1 and 2 in the lower left plan), and their steps are the *pas de basque*.

NOTES TO PAGE 4 OF THE CHOREOGRAPHY

1. As regards the upper right plan, cf. Volynsky: 'The snowflakes form a large star with dancers moving inward and outward.'

2. In the middle right plan, 'P. d. b.' is an abbreviation for *pas de basque*.

3. In the lower right plan, 'R.' is an abbreviation for 'run'.

NOTES TO PAGE 5 OF THE CHOREOGRAPHY

1. Concerning the upper right plan, cf. Volynsky: 'The star is quickly transformed into a large *khorovod*. The circle now opens, now closes.'

2. Concerning the left middle plan, cf. Volynsky: 'The snowstorm twists the huge group . . . into a circle.'

3. Concerning the right middle plan, cf. Volynsky: 'The icicles also wave gently in the air from side to side.'

The Performance Scores of *Sleeping Beauty* and *Swan Lake* in St Petersburg

I. SLEEPING BEAUTY

In the following table, abbreviations of sources are those used in Chapter 5 (see p. 151, above); numbers at the beginning of entries refer to bar numbers; letters at the end of entries refer to the handwriting of an added remark, in accordance with the following table:

A=pencilled additions in the Hol and possibly the Rep, mostly directions for details of performance, mostly in Italian; thought to be Drigo's.

B=pencilled additions in the Rep, mostly assignments of dancers to parts, general criticisms of the music, in French, very similar to verified examples of Petipa's handwriting; thought to be Petipa's.

C=hand in which on-the-spot corrections in pitches and added verbal instructions were made; words are scribbled in large letters, as if the music were still on a music-stand; possibly that of the rehearsal violinists.

D=the hand of a few verbal instructions; large, carefully executed Roman letters, as if written by someone accustomed to writing Cyrillic letters.

E=pencilled additions in PR-I and PR-II, giving names of dancers, directions for details of performance, stage directions, in Russian, very similar to verified examples of Nikolai Sergeyev's handwriting; thought to be Sergeyev's.

PROLOGUE

No. 1, Marche.
16–17, Rep: 'Il faut couper dans ce morceau'—B.
79, Rep: 'trop long'—B.
104, Hol: 'marcato' (above and below the horn parts)—A.
No. 2, Scène dansante.
57, Hol: Tchaikovsky's 'poco meno animato' at top and bottom of the score has been changed to 'poco più animato'; in the middle of the score: 'poco più animato'—A.
57, Rep: 'un poco [meno] animato' ('meno' has been effaced).
73, Hol: dynamic in string parts is '*p*'—unidentified hand.
101, Hol: 'riten'—unidentified hand.
108–9, Rep: 'poco rall.'—A.
110, Rep: 'a tempo'—possibly A.
170, Rep: 'poco rall.'—A.
171, Rep: 'poco rall.'—A.
204–5, Rep: 'un poco allargando'—A.

No. 3, Pas de six.

  50, Rep: 'animando'—A.

  50–3, Hol: 'a poco a poco accellerando ed animato'—A.

  57, Hol and Rep: 'ritenuto'—possibly A.

  58, Hol and Rep: '1° tempo ben marcato'—possibly A.

  62, Hol, above winds: 'attendre'—A; above harp: 'ad libitum'—A.

    Variation V.

      68–71, Hol, Rep, PR-I, PR-II: cut.

    Variation VI.

      1, Rep: first note changed from G$\sharp$ to G$\natural$.

      19–22, PR-I and PR-II: cut.

    Coda.

      52, PR-I and PR-II: 'poco più animato' crossed out.

No. 4, Finale.

  169–71, Hol: 'diminuendo'—A.

  173, Hol: *'pppp'* (string parts); *'pp'* (wind parts)—probably A.

ACT I

No. 5, Scène.

  45–60, Rep, PR-I and PR-II: cut.

  72–3, Rep: 'trop long'—B.

  86–119, PR-I and PR-II: cut (possibly in connection with an English production; in PR-I, 'out' is written at the top of one of the pages of deleted music).

  133–205, PR-I and PR-II: cut (possibly in connection with an English production, for the same reason as the preceding entry).

  133, Rep: 'couper'—B.

  141, Rep: 'ici'—B.

  183, Rep: 'Tâcher de passer à la valse' (written in the margin after the bar)—B.

  184, Rep: 'petite coupe'—B.

  184–205, Rep: cut.

No. 8, Pas d'action.

  (Adagio)

    7–10, Hol: wind parts cut.

  (Adagio maestoso)

    34, Rep: 'animando'—D.

    37, PR-I and PR-II: 'poco stringendo' crossed out.

    74–80, Rep: repeated (on a separate folio bound in between fols. [51] and [52]).

  (Dances of the Maids of Honour and Pages)

    83–4, Rep: 'Cela ne me plaît pas'—B.

    95–110, PR-I and PR-II: cut.

    103, PR-I: 'Meno'—probably E, but in Italian.

    111, PR-I: 'a tempo'—probably E, but in Italian.

  (Aurora's variation)

    184, Rep: 'poco meno'—possibly A.

    216, Rep: repeat sign deleted.

    231, Hol, Rep, PR-I and PR-II: cut. [This is a first ending; in the Hol

Tchaikovsky had written, of the repeat which it begins, 'Cette reprise est facultative.']

All sources modify the ending of Aurora's variation. The Rep preserves alternate readings as follows:

Version 1.

The Hol agrees with this version; the new cadence, written in Hand A, is located at the end of the music of Act I (Hol, Vol. I, fol. 120ʳ).

Version 2.

PR-I follows this version; no new music is added in PR-II, but bars 248–62 are cut. (Coda)

387, PR-I and PR-II: 'Meno'—E.

No. 9, Finale.

1, PR-I and PR-II: 'Allegro giusto' changed to 'Allegro mosso'.

17–18, PR-II: a pause (above the bar-line separating these two bars).

26, PR-II: a pause above the third beat.

69–85, Hol, Rep, PR-I and PR-II: cut.

100, PR-II: a pause above the third beat.

107, PR-I: repeated.

143, Hol: 'Poco meno'—A.

145, Hol: 'riten.'—unidentified hand.

149, Hol: 'più mosso in 2'—A.

159, Hol: 'Meno' . . . 'in 6'—A.

160–75, PR-I and PR-II: cut.

181–2, PR-II: a pause above the bar-line separating these bars.

ACT II

No. 12, Scène.

(Dance of the Baronesses)

   1, Hol: 'in 4'.

   —Rep, PR-I, PR-II: the dance is cut.

(Dance of the Countesses)

   —Rep: the dance is cut.

(Dance of the Marchionesses)

   5–12, PR-I and PR-II: cut.

   31–8, Hol, Rep, PR-I and PR-II: cut. In the Rep the entire dance was cut.

No. 13, Farandole.

   84, Rep: 'Presto' effaced.

No. 14, Scène.

   32, Hol: 'in Sei'—A.

   32, Rep: 'Andante. in 6'—A.

   32–3, Rep: 'Long'—B.

   50–91, Rep: apparently cut at one time, but the cut has been erased.

   76–91, PR-I and PR-II: cut.

No. 15a, Pas d'action.

   42, Hol and Rep: 'poco meno'—A.

   68, Rep: '1° tempo'—A.

   95, PR-I and PR-II: repeated.

   96, Rep, PR-I: pause over rest on beat 4 of first violin part; pause over chord in entire bar in 2nd violin part.

   114, Hol: 'poco meno'—A.

   167, Hol and Rep: cut; 4 additional bars added:

(bar 166)   (bar 167)

No. 15b, Variation.

1–2, Hol: 'Allegro commodo' (cf. 'Allegro con moto' in modern published scores).

—Rep, PR-I and PR-II: cut. Interpolated in its place in the Rep is the first variation of the *pas de quatre*, No. 23. In the Hol: 'Segue Variation Mlle Brianza', written after the last bar of No. 15a. PR-I: 'Go to p. 161 Var' [in English], which is the first page of the Gold Fairy's Variation. PR-II [in Russian and French]: 'The variation is taken from Act III, No. 23, *pas de quatre*, V[ariation] I. Allegro (Tempo di Valse).'

No. 15c, Coda.

90–4, Hol: '(La vision d'Aurore disparait)'—Tchaikovsky's hand.

No. 17, Panorama.

—Hol: Tchaikovsky's final cadence has been altered. He wrote a transition to the next number (the *entr'acte* in C major, with violin solo) which caused the Panorama originally to end on the dominant of C major:

original bar 77   78   79   80

Bars 79–80 were cut and the solo cello part in bars 77–8 was deleted, apparently after the decision to cut all of No. 18. Siloti's arrangement preserves Tchaikovsky's version, but only in imperial period editions; Soviet editions of the piano arrangement (including those attributed to Siloti) and the score (including the Collected Works Edition) preserve the modified cadence, even when No. 18 is restored. The Rep, PR-I, and PR-II were all modified to reflect the changes made in the Hol.

No. 18, Entr'acte.

Hol, Rep: cut.

No. 19, Entr'acte symphonique.

Rep, at the head of the score: 'Long'—B.

47, Hol: 'cantabile' (in wind parts)—A.

54, Hol: 'cantabile' (in wind parts)—A.

96, Hol: 'poco più mosso'—A.

96–9, Rep: possibly cut (symbols of a cut are written in these bars without a connecting line).

100, Rep: 'Allegro [vivace]' ('vivace' effaced).

120, Hol: 'accell.'—unidentified hand.

120, Rep: 'animando'—possibly A.

126–7, Rep: 'animando'—possibly A.

No. 20, Finale.

Rep, at the head of the score: 'Long'—B.

1–10, PR-I: cut.

2, Rep: 'Beaucoup trop long'—B.

22–3, Hol: 'meno mosso'—A.

23–6, PR-I and PR-II: cut.

29, Hol: 'segue 1° tempo'—A.

34–6, Hol: 'accell. un poco'—A.

38–42, Hol: '1° tempo'—A.

38–58, Hol, Rep, PR-I, and PR-II: cut.

ACT III

No. 21, Marche.

3, Rep: 'Couper la marche; tout le monde en Scène. C'est trop long'—B.

16, Rep: 'Rideau' (cf. the same at bar 32 of Hol).

65–72, PR-I and PR-II: cut.

81–8, PR-I and PR-II: cut.

No. 22, Polacca.

10–13, Hol: 'un poco stringendo'—A.

10–15, Rep: 'stringendo'—unidentified hand.

18, Hol: 'un poco ritenuto'—A.

18–21, Rep: 'ritenuto molto'—unidentified hand.

22–30, PR-I: cut.

70, Hol: 'poco meno'—A.

103–10, PR-I: cut.

127–34, PR-I: cut.

Hol, after last bar: 'One bar in case the *sarabande* is to be performed after the polonaise' (in Tchaikovsky's hand), together with a bar of music, crossed out.

No. 23, Pas de quatre.

(*Intrada*)

27–8, PR-II: cut, but the word 'in' is written beneath the bars.

(*Variation I*)

5–20, Hol, Rep, PR-I: cut.

Hol: entire variation cut.

Rep: the variation is present; a copy has been interpolated into Act II in place of No. 15*b*.

PR-I: 'The variation of the ballerina in the nereids (2nd act)' [in Russian]—E.

PR-II: lacks Variations I–III.

(*Variation II*)

Hol, Rep, PR-I: re-numbered '1'.

(*Variation III*)

Hol, Rep, PR-I: cut.

(*Variation IV*)

Hol: re-numbered '2'.

No. 24, Pas de caractère.

Hol, Rep, PR-I: a ten-bar introduction, 'Entrée des chats', added.

No. 25, Pas de quatre.
(Adagio)

    5, Rep: 'rit'—unidentified hand.

    18, Rep: 'rit'—unidentified hand.

    19, Rep: 'rit' (last beat of the bar)—unidentified hand.

    22, Rep: pause above last note.

    27, Hol: modified, with a new bar added:

The Rep has been modified to reflect this change; PR-I ends with bar 27, but a pause has been added above the second quaver of beat three.

(*Variation I*)

   4, PR-I and PR-II: cut.

   5–20, Rep: cut.

   18–33, Hol: cut.

   19–32, PR-I and PR-II: cut.

   45–53, PR-I and PR-II: cut.

   47, Hol: possible cut through bar 56 (the indication is not conclusive).

   47–54, Rep: cut.

   54–6, Hol: cut.

   (*Coda*)

   1, Rep: 'Presto' has been effaced, and replaced with 'Allegretto'—unidentified hand.

   54–69, Rep, PR-I and PR-II: cut.

No. 26b, Cendrillon et le Prince Fortuné.

   21–36, Hol, Rep: cut. In PR-I bars 21 and 37 are marked with an 'X', but no line, indicating a cut, connects them.

   69–70, Hol: 'con grazia' (below the first violin part)—apparently in Tchaikovsky's hand.

   70–1, Hol: 'corni i bassi p'—A.

No. 27, Pas berrichon.

   Hol, Rep, PR-I call for two repeats:

      (1) bars 55–62; after reaching bar 62 the second time,

      (2) bars 27–62, without replaying the repeat of bars 55–62.

   PR-II calls for the first repeat only.

No. 28, Pas de deux.

   (*Entrée*)

   Hol, PR-I: the entire *entrée* (No. 28, bars 6–47) is cut. In the Rep, a cut is opened at the end of bar 5, but left unclosed; bars 6–14, 28–31, 37–8, 41–2 are cut.

   (*Adagio*)

   55–64, Hol, Rep, PR-I: cut.

   (*Variation I*)

   4–7, Rep: 'tempo ad libitum'—unidentified hand.

   (*Variation II*)

   Hol: at the end of the score (Vol. II, fol. 135ᵛ) an introductory bar for this variation:

PR-I also preserves an introductory bar, one without the syncopation:

(introductory bar)   (bar 1)

The Rep preserves no additional music, but symbols, similar to 'I' or '♯', written before the bar, may refer to an added introductory bar.

     43–6, Hol: cut.

     43–54, Rep, PR-I: cut.

     50–7, Hol: cut.

     63–4, Hol, Rep, PR-I: cut.

  (Coda)

     1, Hol: 'Forte' (above first violin part)—A.

     9–10, Hol: 'piano' (above string parts)—A.

No. 29, Sarabande.

     17, Rep: '3 times' [in Russian], a reference, restated at the end of the number, to the playings of bars 17–48.

  PR-I: the entire number is cut.

No. 30, Finale.

  (*Mazurka*)

     9, Rep: 'Ce fine très court sans le galop de la fin. Finir sur la mazurka'—B.

     42–57, Hol, Rep, PR-I: cut.

     90–105, Hol, Rep, PR-I: cut.

     122–37, Hol, Rep, PR-I: cut.

     170–2, Hol: 'poco meno'—A.

201, beat 3—209, beat 3, PR-I: possible cut (the marks are inconclusive).
227–58, Hol, Rep, PR-I: cut.
266–77, Hol, Rep, PR-I: cut.
306, beat 3—384, Hol, Rep, PR-I: cut.

(*Apotheosis*)
393–415, Hol, Rep, PR-I: cut.

II. SWAN LAKE

The two surviving copies of the répétiteur of *Swan Lake* (see Chapter 7, note 37) are in substantial agreement as regards the musical text. But they are different in origin and in richness of supplementary information. Copy 1 appears to have been prepared either from the holograph score or from Kashkin's piano arrangement of 1877; Copy 2 is closer to the *nouvelle version* of *Swan Lake* published by Jurgenson in a piano reduction prepared by Eduard Langer. Of the two, Copy 1 shows far more evidence of use, and contains many more tempo indications and details of stage action than Copy 2.

In the following list, the description of changes in the répétiteur is based on a comparison with the *nouvelle version*, not with Tchaikovsky's original. In counting bars, first and second endings of passages marked by a repeat sign have been counted as one bar. (If, for example, a first ending falls on bar 8 and contains 3 bars, and is followed by a second ending containing two, the entire complex would be numbered bar 8 *a* to *e*; bar 9 would be the first one after the second ending.)

Nouvelle version	Changes in the répétiteur

Introduction—follows the *nouvelle version*.
No. 1—bars 71–2 are repeated.
No. 2—Intrada: bars 35–6 are repeated.
    —*Andante sostenuto*: deleted.
    —*Allegro semplice* (Copy 1): 'Allegro semplice' changed to 'Moderato'.
    —*Moderato*: repeat of the first eight bars deleted; eight bars from the end: 'poco meno' changed to 'meno'.
    —*Allegro* (Copy 1): 'Allegro' changed to 'Allegretto'; in bar 1, 'Lento'.
    —*Coda*: follows the *nouvelle version*.
No. 3—Copy 1: after 'Allegro moderato', 'not slowly' (in Russian).
No. 4—Bars 37–8 are deleted (this corrects what seems to be a printing error in the *nouvelle version*).
    —The répétiteur follows the *nouvelle version* only in part of the episode in F♯ minor (bars 68–75 with its repeat). What would be the first playing of bars 68–75 follows the *nouvelle version*; for its repeat the répétiteur substitutes a variant from Tchaikovsky's original (which corresponds to bars 91–8 of No. 2 in the Collected Works edition of the score and its reprints).
    —bars 168*b*–231, 285–314 are deleted.
No. 5—at bar 17: 'Meno'; at bar 44 (Copy 1): 'Meno'.

No. 6—follows the *nouvelle version*.

No. 7—bars 19–59, 145–54 are deleted.

No. 8—follows the *nouvelle version*.

No. 9—follows the *nouvelle version*.

No. 10—follows the *nouvelle version* to bar 196; three new bars are added at this point which lead directly to bar 245 (that is, bars 197–244 of the *nouvelle version* are deleted).

   —six bars from the end (Copy 1): 'Un poco rit'.

No. 11—bars 77–8 are deleted.

No. 12—at bar 79 (Copy 1): 'un poco meno'.

No. 13—bars 37–8, 58–9 are repeated. At bar 43 (Copy 1): 'rit.' At bar 98: 'a tempo'.

No. 14—follows the *nouvelle version*.

No. 15—transposed from Ab major to A major; above bars 1–2 (Copy 1): 'quickly' (in Russian).

No. 16—tempo modifications (Copy 1): 'Meno' before bar 19; 'più mosso' in bar 35 and again in bar 43; 'poco a poco accelerando' in bars 47–9.

No. 17—follows the *nouvelle version* to bar 49; then bars 2–49 are played again, but without the repeat of bars 3–17 indicated in the *nouvelle version*, and without bars 19–33. After bar 49 has been reached the second time, the remainder of the dance follows the *nouvelle version*.

No. 18—follows the *nouvelle version*.

No. 19—follows the *nouvelle version*.

No. 20—follows the *nouvelle version*.

No. 21—follows the *nouvelle version*.

No. 22—at bar 72: 'Più meno Allo.' (cf. 'Più mosso' in the *nouvelle version*).

No. 23—follows the *nouvelle version*.

No. 24—bars 70–1 are repeated.

No. 25—follows the *nouvelle version*.

No. 26—*Tempo di valse*: follows the *nouvelle version*.

   —*Andante*: follows the *nouvelle version*.

   —*Tempo di valse*: in bar 1: 'in A [major]'. Bars 3–18 are deleted.

   —interpolated variation No. 1 (Op. 72, No. 12): bars 18, 19, the first two beats of 20, and 31 are deleted. At bar 25 (Copy 1): 'accelerando'. N.B. The published version of Drigo's orchestration observes the first cuts, but not that of bar 31.

No. 27—tempo designation at the beginning: 'Allegro Vivace Maestoso'. Bars 19–26 are deleted. At bar 43 (Copy 1): 'Mosso'. At bar 59 (Copy 1): 'Meno'. A pause is introduced over the two quaver rests in the middle of bar 74. Above bar 75: 'tempo'. At bar 91: 'Più mosso'.

No. 28—at bar 29 (Copy 1): 'riten'. Bars 30–91, 98–101, 114–21 (Copy 1), 125–7 are deleted. At bar 134: 'allarg.'

No. 29—harp cadenza follows the last bar, in preparation for

   —interpolated variation No. 2 (Op. 72, No. 11), which follows the *nouvelle version* to bar 119. It then returns to bar 4 and proceeds through the dance until the end. N.B. The published version of Drigo's orchestration corresponds to the performance version.

No. 30—deleted.

No. 31—deleted.

No. 32—follows the *nouvelle version* to bar 51; three new bars are added, leading to a pause over a dominant seventh chord in E major; bars 52–96 of the *nouvelle version* are deleted.

No. 33—follows the *nouvelle version* to bar 26, after which comes
 —interpolated variation No. 3 (Op. 72, No. 15), as presented in the *nouvelle version*. N.B. The published version of Drigo's orchestration corresponds to the performance version. After this the *Allegro agitato* begins (No. 33, bar 27). From this point to the end of the *nouvelle version* bars 139–46 are deleted (in Copy 1), bar 179 is repeated. (At the end of Copy 2 several pages are bound in the wrong order, complicating comparison with Copy 1 and making agreement between the two scores difficult to establish with certainty.)

Select Bibliography

❧

I. BOOKS, ARTICLES, AND MANUSCRIPT SOURCES

Abraham, Gerald, ed., *The Music of Tchaikovsky* (London, 1945).

Asaf'ev, Boris Vladimirovich, *Izbrannye trudy* [Selected Works], 5 vols. (Moscow, 1952–7).

Avtografy P. I. Chaikovskogo v arkhive doma-muzeya v Klinu. Spravochnik [The Autographs of P. I. Tchaikovsky in the Archive of the Home-Museum at Klin. Catalogue], 2 vols. (Moscow and Leningrad, 1950, 1952).

Bakhrushin, Yurii Alekseevich. 'The Ballets of Tchaikovsky and their Stage History', *Chaikovskii i teatr* [Tchaikovsky and Theatre], ed. A. I. Shaverdyan (Moscow and Leningrad, 1940), pp. 80–139, 245–63, 349–54.

Bakst, Léon, 'Tchaikowsky aux Ballets Russes', *Comoedia*, xv/3220 (19 Oct. 1921), p. 1.

Beaumont, Cyril W., *A History of Ballet in Russia (1613–1881)* (London, 1930).

——, *The Ballet Called Swan Lake* (London, 1952).

Benua, Aleksandr Nikolaevich [Alexandre Benois], 'Ivan Aleksandrovich Vsevolozhskii', *Rech'* [Discourse] (1 Nov. 1909), pp. 2–3.

——, *Moi vospominaniya* [My Reminiscences], 2 vols. (Moscow, 1980).

Chaikovskii, Modeste Il'ich, *Zhizn' Petra Il'icha Chaikovskogo. Po dokumentam, khranyashchimsya v arkhive imeni pokoinogo kompozitora v Klinu* [The Life of Peter Ilyich Tchaikovsky. According to Documents Preserved in the Archive named for the Deceased Composer at Klin], 3 vols. (Moscow, 2nd edn 1901–3).

Chaikovskii, Petr Il'ich, *Dnevniki P. I. Chaikovskogo 1873–1891* [The Diaries of P. I. Tchaikovsky, 1873–1891] (Moscow and Petrograd, 1923).

——, *Polnoe sobranie sochinenii* [Collected Works], 62 vols. (Moscow and Leningrad, 1940–71).

——, *Polnoe sobranie sochinenii. Literaturnye proizvedeniya i perepiska* [Collected Works. Literary Works and Correspondence], 17 vols. (Moscow, 1953–81).

Chujoy, Anatole, 'Russian Balletomania', *Dance Index*, vii/3 (March, 1948).

——, trans., 'Writings on Lev Ivanov', *Dance Perspectives*, ii (Spring, 1959), pp. 1–64.

Davydov, N. V., *Iz proshlogo* [From the Past] (Moscow, 1913).

Davydov, Yurii L'vovich, *Zapiski o P. I. Chaikovskom* [Memoirs about P. I. Tchaikovsky] (Moscow, 1962).

Dni i gody P. I. Chaikovskogo [The Days and Years of P. I. Tchaikovsky], ed. V. Yakovlev (Moscow and Leningrad, 1940).

Glebov, Igor', ed., *Chaikovskii. Vospominaniya i pis'ma* [Tchaikovsky. Recollections and Letters] (Leningrad, 1924).

Gorskii, Aleksandr Alekseevich, *Tablitsa znakov dlya zapisyvaniya dvizhenii chelovecheskogo tela po sisteme Artista Imperatorskikh S.-Peterburgskikh Teatrov V. I. Stepanova* [Table of Signs for the Notation of the Movements of the Human Body according to the System of the Artist of the Imperial St Petersburg Theatres V. I. Stepanov] (St Petersburg, n.d.).

Guest, Ivor, 'The Alhambra Ballet', *Dance Perspectives*, iv (Autumn, 1959), pp. 5–72.

Ivanov, Lev Ivanovich, 'Moi vospominaniya. Posvyashchayutsya moim tovari-shcham i sosluzhivtsam' [My Recollections. Dedicated to my Colleagues and Co-Workers] (Leningrad, Leningrad Theatre Museum, ORTs 5430, No. KP 7154/76).

Kashkin, Nikolai Dmitrievich, *Vospominaniya o P. I. Chaikovskom* [Recollections about P. I. Tchaikovsky] (Moscow, 1896).

Khudekov, Sergei Nikolaevich, *Istoriya tantsev* [The History of Dances], 4 vols. (St Petersburg/Petrograd, 1913–18).

Krasovskaya, Vera Mikhailovna, *Russkii baletnyi teatr vtoroi poloviny XIX veka* [Russian Ballet Theatre of the Second Half of the 19th Century] (Moscow and Leningrad, 1963).

Kshesinskaya, Matilde Feliksovna, *Dancing in Petersburg: the Memoirs of Ksches-sinska*, trans. Arnold Haskell (London, 1960).

Larosh, German Avgustovich, *Izbrannye stat'i* [Selected Articles], 5 vols. (Lenin-grad, 1974–).

Leshkov, Denis Ivanovich, 'Personal Reminiscenes of R. E. Drigo' (Moscow, State Central Archive of Literature and Art, *fond* 794, *op.* 1, *ed. khr.* 42), Eng. trans., *The Dancing Times*, lxxii (1981–2), pp. 577–8, 661–2.

Marius Petipa. Materialy, vospominaniya, stat'i [Marius Petipa; Materials, Recol-lections, Articles], ed. Yurii Iosifovich Slonimskii *et al.* (Leningrad, 1971).

Muzykal'noe nasledie Chaikovskogo. Iz istorii ego proizvedenii [Tchaikovsky's Musical Heritage; from the History of his Works], ed. Karl Yul'evich Davydov, Vladimir Vasil'evich Protopopov, and Nadezhda Vasil'evna Tumanina (Moscow, 1958).

'On the Acquisition of the Music and Production of the Ballet *Sleeping Beauty*' (Leningrad, Central Music Library of the Theatre of Opera and Ballet named for

S. M. Kirov, VII $\frac{54154}{delo\ 26093}$).

Pchel'nikov, Pavel Mikhailovich, 'Recollections about P. I. Tchaikovsky', *Moskovskie vedomosti* [Moscow Gazette] (27 Oct. 1900), pp. 3–4.

Petipa, Marius Ivanovich, *Memuary Mariusa Petipa, Soloista E. V. i baletmeistera Imp. Teatrov* [The Memoirs of Marius Petipa, Soloist of His Majesty and Balletmaster of the Imperial Theatres] (St Petersburg, 1906).

Pleshcheev, Aleksandr Alekseevich, *Chto vspomnilos (za 50 let)* [What is Remem-bered (after 50 years)] (Paris, 1931).

——, *Moe vremya* [My Time] (Paris, n.d.).

——, *Nash balet* [Our Ballet] (St Petersburg, 2nd edn 1899).

——, '*Pod seniyu kulis . . .*' ['In the Protection of the Wings . . .'] (Paris, 1936).

——, *Sergei Lifar' ot starogo k novomu* [Sergei Lifar from Old to New] (Paris, 1938).

Romanov, Boris, 'The Dancer's Notes (M. I. Petipa's Work outside the Rehearsal Hall)', *Biryuch Gosudarstvennykh Petrogradskikh Teatrov* [Herald of the Petrograd State Theatres] (1918), vii, pp. 35–9.

Roslavleva, Natalia Petrovna, *Era of the Russian Ballet* (New York, 1966).

Rossiev, P. A., 'The Artistic Circle in Moscow (1865–1883)', *Istoricheskii vestnik* [Historical Messenger], cxxviii (Apr.–June 1912), pp. 482–98; cxxix (July–Sept. 1912), pp. 111–36.

Rozanova, Yuliya Andreevna, *Simfonicheskie printsipy baletov Chaikovskogo* [Symphonic Principles of Tchaikovsky's Ballets] (Moscow, 1976).

Skal'kovskii, Konstantin Apollonovich, *V teatral'nom mire* [In the Theatre World] (St Petersburg, 1899).

Slonimskii, Yurii Iosifovich, '*Lebedinoe ozero' P. Chaikovskogo* ['Swan Lake' of P. Tchaikovsky] (Leningrad, 1962).

——, *Mastera baleta* [Masters of the Ballet] (Leningrad, 1937).

——, *P. I. Chaikovskii i baletnyi teatr ego vremeni* [P. I. Tchaikovsky and the Ballet Theatre of his Time] (Moscow, 1956).

Solyannikov, N[ikolai] A[leksandrovich], 'Vospominaniya' [Recollections] Leningrad, Library of the All-Russian Theatrical Society [LOVTO], Inv. No. 35–r).

Stepanow, W. J. *Alphabet des mouvements du corps humain au moyen des signes musicaux* (Paris, 1892).

Telyakovskii, Vladimir Arkad'evich, *Vospominaniya* [Recollections] (Leningrad and Moscow, 1965).

——, *Vospominaniya 1898–1917* [Recollections, 1898–1917] (Petersburg [sic], 1924).

Tumanina, Nadezhda Vasil'evna, *Chaikovskii, Put' k masterstvu 1840–1877 gg.* [Tchaikovsky. Road to Mastery, 1840–1877] (Moscow, 1962).

——, *P. I. Chaikovskii. Velikii master* [P. I. Tchaikovsky; Great Master] (Moscow, 1968).

Val'ts, Karl Fedorovich, *Shest'desyat pyat' let v teatre* [Sixty-five Years in the Theatre] (Leningrad, 1928).

Volynskii, Akim L'vovich, 'A Wretched Housepainter', *Zhizn'iskusstva* [The Life of Art], vii (20 Feb. 1923), pp. 4–5.

Vospominaniya o P. I. Chaikovskom [Recollections about P. I. Tchaikovsky], ed. Vladimir Vasil'evich Protopopov (Moscow, 2nd edn 1973).

Warrack, John, *Tchaikovsky Ballet Music* (London, 1979).

Wiley, Roland John, 'Dances from Russia: an Introduction to the Sergejev Collection', *Harvard Library Bulletin*, xxiv (1976), pp. 96–112.

——, 'Three Historians of the Imperial Russian Ballet', *Dance Research Journal*, xiii/1 (Autumn, 1980), pp. 3–16.

Yakovlev, M. A., *Baletmeister Marius Petipa. (Ocherk iz istorii russkogo baleta)* [The Balletmaster Marius Petipa. (Essay on the History of Russian Ballet)] (Leningrad, 1924).

II. SELECTED REVIEWS OF FIRST PERFORMANCES

A. *Swan Lake* (Moscow, 1877).

'Theatre Chronicle', *Teatral'naya gazeta* [Theatre Gazette], No. 39 (22 Feb. 1877), p. 178.

N. Kashkin, 'Musical Chronicle', *Russkie vedomosti* [Russian Gazette], No. 49 (25 Feb. 1877), p. 1.

Modest Observer, 'Observations and Notes', *Russkie vedomosti* [Russian Gazette], No. 50 (26 Feb. 1877), pp. 1–2.

Tooth, '*Bénéfice* of Mlle Karpakova I—"Swan Lake", Ballet by Reisinger, Music of Tchaikovsky', *Sovremennye izvestiya* [Contemporary News], No. 55 (26 Feb. 1877), p. 1.

'Moscow Feuilleton', *Novoe vremya* [The New Times], No. 358 (26 Feb. 1877), pp. 1–2.

B. *Sleeping Beauty*

'Theatre Echo', *Peterburgskaya gazeta* [Petersburg Gazette], No. 3 (4 Jan. 1890), p. 3.

N., 'A New Ballet', *Novosti i birzhevaya gazeta* [News and Stock Exchange Gazette], No. 5 (5 Jan. 1890), p. 3.

'Theatre and Music', *Novoe vremya* [The New Times], No. 4976 (5 Jan. 1890), p. 3.

L., 'Theatre Echo', *Peterburgskaya gazeta* [Petersburg Gazette], No. 15 (16 Jan. 1890), p. 3.

M. Ivanov, 'Musical Sketches', *Novoe vremya* [The New Times], No. 4993 (3 Feb. 1890), p. 2.

'Sleeping Beauty', *Nuvellist. Muzykal'no-teatral'naya gazeta* [Nuvellist; Musico-Theatrical Gazette], No. 2 (1890), pp. 3–5.

C. *Nutcracker*

Domino, 'Theatre, Music and Art', *Birzhevye vedomosti* [Stock Exchange Gazette], No. 338 (8 Dec. 1892), p. 3.

N., 'Ballet', *Novosti i birzhevaya gazeta* [News and Stock Exchange Gazette], No. 339 (8 Dec. 1892), p. 3.

V. Baskin, 'Theatre Echo', *Peterburgskaya gazeta* [Petersburg Gazette], No. 339 (9 Dec. 1892), p. 4.

Old Balletomane, 'Theatre Echo', *Peterburgskaya gazeta* [Petersburg Gazette], No. 340 (10 Dec. 1892), p. 4.

M. Ivanov, 'Musical Sketches', *Novoe vremya* [The New Times], No. 6034 (14 Dec. 1892), p. 2.

D. *Swan Lake* (St Petersburg, 1895)

'Theatre and Music', *Novoe vremya* [The New Times], No. 6783 (16 Jan. 1895), p. 3.

B., '*Bénéfice* of Pierina Legnani', *Peterburgskaya gazeta* [Petersburg Gazette], No. 15 (16 Jan. 1895), p. 3.

Veteran, 'The Ballet "Swan Lake" ', *Novosti i birzhevaya gazeta* [News and Stock Exchange Gazette], No. 17 (17 Jan. 1895), p. 3.

B. V., 'Theatre Courier', *Peterburgskii listok* [Petersburg Leaflet], No. 16 (17 Jan. 1895), p. 4.

Ya. D., '*Bénéfice* of Mlle Legnani', *Sanktpeterburgskie vedomosti* [St Petersburg Gazette], No. 16 (17 Jan. 1895), p. 3.

A. B., 'Theatre and Music', *Novoe vremya* [The New Times], No. 6784 (17 Jan. 1895), p. 3.

III. PRODUCTION DOCUMENTS

A. *Sleeping Beauty*

Holograph score: Leningrad, Central Music Library of the Theatre of Opera and Ballet named for S. M. Kirov, Ballet No. 301.

Répétiteur: Leningrad, Central Music Library of the Theatre of Opera and Ballet named for S. M. Kirov, $\dfrac{I\,44154}{Re\ Spyashch}$.

Choreographic notation: Cambridge, Massachusetts, Harvard Theatre Collection, bMS Thr 245 (204).

B. *Nutcracker*

Holograph score: Moscow, State Central Museum of Musical Culture named for M. I. Glinka, *fond* 88, No. 51.

Répétiteurs: Leningrad, Central Music Library of the Theatre of Opera and Ballet named for S. M. Kirov, $\dfrac{I\,44154}{Re\ Shchel}$.

Choreographic notation: Cambridge, Massachusetts, Harvard Theatre Collection, bMS Thr 245 (197).

C. *Swan Lake* (St Petersburg, 1895)

Répétiteurs: Leningrad, Central Music Library of the Theatre of Opera and Ballet named for S. M. Kirov, $\dfrac{I\,44154}{Re\ Leb}$.

Choreographic notation: Cambridge, Massachusetts, Harvard Theatre Collection, fMS 186 (11–13).

Index

424 INDEX